A Line in the Sea

A Line in the Sea

The Qatar v. Bahrain Border Dispute in the World Court

Jawad Salim Al-Arayed

NORTH ATLANTIC BOOKS
BERKELEY, CALIFORNIA

Copyright © 2003 by Jawad Salim Al-Arayed. All rights reserved. No portion of this book, except for brief review, may be reproduced, stored in a retrieval system, or transmitted in any form or by any means—electronic, mechanical, photocopying, recording, or otherwise—without written permission of the publisher. For information contact North Atlantic Books.

Published by
North Atlantic Books
P.O. Box 12327
Berkeley, California 94712

Cover and book design
© Ayelet Maida, A/M Studios.
Printed in Korea.

Cover photograph courtesy the Bahrain Economic Development Board.
Interior photographs and maps courtesy the Office of Agent of the State of Bahrain before the International Court of Justice.
Timeline of Key Events (p. 103): Originally created by the Office of the Agent for the State of Bahrain before the International Court of Justice; reproduced in the *Bahrain Reply* (1999)
Map No. 5 (p. 258): Reproduced in *Bahrain Memorial* as Map No. 2;
Map No. 6 (p. 273): Reprinted from India Office Library & Records, R/15/1/664;
Map No. 7 (p. 274): Reprinted from *Qatar Reply* Map Atlas, Map No. 71, reprinted from *Ameen Rihani, Ibn Sa'oud of Arabia, His People and His Land*. London: Constable, 1928;
Map No. 8 (p. 275): Reprinted from Ward 1965, viii

A Line in the Sea is sponsored by the Society for the Study of Native Arts and Sciences, a nonprofit educational corporation whose goals are to develop an educational and crosscultural perspective linking various scientific, social, and artistic fields; to nurture a holistic view of arts, sciences, humanities, and healing; and to publish and distribute literature on the relationship of mind, body, and nature.

> North Atlantic Books' publications are available through most bookstores. For further information, call 800-337-2665 or visit our website at www.northatlanticbooks.com.
>
> Substantial discounts on bulk quantities are available to corporations, professional associations, and other organizations. For details and discount information, contact our special sales department.

Library of Congress Cataloging-in-Publication Data
Al-Arayed, Jawad Salim.
   A line in the sea : the Qatar versus Bahrain border dispute in the World Court / By Jawad Salim Al-Arayed.
       p. cm.
   Includes bibliographical references and index.
      ISBN 1-55643-464-2 (hc.)
   1. Qatar—Boundaries—Bahrain. 2. Bahrain—Boundaries—Qatar. I. Title: Qatar versus Bahrain border dispute in the World Court. II. Title.
     DS247.Q35A42 2003
     327.536305365'09—dc21   2003000909

1 2 3 4 5 6 7 8 9 / 07 06 05 04 03

Contents

List of Illustrations viii
Preface xi
Introduction xv

Part I—Historical Context

Chapter 1 Early History in the Lower Arabian Gulf 3
    The Setting 3
    Early History 5

Chapter 2 Advent of Western Powers in the Gulf 11
    Portuguese Presence 11
    British Presence and the Emergence of Bahrain
        as a Political Entity 13

Chapter 3 Al-Khalifa Rule of Bahrain, Hasa, and Qatar
Peninsula (Eighteenth and Nineteenth Centuries) 17
    Initial Stages 18
    Authority in the Gulf 20
    External Challenges 27
    Dynastic Struggles 32
    Last Years of Bahrain's Rule in Doha 35

Chapter 4 Life on the Qatar Peninsula 39
    "Human Ecology" of the Qatar Peninsula 39
    The Al-Thani Move toward Prominence 43

Chapter 5 Piracy, the British, and Bahrain's
Emergence as a Political Entity 49
    Piracy and British Moves to Control It 49
    British Recognition of Bahrain as Political Entity 61

Chapter 6 Ottoman Presence and Qatar's
Emergence as a Separate Entity 77
    Ottoman Expansion into Arabia 77
    The Ottomans Arrive in Doha 80
    British–Al-Thani Relations 93
    Ottoman Withdrawal 96
    Establishment of Qatar's Formal Relations with
        Britain—The 1916 Treaty 98
    Minimal Control Characterizes Al-Thani Power
        into the Mid-Twentieth Century 100

Chapter 7 Qatar's Version of Historical Context 105
    Highlights 105
    Qatar's Version of Events 106

Part II—Zubarah

Chapter 8 Founding and Zenith of Zubarah
(1762 to End of Nineteenth Century) 121
  Geography of Zubarah 121
  Founding of Zubarah 123
  Al-Khalifa Take the Bahrain Islands 125

Chapter 9 The Naim: Bahrain's People in Qatar Peninsula 131
  Traditional Way of Life 131
  Nature of Ruler of Bahrain-Naim Relationship: *Ikrimiyyah* 135
  Allegiance to Ruler of Bahrain 136

Chapter 10 Ottoman Attempts to Take Control of Zubarah 141
  Continued Bahrain Rule over Zubarah 141
  Ottoman Attempts to Extend Their Authority to Zubarah 143
  Recognition by Third Parties 152

Chapter 11 Zubarah in the Early Twentieth Century 159
  Zubarah Remains an Integral Part of Bahrain 159
  Emergence of Oil as a Major Force in the Gulf 162

Chapter 12 Qatar Captures Zubarah—July 1937 181
  The Attack on Zubarah 181
  Aftermath of Attack 191
  Mediation Efforts (1944, 1950) 195

Chapter 13 Qatar's Version of Events in Zubarah 203
  Highlights 203
  Qatar's Version of Events 205

Part III—The Hawar Islands

Chapter 14 Dowasir Tribe and Occupation
of the Hawar Islands 221
  Geography 221
  Dowasir Patterns of Living and Economic Activities 226

Chapter 15 Bahrain Authority as Manifested in Hawar 241
  Affirmation of Al-Khalifa Authority 241
  The Dowasir Incident 253

Chapter 16 British and Ottoman Recognition of Bahrain's
Authority over the Hawars 255
  British and Ottoman Recognition 255
  International Treaties (Early Twentieth Century) 261
  British Recognition in Official Reports
    (Early Twentieth Century) 264

Chapter 17 Oil Concessions in the Hawars 267
  Britain and the U.S. Vie for Oil 267

Chapter 18	British Adjudication of Sovereignty over the Hawars	281
	The Oil War Heats Up	281
	The Arbitration	284
	Affirmation of Validity of the 1939 Award	301
	Continued Development of the Hawars	302
Chapter 19	Qatar's Version of the Hawar Situation	305
	Highlights	305
	Qatar's Version of Events	307

Part IV—Resolution of the Dispute

Chapter 20	Steps toward Resolution	325
	GCC Mediation—1976 through 1990	326
	ICJ Jurisdiction Phase	331
	ICJ Merits Phase	337
Chapter 21	The Forged Documents	355
	Discovery of the Forgeries	355
	Preliminary Investigation	357
	Further Verification by International Experts	362
	Submission of Experts' Reports to the Court	386
	Withdrawal of Documents	388
	Qatar Claims Supported by the Forgeries	390
	Wider Significance of the Forgeries	392
Chapter 22	The Judgment	395
	The Court's Decision	395
	Prominent Personalities	407
	Rulers of Bahrain and Qatar	413
	Bibliographical Note	417
	List of References	421
	Index	445

Illustrations

Forgery Graphics

"OK" and Purported British Seal on Forged Document
 QM III.7 364
Floral "G" Seal Attributed to German Ambassador
 on Forged Document QM III.46 376
Script Continuation and Matching Edges on Separate
 Forged Documents QM III.20 and QM IV.9 377
Script Continuation and Matching Edges on Separate
 Forged Documents QM III.201 and QM III.215 378
Script Continuation and Matching Edges on Separate
 Forged Documents QM III.25 and IV.11 378
Matching Edges on Separate Forged Documents
 QM III.100 and QM III.69 379
Detail Showing Matching Edges and Watermark
 Continuation on Separate Forged Documents
 QM III.100 and QM III.69 379
Document with Indented Lines where Writing
 Violates Lines on Forged Document QM III.21
 (Front and Reverse) 381
Comparison of Genuine and Forged Belgrave Signatures:
 Belgrave Genuine Signature Likely Used to Produce
 Forged Signatures, and from Forged Documents
 QM III.140, III.151, and IV.59 382
Comparison of Genuine and Forged Seal Impressions
 by Sheikh Isa bin Ali Al-Khalifa: Seal from Authentic
 Letter and from Forged Document QM III.49 384
Comparison of Houghton's Seal Originally Designed
 in 1990, with a Seal Used on a Qatari Forged
 Document Dated 120 Years Earlier
 (Houghton original and from QM IV.10) 388

Maps

Map No. 1: Disputed Region Showing 1947 HMG Line xvii
Map No. 2: Place Names in India and the Middle East 4
Map No. 3: Bahrain and Qatar 122
Map No. 4: The Zubarah Region with Place Names 134

Map No. 5: Extract from Map by Captain Izzet
   of the Ottoman Imperial Army, 1878 258
Map No. 6: Map Accompanying 1923 Draft Concession 273
Map No. 7: Map Prepared by Major Holmes, 1923 274
Map No. 8: Ward Map, 1924 275
Map No. 9: Bahrain and Qatar—
   Various Maritime Boundary Lines 398

Tables

Timeline of Key Events 103
Rulers of Bahrain: Periods of Rule 415

To the people of Bahrain

Preface

Qatar and Bahrain's border dispute before the International Court of Justice began in 1991 and ended with the Court's final decision on 16 March 2001. But the dispute had simmered—and sometimes boiled over—for more than fifty years before that. Much of the dispute was played out against the backdrop of first discoveries of oil in the Arabian Gulf, and the rush by oil companies, foreign powers, and the leaders of the Gulf nations to find and exploit those lucrative assets. The roots of the dispute lie tangled within the history of British and Ottoman involvements in the Arabian Gulf, and the political destinies of the emerging Gulf States.

This book was written to document some of the historical work done by the staff of my office, and by experts employed by the State of Bahrain, in order to present its case before the International Court. Beginning in the summer of 1996 and continuing until the day the Court rendered its decision in 2001, we carried out historical and other research relevant to this case. The persons whose efforts rendered those years of work into this manuscript were Dr. Beth Olsen, Ms. Iva Kratchanova, Ms. Maisoon Al-Arayed, Dr. Bruce Manzer, and Ms. Jeanette Harding.

I wish to extend my appreciation to all of those involved in research, preparation, and execution of Bahrain's case before the International Court. I am grateful to HE Sheikh Mohammed bin Mubarak Al-Khalifa, the Minister of Foreign Affairs who chaired the Ministerial Steering Committee which guided our efforts throughout, and to the Foreign Ministry staff. I am also indebted for the tireless efforts of all those who joined together in a six-year effort to successfully bring

Bahrain's case before the International Court—my Ministry of State office staff and the many people from various government agencies and Bahraini companies who worked with them, and Bahrain's legal team headed by Jan Paulsson of Freshfields.

I also wish to express my gratitude to the King of Bahrain, His Majesty Sheikh Hamad bin Isa Al-Khalifa, to the Prime Minister, His Highness Sheikh Khalifa bin Salman Al-Khalifa, and to the Crown Prince, His Highness Sheikh Salman bin Hamad Al-Khalifa. It is only through their wisdom, trust, and generous support during the entire duration of this Case that our efforts achieved their aim.

JAWAD SALIM AL-ARAYED

Having acquired for themselves over the past two decades a goodly share of the luxuries and necessities the world has to offer, including the obligatory quota of technological marvels just mentioned, the Qataris have of late been equipping themselves with a history and an indigenous culture, both of noble proportions. The showpiece of this particular enterprise is a "national museum," housed in the former (*c.* 1920) palace of the ruler in Dauhah [Doha]. Largely an inspiration of a public relations firm in London, the museum has been equipped and adorned at a cost of several millions, despite—or perhaps because of—the fundamental limitation of having very little to put into it... It is not the fault of the Qataris that they have no history, nor can it be held against them that they would like to invent one—though it is doubtful whether most of them care one way or another about the past. What is objectionable about these public-relations exercises on behalf of the Qatari regime is that they involve the falsification of the historical record over the past two centuries, notably concerning the nature and length of Bahrain's connexion with Qatar, the relationship between the Al Thani and the Ottoman Turks, and the character and exploits of the best-known member of the line, Jasim ibn Muhammad Al Thani, who was far from being the heroic paragon that modern hagiography has made him out to be.

J. B. KELLY,
*Arabia, the Gulf and
the West* (1980), p. 191.

Introduction

Historically, political affairs in the Middle East have proven to be among the world's most complex and at times contentious. Due in no small part to the nomadic nature of the region's "human geography," numerous territorial disputes between sovereign powers have arisen during the past several centuries. Among the most difficult of these border disputes has been one long festering between the Arabian Gulf nations of Bahrain and Qatar, and recently adjudicated by the International Court of Justice, concerning various Gulf territories, including the Hawar Islands. Within these covers we will endeavor to chart the history of the Bahrain-Qatar controversy and clarify the major issues it precipitated.

Prior to 1971 the Mideast regions of Bahrain and Qatar both were in fact British protected states; that is, Britain was responsible for their international protection and for the conduct of their foreign affairs. This relationship ended in 1971, when Britain decided to terminate its special treaty relations in the Middle East, including those with Bahrain and Qatar, where it had been a dominant power for more than 150 years.

An Exchange of Notes was concluded between Britain and Bahrain on 15 August 1971, and between Britain and Qatar on 3 September 1971. Bahrain and Qatar then accordingly assumed full responsibility for the conduct of their own foreign affairs, becoming members of the United Nations and parties to the Statute of the International Court of Justice on 21 September 1971. The political structures of the two countries, heretofore largely established by Britain, now became susceptible to change.

The Dispute

The British, through their Political Agents and Residents, had mediated disputes within and between the two states up to this point, until their departure in 1971. This included mediations regarding the long-standing territorial dispute between Bahrain and Qatar over the Zubarah region on the Qatar peninsula, the Hawar Islands, and delimitation of the maritime boundary between the two countries including various maritime features in the body of water separating the two countries.

The dispute over ownership of the Hawar Islands became critical in the 1930s, when competitive interest in oil in the Gulf began to simmer. The British government, with the consent of both parties, finally adjudicated this dispute in 1938–39, and found that the Hawar Islands belonged to Bahrain—a decision never accepted by Qatar. Bahrain's Zubarah claim continued to simmer long after Qatar's attack on, and occupation of, Zubarah in 1937. Throughout the 1940s and into the 1950s the Ruler of Bahrain made every effort to redress this grievance—to no avail.

In 1947, when oil production in the region had resumed after World War II, the British were required to make a decision on a maritime boundary between the two states in order to afford oil companies some security. After studying the problems of maritime delimitation and seabed division between Bahrain and Qatar, Britain reaffirmed Bahrain's sovereignty over the Hawars and devised a maritime line, which stood as the de facto boundary until the ICJ judgment of 2001. Neither side accepted all the details of this 1947 decision.

Thus, despite a long history of British mediation and of correspondence involving the two Rulers and various representatives of the British, Bahrain and Qatar entered the 1970s with Qatar's sovereignty over the Zubarah region contested by Bahrain, and Bahrain's ownership of the Hawar Islands and a number of other maritime features contested by Qatar—with no agreed maritime boundary between the two.

But resolution of the problem became imperative by 1990, as failure to resolve it inhibited oil exploration and thus, economic development. By that time, a distinct possibility existed that armed hostilities, which nearly broke out in 1986, might erupt at any time.

In the late 1970s Saudi Arabia and the Gulf Cooperation Council made an effort to mediate the dispute, an effort that ended when Qatar

Note: According to 1947 HMG Line, Qit'at Jaradah and Fasht Al-Dibal were Bahrain enclaves on the east of the Line.

Map No. 1: Disputed Region Showing 1947 HMG Line

took the matter unilaterally to the International Court of Justice in 1991. The case, which became the longest-contested and most extensively documented in the Court's history, concluded with a verdict on 16 March 2001.

This book examines the historical issues and evidence surrounding that dispute. It is not meant to represent a full history of Bahrain, or of the Arabian Gulf region in question; the book does hope to provide illumination about the specific areas involved in the territorial dispute between Bahrain and Qatar.

Following this first chapter, which sets the stage for analysis of the nature of the dispute and efforts to settle it, the work is divided into four broad sections. Each of the first three sections concludes with a summary chapter that includes Qatar's version of events and their arguments presented to the Court.

- The first section, *Historical Context*, examines the historical context of the dispute: the ruling families and the relative scope of their authority in the region, and the influence of foreign powers in the Gulf on the emergence of the political entities of Bahrain and Qatar.
- The second section, *Zubarah*, looks at the issue of the Zubarah region—its historical evolution and Bahrain's continuous exercise of sovereignty there from 1762 until Zubarah's siege and occupation by Qatar in 1937.
- The third section, *The Hawar Islands*, examines in a similar manner Bahrain's occupation and administration of the Hawar Islands to the present time.
- The final section, *Resolution of the Dispute*, deals with various efforts to resolve the dispute—GCC mediations, and the Jurisdiction and Merits phases of the case before the International Court of Justice. It also looks at the forged documents presented to the Court by Qatar in its *Memorial* and *Counter-Memorial* to the ICJ, and with the significance of the Judgment rendered by the International Court of Justice on 16 March 2001.

Historical Context

1 Early History in the Lower Arabian Gulf

The Setting

Climate and water have always been major factors in determining the "human geography" of the Arabian Gulf region. Fresh water is at best scarce for most of the region; and this fact tends to concentrate populations on the coastal regions, and near the few available water sources. Within many areas of the vast inland territories, sparse groups of Bedouin tribes roaming the hinterlands are the only sustainable populations.

The portion of the Arabian coast known as the Qatar peninsula has always been an arid and inhospitable land. The peninsula's south is covered in windblown sands, while the rest of the land is stony and barren, and only a negligible part is arable. Except for desert plants in the north, natural vegetation is nonexistent. Thus, a combination of heat and lack of drinkable underground water, has served to confine human settlement mostly to the coast, where the resources and trade opportunities offered by the sea make survival easier.

In contrast, the main island of Bahrain, with its freshwater springs and natural vegetation, has attracted many a settler. Bahrain island's peculiar hydrological conditions have supported agriculture and—together with Bahrain's strategic location along East-West trade routes and the richness of its fisheries—explain the verdant island's continuous inhabitation throughout the last five millennia.

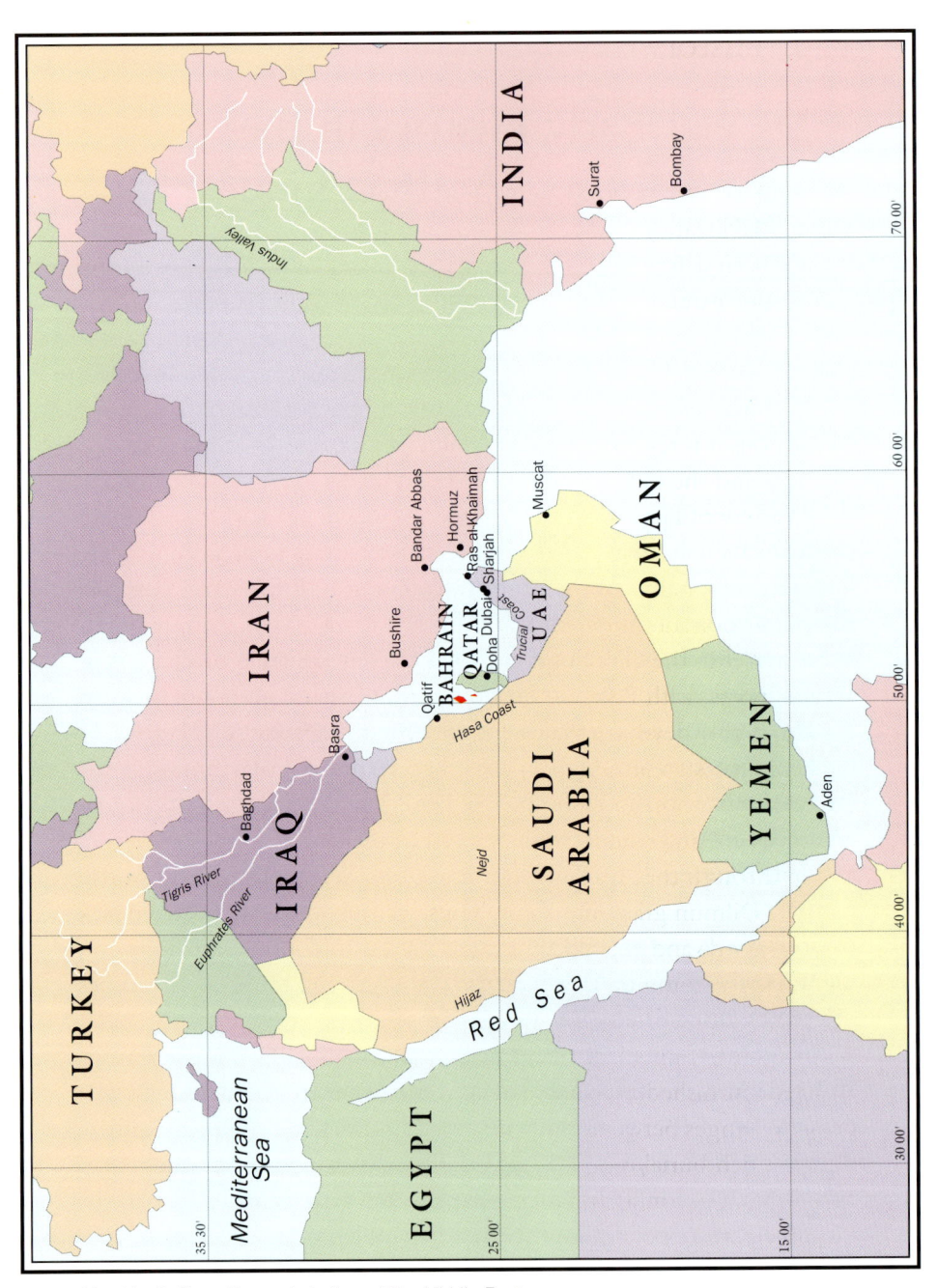

Map No. 2: Place Names in India and the Middle East

Early History

Dilmun

The Bahrain Islands first entered upon the historical stage around 3000 B.C., and for about two thousand years hosted the center of the ancient Dilmun civilization. Although the Dilmun Empire's territorial extent has not been determined with precision, it is known that at various times that empire extended over Bahrain and most of eastern Arabia. The Dilmun Empire was perceived as a sacred land by a number of ancient peoples. In the old Babylonian epic *Gilgamesh*, Dilmun is described as a paradise where the worthiest of people enjoy eternal life. In Sumerian inscriptions it is referred to as the "Land of Paradise," the "Land of the Living," and the "Home of God" (Zahlan 1989, 7).

A variety of factors contributed to such perceptions. Not only did the main Bahrain island enjoy abundant water supplies, fertile soil and lush greenery, but as the center of the Dilmun Empire Bahrain became the center of trade throughout the Arabian Gulf. The intensity of trading activities in the Gulf turned all its main centers into flourishing commercial ports, with Bahrain key among them.

The highly developed civilizations of the Tigris and Euphrates valley created a strong demand for imported goods and stimulated the development of seaborne trade in the Gulf. In the absence of any competing sea or land routes between Mesopotamia and India, commercial traffic through the Arabian Gulf was constantly on the increase. The ports of Dilmun gradually assumed the dual functions of entrepôts for foreign goods and exporters of local merchandise. Dates and pearls—the principal commodities produced by Dilmun—were traded, along with agricultural products from Mesopotamia and spices and raw materials from the Indus Valley and Oman.

Trade furnished a channel not only for commercial, but also for cultural exchanges between Mesopotamia and Dilmun. Archeological evidence—rich burial mounds and monuments in both present-day Iraq and Bahrain—confirms the links between the two civilizations, along with the complex organization of their societies. On the main island of Bahrain, the ruins of an ancient city dating back to those times can still be seen near the village of Saar, and another city, nowadays known as Qal'at Al-Bahrain, existed in the north of the island. Archeologists have discovered streets, houses, workshops, and a temple, all demonstrating that the inhabitants of Dilmun were prosperous enough to look beyond their daily subsistence needs and to develop their cities into busy cultural and religious centers.

In contrast, the Bedouin populations of the Arabian interior were prevented by hostile natural environments from achieving the advanced level of development that characterized coastal trading communities in the Gulf region. Even in the early days, tribes of the Arabian hinterland shared little in terms of economic, social, or cultural patterns with the coastal populations. The Bedouins were insular nomads of the desert; the coastal peoples were sea-oriented merchants living in settled communities. It is easy to understand why in such circumstances inhabitants of the trading cities in Mesopotamia and Dilmun had much more in common, despite their geographical distance, than either had with the tribes wandering in the interior.

Another characteristic of the region has persisted throughout the ages: the domination of sea over land. From the time of the Dilmun Empire, coastal settlements have been the focus of commercial activity and social development, while desert areas have been either sparsely populated by nomadic peoples or uninhabited. Tribes living in the coastal cities and villages have typically enjoyed greater wealth as well as social and cultural interactions with other regions. The coastal tribes have been the ones that defined the identity of larger socio-political units in the region—the territorial extent of such units being determined by tribal and intertribal relations between the settled populations of the coast and the nomadic communities of the desert. The Dilmun Empire represented a classic example of a regional power whose population was concentrated on the main Bahrain Island, and whose mainland possessions included the Qatar peninsula and the Hasa coast of Arabia.

The decline of the Dilmun Empire around 1600 B.C. was related to the emergence of alternative trade routes linking the north and the east. One of those was the Red Sea route that connected India to the Mediterranean Sea via the Red Sea, and gave access not only to the rich markets of Egypt and the Mediterranean, but also to Western markets. Land routes and caravan traffic across Arabia were also developed—owing to the domestication of the camel and the creation of saddles suitable for carrying goods. The period of 1800–1600 B.C. also saw the fall of the

Indus Valley civilization—a development that deprived Gulf traders of an important source of merchandise. Economically weakened, Dilmun became a tributary of Assyria at the end of the second millennium B.C., and, after a brief period of renewed prosperity, Dilmun was absorbed by the Babylonians by about 600 B.C.

Tylos

Recorded history provides little information about events in the Gulf in the two centuries that followed. However, it is known that in the late fourth century B.C. Nearchus (of Alexander the Great's army) established a colony on Failaka Island (in present-day Kuwait), and his explorations of the Gulf reached at least as far as Bahrain. The main island of Bahrain was then given the Greek name of Tylos, by which it was known until the seventh century A.D. Archeological evidence is insufficient to reconstruct the history of the islands during that time. Among the few known facts, however, are that pearling continued to be a traditional occupation and source of income, and that Tylos enjoyed a reasonable level of prosperity.

Following the death of Alexander the Great in 323 B.C. and the breakup of his Empire, Bahrain fell under the influence of one of the Empire's successors, the Seleucid state. The Seleucids' reach extended over the whole of Alexander's eastern territories and encompassed most of the lands between the Indus Valley and the Euphrates. It is not known whether or to what extent Tylos was actually ruled by the Seleucids, or by their successors, the Parthians.

Another power, the Sassanian Empire, succeeded the Parthian state some time in the third century A.D. and, in the fourth century A.D., the Sassanians drew the Bahrain Islands into their orbit. At that time, the culture of Tylos came to reflect a variety of influences—mostly Persian and Greek, and a number of religions co-existed, among which Zoroastrianism, Nestorianism and Judaism were well represented (Savory 1980a, 8–13).

The main Bahrain island continued to exercise its influence over surrounding islands. Sassanian sources mention, for instance, that the city of Darin on Tarut island (off the east coast of Arabia) was considered part of Bahrain. The adjacent coast of the Arabian Peninsula, the Hasa Coast, was also under Bahrain's control. For its part, the Qatar peninsula was perceived to be no more than an extension of the Arabian coast. Both the settlements and the activities of the Qatar peninsula's inhabitants, if any, were so insignificant, they did not provoke a single reference to be made in the recorded history of the times.

Awal

Gulf trade routes regained their importance around the beginning of the seventh century A.D., when Greek influence in the region waned and the faith of Islam emerged as a new force that was to leave an imprint on every aspect of Gulf society in the centuries to come. Armed with their new beliefs, the Arabs who comprised the early Islamic community were able to gain control of Arabia and the Gulf region and to reach as far as the Mediterranean. Religious fervor went hand in hand with economic considerations. The lands conquered by Arab armies were brought into a common commercial sphere; many old trading centers regained their past prominence, while new ones, most notably Basra, were also established.

In those early Islamic times, Bahrain, controlled by the Bani Abdul-Qais tribe, comprised the main island, which had come to be known as Awal, as well the surrounding islands and the eastern coast of Arabia. The Al-Qais converted to Islam in A.D. 640—an event that reaffirmed Bahrain's place in the religious, political, and economic structures in the Gulf. Once again, Bahrain was an important trading hub, its prosperity increasing as Arabs' trading activities expanded to China, the Indian Ocean, and later to Indonesia and Malaysia.

From the ninth to the eleventh centuries Bahrain was controlled by the Umayyad caliphs and, later, by the Abbasids. Initially, strong government in Baghdad ensured stability and favorable conditions for trade. This situation was, however, reversed with the formation of different sects within Islam and by the outbreak of several revolts. The first of these significant events was the insurrection of the Zinj slaves (who claimed to be descendants of the Prophet Mohammed) in A.D. 869. This revolt started near Basra, but the rebels found support among tribes from Iraq and Bahrain, and in 871 their forces sacked Basra and plundered Mesopotamia and Bahrain.

Basra was again sacked in 923—this time by the followers of a religious movement known as the Carmathians. Based in Bahrain, the

Carmathians, who belonged to the Ismaili tradition in Islam, spread their beliefs by both sending emissaries throughout the Muslim world and by waging war on their opponents. Their raids on Basra, Baghdad, Mecca and Medina seriously disrupted the balance in the region, and for most of the tenth century, the Carmathians were considered the ultimate power in the Middle East. They were known to collect tribute from the Caliph of Baghdad and a rival imam in Cairo, and their influence was felt as far south as Oman and as far north as Egypt (Salim A. Al-Arayed 2001, 9–10; Savory 1980, 14–18).

By the beginning of the eleventh century, however, Carmathian control over the region had declined and the old centers of power had reestablished their importance. Bahrain was ruled by a governor who owed nominal allegiance to the Caliph of Baghdad and whose authority extended over a portion of the Arabian mainland. Records of the time testify that trade continued to be the main occupation of Bahrain's local population and their main source of income. Al-Idrisi, an Arab geographer writing in the twelfth century, described the "people of the two banks" as enjoying relative prosperity and being satisfied with their ruler.

Throughout the three thousand years since the beginnings of the Dilmun era, Bahrain enjoyed two important characteristics that kept it both relatively affluent and influential. One was Bahrain's central role in commercial relations with other cities in the Arabian Gulf. Although political and economic configurations shifted constantly, imported goods were always in demand by the population centers. Being strategically located on Gulf trade routes, Bahrain was assured a role as an important element in the web of commercial relations. In addition, Bahraini pearls were a commodity widely traded throughout the Middle East, and pearling continued to be an industry that employed a large percentage of Bahrainis. Thus, whether engaged in trading or pearl fishing, the majority of Bahrain's inhabitants had a source of relatively constant income that enabled them to maintain a certain level of well-being.

The second important characteristic was the concentration of population on both the main island and the adjacent Hasa coast of the Arabian Peninsula. The tribes inhabiting the mainland were an integral part of the social, political, and economic organization of Bahrain and were influenced as much as islanders themselves by developments on the main Bahraini island of Awal. So, regardless of whether Bahrain was independently governed or part of a larger empire, it continued to be perceived as a strategic geopolitical unit encompassing both islands and land territories.

2 | Advent of Western Powers in the Gulf

Portuguese Presence

The Portuguese were the first to reach the Arabian Gulf. Technological advances in shipbuilding that resulted in the creation of vessels equipped for long voyages made this possible. A landmark event—Vasco da Gama's successful 1498 circumnavigation of Africa and arrival in India—ushered in an era of continued European interest in the region. Inspired by the opportunities afforded by the Eastern trade, the Portuguese set about establishing trading stations along the coasts of India and China, and securing a permanent presence in Asia. Gradually, they spread their influence to the Arabian Gulf, thus challenging local Arabs' control of the Gulf trade routes.

To achieve supremacy in the Gulf, the Portuguese seized key strategic points and then maintained a military presence. Following the capture of Aden and Hormuz at the beginning of the sixteenth century, the Portuguese turned their attention to Bahrain and established both a military outpost and a trading station on the islands. Neither the economic nor the military value of controlling Bahrain was lost on the conquerors: pearling was still a profitable industry, while the position of Bahrain halfway between Hormuz and the mouth of the Gulf in the North offered both commercial and military advantages.

But before long a significant challenge to Portugal's position in the region came from the Ottomans. In the aftermath of the 1534 capture of Baghdad by Ottoman Sultan Suleiman the Magnificent, the Ottomans' next logical step was to seek further expansion into the Gulf. They realized—as indeed the Portuguese had a century earlier—that domination over the region necessarily involved control over key trading and military posts. So Bahrain, along with Hormuz and other commercial centers, once again became the focus of imperial rivalries.

In the early 1550s, a number of Ottoman-Portuguese clashes occurred, allowing the Sublime Porte (as the Ottoman government was known, taking its name from the High Gate to the Grand Vezir's offices) to extend its influence over Muscat and, briefly, over Qatif. However, Ottoman efforts to seize the two major strategic ports of Hormuz and Bahrain were unsuccessful. Following their abortive attempt at taking Bahrain in 1556 and a few later confrontations with the Portuguese, the Ottomans acknowledged Portuguese supremacy over the waters of the Gulf.

Yet though the Bahrain Islands were never annexed by the Ottoman Empire, the latter remained an important influence in the region. At times, the Rulers of Bahrain themselves were tempted to switch their allegiance to the Porte. One reason behind such intentions was that the Ottomans and the majority of Bahrainis shared a common religion. Another reason was Portuguese forces' brutality and oppression of the local population. The Portuguese ruled with unrestrained force and missed no opportunity to enrich themselves—whether by maintaining trading activities or by plundering the territories under their control.

The Portuguese conquerors' interest in Bahrain confirmed that Bahrain offered significant opportunities as a trading and pearling center. Its economic development, coupled with its strategic location in the Arabian Gulf, made it a territory coveted by foreign powers, and the Portuguese perceived it as worth the risk of confrontations with competing empires. But the Qatar peninsula remained outside the Portuguese sphere of interest; its lack of resources and uninviting landscape had little to offer to an Empire that was seeking commercial expansion. Significantly, the Qatar peninsula is the only territory in the Arabian Gulf where no ruins related to the period of Portuguese domination have been found.

Throughout the sixteenth century, the attitudes of the Portuguese conquerors met with strong Bahraini opposition. In 1602 this resulted in the Portuguese forces' expulsion from Bahrain. The event triggering this development was the execution of a member of one of the richest local families, after which the victim's brother headed a rebellion against the oppressors and ultimately succeeded in driving them out of Bahrain. In order to secure their newly achieved independence from Portugal, Bahrainis sought the protection of the Persian Empire—a move that brought them back into the Persian sphere of influence (Savory 1980, 20–31; Salim A. Al-Arayed 2001, 22–25; Zahlan 1979, 26–27).

The Portuguese influence, however, did not leave the same indelible impression as did the two succeeding European powers in the Gulf—the British and the Ottomans—for it was within the context of British and Ottoman presence in the Gulf that the political structures, as well as the territorial boundaries, of the present-day states of Bahrain and Qatar took shape. These two powers not only significantly influenced the emergence of the authority systems that characterize the sheikhdoms to the present day; they also provided the mechanisms for Bahrain and Qatar's recognition as international "players."

These developments, however, did not occur by the same means throughout the Gulf. In Bahrain, the already-established political authority of the Al-Khalifa was reinforced by the Ruling family's dealings with the British, while in Qatar the very emergence of the Al-Thani as a Ruling dynasty was only triggered, assisted and given final form by foreign powers.

British Presence and the Emergence of Bahrain as a Political Entity

The eventual end of Portuguese hegemony in the Gulf resulted largely from the increased involvement there of other European powers, most notably Britain. Starting in the late sixteenth century, Britain gradually assumed the role of an important player in the region. Following a number of successful voyages to the Orient and the grant of a Royal Charter to the British East India Company in 1600, British merchants emerged as the principal rival of the Portuguese—initially in respect to the Indian trade, and later, the Gulf trade.

Under the 1600 Charter, the British East India Company was granted a monopoly over trade on three continents, Asia, Africa and America. Its Governor and directors—the latter typically selected from among its stockholders—supervised and managed the company's activities. Throughout the seventeenth century, the Company was mainly interested in maintaining and expanding its commercial presence in the East. An explicit provision existed in its Charter whereby it was prevented from infringing on the trading rights of other European powers in the region. However, Portuguese, Dutch and French merchants soon found themselves outrivaled and displaced from their established spheres of influence.

British economic expansion involved concluding agreements with local rulers in order to secure specific privileges for British operations in the East. After establishing their first trading stations in India, the British moved on to expand their activities into the Arabian Gulf. The Company's main trading posts in the Middle East, called "Residencies," were at Bushire, Basra, and Bandar Abbas, and were subordinate to the Headquarters at Surat and later, Bombay. The British East India Company resorted to military action when required. However, any such military involvement was restricted in scope to protecting British commercial interests from European competitors and from local pirates, rather than to achieving political objectives.

That situation changed at the beginning of the eighteenth century when political domination of the Gulf came as a natural corollary of increased British trading activities. By then, it had become obvious that Gulf trade offered Great Britain fewer opportunities for enrichment than did trade with India. Nevertheless, the importance of the Gulf increased as the British recognized that the success of their Eastern trade depended on the safety of Gulf trade routes; for it was clear that the security situation in the region was affected by two interrelated elements—the stability of local political alliances and the successful suppression of piratical activities.

The security of commercial traffic was a reason for growing British concern at the turn of the eighteenth century. Political developments—most notably, the decline of the Safavid dynasty in Persia—had provided an opportunity for local rulers to seek autonomy, as well as territorial expansion. The resulting breakdown of order in the region led to the departure or restructuring of many European companies. The focus of European commercial activities in the region shifted from the traditional centers of Safavid power—Bandar Abbas and Basra—to areas in modern day Iraq.

Political anarchy on land led to the deterioration of security by sea, as the Safavids sought to reclaim what had belonged to their Empire, and attacked the ports and fleets of newly independent rulers. Bahrain was among the places most bitterly contested. In 1722, it fell into the hands of the Yaaribah tribe of Oman, but was thirty years later recaptured by the Persians. Intertribal warfare also marked a number of other areas in the Gulf that had previously belonged to the Safavids. With these conflicts, commercial traffic suffered and European companies' interests were seriously threatened.

To make matters worse, piracy, which had been present in the Arabian Gulf since at least the eighth century, increased in scale, both Arab and European pirates contributing to this state of lawlessness, thus adding to the dangers of navigation in the region. European pirates' activities reached a peak following the departure of the Portuguese from Oman in the middle of the seventeenth century.

3

Al-Khalifa Rule of Bahrain, Hasa, and Qatar Peninsula (Eighteenth and Nineteenth Centuries)

The emergence of Bahrain as a political entity in the early nineteenth century and of Qatar in the early twentieth century, as well as the definition of their territorial extent, took place in a context of not only British and Ottoman presence in the region but also of shifting tribal alliances and struggles for regional domination. The late eighteenth and early nineteenth centuries were marked by the establishment and initial consolidation by the Al-Khalifa of their control over the Qatar peninsula and the Bahrain Islands—a process that met with a variety of challenges, both internal and external. The Al-Thani, for their part, came to the scene in the late nineteenth century when they transformed from merchants to chiefs of Doha.

This chapter and the following chronicle the rise of the ruling families of Bahrain and Qatar and the development, nature, and geographical extent of their authority. These chapters demonstrate Bahrain's emergence as a political entity much earlier than Qatar, and Bahrain's sovereignty over the areas involved in the dispute. The two chapters also discuss the influence of British and Ottoman presence in the Gulf on these developments and the recognition of Bahrain's status and sovereignty.

Initial Stages

Establishment of Zubarah

In the modern history of Bahrain, special importance is attached to the year 1762—the year in which members of the Al-Utub tribe, led by Mohammed bin Khalifa Al-Khalifa, migrated to the western coast of the Qatar peninsula and founded the town of Zubarah. The Al-Khalifa comprised one of the three Al-Utub tribe branches that had in 1613 jointly established the settlement Kuwait that later evolved into the present day emirate. Responsible mainly for the commercial activities of the new settlement at Kuwait, the Al-Khalifa had attained a level of prosperity and experience that inspired them to seek further expansion and commercial opportunities. Thus in 1762, they left Kuwait and settled in the north of the Qatar peninsula, where Gulf trade and the pearling industry held promise of considerable wealth.

Within a few years, the Al-Khalifa had firmly established their presence in Zubarah. Mohammed bin Khalifa, a shrewd and artful leader, was able to assert both his commercial and political interests. Through a combination of persuasion and monetary incentives, he obtained a significant share of the pearl fisheries in the area, thus acquiring a reliable source of income. In addition, he encouraged the remaining members of his tribe to relocate to Zubarah from Kuwait, and succeeded in uniting them under his leadership. Zubarah then became the Al-Khalifa center of power—a role that it played for three decades.

The Al-Khalifa Sheikh was careful to maintain amicable relations with his former associates in Kuwait, as well as with neighboring tribes. He granted his protection to the Al-Jalahimah, another section of the Al-Utub tribe, who had expressed their willingness to migrate to Zubarah. Shortly after the Al-Jalahimah's arrival, however, tensions arose between the two tribes; the Al-Jalahimah then resettled in a nearby village where they embarked on maritime warfare and were finally defeated by the Al-Khalifa. In their struggle with the Al-Jalahimah, the Al-Khalifa were greatly assisted by local merchants and members of other tribes of the Qatar peninsula.

The Al-Khalifa Sheikh also invited the Al-Naim tribe of Oman to settle in his territories, and with their help he drove away the Al-Musallam, who were in control of most of the Qatar peninsula at the time. By the 1780s, the Al-Khalifa had extended their influence over most of the peninsula. Their power and wealth were rapidly increasing, as merchants and settlers were moving to the flourishing towns under their control. In addition to being a major pearling center, Zubarah had by that time also become the focus of Arab trade with India. Moreover, the Persian occupation of Basra in 1776–79 had provided further impetus to the development of Al-Khalifa territories in the northwest of the Qatar peninsula to counter the Persian strengths.

Bahrain Comes into the Al-Khalifa Sphere

This state of affairs was bound to raise concerns on the opposite shore of the Gulf. As Al-Khalifa power increased, so did the anxieties of the Persian government. By the mid-1770s, Persian rulers grew determined to destroy their Al-Khalifa rivals, and between 1777–81, several unsuccessful assaults were launched on Zubarah under the leadership of Sheikh Nasir bin Madkhur (also known as Nasir of Bushire and Bahrain). The Al-Khalifa retaliated in 1782 by attacking the main Bahrain island.

In the aftermath of Al-Khalifa withdrawal, the Persians prepared a new military expedition. They set up a maritime blockade of the port of Zubarah, and, following the failure of the talks initiated by their rivals, the Persians landed in the Al-Khalifa stronghold. Their forces, combined with those of Sheikh Rashid of Ras Al-Khaimah and of a number of petty rulers on the Arab coast, numbered two thousand men. But the Al-Khalifa had prepared: as soon as the assailants were on shore, they were met with a force much stronger than they had expected. In the fighting that ensued, the Persians and their allies suffered heavy losses and were ultimately defeated and forced to flee to their ships.

On 28 July 1783, with the help of the Naim and other tribes of the Qatar peninsula, and with the assistance of the Al-Sabah of Kuwait, the Al-Khalifa attacked the Persian garrison in Bahrain and expelled the Persians. The threat from the north thus having been removed, the Al-Khalifa ruler—Sheikh Ahmed bin Mohammed Al-Khalifa, who came to be known as Ahmed the Conqueror—returned to his capital, Zubarah.

During the next ten years, a representative of the Al-Khalifa Sheikh governed the Bahrain Islands, and Al-Khalifa rule was quickly consolidated. The Al-Jalahimah, who had been among the Al-Khalifa's allies, were, as earlier in history, dissatisfied with the amount of the compensation granted to them. Leaving the islands, they retired to Khor Hassan and returned to the piratical activities of their predecessors.

In 1796, the Al-Khalifa moved their seat of power from Zubarah to the main island of Bahrain. A primary reason was security: the islands were easier to defend, whereas Zubarah remained vulnerable to overland attacks by Bedouin and other tribes. In addition, the availability of fresh water and natural vegetation, plus a significant population base, made the islands much more attractive than the Qatar peninsula.

With the permanent establishment of the Al-Khalifa Court on the main island of Bahrain, a new structure of governance of Al-Khalifa territories was instituted. The Al-Khalifa Sheikhs ruled the islands, while a governor was appointed to administer Zubarah under Al-Khalifa guidance. In addition, Al-Khalifa control over the remaining portion of the Qatar peninsula continued to be exercised through the allegiance of local tribes. Thus, by the end of the eighteenth century, the Al-Khalifa had consolidated their position as the ruling dynasty of the Bahrain Islands and the Qatar peninsula (Warden 1856, 362–66; A. B. Kemball 1844, 140–41; Lorimer 1908–15, 1:787–88; F. B. Prideaux, 16 July 1905; Khuri 1980, 22–26).

Authority in the Gulf

Until the beginning of the 1870s, when the Ottomans arrived in Eastern Arabia, the Al-Khalifa ruled over the Bahrain Islands, the Qatar peninsula, and the Hasa (eastern) coast of Arabia. Although it would be difficult to apply the concept of sovereignty as understood in Europe to the Gulf region in the nineteenth century, Al-Khalifa authority was exercised in accordance with traditional patterns of governance in the region.

As in Europe, one important characteristic of such authority was the ability to effectively control certain territories. The approach to defining territory differed, however. In the Gulf area, determination of a ruler's possessions focused on the populations loyal to that ruler and the areas such populations inhabited, rather than on fixed physical boundaries per se. Indeed, Gulf rulers' primary consideration was domination over local tribal structures, whereas domination over territory was considered more a derivative and a result of the allegiance of members of loyal tribes. Relations between rulers and their subjects involved varying degrees of control and were, in many cases, rather loosely defined (Joffé 1994, 79–87).

What Does "Control" Actually Mean in the Arabian Gulf Region?
The Ruler of Bahrain maintained ties with the Naim tribe and the Zubarah region despite Ottoman efforts to alter that state of affairs. The difficulty, however, lies in determining the exact nature of that relationship during this period. Did it actually constitute the authority or "sovereignty" of the Ruler of Bahrain over the Naim?

Western notions of sovereignty emphasize that it is:

> The power to do everything in a state without accountability, to make laws to execute and to apply them, to impose and collect taxes and levy contributions, to make war or peace, to form treaties of alliance or of commerce with foreign nations, and the like. (*Black's Law Dictionary,* 6th ed., *s.v.* "Sovereignty")

In addition Westerners stress that

> Sovereignty in government is that public authority which directs or orders what is to be done by each member associated in relation to the end of association. It is the supreme power by which any citizen is governed and is the person or body of persons in the state to whom there is politically no superior. The necessary existence of the state and that right and power which necessarily follow is "sovereignty." By "sovereignty" in its largest sense is meant supreme, absolute, uncontrollable power, the absolute right to govern. The word which by itself comes nearest to being the definition of "sovereignty" is will or volition as applied to political affairs. *(ibid.)*

On the other hand, "sovereignty" as practiced in the Gulf region prior to and during the Ottoman period depended on the concepts of tribal *dirah* (the territory over which a tribe moves) and *ikrimiyyah* (the system of benefits received by important Arab tribes from their Rulers). (For more on *dirah* and *ikrimiyyah,* see Chapter 9.)

Both concepts shared at least one common element—the ability to effectively control certain territories.

Governance of the Bahrain Islands

Al-Khalifa authority took two forms: first, direct administration by members of the ruling dynasty and their allies, and second, rule through coalition with local tribes while the Al-Khalifa maintained the status of supreme political ruler. Examples of direct governance were found mainly on the Bahrain Islands, which were inhabited by merchant and agriculturalist communities. The arrival of the Al-Khalifa and their associates led to an expansion of the population of the islands, and to social and economic restructuring. Though sea trade, pearl production and date palm cultivation remained the primary occupations of local inhabitants, the new organization of economic life resulted in a redistribution of wealth and, consequently, power.

In this region, the ability to project political and economic influence was closely related to control over resources. Direct ruling involvement by the Al-Khalifa depended primarily on their perceptions as to how efficiently resources were used. Thus, whether certain social groups were closely regulated or allowed relative autonomy depended on the segments of the economy with which they were associated.

Agriculture was one area perceived as requiring direct administration and close oversight in order to maximize potential economic benefits, so those communities engaged in palm cultivation and other agricultural activities were therefore tightly controlled. In this sphere, the Al-Khalifa family acted as both rulers and landlords. Although cultivated land was considered the collective property of the regime, estates were distributed to different members of the ruling family for management (Khuri 1980, 43).

Estates were administered through a *wazir* selected by the landlord sheikh, with the help of a number of other proxies. Although no standardized bureaucratic offices existed, the landlord's administration dealt with almost any matter related to the estate. In addition to the *wazir*, the administration also comprised *kikhda*'s (tax collectors) and *fidawi*'s (enforcement officers). The landholder, on his part, acted as a ruler in his estate, collecting taxes, settling disputes and protecting the population.

In his tasks, the landlord was assisted not only by his administrative staff but also by the *majlis,* or local council. The *majlis* represented meeting places for discussions of current affairs, lobbying, and negotiations. Their competence extended over a large array of legal, economic, and political matters, and their role in the management of economic resources was significant. In addition to the sheikh who typically headed a certain council, meetings were attended by relatives, associates, and consultants. Such gatherings frequently went beyond their formally assigned roles as consultation forums and assumed the functions of decision-making bodies.

No centralization or hierarchy existed among different *majlis*. Due to their tribal nature, they comprised a rather diffuse and complex system of authority, in which influence was exercised by the better socially positioned families over less powerful ones. The rank of each individual council was determined by the social status of its head and his standing within or vis-à-vis the ruling dynasty. The *diwan*, i.e. the council of the Al-Khalifa ruler, was most influential and had authority over the distribution of palm groves, the issuance of pearl diving rights, the management of the ports and the collection of taxes. In addition, other matters of importance were referred to it, whenever local councils and the courts proved incapable of resolving them.

There also existed estates that were cultivated by private landowners. Although in such cases the Al-Khalifa were not directly involved in running these estates, they still had the authority to collect taxes, and to settle legal disputes and other conflicts.

Contrary to the direct involvement of Al-Khalifa rulers in governing agricultural communities, pearl production was only loosely and indirectly controlled. This was the preserve of established pearling families—a well-known one being the Al-Dowasir—who inhabited both the islands and the mainland, and who had established their own organizations and structures for the management of economic activities. Within their settlements, the paramount authority was that of tribal sheikhs, who were responsible for maintaining order and settling disputes, in addition to ensuring the smoothness of pearling operations. Tribal sheiks ruled over "extended" tribal communities, which included not only members of their tribe, but also people of a variety of origins participating in the pearling activities.

The administrative bodies of pearling tribes were under the control of the tribal sheik. *Fidawi*'s were used to enforce law and order, and a number of administrators were involved in the running of tribal affairs and commercial activities. As in the case of sheikhly estates, the *majlis* of pearling tribes played the dual functions of consultative and decision-making bodies. However, it was the tribal sheik—similarly to the sheikh in agricultural estates—who had the ultimate authority to sanction or decide on the courses of action to be taken under different circumstances.

As the pearling industry and trade were sufficiently well organized, the Al-Khalifa saw little need for closer oversight of pearling operations, or for stricter control over pearling communities. However, while the Rulers interfered as little as possible in the everyday running of pearling communities' affairs, they made every effort to create favorable conditions for the development of pearling and trade as a whole. Such efforts included providing bases of operation, maintaining port facilities, and instituting a relaxed policy for taxing pearling activities. In addition, the Rulers consulted with pearling communities on matters relevant to their operations, such consultations usually taking the form of invitations directed to the chiefs of tribes to attend the meetings of the Ruler's *majlis*.

Governance of the Qatar Peninsula

Similarly to pearling communities on the islands, considerable autonomy was also granted to the tribes inhabiting Bahrain's mainland possessions. Concentrated mainly in the northwest and the southeast of the Qatar peninsula, the pearling communities of the mainland had attained a high level of organization of their commercial activities, and were subject to little economic regulation by the Al-Khalifa. In the majority of cases, the mainland tribes were related to the pearling families on the islands, and their social organization resembled that of island tribes. Pearling communities were among the region's regular contributors of taxes and religious tithes, and were thus part of the larger economic and territorial unit of Bahrain. Al-Khalifa control in Qatar was exercised mainly through interactions with tribal chiefs, and involved ensuring that tribes enjoyed favorable conditions for their commercial activities, as well as protecting the tribes from raids by hostile neighbors.

The Bedouin communities of the Qatar hinterland were also indirectly governed by Bahrain. While the tribal chiefs ensured that the economic and social needs of their people were met, politically the tribes recognized the supreme authority of the Al-Khalifa Ruler. Their relationship with the Al-Khalifa was mutually advantageous. Generally, the tribes benefited from receiving the favors of the Al-Khalifa, while the latter benefited from having loyal allies helping them control their territories. The paramount example of such Ruler-benefactor ties was the relationship between the Naim of northern Qatar and the Al-Khalifa. As will be discussed in detail in Chapter 9, the Naim served as the main guardians of Al-Khalifa interests in the Qatar peninsula, and benefited as the major recipients of Al-Khalifa support—both financial and political.

Though the Al-Khalifa were involved in the everyday management of mainland affairs to a lesser degree than on the islands, their relationships with the various tribes of the Qatar peninsula entailed an assertion of Bahrain's status as the supreme authority. Particularly in times of trouble, it was the Al-Khalifa who would ensure that law and order were restored and that offenders were punished. While such instances of restoration of law and order occasionally meant suppression of local dissent, they also demonstrated the ability of the Al-Khalifa family to fulfill their functions as rulers in accordance with regional custom. Typically, offenders would be arrested and brought to the main island of Bahrain, or forceful measures would be taken to ensure local tribes' obedience. In addition, a governor would sometimes be appointed with a mandate to prevent further disturbances—as was the case with Doha in the 1840s, and again in the 1860s (Lorimer 1908–15, 1:799; L. Pelly, 13 April 1863).

Although sometimes harsh, the measures taken by the Al-Khalifa generally produced the desired results. Such was the case, for instance, with a rebellion in Doha in 1867. That event had been caused by the local populations' discontent at the high level of taxation imposed by Bahrain Rulers, as well as by the conduct of the Governor of Doha, Ahmed Al-Khalifa. The Ruler of Bahrain, alarmed by the challenge to his authority in Doha and by Wahhabi attempts to take advantage of the situation, was joined by the Ruler of Abu Dhabi in an attack on Doha and Wukra. After the two towns were sacked, local inhabitants launched a retaliatory expedition against the Bahrain Ruler, but obtained no significant results.

As well as maintaining law and order, and the integrity of their interests on the peninsula, the Al-Khalifa ensured that local tribes complied with the general policies and commitments they had undertaken. In the context of foreign power presence in the Gulf, fulfilling the ruling family's international obligations was of particular importance—especially their obligations under existing treaties to suppress piracy. Although the 1867 rebellion described above was interpreted by some, including the

British authorities in the Gulf at the time, as a violation of the Al-Khalifa's anti-piracy commitments, the Rulers viewed that event as an internal matter and felt justified in interfering in order to restore their control over their territories.

Beyond its responsibilities for maintaining economic and social order within its own territories, the Al-Khalifa have shouldered international responsibilities—principally with Great Britain—to protect trade and maintain maritime peace.

Though the Al-Khalifa had to be urged—especially at the beginning of their formal relations with Britain—to enforce observance of their international undertakings throughout their territories, they were recognized as the relevant authority capable of enforcing such commitments. Thus, when the British Political Resident observed, during a visit to Doha in 1823, that certain requirements of the existing Anti-Piracy Treaty with Bahrain had not been met, he sought the Ruler of Bahrain's assurances for the "proper observance of the Treaty in Qatar" (Lorimer 1908–15, 1:793). In later years, the Rulers were known to have interfered on a number of occasions to enforce the terms of similar agreements. A description of one such event, in 1863, is provided by the then British Political Resident:

> ...the Sheikh of Bahrein has, without any urging from me, caused the evacuation of a place named Wukra on his main coast, where ...disreputable characters used to collect and injure Trade, or disturb the peace. The Sheikh has brought the Chief of Wukrah to Bahrein in custody. (L. Pelly, 13 April 1863)

Maintaining law and order and enforcing the terms of international treaties were elements common to Al-Khalifa rule, on both the Bahrain Islands and the Qatar peninsula. Thus, though the chiefs of tribes comprising the Al-Khalifa state were granted varying degrees of independence in dealing with local affairs, they were required to ensure that the political and economic interests of the Rulers were maintained. Whenever such tribes—and particularly, their chiefs—were deemed loyal, capable of handling tribal issues and efficient in organizing their economic activities, central governance was rather relaxed. However, the Al-Khalifa imposed strict measures when those conditions were not met, and typically followed these measures by the institution of direct administration and/or economic management. Thus the exercise of authority by the Al-Khalifa was always undertaken with firmness throughout its territories, despite the turmoils of disputed succession which sometimes occurred.

External Challenges

Al-Khalifa rule over the Bahrain Islands and the Qatar peninsula was also challenged by other powers in the region. At the turn of the nineteenth century, the political situation in the region remained rather unstable, and a variety of tribes and tribal confederations were struggling to define their territories. External challenges to Al-Khalifa authority came mainly from Persia, Muscat, and the Wahhabis, who had firmly established their bases in the region and were now competing for influence over neighboring territories. They were understandably attracted to the resources and location of the Bahrain Islands. In addition, rivalries extended also to various parts of the Qatar peninsula, since the promontory frequently provided refuge to rulers or outlaws from other areas.

The Persians made preparations to retake Bahrain under the leadership of Sheikh Nasir of Bushire and Bahrain as early as 1783. Though Persian interests had been abandoned at the beginning of dynastic struggles in Persia in 1785, their concern with Bahrain affairs remained high, and the Persians sought to reassert their influence whenever suitable opportunities presented themselves. One such opportunity came with a request for assistance from the Ruler of Bahrain when another power, Muscat, launched an assault on the islands in 1799. Yet Persian involvement failed to prevent the Imam of Muscat from succeeding in his next attack and occupying Bahrain in 1800.

In the aftermath of Muscat's invasion, the Al-Khalifa proceeded to Zubarah, where they began preparations to retake their previously occupied territories. There the Al-Khalifa allied with the Wahhabis, adherents to a puritanical reform movement founded by Abdul-Wahhab (1703–92) in the mid-eighteenth century in central Arabia. Initially a purely religious movement known for its strict observance of the teachings of the Qu'ran and the Hadith, it rapidly acquired a secular and political character and was adopted as official doctrine by the tribe of Mohammed ibn Saud and his successors. The Wahhabis embarked on an aggressive campaign of expansion and attracted many followers among numerous tribes in the Gulf—among them the Qawasim, who found in it justification for their piratical activities. Seeking to consolidate their influence in the region, the Wahhabis readily joined the Al-Khalifa's efforts to retake the islands. Together, the Al-Utub, the Wahhabis, and their allies among the tribes of the peninsula drove out the Imam's forces in 1801.

The Al-Khalifa were not, however, able to peacefully enjoy their possessions. Overwhelmed by the superiority of Wahhabi forces, they acknowledged the supremacy of the Wahhabi ruler and accepted Wahhabi control over their territories. The Wahhabis established military outposts on the main island and instituted the payment of tribute. Even so, few changes occurred in the everyday administration of the islands—the Al-Khalifa preserved their positions as governors throughout most of the years of Wahhabi presence and remained the primary force behind the development of the social and administrative structure of Bahrain:

> The Wahabi authority was never actually established in Bahrain excepting for a short period in 1810 when they appointed a Wakil to reside there for the collection of zakat [tribute] but without interfering in the Government of the island which continued to be administered by the Shaikh as before. (Hennell, 30 August 1839)

Al-Khalifa authority over the Qatar peninsula had been weakened, however. New authorities, associated with the Wahhabi state, competed with the Al-Khalifa's previously established domination over the peninsula. The Wahhabi Governor of Bahrain was placed in charge of the collection of tribute from the Bahrain Islands, Zubarah, Khor Hassan, and Qatif. Furthermore, Rahmah bin Jaber, the Jalahimah Sheikh of Khor Hassan who had allied himself with the Wahhabis, assumed possession of Zubarah, and his influence, along with that of his tribe, increased considerably. From Rahmah's new base, he continued his depredations on vessels in the Gulf and became the Wahhabis' chief tool for carrying out their policies at sea.

The Al-Khalifa never resigned themselves to Wahhabi hegemony. Adding aggravation to the presence of Wahhabi military garrisons and tax collectors in their lands were the efforts of Wahhabi teachers to impose a "fundamentalist" interpretation of Islam, plus Wahhabi pressure on Bahrain Rulers to participate in piratical expeditions in the Gulf.

The Al-Khalifa therefore explored a number of opportunities to associate with other powers to overthrow Wahhabi rule; and in 1810 they succeeded in forging an alliance with Sayid Sa'id, the Imam of Muscat, which expelled Wahhabi forces from the Bahrain Islands and the eastern coast of the Qatar peninsula. The following year they were also able to retake their remaining territories on the peninsula and to drive out the Jalahimah.

But after a brief period of friendly relations, tensions again arose between the Al-Khalifa and the Imam of Muscat. The reasons lay mainly in ongoing rivalries for domination over Gulf trade. Due to its geographical position, Muscat enjoyed a significant degree of control over commercial traffic in the region and Rulers of Muscat considered it their established right to collect duties from vessels calling at their ports. However, Bahrain challenged this state of affairs; their subjects, encouraged by increased British presence in the region, began to evade duties payable to Muscat and to make direct journeys to India.

By 1815, relations between Bahrain and Muscat had deteriorated. Bahrain's fears of Muscat were further heightened by the fact that Rahmah bin Jaber, the old enemy of the Bahrain Ruler, had decided to switch his allegiance to the Imam and had declared his willingness to participate in an attack on the Islands. The Al-Khalifa, however, had prepared to repel the expected assault by Muscat, and when, in 1815, Muscat troops landed in Arad, north of the main Bahrain island, they were met with strong Bahraini force. The Imam was defeated and two of his relatives and leaders of the expedition were killed. After failing to enlist the support of the Prince of Shiraz for another attack on Bahrain, the Imam abandoned the idea.

Then in 1828, Muscat renewed its efforts to subject Bahrain. For his part, the Al-Khalifa Ruler embarked on preparations to defend his territories:

> ...the chief...applied all his energies to meet the impending storm, and spared no exertions to place himself in the best posture of defense his resources would admit. (Warden 1856, 378)

After securing the support of the Sheikh of Abu Dhabi, the Imam proceeded to the Islands, and his fleet entered Bahrain harbor in October 1828. The aggressors conquered the fort of Sutteah and threatened Manama. But they were defeated by Bahraini forces under the leadership of Sheikh Abdullah bin Ahmed—a victory achieved with the assistance of Muscat's allies from Abu Dhabi, who had sided with Bahrain's Ruler. Muscat suffered significant losses: five hundred of its soldiers died in the attack and a number of its vessels were destroyed. Following this humiliating defeat and several unsuccessful attempts to secure a peace treaty with the Ruler of Bahrain, Sayid Sa'id returned to Muscat.

The following year, a Bahraini expedition sailed toward the Imam's territories, but achieved no significant results. A formal peace was finally concluded between the two Rulers in December 1829: the Imam officially abandoned any claims for payment of tribute by the Al-Khalifa and Bahrain and the Imam agreed not to interfere in each other's affairs in the future.

No sooner had Muscat's challenges subsided, than the Wahhabis renewed their claims to domination over Bahrain. By the end of the 1820s, they had largely recovered from the blow dealt by Mohammed Ali's expedition from 1812–18 on behalf of the (Ottoman) Porte, and their Ruler, Turki bin Abdullah Al-Saud, had set on a course of territorial expansion. At the end of 1830, Turki demanded the reinstitution of tribute payable by Rulers of Bahrain to the Wahhabis, and the surrender of Al-Khalifa-controlled Dammam to Bushir, the son of Rahmah bin Jaber. Wahhabi support for Bushir derived from the belief that his presence in the region would act as a check on possible future expansions of Al-Khalifa power.

The Ruler of Bahrain, after attempting unsuccessfully to receive British assurances of protection against the Wahhabis, and fearful of a possible alliance of the Wahhabi Amir and the Imam of Muscat against Bahrain, accepted Turki's conditions. His agreement, however, did not result in the Wahhabis' assumption of effective control over the Ruler's territories. Though Sheikh Abdullah did declare that the inhabitants of both the islands and "the coast of Qatar" would pay tribute, his acknowledgement of Wahhabi power was only nominal and Sheikh Abdullah remained as a de facto autonomous Ruler of his territories (LeQuesne 1953, 85 fn 3).

The peace of the islands was again threatened in 1832, when Bushir bin Rahmah undertook another attack on Bahrain, with the encouragement of the Wahhabis. Following his defeat, Bushir quarreled with the Wahhabis and left Dammam for Muscat. This event served as a catalyst to Al-Khalifa plans to recover Dammam, and in 1833–34 the Rulers of Bahrain succeeded in not only reconquering Bushir's former stronghold, but also in extending their rule over Tarut island. Sheikh Abdullah bin Ahmed, who had again received assurances of support by Muscat, then instituted a blockade of Qatif, thus preventing any maritime skirmishes with the Wahhabis.

Relations with the Wahhabis improved in 1836—the year that saw the renewal of Persian claims to Bahrain. Faced with the threat of possible aggression by both Persia and Muscat, Sheikh Abdullah resolved to renew his payment of *zakat* (tribute) to the Wahhabis in exchange for military backing, and the blockade on Qatif was lifted. But, as soon as Al-Khalifa fears that Muscat or Persia might launch an assault on the islands subsided, the payment of *zakat* to the Wahhabis was discontinued.

In 1839, however, Khalid, a pretender to the Wahhabi throne, demanded the tribute formerly paid to Wahhabi Rulers. In the period 1838–40, the forces of Mohammed Ali of Egypt occupied Hasa after a second expedition at Ottoman behest in 1838. Sheikh Abdullah of Bahrain feared that any concessions made to Khalid would only give rise to further demands, but a declaration by Kurshid Pasha of Egypt that he was preparing to subdue the main Bahrain island forced the Bahrain Ruler to submit to Wahhabi pressure.

Wahhabi demands for military assistance by the Ruler of Bahrain against Oman, however, met with resistance, and in 1839, Sheikh Abdullah ordered another blockade of Qatif. After difficult negotiations, the Al-Khalifa Ruler was finally persuaded to sign an agreement whereby he again undertook to pay *zakat* and assist the Wahhabis, while at the same time remaining free to rule his territories. As was stated in the agreement with regard to the Ruler's position:

> In return the Government of Bahrain is to be in my hands or in those of whatever Wakeel [Governor] I may appoint as my Deputy there and no other. In respect to my subjects on the coast of Qatar, &c., [etcetera] no-one is to interfere with them besides myself. This engagement and promise was made before God. (LeQuesne 1953, 87 fn 23)

As in earlier years, however, no tribute was paid to the Wahhabis, despite promises by the Ruler of Bahrain. In fact, as Hennell, the Political Resident, observed in 1839:

> Zakat was never paid by the Utubi Shaikh of Bahrain excepting at those periods when the head of the Wahabi sect was sufficiently powerful to coerce him in case of his refusal. (Hennell, 25 July 1839)

In 1844, the Ruler of Bahrain again undertook to renew payment of tribute, this time to Faisal, the legitimate Wahhabi Amir, who had not long before succeeded in reestablishing his position in the Nejd. In the two years that followed, relations between Bahrain and the Wahhabis were largely determined by internal developments and dynastic struggles in Bahrain, as Sheikh Abdullah and Sheikh Mohammed contested the Ruler of Bahrain's position.

Dynastic Struggles

By the time the Ottomans established their presence on the Qatar peninsula in the 1870s, the system of governance of Al-Khalifa territories — described earlier — had largely taken shape; but that process had been long and painful, and had been disrupted a number of times by challenges from both within and outside the Ruling family. In point of fact, the Ruling dynasty had no firmly established rules of succession, and the death of a Ruler typically signified the beginning of intrafamily rivalries. As descendants and relatives of deceased Rulers competed for influence, new alliances with various tribes, sections of tribes or, not infrequently, foreign powers, were forged and combined in struggles for succession.

The diversity of the population of the Bahrain Islands and the Qatar peninsula made it impossible to ensure an equal footing for different communities in their relations with the Rulers. Furthermore, the tribal nature of Gulf society and the constant movements of large groups of people within the region furnished a setting where different peoples frequently came into contact and, potentially, conflict with each other. Thus, though the ascendancy of the Al-Khalifa family was never seriously questioned by any sources within the Bahrain Islands or the Qatar peninsula, the power of individual members of the ruling dynasty and the stability of their rule suffered numerous challenges.

The first significant event in this respect transpired after the death of Sheikh Salman bin Ahmed in 1825. Sheikh Salman had co-ruled with his brother, Abdullah bin Ahmed, and both Sheikh Salman's political position and his share of Bahrain's economic revenues were inherited by his son, Sheikh Khalifa. The latter then assumed joint powers with his uncle—an arrangement that was to lead, after Sheikh Khalifa's death, to bitter contests between his descendants and Sheikh Abdullah.

This outbreak of dynastic struggles can be traced back to the beginning of the 1830s, when members of the ruling family began to express their dissatisfaction with Sheikh Abdullah. His "misrule, partiality and leniency" had created an atmosphere rife with internal dissensions, and a number of his relatives attempted to assert their own authority over that of Sheikh Abdullah (Warden 1856, 384).

In 1835, the chiefs of Huwailah, who had previously been loyal subjects of the Ruler, sought to break from his control and allied themselves with the Wahhabis. They were joined by two of Sheikh Abdullah's sons, who began inflicting damage on their father's property by engaging in piratical activities and seizing goods and vessels belonging to the Ruler. The Imam of Muscat then interfered and sent his son to mediate between the parties to end hostilities. An agreement was reached whereby contestants were allowed to retain the benefits already acquired; but it was also agreed that the inhabitants of Huwailah would settle on the main Bahrain island, where they would be under stricter control.

However, subsequent attacks on Huwailah, instigated by Sheikh Abdullah's nephews and associates, prevented application of the terms of the agreement and resulted in the secession to Abu Dhabi of Isa bin Tarif, the local chief, and a number of members of the Al bin Ali and Al bu 'Ainain tribes. Isa bin Tarif then sought to secure the support of the Ruler of Abu Dhabi and the British authorities in the Gulf for operations against Sheikh Abdullah's territories, but such support was not extended. On his part, Sheikh Abdullah made every effort to bring the refugees back under his jurisdiction, proposing to allow them to settle on the Qatar coast. In the absence of British guarantees for such a move, the proposal produced no results.

In 1837, alarmed by the unruliness on the main island of Bahrain, Sheikh Abdullah prepared to retire to Khor Hassan on the coast of Qatar north of Zubarah. He dispatched there "two of his wives, with their families, together with the furniture of the houses, even to the very doors" (Warden 1856, 386). Though his intentions were not carried out for some time, they brought about a brief period of calm, as the Ruler's sons and relatives were wary of the chaos that might ensue in Sheikh Abdullah's absence.

A new phase of dynastic struggles began in the 1840s, when a breach occurred between Sheikh Abdullah and Sheikh Mohammed bin Khalifa, who had succeeded his father as co-ruler. In 1842, the dissident Sheikh Mohammed moved to the Qatar peninsula and began to establish pockets of opposition to his grand-uncle's rule. After Sheikh Mohammed returned to the main Bahrain island the following year, actual hostilities broke out between supporters of the two Rulers, provoking Sheikh Abdullah to return to his old base of Muharraq, to head operations against his relative.

Sheikh Mohammed was defeated and fled to the Qatar coast where he had previously established a strong influence. Sheikh Abdullah then conducted reprisals against the towns of Manama and Khor Hassan, whose populations had sided with his rival. In order to reinforce his position on the mainland, and to strengthen the security of his territories, Sheikh Abdullah then began rebuilding Zubarah, which had been largely deserted in the years following the Ruling family's relocation to the islands at the end of the eighteenth century.

After his defeat, Sheikh Mohammed sought to reconsolidate his power and gather sufficient forces for future encounters with his great-uncle. Sheikh Abdullah then began receiving complaints from Qatar chiefs loyal to him of their inability to defend themselves against possible attacks by his rival. Sheikh Mohammed, anticipating actions by the Ruler to check his influence in Qatar, attacked and took possession of the fort of Murair in Zubarah. He further proceeded to Fuwairat, in the northeast coast of the Qatar peninsula, where he established his new headquarters and began preparations for an offensive against the islands.

From Fuwairat, Sheikh Mohammed launched an expedition against his great-uncle. In 1843, his troops landed close to the village of Riffa on the main Bahrain island, but were met by the forces of Nasir, Sheikh Abdullah's son. Though none of the parties prevailed in the fighting that ensued, the arrival of Sheikh Mohammed's brother with reinforcements tipped the balance in Sheikh Mohammed's favor. After their successful attack and occupation of Manama, the joint forces of the two brothers were able to defeat Sheikh Abdullah's troops at Muharraq.

Sheikh Mohammed then assumed possession of the Bahrain Islands, expelling Sheikh Abdullah, but permitting his sons to remain on Muharraq and to preserve their property.

But by the time of his conquest of Bahrain, Sheikh Mohammed had received the allegiance of most tribes on the Qatar peninsula, and this made Sheikh Abdullah's presence in Qatar impossible. The latter therefore settled in Dammam (in today's Saudi Arabia), which was then under the control of his eldest son Mubarak. The decline of Sheikh Abdullah's power then became irreversible, and despite his subsequent attempts to secure foreign support for his claims, his influence over the affairs of the Bahrain Islands and the Qatar peninsula was thereafter insignificant.

Sheikh Abdullah's removal marked the end of a turbulent period. Insofar as the populations of both the islands and the mainland were involved in supporting different contenders, this period of dynastic rivalries produced far-reaching consequences. The commercial activities of the tribes subject to Bahrain Rulers were seriously disturbed. The main Bahrain island

> ...became rapidly the scene of increased anarchy and confusion: as a natural consequence, the trade had diminished to nearly one-half within the last few years [preceding 1842]. (Warden 1856, 392)

In addition, encounters between the forces of the various contestants in the dynastic struggles occurred both on the islands and the peninsula, thus affecting the inhabitants of many areas under Al-Khalifa rule.

Last Years of Bahrain's Rule in Doha

In 1846, yet another blockade of Qatif was justified by Sheikh Mohammed bin Khalifa, the Ruler, "in order to carry into effect [his] desire to annoy the Wahhabis and their dependents"—one such dependent being his rival, Sheikh Mohammed bin Abdullah, who had established himself at Dammam. Hostilities reached a peak when Sheikh Mohammed bin Khalifa's forces blockaded Tarut island and engaged in two battles with the Wahhabis. Friendly relations were restored in 1847 on terms similar to those of all previous agreements with the Wahhabis: promise of payment of *zakat* in return for non-aggression and military assistance.

Again, this arrangement did not last. Dissatisfied with the state of his relations with both the Wahhabis and the British at the time, the Ruler of Bahrain threatened to enter into an agreement with the Porte, as he had been asked to do in an 1847 letter from the Governor of Basra. Though this threat remained unfulfilled, tensions with the Saudi Amir again increased the following year, when the Bahrain Ruler stated his opposition to an impending Wahhabi assault on Oman. Provoked by Bahrain's position, the Wahhabi Amir attacked Araij in Qatar. The Rulers of Abu Dhabi and Muscat came to Sheikh Mohammed's assistance, but after an initial victory over the Wahhabis, they saw their efforts undermined by "the treachery of the Al Thani Shaikh of Doha" (LeQuesne 1953, 89).

Further attempts by the Wahhabis to establish their authority over the Ruler of Bahrain's territories on the Qatar peninsula were, however, prevented by the intervention of the British government. A new peace agreement was negotiated whereby the Ruler of Bahrain was restored his possessions in return for a one-time payment of *zakat*. When in 1852 the Wahhabis sought to impose such payment on an annual basis, their efforts proved unsuccessful.

The two years that followed confirmed an already established pattern of relations between the Wahhabi Amir and the Ruler of Bahrain. Despite the existing agreement to the contrary, the two Rulers constantly engaged in actions against each other—the former supporting Sheikh Mohammed's rival and the piratical activities of the Amair tribe against Bahrain, the latter maintaining a blockade of Qatif ports. In 1854 another Wahhabi assault on Bahrain was repulsed. And though the level of British involvement in relations between the two Rulers had risen, frequent clashes continued to occur, and in 1859 the Wahhabis announced plans for another attack on the main Bahrain island. Preparations were subsequently abandoned under pressure from Britain.

In 1861, the Ruler of Bahrain expressed his dissatisfaction with the foreign powers' partial commitments to the security of Bahrain by flying the Turkish and Persian flags simultaneously. This fact, however, did little to alter his relations with Britain or the neighboring states, and in the same year he again ordered a blockade of the coast of the Wahhabi state. As will be discussed in Chapter 5, a British-sponsored Treaty of that year restored the peace and attempted to regulate the conduct of regional powers. In 1867, responding to renewed assertions by the

Wahhabis of their right to collect *zakat* from Bahrain, British authorities took the view that the Ruler of Bahrain was not subject to the payment of tribute to the Wahhabis in respect of the islands, but that he probably did owe such tribute in respect of Qatar, so as to ensure the protection of his subjects from other tribes.

The arrival of the Ottomans in the Qatar peninsula in 1871 marked the emergence of new political configurations in the Gulf. Relations between local Rulers were henceforth increasingly conducted within the framework of relations between Britain and the Ottoman Empire, and the volatility of alliances among regional Rulers was reduced. This setting contributed to the consolidation of existing Rulers' authority over various areas in the Gulf, as also to the rise to prominence of new ruling dynasties.

4 | Life on the Qatar Peninsula

While Bahrain's history was being written with a broad and bold brush, and the involvement of both local and foreign powers, the Qatar peninsula was relegated to the position of "backwater." Until the mid-1800s, virtually nothing of historical note occurred on the peninsula. It is perhaps useful to review the human and physical ecology of the peninsula to understand the dichotomy between the two areas, and to place the Al-Thani family in the proper context before examining the extent and nature of their authority.

"Human Ecology" of the Qatar Peninsula

As mentioned briefly in the previous section, the populations living in Qatar during the nineteenth century centered on the Zubarah region, on the northwestern coast of the Qatar peninsula, and Doha, on the southeastern coast. In addition to these settled populations, nomadic and semi-nomadic tribes migrated overland between the mainland of Arabia and the Qatar peninsula. The "human geography" of the Qatar peninsula can thus be described as having been divided into three main spheres: the communities of the northwest, those of the southeast, and those of the east of the peninsula.

The Northwest

The tribal confederation in the northwest was comprised mainly of pearling communities and semi-nomadic peoples. It was led by the Al-Naim tribe, who had special relations with the Rulers of Bahrain and ensured that Bahrain's interests throughout the peninsula were maintained; also that the security of the Bahrain Islands was not threatened by hostile groups attacking from the mainland. The population concentrated in the northwest was mainly sea-oriented, and even the tribes that occasionally wandered the desert made arrangements to spend certain periods of the year in coastal settlements, mostly looking after the property of pearlers while the latter were away at sea, but also sometimes participating in pearling activities. On occasion, Bedouin tribes, unable to sustain themselves on the scarce resources of the desert, would attack and plunder the coastal villages. In any case, it was the sea in general—and commercial relations with other population centers in the Gulf of Bahrain in particular—that furnished the main source of living and income to the northwest's inhabitants.

Despite the ability of their inhabitants to participate in pearling and trading activities, the northwest settlements never developed into important population centers, largely due to the fact that the desert prevented their inland expansion, while the seat of governance of the territorial unit to which they belonged was located on the Bahrain Islands. In addition, the harsh climate and the absence of sufficient supplies of fresh water further restricted expansion of their populations.

Thus, although no precise data exist as to the number of people living in the northwest of Qatar during the nineteenth century, it is known that at the beginning of the twentieth century there were only three villages in the northwest of the Qatar peninsula. Those villages were—in addition to Zubarah, which had been destroyed by that time—Abu Dhaluf, Hadiyah and Khor Hassan (or, as it is known today, Khuwayr), and had a total population of fewer than 800 people (Zahlan 1979, 15). The area surrounding them was largely uninhabited, and the closest other settlements on the peninsula were situated on the eastern coast.

Politically, the northwest settlements were subordinate in every respect to developments on the Bahrain Islands. For the greater part of the nineteenth century, they were dominated by the Al-Naim tribe, which had close ties to the Al-Khalifa and indeed represented the Ruler of Bahrain's authority both in the Zubarah region and throughout the Qatar peninsula. Moreover, the territories in northern Qatar frequently served as refuge and power bases of Rulers of Bahrain—in that case particularly during the turbulent period of dynastic struggles in the middle of the nineteenth century, when both Sheikh Abdullah and Sheikh

Mohammed, the two rivals for succession, used the northwest of the Qatar peninsula to build their forces.

The Southeast

The other significant concentration of population in the nineteenth century occurred on the southeast coast of the Qatar peninsula. It centered on the pearl-merchant enclave of Doha and represented a confederation dominated by the more powerful and tribal-based Bahraini and, occasionally, Saudi spheres of influence. Until the Ottomans' arrival in 1871, the formal authority of the Ruler of Bahrain over the settlements in the southeast was recognized by all powers in the region, though it was at times challenged by the Saudi state.

Pearling provided the main means of subsistence to inhabitants of southeast Qatar; thus their communities were eastward-oriented—a tendency characteristic also of the modern-day state of Qatar (which is based primarily on the power structures that emerged in Doha toward the end of the nineteenth century). It has been estimated that approximately 48 percent of the nineteenth century population of the whole peninsula was engaged in pearling—a rather significant proportion, which was probably even higher in the settlements on the coast (Zahlan 1979, 22).

The majority of pearling tribes on the eastern coast of Qatar were related to tribes on the north coast of the Qatar peninsula and on the Bahrain Islands. An example would be the Dowasir, who had a strong presence on the Bahrain Islands, and whose influence was felt as far as Odaid in southern Qatar. Generally, population patterns on the southeast coast of the Qatar peninsula were similar to those observed in the north: mostly settled communities that cooperated with or were harassed by the nomadic tribes of the desert.

Doha, Wukra, Fuwairat, Dhakhira, and Khor Shaqiq were the main settlements on the eastern coast (Zahlan 1979, 15); Adeed [Odaid] is also mentioned (A. B. Kemball 1856, 108). Among them, only three population centers on the southeast coast—Doha, Wukra and Odaid—possessed size and position of any significance in the middle of the nineteenth century. These three localities were noted in an 1845 British survey of the "Arabian Shores of the Persian Gulf." In the survey, which was at the time the authoritative reference book with respect to the geography of the Gulf, Biddah (Doha) is described as a town of "about three hundred houses … a most miserable place: not a blade of grass nor any kind of vegetation near it." "Wukra" is depicted in the survey as a town of about 250 houses, while the following comment is made of Odaid: "In point of appearance it would, perhaps, be difficult to select a more wretched, desolate, and barren-looking spot in the whole of the Gulf" (A. B. Kemball 1856, 108–9).

The South

Certain Bedouin tribes from other parts of eastern Arabia occasionally migrated to the south of the Qatar peninsula. Among them were the Bani Hajir, Al-Manasir, and Al-Murrah. The Bani Hajir originated from Hasa and were presented by Lorimer in his *Gazetteer of the Persian Gulf* as "lawless, troublesome, mischievous and uncivilized," as well as "addicted to piracy," for which purpose they used boats seized from other tribes. The Al-Manasir were from the Trucial Coast (sometimes referred to as Trucial Oman) and wintered in Qatar, where some of them had joined the settled populations of the coast. For their part, the Al-Murrah were described as "the wildest, most dangerous and least civilised of the nomad tribes in their part of Arabia, [who existed], to an appreciable extent, by plunder" (Lorimer 1908–15, 2:612).

The Bani Hajir, as well as the Al-Murrah, allied themselves with the Saudi state, and acted as Wahhabi allies. Frequently they served as the conduit for the extension of Wahhabi influence; for instance, they supported the Wahhabis militarily in their campaigns aiming to challenge the Ruler of Bahrain's authority over the peninsula, and in particular over Doha.

The Interior

The interior of the Qatar peninsula was largely uninhabited. Conditions there in the nineteenth century were as prohibitive as they are today. Palgrave, who visited the area in 1862–63, described the peninsula as "miles and miles of low barren hills, bleak and sun-scorched, with hardly a single tree to vary their dry monotonous outline" (Palgrave 1877, 2:231). Nearly eighty years later, Lt. Col. Hay (who was later to become Sir Rupert Hay), saw nothing different on a trip from the west to the east coast of the peninsula:

> The road lay across stony and uninhabited desert and the going was fairly rough; not a living thing was seen for some 50 miles ... it was strange to travel about these wild parts. (Hay, 19 November 1941)

In this context, it is hardly surprising that, until the advent of the oil age, no permanent settlements existed in the Qatar interior. The majority of the peninsula's inhabitants depended on the sea for their existence, while even the Bedouin communities that ventured into the interior never strayed too far from the coast. That was the situation depicted by a Captain Izzet of the Ottoman army, who in 1878 prepared a map of the region showing only six habitable names: Bahrain Island, Hawar Island, Zubarah, Ras Maroon (Ras Laffan area), the Hills of Biddah (Doha), and in the far southeast corner of what is today the peninsula, Qatar (see Map No. 5, p. 258). All these inhabited areas were either part of the Bahrain Islands, or situated on the Qatar coast, while the rest of the peninsula was shown as empty. That is the situation even today: the infrastructure of the Qatar interior is still undeveloped, and most of the population—indeed a significant 97 percent of it—is concentrated on the east coast.

In sum, Bahrain's sovereignty within the Arabian Gulf region, while occasionally threatened by dynastic controversies and other struggles, seems to have been clearly established well before the dawn of the twentieth century and maintained with relative consistency to this day.

The Al-Thani Move toward Prominence

The Al-Thani family began its rise in importance in Doha in the middle of the nineteenth century. Doha was the largest population center on the east coast of the Qatar peninsula and remained, until the 1870s, under the authority of the Ruler of Bahrain.

The historical record provides little information as to the processes and events that led to the Al-Thani's rise to prominence. In Lorimer's *Gazetteer*, only the following is noted:

> Nothing is known of the manner in which the Al-Thani had attained by 1868 to predominant influence in Qatar; they were Ma'adhid and therefore of the Al bin-Ali, the tribe of Isa bin Tarif. (Lorimer 1908–15, 1:802)

At some point in the nineteenth century, the Al-Thani began to exercise influence in Doha as its principal merchants and tax collectors. At that time, the population of Doha comprised members of a variety of tribes, whose allegiances lay with their tribal leaders and, through them, with the Ruler of Bahrain. (For a detailed breakdown of the population of Doha see Zahlan 1979, 19.) The latter imposed taxes and religious tithes on the inhabitants of the entire peninsula. This formalized taxation of the tribes dependent on the Ruler of Bahrain confirmed him as the peninsula's sovereign authority.

The Al-Thani, however, were never tribal chiefs, nor did they exercise, until the end of the 1860s, the type of authority over local inhabitants that would traditionally qualify them as sovereigns. Rather, their status was that of proxies between the sovereign (Bahrain), to whom taxes were owed, and the population. As such, the Al-Thani did not possess the resources either to act as Rulers or to influence or control events in Doha. Even less were they in position to create, or maintain on their own, any system of governance that would ensure the protection of their interests or the exercise of their political will. In addition, at that time they had at their disposal no means to safeguard the population against tribal incursions or foreign attacks. The Al-Khalifa alone were able to fulfill those functions.

In the 1850s, when the Al-Thani were first mentioned by travelers and authorities in the Gulf, Doha was ruled by an Al-Khalifa-appointed Governor, whose mandate was to ensure the maintenance of law and order, and to check the spread of Wahhabi influence in the region. In 1851, after an attempt to extend the control of the Wahhabi Ruler to Doha, the town was handed back to Sheikh Ali, the Al-Khalifa Governor. However, Sheikh Ali was soon expelled, and an Agent on behalf of the Wahhabis was appointed (the exact circumstances surrounding this event remain murky to this day). Though speculations have circulated that the Agent, who was put in charge of collecting taxes due to the Wahhabis, was actually Mohammed Al-Thani, no specific evidence exists to confirm this assertion (F. B. Prideaux, 16 July 1905). What is certain is this: whether serving under the Al-Khalifa or the Wahhabis, the Al-Thani in the 1860s were far from achieving any autonomous status, and the positions they occupied utterly depended on Rulers of the larger territorial units of the region.

The year 1868 is significant in the history of Qatar, that being when the Al-Thani were formally recognized as Chiefs of the Ma'adhid tribe— and thus, in effect, as Chiefs of Doha. In that year, the Ruler of Bahrain (assisted by the Ruler of Abu Dhabi) undertook a punitive expedition against the insubordinate tribes of Doha and Wukra, and Britain interfered to restore peace (see Chapter 5, in "The Doha Affair: 1867–68"). The visit of Col. Pelly, the British Political Resident, to the region marked the beginning of a new status for the Al-Thani. At the meeting held by Col. Pelly with local chiefs, the Al-Thani were treated as Chiefs of Doha. In that capacity, Mohammed Al-Thani signed two agreements, whereby he undertook certain obligations on behalf of his subordinates.

The first agreement was signed on 12 September by Mohammed Al-Thani alone, and a second agreement was signed on 13 September by all the local chiefs. The document signed on 13 September, entitled, *Agreement between Chiefs Residing in the Province of Qatar and Chief of Bahrain*, read as follows:

> We, the undersigned chiefs, all residing in the province of Qatar, do hereby solemnly agree and bind ourselves to pay to Sheikh Ali bin Khalifa, Chief of Bahrein, the sums of money per annum heretofore paid by us to the Chiefs of Bahrein, as follows: this total sum to be paid by us to Muhammad bin Thani of Doha and by him to the Resident for delivery to the agent of the Chief of Bahrein, at Bushire:
>
> 1,700 Krans on account of the Mahanda tribe,
>
> 1,500 Krans on account of the Al Bu Aainen and Nayim tribes,
>
>   500 Krans on the account of the Semsemieh tribe (i.e. the Al Bu Kuwara, who live at Sumesma),
>
>   500 Krans on account of the Keleb tribe,
>
> 1,500 Krans on account of the Sudan tribe,
>
> 2,500 Krans on account of Muhammad bin Thani (Chief of the Maadhid) and the Musallam tribe,
>
>   800 Krans on account of the Amamera tribe.
>
> ⸻
>
> 9,000 Krans total

> And we, the said Chiefs, understanding that the Bahrein Chief claims from us a total of 15,000 Krans per annum in lieu of 9,000 as above set forth, we do hereby further agree to pay any extra sums not aggregating a total larger than 15,000, which the Resident after judicial investigation may decree.
> Written on the 25 Jamadi-ul-Awal 1285/13th September 1868. (*Agreement between Chiefs Residing in the Province of Qatar and Chief of Bahrain*, 13 September 1868)

The terms and wording of the Agreement reveal a number of significant facts related to the political situation in the region. By undertaking to return to the practice of paying taxes and tribute to the Ruler of Bahrain, the tribal chiefs of the Qatar peninsula formally recognized the continuing authority of the Ruler. Thus, the Al-Thani, like other leaders in the region, acknowledged that they remained subject to the Al-Khalifa.

Another important conclusion deriving from the Agreement is this: while the Al-Thani were clearly placed on an equal footing with other chiefs, they had no prerogative to undertake formal commitments for members of other tribes on the peninsula. A letter addressed by the Political Resident to all tribal chiefs, confirming the terms of the Agreement, further demonstrates that the Al-Thani were held responsible only for the conduct of their subjects in Doha, and not for those of other chiefs (Lorimer 1908–15, 1:802).

The fact that the influence of the Al-Thani family was confined to Doha and its environs is confirmed by other sources as well. In 1864, the *Persian Gulf Pilot* described the Al-Thani as having some authority over the towns of Doha, Little Doha, and Al-Bidah—settlements located within 1 mile of the coast (Constable and Stiffe 1864). No mention was made of their power extending over other settlements on the southeastern coast of Qatar or, even less so, over the entire peninsula. Another source, an Ottoman report of 1871, described the situation as follows:

> [Mohammed bin Thani] residing in [Doha] has no rule over the other villages. The leadership of each village has been left to the local sheikhs. As for [Mohammed bin Thani], in respect of the dependent villages, he holds the position of tax collector and his duty consists of collecting the annual taxes and the taxes from pearl fishing from the people. (*Takvimi Vekayi*, 8 June 1871)

The Al-Thani themselves also admitted at that time that they had no authority over any villages or areas outside of Doha. Jasim Al-Thani, the son of Mohammed Al-Thani, for instance, confirmed in a letter to the British Political Resident in 1881:

> ... I have no power over [the Katar coast]. You are aware of the treaty made in the time of my father [1868] between us and the British Govt. namely that we were only to be responsible for [Doha Town] and Al Wakra.
>
> The Al Katar coast is very large and extensive and I have not the power to forbid anyone from landing or embarking and unless you give strict orders to all the people of Al Katar... to migrate and settle in my country and be subject to me. (Jasim bin Al-Thani, 9 March 1881)

Naturally, the Al-Thani sought to extend their influence over larger territories. The first step toward that goal was to consolidate their position in Doha. In that context, Jasim bin Mohammed, the son of the Ruler of Doha, saw the appearance of the Turks in 1871 as a chance to free himself from the payment of tribute to the Al-Khalifa, as well as an opportunity to strengthen his hand with not only other tribes of the area but also with the Wahhabis and with dissident members of his own family.

However, it was not until the beginning of the twentieth century that the Al-Thani were at last able to achieve a certain degree of control over the greater part of the Qatar peninsula, largely through the skillful exploitation of rival foreign powers in the area, a factor to which we now turn our attention.

5 | Piracy, the British, and Bahrain's Emergence as a Political Entity

Prior to European domination of the Arabian Gulf, Bahrain was often on the geographical fringe of competing empires. As civilizations rose and fell and different powers vied for control over trade, spheres of influence were constantly redrawn. In this ever-changing political environment, cities emerged and declined, the focus of trading activities shifting from one center to another. Significantly, not all regions were equally affected by events, and no single state ever succeeded in establishing its domination over the whole of the Gulf area; but this situation began to change in the fifteenth century with the arrival of the Europeans.

The Portuguese were the first European power to recognize the strategic significance of the Arabian Gulf and in the sixteenth century to establish military and trading stations there. Their interests, primarily commercial, had little influence, however, on the political structures of the Gulf sheikhdoms. It was the British, who first arrived in the late sixteenth century, and their ever-increasing concern to protect the trade routes to India, who eventually largely shaped these structures. In order to achieve their foreign policy goals it became increasingly necessary to become involved in local affairs, particularly dealing with the issues of piracy and the expansionism of the Ottoman Empire.

Piracy and British Moves to Control It

Throughout the Gulf, Britain's primary concern was the safe passage of vessels involved in the Indian trade, and to ensure this, British ships maintained a significant presence in the region. Their East India fleet comprised vessels equipped for both trading and military expeditions. In addition, the warships of the Royal Navy acted to defend British interests, and whenever the need arose, they carried out punitive operations against ships or tribes believed to have committed piratical acts. Conspicuous among these were the operations referred to above, undertaken against the Qawasim pirate fleets based at Ras Al-Kaimah and Sharjah in today's UAE.

European pirate fleets boasted large vessels that enabled them to control commercial traffic entering Gulf waters, and to raid important ports in the region. However, the power of local pirates eventually surpassed the power of European privateers. Among the Arabs, the Qawasim tribal confederation, based at Ras Al-Khaimah and Sharjah in today's United Arab Emirates, were known as a major commercial and military power challenging British supremacy on a number of occasions. Their association with the Wahhabi movement compounded their resentment against British presence. British-Qawasim hostilities began with the establishment of a Qawasim trading station on the island of Kishm, which was in close proximity to Bandar Abbas—a port where the British had strong commercial interests. British losses from customs dues and Qawasim raids (many of these accompanied by massacres of the crews) on British ships further exacerbated the situation. By the beginning of the nineteenth century, the British East India Company appealed to the Royal Navy for assistance.

In 1805, a British naval expedition mounted against the Qawasim achieved a short-lived cessation of piracy. Two years later the pirate activities revived, and the Qasimi Sheikh offered the British a guarantee of safe passage for British ships, against a payment of tribute This led to yet another British attack in 1809 and the destruction of a large part of the Qawasim fleet.

The final British blow to local piracy was dealt in 1819, when they mounted a full-scale campaign against the Qawasim, resulting in the capture of their headquarters at Ras Al-Khaimah. This event ushered in a new era of British political control over the lands that had come to be known as the "Pirate Coast" (later to be known as the "Trucial Coast").

The evolution of British commercial presence in the Gulf into political and military domination was to find its formal expression in the nineteenth century in the treaties between Britain and local rulers. Such treaties were signed in the 1820s, and again in the 1850s (more will be said about these below). These treaties established the so-called "Trucial system," whereby Britain charged itself with the task of suppressing piracy and enforcing stability in the region. Ensuring the safety of navigation was, however, a multifaceted undertaking that in practice amounted to the establishment of a British imperial presence.

Accordingly, Britain's assumption of this new political role in the Middle East reflected on the structure of the "Residencies" of the British East India Company. Initially created to serve as trading stations, they took on increasingly political functions. By the beginning of the nineteenth century, they had been transformed into centers of British political control in the Gulf.

The Residency at Bushire became the heart of British domination, at the top of a complex administrative structure comprised chiefly of numerous British Political Agencies throughout the Middle East. Following the signing of the anti-piracy agreements of the 1820s, the Resident at Bushire was given the title of "Political Resident in the Persian Gulf" and was placed in charge of policing local tribes and maintaining peace in the region. He reported to the Bombay government, which in turn reported to the Governor-General (after 1858, Viceroy) of India. Reflecting the increasing political importance of India and the Gulf, and the declining importance of trade, in 1873 responsibility for the Bushire Residency was taken over directly by the Government of India and a new India Office was created in London to which it reported. This latter office existed until it and the Colonial Office were absorbed by the Commonwealth Office in 1947 where responsibility for Gulf affairs continued to be concentrated until British withdrawal from the Gulf in 1971. (See also, Hay 1959, 12, 13, 20; Tuson 1973, 3, 4, 7, 44–45, 47, 107–8.)

Thus, by the early nineteenth century, the British had laid the foundations of their imperium in the East and had instituted a complex network for the exercise of political and military control in the Arabian Gulf (Salim A. Al-Arayed 2001, 32–33; A. B. Kemball 1844a; Savory 1980, 33–39; Yapp 1980, 70–75; Yapp 1994, 176; Zahlan 1979, 27).

Bahrain as Entrepôt—Early Nineteenth Century

Bahrain, as earlier in its history, was directly involved in and affected by events like these in the Gulf. Although Bahrain's tribes did not participate in piratical activities on a scale with those of the Qawasim, its proximity to both the Qawasim base at Ras Al-Khaimah, and the British base at Bandar Abbas prevented Bahrain from remaining unaffected by Qawasim-British struggles. In addition, Qawasim ships were stationed throughout the Gulf and thus, also in proximity to the Bahrain Islands.

But Bahrain also played a more direct role in the rivalries between the two naval powers—it served as an entrepôt for pirated goods. As a developed trading and financial center, Bahrain had established profitable relations with the Qawasim, whereby goods plundered from British and other European vessels found their way onto the market. Thus, when the British finally took control over the pirate strongholds, they found it essential that Bahrain also fall under their influence.

Consistent with primary British concerns, their involvement in Bahrain was chiefly aimed at ensuring the safety of navigation in the Gulf. However, political struggles among tribal confederations in the region, on the one hand, and the larger volume of commercial traffic on the other, led to an increase in the scale of maritime warfare in the region. At the beginning of the nineteenth century, the deteriorating security situation in the Gulf posed a considerable threat to British commercial interests, and as the British faced prospects of significant losses, they felt compelled to assume a more active role in the region, while at the same time they strove to remain politically neutral with respect to struggles among local rulers.

But in contrast to the states of the Pirate Coast, Bahrain was never the target of British military operations. British naval vessels regularly patrolled Pirate Coast ports, but did not survey Bahraini ports at the beginning of the nineteenth century (Kelly 1968, 162–63, 360–63).

Despite the British naval presence in the Gulf, the main focus of Britain's activities was commercial, and British authorities were opposed to any structured political involvement in the region. The words of the Governor-General of the East India company, although said in relation to events in Muscat, were representative of general British policy at the time:

> Our concern is only with the maritime commerce of the Gulf and as long as that is not molested it matters not to us whether one power or another holds dominion over its shores. (Bentinck 1834)

The British government's objective was thus to remain as detached as possible from internal developments within the Gulf states, including

Bahrain. Specifically, Britain took care not to associate itself with particular Rulers, and not to interfere in any local struggles, except when those were threatening to disrupt trading activities. This attitude found expression in a statement made by the Governor of Bombay, Sir Mountstuart Elphinstone, in 1819:

> We should abstain from all interference... so long as he [the Ruler of Bahrain] restrains his tribes from [piracy]... [I]f any indications of a piratical spirit should manifest themselves, we shall be compelled to adopt the measures of coercions which we are prosecuting against the [Trucial sheikhs]. (Elphinstone 1819)

Prior to the 1820s, despite a number of requests for assistance from the Al-Khalifa, the British government entered into no formal relations with the Ruler of Bahrain. While Britain closely observed political events in the Gulf and, most notably, struggles among local powers that could potentially endanger the safety of navigation in the region, British authorities were reluctant to take sides. Thus, in 1804–5, the Bombay government refused to grant an Al-Khalifa request for protection from the Wahhabis. Though such assistance would have amounted to no more than "a vessel or two for a short time," the Bombay government considered an association with Bahrain undesirable in light of existing Muscat and Persian ambitions to conquer the island (Warden 1856, 366–68).

For his part, the Ruler of Bahrain displayed a friendly attitude toward British authorities and initially acted in a manner consistent with their anti-piracy efforts. Thus, in 1804, for instance, the Ruler refused to commit any of his vessels or subjects for a Wahhabi-led piratical expedition. In 1814, he assured Lieutenant William Bruce, British Political Resident in Bushire, "that [Bahraini] ports were ever open, and should continue so to [British ships], and every aid at all times [would be] rendered to [British] vessels" (Warden 1856, 370).

However, continued threats of invasion by neighboring rulers and Britain's unwillingness to render assistance to the Ruler of Bahrain eventually led to a change in Al-Khalifa attitudes toward the British. Thus, in 1817, Bahrain was reported to have become a major market for pirated goods. Although Bahraini vessels were not involved in piratical activities, the main island had developed close links with piratical tribes from around the region, and most notably, with the Qawasim. In exchange for goods plundered from ships in the Gulf, those tribes were able to obtain in Bahrain a variety of products, such as rice and dates, and naval stores. Under these circumstances, Britain came to regard Bahrain as a piratical port and to perceive a necessity for closer interference in Bahrain's relations with neighboring tribes.

This perception was reinforced in 1819 when Bahrain was believed to be in breach of yet another principle of British policies in the Gulf—namely, of British efforts to stamp out the slave trade. After the British authorities received a report that several Indian women had been sold in Bahrain, Captain Lock of His Majesty's ship *Eden*, in company with five vessels of war, arrived on the main island, only to be convinced by Sheikh Abdullah that the report was unfounded. With the mediation of the Ruler of Bahrain, the British official then secured the release of seventeen slaves who had been captured by pirates at Ras Al-Khaimah.

This event, and the assurance by Sheikh Abdullah bin Ahmed that no pirated goods would be allowed on Bahrain markets did not, however, dispel British fears of possible Bahrain support for pirates and slave traders in the region. The British had also begun preparations for an expedition that would bring an end to the piratical activities in the area.

First Treaties for the Suppression of Piracy
Conclusion of the 1820 Agreements

In late 1819, the British sent a punitive expedition under the command of Sir W. G. Keir that resulted in the capture of Ras Al-Kaimah and the destruction of the Joasmee pirate fleet that was based there. In the aftermath of the expedition against Ras Al-Khaimah, the sheikhs of the piratical tribes of the Gulf concluded a General Treaty with the British government, whereby they bound themselves to see to the "cessation of plunder and piracy by land and sea." Bahrain, which, as described in the previous section, had become associated with different aspects of Gulf pirates' activities, was also affected by this development. Not only were the Rulers of Bahrain pressured into surrendering the ships based at their harbor belonging to piratical powers but they also entered into formal, treaty relations with the British government. This event was the advent of a change in Bahrain's relationship with the British, in which Bahrain was brought into the British sphere of influence as part of the anti-piracy treaties its Rulers signed with the British government.

On 5 February 1820 a representative of Sheikh Abdullah bin Ahmed of Bahrain and his co-Ruler, Sheikh Salman bin Ahmed, signed a

Preliminary Treaty with Britain. Three weeks later this Treaty was signed and accepted also by the two Sheikhs themselves. The main provisions of the Treaty comprised a ban on the sale of pirated goods in "Bahrein or its dependencies" and an undertaking to surrender any Indian prisoners (i.e. slaves) that might be in the Rulers' possession. In addition, the Preliminary Treaty made the Rulers of Bahrain party to the more comprehensive General Treaty between Britain and the Sheikhs of piratical tribes (Preliminary Treaty between Britain and the Sheikhs of Bahrain, 5 February 1820).

By becoming party to the General Treaty, the Rulers of Bahrain entered the British-designed system of relations among Gulf powers. While initially conceived as a tool for achieving the British goals of maritime security and order, the General Treaty, in effect, represented a step toward creating a more predictable political environment in the region. Though Britain was not, at that stage, prepared to institute an elaborate plan for the conduct of Gulf affairs, it did make an effort to define certain basic concepts it considered relevant to maritime activities.

To this end, the Treaty introduced a distinction between "acknowledged war" and "plunder and piracy." While the former was defined as "[war] which is proclaimed, avowed, and ordered by government against government," the latter was described as "the killing of men and taking of goods without proclamation, avowal, and the order of a government." In addition, "the putting [of] men to death after they have given up their arms" and "[t]he carrying off of slaves, men, women, or children from the coasts of Africa or elsewhere" were also deemed to fall under the category of "plunder and piracy" (General Treaty with the Arab Tribes of the Persian Gulf, 23 February 1820, 245–46).

Britain's desire to establish a certain degree of order in Gulf waters was also manifested in the provisions of the General Treaty that required a red-and-white flag to be flown by the vessels of "the pacified tribes." The Treaty also provided for the introduction of ship registers, and described the procedures for the registration of vessels.

The general spirit of the Treaty was particularly well manifested in the wording of Article 4, which stated as follows:

> The pacified tribes shall all of them continue in their former relations, with the exception that they shall be at peace with the British Government, and shall not fight with each other, and the flag

shall be a symbol of this only and of nothing else. (General Treaty with the Arab Tribes of the Persian Gulf, 23 February 1820, 245)

An obvious contradiction contained in that Article illustrates British authorities' desire to see an end to maritime warfare in the region, while at the same time to avoid making a firm commitment to regulate every aspect of intertribal relations. Thus, while the Article stipulated that tribes "shall not fight with each other," it also contained the disclaimer that they "shall continue in their former relations." This qualification was explained by the British government in the following terms:

> Our relations to the Arab States afforded no grounds for interference to restrain their mutual attacks. It is true that Article IV ...mentions peace among themselves... but this appears to have been rather an explanation of the intention of the flag... Government could scarcely pretend to the power of imposing any restraint on the motions of vessels intended for a purpose of lawful warfare. (A. B. Kemball 1844a, 64)

A further attempt at explanation of the meaning of Article IV was made by Major Wilson:

> There is nothing in these Articles which prevents the Arabs declaring war; but whenever they do so, they are required to fight after the manner of acknowledged war... The British Government ...will consider all wars that are not acknowledged as piratical, and treat whoever may be engaged in them accordingly.... (A. B. Kemball 1844a, 65)

Implementation of the 1820 Piracy Agreements

With the signature of the 1820 Agreements Britain assumed a new role in the region. Accordingly, the Residency at Bushire was reorganized: the Resident there, formerly a civil servant concerned with the commercial affairs of the East India Company, took on responsibility for the political affairs of the whole Gulf and was styled "Resident in the Persian Gulf" ("Political Resident in the Persian Gulf" from 1862 onward). His main responsibilities were the permanent suppression of piracy and the conservation of the peace in the Gulf by the "friendly interposition of [British] power and influence" (Hay 1959, 12–13). Employees of the Residency came to be viewed as strictly political figures and were forbidden to engage in any commercial activities. They were given responsibility to formulate and implement British policies on the local level, and were subordinate to the government of Bombay.

After 1820, Britain's policy responses to various events in the Gulf did come to be determined by the distinction between "acknowledged war" and "piracy" introduced in the General Treaty. The general tendency was to treat piratical acts with the utmost seriousness, but to avoid taking sides or undertaking any considerable commitments in instances of "acknowledged war." This attitude derived from the British government's pledge to maintain neutrality with respect to political struggles in the Gulf. With the conclusion of the General Treaty, Britain thus acquired means to exercise its influence over Gulf affairs without placing itself under any formal obligations to regulate all inter-tribal relations.

However, the British government left no doubt about its commitment to enforcing the terms of the General Treaty regarding piracy. In 1822 a ship belonging to a Bahraini merchant was seized on charges of piracy (Warden 1856, 374). In the following year, British authorities instituted a blockade of Sharjah following the attack on a Bahraini boat by two Sharjah vessels, and obtained effective redress by the Chief of the Joasmees (a local tribe) (Warden 1856, 375).

As the Qatar peninsula was at the time considered indisputably part of the territories belonging to the Ruler of Bahrain, the General Treaty was deemed to apply to the peninsula's inhabitants also. This was demonstrated as early as 1821, when Doha was burned by an East India Company vessel as punishment for piracies committed by its inhabitants (Zahlan 1979, 33). Similarly, in 1827–28, Britain was involved in resolving a piratical act committed by members of the Manasir tribe of the Qatar peninsula (Warden 1856, 376–77).

That the Qatar peninsula came under the provisions of the 1820 Treaty was also demonstrated by the following observation made by Lorimer:

> The registration of ships, as observed in the history of Trucial Oman, ultimately proved to be impractical and was abandoned; but in view of the indefinite status, replete with political difficulties into which the Qatar promontory has now lapsed, it is much to be regretted that our officers did not continue to insist, as they did in Trucial Oman, on the use of the Trucial flag. In this there

could have been no real difficulty so long as Qatar remained under the Shaikhs of Bahrain; and the maintenance of the flag might have stereotyped the dependence of Qatar on Bahrain, and with it the principle of British control over Qatar. (Lorimer 1908–15, 1:794 fn)

British authorities increasingly involved themselves in mediating local disputes and sanctioning operations by one tribe against another. Though not perceived as directly stemming from Britain's obligation under the Treaty, such mediation was viewed by the British government as a convenient and relatively cheap means of keeping order on the waters of the Gulf. Thus, in 1822 for instance, Britain agreed to act as mediator in the dispute between the Ruler of Bahrain and Rahmah bin Jaber. Bin Jaber, the Sheikh of Khor Hassan, had allied himself with the Wahhabis and become their chief tool for carrying out their piratical activities. His occupation of Zubarah and alliance with Muscat represented a threat to the Ruler of Bahrain.

Britain, however, refused to commit itself to enforce the agreement reached between the two opponents, as such a step would have led to a greater degree of involvement in intertribal affairs than British interests warranted at the time (Warden 1856, 373).

Despite Britain's reluctance to enforce every aspect of the General Treaty, the Treaty did have the effect of reducing the lawlessness and violence that had prevailed in the region. As Britain unequivocally demonstrated its determination to punish any piratical actions, local tribes increasingly took into consideration the possibility of British punitive measures in response to their operations against one another. In this context, British interference came to be seen—although, in many cases, mistakenly—as yet another channel for resolving local disputes. On some occasions, local rulers approached the British government about acts that could not strictly be considered piratical, but were presented as such in an effort to secure British involvement. Britain, however, was the ultimate arbiter for implementation of the General Treaty, and its officials had the last word in determining whether the actions of various local rulers or tribes constituted "war" or "piracy."

This policy line found expression in Britain's refusal to provide guarantees for a Bahraini-Muscati peace agreement reached in 1829. Although the British government was interested in ending the long-standing conflict between the two powers, it was not yet ready to play the role of guarantor of their relations. Indeed, Britain made considerable effort to mediate between the two opponents but—as in other similar cases—it stopped short of providing British guarantees to enforce the resulting agreement (Warden 1856, 380).

The "Pirate Coast" Transforms into the "Trucial Coast"

British authorities were fast to react to any acts that were considered piracy, but were reluctant to go beyond their Treaty obligations. This resulted in continual maritime warfare—albeit "legitimate"—among local chiefs. When in 1835 a serious violation of the Treaty's anti-piracy provisions by the Bani Yas tribe was added to the number of occasional piratical acts in the Gulf, British authorities decided to expand the scope of British involvement in the region and ban any type of hostilities at sea during the pearling season. In addition to preventing disturbances to the main economic activities of local tribes, such an arrangement was expected to also contribute to the safety of trading expeditions to the Indian subcontinent.

To this end, the British Resident at Bushire secured a Maritime Truce in 1835. The Truce was signed by the tribal chiefs inhabiting the Pirate Coast, and together with the 1820 General Treaty, became the main instrument for the maintenance of peace in the region. What had previously been known as "the Pirate Coast" then came to be called "the Trucial Coast" (Lorimer 1908–15, 1:211).

In 1836, Britain introduced an additional security measure by defining a neutral zone in the Gulf, within which any type of hostilities were forbidden, even outside the pearling season, for as long as the Maritime Truce existed. As the British explained to the chiefs of the Trucial Coast, hostile operations were to be permitted only in certain areas immediately adjoining their coasts. The British government threatened, furthermore, that any breach of this arrangement would trigger the same punishment as piratical acts (Lorimer 1908–15, 1:211).

Britain thus assumed the role of "policeman" of the maritime peace in the region. In accord with the Maritime Truce, Britain became the major arbiter and mediator in local conflicts, as well as the authority whose sanction was required for the conduct of any hostile operations in the region. Since local chiefs were unwilling to go against the wishes of the British government, the security situation in the Gulf soon dramatically improved.

The British government and British traders were not the only parties to reap the benefits of this new arrangement. The Trucial chiefs as well expressed their "undisguised satisfaction" with the "unusual peace and tranquility" that resulted from the signature of the Maritime Truce (A. B. Kemball 1844a, 69). Therefore, they readily agreed to a renewal of the First Maritime Truce of 1835 for one more year, as well as to its subsequent one-year renewals. In 1843, the Maritime Truce was extended once again, this time for a period of ten years. In 1853, a Perpetual Treaty of Peace was signed by the Trucial chiefs.

Bahrain itself did not become party to the Maritime Truce. As the Truce was mainly a response to actions committed by tribes from "the Pirate Coast," Britain did not perceive it necessary to impose its terms on neighboring tribes.

> [The Ruler of Bahrain] was too tangible, and too well convinced how deeply his interests would be affected by any collision with British authority and influence in this quarter to render it probable that he would risk any deviation from that commendable and peaceable line of conduct which had previously distinguished him, as far as his general maritime pursuits had been concerned. (A. B. Kemball 1844a, 69 fn)

The significance of the Truce for Bahrain, however, lay in the fact that through Britain's enforcement of the Truce's provisions, Bahrain's territory was protected from attack by the Trucial Sheikhdoms. In 1836, the extension of the neutral zone to Bahrain gave further meaning to the British government's commitment to the security of the Ruler of Bahrain's possessions. Though Bahrain wasn't assimilated into the Trucial system, Britain effectively assumed the function of guarantor of the Sheikhdom against the ambitions of both its neighbors and its dynastic contenders:

> On the occasion . . . of some irregularities and piratical acts, committed on the Persian Coast by the sons of the Bahrein Chief whilst in rebellion against their father, [the] restrictive line was . . . made applicable to Huailah and Bahrein, by being extended from Hawlool, ten miles north of Ras Reccan, through the island

of El Kraan to Ras Zoor, on the main[land], a measure which was assented to by the Uttobee Chief in a letter dated 26th March 1836. (A. B. Kemball 1844a, 67)

As the above passage indicates, the Qatar peninsula was invariably considered part of the Ruler of Bahrain's possessions, and as such was logically granted the same protections as the Bahrain Islands.

British Recognition of Bahrain as Political Entity

As already discussed in the present section, the early anti-piracy Treaties concluded between Britain and the Gulf Rulers represented a first step toward formalizing Britain's role in the region. In addition, those Treaties gave important evidence of British recognition of the region's Rulers as leaders of separate political entities. As Britain's involvement in the region increased in the following years, the position of those Rulers was strengthened, and the identities and territorial extent of their sheikhdoms were further defined.

Bahrain and the sheikhdoms of the Trucial Coast were the first political units to enter into treaty relations with Britain. And though Britain strove to remain neutral with respect to the sheikhdoms' internal affairs, British efforts toward maintaining peace and order in the Gulf had a significant—though indirect—influence on both the economic activities and the power structures of local tribes. Britain's relationship with local rulers thus had a dual effect: it reinforced particular ruling dynasties' political standing, while at the same time it confirmed the territorial extent of those dynasties' possessions.

In the case of Bahrain, Britain's increasing involvement in Gulf affairs served to cement the position of the Al-Khalifa family. As the Al-Khalifa were the only sheikhdom to deal with Britain directly and be held responsible for the fulfillment of treaty obligations, their paramount status on the Bahrain Islands and the Qatar peninsula was strengthened by Britain's greater involvement. In addition, as early as 1820 Bahrain's Rulers were perceived by British authorities as the leaders of a political entity mature enough to undertake international obligations. Another significant fact: the treaties reflected an expectation that the Al-Khalifa's political authority would possess continuity—insofar as the Rulers undertook, in the

Preliminary Treaty, not to permit certain actions "from henceforth, in Bahrain or its dependencies," and in the General Treaty, to see to the cessation in the Gulf of certain activities "forever."

These limited-effect treaties were soon to evolve into treaties of even greater significance.

Britain as "Protector" of Bahrain Territory: 1840s through 1860s

In contrast to the commercial nature of British activities in the Gulf at the beginning of the nineteenth century, the years following the conclusion of the region's first anti-piracy treaties saw a rapid increase in British military and political involvement. Where in the 1820s British interference was limited primarily to punishing piratical acts, in the 1830s prevention rather than punishment became Britain's main tool for achieving maritime peace. The British-sponsored Maritime Truce, signed in 1835 and periodically renewed, created a framework of numerous "checks" to armed aggression at sea. Britain thus became the guarantor of Gulf sheikhdoms, acting as mediator and arbiter in their disputes, sanctioning their operations against one another and punishing any breaches of the maritime peace.

In the 1840s and 1850s, British relations with Bahrain followed the pattern established earlier in the century. British authorities primarily concerned themselves with the observance of the General Treaty and the Maritime Truce, and their dealings with the Ruler of Bahrain were largely determined by the prevailing security situation in the region. Thus, Bahrain was frequently assimilated into British campaigns formulated in response to events in other parts of the Gulf.

One such campaign, provoked by developments in the Trucial Coast, aimed to suppress slave trade in the region. Because Bahrain was an important maritime power in the region, British authorities felt that its cooperation was required for Britain's anti-slavery efforts to succeed. For this reason, in 1847 the Ruler of Bahrain was made party to an *Agreement for the Abolition of the African Slave Trade*, similar to one concluded earlier with the sheikhs of the Trucial Coast. A further Agreement—supplementing 1847's—was concluded in 1856.

The two agreements represented personal undertakings and were not binding on the Ruler's successors; they aimed merely to resolve immediate problems rather than to define British-Bahraini relations for the future (*Agreement Entered into by Shaikh Mahomed bin Khalifah,*

Chief of Bahrain, for the Abolition of the African Slave Trade, 1847; *Further Engagement Entered into by Shaikh Mahomed bin Khalifah with the British Government for the More Effectual Suppression of the Slave Traffic*, 1856).

British efforts to end the slave trade in the region resulted in no significant changes in the nature of Britain's involvement in Bahrain. Rather, the territorial ambitions of Bahrain's neighbors and internal developments in Bahrain in the 1840s led to increased British interference and to Britain's assumption of political responsibilities. The idea of neutrality in respect to Bahrain's internal affairs was not officially abandoned until the 1860s; but Britain's interests required closer supervision of events in the sheikhdom and greater control over its relations with other powers than a policy of strict neutrality would justify.

Britain had good reasons to view any challenge—external or domestic—to the authority of the Ruler of Bahrain as a potential threat to security in the region. As described in Chapter 3, internal dissensions in Bahrain frequently involved armed operations at sea. In such cases, the degree of the resulting violence could hardly be controlled and maritime traffic suffered.

Wars between other local rulers were also a serious destabilizing factor in the region. But perceived by local tribes as the "normal" means of resolving disputes, such wars were an established feature of relations among powers in the Gulf. Bahrain's location close to the coasts of Persia, Muscat, and the Wahhabi state inevitably caused it to be caught up in such warfare.

In the early 1840s, British efforts focused mainly on enforcement of the neutral zone through the Maritime Truce system. The zone, in which any form of hostilities were outlawed, was viewed by British authorities as their main instrument to control violence in the region and thus to achieve a degree of safety for maritime traffic. As they provided both useful guidelines, and justification for interference, observance of the neutral zone—and of the so-called "Restrictive Line" which marked its limits—became Britain's primary concerns. Under the Trucial System, local rulers were required to seek permission and receive British approval for any armed operations likely to be conducted within the limits of the neutral zone—the absence of such approval likely to trigger punitive measures by Britain. The leaders of local tribes were thus left with little choice but to comply.

Such was the case with Isa bin Tarif who, in 1839, sought permission to attack the territories of the Ruler of Bahrain. Though Sheikh Abdullah, the then Ruler, had at the time fallen out of favor with the British government due to his communications with Egyptian forces in Hasa, Britain refused to give Isa permission to launch operations against the Ruler of Bahrain. Isa was once again restrained in 1841 when the British Resident reiterated his country's position regarding the observance of the neutral zone (Warden 1856, 387–89; Lorimer 1908–15, 1:866–67).

However, Sheikh Abdullah's conduct during the Egyptian occupation of Hasa, as well as his suspected association with a piracy committed in Manama on a boat flying the British flag, finally convinced British authorities to grant their support to a hostile operation by Isa. The latter had in the meantime allied himself with Bushir bin Rahmah, another enemy of the Bahrain Ruler, and in 1843 the coalition was also joined by Sheikh Mohammed bin Khalifa, Sheikh Abdullah's principal rival for the Bahrain succession. Britain's permission for armed operations against Bahrain and refusal to interfere in support of Sheikh Abdullah ultimately determined the outcome of the dynastic contest at that stage (Lorimer 1908–15, 1:869).

However, during the no less turbulent period of 1843–49, when the second stage of dynastic struggles took place, Britain refused to associate itself with a particular contestant and continued to insist on observance of the Restrictive Line. In 1843, British authorities did interfere, to prevent the outbreak of hostilities between two newly formed coalitions: one forged by Sheikh Abdullah's sons with the Rulers of Sharjah and Dubai; the other by their opponents Isa bin Tarif and Bushir bin Rahmah, who had allied themselves with the Sheikhs of Abu Dhabi and Umm Al-Qaiwain (Lorimer 1908–15, 1:871). Fearing that any participation by outside powers in the internal conflicts in Bahrain might result in an unmanageable degree of violence in Gulf waters, Britain refused any of the parties permission to launch hostilities. In the same year, Britain also dissuaded Sayid Sa'id, the Sultan of Muscat, from pursuing his son's plans—formulated upon a proposal by Isa bin Tarif—to invade Bahrain.

Similarly, in 1846 Britain used its political influence to prevent the formation of both a coalition against Bahrain between the Wahhabis and certain Trucial Sheikhs, and of a defensive alliance between Sheikh

Mohammed and the Ruler of Dubai. In 1849, Persian designs to take advantage of the instability in Bahrain and intervene in that power's dynastic struggles were also quashed by British authorities. As the dynastic struggles in Bahrain dragged on, new attempts were made by the deposed Sheikh Abdullah to reclaim his former dominions. Britain's stance, however, remained the same, and British authorities continued to insist on observance of the neutral zone, while at the same time they refused to back any particular contestant. In 1847, Britain intervened militarily following a violation of the Restrictive Line by Sheikh Abdullah and the forces of Isa bin Tarif (who had, in the meantime, allied himself with the former Sheikh of Bahrain, Sheikh Mohammed bin Khalifa). A British ship was dispatched to prevent the outbreak of hostilities; however, a delay in receiving official instructions from the British government caused the struggle to be decided on land between the forces of the two Bahrain Rulers, Sheikh Mohammed bin Khalifa and Sheikh Abdullah bin Ahmed (Warden 1856, 394–420; Lorimer 1908–15, 1:871–72).

These various threats to the security of Bahrain reinforced Britain's commitment to prevent further destabilization by taking a more active role in the sheikhdom's affairs. One short-lived but highly significant development—an attempt by the Ottomans to assert their authority over Bahrain in 1847—further demonstrated the need for a consistent British policy regarding the sheikhdom's political status. As it had become obvious that the enforcement of the Restrictive Line alone was insufficient to achieve the desired measure of stability, Britain grew willing to consider closer political involvement. This evolution of official British policies found expression in the British government's 1847 statement that "any attempts upon Bahrain ought to be resisted by the British naval force" (Lorimer 1908–15, 1:882).

One affair, in which the British chose not to get involved, was the challenge in 1848 to Sheikh Mohammed's throne by Isa bin Tarif, leader of the Al bin Ali tribe living in the Zubarah region, who had formed a coalition of tribes on the Qatar peninsula. This attempt, resulting in the defeat and death of bin Tarif, was largely unsuccessful due to the support of the Naim tribe who had refused to join the coalition.

Bin Tarif had requested from the Ruler of Bahrain the position of governor of Doha, which was granted. Upon assuming the governorship, however, bin Tarif began plotting to remove Sheikh Mohammed from power. According to Mohammed Khalifa Al-Nabhani, a scholar of the history of the region, the Naim were the only tribe not to join bin Tarif in his quest against the Al-Khalifa (Nabhani 1923).

Because the Naim tribe refused to join bin Tarif and his allies, bin Tarif threatened to attack them. The Naim refused to submit, sending instead an urgent message to Sheikh Mohammad Al-Khalifa, in Bahrain, asking for his help and support.

Sheikh Mohammed immediately went to the Qatar peninsula to defend the Zubarah region and the Naim. Together, Sheikh Mohammad, the Naim, and others formed a coalition against bin Tarif and his army. A battle ensued at Umm Suweyya on the peninsula, in which bin Tarif was killed and his army defeated.

In 1848, the British government began an assessment of the advantages of an official protectorate status for Bahrain. The British Political Resident began consultations with Sheikh Mohammed, and in 1849 received the latter's assurances that Bahrain indeed desired such a move. In a letter to the Bombay government, the then Political Resident reported that "the proposition made by Sheik Mahomed, to place himself under the British government, had been debated in an assembly of the principal members of his family, and apparently unanimously agreed to" (Hennell, 28 February 1849). Strategic considerations, however, prevented Britain from proceeding to establish a protectorate in Bahrain. Sheikh Mohammed's proposal was declined, but the Ruler was assured of the British government's continuing support and good will (Lorimer 1908–15, 1:882).

Though Britain was not prepared in 1849 to grant Bahrain the status of British protectorate, it continued to be strongly concerned with the sheikhdom's affairs. Britain's de facto commitment to Bahraini independence was evidenced in a number of successful interventions aiming to uphold the integrity of the Ruler of Bahrain's dominions. Thus, in 1851, when a coalition between the Wahhabis and the forces of the late Sheikh Abdullah's sons threatened the authority of Sheikh Mohammed, a British squadron was dispatched to Bahrain and effectively took the islands under its protection (Lorimer 1908–15, 1:885). Since tensions with the Wahhabis persisted during the two following years, the government of Bombay received authorization "to offer every obstacle to an attack upon [the Bahrain] islands by the Wahhabi Amir."

In this context, Britain acted to stop renewed Wahhabi preparations to take the islands in 1859 (Lorimer 1908–15, 1:887).

The Friendly Convention of 1861

Despite British efforts to maintain the security of Sheikh Mohammed's territories, Britain's refusal to make any further formal commitments was reason for the Ruler's continuing dissatisfaction. In 1859, Sheikh Mohammed announced his allegiance to both Persia and Turkey—which in practice amounted to little more than a mere declaration, but which provoked the British government to take yet another step toward guaranteeing Bahrain's political status.

In 1861, following discussions among a number of government agencies, Britain officially recognized that the integrity of Bahrain was essential to the system of maritime peace in the Gulf. Furthermore, in view of ongoing hostilities between Bahrain and the Wahhabi state, Britain considered it imperative to obtain assurances that the Ruler of Bahrain would observe previous arrangements with Britain "in the interest of commerce, humanity and public security" (Lorimer 1908–15, 1:888). In this context, a Friendly Convention was concluded between Sheikh Mohammed and the British Resident in May 1861. And though obtained without prior express approval by London, it was ratified by the British government in 1862.

The Convention, whose aim was "the advancement of trade and security of all classes of people navigating and residing upon the coasts of [the] Gulf," had a number of political connotations. Like the 1820 Treaty, it acknowledged Bahrain as a separate political entity. Furthermore, Sheikh Mohammed was recognized as the "independent ruler of Bahrein," whose obligations were binding on his heirs and successors. The Convention thus possessed all the necessary characteristics of an international treaty and reflected Britain's understanding of the Al-Khalifa dynasty's political status.

The importance of the Convention also lay in its formalization of Britain's role as guarantor of Bahrain's security against outside aggression. Britain's responsibilities in this respect were spelled out in Article 3, which stipulated that the British Resident would "take the necessary steps for obtaining reparation for every injury proved to have been inflicted, or in course of infliction by sea upon Bahrein or upon its dependencies in [the] Gulf." In addition, "all aggressions and depredations" against Bahrain were to be reported by the Ruler to British authorities, with the British Resident in the Persian Gulf acting as the arbiter in such cases.

In return for British protection, Sheikh Mohammed bound himself and his successors "to abstain from all maritime aggressions of every description, from the prosecution of war, piracy and slavery by sea" as long as the British government guaranteed the security of Bahrain. The Ruler further undertook to provide compensation for any such actions committed by himself or his subjects:

> I, Sheikh Mahomed bin Khuleefa, will afford full redress for all maritime offenses, which in justice can be charged against my subjects or myself, as the ruler of Bahrein. (Terms of a Friendly Convention between Ruler of Bahrain and British Government, 31 May 1861, 235)

Following an already well-established tradition of dealing directly with the Ruler of Bahrain and holding him responsible for the acts of his people, Britain once again confirmed Sheikh Mohammed's status as the sovereign authority in Bahrain.

That Britain had no doubts as to the applicability of the Convention to the Ruler of Bahrain's possessions on the Qatar peninsula was demonstrated shortly after the Convention's ratification. In view of renewed Wahhabi claims to certain territories on the peninsula, the Ruler of Bahrain invoked Article 2 of the Friendly Convention and requested Britain's support in defending his territories. In February 1862, the British Resident sent a letter to the Wahhabi Ruler, reiterating the Ruler of Bahrain's rights in this respect:

> ... credible information has reached the Chiefs of Bahrein that your Highness' Agents are active in sowing dissension amongst the tribes subject to Bahrein on the Guttur coast. Anarchy at all events threatens there and the quiet of the chiefs and the people of Bahrein being thus constantly disturbed some measures on their part seem to them imperative ... I shall I fear be unable to restrain [the Ruler of Bahrain] from the exercise of his legitimate rights and prerogatives ... It will be my duty to respect and even

uphold those rights and prerogatives when they are legitimately proclaimed and put in practice by sea. (Jones, 8 February 1862).

The Doha Affair: 1867–68

But when in the late 1860s the first significant breach of the Friendly Convention occurred, Britain's policy of noninterference in the internal affairs of Bahrain changed. This breach, committed by Sheikh Mohammed himself, was a reaction to internal dissensions in the Doha confederation. The result of Sheikh Mohammed's punitive campaign against the Doha rebels was the sacking of that town with the help of the Ruler of Dubai. When the inhabitants of Doha, in their turn, mounted a retaliatory expedition, and the level of violence at sea escalated, Britain was forced to interfere:

> ...the affair having quickly come to be regarded in the Gulf as a test of British preparedness to maintain peace at sea, it was resolved to inflict an exemplary punishment upon the offending chiefs and not to accept the excuse, which would probably be tendered by Sheikh Muhammad, that he was entitled to punish by any and every means his refractory subjects in Qatar. (Lorimer 1908–15, 1:894)

British authorities then decided to obtain compensation from all the Sheikhs involved in the events; also to secure their guarantees for the restoration of the maritime peace. Learning of British intents and "aware that a reckoning was at hand," Sheikh Mohammed fled from the islands, and his brother, Ali bin Khalifa, became Ruler of Bahrain. In his new capacity Sheikh Ali signed, in September 1868, an undertaking that he would comply with Britain's demands for compensation, and that he would see to the restoration of vessels captured during Sheikh Mohammed's campaign. The new Ruler also declared that Sheikh Mohammed would thenceforth be permanently excluded from the affairs of Bahrain.

Similar conditions were also imposed on the Ruler of Abu Dhabi and the principal sheikhs of the Qatar peninsula. All of them agreed to cease piratical activities and to observe the maritime peace. The agreement signed with the sheikhs of Qatar also ensured a return to the status quo in respect of Qatar inhabitants' relations with the Ruler of Bahrain:

> We, the undersigned, Chiefs, all residing in the province of Guttar, do hereby solemnly agree and bind ourselves to pay to Shaikh Ali bin Khalifeh, Chief of Bahrein, the sums of money per annum heretofore paid by us to the Chiefs of Bahrein... (*Agreement between Chiefs Residing in the Province of Qatar and Chief of Bahrain*, 13 September 1868)

In addition to the Agreement of 13 September 1868 signed by Mohammed Al-Thani (see Chapter 4, in "The Al-Thani Move Toward Prominence"), he himself signed also a separate declaration whereby he promised to "return to Doha and reside peaceably at that port" (*Agreement of Chief of El-Kutr*, 12 September 1868). The very fact that British intervention had been provoked by events in Doha confirmed that British authorities believed the Qatar peninsula to be a dependency of Bahrain. This belief was clearly reflected in the letter inviting Sheikh Mohammed Al-Thani to sign the Declaration. The letter referred to "serious piratical breaches of the maritime truce" (L. Pelly, 11 September 1868). Britain's action was based on an obligation arising from Bahrain's signing of the piracy treaties for its territories, which included Qatar, as no authority from the Qatar peninsula was party to the Truce of 1835 or the Convention with the British government in 1861.

All agreements concluded between the British Political Resident and the Qatar powers involved in the 1867–68 events were personal undertakings and only aimed to confirm existing obligations toward maintaining law and order in the Gulf. As the agreements did not bind the rulers' successors and were only a response to immediate events, they did not amount to recognition of the status of any particular ruler. This is further evidenced by the fact that the 1868 Declaration by the Chiefs of Qatar formalized the Doha confederation's submission to Bahrain.

Increased Involvement with Bahrain's Internal Affairs
Dynastic Struggles and the Ottomans Arrive in Doha: the 1870s

Britain's reaction to events in Doha in 1868 testified to British authorities increasing preparedness to involve themselves in Bahrain's domestic affairs. Britain's actions to resolve the problems between the Ruler of Bahrain and his subjects in Doha were followed by increasing intervention in Bahrain's internal matters.

When another outburst of dynastic struggles occurred in August 1869, resulting in the assassination of Sheikh Ali by the forces of Sheikh Mohammed, Britain felt compelled to take measures to restore law and order. The assistant to the British Political Resident at Bushire was sent to Bahrain, authorized to institute a blockade of the islands of Manama and Muharraq, which had been occupied by the aggressors. Instructions were also given that upon the surrender of Sheikh Mohammed and his allies, then it should be Isa bin Ali, Sheikh Ali's son, who was recognized as the new Ruler of Bahrain. The Political Resident himself proceeded to Bahrain in December of the same year and directed the British naval operation against the islands. Following the defeat of Sheikh Mohammed bin Khalifa's followers, Sheikh Isa bin Ali became Ruler of Bahrain.

Both Persia and the Porte—which was once again becoming an important player in the region—protested against British actions in Bahrain. Responding to Persian complaints, the British government expressed its stance as follows:

> If we are no longer prepared to continue the performance of the tasks we have undertaken, we must withdraw altogether; but the consequences of such a step would be so disastrous, not only to our national honour, but to the peace of the Gulf, to the prosperity of the tribes inhabiting the littoral, and to the lives and property of our subjects... that we cannot contemplate this course as one of which Her Majesty's Government could for a moment entertain. (Government of India, 20 May 1870)

For their part, the Ottomans stated that Britain's involvement amounted to an assertion of British sovereignty over "a portion of Turkish territory" (Lorimer 1908–15, 1:901). The Porte's claims were immediately dismissed. However, two years later, when the Ottomans reached the Qatar peninsula, Britain became aware of the need for a stronger legal basis for its actions in Bahrain.

In 1871, when the Ottomans annexed Hasa, they advanced claims to the Bahrain Islands as well. The strong reaction with which the British government met those claims, however, forced the Ottomans to abandon any plans they might have had to occupy the islands. Assurances of nonaggression against the islands were obtained from the Porte while, at the same time, Britain stressed its continuing commitment to the defense of the Ruler of Bahrain's territories by virtue of the 1861 Convention:

> The decided attitude of the British government and the constant presence of British ships in Bahrain prevented, however, any actual interference... and this result was felt throughout the whole Gulf, to be a salutary and well-timed check to Turkish pretensions and encroachments. (Lorimer 1908–15, 1:904–5)

As will be discussed in detail in the next chapter, the Ottomans established themselves in the southeast of the Qatar peninsula near Doha. Their rule never extended to the north of the peninsula, where the Ruler of Bahrain continued to exercise his authority. A number of attempts were made to assimilate those areas into the Sultan's dominions; however, the forces of the Bahrain Ruler repelled all such attempts (see Chapter 10 for details of these attempts).

Though the Porte continued to seek expansion into Bahrain, and frequently made statements to the effect that the islands were Ottoman territory, no serious steps were taken toward annexing the islands, and any news of possible Ottoman attacks provoked immediate assertions of Britain's commitment to the defense of Bahrain's territories.

The Exclusive Agreements of 1880 and 1892

Turkey's occasional claims to rights in Bahrain and protests against British actions on the islands led British authorities to reconsider the legal basis for their involvement in the region. In addition, strategic considerations—most notably, events related to Ottoman territories in Europe—resulted in an ever more acutely perceived need to define unequivocally what constituted British and Ottoman spheres of influence in the Gulf.

In the 1870s, Britain typically referred to the independence of Bahrain, which, as was stressed in official British communications with the Porte, was in treaty relations with Britain. As a rule, Britain refused to exercise full sovereignty over Bahrain and explained its actions as deriving from its obligations as guarantor of the maritime peace. With the presence of the Ottomans in the Gulf, however, such a position became increasingly untenable, and it became clear that a new legal instrument was needed to justify British interference. Thus, the Exclusive Agreements of 1880 and 1892 were born.

The event immediately provoking British authorities to sign the first Agreement was an Ottoman attempt to establish an Agency and a coal depot in Bahrain. As such actions would have paved the way for the exercise of Turkish influence, Britain took steps to check any further political advances by the Porte. This was done by obtaining the Ruler of Bahrain's promise that Britain would act as the exclusive regulator of his relations with any foreign powers (Ross, 24 December 1880; Government of India, 14 February 1881).

In 1880, the First Exclusive Agreement was signed, wherein the Ruler bound himself and his successors

> ... to abstain from entering into negotiations or making treaties of any sort with any State or Government other than the British without the consent of the... British Government, and to refuse permission to any other Government than the British to establish Diplomatic or Consular Agencies or coaling depots in [Bahrain's] territory, unless with the consent of the British Government. *(Agreement signed by the Chief of Bahrain, 22 December 1880)*

The agreement did not affect customary friendly communications with neighboring states "on business of minor importance."

Britain felt that in addition to serving British interests in the region, such an agreement would also prove useful to the Ruler of Bahrain, by enabling him "to decline, without difficulty or offence, any overtures made to him..." (Government of India, 14 February 1881). Furthermore, the agreement was seen as a tool to counter, not only Ottoman, but also other powers' designs in respect of Bahrain—especially in view of reports of the presence in the Gulf of French, American and Japanese vessels (Ross, 24 December 1880).

In 1892, another Exclusive Agreement was signed with the Ruler of Bahrain, prompted by the appearance of two French adventurers, who in Umm Al-Quwaim opened the prospect of French settlement on the Trucial Coast (Lorimer 1908–15, 1:737–39). As well as reiterating the provisions of the 1880 Agreement respecting relations with foreign governments, the new instrument obliged the Ruler of Bahrain not to "cede, sell, mortgage or otherwise give for occupation any part of [his] territory save to the British Government" (*Exclusive Agreement of the Shaikh of Bahrain with the British Government*, 13 March 1892). This provision was to prove crucial in negotiations with oil companies in the early twentieth century.

The two Exclusive Agreements made Britain's responsibility for the security of Bahrain "nearly total" (Anscombe 1994, 103), and transformed the latter into a protected state. While the prerogatives of the British government with respect to international representation were clearly defined, no mention was made of regulating the internal affairs of Bahrain. However, Britain's need to enforce the foreign policy provisions of the two treaties led it to assume, as of the end of the nineteenth century, the de facto administration of the islands:

> ... the attention of the British Government, whose influence in Bahrain was now more powerful than before, was turned chiefly to schemes of internal improvement and reform, and to precautions against political competition on the part of European powers. Any distinction between British policy and the general course of events in Bahrain is henceforth impracticable.... (Lorimer 1908–15, 1:926)

Formally, the administration of Bahrain became the responsibility of a British Political Agent who was to be permanently present in the country, to oversee day-to-day matters, and to communicate with the Ruler on behalf of the British government. The Political Agent was to report to the Political Resident in the Persian Gulf; the latter would remain in charge of supervising the whole region. The appointment of the first Political Agent in 1904 marked the institutionalization of British control over Bahrain. Another event that formalized that control was the proclamation of the 1913 Bahrain Order in Council—a document providing the framework for the administration of Bahrain's legal affairs (Saldanha 1904, 131; *Bahrain Order in Council*, 12 August 1913). In 1946, the Political Residency itself was transferred to Bahrain.

Bahrain, whose status as a separate political entity had been recognized by the British as early as 1820—had thus been firmly absorbed into British administrative structures. Starting as an attempt to improve the security situation in the region, the relationship between Britain and Bahrain went through a number of stages before culminating in the signature of the Exclusive Agreements. Thereupon, Britain—while continuing to formally treat Bahrain as an independent entity—became the exclusive regulator of its international relations, and also placed itself in a position to oversee every aspect of Bahrain's internal administration.

6 Ottoman Presence and Qatar's Emergence as a Separate Entity

Although by the end of the eighteenth century Britain had assumed the role of a dominant maritime power in the Middle East, the mainland of Arabia was largely unaffected by British influence. That the British never sought to extend their presence inland can be explained by the fact that Arabia had little to offer in terms of economic potential. The India trade, which had emerged as the paramount British concern in the East, depended on maritime traffic rather than on land routes. Ensuring the safety of commercial navigation had thus become Britain's paramount task, and one which required serious military, financial, and political involvement in the Gulf. Thus the British were prevented from directing their resources toward the conquest of territories of doubtful value to their Empire. But for the Ottoman Empire, control of the arid and desolate lands of Arabia was paramount.

Ottoman Expansion into Arabia

The Ottomans had a number of reasons to seek expansion into Arabia. They were motivated chiefly by perceived threats to their Empire posed by European powers in the Gulf—by the Portuguese in the sixteenth century, by the British in the nineteenth. Ottoman sensitivities were further aroused by events in the European territories of the Empire, where the European powers were providing support to peoples struggling for autonomy from Istanbul. Ottoman fears about political developments in the Ottoman European territories were projected onto the situation in the Gulf, resulting in an unrealistic assessment by the Porte of British interests in the region. Fearing encroachment into their territories from British bases in the Arabian Gulf, the Ottomans thus embarked on a program of expansionism that aimed at securing the southern borders of their Empire (Anscombe 1997, 11, 21; Fromkin 2001).

Ottoman rule in the Arabian Peninsula and Qatar came at an increasingly delicate time for the Ottomans. No longer the mighty power it had been in the fifteenth and sixteenth centuries, the Porte was forced to rely on British and French assistance to protect it from Russian encroachment during the Crimean War (1854–56). The Porte's Balkan provinces of Bosnia, Herzegovina, and Bulgaria had risen up in rebellion. To add insult to injury, the situation in its North African and Asian provinces was unhelpful: Mehmet Ali's reign in Egypt (1805–48) was independent of the Porte; France had occupied Algeria in 1830; and the British had been in control of Aden since 1839. The symbolism of a growing British presence in the Arabian Peninsula, the heartland of Islam, damaged the Ottomans' image as "protector of the Islamic world." They desperately needed to regain a foothold in the Gulf, and their efforts in Arabia and the Qatar peninsula were a part of that plan.

Another factor precipitating Ottoman involvement in the Gulf was the emergence of the Wahhabi movement. Abdul-Wahhab taught a "puritanical" version of Hanbali Sunni beliefs, which had taken on political connotations and had been adopted as official doctrine by the tribe of Mohammed ibn Saud. His successor, Abdul-Aziz ibn Saud, had launched a number of successful campaigns on the coast of the Arabian Gulf, reaching as far north as Iraq. As a result, the Gulf had by the beginning of the nineteenth century become a place where Wahhabism was developing into an ever more formidable religious and political force.

Ottoman fears derived mainly from two aspects of Wahhabism, first, violence, which constituted an essential part of its doctrine; and second, Wahhabism's rejection of the Ottoman Sultan's claim to be the supreme ruler of all Muslims. In 1802 the Wahhabis took control of Mecca, and then continued their expansion to territories which until then were considered to be under the nominal suzerainty of the Sultan. As a result, the Sublime Porte invited Mohammed Ali, the Viceroy of Egypt, to reassert Ottoman authority over Wahhabi-controlled areas. Mohammed Ali's expedition from 1812 to 1818 resulted in the occupation of the Nejd (central), Hasa (Eastern), and the Hijaz (Western) areas of the Arabian Peninsula. The Wahhabi strongholds were thus shortly brought back into the Ottoman orbit. After a second expedition to the Nejd in 1838, Egyptian forces withdrew from the area in the 1840s—an event that marked a return to the previous state of affairs in the region and the restoration of Saudi power (Yapp 1994, 174–75; Yapp 1980a, 46).

Though for all practical purposes the Saudis were the rulers of Eastern Arabia, they continued to acknowledge the formal suzerainty of the Sultan. This fact enabled the Porte to intervene following the 1865 outbreak of a dynastic succession conflict between the two sons of the Wahhabi Amir. The Porte's restoration of order in 1871 marked the formal beginning of the second period of Ottoman imperial presence in the region. During this new wave of assertion of Ottoman authority in the Gulf, the Bahrain Islands remained essentially unaffected because the British had so firmly established their hold over it. However, the Ottomans reached as far as the southern portions of the Qatar peninsula, and in 1871 the Chief of Doha formally recognized their authority. The only problem was, they also had to deal with the local balance of power in the Qatar peninsula during the late nineteenth century; in other words, the Rulers of Bahrain in the Zubarah region, the Al-Thani in Doha and its environs, and occasionally the Al-Saud of the Arabian Peninsula, who used the Qatar peninsula as a base for raids.

The lands acquired in 1871 were duly incorporated into the Ottoman administrative system. The *Sanjak* (subprovince) of Nejd was formed, ruled by a *Mutasarrif* (governor) and comprising four *kaza*'s (districts); there also were *nahiye*'s (subdistricts) and *koy*'s (towns, villages) (Bahrain 1996, 23 ¶ 65, 84 ¶ 191). The Ottomans, however, failed to develop their presence into fully fledged domination of the area, due to the difficulties associated with controlling diverse and rather unruly tribes. Another event having a negative effect on the Porte's ability to establish effective control was the 1872 departure of the architect of the Ottoman administrative system in the area, Midhat Pasha (Anscombe 1997, 68–73).

Britain remained largely uninvolved in the events that were unfolding on the mainland; official British policy called for non-interference in the affairs of tribes whose activities fell outside the scope of Britain's maritime and security interests. The Ottomans assured Britain that no attempts would be made at extending Ottoman control to Bahrain or the Trucial states; this further contributing to Britain's willingness to accept the outcome of the 1871 Ottoman campaign.

Thus, during the last half of the nineteenth century, the British and Ottoman spheres of influence in the Gulf took shape according to the principle of British control over the sea and Ottoman control over the land, the two empires being equally unwilling to infringe on each other's possessions. Britain took advantage of the strategic and economic benefits of controlling the Gulf's key trading ports, and was mainly interested in ensuring the safety of navigation and protecting its profitable Eastern trade. The Porte was mostly concerned about maintaining a presence in the Gulf in order to deal with the security challenges posed by the Wahhabi movement, and to defend itself from a potential European threat to its southern borders. This division of the Gulf region into British and Ottoman spheres of control furnished the framework within which the modern political entities of Bahrain and Qatar were to emerge.

The Ottomans Arrive in Doha

Prior to the Ottoman arrival on the Qatar peninsula, no indigenous authority existed there. The peninsula was effectively ruled as a dominion of the Ruler of Bahrain and was recognized as such by all relevant powers in the region and, most notably, by Britain. This situation changed in the early 1870s when the Ottoman Empire extended its influence over parts of Qatar—a fact that resulted in the emergence of new power configurations and in the separation of the Ottoman-ruled portions of the peninsula from Bahrain.

The Ottomans expanded into the southeast of the Qatar peninsula after their successful campaign in Hasa. That move was made possible by the invitation of the Al-Thani chiefs of Doha, who viewed the establishment of Ottoman rule as an opportunity to wrest themselves from the control of the Al-Khalifa, as well as to secure for themselves protection from Wahhabi ambitions. Furthermore, in view of their limited influence in the peninsula, the Al-Thani perceived an association with the Porte as a way of possibly expanding the area under their control to include additional territories outside of Doha.

Mohammed Al-Thani, the chief of Doha town, was initially uncertain of the advantages of acknowledging the supremacy of the Porte and fearful of the possible reaction such insubordination to the Ruler of Bahrain might trigger. However, his opposition was overcome by his son Jasim, who in 1871 allowed an Ottoman garrison to be established in Doha and accepted Ottoman control over his territory.

The limits of that territory became evident when Jasim was given four flags by the Ottomans and instructed to raise them on their territory (Smith, 20 July 1871), as a sign of his submission to the Porte. One of the flags was accordingly placed above Jasim's house in Doha town, while the other three were sent to Wukra, Khawr, and Odaid—places not far from Doha. As the flags "marked the important and most distant points of Al Thani territory" (Anscombe 1994, 42), they also defined the territorial extent of Ottoman sovereignty in the peninsula (Smith, 20 July 1871).

Thus, from the early days of their presence in the Qatar peninsula, Ottoman authority was confined to the territories over which Sheikh Jasim perceived himself as having some influence—southeastern portions of the Qatar peninsula. Despite their later ambitions to push into the north, the Ottomans were never successful in establishing themselves in any other areas of the promontory.

Britain's view of the situation in southeastern Qatar confirms this. British authorities were well aware of the fact that the Ottomans had carried out their expansion through the chiefs of Doha, and their evaluation stated as follows:

> ...whatever foothold the Turks may have acquired in El-Katr was obtained... by the invitation of the local chiefs of El Bidaa [Doha]. (Government of India Foreign Dept., 22 May 1879, 5)

The Ottomans themselves had no illusions about the extent of the areas such a "foothold" comprised. In their *Official Gazette*, the following was stated in 1871 with respect to Al-Thani control:

> ...the leader residing in Bida [Doha] has no rule over the other villages. The leadership of each village has been left to the local sheikhs. (*Takvimi Vekayi*, 8 June 1871)

Whatever territories the Al-Thani did control became the Ottoman *kaza* (district) of Qatar. This administrative unit was part of the *Sanjak* (sub-province) of Hasa, and was thus incorporated into the larger Ottoman administrative system in Arabia (Anscombe 1994, 68).

Ottoman Control Extended only to Doha Area

The population concentrated in the *kaza* of Qatar was comprised primarily of pearl merchants and traders. Before the arrival of the Ottomans, the southeast coast was subordinate to the Ruler of Bahrain and maintained relations with the inhabitants of north Qatar. It was also the frequent target of Wahhabi attacks and Bedouin raids from the southeast. Its activities focused on the sea, and it felt little need for any expansion into other sections of the peninsula. Thus, far from exercising influence over any other areas, the Doha population was mainly concerned with defending itself from attacks from the interior, and with pursuing its seaward-oriented activities.

The human geography of the Qatar peninsula prevented the extension of Ottoman control beyond the areas inhabited by the merchant communities in the southeast. The Ruler of Bahrain's established influence over the pearling communities and the semi-nomadic peoples in the northwest, the threat of the Wahhabi Ruler and the Bedouin tribes from eastern Arabia in the south, along with the existence of an "empty quarter" in central Qatar—all served as powerful checks on any attempts at Ottoman or Al-Thani expansion. Mention should also be made of the British, for whom keeping the peninsula's coastal waters free of any pirate activities was high on their list of concerns.

With the Ottoman arrival in the Qatar peninsula in the late nineteenth century, yet another player was thrown into the mix of actors. In some ways, the Ottoman presence did not alter the human geography of the Qatar peninsula. Rather, under the Ottomans, Jasim bin Mohammad Al-Thani simply consolidated his position in the Doha enclave.

The Ottomans recognized the northern limits of the *kaza* of Qatar throughout the period of their presence in the peninsula. Ottoman officials distinguished between the *kaza* of Qatar—a term that applied to Doha and its environs—and the Odaid and Zubarah regions, to the south and north respectively. Although the Ottomans certainly coveted the latter two areas, Istanbul never succeeded in extending its rule there. This fact was recognized in a letter from the Office of the Assistant *Kaimakam*, who dwelt on the advantages of the possible inclusion of Odaid and Zubarah into the *kaza* of Qatar:

> If a government is now established in Udaid and Zubarah then the Kaza of Qatar will be able to benefit from the pearl fishing in this area. (*Report from the Office of Assistant to the Governor of Katar,* 7 November 1891)

This state of affairs was also reflected in an Ottoman map prepared in 1878. The map featured three political entities on the Qatar peninsula: Qatar, Zubarah, and Odaid (Extract from Ottoman map entitled *The Velayat of Basra* by Captain Izzet of the Imperial Army of the Ottoman Empire, 1878).

The British also viewed Odaid and Zubarah as areas outside of Ottoman control, and expressed that view to the Ottoman government on numerous occasions. Thus, in 1909, the Ottoman Foreign Minister himself observed:

> The British Government has always repeated her right to protect the shores of Zubarah and Udaid. (*Ottoman Arabic Report,* 27 January 1909)

In the last quarter of the nineteenth century and in the early twentieth century, the Ottomans and the Al-Thani carried out no less than seven campaigns whose aims were to extend Ottoman control to the north of the peninsula, particularly Zubarah. As will be discussed in greater detail in Chapter 10, they all proved failures. In addition to military operations, attempts to establish Ottoman authority in those areas by appointing administrators were equally ineffective. Between 1895 and 1912, four *mudir*'s (subgovernors or local administrators) were appointed to Zubarah and six to Odaid. None, however, effectively assumed his official functions:

> Istanbul maintained its right of appointment ... by continuing to name the officials ... even if they had to stay in Hufuf instead of their posts. (Anscombe 1994, 221)

It became clear, however, that the Rulers of Bahrain had no intention of giving up Zubarah, and that they had British support in this. So the Ottomans abandoned their plans to extend their authority to Zubarah, thus preserving the Ruler of Bahrain's control there.

Ottoman Administration

Overall, the years of Ottoman presence in Qatar were marked by the absence of any authority that could either unify the tribes of the peninsula or maintain some measure of law and order. Neither Ottoman officials nor the Al-Thani were able to significantly alter the existing power vacuum. (For details of Ottoman governance and their relations with inhabitants of the peninsula see especially Anscombe 1997, 49–53; and Lorimer 1908–15, 1:970–72, 979–87, 1130, 1439–46, 1502–5.) As the Ottomans at the end of the nineteenth century faced numerous challenges to their position (mainly in Europe), and as the Empire's resources—both military and financial—were limited, the *kaza* of Qatar never received the attention that would have allowed for the establishment of effective administration. Ottoman attempts to institute an effective system of governance were sporadic and half-hearted. The situation was further compounded by financial crisis in the Empire:

> As a result of the empire's extreme financial troubles in the period [the 1870s–1890s], anything that was to be attempted in Hasa was to be done cheaply. Money was not to be invested there, it was to be extracted. (Anscombe 1994, 74)

Thus, the local population was subjected to the payment of taxes to the Ottomans while its main concerns remained largely unaddressed. Among these concerns were the numerous raids by tribes inhabiting the southern parts of the peninsula. Due to the inability of either the Al-Thani or the Ottomans to guarantee the security of the population, violence prevailed.

Britain's concern for the preservation of maritime peace made it monitor closely the situation in the Qatar peninsula. The weakness—or, in certain areas, the outright absence—of effective administration there soon became evident. In 1874–76, a number of piratical acts committed by the Bani Hajir tribe remained unpunished due to the absence of any responsible authority in the Qatar peninsula. The Ottomans were unable to control even the parts of the Qatar peninsula that they occupied, nor did they have much influence on the activities of local chiefs. British authorities in 1874 reported on the situation as follows:

> The chief cause of embarrassment as regards the maintenance of peace and neutrality by sea between Bahrein and Katar lies in the

present uncertainty as to the question with who responsibility rests. The various mainland Sheikhs may shelter themselves under Turkish protection whilst the latter power has not formally assumed Government duties. Were the responsibilities more decidedly fixed the constant inconvenient anxiety about Bahrein would disappear. (Ross, 19 December 1874)

As the situation did not improve in the years that followed, British authorities went as far as to conclude that Ottoman sovereignty over the "sea coast of Katar" could not be recognized. The British Political Resident observed as follows:

> ...after his further experience and observation of the mode of procedure and policy of the Turkish authorities on the Arabian side of the Gulf, it seemed hopeless to expect a state of security to result from Turkish exclusive control, even where they were firmly established. (Ross, 24 December 1887)

A report produced by the Ottomans in 1917 after their departure from the Qatar peninsula blamed "indifference on the part of Ottoman authorities, coupled with England's desire for control" as the main causes for the failure of the Porte to establish effective administration. Referring to the Ottomans' alleged presence in the Qatar peninsula in the sixteenth century, the Report assessed Midhat Pasha's 1871 expedition as the event that had again brought the peninsula into the Ottoman orbit, but mentioned that his subsequent departure had allowed Britain to seize the peninsula indirectly. In this respect, the report noted:

> England's categorical language and its determination to prevent our mudirs [local administrators] from settling in their posts, by force if necessary, deterred the imperial Government from resuming [as in the sixteenth century] effective administration of the aforesaid peninsula. (*Ottoman Report concerning Bahrain, Qatar, Nejd and Basra*, 29 May 1917)

The Ottomans' analysis concluded with the observation that the Ottomans themselves had no information of a time when they had exercised genuine control over Qatar. Furthermore, they pointed out that the best information they had derived from assuming that no effective administration over the coast of Qatar had existed since the early nineteenth century "at least." This same report went on to admit that the Ottomans' policy in the Zubarah region had been one of "indifference" (*Ottoman Report Concerning Bahrain, Qatar, Nejd and Basra*, 29 May 1917).

Ottoman–Al-Thani Relations

Mohammed Al-Thani and his son Jasim seized upon an alliance with the Ottomans in Doha in 1871 as an event that might free him from paying tribute to the Al-Khalifa, as well as from persistent attempts by the Al-Saud, the Wahhabis, and Bedouin tribes to infiltrate the peninsula. Additionally, he was able to remove his main competitors in Doha, the Indian community.

In terms of securing himself in Doha and its environs, Jasim's plan worked. Ever since the 1868 Agreement, the British had discouraged the Ruler of Bahrain from the Qatar peninsula, while at the same time, the British continued to recognize that the Bahrain's rights in the Zubarah region remained (see Chapter 10, in "Recognition by Third Parties").

The Al-Thani family started out as a merchant family centered in Doha and its surrounding areas and was not always in complete control over that territory. Its main competitors in Doha were Indian traders.

Jasim Al-Thani used Ottoman support to oust the Indian traders from the date and pearl trades, in order to dominate these himself. He had to walk a fine line in this endeavor, however. The Indian community in Doha were British subjects and as such enjoyed British protection. As Crystal notes, this point did not put too much of a damper on Jasim's ambitions:

> In the 1870s and 1880s, he took every opportunity, formal and informal, to harass the Indians. He raised their taxes. He encouraged his tribal supporters to attack Indian ships and shops. He closed their businesses. He did everything but obtain Ottoman support, although this too he tried. (Crystal 1990, 31)

Perceived as competitors in Doha's lucrative pearling trade, the Indians were frequently mistreated by the local chief. In 1883, an Al-Thani campaign (with Ottoman support) to expel the Indians from Doha triggered immediate British intervention. The Political Resident personally went to Doha and threatened Jasim with punitive measures if the Indians were not allowed back into Doha and paid compensation. Realizing the seriousness of the threat, Jasim complied with British demands (Zahlan 1979, 56; Lorimer 1908–15, 1:812). Further disturbances in the late 1880s compelled additional involvement by the British to support the rights of the Indian and Bahraini residents of Doha.

Eventually the Indian community had enough, closed up shop, and with British aid left Doha to Al-Thani and his entourage.

It will be recalled that the Ottomans and the British were engaged in a delicate relationship at this period. They were competitors in the Gulf region, but in European affairs they were unspoken allies, with Britain dictating the terms.

This tacit balance between the Ottomans and the British had important consequences for Al-Khalifa and Al-Thani power in the Qatar peninsula. The British tolerated the Ottoman presence in the Qatar peninsula as long as it was confined to Doha, its environs, and the south of the peninsula. Thus, they limited, yet at the same time, strengthened, the influence of the Al-Thani there. The net effect of this was a lessening of the Rulers of Bahrain's traditional influence in those areas.

But the Chief of Doha's submission to the authority of the Ottoman Empire weakened, rather than strengthened, his political status. Although he acquired Turkish protection, in reality neither he nor his ambitious son, Jasim, had much power to control the workings of the Ottoman administrative and military machine—however weak and efficient that might have been. Other chiefs of the peninsula were equally unable to exercise such control. Thus, in 1873 when the Ruler of Dubai complained about piratical acts committed by Ottoman soldiers, the British Political Resident observed that "the robberies were apparently committed by disorderly Turkish soldiers over whom the Arab chiefs of Guttur themselves have no control" (Ross, 13 September 1873).

Realizing that their power in Doha had diminished rather than increased following the arrival of the Ottomans, the Al-Thani became disillusioned with their new status. They were, however, trapped in relations from which they were also afraid to break free:

> Mahomed bin Thani, though now averse to, and desirous of freeing himself from the thralldom of Turkish control, is afraid of exhibiting outward symptoms of disaffection, which would

probably result in his removal to Constantinople and detention there for an indefinite period.

Jasim Agha, the Turkish officer, is consulted in all matters connected with the Chief's policy and administration and nothing can be done without his concurrence. Such curtailment of power is extremely irksome to Mahomed bin Thani, and also to his ambitious son Jasim. (Fraser, 1875)

In 1876, Jasim was appointed *Kaimakam* of Qatar. As the term *kaimakam* was used to designate the governor of a *kaza*, Jasim's authority can be viewed only in the context of the limited geographical extent of Ottoman authority in the peninsula. As demonstrated in the previous section, the *kaza* of Qatar included only Doha and its environs. In 1879, Jasim Al-Thani was reconfirmed as *Kaimakam* of the *Kaza* of Qatar, or "Governor of Doha" (Lorimer 1908–15, 1:804).

In addition to resulting in the Al-Thani's subjection to Ottoman administrative procedures, the alliance of the Doha chiefs with the Porte led also to the alienation of a number of tribes who had previously acknowledged the Al-Thani's influence. Such were the Al-bu-Kawarah, who left Doha in 1879 to escape from the Al-Thani. British records give the following account of that event:

> Dissentions have, during the past few years, been rife amongst the Arabs residing under the jurisdiction of Shaikh Jasim of El-Bida'a, and bodies of seceders first settled at El-Foweyrat on the Katr Coast, where they are to some extent under the protection of the Noeym tribe who maintain intimate friendly relations with the Chief of Bahrain. (Ross 1886–87, 7)

In addition to providing a useful account of events in 1879, the above passage furnishes yet another proof that the authority of the Doha confederation did not extend outside the commercial enclave on the southeast coast. Obviously, the Al-bu-Kuwarah were well aware of that fact when they decided to leave the Al-Thani's authority and to move to Fuwairat in the north of the Qatar peninsula.

In 1885, about one hundred people left Wukra for similar reasons and settled in Ghariyeh, on the northeast coast of the peninsula (Zahlan 1979, 51). Rivalries then ensued between Jasim Al-Thani and the leader of the Ghariyeh settlement (who was, incidentally, a son of the Ruler of

Bahrain) for influence over the Ottoman-dominated parts of the peninsula. When it became clear that Jasim was not going to let the argument subside, the settlement group—with Ottoman approval—moved to Tarut Island, a small island near the coast of the Arabian Peninsula nearly opposite Bahrain, and the Ghariyeh area remained unsettled thereafter (Lorimer 1908–15, 1:805–6).

But Jasim's relations with his Ottoman overlords were already deteriorating. In the period 1885–89, Jasim Al-Thani resigned from the *kaimakamlik* several times but his resignation was not accepted. Thus, when in 1887 the Turks announced plans to build a customs house in Doha—a development that was perceived by the Al-Thani Sheikh as directly undermining his authority—he withdrew from Doha. In his words, the affairs of that town were thereafter to be "first referred to God and then to the Turkish Government" (Lorimer 1908–15, 1:806). Sheikh Jasim then tried to destabilize his former territories and was believed to have instigated a number of attacks on and disturbances in Doha and its vicinity (Lorimer 1908–15, 1:806).

Ottoman authorities were equally dissatisfied with Sheikh Jasim's conduct and position. In 1887, the Department of Internal Affairs of the Ottoman Council of State assessed the situation as follows:

> Sheikh Jasim has for a long time functioned only in name as provincial governor in the Qatar district between Oman and Bahrain. He stays in Qatar two or three months a year...and he spends the rest of his time with the tribes in the desert...It is essential that you...immediately relieve Sheikh Jasim of his authority and appoint in his place a different governor. (*Report from Ottoman Council of State Department of Internal Affairs*, 18 January 1887)

One year after the above events, however, Jasim had returned to Doha and resumed his previous duties. Nevertheless, he lived in fear of the Ottomans and was acutely aware of the fact that his continuing association with the Porte might further erode his position and cause local inhabitants to leave his lands:

> ...he does not know what the Turks may do to him and the inhabitants of El Katar; the latter are Bedouins and own no date plantations or other landed property, that might compel them to

patiently bear any oppression; and possibly they may leave the place and go elsewhere, as it is intimated. (Rasul, 27 June 1888)

Al-Khalifa Influence in Ottoman-Dominated Qatar

While the Ottomans made southeastern Qatar part of their dominions, Al-Khalifa influence did not disappear overnight. The century-old tradition of relations with the Ruler of Bahrain could not be easily destroyed by the Al-Thani. In 1874, Sheikh Jasim complained to the Ottomans that Doha effectively remained under Bahraini authority. That fact caused significant anxiety among the Al-Thani—a family that had just undergone a transformation from local tax collectors to chiefs of the Ottoman-dominated Doha confederation (Bahrain 1996, 58–60 ¶ 131–35).

In view of Al-Thani complaints, the Ottomans decided to strengthen their political position by sending Sheikh Nasir bin Mubarak Al-Khalifa to Doha. An enemy of the Ruler of Bahrain, Sheikh Nasir was expected to counter any Bahraini influence in Doha. To this end, he set to expanding ostensibly Ottoman (but actually his own) interests in achieving domination over Bahrain. As will be described in Chapter 10, those attempts met with strong resistance on the part of both Britain and Bahrain and ultimately proved futile.

When Sheikh Nasir arrived in Doha, Jasim Al-Thani publicly relinquished his title of Governor to Sheikh Nasir, and placed himself in the position of his Assistant (News Agent, Bahrain, 14 October 1874).

Sheikh Nasir explained his relationship with Jasim Al-Thani in the following manner:

> Jasim in his own heart does not like that I should acquire independence and power and he has understood, the cause is this, that should I in the meantime obtain my object [he fears] he would have no escape from my clutches[. A]s you know Guttur and its environs were formerly under the administration of the Shaikhs of Bahrain, and [the people] were regarded as subjects, but it is some time now that they have gone under the authority of the Ottoman Govt. and are now repentant of their conduct and are very desirous of escaping from and getting out of the authority of that Government. (Ross, 1881)

Whatever his actual ability to control events in Doha might have been, Sheikh Jasim himself did not feel he had achieved a status placing him on equal footing with the Al-Khalifa Sheikhs. Illustrating this fact is a small episode that occurred in 1881. In that year, the brother of the Sheikh of Bahrain visited the west coast of the Qatar peninsula. An account of this event given by Captain Prideaux relates as follows:

> In December [1881], Sheikh Ahmed, the brother of Sheikh Isa [of Bahrain], landed on the west coast of Katr with about 200 followers for the purpose of sport. Sheikh Jasim [of Qatar] sent a deputation from Bida to welcome him and invite him to an entertainment in the interior. Sheikh Ahmed insisted upon Jasim's coming himself to greet him where he was, which the Bida chief accordingly did, and subsequently Sheikh Ahmed accompanied him to his camp. (F. B. Prideaux, 16 July 1905, 8)

This event raises serious doubts as to the actual authority of Sheikh Jasim in the western part of the peninsula. Had Jasim been the recognized chief of that area, it would have been unthinkable for a foreigner—and one, moreover, not himself a sovereign—to require the appearance of the local ruler.

The Rebellion of 1893

As events in the 1880s demonstrated, the Al-Thani were far from achieving a significant measure of autonomy in Ottoman-controlled Qatar. Since they had come to prominence in Doha in the late 1860s, the Al-Thani had anxiously striven to consolidate their position in the merchant confederation and possibly to expand also to other areas in the Qatar peninsula. However, they were too weak to rely on their own resources in such an undertaking, and while the Al-Thani eagerly desired independence, they were also well aware that they could not afford it.

The Al-Thani's anxiety over their position vis-à-vis the Ottomans led to the deterioration of their relations with the sovereign power. Tensions culminated in 1893, when the *Vali* of Basrah paid a visit to the Qatar peninsula, attempting to resolve tensions that had resulted from the power vacuum in Doha. Jasim, who had withdrawn from Doha, was invited for talks by the *Vali*. But the Al-Thani sheikh refused to appear before the Ottoman official for fear of being arrested. Negotiations began with Sheikh Ahmed, Jasim's brother, acting as intermediary. By the end of the month, no solution had been reached, and the *Vali* decided to resort to military action.

On 18 March 1893, Ahmed and twelve other influential men were arrested, and an Ottoman attack was launched on the forces of Sheikh Jasim. Jasim's army of Bedouins, however, prevailed and the Ottomans were forced to withdraw to Doha. The Al-Thani sheikh's forces then followed them to the coast, where they besieged Ottoman ships and seized the wells around Doha, thus compelling the *Vali* to order the release of Ahmed and the other prisoners.

After attempting unsuccessfully to obtain British protection, Sheikh Jasim reached an agreement with the Turks in June 1893. He promised to resume payment of taxes to the Ottomans and to surrender the weapons captured during the fighting, in return for a full pardon by the Porte.

Jasim then resigned his official position. The Ottomans once again refused to accept his resignation, for they preferred to have Jasim on their side rather than sowing dissent in their territories:

> The refusal of the Turks to accept Jasim's resignation was probably due to the consideration that he was less dangerous as an official than he might be as an irresponsible free-lance. (Lorimer 1908–15, 1:824)

Jasim retired nevertheless, and the *Kaimakamlik* was then assumed by his brother Sheikh Ahmed Al-Thani.

Then in 1898, despite his apparent withdrawal from politics, Jasim led another attack on the Turkish, this time against the Ottoman garrison in Doha. It failed, yet the only punishment Jasim suffered was the confiscation of his property (Commander of the Sphinx, 1898).

In the early 1900s, Jasim risked antagonizing the Ottomans even further by entering into relations with Ibn Saud, who had just established himself in Riyadh. In 1902, Jasim began to make annual payments and send gifts to Ibn Saud — actions to which his brother Ahmed was strongly opposed (Lorimer 1908–15, I:835).

Generally, events in the 1890s and early 1900s demonstrated the decline of Ottoman power in the Qatar peninsula and the inability of the Ottomans to take effective measures to counter internal challenges to their authority. For their part, the Al-Thani had turned from being the Ottomans' principal allies in the peninsula into insubordinate local chiefs. Their ability to mobilize the forces of belligerent Bedouins in

Qatar, and to stand up to Ottoman attempts to reduce their power, became increasingly obvious. Unprepared to devote any further resources to reinforcing their positions in the Qatar peninsula, the Ottomans then accepted the situation for the time being.

British–Al-Thani Relations

Britain's initial policies in response to Ottoman activities in Hasa emphasized restraint and non-interference. Considering the insignificant economic potential of the territories conquered by the Ottomans and the existence of guarantees by the Porte that no invasion of Bahrain would be undertaken, Britain did not seek to expel Ottoman forces from the southeast of the Qatar peninsula.

As the Ottoman's failure to establish effective administration in the southeast of the peninsula became obvious, the British were, however, forced to interfere on numerous occasions, to counter threats to their interests in Qatar. One such threat was the attitude of the Al-Thani sheikhs toward the Indian residents of the peninsula, who enjoyed a special status as British subjects. An Al-Thani attempt in 1883 to expel the Indian traders resulted in direct intervention by the Political Resident, and eventual Al-Thani compliance with the British demands (see also "Ottoman–Al-Thani Relations" earlier in this chapter).

But Britain's interference in support of the rights of its subjects did not produce lasting results. During the disturbances of the late 1880s, it was the Indians—together with Bahrainis residing in Doha—who experienced the most serious property damage. Once again, the Al-Thani were forced to apologize and pay compensation.

Though British actions in both cases provoked expected protests on the part of the Ottomans, Britain, being the only power capable of resolving the situation, had felt compelled to interfere.

In the 1890s Britain again became involved in the internal affairs of Ottoman-dominated Qatar. A breakdown of law and order in that period, coupled with the absence of any identifiable authority in the Ottoman-dominated part of the peninsula, resulted in yet another British intervention. In 1893, Col. Adelbert C. Talbot, the Political Resident, arrived in southeastern Qatar and made an attempt to mediate between the Al-Thani and the Ottomans, who were at the time engaged in heavy fighting.

When the Ottomans declined Talbot's proposal, he proceeded to conduct an interview with the Al-Thani's Sheikh Jasim, meant to assess Jasim's preparedness to switch his allegiance to Britain. Jasim had expressed such a wish in a letter to the British government earlier that year. He had also applied to the Ruler of Bahrain for "leave to settle, under his jurisdiction, in the northern part of Qatar" (Lorimer 1908–15, 1:824). As a result of the deterioration of his relations with the Ottomans, Jasim had come to see association with the British and Bahrain as an opportunity to escape his dependence on the Ottomans. Regardless of the possibility that submission to Britain might signify acceptance of Bahrain's sovereignty over Doha (or possibly, of the entire Qatar peninsula), Jasim was eager to release himself from his ties to the Ottomans (Talbot, 7 May 1893). Thus, in the interview held in Wukra between the British Political Resident and the Chief of Doha, the latter went as far as to agree to resume payment of tribute to the Ruler of Bahrain.

> Shaikh Jasim at once acknowledged the rights of Bahrain and expressed his willingness to pay tribute as before. (Talbot, 7 May 1893, ¶ 7)

In return for obtaining British protection, Jasim promised to expel the Ottoman garrison from Doha. However, Britain decided an alliance with the Al-Thani would be inexpedient at that stage and discontinued the negotiations (Talbot, 7 May 1893).

Nevertheless, contacts between Britain and the Al-Thani were not severed. As the Al-Thani's relations with the Ottomans continued to deteriorate, Jasim once again considered the advantages of changing to a different protecting power. In 1898, Ahmed, Jasim's brother reiterated his family's wish that the Ottomans be expelled and expressed the Al-Thani's willingness to "enter in the same treaties with the British Government as [had] the Trucial Chiefs" (Commander of the Sphinx, 1898). Sheikh Ahmed's failure to confirm his requests in writing, however, prevented the British from addressing the issue (Lorimer 1908–15, 1:829).

At the turn of the twentieth century, the power vacuum in Doha gave the British reason for continued concern. On numerous occasions, faced with the inability of any authority in Doha to exercise government functions, Britain itself intervened to restore law and order in the southeast of the Qatar peninsula. Thus, when in 1900 members of the Bani Hajir tribe violated the maritime peace, it was Britain that had to intervene to resolve the situation. Similarly, that same year Britain punished the Al bin Ali merchants involved in an attack on a group of pearl fishers. In none of these cases was the Al-Thani family, ostensibly the local authority, involved in dealing with the two incidents (Lorimer 1908–15, 1:834).

By this time, it had become evident that Ottoman interest in the Qatar peninsula was decreasing, and British authorities began to contemplate a permanent arrangement with the Al-Thani sheikhs (Saldanha 1904a, 48). When in 1902 the Al-Thani renewed their offer to switch allegiances to Britain, the British reasoned as follows:

> ...if [the chief of Doha] were taken under the protection of His Majesty's Government, he would reside at any place in Katar approved by the Government and...he would hold himself responsible to keep the seas round Katar free from pirates and would co-operate with His Majesty's Government and the Chief of Bahrein in any matters which might concern them on the main land. (C. A. Kemball, 26 April 1902)

Intragovernmental consultations ensued. While the future of British policy toward Qatar was being contemplated, the question of the Al-Thani family's uncertain status re-emerged. Needing clarity on this issue, the British Political Resident proposed to make enquiries as to the precise extent of the Al-Thani's jurisdiction and influence. Authorization for such a step was granted by the British government, accompanied by the following observation:

> ...should it prove that the Sheikh is established as Chief of Katar, we would propose to authorize Colonel Kemball [the British Political Resident] to conclude with him an Agreement similar to those which have been executed with the Trucial Chiefs of the Arab Coast. (Government of India, 10 July 1902)

But further investigation by British officials led to no conclusive opinion. In 1903, the Assistant British Political Resident reported that

> ...the influence of the Al-Thani family was likely to decrease in Katar because most of the Arabs being pearl divers, who had

grown rich by the bounty of Sheikh Jasim, would soon be less dependent upon his bounty. (Saldanha 1904a, 55)

Despite the fact that the Political Resident himself was in favor of granting protection to the Al-Thani, the final decision was against such an alliance with the Al-Thani. The Government of India explained that decision in the following terms:

> The decision of His Majesty's Government that no agreement should at present be concluded with the Chief, appears to have been based on two main considerations, first, that such a Convention would constitute a disturbance of the *status quo*... and, secondly, that the influence of Sheikh Ahmed was on the wane, and that an arrangement with His Majesty's Government would only be used by the Chief to retrieve his diminishing influence. (Government of India, 31 March 1904)

Ottoman Withdrawal

The Unratified 1913 Anglo-Ottoman Convention

In 1911, Britain and the Ottoman Empire entered into negotiations regarding their relations in Arabia. A number of issues discussed had direct bearing on the Qatar peninsula; however, the agreement reached two years later was only provisional and partial. And, significantly, it was never ratified.

The importance of the agreement (which came to be known as the Anglo-Ottoman Convention) to the present discussion is this: the State of Qatar consistently relies on this unratified agreement as proof of the recognition of Al-Thani sovereignty over the entire Qatar peninsula. So it will be relevant at this time to examine the two parties' positions in the course of the negotiations preceding the agreement, and also the provisions in the agreement that deal with the Qatar peninsula.

The clause relevant to Qatar is Article 11 of the Convention, which provided for the establishment of a line separating the Nejd from the Qatar peninsula, and announced the renunciation by the Ottoman government of "all their claims with regard to the El Katr peninsula." The clause further stated that the peninsula was to be governed, as before, by Sheikh Jasim Al-Thani and his successors, and that Britain would not permit the Sheikh of Bahrain "to interfere in the internal affairs of El Katr, to infringe the authority of the country or to annex it" (Convention between United Kingdom and Turkey, 29 July 1913).

At first glance, such stipulations seem contrary to official British policies of protecting the Ruler of Bahrain's interests in the Qatar peninsula:

> . . . any lasting settlement between the two powers must provide for the definite renunciation by the Ottoman Government of Bahrain and adjacent islands and of the whole of the Peninsula of El Katr (including El Bidaa), where the Sheikh of Bahrain has important rights. (*Draft memorandum*, July 1911, 4)

The contrast between this stance and the final text of the Convention is explained by the maneuvers of the Ottoman Minister in London in 1913. As he himself reported, he took those steps by his own initiative when he realized the futility of Ottoman attempts to preserve the Sultan's sovereignty in the region:

> I provided information that we could give up our claims in El-Katar with some conditions; *these suggestions were my own ideas*—e.g. that (Katar) should not be part of Bahrain, or be loyal to England or under its rule . . . (Hakki Pasha, 25 February 1913) [Emphasis added.]

Thus, the provisions included in Article 11 did not reflect an explicit policy decision of the Ottoman government, but were, rather, the result of last-minute actions by the Turkish representative.

As already mentioned, the Convention was never ratified and was not viewed by the parties as a landmark in the history of the area. This is proven by the report on the new instrument prepared by the Ottoman Council of Ministers:

> The agreement and declaration of 29th July 1913, signed by Sir Edward Grey and Hakki Pasha, concerning the temporary nature of the documents, which will, under the condition of the diplomatic note, allow for amendments or reciprocal exchange of ideas, have all been submitted to the General Council of Ministers for their consideration. (Official report of the Ottoman Council of Ministers, 1 February 1914)

Events were, however, rapidly developing, and the applicability of the Convention to the changing situation in the Gulf became increasingly dubious. As the Ottomans lost Hasa and the Ruler of Bahrain remained in possession of the northern parts of the Qatar peninsula, negotiations over the Convention were abandoned:

> The non-ratification of the Convention became a permanent fact of history. (*The Buraimi Memorials* 1987, 1:389; Wilkinson 1991, 99)

Ottoman Withdrawal

As the events of the First World War overtook the Ottoman Empire, in August 1915 Major Keyes, the British Political Agent, met with Sheikh Abdullah bin Jasim to discuss surrender of the Turkish Fort and requested that the Sheikh present surrender terms to the Ottoman commander. The flight of the remaining Ottoman soldiers and the formal handover of the Fort to the Chief of Doha marked the end of almost half a century of Ottoman presence in the Qatar peninsula (Keyes, 23 August 1915).

Establishment of Qatar's Formal Relations with Britain—The 1916 Treaty

British protection was finally granted to the Al-Thani in 1916, when a Treaty was signed between Britain and Sheikh Abdullah, the son of Jasim Al-Thani. The Treaty was written in the first person, from the point of view of the Chief of Doha, who was styled "Ruler of Qatar." In the Treaty there was no statement to the effect that the obligations undertaken by Sheikh Abdullah were to be binding on his successors. The new instrument simply referred to the Agreement between Mohammed Al-Thani and the British government and stated that the duties undertaken then were to be fulfilled by Sheikh Abdullah as successor to Sheikh Mohammed. A number of provisions followed which effectively represented a compilation of the conditions imposed by the British government on the Trucial Sheikhs through the Maritime Truce of 1835, the Perpetual Treaty of Friendship of 1853 and the Exclusive Agreements (similar to those signed with the Ruler of Bahrain) of the 1880s and 1890s:

> ...the Political Resident in the Persian Gulf, has favoured me with the Treaties and Engagements, entered into between the [Trucial] Sheikhs...and the High British Government, and I hereby declare that I will abide by the spirit and obligations of the aforesaid Treaties and Engagements. (*Treaty between the British Government and Sheikh of Qatar, 3 November 1916,* 258)

Qatar thus was assimilated into the system of British-protected states, and the establishment of a de facto British protectorate in the peninsula became a reality. Under the Treaty, the "Ruler of Qatar" and his subjects received "all the immunities, privileges, and advantages" that had been applicable to the Trucial Sheikhs and their subjects. For his part, the Ruler undertook to have no dealings with—and, particularly, cede no territory to—any foreign powers without the consent of the British government. The Treaty also contained a provision related to the suppression of piracy and the slave trade. Last but not least, it pointed to British responsibilities for the protection of Qatar's territory from aggression by sea, and to Britain's obligation to mediate in instances of land attacks and seek redress for any losses suffered by Qatar.

Three Articles—VII, VIII, and IX—were suspended after the conclusion of the Treaty "since Abdullah did not feel sufficiently strong internally to impose them on his people." Those particular Articles concerned the protection of British subjects, the appointment of a British Agent and the establishment of postal and telegraphic services (Zahlan 1979, 60).

Though the Treaty made references to the territory under Sheikh Abdullah, it contained no geographical definition of that territory. Rather, the Treaty implied that the territorial extent of the new political entity coincided with the limits of the *kaza* of Qatar. As the area controlled by Sheikh Abdullah was very limited, and no mention was made in the Treaty of extending his possessions, it can safely be assumed that the Treaty was deemed to apply to the Doha confederation and its environs.

The fact that Sheikh Abdullah's dominions were not explicitly defined, however, has sometimes caused confusion over the terms used to refer to his territories. Thus, in a 1934 meeting with the Political Resident, the Sheikh of Qatar clearly expressed his understanding that the Treaty covered only the coast of the Qatar peninsula:

> The Treaty does not include the interior but only the coast. (Fowle, 12 March 1934, 2)

The British Agent then corrected him, saying that the Treaty covered the whole of his country (Fowle, 12 March 1934, 2). Whatever that "whole" of Sheikh Abdullah's territories might have meant at the time, however, it certainly could not have comprised more than those interior areas the Al-Thani might have occasionally controlled in addition to coastal areas. As the Ruler of Bahrain was the sovereign authority in the north of the peninsula while the Wahhabis were exercising a very strong influence in the southeast, it cannot be assumed that those territories were viewed by the British as belonging to the Al-Thani. Furthermore, Britain had not undertaken under the Treaty to protect Qatar by land—a fact that is clearly demonstrated in the explanation Sheikh Abdullah was given when soliciting British protection from the Wahhabis:

> [The British] Government... might perhaps if Doha is threatened and British subjects and property endangered send a ship there. (Trevor, 13 May 1921 ¶ 4)

Minimal Control Characterizes Al-Thani Power into the Mid-Twentieth Century

As Bahraini and Wahhabi influence over the northern and the southeastern part of the peninsula persisted, Sheikh Abdullah was no more capable of extending his influence in the decades that followed the conclusion of the Convention than he had been at the time of its signature. Thus, in 1922 the British Political Resident expressed his fears about the security situation in Qatar and even acknowledged the possibility that Qatar might cease to exist:

> I think it would be a pity if Qatar disappeared as a separate entity; from our point of view it is convenient to have the rulers of the coastal districts on the coast, but I do not see any practical means of preventing peaceful penetration of the country by Akhwan [Wahhabis] or Bin Saud's adherents. (Trevor, 10 November 1922)

A 1923 British Report described the situation in similar terms:

> In his own territories, the [Ruler of Qatar] is now powerless. Any attempt to enforce his rule is frustrated by malcontents appealing to the Sultan of Nejd [Ibn Saud], whose power the [Ruler] fears. Cases have occurred of persons being arrested by armed followers sent by the Sultan, not merely within Qatar, but actually in the Town of Doha, where the Ruler resides. (Administration Report for Bahrain Political Agency for the year 1923, 72)

The Al-Thani's inability to effectively control their territories became an established feature of their rule. As Britain's responsibilities toward Qatar lay mainly in ensuring its protection from attack by sea, and in exercising some control over its foreign policy rather than its domestic affairs, the lack of effective government in Qatar became chronic. In the context of oil negotiations in the 1930s, Britain again recognized this situation and explained their policy in Qatar as follows:

> Presumably we do not want to add to the hinterland of Qatar large areas which the Sheikh may not be able to protect and which we should find it difficult to make secure for oil concessionaires. (*India Office Memorandum,* 11 January 1934)

Continuing discussions within the British government about the advisability of granting protection to Sheikh Abdullah in exchange for his granting an oil concession to a British company generally produced the same conclusion:

> The only dangers against which the Sheikh might need to be protected would come from either (a) Ibn Saud or (b) the tribes of the hinterland....
>
> [The Sheikh protecting himself] would probably in any case be impossible, since our accounts of the Sheikh are that he is little more than a large merchant and his territory is very sparsely inhabited by tribesmen over whom he appears to exercise a very loose control. (*India Office Memorandum,* 21 February 1934)

The similarities between the above statement and the first official accounts of affairs in Qatar—account produced seven decades earlier—speak for themselves.

It will be recalled that the lack of effective control by the Ruler over his territories manifested itself, among other ways, in suspension of the

Articles of the Treaty pertaining to the appointment of a British Agent in Qatar, because the security of such an official could not be guaranteed by the Ruler. Not until 1953 was such an Agent appointed. Until then, Britain exercised its control over Qatar through the Agency or the Residency in Bahrain. Thus, despite the signing of the 1916 Treaty, Britain initially and for some time thereafter maintained quite a low level of involvement with the affairs of the Al-Thani. And though the oil concession negotiations of the 1930s changed that situation, even those negotiations were directed through British representatives based in Bahrain.

Thus the Qatar state, though recognized in the Anglo–Al-Thani Treaty, continued to be characterized by rather shaky Al-Thani authority. The Qatar state that formally emerged in 1916 did not in effect come to possess the attributes of a state for at least another 30 years. Its small population base, political instability, and natural conditions precluding the establishment of effective authority—all were reasons behind the Al-Thani's inability to consolidate their position for many years after the British had recognized their state.

7 Qatar's Version of Historical Context

Highlights

In 1971, both Bahrain and Qatar proclaimed their independence. Their "special treaty relations" with Britain terminated with exchanges of letters between the British Political Resident and the Rulers of Bahrain and Qatar respectively. The letters, dated 15 August 1971 and 3 September 1971 announced respectively the assumption by "the State of Bahrain and its Dependencies" and by the "State of Qatar" of "full international responsibility" as sovereign and independent states, marking the end of an important period in both states' evolutions. But Bahrain and Qatar had gone quite different ways to reach that stage:

Bahraini Events
- The Al-Khalifa—the ruling family of Bahrain—established themselves in Zubarah in 1762; by the 1780s they extended their authority over the entire Qatar peninsula; in 1783, they conquered the Bahrain Islands, where they moved their seat of government in 1796; they maintained their authority over the entire Qatar peninsula until 1871.

Qatari Events
- The Al-Thani—the ruling family of Qatar—emerged to significance in Doha in the 1860s; their authority in southeastern Qatar was confirmed in 1871–1915 while under Ottoman suzerainty.

Bahraini Events	**Qatari Events**
• Al-Khalifa rule was consolidated in the face of internal and external challenges throughout the nineteenth century.	• Al-Thani rule remained precarious through the early twentieth century.
• Bahrain was first recognized as a political entity under the Al-Khalifa in 1820, when it signed its first treaty with Britain.	• Qatar was first recognized as a separate entity under the Al-Thani in 1916, when it signed a treaty with Britain, after Qatar achieved independence from the Ottoman Empire.
• Bahrain came under British protection in 1861, and entered into "special treaty relations" with Britain by virtue of the Exclusive Agreements of 1880 and 1892. Thereupon, Britain assumed responsibility for the conduct of its international relations and closely supervised its internal affairs.	• Qatar entered into "special treaty relations" with Britain by virtue of the Anglo–Al-Thani Agreement of 1916. Thereupon, Britain assumed responsibility for the conduct of its international relations and closely supervised its internal affairs

Plainly, Bahrain emerged as a political entity almost a century earlier than did Qatar. Thus, Bahrain's history has abounded in clear acts of sovereignty over all its Rulers' territories. In contrast, Qatar's history has been marked by a relative dearth of such events—a fact clearly visible from the timeline included on page 103, which demonstrates that instances of Bahrain's exercise of sovereignty far outnumber those of Qatar. The territorial implications of this fact will be demonstrated in the next chapters. Yet despite this objective evidence, Qatar holds to a different version of historical events.

Qatar's Version of Events

The events discussed in Chapters 2 through 6 have illustrated the general background against which Bahrain and Qatar have built their cases before the International Court of Justice. However, the two states' *interpretations* of those events differ considerably. While Bahrain's arguments have remained consistent with the facts as set out so far, Qatar sees the region's history in a quite different light.

Qatar Peninsula

Al-Thani Authority

The main difference between the two powers' views has lain in the disproportionate importance Qatar has attached to the purported power of the Al-Thani family prior to 1871. In one of the forged documents Qatar submitted with their pleadings (and later retracted), Qatar's forgers elevated the Doha chiefs to the status of recognized masters of the Qatar tribes even before the arrival of the Ottomans:

> In Qatar, the 1850's saw the rise of Mohamed bin Thani bin Ali bin Jassim Al-Bin-Tamim, who increasingly asserted his authority over the tribes of the peninsula and upheld their independence. (Qatar 1996, 24 ¶ 3.22)

The Al-Thani were consistently portrayed as the more or less independent rulers of "the entire province of Qatar" as early as the 1860s (Qatar 1997, 22 ¶ 2.25; Qatar 1999, 8–9 ¶ 1.24). The Al-Thani were said to have "gradually" expanded their influence till it came to encompass the entire peninsula just before the Ottomans' arrival.

The main flaw in this position is that it treats the Qatar peninsula as an integrated socio-political unit. Yet as has already been mentioned, the Doha confederation (over which the Al-Thani were beginning, in the mid-nineteenth century, to exercise some influence as local tax collectors for the Al-Khalifa), was only one of three regions that determined the human geography of the peninsula. Isolated from the northwestern areas (which were integrated into the Gulf of Bahrain and under the authority of the Ruler of Bahrain) and the southern areas (dominated by the Wahhabis), the Doha confederation had rather limited exchanges with the other communities in the peninsula.

Politically, the Doha region was part of the Al-Khalifa state (although it was not closely regulated). But the Al-Thani had not yet attained any position of political significance such as could enable them to focus the loyalties of neighboring tribes; rather, their influence, whatever its precise scope, was limited to the town of Doha. And while that town and its environs were not infrequently, *collectively* referred to as Qatar, the territory associated with them was *not coextensive* with the entire peninsula. In fact, the socio-economic unit of Qatar was only one of three such entities on the peninsula of Qatar.

Throughout the Court pleadings, however, Qatar made every effort to ignore these facts. Its *Memorials* typically—and self-servingly—treated the word "Qatar" as if it described a political entity whose territory coincided with the entire Qatar peninsula. Whenever the word "Qatar" appeared in historical documents, Qatar interpreted it without regard to the context in which it had been contemporaneously used (e.g. Qatar 1996, 29–30 ¶ 3.36–3.38). Thus, Qatar's attempts to present the Al-Thani as having exercised their authority over the entire peninsula were, in effect, limited to reiterating that the Al-Thani had some influence over "Qatar." Yet historically that region did not extend beyond the vicinity of Doha, or at most, beyond an area encompassing a limited stretch of the southeast coast of the peninsula. So, reliance on the word "Qatar" could do little to prove that the Al-Thani had ever been the political authority of the entire peninsula.

Though based on dubious premises, the thesis of the Al-Thani projecting their political influence from coast to coast was central to Qatar's case. Even so, this thesis itself was inconsistently developed throughout the pleadings. Thus, for instance, Qatar's oral pleadings contained numerous contradictions about the precise date when the Al-Thani supposedly extended their influence over the entire peninsula. Different speakers placed that development in the "beginnings of the 20th century" (Salmon, 30 May 2000, 28 ¶ 15(a)) in "roughly 1870" (Bundy, 31 May 2000, 9 ¶ 7), and in "the middle of the nineteenth century" (David, 5 June 2000, 53 ¶ 12). A reference to Qatar's written pleadings will demonstrate yet further contradictions. The *Counter-Memorial* submitted by Qatar, for instance, described the situation in the following terms:

> [In the nineteenth century t]here were only tribal chiefs who endeavored to consolidate their position by developing their relations with other tribes and controlling the trade networks. (Qatar 1997, 17 ¶ 2.14)

Al-Khalifa Authority

The argument just referred to above implied that neither the Al-Thani nor any other power was recognized in the nineteenth century as having authority over the entire peninsula. Significantly, such an argument also meant that—similarly to the Al-Thani—the Al-Khalifa were in no position to act as sovereigns over the tribes of Qatar. The historical record, however, demonstrates otherwise. Contemporary visitors to the area confirm that the Al-Khalifa were the sovereign power in the Qatar peninsula. For instance, Captain George Brucks of the British Indian Navy, who conducted a meticulous survey of the Arabian coast in 1821–29, observed:

> From the point [of Ras Rakkan, the northernmost point of the Qatar peninsula] to al Bidder [Doha] southward, and to Warden's Islands [the Hawar Islands] westward, the authority of the Shaikh of Bahrein is acknowledged. (Brucks 1856, 561)

The authority exercised by the Al-Khalifa with respect to both the Bahrain Islands and the Qatar peninsula was also different in nature to that of the Al-Thani in Doha. The Al-Khalifa claimed the allegiance of the majority of Qatari tribes (most notably, those inhabiting the peninsula's northwestern and southeastern areas), and were recognized by those tribes as the paramount political authority. Such recognition manifested itself, among other things, in the payment of taxes to the Al-Khalifa rulers. By the time the Ottomans reached the Qatar peninsula, Al-Khalifa rule had undergone a century-long evolution, while the Al-Thani were only emerging as a power in Doha and did not represent, at that stage, any significant threat to Al-Khalifa sovereignty.

That the Qatar peninsula belonged to the Ruler of Bahrain's dominions was a fact also recognized by all relevant players in the region. British authorities call Doha part of the Ruler of Bahrain's "main coast" (L. Pelly, 13 April 1863), and they expected their political arrangements with the Al-Khalifa to be observed also in the Qatar peninsula (Lorimer 1908–15, 1:793). In its Application to the Court in July 1995, Qatar itself mentioned this fact:

> Until 1868, the Qatar peninsula was considered by the British as a dependency of Bahrain. (Qatar 1991 ¶ 5)

Palgrave, a British traveler in 1877, was extensively relied on in Qatar's oral pleadings (*cf.* Pilkington, 29 May 2000, 49 ¶ 17 *et seq.*). He pointed out that the Ruler of Bahrain had "a sort of control or presidential authority in Katar" (Palgrave 1877a, 2:232–33). As for the Al-Thani, Palgrave's description was rather contradictory. Qatar relied in its pleadings on the fact that Mohammed Al-Thani had been described as the governor of Doha who had been "generally acknowledged for head of the entire province"; however, as Bahrain pointed out, Palgrave also mentioned that Mohamed bin Thani had "in matter of fact very little authority over the other villages . . . Ebn-Thanee is for those around only a sort of collector-in-chief, or general revenue-gatherer." (Palgrave 1877a, 2:232–33) Thus, again, the "province of Qatar" was placed in its proper geographical context—i.e. as the immediate vicinity of Doha town, where the Al-Thani were based.

The Qatar peninsula—including the Doha enclave—was also recognized as a dependency of Bahrain by the other powers in the region. The Wahhabis, for instance, uniformly dealt with the Ruler of Bahrain to settle matters over the payment of *zakat* by Qatar tribes. Moreover, the Rulers of Bahrain viewed the Wahhabi incursions on Doha as challenges to Al-Khalifa authority (LeQuesne 1953, 87). Rulers of Abu Dhabi were also aware of Bahraini authority in Doha—as demonstrated, for instance, in 1835, when they granted asylum to Isa bin Tarif (then based in Huwailah in Qatar), who was fleeing from the Al-Khalifa.

Throughout the nineteenth century, the actions of the tribes inhabiting the Qatar peninsula typically reflected recognition of the Al-Khalifa's political status. The most notable cases occurred in times of political turmoil when the policies of the Al-Khalifa sometimes provoked dissatisfaction among the tribes on the peninsula. Such was the case in the 1830s, when members of the Al bin Ali and Al bu 'Ainain tribes left for Abu Dhabi in protest against events associated with Al-Khalifa dynastic struggles. Such was the case also in 1867, when the inhabitants of Doha expressed their dissatisfaction with the succession of Bahraini governors and the new tax policies of the Al-Khalifa by rising against the Rulers. Thus, far from confirming Qatar's argument that by the 1850s the Al-Thani had displaced the Al-Khalifa as the dominant authority in the peninsula, the historical record shows that the Qatar peninsula was an integral part of the political entity of Bahrain. And though the Al-Thani did begin to exercise some influence in Doha, that influence was of limited geographical scope and of such a quality that it amounted to nothing approaching territorial sovereignty over Doha, much less over the entire peninsula.

1868 Agreements

Qatar has interpreted the signing of the 1868 Agreements as a landmark event. Disregarding basic historical facts, Qatar has asserted throughout its pleadings that the Agreements recognized the attainment by the Al-Thani of a status comparable to that of the Al-Khalifa:

> In the Agreements of 1868, the position of Sheikh Mohamed bin Thani as Chief of Qatar was acknowledged, and the two Agreements treated the Chief of Bahrain and the Chief of Qatar on an equal footing. (Qatar 1996, 30 ¶ 3.38)

> ... the Al-Thani Ruler was, for the first time, recognized as a sovereign in his own right possessing territorial rights in the Qatar peninsula. (Bundy, 20 June 2000, 43 ¶ 5)

> This was the first time that the British had recognized Qatar as a separate entity from Bahrain, under the authority of Mohamed bin Thani, who was described as the 'Chief of El-Kutr.' (Pilkington, 29 May 2000, 52 ¶ 32)

Qatar further asserted that under the 1868 Agreements the sea between the Bahrain Islands and the Qatar peninsula was to act as a buffer between Bahrain and Qatar—a conclusion that was, interestingly, based on the fact that Sheikh Mohammed had promised not to put to sea with hostile intentions (Qatar 1996, 30 ¶ 3.39). This unwarranted interpretation also served as the basis of Qatar's statement that the Agreements, in effect, recognized the separation of Qatar from Bahrain (Qatar 1999, 7 ¶ 1.21; Qatar 1996, 30 ¶ 3.38; Qatar 1997, 23 ¶ 2.26). The only "sea" that could have been implied by that was on the southeast coast of the Qatar peninsula, since no Qatari vessels plied the waters of the Western Coast.

However, history shows that neither the wording of the Agreements nor the events surrounding their signature implied such recognition. Rather, the Al-Thani themselves acknowledged the limited territorial extent of their own influence, and also their political subordination to the Rulers of Bahrain. As has already been shown, in the Agreements,

Mohammed Al-Thani promised to return to the Bahraini fold. He was, furthermore, described as only one of a number of chiefs from the Qatar peninsula (*Agreement of Chief of El-Kutr,* 12 September 1868). Thus, far from acquiring any measure of political independence by virtue of the 1868 Agreements, the Al-Thani chief had in effect promised to maintain his dependency on Bahrain.

Bahrain Islands

Qatar's claim that the Al-Thani were acting by the mid-nineteenth century as the unchallenged authority in the Qatar peninsula was supported by their argument that, in the period 1780–1860, Al-Khalifa control over the Bahrain Islands was ineffective (Qatar 1997, 10 ¶ 1.34). Though only the authority of the Al-Khalifa dynasty in the Qatar peninsula rather than the Bahrain Islands was important to the case, Qatar did not fail to mention the initial difficulties associated with the establishment of the Al-Khalifa state.

Those difficulties, however, did not significantly affect the formal standing of the Al-Khalifa as the paramount power in both the Bahrain Islands and the Qatar peninsula. The dynastic struggles that the Al-Khalifa faced throughout the nineteenth century were used by Qatar to describe the "confused state of affairs in Bahrain" (Pilkington, 29 May 2000, 49 ¶ 14). However, it is important to note that those conflicts exclusively involved members of the Bahrain ruling family. It is true that the authority of particular Al-Khalifa rulers was challenged at different points in time, but the authority of the Al-Khalifa dynasty as a whole was never at issue.

Moreover, despite attempts by external powers—such as the Wahhabis, Muscat, Persia, et al.—to displace the Al-Khalifa family's authority in the Bahrain Islands and the Qatar peninsula, the Al-Khalifa succeeded in preserving their possessions, even at the cost of entering into different political alliances and committing significant resources to military campaigns. Nevertheless, the supremacy of the Al-Khalifa was maintained, and as early as 1820, when Bahrain signed its first treaty with Britain, the British government recognized the Al-Khalifa as the leaders of the political entity of Bahrain.

About the nature of Al-Khalifa rule, Qatar stated, "the Al-Khalifa at no time had any effective control over autonomous tribal groupings engaged in fishing and pearling activities" (Qatar 1997, 44 ¶ 2.63).

Those communities were indeed granted a significant degree of autonomy. But this did not in itself amount to political independence, and those tribes did clearly recognize the political supremacy of the Al-Khalifa. Such arrangements were consistent with local traditions of political governance and intertribal relations and cannot be equated with formal independence.

Other differences between the views of Bahrain and Qatar concerned the extent of Al-Thani authority during the period of Ottoman domination, and the significance of the treaties associated with the Ottomans' departure from the peninsula. In presenting its version of history, Qatar aimed to prove that by the end of the nineteenth century the Al-Thani had "consolidated" their rule in Doha and throughout the peninsula, and that that fact had been recognized in the treaties of the early twentieth century. Qatar's interpretation of those events was, naturally, related to its attempts to show that the Al-Thani's authority had extended from coast to coast even before the end of the nineteenth century, and that the formation of the political identity of Qatar was rather advanced by the time the Ottomans left.

The Ottomans and the Al-Thani

In line with its assertions about the extent of Al-Thani authority in the middle of the nineteenth century, Qatar depicted the chiefs of Doha as having used the Ottoman presence to consolidate their rule over the peninsula (Qatar 1996, 24, 26–28 ¶ 2.28–2.29, 2.34–2.35). Most notably, the fact that Jasim Al-Thani had been appointed *kaimakam* of the *kaza* of Qatar was interpreted as confirming his paramountcy in the peninsula:

> ...during the Ottoman period Al-Thani authority was gradually extended and consolidated throughout the whole of Qatar. Sheikh Jassim skillfully played off the two major Powers in the region (Turkey and Britain) against each other... He was now, and remained until his death in 1913, the dominant figure in Qatar. (Qatar 1999, 23 ¶ 2.10)

And a more cautious statement:

> ...Sheikh Jassim bin Thani of Qatar was appointed by the Ottomans as kaimakam over the kaza of Qatar. The documentary evidence shows that, while Sheikh Jassim paid nominal

allegiance to the Ottomans and tolerated an Ottoman military presence in Qatar, he also acted independently at times on the peninsula and was suspicious of Ottoman designs. (Al-Meri, 30 May 2000, 3 ¶ 7)

However, Chapters 3 and 6 showed that, far from being the "dominant figure in Qatar," Sheikh Jasim held a rather shaky position. His reign was plagued by significant instability, with threats from the Wahhabis and intertribal rivalry. His subordination to the Ottomans and fear of punishment frequently prevented him from asserting his political will (Fraser, 1875). By 1888, he lived in fear of his overlords while also being aware that his power was eroding among local inhabitants (Rasul, 27 June 1888). Despite several instances when he received local tribes' backing against the Ottomans (most notably, during the 1893 rebellion), Jasim failed to mobilize the kind of support that would have allowed him to overthrow Ottoman rule. Moreover, whether acting with the approval of or acting against the Porte, he was unable to establish effective administration of the *kaza*—the resulting power vacuum that led on certain occasions to British interference (see section on "British–Al-Thani Relations" in Chapter 6).

As for the territorial extent of the *kaza,* Qatar has maintained in its pleadings that it encompassed the entire peninsula. Most importantly, Qatar claimed the *nahiye*'s of Zubarah and Odaid had been part of the *kaza* and subject to Al-Thani/Ottoman control; Qatar also made references to Ottoman administrative records that apparently supported their thesis (Al-Meri, 30 May 2000, 5–6 ¶ 17, 19, 21).

However, Qatar's evidence needs to be placed in context. A common feature of the records Qatar cited was this: while some did appear to include Zubarah and Odaid among the territories under Ottoman control, they provided no examples of the actual exercise of Ottoman or Al-Thani control in those areas. Rather, these territories' inclusion amounted to only a bold statement, a mere expression of Ottoman officials' wishful thinking and not a reflection of true facts. More trustworthy sources describing the situation in Zubarah and Odaid were the accounts of those Ottoman officials who were directly involved in attempts to extend Ottoman authority in those areas: their reports and statements consistently recognized the fact that the Porte's authority was limited to Doha and its surroundings. Typical are the following comments:

> [Britain] does not recognise that the Ottoman State has any rights of control over these shores [Zubarah]. (*Ottoman Report on Bahrain,* 16 September 1895);
>
> Britain claims that Zubarah is under the control of Bahrain... (*Ottoman Arabic Report on Zubarah Affair,* 3 May 1897);
>
> ...Britain insists that the Ottoman State has no rights of sovereignty over [Zubarah]...(*Ottoman Arabic Report on Zubarah Affair,* 3 May 1897);
>
> ...England will not give up claims on Zubara...(*Ottoman "Report on Bahrein" from the Ottoman Council Chamber,* 22 April 1900);
>
> [I]t is vital to end disagreements [with Britain] by putting an end to fruitless efforts to impose sovereignty in the Katar peninsula (*Projected Ottoman Council of Ministers Decision,* 11 March 1913)

Further confirmation of this was also given by Jasim Al-Thani himself in 1880, when he unambiguously stated in respect of Fuwairat (in the north of the peninsula):

> I have nothing to do with...the northern countries, for they belong to the parts of Bahrain. (Jasim bin Al-Thani, 24 November 1880)

International Treaties

Qatar's eagerness to find support for the supposed peninsula-wide integrity of the Qatar state also colored its discussion of the treaties of the early twentieth century. As was the case with the 1868 Agreements, the interpretations offered of the later treaties were rather strained and unconvincing. Despite assertions that the agreements "repeatedly and consistently" recognized Al-Thani "sovereignty...as encompassing all of the areas included in the Qatar peninsula" (Bundy, 21 June 2000, 9 ¶ 57; Sinclair, 21 June 2000, 24 ¶ 2(4)), no such recognition can, in fact, be reasonably derived from those documents.

Thus, for instance, the unratified 1913 Anglo-Ottoman Convention—considered as a "fundamental document" by Qatar in its pleadings (Pilkington, 29 May 2000, 57 ¶ 64)—was said to have recognized "the autonomy of the Qatar peninsula under Al-Thani rule" (Qatar 1996, 37 ¶ 3.57). It will be recalled that the Convention was never ratified, and never defined the geographic limits of "Qatar." Nevertheless, Qatar saw it as important because it "must be regarded as an expression of the thinking of the British and the Ottomans at the time" (Pilkington, 29 May 2000, 58 ¶ 67). In order to make its thesis more credible, Qatar pointed also to a subsequent, ratified, Anglo-Turkish Convention of 1914:

> Qatar acknowledges that the 1913 Anglo-Ottoman Convention was not ratified. It was, however, signed by both parties, and Article 11 of the Convention must have been regarded by both of them as declaratory of an existing state of affairs, since it was expressly referred to in Article III of the 1914 Anglo-Turkish treaty, which was ratified. (Qatar 1999, 33 ¶ 2.36)

Article III of the 1914 Convention, however, referred only to Qatar's southern border and stipulated that the delimitation to be carried out there would be "in conformity with Article 11 of the Anglo-Ottoman Convention [of 1913]." The purpose of referring to Article 11 was thus somewhat limited. In other words, Article 11—essential as it is to Qatar's thesis—did not apply to any part of the Qatar state other than its southern border; it certainly contained no recognition of the political status of the entire peninsula. Thus, though the 1913 Convention did contain a provision that "the peninsula" would be governed by the Al-Thani, that idea did not outlive the 1913 Convention and was not carried over to the 1914 Convention.

Nor was that notion reflected in the 1916 Treaty between Britain and Abdullah Al-Thani. Qatar, nevertheless, chose to see things otherwise:

> The Treaty does not specifically define the territory of Qatar, but it was implicit: the Treaty was signed only three years after the 1913 Convention, which expressly referred to the *whole peninsula* being governed by the Al-Thani. Furthermore, its language clearly indicates that Qatar's territory covered much more than the Doha area: it speaks of "territories," "frontiers" and "ports." (Pilkington, 29 May 2000, 59 ¶ 75)

Bahrain's interpretation of this position was as follows:

In other words, or so Qatar suggests, the 1916 agreement must mean more than what it says because one of the parties to it had been involved in negotiations of another document, with a third party, which, if it had been ratified, might have included the thing Qatar would have liked to see in *this* agreement. Such an argument does not require refutation. (Paulsson, 9 June 2000, 9 ¶ 38)

It will be recalled that Qatar's Sheikh Abdullah himself observed in 1934 that the 1916 Treaty did not cover "the interior but only the coast" (Fowle, 12 March 1934, 2).

Thus, a closer examination of Qatar's arguments to support its contention—that from 1868 onward it was a recognized political unit stretching from coast to coast—inevitably leads to the conclusion that such an assertion was and is unfounded. The treaties of the early nineteenth century contained no such recognition—as is also the case with the Agreements of 1868. This should come as no surprise, in view of the fact that the Al-Thani's control was at the time of the treaties still limited to Doha and its vicinity.

Zubarah

8

Founding and Zenith of Zubarah (1762 to End of Nineteenth Century)

As noted in Chapter 3, the Al-Khalifa family arrived on the western coast of the Qatar peninsula in the eighteenth century and established the town of Zubarah as their capital. Soon afterward they invited the Naim tribe to live in Zubarah, promising the Naim protection from other tribes in the area in exchange for their allegiance.

This arrangement continued even after the Al-Khalifa relocated their base to Bahrain's main island and Zubarah developed into an important trading area. The Al-Thani never occupied the Zubarah region, despite seven attempts to do so from 1873–1903. Zubarah continued under Al-Khalifa sovereignty with international recognition until the attack by Qatar and Zubarah's occupation in 1937. The issue of Qatar's occupation of the Zubarah region has never been adjudicated, despite numerous protests by Bahrain, until now.

This section will examine these issues in detail.

Geography of Zubarah

The Zubarah region, located on the west coast of the Qatar peninsula, comprises about 193 square kilometers (74.52 square miles) in area, or approximately 1 percent of the total land area of the Qatar peninsula, and 27 percent of Bahrain's land territory respectively. Today it is virtually uninhabited. But there do exist remnants of its various settlements that serve to delineate its borders.

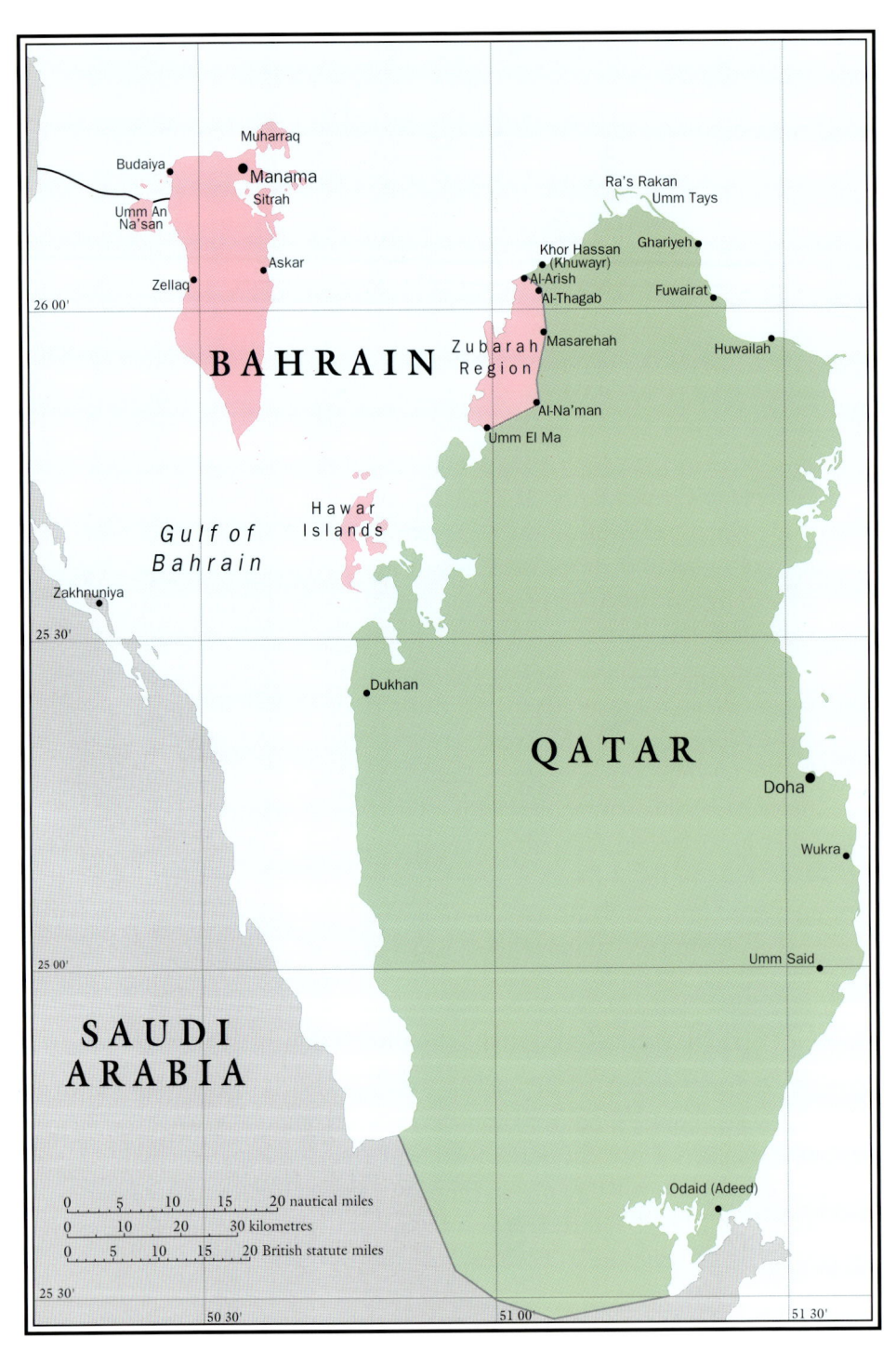

Map No. 3: Bahrain and Qatar

The Bahrain–Qatar map (Map No. 3, p. 122) shows that Al-Arish lies at Zubarah's northernmost point, about 10 kilometers (6.21 miles) north of its principal town, Zubarah, on the coast. Its southernmost settlement is Umm el Ma, about 20 kilometers (12.43 miles) south of Zubarah. Al-Na'man lies on its easternmost border, about 13 kilometers (8.08 miles) inland. Its remaining settlements include: Umm Al-Ghubbur, Masarehah, Al-Thagab, Umm Al-Shuwyyl, Al-Rubayqah, Fuhaihel, Al-Muharaqa, Al-Judadah, Al-Ham, Hulwan, Lisha, Furaiwah, and Rakiyat.

As seen from the map, this is a small and self-contained area, as a large, empty desert separates it from the peninsula's only other significant population base, the port of Doha and its environs on the eastern coast of the peninsula. As such, this region traditionally maintained close social, economic and political ties with the Bahrain Islands, which are only a short boat-ride away.

Founding of Zubarah

Pre-1762 History

The history of Zubarah prior to the eighteenth century—like that of the Qatar peninsula itself—has yet to be written. For now, all historians can do is speculate based on the little information there is about how the men and women of the Zubarah region lived (how they were governed, how they made their livelihoods, how they organized their social structure, et cetera). Prior to the European traveler accounts of the eighteenth century, Qatar made no mention of any historical documents or histories of the region. Other than forged documents, the only legitimate documents which Qatar could dredge up to support its version of the history of Zubarah were three fragmentary references to people wearing Qatari turbans or gowns (Al-Hafidh; Ibn Al-Athir; Ibn Saad).

In all likelihood, the region never had more than temporary settlements during this period. Its location on the coast was certainly more hospitable than the interior and might have attracted people to build small villages; but even as late as the eighteenth century, life there was transient:

> The only settlements that existed... were small, poor fishing villages oriented towards the sea or towards the desert of their tribes' original ranges. These settlements were ephemeral. Often populated by clans made temporary refugees through tribal disputes, the towns of Qatar could disappear overnight as their few families packed belongings on camels or boats and headed for the desert or the sea. (Crystal 1990, 26–27)

Zubarah Town is the principal settlement in the Zubarah region. It lies at the foot of a deep bay, thus making it an attractive location for a port. Its vicinity is relatively rich in pasture, with access to wood, and the tribes of the peninsula used it to graze their animals. It is, however, poor in water; the closest water supplies lie east and southeast from the town, where the wells of Halwan, Masarehah, and Lisha are located.

The principal sheikhs of the Qatar peninsula prior to the arrival of the Al-Khalifa in the 1760s were the Al-Musallam, a section of the larger Bani Khaled tribe. At the height of its power, Bani Khaled influence ran from Basra, to Kuwait, to the Qatar peninsula and into the Nejd. In the Qatar peninsula itself, the Al-Musallam, were centered in Huwailah, then the largest settlement on the east coast. There were also two other important tribes in the peninsula at this time—the Ma'adhid in the village of Fuwairat and the Sudan in Doha (Lorimer 1908–15, 1:787; Crystal 1995. 16).

By the time the Al-Khalifa reached the western coast of the Qatar peninsula in the 1760s, the Bani Khaled tribe's hold had weakened. This eased Al-Khalifa's entry into the region.

Al-Khalifa Arrival

As detailed in Chapter 3, the Al-Khalifa arrived in the north of the Qatar peninsula in 1762. They, along with the Al-Jalahimah and Al-Sabah families, formed a division of the Utub tribe that had established Kuwait in 1716.

The Al-Khalifa had been the preeminent merchants in Kuwait, and after about five decades of steady growth there, they decided to expand their pearling business beyond its borders. Their first choice was to move to the Bahrain Islands, as these were close to the center of the pearling industry in the Gulf. The islands were then, however, under the control of the Persian Empire. Rather than try to fend off the Persians, the Al-Khalifa decided to settle at Zubarah instead.

Other tribes decided to join the Al-Khalifa in their move, most notably the Al-Jalahimah. It is at this point, the arrival of the Utub in 1762, that the history-proper of Zubarah begins.

Securing Zubarah

Despite the declining Bani Khaled influence in the area, the Al-Khalifa knew they would not be able to maintain their position in the Zubarah region were they to depend on economic wealth alone. Thus, from almost the very beginning, the Al-Khalifa worked to add political authority to their already solid economic base.

One of their most effective strategies was to invite the Naim tribe (originally from Oman) to settle in the Zubarah region. The two groups worked out an alliance whereby the Naim would pledge their allegiance to the Al-Khalifa and defend Al-Khalifa interests in the Zubarah region. In return, the Naim would enjoy protection from attack. The arrangement was a mutually advantageous relationship of Ruler and benefactor: the Al-Khalifa maintained their control over territory through a loyal ally, and the Naim enjoyed the protection and favors of the Al-Khalifa.

The new wealth generated from the pearling trade made Zubarah a tempting target for those wishing to share in the region's prosperity illicitly. It became the subject of attack, particularly by the Persians. To fortify their position, the Al-Khalifa built the Murair Fort, near the edge of the town of Zubarah, in 1768.

This did not stop the attacks, however. In the early 1780s, at least two attacks—neither successful—were launched against Zubarah by Nasir bin Madhkur of the Matarish tribe of Oman. Madhkur was then governing the Bahrain Islands as a dependency of the Persian Empire (Khuri 1980, 24).

Al-Khalifa Take the Bahrain Islands

The Al-Khalifa recognized that they needed to gain control of the Bahrain Islands in order to secure the Gulf of Bahrain and the lucrative pearling industry there. And they would need help to take control of these islands, heavily protected as they were by Persian forces.

So in 1783, the Al-Khalifa set about forming a coalition. They called upon their subjects, the Naim, and also remembered their cousins, the Utub, in Kuwait.

On 28 July 1783, having gathered their forces, the Al-Khalifa attacked the Persian garrison on Bahrain and succeeded in expelling the Persians (A. B. Kemball 1844, 141).

It was not a quick victory. As Brucks relates, after several months of fighting people were tiring of war to the extent that several of the allies of both the Persians and the Al-Khalifa began to withdraw. Consequently, the two parties entered into a treaty, by which the Persian troops were withdrawn, and the head of the Al-Khalifa family, Sheikh Ahmed, agreed to pay tribute to the Persians. This arrangement continued until about 1790, when the Persians finally retreated to Persia altogether (Brucks 1856, 565).

In 1796, the Al-Khalifa moved their seat of government first to the main island of Bahrain and then to Muharraq island. As Rulers of Bahrain, the Al-Khalifa were able to control almost the entire pearl trade coming in and out of the Arabian Gulf (Lorimer 1908–15. 1:841). The decision was a good one, for Bahraini pearls were soon renowned for their shape and color:

> The pearls taken at Bahrein, though not so white as those of Ceylon and Japan, are much larger than those of the former place, and of a more regular shape than those of the latter. They are of a yellowish cast, but have this recommendation, that they preserve their golden hue; whereas the whiter kind lose much of their luster by keeping, particularly in hot countries. (Justamond 1776, 25–26)

However, the wealth of the Bahraini pearl trade made them the envy of other Gulf leaders. In 1800, the Imam of Muscat attacked the main island of Bahrain, captured all the headmen and forced them to go to Oman. The Al-Khalifa returned to Zubarah, where they solicited the protection of the Wahhabis (Warden 1856, 366). In 1801, the Al-Khalifa and the Wahhabis engaged in a joint attack against the Imam of Muscat and retook Bahrain.

Bahraini Ties with Zubarah Remain

But even after moving their capital to Bahrain, the Al-Khalifa did not let go of Zubarah. They found Zubarah a useful buffer against attacks from the Qatari mainland. Thus, they appointed a governor in the town to rule on their behalf and spent their winters in the Zubarah region, reserving the summer months for the cooler Bahrain climes.

To strengthen their defenses in the region, the Al-Khalifa fortified Zubarah town between 1783 and 1796. A channel was constructed from the sea to the entrance of Murair Fort. Towers along each side of the channel were put up to protect vessels on their way to the fort. In addition, walls were built to protect road access to the fort from the city gate.

The Rulers of Bahrain also saw to it that the civilian amenities of the town were improved: a mosque, several freshwater wells, and additional houses were constructed.

Yet despite the added fortifications Zubarah was attacked again, this time by the Wahhabis. In 1810,

> The Wahabee ruler assume[d] the government of Bahrein and Zobara, and appoint[ed] Abdoolla bin Oofeysan Vukeel over those places, and the Kateef and Gutter districts ... the Uttoobees continue[d] in administration but pa[id] tribute to the Vukeel. (Warden 1856, 368)

Then, in 1810–11,

> The Imaum [of Muscat], taking advantage of the attention and resources of the Wahabee ruler being engaged in checking the invasion of the Turkish troops under Ibrahim Pasha, attack[ed] Zobara and Bahrein, burn[ed] the former and land[ed] on the latter. The Wahabee Vukeel, Oofeysan, [was] made prisoner, and the Uttoobees recover[ed] the island. (Warden 1856, 368)

These destabilizations were temporary, however, and the Rulers of Bahrain continued their administration of the Zubarah region even, as seen above, when under a short period of Wahhabi rule.

Throughout the rest of the nineteenth century, the prosperity of the Zubarah region declined. Nonetheless, the Rulers of Bahrain maintained their ties to the Zubarah region and the Naim continued to live there as Bahrain subjects. Captain Brucks, who conducted a survey of the region in the 1820s verified:

> Zobara... is a large town, now in ruins... the inhabitants are ... subject to Bahrein.... (Brucks 1856, 562)

This situation remained unchanged in the 1880s, when disturbances broke out on the east coast of the peninsula. As the British observed:

> Dissensions have, during the past few years, been rife amongst the Arabs residing under the jurisdiction of Sheikh Jasim of El-Bida'a, and bodies of seceders first settled at El Foweyrat on the Katr Coast, where they are to some extent under the protection of the Noeym tribe, who maintain intimate friendly relations with the Chief of Bahrain. (Ross 1886–87, 7)

In the 1890s, the Ottomans, as acknowledged by Sheikh Jasim of Doha, also recognized Bahrain authority over the Naim. Toward the end of the nineteenth century, Sheikh Jasim's control over Doha and its surrounding settlements had weakened considerably. He informed the Ottomans that:

> He would no longer be capable of performing the duty of Kaymakam, and requested that his resignation be accepted: and that on the other hand, the greater part of the weapons and things lost by the Imperial Troops were in possession of the Naim tribe, and that this tribe was in Bahreyn. (*Ottoman Report on Qatar*, 22 September 1893, 5)

The Rulers of Bahrain maintained their position in Zubarah because it was key to protecting the Bahrain Islands. It provided them with a sense of control over the affairs of the often unstable Qatar peninsula. For example, in 1869 an understanding was reached between the representative of the Ruler of Bahrain and the representative of the Sheikhs of the Doha confederation in which "... the sum of 4,000 Krans will be paid to Rashid bin Jabbur Shaikh of the Naim for his protecting Guttur" (Understanding between Ruler of Bahrain and Sheikhs of Doha, 10 April 1869).

Similarly, the Naim maintained their loyalty to the Rulers of Bahrain because the Rulers of Bahrain, as will be seen below, also provided the Naim with stability, giving them food and arms when necessary. These were precious commodities in a time where raids could occur at any moment.

Prosperous Trading Center

The situation in the Zubarah region changed dramatically under Al-Khalifa governorship. As mentioned earlier, the only settlements in the area in the early eighteenth century were probably transient. After 1762, however, Zubarah was transformed from a virtually uninhabited area into one boasting approximately 3,000 people at its height (1762–83). This is significant, given that only 3,500 people lived in the whole Qatar peninsula at that time (Paulsson, 9 June 2000, 28 ¶ 131).

As indicated earlier, the Qatar peninsula has traditionally been one of the least populated areas on earth. Even as late as the 1940s, the population of the entire Qatar peninsula was estimated to be ten thousand, or perhaps up to double that number at most (Paulsson, 9 June 2000, 10–11 ¶ 45). Thus, that the Al-Khalifa were able to attract three thousand people to the region during the eighteenth century is astonishing.

People came to the town of Zubarah for several reasons. First, as mentioned previously, the Al-Khalifa were associated with stability of rule:

> The one who established Al-Zubara and entered it into history was Shaikh Mohammed bin Khalifa. Then it was finished and enlarged and many people came to it due to the good character of its establisher and Amir, Shaikh Mohammed bin Khalifa Al-Khalifa and after him, his respected sons. They were brave, kind, generous and wise. (Abdulla Al-Khalifa and Hussein 1984, 2)

Second, the Al-Khalifa combined sound economic policy with political authority. They made sure foreign merchants enjoyed complete protection. They also implemented a system of no customs duties to encourage trade (Lorimer 1908–15, 1:789). These procedures enabled the Al-Khalifa to turn Zubarah into "the cosmopolitan centre of the peninsula of Qatar and Bahrain, with no rival" (Abdulla Al-Khalifa and Hussein 1984, 2).

Archeological Evidence

Much archeological evidence shows that it was the Al-Khalifa who founded Zubarah. In his book *Looking for Dilmun,* Geoffrey Bibby, leader of the Danish archeological team that visited Zubarah in 1956, says:

> We had been rather chary of visiting Zubara, for our motives might well be misunderstood, both by Sheikh Sulman of Bahrain and by Sheikh Ali of Qatar. For Zubara is the ancestral home of the sheikhs of Bahrain, a town in which the Al-Khalifa family had settled when, in the middle of the eighteenth century, they had moved south from the neighbourhood of Kuwait....
>
> We had to see it. Although we ran the risk of being deemed Bahraini spies, there was a possibility that Zubara was an ancient town.
>
> [A]fter lunch we collected potsherds, though we could already see that Zubara was no ancient city. There was no tell [a mound created by the remains of ancient settlements], except one in the making. The buildings that were crumbling to ruins about us and being covered with sand would one day be an even flattish mound that future inhabitants of Qatar might well choose as a site for a new city. But these buildings were themselves built upon the naked rock and sand of the foreshore—*there had been no city before the Zubara of the Al-Khalifah.* (Bibby 1970, 122–23) [Emphasis added.]

9 The Naim: Bahrain's People in Qatar Peninsula

The Naim originated in Oman. Tradition holds that a section of the tribe was invited by the Al-Khalifa to settle along the western coast of the Qatar peninsula when the Al-Khalifa moved there in the eighteenth century. Over time, the Zubarah Naim became completely detached from the main body of the tribe in Oman.

No definite figures tell how many Naim actually left Oman to join the Al-Khalifa. Lorimer estimates that about two thousand Naimi tribesmen lived outside of Oman while the Al-Khalifa had their base in the Zubarah region (Lorimer 1908–15, 2:1305).

Because of their special relationship with the Al-Khalifa, the Naim's standing vis-à-vis the other tribes in the Zubarah region rose; after the Al-Khalifa, the Naim came second in the area. The Al-Khalifa appointed them as governors of the town, and they received favors from the Rulers of Bahrain. In addition, as will be seen below, they defended the town from outside attack, which no doubt earned them the gratitude of the other inhabitants of the Zubarah region.

Traditional Way of Life

After settling in Zubarah, some of the Naim became pearl divers, but the majority were pastoral, depending on their livestock for subsistence. Contemporary estimates were that they owned about 100 horses, 600 camels, 1,000 sheep, and 1,000 goats (Lorimer 1908–15, 2:1305; Ferdinand 1993, 41).

The Naim followed a seasonal migration pattern. In winter, they resided in the Qatar peninsula, mainly in the Zubarah region; during the summer, most Naim migrated to Bahrain and formed camps in the northern part of the main island, though some did take up quarters near Doha, on the western coast (Lorimer 1908–15, 2:1305; Ferdinand 1993, 41).

When in Bahrain,

> ...they stayed in palm leaf huts (barasti) close to wells where they had traditional rights or near the sea, e.g. on small uninhabited islands. They grazed their animals in the southern desert, as well as in the palm grove area of the north. (Ferdinand 1993, 41)

Tribal Dirah

As mentioned above, the Qatar peninsula is sparsely populated, and villages sometimes disappeared overnight due to tribal disputes. As such, there were few indications of the exercise of sovereignty by means of a fixed presence in the eighteenth and nineteenth centuries. This does not mean, however, that there were not ways through which a ruler might establish title to his territories or possessions.

In the nomadic areas of the Gulf, a ruler established sovereignty through a concept known as tribal *dirah*. Again, a tribal *dirah* is generally defined as the territory within which a tribe moved.

As noted earlier, among the privileges granted to the Naim was the right to use certain grazing grounds, wells, and oases in and around the Zubarah region. As they owed their allegiance to the Al-Khalifa, the area in which the Naim moved defines the territory over which they exercised their sovereignty.

Contemporary documents and the recollections of the former inhabitants of Zubarah now resident in Bahrain establish the following wells and places (none of which are inhabited today) to be subject to the sovereignty of the Ruler of Bahrain as part of the tribal *dirah* of the Al-Jabr section of the Naim tribe:

- Al-Arish
- Rakaiyat
- Furaiwah
- Al-Thagab
- Ain Muhammed
- Masarehah

- Lisha
- Zubarah
- Umm Al-Shuwyyl
- Hulwan
- Al-Rubayqan
- Umm Al-Ghubbur
- Al-Maharaqa
- Al-Judaydah
- Al-Na'man
- Umm El Ma (Bahrain 1996, 41 ¶ 102)

In its written pleadings to the Court, Bahrain presented a map showing the tribal *dirah* of the Al-Jabr branch of the Naim tribe (see Map No. 4, overleaf). Therefore, the line that links the wells, oases and place-names along the edge of the *dirah* of the Al-Jabr section of the Naim tribe constitutes the boundary between the Zubarah region, over which the Ruler of Bahrain maintained his authority and the State of Qatar.

International law recognizes that the concept of tribal *dirah* and ties of allegiance can form the basis for sovereignty. For example, in 1981, the International Court of Justice accepted as its premise the regional norm that territorial sovereignty over desert areas that are or have been occupied by Arab tribes is directly linked to the question of tribal allegiance, as reflected in the *Dubai/Sharjah* arbitration. The ICJ observed:

> ...that until the mid-twentieth Century this region was largely desert and sparsely populated. Except for the coastal fringe, the population was nomadic or semi-nomadic and for such people the modern concept of "boundary" or "frontier" had no meaning. They were concerned only with areas or localities within which they moved from place to place....
>
> The tribes owed allegiance to a Ruler. The form of allegiance varied, but might, for instance, involve the payment of the religious tax known as "zakat." The link between a tribe and a Ruler might be close or tenuous, dependent on the degree of independence manifested by the people concerned. It was, however, by way of this allegiance that a Ruler was able to exercise a form of sovereignty over a region where nomadic tribesmen were regularly moving from place to place." (*Dubai/Sharjah Arbitration Award*, 19 October 1981, 543)

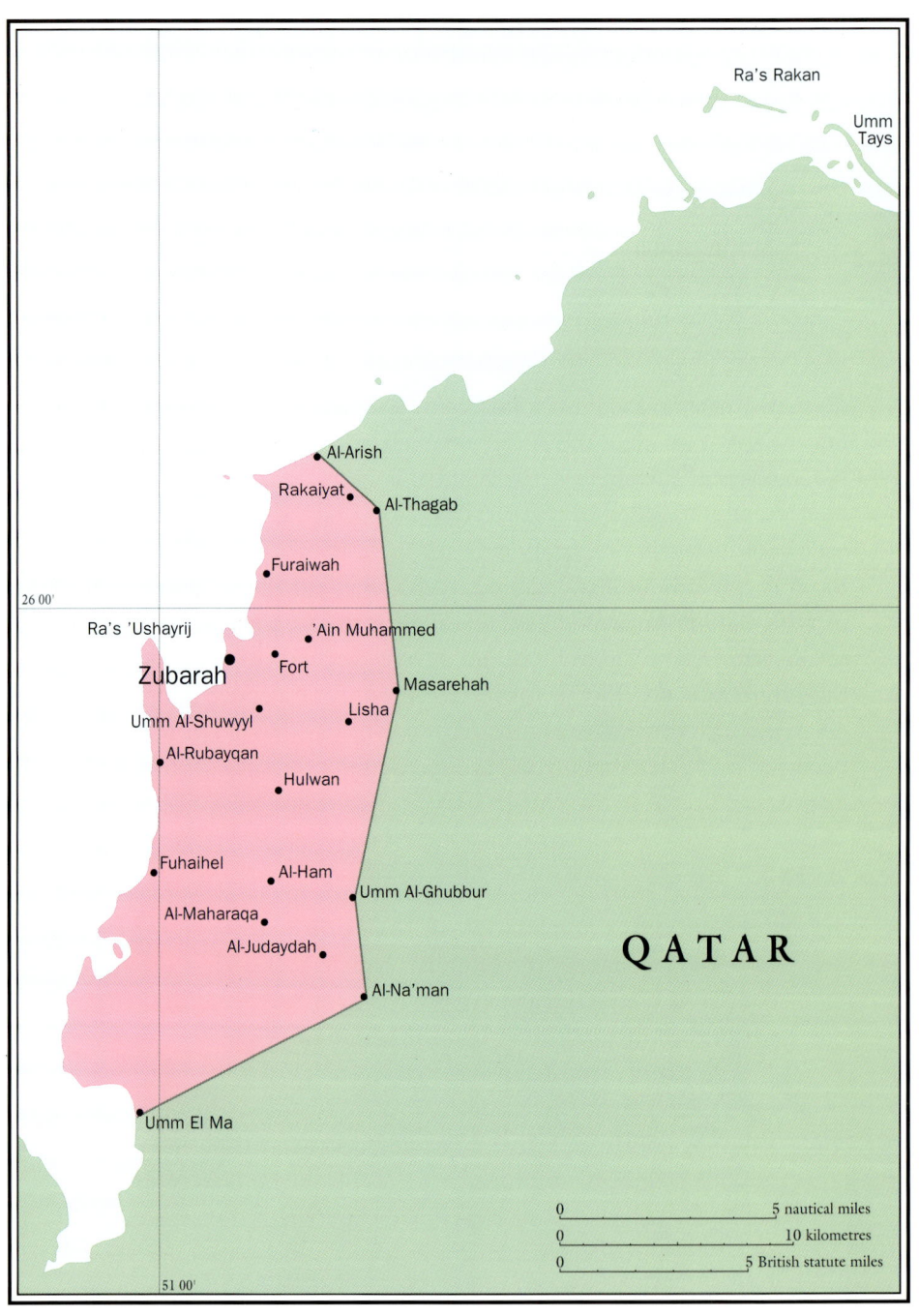

Map No. 4: The Zubarah Region with Place Names

Nature of Ruler of Bahrain-Naim Relationship: *Ikrimiyyah*

When the Al-Khalifa arrived in the Qatar peninsula, they worked to create a reliable and armed power base of their own through the Naim tribe. As already noted, the Zubarah region was attacked by Persia, Muscat, wandering Arab tribes, and later by the Ottomans. It was particularly vulnerable during the summer months, when many of its able males were away for the pearling season.

The Al-Khalifa, therefore, needed a more permanent presence on which they could depend. As mentioned above, the majority of the Naim tribe were pastoral nomads. They were the ideal source of the needed presence.

To encourage the Naim to settle in Zubarah, the Al-Khalifa granted them the use of grazing grounds, wells and oases in and around Zubarah.

This arrangement was based on *ikrimiyyah*—the system of benefits received by important Arab tribes from their Rulers. There are various instances of the benefits the Al-Khalifa bestowed on the Naim tribe.

As noted above, an understanding was reached between the Ruler of Bahrain and the Sheikhs of the Doha confederation that the Naim tribe was to be paid the sum of 4,000 krans a year. This amount was taken from the taxes and tribute payable to the Ruler of Bahrain from the Doha confederation (Understanding between Ruler of Bahrain and Sheikhs of Doha, 10 April 1869). In 1875, the British Political Resident asserted:

> Sheikh Esau is said to spend three to four thousand kran every month on the people of Zobarah, and gives Nasir bin Jabar 300 krans per mensem. (News Agent, Bahrain, 16 March 1875)

The British Political Resident clearly noted that this was Nasir bin Jabar's salary (News Agent, Bahrain, 16 March 1875). In 1887, a *Persian Gulf Administrative Report* again affirmed the benefits accrued to the Naim from the Ruler of Bahrain:

> The Chief, Shaikh Esea-bin-Ali, continues to maintain intimate friendly relations with the Na'eem of the mainland, to whom, and to other Arabs of the mainland, he makes yearly presents of considerable value. Indeed a large portion of the revenues of

> Bahrain are dissipated in this manner without any ostensible compensating advantage. (Ross 1886–87, 6)

As will be seen in Chapter 11, this system continued into the twentieth century.

Contrary to the *Administrative Report*, the Ruler of Bahrain did gain certain advantages from the Naim's allegiance. Though speaking in 1874, the Political Resident's remarks as follows pertain to the rest of the nineteenth and early twentieth centuries:

> Shaikh Esau necessarily relies much on the Naeem tribe of Zubarah who came to his aid in his late dangers, and if he were to be deprived of their support, his means of defence would be greatly weakened. (Ross, 10 November 1874)

Thus aided, the Ruler of Bahrain was able to maintain control over his territory in Zubarah.

Allegiance to Ruler of Bahrain

The Naim demonstrated their allegiance to the Rulers of Bahrain in several ways: they paid taxes, they acted as guards, and they defended the Zubarah region from outside aggression.

Payment of Taxes

As previously indicated, the Al-Khalifa were sovereign over much of the Qatar peninsula during the eighteenth and nineteenth centuries. As sovereigns, they collected tribute and taxes from the other tribes of the Qatar peninsula.

As noted in Chapter 5 in "The Doha Affair," the Doha confederation, led by Muhammad Al-Thani, attempted a rebellion in 1867, which was put down by the British. Not having succeeded, Al-Thani bound himself to "maintain towards Sheikh Ali bin Khalifeh, Chief of Bahrain, all the relations which heretofore subsisted between me and the Sheikh of Bahrain" (*Agreement of Chief of El-Kutr*, 12 September 1868).

Part of Al-Thani's obligations was to collect taxes and tribute payable to Bahrain from all the local chiefs on the Qatar peninsula. The taxes owed by the Naim and Al Bu Aainen tribes combined were 1,500 krans (*Agreement of Chief of El-Kutr*, 12 September 1868).

Acting as Guards

The Naim showed their loyalty to the Rulers of Bahrain by providing a variety of services for them, one of the most important of which was to act as their guards. This service was specifically acknowledged in the 1869 Understanding noted above, which awarded the head of the Naim the sum of 4,000 krans annually for protecting Qatar (Understanding between Ruler of Bahrain and Sheikhs of Doha, 10 April 1869).

Defending Zubarah

The Naim tribe further demonstrated their allegiance to the Ruler of Bahrain by defending the Zubarah region from outside aggression. As described previously, the Zubarah region was a thriving commercial center from 1762–83. Among the first "outsiders" to be attracted to the wealth centered in the Zubarah region were the Persians, who had a base nearby in the Bahrain Islands (which were then governed by Nasir bin Madhkur).

In the early 1780s at least two attacks—none successful—were launched against Zubarah by Madhkur; the Naim participated in the force that defeated him.

Also described previously (Chapter 5, section "Britain as 'Protector' of Bahrain Territory: 1840s through 1860s") was the help given in 1848 by the Naim to the Ruler of Bahrain, Sheikh Mohammed bin Khalifa, to defeat the coalition of tribes formed by Isa bin Tarif in an attempt to overthrow him.

These events illustrates not only the Ruler of Bahrain's commitment to the Zubarah region and the Naim, but also his sovereignty over most of the Qatar peninsula, as it was he who had appointed bin Tarif as governor of Doha. Similarly, the Naim's refusal to join bin Tarif shows that they were loyal subjects of the Rulers of Bahrain.

In 1870, British dispatches reported that the Naim had defeated the Bani Hajir, a tribe from Nejd on the Arabian Peninsula which had been plotting against the Ruler of Bahrain (*Report to British Political Resident*, 1 May 1870).

The Bani Hajir tried once more in 1875. Again, the Naim headed off Bani Hajir encroachment on the Zubarah region, carrying off some head of cattle (Saldanha 1904a, 8).

The Bani Hajir tried yet again in 1876. Together with another tribe called the Monasoor, they positioned themselves about half a day's distance from Zubarah to see how the Naim would react. Upon learning of their presence, the Naim sent intelligence scouts, but these were discovered by the Bani Hajir, who killed three of them. The Naim then asked help from the Ruler of Bahrain, who sent boats to convey their camels, sheep and cattle to Bahrain (News Agent, Bahrain, 9 February 1875). After regrouping, the Naim repositioned themselves at Zubarah, armed with provisions from the Ruler of Bahrain (W. F. Prideaux, 7 October 1876).

Their intent was to defend the Zubarah region. As the Ruler of Bahrain maintained to the British in 1877:

> ... the only people, who left Bahrein for Zobarah, were those of the Naim tribe ... who returned of their own accord upon hearing that a hostile force had come to attack Zobarah. ... (Isa bin Ali Al-Khalifa, December 1877)

Ruler of Bahrain Authority Confirmed to British

The Ottomans arrived in the Qatar peninsula in the second half of the nineteenth century. They almost immediately set their eyes on the Zubarah region. Perturbed by this possibility, the Ruler of Bahrain went to the British for help in putting them off.

At the time, the British were engaged in a delicate relationship with the Ottomans. (For more on the nature of this relationship see Chapter 6.) They, therefore, asked the Ruler of Bahrain whether there was anything on record to prove that the Naim were his subjects.

The Ruler of Bahrain said yes:

> When Colonel Pelly was here at the time when I became Chief of Bahrein, Nasir bin Jubbur acknowledged in Colonel Pelly's presence that he was my subject, and under treaty to me. (Grant, 16 August 1873)

On 2 September 1873, the Ruler of Bahrain reaffirmed his rights over Zubarah:

> The Naim tribe and their dependents have ever been my subjects since they were at Guttur and paid religious tithes until three years ago.... Subsequently the Gutterees and their chief Mahomed bin Sanee [Mohammed bin Thani] rebelled and went under the

protection of [the Ottoman Empire] but the tribe of Naim and their dependants remained my subjects and paid their annual tribute.... Zobareh is a property under the rule of Bahrein and which belonged to the Uttoobees [i.e. the tribe of the Al-Khalifa]. On referring to the [1868] Treaty you will perceive that Zobareh is a dependency of this Island. (Isa bin Ali Al-Khalifa, 2 September 1873)

Al-Jabr Branch

The section of the Naim tribe that moved to the Qatar peninsula was composed of several branches. The two most important branches of the Naim within the Qatar peninsula were the Al-Jabr and the Al-Ramzan, with the Al-Jabr assuming a more senior position than the Al-Ramzan (Montigny-Kozlowska 1985, 136).

In the beginning, both branches owed their allegiance to the Al-Khalifa. As will be seen in the Chapter 12, however, the Al-Ramzan switched their allegiance to the Al-Thani family, due to an internal dispute with the Al-Jabr in the 1930s. Through it all, the Al-Jabr remained loyal to the Ruler of Bahrain.

10 Ottoman Attempts to Take Control of Zubarah

As will be recalled from Chapter 6, the Ottomans set up camp in the Doha region of the Qatar peninsula in 1871, thereby changing the relationship between the Al-Khalifa and the Al-Thani families. Traditionally, the Rulers of Bahrain had been responsible for the entire Qatar peninsula as well as the Bahrain Islands. With the Ottoman arrival, however, their grip on the eastern and southern parts of the promontory loosened, as the Al-Thani of Doha found their position temporarily strengthened by the power of the Porte.

Bahrain remained in control of the northern area of the peninsula, though from time to time the Ottomans and Al-Thani exhibited their desire to expand their control into the Bahraini regions, especially Zubarah. This was evidenced by the Ottoman's seven attempts between 1873 and 1903 to establish their authority there. Throughout, these attempts were consistently resisted and Bahrain's hold on the Zubarah region remained unaffected.

Continued Bahrain Rule over Zubarah

The Zubarah region was important to Bahrain for two basic reasons. The first was historical: Zubarah had been home and seat of government for the Al-Khalifa tribe from 1762 until they moved their capital to the Bahrain Islands in the 1790s. Even after this event, the Zubarah region was closely tied to the islands, with frequent travel and close economic and family ties between the islands and the Zubarah region. The second reason was strategic: Zubarah served as an effective buffer against attacks from the peninsula. For the Al-Khalifa, and others, Zubarah had served as a staging post for attacks on the Bahrain Islands, and the Al-Khalifa wanted to ensure that this critical area remained in their control.

Bahrain Supplies Resources to Zubarah

During the Ottoman presence, the Ruler of Bahrain maintained his control over Zubarah. This control took several forms, in addition to the continuing close relationship with the Zubarah residents. One significant expression of Bahrain's authority was in the supply of resources. The Ruler of Bahrain financed various construction projects in the Zubarah region and provided essential supplies to the residents during the Ottoman presence.

The Turkish period in the Qatar peninsula was a turbulent one for the inhabitants of the Zubarah region. Ottoman troops, having only arrived in the Qatar peninsula in 1871, were at Zubarah's doorstep, trying to take over land that Bahrain's people had inhabited for more than 100 years. The Ruler of Bahrain and the Naim supported each other because both were in need—the Ruler of Bahrain depended on the Naim to guard the Zubarah region against potential attacks, and the Naim tribe depended on the Ruler of Bahrain for his annual gifts of food and supplies to survive in a spot limited in water supplies and grazing areas (see Chapters 4 and 9).

When it became increasingly clear that the Ottoman threat against the Zubarah region was growing more menacing, the Ruler of Bahrain fortified the defenses of the town of Zubarah. In 1874, he sent several masons to carry out necessary repairs to the fort. He supplied the required materials and bore all the expenses. He also made sure that the residents had adequate food provisions. According to a British government report, the inhabitants of the Zubarah region were "in a great measure subsisted by him and boatloads of rice, dates and other provisions are continually dispatched" (Fraser, 18 December 1874).

In a letter to the Secretary of the Government of India, the Political Resident recognized that Sheikh Isa was within his rights:

> My reply to the Chief was to the effect that... I would not interfere with the dispatch of reinforcements as a purely defensive measure; but that it was for the Chief himself to judge as to the necessity for, or expediency of, the measure. (Ross, 10 November 1874)

Not only did the Resident acknowledge the Ruler of Bahrain's authority in the Zubarah region, he also left it up to the Ruler to decide on what measures would be most appropriate to take to build up the defense of the area. In other words, Sheikh Isa was free to exercise his sovereignty there.

Nonetheless, it is important to note that, given the Ottoman presence in the Qatar peninsula, the British were willing to recognize such sovereignty over the Zubarah region only. Thus:

> You [the Political Resident] intimated there would be no objection provided I did not go beyond [Zubarah] and this course I have pursued. (Isa bin Ali Al-Khalifa, 17 December 1874)

Administrative and Executive Control

The Ruler of Bahrain's powers in the Zubarah region were also evidenced in his changing the Governor of Zubarah Town during the Ottoman period. On 1 October 1874, Sheikh Isa replaced Nasir bin Jabar with Khalifa bin Ghatam (Fraser, 18 December 1874).

Bahrain involvement in the administrative affairs of the Zubarah region did not stop in 1874. British reports for the period 1886 to 1887 stress that:

> The Chief, Shaikh Easa-bin-Ali, continues to maintain intimate friendly relation with the Na'eem tribe of the mainland, to whom, and to other Arabs of the mainland, he makes yearly presents of considerable value. (Ross 1886–87, 7)

Ottoman Attempts to Extend Their Authority to Zubarah

The Ottomans recognized the close ties between the British and the Al-Khalifa, but not to the extent that this prevented them from testing how far that relationship would go. After all, the British were apparently adopting a "hands off" policy to areas outside the Zubarah region.

Al-Thani's efforts to spread out into the northwest of the peninsula did not go as well, however. The Ottomans certainly wanted to expand into Zubarah, and they tried. But when they came up against British resistance, they stopped. Between 1873 and 1903, the Ottomans and their Al-Thani clients made a series of seven attempts to extend their authority to the Zubarah region.

While Ottoman motives to push into the Arabian Peninsula involved larger geopolitical concerns, the reasons they expanded into the Zubarah region were mostly financial. An Ottoman report describes their interest in the pearling money that the Zubarah region generated:

> If a government is now established in Udaid and Zubarah then the Kaza of Qatar will be able to benefit from the pearl fishing in this area. (*Report from the Office of Assistant to the Governor of Katar,* 7 November 1891)

Additionally, the Ottomans also knew that Zubarah could be used as a base from which to attack Bahrain, which had an even more developed pearling trade.

First and Second Attempts (1873 and 1874)

The first Ottoman attempt to control Zubarah occurred in 1873, when Hossein Effendi, an Ottoman official, accompanied by one hundred men, sailed to the port in Zubarah to convince its residents to switch their allegiance to the Ottoman Sultan. The Bahrain-appointed Governor of the town and Chief of the Naim tribe, Nasir bin Al-Jabar, greeted the Porte's representative but rejected his proposal, informing him he was

> . . . a Bahrein subject, and that if the Effendi had anything to say in the matter he had better address himself to the Chief of Bahrein. (Grant, 16 August 1873)

In correspondence with the Political Resident, Sheikh Isa Al-Khalifa provided the British with the Naim headman's statement made at the time of his accession in 1869, in which Nasir bin Jabar, "acknowledged in Colonel Pelly's [the Political Resident] presence that he was my subject, and under treaty to me" (Grant, 16 August 1873). He further pointed out that even after some tribes of the Qatar peninsula, like the Al-Thani, rebelled against him in 1867, "the tribe of Naim and their dependants remained my subjects and paid their annual tribute . . ." (Isa bin Ali Al-Khalifa, 2 September 1873).

Having failed to convince the residents of the Zubarah region to join them voluntarily in 1873, the Ottomans turned to local Bedouin tribes to carry out attacks against the Bahrain Islands and Zubarah. Their first attempt using force took place in 1874.

The Al-Thani enlisted two hundred mercenaries of the Bani Hajir tribe, Bedouins from the mainland of Arabia, to help the Ottomans carry out the attack. It ultimately failed, and describing the incident, the Political Resident said:

> ...the small summer garrison of Zubarah held out gallantly until relieved by their fellow tribesmen, who suddenly returned in strength from Bahrain and the pearl banks and inflicted a severe defeat upon the assailants. (Lorimer 1908–15, 1:906)

In a letter to the Government of India about the affair, the Political Resident acknowledged that the Ruler of Bahrain was protecting the Naim tribe:

> Zobarah is held by the Naim Tribe who are allies and in some degree dependants of the Bahrain Chief. The sovereignty over all this Coast in undefined, but the Chiefs of Bahrain have always looked on Zobarah as a feudal dependency of Bahrain. Sheikh Esau [the Ruler of Bahrain; usually spelled "Isa"] accordingly allowed the body of the Naim Tribe who had come to his assistance to return to the relief of their comrades at Zobarah. (Ross, 12 September 1874)

Third, Fourth, and Fifth Attempts (1878, 1888, and 1891)

The next two attempts by the Ottomans and the Al-Thani to take over the Zubarah region utilized the animosity of Nasir bin Mubarak, a renegade member of Bahrain's ruling Al-Khalifa family, who spent most of his life unsuccessfully trying to overthrow the Al-Khalifa regime.

The first of these attempts was in 1878. The chief of Doha, now Sheikh Jasim bin Thani, recruited the help of Nasir bin Mubarak, and tried to take the area by force (Saldanha 1904a, 13). During this attack, the town of Zubarah was destroyed.

Not until ten years later did the Ottomans again decide to attempt to gain control of the Zubarah region, this time in the form of settlement. In 1888, the Ottomans drew up a plan to rebuild the town of Zubarah and have Nasir bin Mubarak Al-Khalifa inhabit the region with his followers. The *Vali* of Basra, an Ottoman official, noted the intent was to divert the lucrative pearl trade away from Bahrain and "secure an income for the Treasury..." (Vali of Basra, 12 April 1888).

The Ruler of Bahrain alerted Britain about the Ottomans' intended move and Britain concurred with his concerns:

> The Chief apprehends that Nasir-bin-Mubarak the refugee from Bahrein, will be instigated to settle at Zobarah with his followers of the Beni Hajir tribe, and supported in doing so by the Turks, either directly or indirectly.
>
> There can be no doubt that if this measure were carried out it would constitute a menace and standing danger to Bahrein, and the objection raised by the Chief of Bahrein is, assuming his information correct, reasonable. (Ross, 12 March 1888b)

The Political Resident warned Sheikh Jassim and Nasir bin Mubarak that no settlement would be permitted, and the plan was rescinded (Ross, 12 March 1888; Ross, 17 March 1888; Saldanha 1904a, 35).

Despite warnings from the British and Bahrain not to settle the Zubarah region, the Ottomans and Al-Thani resumed their settlement program in 1890–91. On this attempt, the Ottomans tried to appoint sub-Governors *(Mudir's)* for the regions of Zubarah and Odaid, in order to "benefit from the pearl fishing in the area" (*Report from the Office of Assistant to the Governor of Katar,* 7 November 1891). But as they had done on all previous attempts, the residents of the Zubarah region warned the Ruler of Bahrain and "... refused occupation by the Ottomans" (Ottoman Ministry of the Interior, 30 November 1911).

Sixth Attempt (1895)

The situation over Zubarah flared up again a few years later, due to a dispute between the Ruler of Bahrain and the Al bin Ali tribe. In early March 1895, the Al bin Ali left the main islands for Zubarah. Sheikh Sultan bin Mohamed Salamah, head of the Al bin Ali tribe, asked Sheikh Jasim bin Thani to mediate the dispute with the Ruler of Bahrain.

The British were wary of this move, however. Colonel F. A. Wilson, the Political Resident reported:

> There can... hardly be a doubt that Jasim, whether or not he fostered the quarrel from the beginning, very soon saw in it a means to further his own aims and to carry out a design which he has

before attempted, of a settlement at Zobarah. (Wilson, 4 May 1895)

The Ruler of Bahrain

> ...intimated that though he had not been seriously concerned at the alienation of Sheikh Sultan, the object now declared, of a settlement at Zobarah, was a serious menace and injury to his position at Bahrein. (Wilson, 4 May 1895)

The Political Resident agreed that the settlement "should be forcibly stopped" (Wilson, 17 April 1895). The British Foreign Secretary supported the Resident: "send [a] strong warning to Jasim that settlement [of] Zobarah will not be allowed" (Foreign Secretary, 20 April 1895).

Thus, the British decided to hit the Al bin Ali where it mattered the most—their share of the pearling trade. They ordered the Al bin Ali tribe to vacate the Zubarah region, thereby cutting off their access to the region's pearling banks. Since they were already prevented from access to the pearling banks near the main islands of Bahrain due to their dispute with the Ruler of Bahrain, all avenues to pearling banks were effectively blocked.

Sheikh Sultan pleaded with the British government to allow them to remain, at least until the end of the pearling season (Sultan bin Mohamed bin Salamah, 25 April 1895), but the Political Resident would not budge in his demand for their immediate departure (Wilson, 2 May 1895).

Indications were that the Ottomans had cooperated, in either a direct or indirect manner, with the Al-Thani and the Al bin Ali efforts to settle the Zubarah region. For example, Sultan bin Mohamed bin Salamah raised the Turkish flag over Zubarah (Wilson, 4 May 1895), and the Mutassarrif of El-Hasa, after a stay or more than a week at Zobarah, and after having given assurances of support and full protection to Sheikh Jasim bin Thani and Sultan bin Salamah, promised to send a Mudir or Governor with some soldiers to Zobarah (Wilson, 18 May 1895).

The result was a standoff between the British and Bahrain on the one hand, and the Ottomans and the Al-Thani on the other.

By July, the situation had not improved, so the British determined to take more emphatic action. A team headed by Lieutenant Kirke seized the boats of the Al bin Ali, taking seven. The boats were turned over to the Ruler of Bahrain for "safe custody." However, despite the seizure of boats, Sheikh Jasim remained in Zubarah (J. H. Pelly, 9 July 1895).

In September 1895, word reached the British that Sheikh Jasim bin Thani at Zubarah had reasserted his resolve to attack Bahrain. They also learned that the Ottomans were to join the Al-Thani forces (J. H. Pelly, 7 September 1895). Captain Pelly, the British Commander, decided to give Sheikh Jasim a chance to respond to these accusations (J. H. Pelly, 7 September 1895a). No reply was forthcoming, however, so Captain Pelly opened fire on the Al-Thani fleet, and forty-four dhows were destroyed.

Captain Pelly reported that the morning after the attack:

> A flag of truce was flying on shore this morning, and I received a letter from Jasim, to which I sent a reply stating my terms for his surrender. Later in the day I received his answer, complying with my demands. (J. H. Pelly, 7 September 1895)

The Ottomans and Sheikh Jasim withdrew the next day, and Zubarah returned to the authority of the Rulers of Bahrain and the Naim tribe.

Seventh Attempt (1903)

The last attempt occurred in 1903, when Jasim bin Thani tried once again to persuade the Ottomans to set up an administrative unit in Zubarah. Lt. Col. Kemball, the Political Resident reported that:

> Sheikh Jasim-bin-Thani had asked the Porte to establish administrative units at Zobara, ... and that Arabi Effendi, who had gone to Bahrein by the preceding mail-steamer, was nominated to the Zobara Mudirieh [subgovernor]. (C. A. Kemball, 23 March 1903).

Kemball underlined that in his opinion:

> It is ... absolutely essential for the security of the Bahrein islands that Zobara should not be occupied by the Turks. Apart from the fact that the occupation of Zobara would be viewed with the greatest concern by the Chief of Bahrein, who considers the place to be an appanage of his, and whose rights we are bound to maintain. (C. A. Kemball, 23 March 1903)

The Viceroy concurred that it was "necessary to prevent Turkish occupation of Zubarah..." (Viceroy of India, 19 January 1903). Thus,

Britain warned the Ottomans, the Ottoman plans were effectively foiled, and Zubarah was returned once again to the Naim and Bahrain.

The Ottomans made no further attempts at control of the Zubarah region during their tenure. After the destruction of Zubarah town in 1878, the only permanent inhabitants of Zubarah were the Naim tribesmen, who continued their pastoral existence, closely tied to Bahrain and its economy, and serving as the protectors of the area for Bahrain's Rulers. It was not until 1937, when oil issues had become paramount, that the Al-Thani made their final move to obtain Zubarah.

Reasons for Ottoman Failure

By making seven attempts at Zubarah over the course of thirty years, it is clear that the Ottoman and Al-Thani were both sorely tempted and unfailingly incapable of wresting control from Bahrain's rulers. One significant reason for these failures can be traced to international geopolitics — the repeated interventions of the British were always met with an Al-Thani/Ottoman withdrawal. It will be remembered that Britain and the Ottomans kept to an uneasy balance of power in Europe — with both wary of the others motives and not wanting to escalate tensions over minor breaches in remote areas. Whenever the British gave a serious warning that they would not put up with any expansionist plans for Zubarah, the Ottoman/Al-Thani forces retreated.

But there are also several more local factors which explain the Ottomans' inability to penetrate the Zubarah region.

Geography

The desert separating the two coasts prevented the Ottomans from gaining effective control over the entire Qatar peninsula. With no road across the peninsula, the only means of getting from one coast to another was via caravan, a journey of several days that was often fraught with danger. Their only alternative was to go around the peninsula by sea. These logistics made any military campaign (securing supplies, arms, food, water, etc.) by the Ottomans to push forward into the Zubarah region difficult.

One can appreciate the significant role geography played in the Qatar peninsula when one compares the Ottoman experience in the eastern part of the Arabian Peninsula, which has historically had a more hospitable natural environment than its Qatari counter part. Midhat Pasha, the Ottoman official assigned to bring the Arabian and Qatari peninsulas within the orbit of the Porte, exulted that in Hasa, "the date groves roughly equaled in size those of Baghdad and Hilla in Iraq, while exceeding them in productiveness" (Anscombe 1997, 36).

Nonetheless, along the Hasa coast, the harbor at Ras Tanura had no fresh water supply. Water had to be brought from a spring two to three hours away or could be distilled from seawater. In addition, in 1871 Ottoman troops suffered from fever in the Qatif region, to be only worsened by surrounding shallows that made getting medical supplies to them difficult (Anscombe 1997, 34–35).

How were the Ottomans to fare any better in the Qatar peninsula, which has been described as a spot "antagonistic to life" (Herbert 1924, 87)?

Unreliable Partners

With vast experience in territorial expansion behind them, the Ottomans realized that, for their expansion to have better chances of success in the long run, they could not just enter a territory and take it over. It would be much more practical to work through local allies.

The Ottomans' main partner in their expansion into the Qatar peninsula was the Al-Thani family. But, as noted earlier, the Al-Thani were barely in control of the Doha area, much less in control of the entire Qatar peninsula.

Ottoman plans were further complicated by the fact that the Al-Thani were not really interested in Ottoman suzerainty. The Al-Thani's main concern was lessening the influence of the Ruler of Bahrain and other Arab tribal leaders:

> [The Al-Thani were] pushed on one side by their sometime overlord and rival, the shaikh of Bahrain, who still controlled the small port of Zubara on the northwest coast of the Qatar peninsula, and who still expected yearly tribute payments from Doha. On the other side, Sa'ud and his allies plundered the Al Thani domains and even cut off Doha's water supplies. The natural source of help for the Qataris in that situation was the Ottomans, who were seeking to capture Sa'ud and were known to disapprove of an independent, British-protected Bahrain. (Anscombe 1997, 31–32)

As noted in Chapter 6, section "Ottoman–Al-Thani Relations," the Al-Thani quickly tired of the Ottoman presence, complaining that the Ottomans insisted that the Al-Thani consult them on every matter and demanded large sums of money (Crystal 1990, 32; Lorimer 1908–15, 1:804).

The Ottoman demands, and the Al-Thani reluctance to meet them, strained relations between the two parties, eventually resulting in the Rebellion of 1893 and the Al-Thani plea for British assistance. Such a situation clearly prevented the Ottomans from maximizing their authority in the Qatar peninsula.

Other local allies proved themselves no more dependable. The Bani Hajir were, for all intents and purposes, a pirate-tribe, and Nasir bin Mubarak was a renegade. Neither was interested in following any structure and hierarchy of the Porte.

Nature of Ottoman Military Presence and Administration

As stated in Chapter 6, the Ottomans were unable to take effective measures to counter internal challenges to their authority. Anscombe points out that while Midhat Pasha devised a plan of administration that could have been the basis of good government, his was frustrated by lack of money and other resources, including, at times, military manpower. Unfortunately for the Ottomans, Midhat Pasha left his post before his plans could be fully implemented (Anscombe 1997, 6–7).

All these problems were compounded by the Ottomans' pressing lack of Arabic-speaking officials on the peninsula. It goes without saying that the Ottomans would have no chance of communicating well with the Arabs in the Qatar peninsula if they couldn't speak their language. Thus, the Porte was sent the following message:

> To ensure the control of passengers at the port of Qatar, it is necessary that an Arabic speaking harbour master be sent. It is also necessary for an Arabic speaking individual to be appointed assistant to the Kaimmakam of Qatar, Jasim al Thani . . . (*Ottoman Arabic Cabinet Minutes,* 27 November 1889)

Failure to Win the Loyalty of the Tribes of the Peninsula

In 1900, the Ottomans admitted that in addition to the delicate situation with Britain that constrained their moves, part of their weakness in the Qatar peninsula was a lack of loyalty among the tribes:

> Even if it is not wise at present to use force, we need to try to win over the sheikhs and to show great care in this situation. (*Ottoman "Report on Bahrein" from Council Chamber*, 22 April 1900)

In 1909, the Ottomans admitted to administrative problems, noting that their self-appointed district of Zubarah

> ... never had official administration representing the state nor [has it] undergone any development or improvement. (*Ottoman Arabic Report from Province of Basra to Ministry of Interior*, 25 September 1909)

Despite numerous attempts to gain some toehold in Zubarah, neither the Ottomans nor Al-Thani ever succeeded in gaining any control over the area.

Recognition by Third Parties

Great Britain

The British responses during each of the seven attempts by the Ottoman and Al-Thani to expand their control into Zubarah provide ample evidence of British recognition that the Zubarah region remained under the suzerainty of the Ruler of Bahrain during the Ottoman period. For example, it will be recalled that the first attempt by the Ottomans to militarily take over Zubarah took place in 1874, during which the Ruler of Bahrain sent assistance to the Naim. The British were monitoring the situation carefully, wary of upsetting Ottoman sensibilities in the area. Thus, the Assistant Political Resident asked the Ruler of Bahrain "if he fully comprehended that he was running a great risk by taking action against Zubara which was situated on the main land." Lt. Fraser noted that Ruler of Bahrain "... remarked that Zubarah was one of his dependencies and the Naeem this [*sic*] subjects." Fraser admitted, "In this he is right and it is difficult to see why or how we can prevent his sustaining sovereignty" (Fraser, 18 December 1874).

In addition, when it became clear that the Ottomans planned to settle people in the Zubarah region, which had lain in ruin following the destruction by Sheikh Jasim's forces in 1878, the British rejected the move on two grounds, the first for purely practical reasons. As mentioned earlier, the Ottomans were planning to have Nasir bin Mubarak head the settlement program. But Nasir's reputation as a renegade preceded him, and the British feared that "...the place would, in all probability, become a nest of pirates, and the interests which the British Government have at heart would undoubtedly suffer considerably..." were the plan put into force (Ross, 17 March 1888).

The second reason was "moral." The British had no doubt that the Rulers of Bahrain had enjoyed a long history in the Zubarah region. This was the spot they had chosen as their capital when they first left Kuwait in 1762; and even after moving their seat of office to the Bahrain Islands, the Rulers had maintained their ties to the area through the Naim (see Chapter 9). Thus, the Political Resident recommended:

> If Zobarah is to be rebuilt and peopled, this should be, I think, in justice, done only in a manner acceptable to the Chief of Bahrain. The settlers should be people friendly to him and not his enemies. (Ross, 17 March 1888)

British recognition of the Ruler of Bahrain's authority in the Zubarah region continued into the twentieth century. As noted previously, the relationship between the Al-Thani and the Ottomans was an uneasy one—one the Al-Thani determined was no longer worth keeping in 1902, when they expressed to the Political Agent in Bahrain, that they were "anxious to come under the protection of His Majesty's Government." The Ruler of Qatar added at that time that he would be willing to cooperate with the British government and the Ruler of Bahrain in any matters which might concern the mainland (Gaskin, 22 March 1902).

Foremost on the agenda, of course, was to determine the extent of territory under Al-Thani control. J. C. Gaskin, the Assistant Political Agent in Bahrain, was assigned this task, and based on interviews with the Ruler of Qatar, Gaskin reported that the Qatar Ruler's claim extended to all parts of the Qatar peninsula except for the Zubarah region, where even the Ruler of Qatar admitted that "Zobara is the only place in Katr to which he [Ruler of Bahrain] can lay claim." Thus, Gaskin recommended that Bahrain should have Zubarah, and then suggested placing an Al-Khalifa representative there (Gaskin, 22 March 1902; Gaskin, 29 March 1902).

However, the Ruler of Qatar was not dissuaded from trying to claim Zubarah. It will be recalled that in 1903 Sheikh Jasim, trying to play both sides, attempted to settle the Zubarah region, with the assistance of the Ottomans. But in this, the British refused to cooperate, stressing instead that they were bound to maintain the Ruler of Bahrain's rights in Zubarah (C. A. Kemball, 23 March 1903).

Apparently the British realized that they could probably not rely on the Al-Thani to best represent their interests in the Qatar peninsula. In 1905 the British Defence Committee, at the behest of the Secretary of State, undertook an examination of the question of the policy to be pursued by it's government in the Gulf. Captain Prideaux, the Political Agent in Bahrain, concluded in his report to Major Cox, the Officiating Political Resident, that one of three alternative policies should definitely be decided upon.

(1) That the suzerainty of the Ruler of Bahrain should be reasserted over the whole of the Katr peninsula, except the Al Bidaa Chiefship, the limits of which should be reduced to the narrowest possible limits.

(2) That for reasons stated we should declare the complete independence of the maritime Arab tribes and maintain a post and Native Agent on the Katr coast so long as the Turks remain at Al Bidaa.

(3) That we should agree to recognize the sovereignty of the Turks over the whole of the Katr peninsula on certain conditions, namely (a) that we should be given a lease by the Porte of the whole maritime strip to a distance of 5 miles back from the Coast, or (b) that the Porte should entrust the administration of the tract in question to British officers. Either arrangement to remain in force for a period of 50 years." (F. B. Prideaux, 16 July 1905, 1)

It is important to note that the first option, reasserting the Ruler of Bahrain's suzerainty over the whole of the Qatar peninsula, retained Al-Thani's traditional rights in Doha but "reduced [them] to the narrowest possible limits" (F. B. Prideaux, 16 July 1905, 1).

The British eventually decided not to pursue this course of action, but just a few months after they were contemplating it, they reiterated their commitment to Bahrain and Zubarah, by informing Sheikh Ahmed Al-Thani, when he expressed an interest in re-populating the area, that they would never allow the settlement of a party hostile to Bahrain at Zubarah (F. B. Prideaux, 23 December 1905).

Bahrain continued to exercise authority over the Zubarah region through the end of the Ottoman period in 1915, while Sheikh Jasim Al-Thani's authority continued to be limited to Doha Town (*Ottoman Arabic Report by Governor of Sanjak of Akka*, 24 December 1907; Muharram Pasha, 5 December 1908; *Ottoman Arabic Report*, 27 January 1909; *Ottoman Arabic Report from Province of Basra to Ministry of Interior*, 25 September 1909).

Ottoman Empire

Despite Ottoman attempts to expand their influence in the Qatar peninsula, they were aware that their efforts would aggravate their relationship with Great Britain, as they could be potentially be viewed as a danger to Bahrain. An Ottoman report recognized that the Porte's sending troops to the Zubarah region was a risk because Britain "... does not recognize that the Ottoman state has any rights of control over these shores," and that, therefore, the Ottoman government "must gather together its evidence" (*Ottoman Report on Bahrain*, 16 September 1895; Ottoman Minister of the Interior, 11 December 1908).

However, in 1896, the Ottomans complained that they could find "... no strong proof to help [them] ... completely refute the British claim" that the Zubarah region was territory of the Ruler of Bahrain and thus merited British protection (*Ottoman Report Concerning Zubarah and Bahrain*, 12 February 1896).

In addition, the Ottomans could never fully escape the fact that they needed British support to counter their problems in Europe. In 1897, they ascertained that Zubarah was probably not worth the risk:

> Britain claims that Zubarah is under the control of Bahrain which it claims is under British protection, and Britain insists that the Ottoman state has no rights of sovereignty over it. However the Ottoman government has not yet given any recognition of Britain's claims that it has the right to protect Oman and the islands of Bahrain. To try and sort out boundaries at this point would not

be appropriate, but would raise new problems. Discussions between the London Embassy and the British Foreign Ministry will give no results and it is better for the present to leave the matter alone and say nothing. (*Ottoman Arabic Report on Zubarah Affair*, 3 May 1897)

In 1911, the Ottomans admitted, "there will be no disregarding the expansion of England's influence," and that their persistence in the Qatar peninsula, "greatly offends the English" (Ottoman Ministry of the Interior, 30 November 1911). Thus, in 1913 an Ottoman official recommended giving up claim to Qatar on certain conditions, among the most important of which was that "Katar" should not be a part of Bahrain, or under British rule (Hakki Pasha, 25 February 1913).

Just a few days later, however, the Ottoman Ambassador to London noted that "the legal rights we drafted for there [Qatar peninsula] are very sketchy and unclear." He added that

> Since English opposition continues it is evident we shall not be able to send fresh troops.... In these circumstances there is no advantage to us in prolonging disagreement. (Ottoman Ambassador to London, 28 February 1913)

Al-Thani

The Al-Thani, too, admitted their weakness on the eastern coast of the Qatar peninsula. As late as 1874, Jasim bin Thani complained to the Ottomans that, despite everything, even the Doha confederation remained subject to the effective exercise of Bahraini authority (News Agent, Bahrain, 14 October 1874). And, in 1880, Sheikh Jasim acknowledged that the northern sections of the peninsula also "belong to the parts of Bahrain" (Jasim bin Mohammed Al-Thani, 24 November 1880).

In his letter, cited earlier, of 9 March 1881 to Col. Ross, the Political Resident, Al-Thani acknowledged again, but this time to the British, that they were in control of only Doha:

> You write to me that I should keep guard over the whole of the Katar Coast but I have no power over it. You are aware of the treaty made in the time of my father between us and the British Govt. namely that we were only to be responsible for Dohat al Bidaa and Al Wakra.

> The Al Katar Coast is very large and extensive and I have not the power to forbid anyone from landing or embarking... (Jasim bin Mohammed Al-Thani, 9 March 1881)

Sheikh Jasim's troubles discouraged him. Aware that Ottoman involvement in the Qatar peninsula could not secure his position any more, he told the British that he no longer desired to be involved in the politics of the peninsula. Rather, he wished British protection and a place of safety to which he could retire (Talbot, 7 May 1893).

The Political Resident explained to Sheikh Jasim that even if "the Turks could be induced to waive their claims, those of Bahrein to Katr could not be ignored." Sheikh Jasim "at once acknowledged the rights of Bahrein, and expressed his willingness to pay tribute as before" (Talbot, 7 May 1893).

Sheikh Jasim was eventually replaced by his son, Sheikh Abdullah, who, though not as conciliatory toward the Ruler of Bahrain as Sheikh Jasim may have been, also admitted the lack of Al-Thani control over the entire Qatar peninsula. In 1922, he complained to the British of dissident family members going over to Al-Saud in defiance of his authority (Trevor, 10 November 1922).

He explained that this was encouraging villages traditionally under his control to ignore his demands for tribute:

> ...there are one or two petty villages on the coast, which have refused to pay customary tribute, and are fighting amongst themselves and will neither come in to his Capital when called, nor obey his orders. (Trevor, 10 November 1922)

Ten years later, things had not improved. When the British wished to obtain landing ground in the peninsula for the British Royal Air Force, the Political Resident conceded that the Ruler of Qatar's authority within the town of Doha might have to be boosted, as there was still a chance that the Ruler might be murdered by dissenting family members (Biscoe, 7 June 1932).

If Sheikh Abdullah barely controlled Doha and its environs, he was clearly not in control of the Zubarah region, all the way on the other side of the peninsula.

11 | Zubarah in the Early Twentieth Century

Zubarah Remains an Integral Part of Bahrain

Bahrain continued to exercise authority over the Zubarah region in the 1920s and well into the 1930s. The period was essentially quiescent until about 1933, when oil companies began to compete for concessions in Bahrain and Qatar. Amid this competition came Qatar's armed attack on Zubarah in 1937—an attack which precipitated the dispute that culminated in the 2001 Judgment of the International Court of Justice in The Hague. Several factors, however, serve to point to the continued sovereignty of Bahrain in the Zubarah region.

Zubarah was not Granted to Al-Thani by 1916 Agreement

It will be recalled that Qatar finally came within the orbit of British protection by virtue of the 1916 Treaty. As noted in Chapter 6, in "The 1916 Treaty," while the Treaty made references to the territory under Sheikh Abdullah, it contained no geographical definition of that territory. Rather, the Treaty implied that the territorial extent of the new political entity coincided with the limits of the *kaza* of Qatar.

From the analysis above, it is clear that the Zubarah region did not fall within the *kaza* of Qatar. The Ottomans acknowledged as much; so too, have the Al-Thani themselves.

Despite his efforts to do otherwise, the Ruler of Qatar failed to gain a foothold in the Zubarah region after the signing of the 1916 Treaty; and his failure served to confirm the Ruler of Bahrain's authority there. As we have seen, he lacked British support in this effort; and he barely had control of Doha itself, the capital of his new state. The British did not wish to waste time and effort in extending the Qatar Ruler's hand to control Zubarah, when it was highly unlikely that the Ruler would be able to maintain a sustained presence there.

As will be shown later in this chapter, not until the possibility surfaced of finding significant reserves of oil in the Qatar peninsula did the British attitude toward Zubarah and the Ruler of Qatar change. In the interim, the Ruler of Bahrain kept his hold on the Zubarah region, much as he had done before.

Ruler of Bahrain Plans to Build Port (1919)

Of course, British unwillingness to help the Ruler of Qatar in Zubarah did not mean that the Ruler of Bahrain could rest easy. The danger to Zubarah from Doha might have been temporarily lessened by this lack of British support, but threats from a bigger, more powerful neighbor, the Al-Saud in the Arabian Peninsula, were also increasing in strength at the time.

In 1919, rumors reached Sheikh Isa of Bahrain that Ibn Saud planned to build a port in Jubail (north of Qatif). The site was ideal as its water was deep close to the shore at all tides. The plan made the Ruler of Bahrain apprehensive. He feared

> ...that should such port be opened, then Bahrein was doomed, for all its present trade with the mainland would go direct by steamer to the new port and leave Bahrain out. (Dickson, 17 January 1920)

Instead, the Ruler of Bahrain proposed building a port of his own in Zubarah, hoping that if one was built there, no need would exist to build another port in Jubail. But Major Dickson, the Political Agent in Bahrain, refused the Ruler of Bahrain's wish to build a port in Zubarah, stating that:

1. Sheikh Abdullah bin Jasim of Qatar would strongly resent it;
2. It would at once divert all trade from Doha to Zubarah, and Doha would, therefore, disappear as the seaport of Qatar;
3. The Al-Saud similarly would take offence
   (Dickson, 6 December 1919)

The British were clearly thinking about their larger geopolitical concerns in the area rather than the Ruler of Bahrain's rights in the

Zubarah region, though the British themselves had repeatedly acknowledged those as valid. But the British interests regionally prevailed, despite the fact that, "the harbour of Zubara is naturally much better than that of either Doha or O'Jair" (Dickson, 6 December 1919).

Inclusion of the Naim Tribe in Bahrain Civil and Pension Lists (1920s)

It will be recalled that it was the practice of the Ruler of Bahrain to make monthly payments to certain family members and other subjects in return for their allegiance. The names of such individuals were recorded on what were referred to as "the Bahrain Civil List" and "the Bahrain Pension List."

In the 1920s, members of the Al-Jabr section of the Naim tribe living in Zubarah continued to be a part of these lists. For example, the 1925 Civil List contained the names of "Rashid bin Mohammad Al Jabar," "Khalid bin Mohammad Al Jabr," and "Rashid and Abdulla, sons of Nasir bin Jabbar" (Hendry, 15, 19 September 1925).

1930s—Population Migration to Bahrain

The 1930s saw the migration of a significant proportion of the population of Zubarah to Bahrain. This response came mainly to economic developments in the 1930s that transformed Bahrain into one of the most prosperous powers in the Middle East.

The most significant such event was the discovery of oil. It was in Bahrain that oil was first found in commercial quantities in the Gulf, when the Bahrain Petroleum Company struck oil in 1932. With the development and expansion of the oil industry in Bahrain, the country's population began to enjoy numerous new benefits and employment opportunities. New infrastructure projects were launched and schools, hospitals, and roads were built with the oil revenue. The welfare of Bahrain's inhabitants increased significantly, and Bahrain came to be known as a place where the streets were "paved with gold" (Belgrave 1960, 103).

Most notably, oil helped Bahrain to avoid the economic crisis associated with the sharp 1920s decline of the pearling industry in the region. This crisis was caused by the development of Japanese cultured pearls, "wreaking havoc" on a society that had traditionally relied on pearling for its living (Hamad bin Isa Al-Khalifa, 3 May 1930). Many of Bahrain's

Arab neighbors experienced serious economic difficulties at the time, as large proportions of their populations—like Bahrain's population until then—were engaged in pearling.

The Qatar peninsula was seriously hit by the demise of pearling. The coastal areas—practically the only inhabited areas of the peninsula—slid into desperate poverty. Many of the region's inhabitants sought to move to Bahrain, where life had become much more comfortable. Immigration became a serious problem for the Al-Khalifa state, and measures were instituted by Bahrain to stop the waves of immigrants who threatened to flood the country. But unlike the inhabitants of other regions in the Qatar peninsula, the Naim, who were considered subjects of Bahrain, were encouraged to relocate to the main Bahrain islands, and many did so to take advantage of the educational, economic, and health benefits that were coming to Bahrain as a result of the oil development.

Those Naim who continued to reside there moved freely between Zubarah and the main Bahrain island—as they had always been able to do. And many who had established themselves on the main island continued to use Zubarah as winter residence, thus maintaining their emotional ties with the region (Bahrain 1996, 98–99 ¶ 226–29; Belgrave 1960, 103–4).

Emergence of Oil as a Major Force in the Gulf

The history of the Zubarah region in the 1930s cannot be separated from what was happening worldwide at the time. Internationally, Great Britain's dominance was slipping, and a new player in the game of international relations—the United States—had emerged to further diminish Great Britain's global position.

Foremost among Great Britain's concerns was protecting its most prized possession—India. The Middle East—the Gulf Region in particular—was integral to Britain's access to India's trade routes, so Britain was determined to ensure that the region remained in its hands.

Furthermore, the discovery of oil in the Gulf in the 1930s encouraged oil companies from Britain and, more notably from the United States, to come to the Gulf. Despite its best efforts, Britain could not prevent American oil companies from competing and sometimes winning the oil concessions Britain was after.

For these reasons, the Zubarah region fell victim to wrangling between the British and Americans over oil concessions. As part of its treaty relations with Bahrain, Great Britain had pledged to protect its territory from outside aggression. In return, Bahrain had promised to refrain from engaging in any pirate activity. And until the issue of oil arose, Britain had to a large extent maintained a consistent policy in Bahrain and the Qatar peninsula. But when British oil companies lost the Bahrain Concession to an American company in 1925, Britain began to re-evaluate its policy on the Qatar peninsula, fearful that it might also lose this territory to an American oil company.

The Ruler of Bahrain's Agreement not to Grant Oil Concessions without British Approval

Western involvement was not anything new in the Gulf region, but for most of the nineteenth century the area had been dominated by the British. The situation had started to change toward the end of the century, when the Germans started to show an interest beyond Iraq. But soon Britain's concerns led them to take steps to avoid sharing oil concessions if that could be avoided. Thus, Britain made agreements with regional sheikhs, including those of Kuwait and Bahrain, that oil development should be handled by British principals only, and that the British government should be in charge of these nations' foreign relations.

But as the new century dawned, the Americans were also looking toward the Middle East. Now London insisted on a "British nationality clause" in any concession agreement that was made, requiring that oil development be carried out by "British interests" only. Thus the Ruler of Bahrain agreed on 14 May 1914 not to grant any oil concession in his territory without the prior approval of the British government (Isa bin Ali Al-Khalifa, 14 May 1914; Haworth, 2 April 1928). The Ruler of Kuwait had signed a similar agreement in 1913.

A small state like Bahrain had little choice but to comply with Great Britain's demands: Bahrain needed protection from its larger and stronger neighbors, particularly Persia and other rival forces in the Arabian Peninsula. The threat of attack from the Qatar peninsula was also of concern.

Decline of British Political and Economic Influence

It appeared at first that the discovery of oil in the Gulf would serve to strengthen Britain's position, particularly in view of the above-mentioned "British nationality clauses." Paradoxically, however, the decline of British political and economic influence in the Gulf region in fact coincided with the discovery of oil in the region in the 1930s.

Several factors led to the deterioration of Britain's position during this period. The first was Britain's contradictory policy in Palestine. In 1915–16, through the Hussain-McMahon correspondence, the British promised the Arabs independence in return for revolting against the Turks. At the same time, however, the British entered into a series of secret negotiations with France, the Sykes-Picot Agreements, promising to divide and rule the Middle East with its allies. In addition, the British committed themselves to the Balfour Declaration of 1917, which promised the Jews—whose help the British needed in the World War I war effort—a Jewish homeland in Palestine.

While Britain did manage to keep its conflicting promises to the Arabs and Jews under control during World War I, the situation unraveled once the War had ended. The Arabs expected independence; while on the other hand, the Jewish community stepped up its immigration into Palestine—and some Jewish organizations spoke of a Jewish state comprising all of Palestine. Clashes between the two communities were inevitable, and in 1936, an Arab rebellion in Palestine broke out against the British.

Subsequent British efforts to calm the situation diverted valuable resources away from the Gulf. Moreover, the Arabs in the Gulf region supported the Palestinians, and Britain's contradictory policy greatly tarnished Britain's image in their eyes.

Second, disagreements arose between the British Foreign Office and the Government of India Office about appropriate policy in the Gulf. The British Foreign Office was concerned with British policy in the Middle East on a more general scale. Foremost among its concerns was appeasing the situation in Palestine. Under such conditions, Britain was willing to set aside pending border disputes, to win powerful Gulf leaders to its side. Kelly explains that the Foreign Office, convinced that Ibn Saud . . .

was a figure of some consequence on the Middle-Eastern stage, were anxious to remain on good terms with him, in the hope that his influence might be brought to bear to help to resolve the difficulties into which Britain had gotten herself in Palestine. (Kelly 1980, 66)

They therefore were willing to give him territory—which the India Office felt should have gone to Abu Dhabi (Kelly 1980, 66–67).

The result of all this was an inconsistent, and oftentimes confusing, British policy in the Gulf.

The Discovery of Oil and Regional Development

The outbreak of World War II temporarily suspended British negotiating activity regarding borders in the Gulf region. Only when the war had ended could Britain once again return to Gulf issues. But they faced a major problem: the India Office, which traditionally had been responsible for Gulf region affairs, had been dismantled at the end of the war.

The postwar era had ushered in a New World Order in which the United States and the USSR were now the world's number one and number two leading powers. Great Britain had fallen to a distant third at best.

Britain's position was impeded especially because it had been forced to let go of India, as the persistence of colonialism had become the subject of intense moral and political controversy after the Second World War. The loss of India in 1947 meant that Britain's Government of India Office—the body responsible for Gulf affairs—was now effectively defunct. The British Foreign Office (FO) stepped in to fill the India Office's role, but adopted a rather different Gulf policy than its predecessor's.

According to Kelly, the Foreign Office never really felt comfortable about its role in the Gulf. He explains that it inherited the custodianship of British interests, but that the duties and responsibilities Britain shouldered in the Gulf now were more of a colonial rather than a diplomatic nature. He argues that this had important consequences for the Gulf region because:

> Diplomacy of its nature is a process of bargaining, of the reconciliation of different and often opposing interests, a process in

> which the completion of a negotiation is all too frequently considered of greater consequence than what transpires during it. In such circumstances, peoples and territories are apt to be regarded somewhat distantly, as concepts or symbols. Imperial or colonial rule, on the other hand, breeds a deep sense of responsibility towards the peoples and lands ruled, along with a habit of authority over them; so that there is a natural resistance among imperial administrators to the notion that the fate of these peoples and lands is to be bandied about in transactions in far-off capitals. (Kelly 1980, 98–99)

He adds:

> When the Foreign Office assumed charge of Britain's interests and obligations in the Gulf from the India Office and the Indian empire, it did not inherit along with it the spirit and outlook of the Indian Civil Service. Herein lay the essential difference between the two players in their approach to the Gulf, a region where Britain had always played an imperial rather than a diplomatic role. (Kelly 1980, 99)

This change in the nature of the decision-making body responsible for Gulf affairs coincided with the discovery of oil in the region. Together, these two factors proved to have far-reaching consequences for the drawing of borders between the various Gulf sheikhdoms.

1925 Bahrain Oil Concession

No discussion of the history of oil concessions in Bahrain and Qatar would be complete without mention of Major Frank Holmes, a man described as "a ruddy, genial, hearty, energetic, undiscourageable ... adventurer" (Stegner 1971, 6). Holmes was born on a farm in New Zealand in 1874 and was trained as a mining engineer. His profession caused him to travel all over the world, finding him work in South Africa, Australia, Malaya, Mexico, Uruguay, Russia, Nigeria, and, more significantly for our story, the Gulf. Perhaps Stegner describes his role best:

> Holmes was one of those who, as Bernard De Voto once said, awake alertly in the night, hear history's clock strike at a critical time — but count the strokes wrong. He was on the trail of a big

idea very early, but as it happened, arrived just a little too early and in not quite the right way. (Stegner 1971, 6)

Holmes first heard about oil seepages in the Gulf while in Ethiopia in 1918 and "as a mining engineer, found his interest piqued" (Yergin 1991, 280). Later, when stationed in Iraq by the British Army after World War I, Holmes had access to petroleum maps, which left him even more intrigued (Stegner 1971, 6).

In the early twenties, Holmes went to Bahrain to work on the water system there. "He was such an agreeable fellow, so uniformly good-natured and so full of bustle and steam, that he made many friends among both the British and Arabs" (Stegner 1971, 6). Thus, when in 1925 a group of London financiers formed the Eastern and General Syndicate (EGS) to acquire and operate oil concessions in the Middle East, "Holmes was their natural choice as Bahrain agent" (Stegner 1971, 6).

Holmes put every effort into finding oil in the Gulf. As Yergin says:

> He was convinced that the Arabian coast would be a fabulous source of petroleum, and he pursued his dream with unswerving stamina. A promoter par excellence, with a gift for making people believe in him, he traveled up and down the Arabian side of the Gulf, from one impoverished ruler to the next, spinning his vision, promising them wealth where they saw only poverty, seeking always to put another concession in his kit. (Yergin 1991, 281)

In contrast, several British oil companies noted that the geological reports of the area "leave little room for optimism," for oil to ever be found in Arabia (Chisholm 1975, 555). Additionally,

> The Tertiary reservoir-rocks, so rich in south-western Persia, were in Bahrain exposed on the surface, nor was there, as yet, in the region any evidence which suggested the existence of pre-Tertiary oil. (Longrigg 1968, 103)

In addition, Holmes's actions inspired the wrath of the British Foreign Office. To them, he was "an unscrupulous troublemaker with a "capacity for mischief," who was trying, in pursuit of a quick profit, to undermine British influence in the area" (Yergin 1991, 281).

Holmes did enjoy the support of the Ruler of Bahrain, however. As noted earlier, Holmes's original mission in Bahrain was to work on the water supply. Fresh water then was in short supply, and part of Holmes's work was to find it, which he did. In return, the Ruler granted Holmes the Bahrain oil concession, with the approval of the British, in 1925.

The Bahrain concession provided an option to select a 100,000-acre area from Bahrain's total surface area for an oil lease. Bahrain's main island alone constituted 142,000 acres; thus, the 1925 concession did not cover all Bahraini territory. The remaining area was commonly referred to as the "unallotted area," and, as will be seen below, eventually became the subject of much controversy.

Holmes had no guarantee, of course, that he would find oil. And even if he could, he had no assurances that revenues from sales would flow immediately. Thus, as an incentive to allow his company to keep searching for oil, Holmes and the Ruler of Bahrain reached an understanding, under which the Ruler would be given "option payments," or royalties, until commercially exploitable quantities of oil were found.

1930 Assignment of Concession to BAPCO

There was one difficulty in the Syndicate's winning the Bahrain concession, however, which stemmed from the nature of EGS—it was not an oil exploration company. Rather, its role was

> ... either to act as negotiator for oil companies which wanted concession but lacked contacts for making them, or to obtain the concessions first and then sell them to companies which would explore and develop them. (Stegner 1971, 6)

Clarke adds that:

> Since it had neither the funds nor the technical experience to exercise its option on the Bahrain concession, the directors decided to sell the option instead. (Clarke 1990, 62)

However, according to the "British nationality clauses," EGS was required to sell the option to a British oil company. But none was interested. Among the reasons:

> No one seemed willing to consider Bahrain on its own, the general feeling being that oil exploration on the islands would only be attractive to an oil company, if conducted in association with similar exploration on the mainland. (Clarke 1990, 63)

The attitude of Anglo-Persian and other British oil companies placed Holmes in a desperate situation:

> By 1926, the syndicate was in deep financial trouble. Holmes was continually obliged to fork out money for travel expenses, gifts and gratuities, and entertainment. So bleak was the syndicate's financial predicament that it was driven to try to sell all of its concession to Anglo-Persian, but the company said no. After all, there was no oil in Arabia. (Yergin 1991, 282)

To make things worse,

> ...Holmes met a decidedly frigid reception when he tried to obtain capital in the City of London. Despite his persistence and salesmanship, he could not get anywhere. "Holmes was the worst nuisance in London," one English businessman recalled. "People ran when they saw him coming." (Beatty 1939)

So Holmes set sail for New York in the hopes of finding better luck there. He knew, however, that he would have a difficult time convincing what he referred to as "the really big New York Sheikhs" with no encouraging geological reports in hand. So he pressed one of his geologist associates, T. George Madgwick, Professor of Oil Mining at Birmingham University, to write a report on what he had seen in Bahrain.

On 23 September 1926, Professor Madgwick issued the following opinion:

> In the centre [of Bahrain island] is a depression 12 miles long [19.3 km] and four [6.4 km] wide... This is enclosed by an almost perfect low escarpment of Middle Eocene rocks so that we have an ideal "dome." In the centre of this depression rise the only prominent hills in the Islands, the principal one know as Jebel Dukan whose height is marked as 440 feet [134 m]... There is some faulting... but so far as can be judged not of great magnitude... Where the southern steepening of the dip begins to make itself felt... about where the crest of the fold would be, is an occurrence of asphaltic material connected with vertical fissuring... The structure is so striking that in conjunction with the asphalt—which is regarded as a desert seepage—there can be no hesitation in saying that test drilling is called for.... (Madgwick 1926)

With Madgwick's report in hand, Holmes, along with a friend intimately connected to U.S. oil circles, Thomas Ward, planned a series of visits to potential backers.

One of the first of those visits was with Major Thomas R. Armstrong, an executive from Standard Oil of New Jersey. In preparation for the visit, Armstrong purchased the only available map in New York that showed the Red Sea and Arabian Gulf areas. When he saw the size of Bahrain on the map, Armstrong declared:

> Since Bahrain, when viewed on a world map, is small enough to fit under the tip of my pencil, it is not big enough for us. (Clarke 1990, 65; Yergin 1991, 282)

Once again, the door was closed for Holmes. To his credit, however, he did not give up. Holmes had Professor Madgwick prepare another report in 1927 stating:

> I have had a good look over the area surrounding the seepages, and the dome formation is exceedingly attractive... The oil indications... are more promising and extensive than I had conception of. (Madgwick, 16 January 1927)

Finally, one American concern, Gulf Oil, showed serious interest in Holmes and EGS. To push Gulf Oil into a firm commitment, Holmes provided the company with rock samples and a "greasy substance" along with the recent report on his findings in Bahrain. His tactics worked. On 30 November 1927—just three days before his option payment to Bahrain was due—EGS assigned the Bahrain concession to Eastern Gulf Oil, a subsidiary of the Gulf Oil Corporation.

But EGS's problems didn't end there. In 1928, Gulf Oil became part of the American group in the Turkish Petroleum Company, a signatory to the Red Line Agreement. An important aspect of the Agreement was the "self-denying" clause in which the signatories (Royal Dutch/Shell, Anglo-Persian and the Near East Development Company, among others) agreed to work jointly—and only jointly—in the Gulf region. The object was to stop competition between these shareholding companies. That meant that Gulf Oil could not work in Bahrain, as its new British partners were not part of the deal Holmes had secured (Clarke 1990, 80; Yergin 1991, 204).

Holmes's problems were compounded by the fact that around the same time, the Secretary of State for the British Colonies, L. S. Amery, wrote a confidential memo to the Political Resident stipulating that in regards to the Bahrain Concession:

> Neither the Company nor the premises, liberties, powers, and privileges, hereby granted and demised, nor any land occupied for any of the purchases of this lease, shall at any time be, or become directly, or indirectly controlled or managed by a foreigner or foreigners or any foreign corporation or corporations, and the local General Manager of the Company, and as large a percentage of the local staff employed by them as circumstances permit, shall at all times be British subjects. (Amery, 19 June 1928)

Toward the end of 1928, EGS was able to solve one of its problems—finding a company, Standard of California (Socal), that was not party to the Red Line Agreement. Like Gulf Oil, Socal was committed to drilling for foreign oil. Unfortunately, however, it was a complete newcomer to the Middle East and "did not have one drop of foreign oil to show for its efforts" (Stegner 1971, 7; Yergin 1991, 282).

When Holmes and his colleague, Edward Janson, informed the British Secretary of State that they were negotiating with Socal, Amery immediately asked if that meant most of the funding would be American. Janson conceded that "the real control would pass into American hands and that the Eastern and General Syndicate would be kept alive in some way but only as nominal concessionaires" (Clarke 1990, 82).

When the Secretary of State reminded Holmes of the "British nationality clauses" in the 1914 Agreement signed with the Ruler of Bahrain, Holmes and his partners realized the urgency of finding a solution.

Their solution was to set up a Canadian subsidiary to Socal, the Bahrain Petroleum Company Limited (BAPCO). Surprisingly, the British government did not object to this arrangement, but stipulated:

> ...that the company developing Bahrain must be a British company, registered in Canada, and must establish an office in Great Britain, in the charge of a British subject, for maintaining communications with His Majesty's government; one director must be a British subject, persona grata to the British government; as many of the company's employees as was consistent with efficient

operation must be British or Bahrainis; and the company must maintain on Bahrain Island a "chief local representative" whose appointment must be approved by the British government and who must, in all his dealings with the Shaikh of Bahrain, work through the British Political Agent. (Stegner 1971, 8)

EGS agreed, and on 12 June 1930 formally assigned the Bahrain Concession to BAPCO. Despite the above safeguards, however, the British could not deny that BAPCO was a 100 percent U.S.-owned company.

1932 Discovery of Oil in Bahrain

On 31 May 1932, BAPCO struck oil in Bahrain, the first such strike on the Arab side of the Gulf. Most of the major oil companies were caught off guard, especially since some of their directors had until that moment scoffed at Holmes's suggestion that the Gulf was a possible site for oil reserves. Now, suddenly, Bahrain was being hailed as "the outstanding development in the eastern hemisphere since Iraq" (*Industrial City on a Tropical Island* 1937). Major Holmes, the "worst nuisance in London," had been vindicated.

In the end, though, the Bahrain oil discovery proved to be quite small. Nonetheless, BAPCO's discovery came at an opportune time for Bahrain, whose economy was reeling from the aftermath of the worldwide depression and further crippled by the aforementioned introduction of artificial pearls from Japan into the international market, which hit hard at Bahrain's main source of revenue—the pearling industry.

When oil was struck, men unable to find jobs as pearl divers now found jobs at the oil refinery, which paid them a regular salary and even took care of their medical needs. Longrigg states:

> The social effect of the well-provided employment offered to the Bahrainis, the increase of spending power among the public, and the direct benefit to the Shaikh's Treasury were all the more notable since the pearl trade, traditionally the island's chief occupation and asset, had some years before entered a period of severe depression. No community or government, indeed, has been more suddenly and timely rescued from economic disaster than those of Bahrain in 1932. (Longrigg 1968, 103)

Zubarah to Be Possibly Included in Unallotted Area

As stated earlier, the 1925 Bahrain oil concession did not cover all Bahraini territory; thus, the fate of "the unallotted area" was left undecided. But encouraged by what had been found on the main island of Bahrain, BAPCO sought to extend its license to other parts of the territory. In 1934, a lease was signed between BAPCO and the Ruler of Bahrain.

According to the lease, BAPCO was permitted to prospect and drill for, extract, treat, refine, manufacture, transport and deal with petroleum products "within the area or areas of the "First Schedule," or in other words, the territory defined in the 1925 concession. It also called for additional areas to be delineated as set out in a "Second Schedule" attached to the new lease (*Lease between Ruler of Bahrain and BAPCO*, 29 December 1934).

In 1936, K. Skinner of BAPCO tried to determine exactly what areas fell under the " Second Schedule." He noted with interest that "the Khalifa family at one time lived in Zubarah and still have some claim to that town and its environs." He raised the possibility of adding it to the as-of-yet-undetermined Bahrain "unallotted area," but cautioned that "just what its environs amount to I do not know," because there was the possibility that the land claimed might extend too far south. He therefore recommended finding out the precise status of Zubarah first (Skinner, 5 December 1936).

British vs. U.S. Oil Companies' Interests

Whether or not the Zubarah region fell under the Bahrain unallotted area is a question that must be seen in the context of British commercial interests versus those of U.S. oil companies. Beginning its economic relationship with the Gulf region in the late seventeenth and early eighteenth centuries, Britain enjoyed a position as the dominant foreign economic power in the region (see Chapter 2). As previously pointed out (p. 162), the aftermath of World War I and the resultant emergence of American influence in world affairs, however, threatened to shift the balance out of Britain's favor.

American influence in the Gulf region was felt very early in the twentieth century, when American missions set up operations in various Gulf sheikhdoms, building schools and hospitals. The first missionaries in

Bahrain, from the Dutch Reformed Church of America, came in the early 1890s.

As early as 1932, the British government described as "unfortunate" that American interests had secured such a strong foothold in an area most important to British interests, and recommended that "that no steps be neglected that enable the Anglo-Persian Oil Company to bring the area within their sphere of influence" (Bahrain 1996, 102–3 ¶ 235–36; Bahrain 1997, 92 ¶ 204–5; Belgrave, 16 August 1933).

World War II heightened British concerns even further. Britain was determined to protect British oil interests so as to protect communication with India. Securing Arab Gulf oil was an essential component in its strategy. And after losing to BAPCO in Bahrain, Britain was determined not to risk also losing part of the Qatar peninsula, Zubarah, to BAPCO.

In addition to Bahrain's standing claims to the Zubarah region, Britain faced a more immediate problem on the Qatar peninsula—the instability of Al-Thani power and influence. The British perceived Qatar's weakness as stemming from numerous sources. First among these: the encroachment and territorial claims on the peninsula by Ibn Saud. This represented not only a destabilizing influence to the ruling Al-Thani family (thus jeopardizing any oil concessions); it also represented an indirect threat of American oil competition, since Standard Oil (which hoped to penetrate Qatar) had influence with Ibn Saud. A second factor troubling the British was the open hostility of many of the Bedouins (many were Wahhabis) of the peninsula to the Al-Thani (Crystal 1990, 114–15).

As part of its efforts to prop up Al-Thani authority in the peninsula, Britain advised Anglo-Persian Oil Company officials to "let sleeping dogs lie" when it came to the Zubarah issue. The situation on the ground, however, did not always work the way Britain wished it would. As will be seen below, the Ruler of Bahrain continued to maintain his claim to the Zubarah region, and its inhabitants continued to pledge their loyalty to him.

Thus, the British were in a difficult position. Acknowledging the Ruler of Bahrain's authority over Zubarah risked losing the area to an American oil company. On the other hand, propping up the Al-Thani family risked harming its relationship with the Al-Khalifa family, one of its most loyal allies in the region. The result is a historical record replete with contradictory British policy towards Zubarah. And while Britain's "balancing act" may have staved off American oil companies in the short run, in the long run it only served to exacerbate feelings between Bahrain and Qatar.

1935 Qatar Oil Concession

Britain's relations with Qatar were formalized through the 1916 Treaty (see Chapter 6). Like the treaties signed with other Gulf sheikhdoms (Kuwait [1913] and Bahrain [1914]), Britain stipulated a "British nationality clause" for all oil concessions.

In order to secure the Qatari concession, Britain tied the issue to offering the Ruler of Qatar protection. As mentioned earlier, the borders between Qatar and present-day Saudi Arabia were not yet delineated in the 1920s. Dissident Al-Thani family members took this as an opportunity to ask Ibn Saud for help. In 1921, in the wake of trouble with his brothers, the Ruler of Qatar wrote to the Political Resident:

> Qatar is a wide (district), has many villages some of which are far apart, and I am responsible for anything that happens in them. But if any one rebels and creates trouble and disturbance, and if I ask for the moral help of the Government such as a ship or anything like it, by which I may frighten people, or use it as circumstances may demand, (will they give me?). (Trevor, 13 May 1921a, 16–17)

The Deputy Secretary to the Government of India responded in the negative, saying "...the Government of India are not prepared to promise anything further than diplomatic assistance..." (Trevor, 13 May 1921a, 17).

The situation for Sheikh Abdullah only got worse:

> During the last year disaffected members of his family and other shaikhlings have been in constant communication with Bin Saud, and go to pay him visits which are generally followed by some form of defiance to his authority.
>
> This has become so marked, and persons who would never before have attempted to dispute his authority have become so turbulent, that it is obvious that they are receiving moral support, and in all probability pecuniary assistance. (Trevor, 10 November 1922, 1–2)

The British government felt constrained by the fact that Ibn Saud was a powerful ally, and did not want to risk alienating him, especially as American oil companies like Standard Oil were already making inroads into his territory. In addition, it is important to note that it was not all that clear what Sheikh Abdullah had to offer the British—it had not yet been confirmed that the Qatar peninsula contained any significant oil deposits.

In any event, all it took to change the attitude of the British government toward Qatar was the possibility of finding oil in the Qatar peninsula. The Ruler of Qatar had already granted exploratory rights to the D'Arcy Exploration Company, a subsidiary of the Anglo-Persian Oil Company, in 1926. When Bahrain and Saudi oil concessions went to American oil companies in the 1930s, British interest in Qatar was invigorated.

With American oil companies growing increasingly more competitive in the region, one might have expected the British Foreign Office to speed up negotiations over national borders so that it could best take advantage of the territory under its control. When it came to sovereignty over the Zubarah region, however, the British were inclined to let the issue lie low.

In 1933 the Political Agent in Bahrain cautioned against investigating the extent of Al-Thani territory on the Qatar peninsula:

> ...it would advisable in any matter of boundaries to avoid reference so far as possible to the western coast of Qatar as there were certain places on it which were claimed by Bahrain. (Loch, 13 June 1933, 1)

This reluctance to discuss the boundaries remained despite the requests of Petroleum Concessions Limited (PCL), the British oil company favored by the British Foreign Office, which needed to know the exact borders in order to start its drilling operations:

> Mr. Sampson [PCL representative] pointed out the importance of knowing exactly where these places were, but I explained that it was quite impossible to say anything definite and that one could only hope that the question would not arise. (Loch, 13 June 1933, 1)

A few days later, Mr. Sampson asked again about the limits of Al-Thani rule on the peninsula. The Political Agent reported once again that he took

> ... [the] opportunity on another occasion of advising Mr. Sampson to keep clear of the Western coast of Qatar, so far as might be. (Loch, 25 June 1933, 1)

The PAB added:

> He [Mr. Sampson] asked ... about the Bahrain claims, but I said that I could tell him little except that they were considered locally to be live claims, and that I thought that, unless they found that they definitely required to operate there, it would be best, at any rate at this stage, to let sleeping dogs lie. (Loch, 25 June 1933, 2)

The British Foreign Office wanted to secure the Qatar peninsula for their own commercial interests. Indeed, in order to secure the concession, they informed the Ruler of Qatar that they would afford him protection, but only if he assigned the concession to a British company. However, since they were not yet convinced the Qatar peninsula contained any fruitful oil reserves, they at the same time "... made it clear that they were anxious to walk very carefully in this part of the world, so as to avoid an oil war with American oil interests over what was on a long view a relatively unimportant area" (Laithwaite, 15 December 1933, 11).

So Britain embarked on its oil concession negotiations with Qatar at a comfortable pace, not finalizing them until 1935 (Fowle, 11 May 1935; *Qatar Oil Concession* 1935).

PCL's Interest in Bahrain Unallotted Area

In September of 1936, the Qatar concession was transferred to Petroleum Concessions Limited (PCL), a subsidiary of the Iraq Petroleum Company, of which Anglo-Persian was a major shareholder. Almost immediately, PCL investigated the exact status of the Zubarah region and Bahrain's unallotted area, hoping, of course, to gain exclusive drilling rights in both territories.

In the short run, Britain's policy of ignoring the Zubarah issue might have afforded them some "breathing room," but once the concession was signed, with the status of Zubarah still undecided, it was asserted

"...it was most inconvenient for Petroleum Concessions Limited not to have clear information about the frontiers," especially since "the indications of oil in Qatar were very promising" (*Foreign Office Minutes* entitled *"Eastern and Southern Frontiers of Arabia,"* 25 June 1937).

Now PCL was caught in a particularly delicate position, because in order to be able to drill in the Zubarah region and Bahrain's unallotted area, they were forced to bargain with both the Ruler of Bahrain *and* the Ruler of Qatar.

From the Ruler of Bahrain they received this notice:

> We have heard news that the Petroleum Concessions Company have an idea of opening a harbour.
>
> If the Company wishes to open conversation with us about opening a harbour at our sea port at Zobara we will be pleased to give all facilities and agreement. (Hamad bin Isa Al-Khalifa, 14 April 1937)

Later, the Ruler of Bahrain indicated that he would be willing to give PCL all of the unallotted area provided that a clause be inserted in the concession agreement that stated "no effort would be made to develop the oil resources of the Zubarah area" (Longrigg, 16 August 1937).

On the contrary, the Ruler of Qatar refused to acknowledge that the Ruler of Bahrain had any say in the matter, since the former considered *himself* to be in control of *all* the mainland of Qatar (Longrigg, 16 August 1937).

But PCL felt that the Ruler of Bahrain had more say over the Zubarah issue, and suggested a compromise that would avoid antagonizing him:

> ...we remain anxious to obtain the unallotted portion of the Bahrain Islands, and we feel that a formula for these could perhaps be found which would leave the Zubarah question completely on one side. (Longrigg, 16 August 1937, 2)

But as the PAB pointed out, matters were complicated by the fact that "there [was] no decision made by His Majesty's Government with regard to the ownership of Zubarah" (Hickinbotham, 16 September 1937, 1).

Since the issue had such potential to disrupt the delicate oil concessions negotiations, the Political Agent advised against actively investigating the matter, for, as he said, "if the Shaikh of Bahrain eventually succeeds in proving his claim to the area know as Zubarah then *ipso facto* the Shaikh of Qatar cannot be said to rule over that area and, therefore, that area cannot be considered as part of the state of Qatar" (Hickinbotham, 16 September 1937, 3).

Thus, despite PCL's wishes to obtain as much territory as they could, the British government found it more convenient to keep temporizing.

Change of the Ruler of Qatar's Attitude toward Zubarah

The Zubarah question had remained dormant for so long simply because the Ruler of Qatar had expressed no interest in it before 1937. It was known that the Ruler of Bahrain traditionally had been responsible for the area, and even if his activities there were less now than they had been before, it was assumed that Zubarah was still under his control. The main inhabitants of the region, the Naim tribe, certainly thought so.

But with the prospect of oil in the Zubarah region, everything changed. Now, the Ruler of Qatar was claiming Zubarah as part of the territory under his control. As the Political Agent, Bahrain noted, "... owing to the development of petroleum, Zubarah has become a place of [Qatari] interest" (Loch, 13 March 1937).

12 | Qatar Captures Zubarah— July 1937

The Attack on Zubarah

The possibility of finding oil in the Zubarah region aggravated a situation that was already complicated. While the Ruler of Bahrain insisted on asserting his claims to Zubarah, that the British no longer cooperated with him on this issue no doubt negatively affected his feelings toward Sheikh Hamad Al-Thani. On the Ruler of Qatar's part, the British position emboldened him to take more aggressive action, thus serving to further heighten friction between the two Rulers. The situation did not go unnoticed by the British. The Political Agent in an official note dated March 1937 warned that

> [Zubarah] is going to be the subject matter of a tensible feeling between the Al Khalifahs and Al Thani. Al Khalifahs think that the tract belongs to Bahrain whereas... Al Thani thinks that it is a part of Qatar territory... owing to the development of petroleum. (Loch, 13 March 1937)

In July 1937, the situation between the two sides exploded.

Chronology of Events

In order to make a credible claim to the Zubarah region, the Ruler of Qatar had a serious obstacle to overcome: he needed to procure evidence of his authority over it and its inhabitants—of which up until 1937 none existed.

| 181

The Ruler of Qatar Plans to Build Port

Among the first measures the Ruler undertook was creating physical "evidence" of Qatari control over the Zubarah territory by constructing a Qatari port and pier in Zubarah. Evidence suggests that oil played a significant part in the Ruler of Qatar's decision:

> I consider that the possibility of the [Qatari] Oil Company making a port at the west coast of Qatar caused certain persons... to influence the Shaikh to proceed... It is probable that this tour of the Ruler of Qatar was simply and solely so that he could show to the world in general and the Na'im in particular that he was the ruler of the territory. (Hickinbotham, 3 May 1937, 5)

Bahrain's previous failure to get British support for a Bahraini port in Zubarah in 1919 (see Chapter 11) offered added incentive for the Ruler of Qatar to try and build one of his own.

The Ruler of Qatar Plans to Tax Zubarah Inhabitants

A Qatari port and pier in Zubarah would mean little if the Ruler of Qatar could not show that the people of Zubarah owed their allegiance to him. The Qatari Ruler needed more direct evidence of his claim, so he undertook a tour of Zubarah in March 1937, during which he announced that its inhabitants would now have to pay taxes to him—something they had never done before (Hickinbotham, 3 May 1937).

At that moment he was fortunate to find a rift unfolding between the two main sections of the Naim tribe—the Al-Jabr and the Ramzan. Of this, he took full advantage. The Political Agent explains the course of events like this:

> Sometime ago a man called Ramazan of the Ramazin sub-section of the Na'im tribe divorced his wife. The woman remarried into the Al Jabor section of the Na'im tribe. As a result of this there was friction between Ramazan and Shaikh Rashid bin Mohammad [Al-Jabr], the alleged leader of the Na'im. (Hickinbotham, 3 May 1937, 1)

Amid this falling-out between Ramzan and Sheikh Rashid, the Ruler of Qatar sent a letter in April 1937 to Sheikh Rashid, as head of the Al-Jabr branch of the Naim tribe, claiming all Qatar and giving Al-Jabr seven days to state his loyalty. The Ruler warned that if he did not receive

Al-Jabr's pledge of allegiance, Al-Jabr would be punished (Hickinbotham, 23 April 1937). Among the men the Ruler of Qatar chose to deliver the letter was Ramzan.

Reflecting on the issue, the Political Agent said:

> I think that Ramazan was specially chosen to be one of the party of tax collectors who were sent to Faraihah, *et cetera*, because he was known to be at enmity with the Na'im who inhabited those villages. (Hickinbotham, 3 May 1937, 5)

But the letter did not have the desired effect. Al-Jabr passed the letter on to the Ruler of Bahrain and in turn, the Bahraini Ruler informed the Political Agent. In a telegram to the Political Resident, the Political Agent noted that Rashid Al-Jabor was a Bahrain subject, and enjoyed an allowance from the Bahrain Civil List (Hickinbotham, 23 April 1937). This telegram attests that British officials in the area understood the relationship between the Naim tribe and the Rulers of Bahrain to be that of sovereign and subject.

It should be noted, however, that the Naim's allegiance was not a "given." As previously mentioned in Chapter 9, the relationship between the Naim tribe and the Al-Khalifa rested on the *ikrimiyyah* system, which was by definition mutually beneficial; the Rulers of Bahrain provided the Naim with foodstuffs, gifts, and, most important of all, protection, while in return, the Naim defended Bahraini interests in the Zubarah region. Were the system to break down in any way—for example, if the Rulers of Bahrain were no longer able to protect the Naim from outside aggression—nothing stood to prevent the Naim from looking for another benefactor. It was of just such a situation that the Political Agent was most fearful. In his telegram, he said:

> Serious point if true is that the Naim are reported to have said that if they do not get support from Bahrain they will adhere to Bin Sa'ud. (Hickinbotham, 23 April 1937)

In order for the Ruler of Bahrain to maintain his relationship with the Zubarah region, which was important to him not only for emotional reasons but practical ones—it could be used as an effective launching point for attacks against the main island of Bahrain—he had somehow to show the Naim tribe that he could still protect and take care of them.

And for all intents and purposes, the Bahraini Ruler did satisfactorily keep his commitment to the Naim, right up until the attack. A member of the Naim tribe and a resident of the Zubarah region, Mohammed bin Mohammed bin Theyab Al-Naimi, recalls the Ruler of Qatar's efforts to try to tax Zubarah residents:

> In the late 1930s, Ibn Thani wanted to put a guard post in the north of Qatar and impose taxes on the Naim. Until that time, Ibn Thani did not try to collect *zakat* (religious taxes) from us, and he did not have any *fidawi*'s (guards) in the area. The Al Jabr Naim refused to accept the guard post or the taxes because we considered ourselves to be subjects of Sheikh Hamad bin Isa of Bahrain. (Mohammed Al-Naimi, 6 September 1996 ¶ 10)

Another member of the Naim says:

> ...there had been a lot of trouble with the Al-Thani Sheikh of Qatar who wanted to tax the Al Jabr Naim, for example by charging customs duties on the dhows which brought food from the main island of Bahrain and setting up a guard post in our tribal territory. Another section of the Al Naim tribe, the Al Ramzan, had switched allegiance to the Al-Thani Sheikh and had been appointed to collect taxes from the Al Jabr section of the tribe.
>
> This caused a great deal of bad feeling within the Al Naim tribe and our leader Rashid bin Mohammed Al Jabr argued with the Al Ramzan section and refused to pay any taxes. He made it clear to the Al-Thanis that the Al Jabr Al Naim were subjects of the Ruler of Bahrain and that we would have nothing to do with the Al-Thani. We were afraid that the Al Thani would demand allegiance by force and many of the Al Naim tribe gathered at the ruined town of Zubarah from the outlying towns and villages in fear of an attack. (Saleh Al-Naimi, 14 September 1996 ¶ 9)

Throughout, the Al-Jabr section of the Naim remained steadfast in their loyalty to the Ruler of Bahrain.

Heightening of Tensions

To help bolster the defenses of the Naim, the Ruler of Bahrain sent them food and arms—which, it is important to note, was done at the request of the Naim:

> Our leader, Rashid bin Mohammed Al Jabr, had gone to the Ruler of Bahrain, Sheikh Hamad bin Isa and his son Sheikh Salman, seeking weapons in fear of an attack from Ibn Thani. He had sought the weapons from the Ruler of Bahrain because they were our Rulers, and because the Naim were fighting on behalf of the Al Khalifa. (Mohammed Al-Naimi, 6 September 1996 ¶ 10)

But it was only after their invasion on 1 July 1937 that the Ruler of Qatar complained to the British about the provisions that Bahrain had supplied:

> I regret to mention the acts committed by Bahrain during this time, by reinforcing the rebels of my subjects by supplying them with provisions, money, arms and ammunition... I have found amongst them arms possessed by the rebels of my subjects, arms which bore the Bahrain Government mark. (Abdullah bin Jasim Al-Thani, 11 July 1937, 1)

By April of 1937, tension levels were high. Fearful of an attack from Al-Thani, around one thousand armed Naim tribesmen formed a camp in Zubarah. When the Political Agent enquired why they had so gathered, they assured him

> ...they had collected with no evil intent, but only becauxe [sic] they have been threatened with taxation and having objected they feared that Shaikh 'Abdullah bin Qassim would take actions against them. They stressed that [they] were subjects of the Sheikh of Bahrain. (Hickinbotham, 3 May 1937)

In a separate telegram to the Political Resident, the Political Agent reiterated that the "concentration [was] owing to fear," and the "cause of discontent [was] Qatar's threat of taxation" (Hickinbotham, 30 April 1937).

Not only were the Naim agitated, great concern had arisen also among the ruling circles on the main island of Bahrain, and they decided to take more aggressive action:

> A party of the Al Khalifa consisting of three of His Highness' guards landed at Zubarah with a quantity of materials and planted the Al Khalifah flag on the beach. The materials were apparently for the repair of the fort. (Hickinbotham, 3 May 1937, 2)

Compromise Proposal

At this point the British decided to take more decisive action. On 1 May 1937, the Political Agent conducted an interview with Sheikh Abdullah of Qatar. The Political Agent noted that:

> The Ruler was at first disinclined to discuss the matter [Zubarah] ... He pretended to know nothing about the events ... however, after a little persuasion, he decided to discuss the matter of the Na'im. (Hickinbotham, 3 May 1937, 3)

The Political Agent and the Ruler of Qatar agreed that the matter would be referred to the Resident and that

> ... there would be perfect security ... from now onwards and that the Na'im were at liberty to depart to their normal places without fear of any interference from him or his people [the Ruler of Qatar] until such time as the Resident had given his decision. The Political Agent noted the Na'im "were obviously gratified and relieved" by this decision. (Hickinbotham, 3 May 1937, 4)

In the interim, the Political Agent proposed a compromise: the Sheikh of Qatar would agree not to impose taxes on the Nai'im, would not enforce any import dues in Zubarah and on the northwestern coastal villages in the Zubarah region, would not require travel papers of persons passing between Bahrain and the west and northwest coasts of Qatar, and would acknowledge the Sheikh of Bahrain's right to the ownership of the Zubarah area as his personal property. In return, the Ruler of Bahrain would resign all oil and commercial rights in the area to the Sheikh of Qatar (Hickinbotham, 3 May 1937, [9]).

It is important to note that the compromise proposal did *not* deal with the issue of sovereignty directly; rather the proposal described the rights of both Rulers in terms of personal property (Bahrain 1996, 117 ¶ 271).

About a month later further negotiations took place, in which Qatar agreed to maintain the status quo (abstaining from taxation, immigration, and import control) in Zubarah, provided that Bahrain withdraw its claim to Zubarah and the Naim tribe. The Ruler of Bahrain expressed that he was prepared to make a modified renouncement:

As long as the above conditions are carried out without alterations I (the Sheikh of Bahrain) agree to withdraw my claim to Zubarah and the Naim but should there happen anything contrary to the conditions my claim returns as before. (Fowle, 23 June 1937)

After further reflection, however, the Ruler of Qatar changed his mind. On 9 June 1937 he explained to the Political Resident that "[his] proof is clear" in regards to Qatari sovereignty over Zubarah, adding that the 1916 Treaty authorized his assigning oil drilling rights to the Zubarah region to PCL (Abdullah bin Jasim Al-Thani, 9 June 1937, 2).

It bears mentioning that the Ruler of Qatar was incorrect in his interpretation of the 1916 Treaty. It will be recalled that the 1916 Treaty contained no geographical definition of the territory of Qatar. Furthermore, nothing in the Treaty indicated that "Qatar" should include anything more than what had been the Ottoman administrative unit of Qatar, basically the region around Doha.

Naim Maintain Loyalty to the Ruler of Bahrain

In their assessment of the strength of Qatar's claim vis-à-vis that of Bahrain's, Britain also noted that Bahrain had the upper hand. In a memorandum to the British Secretary of State for India dated 5 May 1937, the British Political Resident communicated Bahrain's case to the Secretary of State for India, admitting:

(1) that for many years past the Naim tribe of Bahrain origin, and members of whom live in Bahrain are practically the sole inhabitants of Zubarah

(2) and the Naim at Zubarah pay no taxes, including customs to the Shaikh of Qatar. Nor does the Shaikh of Qatar insist on travel papers for Bahrain subjects visiting Zubarah

(3) that the Naim tribe obey the orders of the Shaikh of Bahrain, in support of which statement the Bahrain Government quote that many years ago the tribe obeyed the orders of Shaikh 'Isa, then Ruler of Bahrain, not to occupy the Zubarah fort, which they wished to do. Further, that the Naim tribe generally obey the orders of the Ruler of Bahrain.

The Bahrain Government, however, admit that they do not administer or take taxes at Zubarah. (Fowle, 5 May 1937, 2)

During these critical months of negotiation between Bahrain and Qatar, the Naim tribe maintained their loyalty to the Ruler of Bahrain, and they registered their land in Bahrain (*Request for Registration of Property in Zubarah Region*, 23 April 1937).

In addition, the Chief of the Naim tribe repeated his request for arms from the Ruler of Bahrain. He underscored the fact that "[w]e have not risen in the matter except for preserving your boundaries..." (Al-Jabor, 24 April 1937). The very next day, he wrote again to the Ruler of Bahrain, saying:

> We have not come forward in this matter but for the fact that we are within your boundaries and we will not let them [the Qataris] take your territory. (Chief of Naim tribe, 25 April 1937)

In June 1937 more than three hundred Naim inhabitants signed a petition to the Ruler of Bahrain affirming that they and their families had lived in the Zubarah region for more than one hundred years, and that they had never been under any rule other than that of the Al-Khalifa (Belgrave, 20 June 1937).

The Ruler of Qatar's position was further weakened when Doha residents, including members of his own family, joined with the Al-Jabr branch of the Naim. Assessing the Ruler of Qatar's situation the Political Agent said:

> My general impression is that the Shaikh of Qatar's position is being daily weakened by defections not only of outside notables but from his own family. He will very shortly not be in a sufficiently strong position to make any terms whatsoever and indeed rumors are circulating that he goes daily in fear of his life. (Hickinbotham, 29 May 1937)

The situation was looking less positive for the Ruler of Qatar: the project for building a port never got off the ground; the inhabitants of the Zubarah region refused to pay taxes; and the British put forward a plan that preserved the status quo. In frustration, the Qatar Ruler encouraged Bedouins to attack Zubarah. Abdullah bin Hasan, a messenger for the Ruler of Bahrain reports:

> I heard that on the 20th June 1937 the Bedouins of Qatar plundered 18 she-camels and 7 young male camels from the Naim at

Zuabarh [sic] ... The Bedouins brought the booty to Qatar and they were immediately branded with the Qatar "wasm" (brand). On the 21st June 1937, in the afternoon, certain Bedouins of Qatar brought 7 camels which they had plundered either from the Chaban or Naim tribes. While at Rayan, I used to notice a lot of Bedouins coming to Shaikh Abdullah [of Qatar] daily getting arms and ammunition ... (Abdullah bin Hasan, 22 June 1937)

Despite the deterioration in relations between Bahrain and Qatar, Britain determined that any outbreak of hostilities "... does not call for our active intervention" (Fowle, 23 June 1937). Britain's position had been to ignore the Zubarah question for some time now, but never had it so openly refused to protect Bahraini property there.

Second Round of Negotiations Leads to Attack

Hope of finding a negotiated settlement was not lost, however. In late June 1937 a second round of negotiations took place in Ghariyeh, a northern village on Qatar's east coast. At first, the negotiations seemed to be going well. During the evening, however,

> It appeared that the meeting was not altogether a cheerful one as the party sat for exactly an hour without making any remark and at the end of this period the Shaikh of Qatar left. (Hickinbotham, 1 July 1937)

In this event, the Bahraini delegation requested that the talks be temporarily suspended so they could go back to Bahrain to obtain further instructions from their Ruler. The quickest way back was by boat, and just as the Bahrainis turned from the coast of Zubarah, they saw the town being attacked—the Ruler of Qatar had hired armed Bedouin mercenaries to take the region by force.

Charles Belgrave, the Adviser to the Ruler of Bahrain and member of the Bahrain delegation, described the following scene:

> Some unusual activity had been sighted on the coast [from the boat]. Motor lorries, loaded with men, were moving in the direction of Zabara and bodies of men were deploying. Then, as we watched, the fighting started. The Naim tribesmen who lived at Zabara were being attacked by Shaikh Abdulla bin Jasim's Bedouin ... (Belgrave 1960, 156)

According to an interview with the Political Agent that very day, Belgrave estimated the Qatar force at five thousand to seven thousand men, three trucks adapted for carrying troops, and six automobiles. One hundred Naim and adherents of the Ruler of Bahrain were reported to have died in the fighting (Hickinbotham, 1 July 1937; Hickinbotham, 2 July 1937).

Eyewitness accounts of Naim tribesmen living in the Zubarah region show that the attack had been planned in advance, for assaults by Al-Thani's men on other Naim villages took place at the same time as the attack on Zubarah. Saleh bin Muhammed Ali bin Ali Al Naimi says:

> On 1 July 1937, early in the afternoon, I saw a large body of tribesmen, some Qatari, some Bedouin from the Manasir and Beni Hajir tribes, approaching our *dirah* (tribal area) near Lisha. Some were on foot and some were in lorries. There were maybe three or four thousand men in total and most of them had guns. It was clear that they were intending to attack us. One of our tribesmen shouted the battle cry. We went to join the other members of our tribe who had assembled to defend our tribal area against the attack.
>
> A front line of our tribe went ahead on camels and horses and the rest of us followed on foot. They reached the site of the battle before us. Meanwhile, the women and children took down the tents to move away from the area of fighting. I heard a lot of gunfire but by the time I arrived on foot, the Qataris had retreated to the east. We found the injured and brought them back to Lisha for treatment.
>
> That day three of our tribe died in the fighting, Majd bin Nasr, Isa bin Ahmed Al Sayed and Ahmed bin Mohammed, the brother of Rashid bin Mohammed. Majd bin Nasr was at first seriously injured but subsequently died of his wounds at the American Hospital on the main island of Bahrain. (Saleh Al-Naimi, 14 September 1996)

When he learned of the attack, the Ruler of Bahrain made a formal request to Britain for help in protecting the Zubarah region:

> We have to inform you that all our efforts to arrive at a compromise with the Ruler of Qattar regarding the matter of Zubara and

the Naim have been without success... Shaikh Abdullah bin Jasim refused to agree to any terms except his own.

> We wish to prevent a war and the shedding of blood. We request the British Government to restrain [the Ruler of Qatar] from making war against our subjects who live within our boundaries at Zubarah. (Hamad bin Isa Al-Khalifa, 1 July 1937)

Britain refused Bahrain's request. A statement by the British Political Resident at the time clearly indicated where Britain's interests lay:

> [The Qatari PCL] Oil Company... will not resume operations until autumn and before that dispute between Shaikh of Qatar and Naim should have been settled. (Fowle, 2 July 1937)

Aftermath of Attack

Naim Tribe Forced to Migrate to Bahrain

Abdullah Al-Thani's men did not stop at the town of Zubarah, but attempted to capture the entire Zubarah region from the Ruler of Bahrain. On 2 July the Adviser to the Ruler of Bahrain, Charles Belgrave, informed the Political Agent that the village of Furaiwah, 5 kilometers north of the now ruined town of Zubarah, had also been captured, in particularly fierce fighting. An eyewitness to the battle relates:

> ... they [Al Thani's men] have a machine gun on a lorry which fires hundreds of shots and wings round in a circle. (Belgrave, 2 July 1937)

Boatloads of women and children from Zubarah, Furaiwah and other small villages fled to Bahrain. Bahrain police patrols were sent to receive the refugees, and medical arrangements were made to treat the wounded (Hickinbotham, 2 July 1937).

Encouraged by the British stance—or rather, lack thereof—toward his attack, the Ruler of Qatar gave the Zubarah region's inhabitants a choice: they could either stay in Zubarah but under his authority, or leave the area entirely. The leaders of the Al-Jabr section of the Naim tribe held a meeting to decide what course of action they should take.

Saleh bin Mohammed Ali bin Ali Al Naimi relates the decision they took:

> The Al Jabr Al Naim conferred and the elders decided that allegiance lay with Bahrain. A letter was written to Sheikh Hamad bin Isa, asking him to transfer us to the main island of Bahrain, which he did. (Mohammed Al-Naimi, 6 September 1996)

Not all the Naim chose to go to Bahrain; some decided to accept the authority of the Ruler of Qatar. The majority of the Al-Jabr branch, however, including its Chief, Rashid bin Mohammed, maintained their loyalty to the Ruler of Bahrain and sought refuge on its main islands. Approximately twelve hundred to thirteen hundred Naim tribesmen made the journey over from Zubarah (Bahrain 1996, 128 ¶ 290).

As the British Political Agent later noted:

> The tribesmen who came over to Bahrain in 1937 must have regarded themselves as subjects of the Sheikh of Bahrain or they would have remained in Qatar and submitted to the authority of the Sheikh of Qatar. (Wakefield, 11 January 1948)

The Ruler of Bahrain Has Maintained His Claim

Badly outnumbered, the Naim surrendered to Abdullah Al-Thani on 5 July 1937. Just one day after the Naim ceasefire, the Ruler of Bahrain protested to Britain, saying, "Sheikh Abdullah has occupied our country" (Hamad bin Isa Al-Khalifa, 6 July 1937a).

He also repeated his request for assistance, but received no reply. British oil interests would be better served by a Qatari victory in Zubarah.

Nevertheless, the Ruler of Bahrain has continuously asserted his claim to the Zubarah region ever since.

Bahrain Sanctions on Qatar

Frustrated at receiving no response from the British, the Ruler of Bahrain expressed his displeasure at the situation more forcefully: he informed the British government that ". . . for the time being we wish to eliminate all intercourse and commerce with the State of Qatar."

As part of the sanctions imposed, no Qataris except bearers of official messages from the Sheikh of Qatar to the Political Agent were to enter Bahrain. No exports of any kind were permitted from Bahrain to

Qatar, with the exception of water and stores for the Petroleum Concession Limited, for which special permission was given by the Bahrain government. In addition, transit dues privileges were revoked (Hamad bin Isa Al-Khalifa, 6 July 1937; Belgrave, 11 June 1942; *Representations on Zubarah to Foreign Office*, 4 August 1949).

Qatar protested the sanctions, writing to the Political Resident:

> I do not yet know the grounds on which the Bahrain Government have based the prohibition upon Qatar subjects... I am now reporting my complaint and protest to you for this attitude which the Bahrain Government have adopted towards me without any justification. (Abdullah bin Jasim Al-Thani, 17 July 1937)

About then Qatar was enduring very difficult economic times. In the 1920s, competition from Japanese cultured pearls had wrecked the market for natural pearls throughout the Gulf, including Qatar. In addition, the area was still recovering from the worldwide depression. The Ruler's fractious relationship with his brothers had not helped matters, either. They and the villages under their control refused to pay tribute to the Qatar Ruler. That the Ruler of Bahrain had now imposed his embargo on top of all this was devastating (Crystal 1990, 117).

Regardless, Bahrain's sanctions on Qatar continued until virtually the end of World War II.

Factors Influencing British Reaction to Bahrain Protest

Immediately after the attack, the Ruler of Bahrain insisted that his rights in the Zubarah region not be ignored, and on 6 July 1937, his Adviser wrote to the Political Agent:

> I have the honour to inform you that His Highness Shaikh Sir Hamad bin Isa al-Khalifa... has asked me to ascertain from you when his claim to the Zubara area will receive consideration and by whom the matter will be examined. (Belgrave, 6 July 1937)

Initially, the Resident was open to hearing the Ruler of Bahrain's position and suggested a framework to his superiors in which hearings over the Zubarah region could be heard. He said that due to the treaty relations between Britain and Bahrain and Qatar respectively, Britain was naturally the only competent authority to hear the case. Thus, he recommended informing the Ruler of Bahrain that His Majesty's

Government noted his request and asking him when his case would be ready for submission (Fowle, 9 July 1937).

However, the India Office disagreed with Lt. Col. Fowle's recommendation. Its main objection stemmed from geopolitical concerns:

> I have pointed out on another paper that if we allow the Sheikh of Bahrain to establish claims on the mainland of Qatar we shall greatly weaken our case for maintaining the integrity of the Peninsula against Ibn Saud. I think therefore we shall have to be careful not to do or say anything implying that we might recognise the Sheikh of Bahrain's claims. (*India Office Memorandum*, 14 July 1937)

To back up its stance, the India Office advocated a reinterpretation of the 1875 Treaty, which stipulated that the Ruler of Bahrain should avoid entanglements on the Qatar peninsula. Now, however, the Treaty was to be understood as recognizing the Sheikh of Qatar's rights over the whole of the Qatar peninsula (*Draft Telegram*, 10 July 1937).

Captain Hickinbotham, Political Agent in Bahrain, noted:

> ...on further consideration I think you will find that in the correspondence referred to by you, that is, the correspondence which took place in 1875, there is no decision made by His Majesty's Government with regard to the ownership of Zubarah.
>
> From re-reading the letters it appears to me that the Government of India were at that time anxious to avoid complications on the mainland and at the same time they were not disposed to give a definite decision regarding the ownership of Zubarah. The same situation appears to have arisen this year.
>
> As I have said above I can find no specific decision by the Government of India. In fact they appear to have avoided giving a decision... (Hickinbotham, 16 September 1937)

Once again, Kelly's argument about the tension between the colonial and diplomatic strains of British foreign policy was coming into play. However, in this case, the tension between the two strains was present in the India Office itself and not just between the India Office and the Foreign Office, as mentioned previously. For his part, Captain Hickinbotham, the Political Agent, represented the colonial strain, which was more in tune with what was actually happening on site, while Lt.-Col. Fowle, the Political Resident, represented the diplomatic strain, which was more interested in geopolitical and commercial concerns.

These differences proved insurmountable, and no hearing over the Zubarah issue was held.

Mediation Efforts (1944, 1950)

Britain's stance encouraged the Ruler of Qatar to try to consolidate his authority in the Zubarah region after his attack in 1937. To effect this, he built a fort there in 1939. The Ruler of Bahrain took this as a provocative action, saying,

> [W]e regard this action as illegal because Zubara is our town and contains our cemeteries and mosques. (Hamad bin Isa Al-Khalifa, 26 April 1939)

The two years since the attack had not calmed the situation between the two leaders. While the India Office was apparently still willing to let things take their course absent their involvement, the British Political Agent, Captain Hickinbotham, decided to take more proactive action by offering to mediate the issue of Zubarah between the two sides.

Britain's 1944 Mediation

Points listed in Hickinbotham's proposal include the following:

- the Ruler of Bahrain has certain personal property rights,
- the Ruler of Qatar relationship with PCL in Zubarah not affected,
- the Ruler of Bahrain has jurisdiction over his own subjects in the area but not over subjects of the Ruler of Qatar,
- the Ruler of Bahrain supplies sugar, grain, clothing, etc., to his subjects only,
- the Ruler of Qatar can have customs official there if he wants,
- no new buildings built by either side (Hickinbotham, February 1944).

Regardless of the merits of these points, the Rulers of Bahrain and Qatar both had much to gain from a settlement of the Zubarah dispute, and Hickinbotham's proposal at least represented a starting point on which they might build. It was no easy process, however, convincing the two Rulers to come to the bargaining table.

Trying to entice the Rulers of Bahrain and Qatar into the mediation efforts, Hickinbotham stressed that the ideas he was presenting to them were merely his "personal suggestions." Discussing the matter with the Ruler of Qatar, he said:

> It is unnecessary for me to stress the benefits which will accrue to your country by a settlement of this dispute nor do I deny for one moment that Bahrain will not benefit. (Hickinbotham, 8 February 1944)

As added incentive, Hickinbotham reminded the Ruler of Qatar of the negative effects the Bahrain embargo was having on Qatar's economic situation:

> ...the difficulty and danger of supplying Qatar with grain and sugar from Dubai will be overcome. (Hickinbotham, 8 February 1944)

But when Hickinbotham showed the Qatari leadership the draft, the son of the Ruler refused to affix his seal to it and tore up the document. During discussions lasting far into the night, the Ruler of Qatar was finally convinced to sign on 18 June 1944. His son was still unhappy, however, declaring "his father has sold the country to the Al Khalifah" (Prior, 18 June 1944).

The Ruler of Bahrain signed the document a little less than a week later and subsequently lifted the embargo on Qatar.

But the 1944 Agreement did not produce the effects Hickinbotham desired, largely because the Rulers of Bahrain and Qatar both interpreted the Agreement to their own favor.

The Ruler of Bahrain understood the agreement as preserving the status quo prior to the 1937 attack:

> As you are aware that according to the agreement, everything in Zubarah should return to its original condition...You have promised during our two conversations that you will take the matter into consideration and make the condition of Zubarah as it was before. (Salman bin Hamad Al-Khalifa, 14 September 1944)

The Ruler of Qatar, on the other hand, thought the agreement preserved the status quo as it stood in 1944:

> ...we have been surprised to see Your Highness using for Zubarah the word "Your country." Zubarah, as everybody knows, is an inseparable part of Qatar. It is my country and not yours as you mentioned. (Abdullah bin Jasim Al-Thani, 30 January 1945)

Given the Ruler of Bahrain's strong feelings on this matter, he immediately complained to the British government:

> [He] Sheikh Abdulla mentions... that Zobarah is his country. It is strange for Sheikh Abdulla to mention this while he is aware of the existence of our houses, forts, mosques and graves of our people and that it had been in our possession till the trouble started eight years ago when he occupied it and built on it. (Salman bin Hamad Al-Khalifa, 3 February 1945)

So, despite Hickinbotham's best effort, his proposal was a failure. Seeing that the wrangling between the two Rulers had continued almost a year after the signing of the Agreement, the Political Agent advised the Ruler of Bahrain to talk directly to the Ruler of Qatar (Hickinbotham, 6 March 1945).

In 1946, a new Political Agent, Arnold Galloway, was assigned to the Gulf, in Bahrain. He had no better luck finding a solution to the Zubarah issue than had his predecessor. As he explained, part of the problem involved the nature of the 1944 Agreement itself:

> A difficulty which I am faced in approaching the problem is the vague wording of the agreement under which it is almost impossible to tie any one party down to any one thing. I, myself, do not know what was really intended nor what reading the two sheikhs actually place on it. (Galloway, 11 June 1946)

Thus, a major problem with the 1944 Agreement was that it tried too hard to please both sides. It took no firm stance one way or another.

Qatar Attempts Settlements in Zubarah, 1946

In 1946, the Ruler of Qatar tried to settle some of his followers in Zubarah. Predictably, Bahrain protested this action. The Ruler of Bahrain expressed his clear frustration: "O' Your Excellency, how often aggressions and troubles are done by Qatar people against us, which we refer to you one after another" (Salman bin Hamad Al-Khalifa, 5 March 1947).

Yet according to the British government, nothing in Qatar's actions violated the 1944 Agreement.

In 1948, the Ruler of Bahrain asked again, "whether the PRPG was 'going to make any decision regarding the dispute between Bahrain and Qatar' and 'whether or not the matter is going to be dealt with.'" (*Report* entitled *"Note on Developments in the Zubarah Case,"* 1948).

This time the Resident asked the Ruler of Bahrain to submit a clear statement of exactly what he was claiming in Zubarah. The Ruler of Bahrain submitted an extensive reply on 2 March 1948 (Salman bin Hamad Al-Khalifa, 2 March 1948). But this brought no tangible results from the British.

Fast Turnover in PABs

In 1948, yet another Political Agent, C. J. Pelly, was appointed to Bahrain. He asked the Bahrain Ruler to define—again—the precise extent of the properties he claimed in Zubarah. The Ruler's reply to Pelly's query referred to the old Murair fort, the mosque, the wells, and various houses. The Ruler pointed out that never till the dispute had he experienced any interference from the Al-Thani over Zubarah:

> Never, before the dispute, were our privileges questioned and our authority at Zubara was similar to that in Bahrain. (Salman bin Hamad Al-Khalifa, 2 March 1948, 1–2)

Yet again, no satisfactory resolution of the matter was in sight, in no small part due to the fact that three appointments had been made to the Political Agency in just four years—Hickinbotham, then Galloway, and then Pelly. As every new appointment required an extensive period during which the Agents had to acquaint themselves with the case before proceeding to its resolution, much precious effort was wasted, and attempts to resolve the conflict were carried out in rather intermittent fashion.

Ruler of Bahrain's Legal Efforts

Thus, in 1948, The Ruler of Bahrain hired BAPCO's London solicitor, H. Ballantyne, to present his case to the British government. It was stressed that Ballantyne was working in his personal capacity, and not in any way representing the oil company.

Ballantyne proposed that the Ruler of Bahrain and his family be regarded as the "Freeholders" of the Zubarah region, with the mineral rights to the area resting with the Ruler of Qatar. For all intents and purposes, his proposal seemed to be in accord with the 1944 Agreement. Nonetheless, the British government rejected it (Ballantyne, 2 June 1948; Ballantyne, 2 June 1948a).

The British response notwithstanding, the Ruler of Bahrain protested once again to the British government, expressing regret over its "evasive and non-committal replies." The Ruler of Bahrain admitted that his "only hope of obtaining a settlement of this dispute is by making a direct appeal..." to the British Foreign Secretary. The Ruler of Bahrain then presented a clear and detailed statement of what he was prepared to do:

(a) To define, as is shown on the map herewith, the area of Zubarah. To hold this land and what is on it in free use by my family, my adherents and my subjects.

(b) To hold the land so defined as in private ownership for ever.

(c) To surrender to the Shaikh of Qatar or otherwise renounce all oil rights in the Zubara area; in this connection I would like to point out that I have never at any time claimed such rights there.

(d) Subject to my seeing the oil concession Agreement between the Shaikh of Qatar and the Petroleum Concessions Limited to respect the provisions of that Agreement so that all its benefits, entirely, go to the Shaikh of Qatar.

(e) To obtain the surrender by the Bahrain Petroleum Company of any claims they have or may have in Zubara under the concession which they hold from me in my territories.

(f) To continue, as now and as before, to [give to] Petroleum Concessions Limited freedom to conduct its business in my country and to buy water from here and carry it to Qatar....

(g) In return for this fair offer I require to obtain the rights of my family, my adherents and my subjects at Zubara including freedom and security for their lives and property similar to the conditions which they enjoyed at Zubara prior to the dispute in 1936 [*sic*]. (Salman bin Hamad Al-Khalifa, 24 June 1948)

The British Foreign Office felt that it now had no choice but to discuss the matter, since "[t]he Sheikhs of Bahrain have persistently and periodically during the last 60 or 70 years claimed sovereign rights in the Zubarah area" (*Foreign Office Discussion Paper*, 21 July 1948).

Once again, though, British oil interests proved to be of paramount concern:

> It seems fairly clear that the Sheikh of Bahrain is being encouraged to raise once again this long standing dispute by the American Oil Company (BAPCO) who have a concession in Bahrain and if we allow it to continue there is some danger that the British Oil Company, who have the concession in Qatar, may become involved in support of their Sheikh. We would then see a deterioration in relations between the two oil companies as well as the two Sheikhs. For this reason I feel that we should not, as suggested by the Resident, temporise any longer.... (*Foreign Office Discussion Paper*, 21 July 1948)

The major problem the British government had was defining exactly the nature of the rights the Ruler of Bahrain did have in the Zubarah region:

> He has undoubtedly some private or tribal rights in Zubarah which local custom would admit though they may be contrary to modern ideas of territorial sovereignty. (*Foreign Office Letter*, 3 September 1949)

1950 and Afterwards

In 1950, with assistance from British officials resident in the Gulf, the Ruler of Bahrain and the Ruler of Qatar reached an oral agreement over Zubarah. The Political Resident joyfully reported, "You will be glad to hear that the situation regarding the Zubarah case which I last discussed ...at last looks a bit brighter" (Hay, 7 February 1950).

According to the agreement, the Ruler of Qatar agreed that the Ruler of Bahrain might send his followers and tribesmen to Zubarah to graze without passport or customs formalities, and also that the Ruler of Qatar would leave the fort vacant, provided that in return the Ruler of Bahrain would allow goods for Qatar the same privileges enjoyed by Saudi Arabia regarding the payment of transit duties as goods (Hay, 7 February 1950).

The Political Resident stated that the Ruler of Bahrain had accepted this and was making arrangements to send one hundred fifty to two hundred of his people to Zubarah, along with the necessary rations to support them. In an inspection visit to Zubarah, Pelly reported that all was calm in the area, with "no one carrying a rifle" (C. J. Pelly, 20 March 1950).

Thus, on 26 June 1950, 120 Naim tribesmen returned to Zubarah. Accompanying the tribesmen were their wives and children (Belgrave, 26 June 1950).

For two years all was well. But in 1952, the Ruler of Bahrain reported a breach in the status quo. The Adviser to the Ruler of Bahrain explained:

> I have the honour to inform you that His Highness has instructed me to write to you on the subject of the fort at Zubara, when friendly relations were established between Bahrain and Qatar, two years ago, the main factor which contributed to His Highness's agreement was the fact that the Shaikh of Qatar withdrew the garrison of the fort and left it closed and empty. It has now been reported to His Highness that stores of food are being placed in the fort and the followers of the Shaikh of Qatar are constantly going in and out of the fort by day and by night. (Belgrave, 15 April 1952)

The Political Agent therefore "... spoke to Shaikh Ali bin Abdullah al Thani and asked him to remove this hay from the fort and to leave it completely empty" (Laver, 19 May 1952).

Things returned to normal for a while, but little less than a year later, Qatar reestablished a guard post at the fort in Zubarah. Their actions elicited immediate protest from the Ruler of Bahrain (Salman bin Hamad Al-Khalifa, 18 March 1953).

The Ruler of Qatar seemed determined not to lessen his influence in the region, and for this reason the spiraling of tension between the Ruler of Bahrain and the Ruler of Qatar began once again.

The agreement reached in 1950 had not put an end to the dispute. On 5 May 1954, the British government proposed another agreement, but both parties rejected it (Burrows, 5 May 1954).

Bahrain continued to claim sovereignty over the Zubarah region and in February 1961, the Ruler of Bahrain drafted a letter to the Political Resident in which he set out fully the history of the matter and the precise nature of Bahrain's claim (Salman bin Hamad Al-Khalifa, 8 February 1961).

Following distribution by Bahrain at a UNESCO Conference in 1966 of a booklet showing the Zubarah region to be part of Bahrain, in the interests of regional stability, international peace and security, and the general promotion of brotherly relations between the two states, Bahrain refrained from confrontational assertion of its sovereignty to the Zubarah region, while continuing to reserve its rights and make the United Kingdom and Qatar aware of them.

The situation continued unresolved despite numerous attempts at settlement until 1976 when King Khalid bin Abdul-Aziz Al-Saud of Saudi Arabia undertook efforts to mediate the dispute, as outlined in Chapter 20.

13 Qatar's Version of Events in Zubarah

Highlights

About the 1937 invasion of Zubarah, Belgrave wrote in his memoirs, "When Shaikh Hamed [Al-Khalifa] died, in 1942, I remembered the words which were attributed to Queen Mary Tudor: 'When I am dead ...you shall find "Calais" lying on my heart,' but in this case the word would have been 'Zabara'" (Belgrave 1960, 156).

The Al-Khalifa's ongoing claim on Zubarah can be explained by the following summary of historical events preceding Zubarah's occupation by the Al-Thani in 1937:

Bahraini Events
- Zubarah is the ancestral home of the Al-Khalifa. The Al-Khalifa arrived there in 1762 and made it their headquarters. They maintained their ties to and sovereignty over Zubarah after they established themselves on the Bahrain Islands.

Qatari Events
- No competing authority ever originated from the Qatar peninsula that could displace the Al-Khalifa in Zubarah.

Bahraini Events	Qatari Events
• After the center of the Al-Khalifa state moved to the main Bahrain island in 1796, the Al-Khalifa continued to exercise their authority over Zubarah through the Naim tribe, particularly its Al-Jabr branch. The Naim recognized the paramountcy of the Al-Khalifa and consistently defended Al-Khalifa interests in the Qatar peninsula.	• The Al-Thani, who emerged to prominence in Doha in the 1860s, had no tribal backing in the northwest of the Qatar peninsula.
• The Al-Khalifa's full title to Zubarah was internationally recognized until 1937.	• The Al-Thani—with Ottoman support—made six unsuccessful attempts to extend their authority to Zubarah during the period 1874–1903. The 1916 Treaty marking their independence from the Ottoman Empire did not include recognition of control over Zubarah.
• Oil was discovered in Bahrain in 1932, and at that time Zubarah was possibly to be included in the unallotted area.	• The motive behind the 1937 Al-Thani attack was oil, which was not discovered in Qatar until 1939. In the 1930s Qatar was a place of desperate poverty, and Qatar desired whatever oil might be discovered in the Zubarah region.
• Bahrain granted its oil concession to a U.S. company.	• Qatar granted its oil concession to a British company. So British interests were served at this time by supporting Qatar's claim over Zubarah.

Bahraini Events	Qatari Events
• The Al-Khalifa have maintained their claim since 1937.	• To this day, the Al-Thani have not established effective government in the northwest of the Qatar peninsula.

Until recently, the status of Zubarah had never been finally adjudicated. In 2001, it fell to the International Court of Justice to issue a ruling about the question of sovereignty over the Zubarah region. For a complete discussion of the *ICJ Final Judgment* see Chapter 22.

Qatar's Version of Events

Qatar has called the issue of Zubarah "not a serious dispute" (Shankardass, 5 June 2000a, 26). It has denied both the historical and the legal bases for Bahrain's claim, and accused Bahrain of pursuing "essentially tactical purposes" (David, 21 June 2000, 17 ¶ 3). Here, Qatar directly referred to Bahrain's alleged use of Zubarah to counterweigh Qatar's claim to the Hawar Islands. Bahrain, however, has reminded the Court that it is Qatar rather than Bahrain that has employed such "leveraging" techniques over the years (Paulsson, 28 June 2000, 32 ¶ 37). As early as 1961, for instance, John C. Moberly, the British Political Agent in Doha, reported of a meeting with Sheikh Ahmed Al-Thani:

> He said that if [Sheikh] Salman [of Bahrain] persisted in pursuing his claim to Zubarah he [Sheikh Ahmed] for his part would raise the question of Hawar Island. (*Qatar Diary No. 2 of 1961*, 3–4)

Origins of Zubarah

What were later discovered to be forged documents were presented in Qatar's written pleadings as purported "evidence" that settlements existed in Zubarah before the arrival of the Al-Khalifa in 1762:

> [A] town existed at Zubarah on the northwestern coast of the Qatar peninsula in early Islamic times, and there are also references to Qatari products dating from those times. Further evidence shows that at least by the beginning of the seventeenth century Zubarah was already a fortified town, with its own Sheikh and administration. (Qatar 1996, 22 ¶ 3.16)

Even after abandoning these forged documents as "evidence" on which to base its statements, Qatar continued to claim that important communities "might have existed" in the region (David, 5 June 2000, 52 ¶ 7). However, Bahrain has viewed Qatar's references to such supposed communities as entirely valueless and obviously irrelevant to the task of establishing the extent of *Al-Thani* authority in the north of the Qatar peninsula.

> These speculations may be true, but it cannot seriously be proposed that the modern State of Qatar somehow succeeded to a ghostly ancient principality whose existence is uncertain, whose time is entirely speculative, whose borders are unknown, and whose rulers cannot be identified. (Paulsson, 8 June 2000, 46–47 ¶ 21)

Al-Khalifa and Al-Thani Claims of Authority

Qatar's presentation of the history of Zubarah centered on two main assertions: that the nature of the Al-Khalifa's occupation of the region justified no claims to territorial rights there, and that the Al-Thani had in fact extended their authority to Zubarah in the late 1860s.

Qatar portrayed the Al-Khalifa as leaders of a tribe whose presence in and therefore, association with, Zubarah had been only sporadic. Qatar stressed that the Al-Utub, the tribe of which the Al-Khalifa were a branch, had been in Zubarah only in the years 1766–83, 1800–1 and 1842–43, and that their occupation of the area had been "both intermittent and of short duration." Qatar pointed out that other powers, such as the Wahhabis in 1809 and Muscat in 1811, had reached Zubarah as well. The latter had destroyed the town, from which time it had "ceased to exist as such" (David, 5 June 2000, 53 ¶ 10).

But Bahrain disagreed with Qatar's selective interpretation of historical events. For one thing, Bahrain's pleadings presented sufficient evidence to show that the Al-Khalifa did not indeed abandon Zubarah after they moved their seat of government to the Bahrain Islands. For though the Ruling dynasty's official headquarters were removed from Zubarah, the Al-Khalifa continued to spend the winters in the region, and thereby confirmed Zubarah's importance as one of their principal possessions. They also did not abandon responsibility for the development of the area: in the period 1783–94, the Al-Khalifa ordered the construction of a channel, fortifications, a mosque, and several freshwater wells in Zubarah. The Al-Khalifa's commitment was also demonstrated by the appointment of a governor in Zubarah as soon as it had become clear that the Al-Khalifa's Court was to remain permanently on the Bahrain Islands (Bahrain 1996, 45–46 ¶ 111–12).

Bahrain has acknowledged that the town of Zubarah declined economically in the early nineteenth century, and that the resulting scattering of its population weakened its position. And Bahrain has admitted that the situation in Zubarah further deteriorated following attacks by neighboring powers (Bahrain 1996, 46 ¶ 113).

But Bahrain has also pointed out that none of those events led to an outright loss of the Al-Khalifa's rights in the region. It will be recalled from Chapter 3 that traditionally in the Arabian Gulf, the paramount criterion for determining sovereignty over areas was the allegiance to a ruler held by local tribes. Whether such tribes were governed directly or indirectly through their chiefs, it was the tribes' submission to and recognition of the authority of a ruler that defined the latter's possessions. In the case of Zubarah, the population that remained in the region continued to recognize the Al-Khalifa as supreme political leaders—particularly in the absence of any competing authority in the Qatar peninsula. The historical record amply confirms this fact; as Captain Brucks, for instance, wrote in the 1820s:

> Coast from Ras Reccan to Zobara.—The coast runs south-westerly ... The villages are all subject to Bahrain ... (Brucks 1856, 562)

Bahrain's pleadings also made reference to the fact that until the Ottomans reached the Qatar peninsula in 1871, the Al-Khalifa were the recognized authority over not only the Zubarah region but also the entire peninsula (Bahrain 1996, 42–58 ¶ 104–30; Bahrain 1999, 99 *et seq.* ¶ 193 *et seq.*). Qatar itself confirmed that as fact up to the period prior to 1868. As Qatar stated in its 1991 Application to the International Court of Justice:

> Until 1868, the Qatar peninsula was considered by the British as a dependency of Bahrain. (Qatar 1991 ¶ 5)

Yet Qatar's interpretation of the events following Mohammed Al-Thani's signing of the 1868 undertaking differed from Bahrain's. As was pointed out in Chapters 4 and 7, Qatar claimed that, in effect, the

1868 document recognized the Al-Thani's attainment of coast-to-coast sovereignty. Naturally, Qatar argued, that had meant the extension of Al-Thani authority to Zubarah also:

> The basis of Qatar's title to Zubarah is bound up with the establishment of the authority of the Al-Thani over the whole of the peninsula. Recognized from the middle of the nineteenth century, this authority was officially confirmed by the separate treaties the British signed with Bahrain and Qatar in 1868, and also at the time of Qatar's submission to the Ottomans in 1871. (David 5, June 2000, 53–54 ¶ 12)

As has been demonstrated in previous chapters, and as became abundantly clear from the evidence submitted as part of Bahrain's pleadings, such assertions are groundless. Far from exercising any authority over the entire Qatar peninsula by 1868, the Al-Thani were barely emerging to some status in Doha alone. Almost seventy years were to pass until in 1937, the Al-Thani invaded Zubarah and extended their control to that region. Throughout the almost ten years of the ICJ proceedings and the thousands of pages of evidence, Qatar never presented any evidence of their administration or control of the Zubarah area until their invasion of 1937.

The Naim's Consistent Loyalty to Bahrain

Qatar also has sought to challenge Bahrain's claim to the Zubarah region by raising doubts as to the nature and relevance of the ties between the Rulers of Bahrain and the Naim tribe. Qatar's pleadings mentioned that the Naim's *dirah* was not sufficiently well defined and that the tribe's loyalties were inconstant (Qatar 1997, 153–64, 179–83 ¶ 5.12–5.20, 5.45–5.56; Qatar 1999, 254–66 ¶ 6.34–6.58).

As Bahrain (and this book) have pointed out, however, the attitudes and the activities of the Naim—particularly of the Al-Jabr section of the tribe—exhibited all the characteristics of a loyal tribe. They paid taxes to the Al-Khalifa and acted as the rulers' tax collectors and guards. The Naim have also been the recipients of financial support, provisions and cattle from the Rulers of Bahrain, as well as of Al-Khalifa protection in times of trouble. Their contacts with the Bahrain Islands have been constant, and the Naim have frequently traveled to the main Bahrain island (Bahrain 1999, 124–26 ¶ 234; Bahrain 1996,

8–9, 28–35, 91–93 ¶ 25, 75, 77–88, 207, 210; Bahrain 1997, 19–20, 22–26, 39–40, 42–43 ¶ 43, 45, 47–57, 85, 92). The Naim's continued integration into and loyal association with Bahrain are, furthermore, clearly although tragically demonstrated by the fact that most of the Naim in Zubarah left for the Bahrain Islands when Al-Khalifa authority over Zubarah was displaced following Qatar's 1937 armed attack (see Chapter 12).

Extent of Ottoman/Al-Thani Authority

In line with its theory of having achieved coast-to-coast integrity as of 1868, Qatar claimed that the Ottoman presence in the peninsula had helped the Al-Thani to consolidate their rule over Zubarah. Qatar asserted that during the years of Ottoman domination, there had been "no interference by Bahrain anywhere in the peninsula" (Pilkington, 29 May 2000, 54 ¶ 45), and that Zubarah—just like other areas of Qatar—had undoubtedly been under Ottoman control:

> Between 1871 and 1913 (when they relinquished their rights in favour of the Al-Thani), the Ottomans regarded the entire peninsula of Qatar including Zubarah as part of Ottoman territory, with Sheikh Jassim bin Thani exercising authority over the whole territory as their *kaimakam*. (Qatar 1999, 238 ¶ 6.5)

Such a claim was unfounded, in view of the fact that the Ottomans' jurisdiction over certain areas in the Qatar peninsula had been defined by the extent of Al-Thani control prior to the Ottomans' arrival. Because the Doha chief's influence was confined to the areas immediately surrounding Doha, or at most the southeast coast of the peninsula, it would be impossible to assume that Zubarah had become part of Ottoman territories in 1871. It will furthermore be recalled from Chapter 6 that the Ottoman *kaza* of Qatar was co-extensive with Doha and its environs, and also that—despite occasional bold assertions to the contrary—the Porte never succeeded in incorporating the peninsula's northern regions into its administrative structures.

Qatar also maintained that not only had the Al-Thani (and the Ottomans) acquired sovereignty in Zubarah in 1871, numerous events attested to the consolidation of their rule there throughout the years of Ottoman presence. Qatar called those events the "best-known examples of Qatar's exercising authority in Zubarah" (David, 5 June 2000,

7 ¶ 26). But in truth, Qatar was referring to the *failed* attempts by the Al-Thani and the Ottomans to bring Zubarah under their control (see Chapter 10 for details on each of these attempts).

For instance, the 1878 attempt, which ended in the sacking of Zubarah by the Al-Thani's forces, Qatar claims affirmed Zubarah's status as a dependency of the Al-Thani. Yet, that incident was not followed by the establishment of Ottoman administration in Zubarah. Nevertheless, Qatar stated:

> After 1878, however, the Turks did not occupy Zubarah, and subsequently the British did not accept Zubarah's being occupied by them when they wanted to appoint representatives there. However, this in no way alters the fact that Sheikh Jassim Al-Thani exercised his authority at Zubarah in 1878...[T]he British confirmed that their opposition to the Turkish presence in Zubarah did not in any way entail recognition of the rights claimed by Bahrain. (David, 5 June 2000, 4 ¶ 18)

Likewise, the 1895 Qatar attempt on Zubarah, and particularly the destruction of the fleet of Al-Thani boats by Britain, Qatar interprets as demonstrating that the British acted in fear that the Al-Thani might invade the Bahrain Islands, rather than Britain acting in support of the Al-Khalifa's rights to the region (David, 5 June 2000, 7 ¶ 26). This, however, was not reflected in the terms of the Al-Thani's surrender, which provided for the dispersal of the tribes that had supported the Al-Thani in their attack—or in affirmations about the incident made by British officials themselves:

> ...the Shaikh of Bahrain, who is on friendly terms with the British Government, and Zubarah being one of the towns belonging to him, also the Albin-Ali being his subjects.... (J. H. Pelly, 23 July 1895)

Qatar also cited other incidents where tribes were sent to Zubarah as part of Ottoman and Al-Thani attempts to conquer the region (David, 5 June 2000, 2–4 ¶ 13–15). For its part, Bahrain acknowledged that indeed challenges had been made to Al-Khalifa authority in the northern parts of Qatar, and that the Al-Thani had indeed reached the north of the peninsula on several occasions. But their attempts to establish any permanent authority in the north were unsuccessful. And while such incidents led to an increase in Anglo-Ottoman tensions, no annexation of the Zubarah region occurred prior to 1937 (i.e. 20 years after the Ottomans left). So, as title to Zubarah in the years preceding 1871 unquestionably rested with the Al-Khalifa, and as the Al-Thani failed to take control of the region in the period 1871–1916, the Al-Khalifa remained in possession of Zubarah during the period of Ottoman presence in Arabia. As Bahrain stated during the Oral Hearings in The Hague:

> Bahrain's case may have its *difficulties,* but Qatar's case is *impossible* unless one accepts the notion of instant inherent natural borders. There is no proof of any allegiance to Qatar in the Zubarah region before the Al-Thani attack of 1937. (Paulsson, 9 June 2000, 19 ¶ 84)

Recognition

Qatar asserted in addition that throughout the period of Ottoman domination over the southeastern portions of the peninsula a variety of outside powers had acknowledged the rights of the Al-Thani in Zubarah, and also the absence of any such rights belonging to the Al-Khalifa.

Britain

Qatar's pleadings described British attitudes toward the region as determined mainly by concerns for the security of Bahrain—concerns that had sometimes caused British officials to express ambiguous positions. Nevertheless, Qatar stated, what emerged from a detailed examination of the historical record was the fact that the British were well aware of the Al-Thani's exercise of authority in Zubarah (*cf.* Qatar 1996, 33–36, 192–98 ¶ 3.46–3.54, 8.12–8.30). Qatar identified the main characteristics of British policy toward Bahrain and Qatar as follows:

> British policy towards Bahrain during this period continued to be directed at isolating Bahrain from the problems of the mainland and protecting it from claims of other powers. (Qatar 1996, 33 ¶ 3.46)

> British relations with Qatar following the arrival of the Ottomans were marked by a desire to continue to enforce the maritime peace against acts of piracy stemming from Qatari ports and to protect

the local Indian traders from Sheikh Jassim's continuous harassment. At the same time the British recognised that the Ottomans had *de facto* control of the peninsula, and they were prepared to acknowledge this control. (Qatar 1996, 33 ¶ 3.47)

Bahrain showed, however, that British policies had been determined by larger geopolitical concerns, rather than by any recognition of supposed Al-Thani rights in the north of the Qatar peninsula (Bahrain 1997, 46 *et seq.* ¶ 98 *et seq.*). Paramount among such concerns had been the maintenance of the delicate balance of British relations with the Porte. In their efforts not to antagonize the Ottomans in the region, British authorities had frequently been prevented from supporting the Al-Khalifa's claims to Zubarah. Britain's position was succinctly expressed in an 1874 letter from the British Political Resident to the Ruler of Bahrain:

> I took the opportunity to repeat to you the advice you have so often received from the British Resident to keep clear of the feuds on the mainland, *and especially to avoid giving offence to the Turkish Government.*
>
> Having reported the nature of this conversation to the Government of India, I am instructed by Government that if you should take any part in complications on the mainland, the British Government will not guarantee you protection. (Ross, 12 December 1874) [Emphasis added.]

As a reaction to Britain's position, the Ruler of Bahrain asserted that although he had been instructed "to abstain from interference on the mainland; that he had carried out the wishes of Government in this respect, but that he had never been expressly forbidden to throw up connection with Zobarah" (Fraser, 8 March 1875).

Britain had thus been caught in a situation where, on the one hand, it was committed to protect the Al-Khalifa's possessions while, on the other hand, its larger strategic interests dictated that it must abstain from interference in the peninsula. Thus, Britain's recognition of the Ruler of Bahrain's rights failed, in certain cases, to translate into active support. Nevertheless, its position was well known, and as the Ottoman government explained the British position:

England claims that Zubarah is under the control of Bahrain which it claims is under English protection, and England insists that the Ottoman State has no rights of sovereignty over it. (*Ottoman Arabic Report on Zubarah Affair*, 3 May 1897)

Qatar also made reference to the treaties of the early twentieth century, as yet another proof of British recognition of Al-Thani authority in Zubarah (*cf.* David, 5 June 2000, 9 ¶ 29). As has been discussed in Chapter 6, however, those treaties contained no such recognition.

Regional Powers

In its *Memorial*, Qatar stated that the "separation of Qatar and Bahrain"—which supposedly had been recognized by Britain—had also been confirmed by a number of regional rulers, most notably by Sheikh Zayed of Abu Dhabi (Qatar 1996, 192–93 ¶ 8.13). Qatar later abandoned that assertion, after the documents on which it had been based were exposed by Bahrain as forgeries.

Maps

Qatar devoted special attention to cartographic evidence that supposedly demonstrated that the Zubarah region had been recognized as integrated with the rest of the Qatar peninsula as early as 1870. The International Court was inundated with numerous maps produced by publishing houses in "France, Great Britain, Germany, Russia, the United States, Italy, Turkey, Poland, Austria, Iran and even Australia," and which Qatar saw as confirming its version of the history of the region (Bundy, 31 May 2000, 10 ¶ 5).

All such maps were, however, inconclusive. Bahrain did not fail to point out that a much more relevant map, the Izzet map of 1878 (see Map No. 5, p. 258)—one produced by a person who had actually been in the region—clearly distinguished between Zubarah and the area called Qatar in the southeast of the peninsula (see Chapter 4, section titled "Human Ecology of the Qatar Peninsula"). Bahrain furthermore pointed out that the "map game [could] be played in infinite permutations," and gave as examples numerous maps published in the early 1850s, none of which showed even the existence of the Qatar peninsula at a time when, as Qatar had asserted, it had allegedly become a single political unit under the Al-Thani (Paulsson, 8 June 2000, 12 ¶ 50).

Internal Affair

In its pleadings, Qatar denied that its 1937 attack on the Zubarah region had been an act of international aggression. Rather, Qatar maintained that it had acted out of internal considerations: the Naim tribe had been "engaging in smuggling from Bahrain into Qatar," and had not proven loyal to the Ruler of Bahrain. Qatar therefore justified its action by saying that all the Ruler of Qatar did in 1937 was "impose his authority over the dissenting Naim by force and put an end to the smuggling and other unlawful activities" (Qatar 1997, 172–73 ¶ 5.35).

"Exercise of Al-Thani Sovereignty"

Qatar's version of the 1937 attack rested on statements made by Sheikh Abdullah bin Jasim Al-Thani in the aftermath of the attack. The Ruler of Qatar, who was determined to inform the Political Agent of his view as to what had taken place in Zubarah in 1937, claimed that "whoever intimated the case . . . [to the Agent], did not disclose the whole facts. . . ." According to Sheikh Abdullah, ". . . all what had happened were considered to be of pure internal affairs to which no one else has any right to protest to us against them." Sheikh Abdullah further explained that

> It has been reported to me that the northern coasts of Qatar have become a landing place for those boats which smuggle goods and that many things come from places and run out from there to all sides of Qatar which causes a great harm to the income of the country and affected its imports. (Abdullah bin Jasim Al-Thani, 23 April 1937)

As a remedy, Sheikh Abdullah had supposedly ". . . appointed guards to guard the coasts and to observe all what arrives with the intention of smuggling" (Abdullah bin Jasim Al-Thani, 23 April 1937).

Thus, according to the Ruler of Qatar, Qatar's actions in 1937 were simply an expression of Qatari sovereignty over the Zubarah region.

Qatar's lawyers also shared that interpretation of events; they presented the 1937 invasion of Zubarah as yet another example of the exercise of authority by the Al-Thani:

> Finally, 1937: The Ruler of Qatar's action, aimed at asserting his authority over the Naim in Zubarah, is again a typical act of sovereignty. (David, 5 June 2000, 9 ¶ 26)

Qatar went on to claim that—"quite unjustifiably"—the Ruler of Bahrain had turned what had been an instance of legitimate action by the state of Qatar toward its subjects into a crisis. Surprisingly, as Qatar stated, that action had caused Sheikh Hamad of Bahrain to feel "affronted" (Shankardass, 5 June 2000a, 28 ¶ 7).

Bahrain, for its part, observed that Qatar had no choice but to couch its actions in that manner because to do otherwise would have been to admit that it had knowingly violated the international norms of the time—most notably the Covenant of the League of Nations and the Kellogg-Briand Pact, which precluded nations from using force as an instrument of international policy (Lauterpacht, 8 June 2000, 39 ¶ 92). As Bahrain observed on numerous occasions, international law held that aggression did not constitute a legal means for acquisition of territory and therefore did not create title. Obviously, the implications of that principle for Qatar were that its expansion to the Zubarah region had been unlawful (*cf.* Bahrain 1996, Section 4.2, 226 *et seq.* ¶ 509 *et seq.*).

The Naim

In support of its claim that the events of 1937 had been an internal affair for Qatar, Qatar once again stated its rejection of the special relationship between the Rulers of Bahrain and the Naim tribe, the Al-Jabr branch in particular. It maintained that even in 1937, when the Ruler of Qatar took action to stop smuggling activities in Zubarah, the Naim had been concerned solely with their own interest and not with their relationship with the Ruler of Bahrain. Qatar presented as evidence a telegram from the Political Agent to the Political Resident which read:

> Serious point if true is that Naim are reported to have said that if they do not get support from Bahrain they will adhere to Bin Sa'ud. (Hickinbotham, 23 April 1937)

Qatar concluded from that,

> ...the only concern of Bahrain and the British as regards Zubarah was the security of Bahrain; and that Bahrain's relations with some of the Naim consisted essentially of the Ruler of Bahrain periodically making gifts to them to keep them in good humour in the interests of the security of Bahrain. There was nothing in this relationship to support any Bahraini territorial claim to Zubarah. (Qatar 1997, 164 ¶ 5.20)

Qatar tried to bolster its position further by saying that even Rashid bin Jabor, the head of the Al-Jabr branch of the Naim—much less the Ramzan—was a subject of Sheikh Abdullah Al-Thani. In his letter to the Political Agent, the Ruler of Qatar said

> ... Rashid bin Muhammad al Jabbur is one of my subjects and if he interferes in a matter which leads to rebellion and disobedience and causes agitation it is my duty and it is necessary to restrain and punish him. (Abdullah bin Jasim Al-Thani, 23 April 1937)

That, according to Qatar, offered further proof that its actions in 1937 had been an internal affair, since Bahrain had not been in possession of Zubarah territory for at least seventy years, and the inhabitants there had been loyal to the Ruler of Qatar.

But in addition to Qatar's having failed to establish during the pleadings how or when it had extended its authority to Zubarah prior to 1937, Bahrain pointed out numerous other weaknesses in Qatar's position, one of the most ludicrous of which was Qatar's depiction of the Al-Jabr branch as loyal to the Al-Thani. As has already been mentioned, far from professing any allegiance to the Rulers of Qatar, the Al-Jabr adamantly maintained their status as Bahraini subjects. For example, Rashid bin Jabor himself was included in the Bahrain Civil Lists from the 1920s and 1930s (Hickinbotham, 23 April 1937; Hendry, 15, 19 September 1925). Moreover, the Al-Jabr's reaction to the 1937 Al-Thani attack was to seek the help of the Al-Khalifa, and to eventually move to the Bahrain Islands after the Al-Thani's ultimatum.

Answering Qatar's claims as to the uncertain loyalties of the Naim, Bahrain also pointed out that in the course of the negotiations preceding the Al-Thani attack on Zubarah, Bahrain had proposed a plebiscite among the Naim—an event which never came to pass. As Hickinbotham, the British Political Resident, described it, the real situation in those days had been as follows:

> We [the British Government] were agreed that *provided any vestige of power remained with Shaikh Abdullah* [of Qatar], there was no reason why a compromise should not be satisfactorily arrived at in this form—whilst the Na'im should be given the right to decide by plebiscite as to which ruler they desire to serve, and of course should they move into *any portion of Qatar belonging to*

the Shaikh of Qatar, after having admitted, for example, Bahrain nationality, they would then *ipso facto* be liable for payment of all taxation that at the time had been imposed upon other adherents to Qatar. (Hickinbotham, 29 May 1937) [Emphasis added.]

British Recognition

Qatar was understandably pleased with the failure of British authorities in 1937 to uphold the rights of the Ruler of Bahrain in Zubarah. With regard to Britain's attitudes in the aftermath of the attack, Qatar held that the British were involved in efforts to improve the relations between the Rulers of Bahrain and Qatar, while continuing to acknowledge Qatar's sovereignty over Zubarah. A specific reference was made to the 1944 Accord, which was seen by Qatar as "[p]erhaps the most formal disclaimer of any Bahraini sovereignty over Zubarah and recognition of Qatar's sovereignty" (Shankardass, 5 June 2000a, 28 ¶ 8).

The 1944 Agreement, however, contained no such disclaimer. Rather vague in its formulations, the Agreement mentioned only "the restoration of friendly relations" between the Al-Khalifa and the Al-Thani. As Bahrain pointed out:

> This text is sufficiently ambiguous that one has the strong sense that it was the result of arm-twisting by the British, who wanted peace and whose real interest was in the last sentence. This was a standstill agreement to help the oil men. (Paulsson, 9 June 2000, 23 ¶ 102–103)

The "last sentence" referred to above read:

> This agreement does not affect the agreement with the Oil Company operating in Qatar whose rights are protected. (*Agreement signed by Ruler of Qatar and Ruler of Bahrain on 17 June and 23 June 1944* respectively)

The Hawar Islands

14 Dowasir Tribe and Occupation of the Hawar Islands

The Hawar Islands are an integral part of Bahrain and have been under uninterrupted Bahraini sovereignty for more than two centuries. Bahrain has over the years regulated their economic activities and legal affairs and carried out public works and services there, and continues to do so. Bahrain's sovereignty over the Islands has been recognized both by the Ottomans and the British, and during the awarding of oil concessions in the 1920s and 1930s, the Hawars were considered part of Bahrain's territory. Further, the British adjudication of 1938–39 concluded that the Hawar Islands belong to Bahrain. The chapters in this section examine these issues in detail.

Geography

Though close to the shores of the Qatar peninsula, the Hawar Islands are an integral part of the Bahrain archipelago. They consist of a cluster of some eighteen islands and islets, lying at the closest point about 11 nautical miles southeast of the main island of Bahrain, and extending for a further 8 miles in various directions.

Composition of the Hawars

The Hawars consist of the following islands:

Ajirah	< 0.03 km²
Rabad Al-Gharbiyah	< 0.90 km²
Rabad Ash Sharqiyah	< 1.43 km²
Jazirat Rabad Al-Gharbiyah	<0.01 km²
Jazirat Rabad Ash Sharqiyah	<0.01 km²
Qassar Rabad	<0.01 km²
Umm Alchen	0.03 km²
Hawar	38.56 km²
Juzur Alhajiyat (Island Group)	0.06 km²
Suwad ash Shamaliyah	2.72 km²
Umm Jini	0.06 km²
Umm Haswarah	0.49 km²
Juzur Al-Wukur (Island Group)	0.02 km²
Suwad Al-Janubiyah	7.19 km²
Juzur Bu Saada (Island Group)	0.16 km²
Janan	0.10 km²
Hadd Janan	< 0.01 km²
Qassaseer Busadad	< 0.01 km²

The Hawars also include the following low-tide elevations:

Qit'at Umm Albugarr
Qit'at Al-E'ddah
Qassar Al-Ali

Note that the word *Jazirat* means island in Arabic, while *Jazur* is the plural, or islands. The Hawar Islands comprise approximately 51 km², or more than 7 percent of Bahrain's total land area (approximately 701 km² surface area).

The southern boundary of the Hawars, Janan, is in fact two islands—Janan and Hadd Janan. Situated about 1 nautical mile off the southern coast of Hawar Island, the two islands merge into a single island at low tide, with a combined area of approximately 0.1 square kilometer. Janan and Hadd Janan are in general simply referred to as "Janan." While the British arbitral decision in 1939 confirmed the ownership of the Hawars (including Janan) by Bahrain, a further set of British letters in 1947 demarcated Janan as separate from the other Hawars. Accordingly, these two islands—Janan and Hadd Janan—have been occupied by Qatar since 1947.

Status of Janan

Janan—i.e. the two Janan islands—were included in the British decision of 1939 by virtue of their forming an integral part of the Hawar group of islands (see Chapter 18).

But the association between Janan and the main Hawar Island was not just geographical. The patterns of habitation in the region were such that, like the other Hawar Islands, Janan was used by Bahraini subjects in their economic activities. As one former Hawar resident recalls:

> Apart from the main Hawar Island, there were many fish traps on the other islands. Just north of the island of Janan, there were many reefs which were dangerous for fishing dhows. A pipe was therefore built there by the Bahrain Government to lead the dhows away from the reefs. I remember that a fisherman from Muharraq once accidentally hit the pipe and broke his dhow. He was compensated by the Bahrain Government, by Sheikh Salman. (Hamoud Al-Dosari, 7 September 1996)

Another Hawar islander describes the situation in similar terms:

> Many of the Hawar Islanders also had fish traps on the other [Hawar] islands. They would sail there to check the traps and put up makeshift shades. Janan Island and Hadd Janan were particularly rich in fish and many Hawar Islanders had fish traps there, including my father and Muhanna bin Hazeem from the South Village. (Salman Al-Dosari, 15 September 1996)

In the course of the 1938–39 adjudication, British officials referred to the territories under consideration as the Hawar Islands. No reservations with respect to Janan were at any point made by any of the participants in the adjudication, so Janan must necessarily have been included. This would explain, for instance, the British Political Agent's letter of 20 May 1938, notifying the Ruler of Bahrain of the Ruler of Qatar's claim, and describing the latter as having laid a "claim to the *Hawar Islands*" (Weightman, 20 May 1938a). [Emphasis added.] The

Political Agent also defined the scope of the dispute in the same terms when forwarding the Ruler of Qatar's claim to the Political Resident:

> ...in reply to the present communication from Shaikh Abdullah bin Qasim I should write and inform him that though the Bahrain Government possess a prima facie claim to *the Hawar group of islands* which is supported by their formal occupation *of them* for some time past, [Britain] would be prepared to give consideration to a formal claim by him.... (Weightman, 15 May 1938) [Emphasis added.]

The Foreign Office and the India Office also understood the scope of the dispute to be with respect to the Hawar group of islands:

> I am replying to your letter...in regard to the rival claims of the Sheikh of Qatar to the *Hawar group of islands*. (*Foreign Office Letter to India Office,* 12 July 1938, 1). [Emphasis added.]

The context of the adjudication—i.e., the oil concession negotiations of the 1930s—is also significant in this respect. As British officials were aware of the dangers of any unresolved territorial issues, they were careful to use the proper definitions to refer to territories estimated to contain oil deposits. As the person charged with monitoring the negotiations in the region, Hugh Weightman himself (the Political Agent) had numerous opportunities to review concession maps and draft agreements. Undoubtedly, he would have understood that "the Hawar group of islands" included Janan. Had he thought Janan should remain outside the scope of the 1939 award, he would have said so in his detailed analysis of the dispute between Qatar and Bahrain. Not only did Weightman make no such reservation with respect to Janan, he consistently referred to the group of islands as a whole throughout the proceedings. Thus his Report of 22 April 1939 stated:

> The small barren and uninhabited islands and rocky islets which form the complete *Hawar group* presumably fall to the authority of the Ruler establishing himself in the Hawar main island, particularly since marks have been erected on all of them by the Bahrain Government. (Weightman, 22 April 1939) [Emphasis added.]

The decision taken by the British government in July 1939 reflected the same general understanding:

> ...on the subject of the ownership of the Hawar Islands I am directed by His Majesty's government to inform you that, after careful consideration of the evidence adduced...they have decided that these Islands belong to the State of Bahrain and not to the State of Qatar. (Fowle, 11 July 1939; Fowle, 11 July 1939a)

Notably, the decision did not exclude any particular island.

The Gulf of Bahrain

As mentioned above, the northernmost island of the Hawar group is situated only 11 nautical miles from Ra's Al-Barr, the southern tip of Bahrain's main island. The intervening waters—the Gulf of Bahrain—contain several other islands (Halat Noon, Qasar Noon, Jazirat Mashtan and Al-Mu'tarid), distributed evenly between the main Bahrain island and the Hawar group. Moreover, the Gulf of Bahrain is very shallow; the depth is mostly less than 6 meters and rarely exceeds 9 meters.

Sheltered in the west by the main island of Bahrain and in the east by the western coast of the Qatar peninsula, and abundant in pearl oysters and fish, the eastern reaches of the Gulf of Bahrain have for many centuries been a major source of income for the Bahraini people. Hawar can be reached from the main island of Bahrain by helicopter in a few minutes. By motorboat the journey is less than an hour, and by sailboat the journey is no more than three or four hours. The main islands comprising Bahrain, the Hawar Islands and Zubarah can historically be seen as a socio-economic unit bound together by the waters of the Gulf of Bahrain.

While only 11 nautical miles of shallow sea separate the southern tip of Bahrain's main island at Ra's Al-Barr from the Hawar Islands, in comparison more than 80 kilometers of barren desert wasteland separate Doha from the Gulf of Bahrain and the Hawar Islands. The main island of Bahrain, the Zubarah region and the Hawar Islands have historically formed a triangle of populated territory under Bahraini sovereignty, interconnected by easy passage over the shallow waters of the Gulf of Bahrain.

Establishment of Al-Khalifa Authority

As has been described in previous chapters, the authority of the Al-Khalifa over the Bahrain Islands and the Qatar peninsula was recognized and maintained despite numerous external challenges and domestic problems. The arrival of the Ottomans in 1871 did curtail Al-Khalifa control over certain areas in the southeast of the peninsula. Yet no competing authority emerged in the north of Qatar, and the integrity of the socio-economic unit comprising the Gulf of Bahrain remained undisturbed. Not until 1937, when the Al-Thani forcibly acquired the Zubarah region, was the domination of the Al-Khalifa over northern Qatar formally questioned. Even then, the expansion of Al-Thani authority was not accompanied by the establishment of effective government or infrastructure anywhere in the north; only in the oil-rich Dukhan region on the western shore. The Hawar Islands and other numerous features of the Gulf of Bahrain remained—both formally and effectively—outside the scope of Al-Thani authority.

Arrival of the Dowasir

Historically, the Hawar Islands have been under Al-Khalifa control ever since 1783, when Sheikh Ahmed the Conqueror's forces expelled the Persian garrison from the main island of Bahrain. The establishment of Al-Khalifa authority on the Bahrain Islands marked the culmination of a stage of territorial expansion that resulted in the transformation of the entire Gulf of Bahrain into an Al-Khalifa dominion. As various population groups in the Qatar peninsula and the Bahrain Islands acknowledged the paramount authority of the Al-Khalifa family, what was to become the political unit of Bahrain acquired its territorial definition.

Soon after the incorporation of the Bahrain Islands into the territories under Al-Khalifa control, a branch of the Dowasir tribe from Al-Hasa on the Arabian mainland requested permission to settle on the Hawar Islands. Around 1800, such permission was granted by the Qadi of Zubarah. As the highest ranking religious and legal official of the Al-Khalifa family, the Qadi extended the Al-Khalifa's sanction to the Dowasir's presence on the Hawars—islands that were at the time already part of the Al-Khalifa's possessions.

This event marked the beginning of a typical ruler-benefactor alliance between the Al-Khalifa and the Dowasir. The Al-Khalifa confirmed their authority over the Hawars by permitting the Dowasir tribe—whose allegiance they thereafter claimed—to settle in their territories. For their part, the Dowasir acknowledged the Al-Khalifa as their rulers and became Al-Khalifa subjects. As with the Ruler of Bahrain's relationship with a number of tribes on the Bahrain Islands and the Qatar peninsula (described in Chapter 3), the coalition between the Al-Khalifa and the Dowasir was an example of indirect governance. As a tribe the Dowasir regarded the Hawars as their territory, while at the same time they recognized the Ruler of Bahrain's paramount political authority there. This state of affairs was reflected in a 1909 letter from Captain Prideaux, British Political Agent in Bahrain, to Major Cox, British Political Resident:

> ...the Dowasir especially as regards Hawar are inclined to consider themselves the independent owners on the strength of a century-old decision of a Kazi of Zubara (who however of course was an official under the Al Khalifa)...(F. B. Prideaux, 20 March 1909)

In another letter sent the same year, Prideaux described the situation similarly:

> ...the Dowasir regarded Hawar as their own independent territory, the ownership of this island having been awarded to the tribe by the Kazi of Zubara more than 100 years ago, in a written decision which they still preserve. (F. B. Prideaux, 4 April 1909)

Prideaux continued:

> ...as the Kazi of Zubarah was in those days an official of the Al Khalifa, the [main Hawar] island would seem to be a dependency of the mainland State, which the Chief of Bahrain still claims as morally and theoretically his. (F. B. Prideaux, 4 April 1909)

Thus, beginning in the early nineteenth century, the Dowasir became the main inhabitants of the Hawars. Following the approval of their settlement by the Al-Khalifa official at Zubarah, they established themselves on the islands, where their lives began to revolve around the typical economic activities in the region—pearling, fishing, and trading. Though they were not directly governed by an Al-Khalifa official, politically they remained a dependency of the Ruler of Bahrain. This fact was also recognized in the first comprehensive official British survey of the Arabian Gulf, conducted between 1821 and 1829 by Captain George Brucks, a British Indian Navy officer. About the Hawars—referred to as "Warden's Islands" at the time—Brucks observed:

> Warden's Islands is a group of eight or nine islands and rocks extending from lat. 25–46-25N, long. 50–55E to lat 25–33N, long 50–53-20E. The principal is called Al Howahk, and is about four miles long. It has two fishing villages on it, *and belongs to Bahrein*. (Brucks 1856, 563) [Emphasis added.]

This statement resulted from thorough research by Brucks, who shared the following in his introduction:

> ...What I have done is to try and place the situation, numbers and manners of the people I have visited, and who are little if at all known, in as clear a point of view as my information and abilities would permit.
>
> My information has been obtained in the following manner: I have proposed to the chiefs certain questions relative to the tribes, and their localities, of the revenues, trade, &c [etcetera] which I have noted, with their replies. This I have done to several other persons at different periods, and then taken such of the substance as appeared to agree the best...(Brucks 1856, 532)

Further Political Integration of the Dowasir

The middle of the nineteenth century saw the strengthening of the allegiance of the Dowasir to Bahrain. Indeed, their political relationship with the Ruler of Bahrain was reinforced in 1845, when the Dowasir were invited to settle also on the main Bahrain island. There they founded the towns of Budaiya and Zellaq on the west coast. As reported by Lorimer in his *Gazetteer*, at the beginning of the twentieth century, the Dowasir had a firmly established presence on the island:

> [The Dowasir] have now about 800 houses at Budaiya' and 200 at Zallaq, both places on the west side of the Bahrain Island. (Lorimer 1908–15, 2:391)

The Dowasir were not passive inhabitants, nor did they live in isolation from the rest of Bahraini society. Their economic activities and their loyalty to the Rulers of Bahrain allowed them to rise in political importance as well, and by the beginning of the twentieth century, they had become a significant political force in Bahrain. Lorimer noted in this respect:

> In Bahrain the Dowasir are the most numerous Sunn'i tribe after the Utub [Al Khalifa], and are the second of all the Bahrain tribes in political importance, being inferior in this respect to the Utub only. (Lorimer 1908–15, 2:391)

The close relations between the Al-Khalifa and the Dowasir were confirmed also by marriages between members of the ruling family and Dowasir families—including families from Hawar. One such case was reported by the British Political Agent, Captain Prideaux, in relation to a trip he took to Hawar in 1909. The British official described one of the localities on the main Hawar island as

> a collection of 40 large huts under the authority of a cousin of the tribal principal Shaikh. This individual is... related by marriage to Shaikh Isa bin Ali [the Ruler of Bahrain]. (F. B. Prideaux, 4 April 1909, 3)

Dowasir Patterns of Living and Economic Activities

Following their arrival on the Hawar Islands and later on the main Bahrain island, the Dowasir became not only part of the political entity of Bahrain, but also participants in Gulf economic activities. As the Bahrain Islands, the northern areas of the Qatar peninsula, and the numerous islands and islets in the Gulf of Bahrain constituted an integrated socio-economic unit, the Dowasir soon entered that complex web of social and commercial relations.

Logically, the main Bahrain island and the island of Muharraq were the focus of those relations, providing the main markets where produce from around the region was sold, and where basic supplies could be obtained. The Dowasir dhows often made the easy crossing to the main island of Bahrain—11 nautical miles (20.37 km) away—taking fish and gypsum from the Hawar Islands to sell on the markets. They returned with goods and supplies, particularly fresh water. This pattern of Hawar Islanders' commercial activity continued until the discovery of oil in the region.

Though the Dowasir moved freely back and forth from the Hawars to the markets of Manama and Muharraq and the settlements of Budaiya and Zellaq, they cultivated virtually no contacts with the inhabitants of eastern Qatar. To visit the settlements around Doha would have meant a 150-kilometer sail around the peninsula, or 80 kilometers across the barren and hostile desert. The Dowasir found little incentive to undertake such journeys—much less regular trips—because those settlements had little to offer compared with the expansive trading centers in the Gulf of Bahrain. Thus, the Hawars' inhabitants concentrated exclusively on developing their ties with the main Bahrain island and other centers in the Gulf of Bahrain.

Patterns and Evidence of Habitation

Seasonal Migration

The Dowasir's living patterns were shaped in response to seasonal economic activities in the Gulf of Bahrain. Following the invitation of Sheikh Mohammed bin Khalifa Al-Khalifa, the Ruler of Bahrain, to settle on Bahrain's main island, the Dowasir were able to follow the seasons and the resources of the Gulf while enjoying a settled pattern of life. They spent five months of the year on the main island of Bahrain during the pearling season, and the remainder of the year in regular habitation in their villages on the Hawar Islands. Despite their seasonal migration, the Dowasir were not nomads and their settlements on both the main Bahrain island and the main Hawar island were permanent in nature. As a former Hawar Islander related in his testimony submitted to the International Court of Justice:

> Everyone lived with their families and cattle and property on the Islands. They would come every year with their families, their servants and their belongings from Zellaq after the summer pearling season...

> ... I do not know exactly how long the Dowasir had been in the Hawar Islands. When I was a child, I served coffee in the Majlis [the village meeting place] to people who were 80 and 90 years old. They used to tell stories of living in the Hawar Islands when they were young. (Hamoud Al-Dosari, 7 September 1996 ¶ 6)

As the author of this statement is eighty years of age now and was referring to his childhood in the late 1920s or early 1930s, the approximate period to which the stories can be related is easily estimated as the mid-1800s.

Other testimonials provide further details of the seasonal migration of Hawar inhabitants. They would leave the main island of Bahrain and then sail from island to island until they reached the Hawars. The journey from their homes in Budaiya and Zellaq to their homes in Hawar was a routine part of their lives. Another former resident of the Hawar Islands, now resident in the main island of Bahrain, has described the Hawar Islanders' former traditional route thus:

> When we travelled from Zellaq to the Hawar Islands, we used to sail to Ra's al Barr on the southern tip of the main island of Bahrain and then towards the east until we reached Halat Noon, a very small island. After Halat Noon we sailed on to Al Mu'tarid. Then we sailed east until we arrived from a northerly direction at the two Rabad islands which are to the north of the main Hawar Island. We would pass to the west of the Rabad Islands and enter the main Hawar Island from a bay in the north. We would put a stick in the seabed to tie the dhows in the bay of the North Village because we didn't use anchors. (Al-Ghattam, 15 September 1996 ¶ 3)

The Dowasir were not the only permanent residents of the Hawars. Another prominent Bahraini family that lived on the islands was the Al-Ghattam. The ruins of their home in the North Village of the main Hawar island may still be seen.

The lifestyle of the islanders appears to have remained virtually unchanged from 1845 until the 1940s, when the oil era dramatically changed Bahrain society.

Evidence of Permanent Habitation

The Hawars contain physical evidence of permanent human habitation dating from the beginning of the nineteenth century to the present day. The remains of at least two villages can still be seen, one in the northern part of the main Hawar Island, another in the south. Remains of houses built of locally extracted gypsum are evident in both places.

The existence of the two villages is well documented. They were mentioned in Captain Brucks's survey of the Gulf of the 1820s, as well as in Lorimer's *Gazetteer* of 1908–15. In addition, numerous other sources provide descriptions of the villages that leave no doubt as to their permanent nature. One such description is contained in Bahrain's Counter-Claim in the course of the 1938–39 British adjudication (to be discussed in Chapter 18) concerning Hawar. That document referred to

> ...a long established settled community of Arabs living in permanent stone houses with their wives and families and their cattle, sheep and donkeys... The villages of Hawar consist of stone houses, permanent buildings not palm huts, built by Bahrain subjects. There are also in the various islands ancient stone cisterns constructed by the ancestors of the present inhabitants who were permitted to build them by the Shaikhs of Bahrain in the past. The inhabitants of Hawar reside there permanently keeping their goods and chattels in their houses and their boats, when not in use, on the shore of the islands. (Belgrave, 22 December 1938)

When in April 1939 Hugh Weightman, the British Political Agent, undertook a fact-finding mission to the Hawars, he also noted "two villages in the main Hawar Island... [which were] quite small villages, occupied by about 35 and 20 families respectively" (Weightman, 22 April 1939, 4). Weightman further reported that the families of the Hawar islanders lived

> ...in houses of the type known as "kubara," i.e. built of unfaced stone and held together with mud and roofed with date palm. These are definitely more permanent constructions than fishermen's "barasties" (palm huts) and some at least of them are occupied throughout the year. (Weightman, 22 April 1939, 4)

Having personally seen the physical evidence on the Hawars, Weightman then concluded:

> I am not able to state definitely that these Dawasir have for the past 150 years occupied Hawar at all seasons of the year, though those now in residence there claim that this is so. On the other hand the cemeteries, the water cisterns, the ruins of the old fort which I have myself seen and the type of house in use all provide evidence of consistent occupation for at least the greater part of the year. (Weightman, 22 April 1939, 8)

In 1995, a survey conducted by archeologist Professor Paolo Costa of the University of Bologna reached the same conclusions. Professor Costa's research revealed the existence of three ancient villages on Hawar—one in the north and two in the south. The North Village was estimated to have comprised about thirty houses and two mosques. It was established that the two villages in the south of the main Hawar island were smaller but also contained remains of mosques (Costa 1995).

In addition to the houses and mosques, Professor Costa noted no fewer than six cemeteries, including a children's cemetery. He also observed a large number of dams and water cisterns, animal-powered millstones, pottery shards, three gypsum quarries, and other evidence of human habitation. Professor Costa's findings led him to the following conclusion:

> I cannot refrain from expressing the belief that what results is definitely the picture of settled people and not of wandering fishermen or occasional visitors. (Costa 1995)

Water Supplies

The Hawar Islands had no natural water wells, but numerous water cisterns were used to retain rainwater. Lorimer noted this fact in his *Gazetteer*:

> [Jazirat Hawar is about] 10 miles long, north and south, and roughly parallel to the Qatar coast. There are no wells but there is a cistern to hold rainwater built by the Dawasir of Zellaq in Bahrain who have houses at two places on the island and use them in winter as shooting boxes... (Lorimer 1908–15, 2:399)

Cisterns were constructed throughout Hawar to catch and store water during the rainy season. These cisterns' design reflected the Hawar residents' ingenuity in collecting the precious liquid. Some of the eight cisterns to be found in Hawar were built at the confluence of natural drainage beds in order to obtain a maximum flow of water after a rainfall. One of the cisterns filtered water collected in another cistern, and the resulting drinking water was covered to prevent evaporation. Also, in the southern part of Hawar a dam was built to control the flow of water.

Many islanders also used the water tanks of their pearling boats as water cisterns for their families. When water supplies ran low, water was brought and bartered by the fish merchants from Muharraq when they came to the islands to pick up fish to take to market. Bahrainis still living who grew up and lived on the Hawar Islands recall:

> When there was not enough water in the cisterns, the boats which would come from the islands of Bahrain and Muharraq to pick up the fish to take to market would bring water. They would usually go to Muharraq to a place called Halat Abu Mahir, where there was a spring called Ain Fakhro to bring supplies of fresh water in the tanks. Additionally, if we were fishing near the west coast of the Qatar peninsula we would go to Zekrit. There was a spring there where we could get fresh water. (Hamoud Al-Dosari, 7 September 1996 ¶ 16)

Thus, from about 1800, when members of the Dowasir tribe obtained permission from the Qadi of Zubarah to settle on the Hawar Islands, occupation by Bahraini subjects has been open and continuous. No rival presence has appeared there at any time. Consequently, Bahrain has exercised more than the contextually appropriate level of occupation required by international law in the Hawar Islands, while Qatar has exercised none.

Economic Activities

The Hawar Islanders depended for their living mainly on the resources of the sea. As elsewhere in the Gulf of Bahrain, their primary occupations were fishing and pearling. In addition, considering the significant deposits of gypsum on the islands, gypsum mining was an important economic activity. Fish, pearls, and gypsum were thus the main commodities that enabled the Dowasir to participate in economic interactions with other tribes of the Gulf of Bahrain.

Fishing

Fishing was the Hawar Islanders' most important traditional source of income. The waters of the Gulf were rich in resources, and the markets of Manama and Muharraq, where the islanders sold their catch, were only a short boat ride to the north.

As the settlements on the Hawar Islands were permanent, so were the fishing nets that the inhabitants of the Hawars built off the islands. Thus, a 1938 affidavit sworn by Hawar islanders offered the following description:

> We have our fishing nets built of stones from long built by our fathers, grandfathers and their predecessors which we are repairing when there is a need for such repair [*sic*]. These are in addition to the temporary nets which we put up in Hawar sea near our houses for fishing during the fishing season. (Belgrave, 22 December 1938)

This affidavit was given in the course of the adjudication initiated by Britain following Qatar's first claim to the Hawar Islands. Qatar was seeking at that time to present Hawar islanders as itinerant fishermen who occasionally used the islands for shelter, but Bahrain then further stated in its Counter-Claim:

> …the fishermen who are referred to [by Qatar] are some of the inhabitants of Hawar who live in the islands and who go fishing from their home [on the Hawar Islands] bringing back their fish to Hawar or sometimes sending it to Manama for sale. (Belgrave, 22 December 1938, 2)

The central role of fishing in the life of Hawar communities is further revealed by the testimonials of former Hawar Islanders submitted to the International Court of Justice. One such islander, a Dowasir man who had spent his childhood on Hawar, stated:

> I earned my livelihood from the sea. During the winter we would fish using fish traps and nets. If the weather was good, fish traders would come from Muharraq and the main island of Bahrain to buy the fresh fish. The traders would buy it straight off the pier, fill up their boats and take it back to sell in Muharraq. They would often bring provisions which we could not get in Hawar such as

> lemons, coffee and rice which we would trade for our fish. If the weather was bad, everyone—the men, the women, the servants, the children—would clean the fish and when it had dried we would store it in straw sacks that had been used previously for dates. Everyone used to help each other. Then we would take it and sell it in Muharraq for one or two rupees. (Hamoud Al-Dosari, 7 September 1996, ¶ 18)

Another former Hawar resident recalls:

> Our livelihoods on the islands depended on our fish traps, nets and God...At the end of winter and the beginning of spring, the fish season is at its best. Many types of fish such as safi, janam, subaitis, hammour and faskar were available in abundance in the Hawar Islands. (Nasr Al-Dosari, 16 September 1996 ¶ 16)

As well as in the waters off the main Hawar island, fishing also took place in the vicinity of the smaller islands in the Hawar group, such as Janan and Hadd Janan:

> Many of the Hawar Islanders also had fish traps on the other islands. They would sail there to check the traps and put up makeshift shades. Janan Island and Hadd Janan were particularly rich in fish and many Hawar islanders had fish traps there, including my father and Muhanna bin Hazeem from the South Village. (Salman Al-Dosari, 15 September 1996 ¶ 7)

Pearling

Pearling was another traditional occupation of the Hawar Islanders. Those who earned their livelihood from fishing, animal husbandry, and gypsum mining in the winter months typically participated in pearling activities during the summer season. That situation remained unchanged until the decline of the pearling industry following the development by the Japanese of cultured pearls in the 1930s (Crystal 1990, 116–117).

Pearling season in the Gulf began in May, when the boats belonging to pearling families would leave their harbors and head for the offshore pearl banks. The Dowasir were among the best-known pearlers in the region, and those who lived on the Hawars were both owners of pearling dhows and regular participants in the pearling trade. In the words of one:

> There were many boats of the Dowasir that would go pearling. The pearling captains from the North Village were Ali bin Thamer, Mohammed bin Ahmad, Rashid bin Mohammed and his brothers Saad and Majid. They all had pearling dhows. The families of Hassan bin Thamer, Bumaid, Khalifa bin Juma, Sabah bin Snan all dived for pearls. Even the Al-Ghatam, who were not Dowasir, dived for pearls. From the South Village, Rahma bin Rashid had three or four large dhows with 150 to 250 men. One of his assistants was Muhanna bin Hazeem. Saeed bin Rashid also had boats. (Hamoud Al-Dosari, 7 September 1996 ¶ 20)

The importance of pearling as a traditional occupation of the permanent inhabitants of Hawar was noted also by Hugh Weightman, the British Political Agent, who made a visit to the Hawars. Weightman noted the pearling boats near the Northern Village and drew the following conclusion:

> ...were the Dawasir purely temporary visitors to the island, with their permanent habitations in Zellaq, their pearling boats would not be beached in Hawar. (Weightman, 22 April 1939, 6)

Animal Husbandry

Though the survival of Hawar islanders depended on the sea in large measure, conditions on the Hawars allowed animal husbandry to develop as yet another traditional occupation. While men were away fishing or pearling, women took responsibility for the animals. The small size of the islands, the flat terrain and the existence of sufficient vegetation made it easy for local inhabitants to graze their animals:

> We also kept cattle, sheep, goats, cows and donkeys. The cattle wandered the island without any shepherds. They would eat the vegetation and come back to the village by themselves. There was good pasture in the winter, better than in the main island of Bahrain. (Al-Ghattam, 15 September 1996 ¶ 13)

In his 1939 Report, Weightman, the British Political Agent observed as follows:

> After good rain the island provides better pasturage than Bahrain itself and even this year, when the rain was very late, there are still

to-day between 50 and 100 animals in Hawar. (Weightman, 22 April 1939, 5)

In times of water shortages on the Hawar Islands, animals were occasionally sent to the main Bahrain island (Weightman, 22 April 1939, 5).

In addition to making use of natural conditions on their island, local inhabitants also made efforts to increase the available pasture area. To this end, they built a number of dams in various areas of the main Hawar island, thus creating basins that improved the quality of grazing grounds. As suggested by archeologist Professor Costa, the additional yield thus obtained would have enabled the production of dry fodder for the animals (Costa 1995, 10).

Gypsum Extraction

The gypsum rock found in Hawar was an important natural resource furnishing yet another source of income for Hawar residents. Hawar gypsum was quarried throughout the nineteenth and twentieth centuries and was used in construction on the Hawar Islands, the main Bahrain island and Muharraq island.

Hawar had three extraction sites. One in particular yielded considerable quantities of gypsum and provided material mainly for export to the rest of Bahrain. As explained in Professor Costa's report:

> Of the three, the two smaller quarries of about 2 hectares are located close to areas where there are buildings which required plastering: the gypsum was therefore quarried mainly for local use: the third quarry, on the contrary, is very large in size (over 10 hectares) and lies far from local settlements. It seems clear that the exploitation of this quarry does not depend upon local demand and that the gypsum was extracted to be used elsewhere. (Costa 1995, 16–17)

Typically, gypsum was brought from Hawar to the main island of Bahrain and used in the construction of traditional houses. A fine example of such a building is Sheikh Isa bin Ali's palace in Muharraq; this was built in the mid-nineteenth century and features intricate gypsum detailing (*Recent Photographs of the Hawar Islands,* 138). As His Highness Sheikh Hamad bin Isa Al-Khalifa himself observed:

Visitors to Bahrain remark on the beauty of our traditional buildings. The best gypsum for these buildings came from Hawar. . . Our government issued licenses for gypsum extraction in the Hawar Islands beginning in the early part of the 20th century. (Bahrain 1996, 205–206 ¶ 456–457)

15 | Bahrain Authority as Manifested in Hawar

The Al-Khalifa's exercise of jurisdiction over the Hawar Islands from the beginning of the nineteenth century was uninterrupted and exclusive. The local population—belonging mainly to the Dowasir tribe—was subject to Bahrain and was continuously present on the islands following the granting of permission to settle by the Qadi of Zubarah (an official of the Al-Khalifa family) in about 1800. Not only did Hawar inhabitants owe their allegiance and their right to reside in Bahrain to the Al-Khalifa, they were also subject to the operation of Bahrain laws and regulations. Governmental authority was continuously displayed on the islands, and every significant aspect of Hawar residents' activities was regulated in accordance with local custom.

The Dowasir were subject to the same degree of Al-Khalifa regulation as were other pearling and fishing communities on the Bahrain Islands. On the local level, the tribal Sheikh was the main authority, responsible for the organization of tribal—most notably, economic—activities. Despite relaxed government control, however, the paramount authority of the Al-Khalifa was recognized and affirmed on numerous occasions. As the social and political system of Bahrain evolved, a trend toward expanded central regulation of all aspects of local affairs emerged.

Affirmation of Al-Khalifa Authority

The Rulers of Bahrain affirmed their authority over the Hawar Islands on numerous occasions. They are recorded to have made annual visits to the islands as far back as the nineteenth century. During one such visit (in 1873) by Sheikh Isa bin Ali, some passing Ottoman soldiers were shipwrecked there. The Ruler ordered that they be transferred to the main island of Bahrain and from there, onward to their intended destination. The Ruler acted as the highest authority on Hawar by extending his help to the shipwrecked seamen, and by arranging for their evacuation via his capital on the main Bahrain island (Belgrave, 22 December 1938, 7).

No authority related to the settlements around Doha ever visited the Hawar Islands in a Ruler's capacity. The first recorded visit of a Ruler of Qatar anywhere close to the Hawar Islands took place in 1938, when the then-Ruler on an inspection tour visited the new oil works in Zekrit in the west of the Qatar peninsula (Pilkington, 29 May 2000, 61 ¶ 82). No records exist of any contact between the Hawar Islanders and the people of Doha. In their testimonies submitted to the International Court of Justice, Hawar residents uniformly denied that any such contact ever took place:

> I never heard about any Al-Thani ever coming to Qatar. No-one from Qatar ever lived or settled on the main Hawar island. (Salman Al-Dosari, 15 September 1996 ¶ 10)

> No one from the Qatar peninsula ever came to visit or settle in Hawar. (Nasr Al-Dosari, 16 September 1996 ¶ 23)

> No-one ever left the Hawar Islands to go to Qatar. There was no reason to leave Bahrain. I never heard of a Qatari coming to the Hawar Islands. No Qatari person or anyone with any allegiance other than to Bahrain and the Al-Khalifa ever had houses on the Hawar islands, lived there, fished there, or visited there. (Hamoud Al-Dosari, 7 September 1996 ¶ 29)

In contrast, the Hawar Islanders consistently displayed their awareness of being Bahraini subjects, and they readily affirmed the paramount authority of the Al-Khalifa. For instance, they found ways to fly the Ruler's flag though the islands had no proper flagstaff before the police fort was built in 1937–38:

> We always considered ourselves to be part of Bahrain. We had the Bahraini flag even before the fort was built. We didn't have a flag pole but on special occasions, such as Eidd, we would fly the

Bahraini flag over the houses and on the dhows. (Al-Ghattam, 15 September 1996 ¶ 17)

The same former Hawar resident further describes the festivities on Hawar as follows:

> I also enjoyed many Eidd festivals in Hawar. During the Eidd, we would fly the flag of Bahrain from the dhow and the roofs of the houses and the young children would wear daggers and someone would beat the drum for them. (Al-Ghattam, 15 September 1996 ¶ 11)

Regulation of Economic Activities

For most of the nineteenth century, the inhabitants of the Hawar Islands enjoyed virtual autonomy in their commercial activities. The tribe was the primary unit for the organization of economic life, and Rulers of Bahrain exercised little centralized supervision over the actions of local inhabitants. Hawar Islanders' exchanges with the Bahrain Islands were determined by economic forces and by family and tribal ties rather than by centrally imposed rules.

The beginning of the twentieth century, however, was marked by increased government involvement in the economic activities of Bahrainis. As political and social structures became more complex, the need for standardization became more acute. New rules were introduced, and major economic activities were gradually brought under formal regulation.

Fishing

Fishing rights were originally granted to the Hawar islanders by the Ruler of Bahrain (Belgrave, 29 May 1938, 1). Other than that, however, no direct Al-Khalifa regulation was enforced controlling the fishing activities of the islanders—just as there was generally no regulation over the fishing activities of any Bahrainis. The abundance of fish in the waters around the Hawars and the well-functioning channels of economic interaction between the Hawar Islands and the Bahrain Islands provided for the efficient operation of the fishing industry.

Though the everyday fishing activities off the Hawars followed no centrally imposed pattern, the islanders were subject to the same registration procedures that applied to all Bahrainis. Thus, permanent fish traps were registered in the Land Department of the Bahrain government similarly to "all other fish traps in Bahrain waters" (Belgrave, 29 May 1938, 4).

Hawar Islanders also recognized the Bahrain government as the relevant authority able to represent them or assist them in resolving their problems and occasional conflicts related to fishing activities. The active protection of the Bahrain government was manifested on a number of occasions. For instance, the Bahrain government complained in January 1938 about the theft of fish from the traps of Hawar Islanders: in a letter addressed to the Manager of Petroleum Concessions Limited, the people suspected of the theft were advised "to steer well clear of the traps" (Belgrave, 31 January 1938).

Hawar islanders also relied on the Ruler of Bahrain to resolve their disputes over fishing rights or fish traps. Consistent with the pattern of authority described in Chapter 3, they first referred such disputes to their tribal elder, and if no solution could be reached, to the Ruler himself:

> If two Dowasir men in the Hawar islands had a dispute they went to the tribal elder to solve it. If he did not solve it, they went to our Ruler, Sheikh Isa bin Ali or his descendants and asked him to solve it. The disputes were usually about fishing rights and fish traps. (Hamoud Al-Dosari, 7 September 1996 ¶ 24)

Pearling

As mentioned in Chapter 3, pearling was an industry that throughout Bahrain was only indirectly regulated by the Al-Khalifa. The Dowasir, as one of the major pearling tribes of the Gulf, had in place an elaborate organization and managed their economic activities tribally. The Al-Khalifa provided them with pearling rights, but did not interfere in their economic affairs. Throughout the nineteenth century, no license fees or taxes on the catch were imposed anywhere in Bahrain; as a result, the development of the pearling industry was strongly stimulated, and export taxes as well as a variety of other sales dues payable to the Rulers of Bahrain were maximized (Khuri 1980, 66).

However, the drive toward increased government involvement at the beginning of the twentieth century led to the introduction of more uniform economic practices in Bahrain. The complex system of contracts and debts that formed the basis of relations between different people engaged in the pearling industry came under government regulation. Particular emphasis was placed on the protection of the pearl divers' interests, and a requirement was introduced that pearl boat captains record the accounts of every diver in a special book. General record-keeping standards for pilots were also established (Khuri 1980, 106–8).

Naturally, the inhabitants of the Hawars—like other Bahrainis—were affected by the new regulations. The government of Bahrain distributed diving books to the divers and log books to the captains. As a former Hawar resident recalled:

> Every diver had a log book and the log books were issued by the Bahrain Government. The log book kept a record of the diver's name, credits, debits and possessions. When the time came for diving, we submitted our log books and after we returned they checked out how much we owed or were owed. If there were no debts, the diver was given a release and was free to stay with the Captain or to go to work for somebody else. (Hamoud Al-Dosari, 7 September 1996 ¶ 21)

The requirements related to the registration of pearl boats were also standardized. A system was introduced whereby boat certificates were to be validated annually by the Bahrain government. The registration formalities were described by another former Hawar islander as follows:

> The boats used by the Hawar Islanders were registered in Bahrain. The registration books were called "passes." They were issued by Saad bin Samra, a Bahrain Government official, who would charge 100 rupee per dhow. No dhow could leave Bahrain for the pearling banks without a pass. (Al-Ghattam, 15 September 1996 ¶ 23)

Gypsum Extraction

The government of Bahrain also regulated gypsum extraction on the Hawars. As quarrying significantly increased in volume in the 1920s, so did the government of Bahrain's regulation of the industry.

Some of the measures taken by the government were in response to specific requests made by the Hawar Islanders themselves. Typically, local inhabitants' complaints had to do with the increased quarrying perceived as taking place too close to their villages, and therefore disturbing their families. As one former Hawar resident recalls,

> ... the older Dowasir complained that there was too much gypsum cutting near the homes and the women. (Hamoud Al-Dosari, 7 September 1996 ¶ 23)

The islanders were also concerned that the quarrying would deplete their gypsum resources too quickly. As a result, the government of Bahrain imposed a requirement that gypsum quarrying on the Hawar Islands could be carried out only under a license issued by the government. The same Hawar Islander explained in his testimony submitted to the International Court of Justice:

> ... the Bahrain Government regulated the cutting by requiring the cutters to carry permits. The permits were issued by the Bahrain Chief of Police, Sheikh Khalifa bin Mohammed. He used to stay on the main Hawar Island in the police fort and meet the Dowasir. He issued the permits after there had been several quarrels. Only people who had a permit were allowed to cut the gypsum. (Hamoud Al-Dosari, 7 September 1996 ¶ 23)

This licensing system was recorded in a 1939 report from the British Political Agent to the Political Resident (Weightman, 22 April 1939, 5). Charles Belgrave, the Adviser to the Bahrain government, mentioned it on a number of occasions (Belgrave, 29 May 1938). Furthermore, Bahraini government officials consistently documented the regulation of gypsum quarrying on the Hawar Islands. The *Annual Report of the Government of Bahrain, March 1937–February 1938,* for instance, described the manner in which gypsum was brought from Hawar to the main island of Bahrain and Muharraq Island for construction there, by boats working as ferries, before the construction of the Manama-Muharraq causeway:

> ... small sailing boats [based on the main island of Bahrain and on Muharraq Island] ... bring building stone from the reefs out at sea and [gypsum] from Hawar. (*Annual Report of the Government of Bahrain, March 1937–February 1938,* 16)

Public Works and Services

In addition to regulating economic activities, the government of Bahrain provided a number of services related to the welfare of Hawar residents.

Due to the absence of natural water springs on the Hawars, water was collected in cisterns built by local inhabitants or sometimes brought from the Bahrain Islands. In the 1930s, the Bahrain government made efforts to establish permanent local drinking water supplies on the Hawars. The government began drilling for water on the Hawars in 1937, and commissioned a number of subsequent surveys of the islands (Weightman, 15 May 1938, 1; Fripp, 10 August 1941, 1; PCL, 30 June 1939, 2). In 1939, BAPCO, the Bahrain oil concessionaire, undertook further geological mapping of the islands under the authority of the government (Fripp, 10 August 1941). The government also maintained existing dams, and in 1938 and 1939 made structural repairs to the water cisterns (*Expenditure Summary for the Government of Bahrain for 1358H [1939]*, 4).

The residents of Hawar also relied on the government of Bahrain to reconstruct old buildings on the islands. A number of damaged houses were thus repaired at the request of local inhabitants (Hamoud Al-Dosari, 7 September 1996 ¶ 8). The government's activities on the Hawars also typically involved constructing new buildings and facilities. From 1937–38, a fort, a pier and a police post were constructed on the Hawars (*Annual Report of the Government of Bahrain, March 1937–February 1938*, 16–17; PCL, 30 June 1939, 2).

In 1939, a new mosque was built in the North Village on the orders of the Ruler of Bahrain (PCL, 30 June 1939; *Expenditure Summary for the Government of Bahrain for 1358H [1939]*, 8). Before, the residents of the Hawar Islands had had only prayer walls and unroofed mosques. A former Hawar Islander recalled the earlier mosque in the North Village "which had been built, like the houses, out of the local gypsum stones" (Hamoud Al-Dosari, 7 September 1996 ¶ 9). A former resident of the South Village also recalled a small open-air mosque in his village (Nasr Al-Dosari, 16 September 1996 ¶ 4).

> Due to the small size of the Hawars' population, no schools or hospitals existed on the islands. Hawar residents used the medical facilities on the Bahrain Islands, and their children were educated in Bahraini schools. It is notable that those facilities were

located in the main population centers of Manama and Muharraq and—until the late 1940s–early 1950s, when the first schools and hospitals were built in Qatar—were also used by the inhabitants of the peninsula, including members of Qatar's Ruling family. (Volterra, 28 June 2000, 47–48 ¶ 54–59)

Judicial Authority

Residents of the Hawar Islands stood under the civil and criminal jurisdiction of the courts of Bahrain. As already mentioned, tribal elders settled minor disputes among islanders, while more serious ones were referred to the Ruler of Bahrain. For his part, the Ruler referred the disputes to the relevant courts, whose *Qadi*'s were officials under his authority.

The majority of the disputes concerned land and fishing rights. One example was the case between four Hawar Islanders, decided in 1909 by the *Qadi* (Islamic Court System Judge) of the Sharia Court in Bahrain. In the judgment the *Qadi*, Sharaf bin Ahmad, stated as follows:

> Be it known that Ahmad bin Shahin Dosari and Bati bin Salman and Jabr bin Muhanna and Hamad bin Saeed have appeared before me and disputed the ownership of land and sea properties in Hawar. Ahmad bin Shahin claimed these to be his property inherited from fathers and forefathers; Jabr and Bati claimed them to be their properties and that they held document.... (Sharaf bin Ahmad, 1909)

In another case, in 1910, the judgment of the Court begins:

> By the order of Shaikh Abdulla bin Isa Al Khalifah, Ahmad bin Shahin Dosari and Isa bin Ahmad Dosari appeared before me in a dispute about land and sea properties in Hawar.... (Sharaf bin Ahmad, 1910)

The judgment was sealed by the Ruler of Bahrain, Sheikh Abdulla bin Isa Al-Khalifa, and signed by Judge Sharaf bin Ahmad. Both judgments show clearly that the Hawar Islanders recognized and accepted the authority of Bahrain courts, and thus, also the authority of the Al-Khalifa.

Further evidence of Bahrain's exercise of judicial authority over the Hawar Islands can be found in official 1911 British records. These records tell of a request from the British Political Agent to the Ruler of Bahrain to compel a resident of the Hawar Islands, Isa bin Ahmad Al-Dosari, to appear before the courts in a civil case. Responding to the British request, the Ruler stated that he would ensure the islander's presence if it was required (Isa bin Ali Al-Khalifa, 15 January 1911).

That subpoena powers were exercised by both the Ruler of Bahrain and the Bahrain courts over the Hawar islanders can be demonstrated once again from a 1931 case involving a Hawar resident who failed to appear before the court when summoned. To compel the defendant to attend the case, the court turned to the Ruler of Bahrain, "informing him of the case and asking him to order his servant to produce [the] defendant from Hawar" (*Particulars of Case no. 264/1351*, 1932). An order was issued, and the Bahrain police were finally directed to produce the defendant from the Hawars (*Bahrain Court Record for Case no. 264/1351*, 1932).

Court records also contain information of another case from 1932 where the parties were cited as follows:

> Plaintiff: Hamad bin Jasim *of Bahraini origin, living in Hawar, a Bahraini subject*
>
> Defendant: Ali bin Thamir *of Bahraini origin and living in Hawar, a Bahraini subject (Bahrain Court Record for Case no. 264/1351, 1932)* [Emphasis added.]

Yet another case concerning fish traps in the Hawar Islands was heard by the Bahrain Sharia Court in 1939. The case was mentioned by both the British Political Agent in his 1939 report in the form of a letter on the ownership of the Hawar Islands and by the Adviser to the Bahrain government (Weightman, 22 April 1939, 6; Belgrave, 20 April 1939).

Law Enforcement, Defense and Regulation of Immigration

As the Hawars were considered an integral part of Bahrain, Bahraini laws naturally applied to the islands and were enforced as a matter of course. To the islanders, the laws were announced by public displays of official proclamations (Belgrave, 22 December 1938, 6; Belgrave, 29 May 1938, 3). Violations of the laws were punished and Bahrain's *fidawi*'s (members of a sheikh's staff concerned with keeping law and order), *nature*'s (a type of civil police), notice servers, and police on the islands insured the appearance of malefactors before the authorities of the government of Bahrain on Muharraq island and the main Bahrain island (Bahrain 1996, 1:217 ¶ 479; Belgrave, 29 May 1938, 3).

The Adviser to the Government of Bahrain confirmed this fact in a 1938 note:

> Recently, in connection with a quarrel between some of the people in Hawar, the Bahrain police had occasion to make several arrests in Hawar and to produce the persons in the Bahrain Court. (Belgrave, 28 April 1936, 203)

In certain cases, the police themselves would simply take action and then appraise the courts of events on the islands. Such a case occurred, for instance, in 1936, concerning a violation of property rights over fishing grounds. In the conclusion of the Memorandum addressed by the Bahrain Police Directorate to the Bahrain Courts, the following was stated:

> Having informed you thus, we leave the matter to you. Hajj Abbas, Chief of Police. (Abbas, 14 April 1936)

A postscript at the bottom of the Memorandum further indicated that:

> The two parties were present and we informed them that the fishing areas were not theirs this year. We said that if they caused a problem, the Court would lock them all up and that if any of them had a petition to make, he should present it and the Courts would look into it. (Abbas, 14 April 1936)

Before a regular police force was institutionalized in the late 1930s, guards appointed by the Ruler of Bahrain policed the Hawars. A former Hawar resident born in the 1920s recalls:

> When I was young, I used to help the guards of the islands before the police fort was built. We were acting under the authority of Sheikh Hamad, the Ruler of Bahrain. We used a small straw hut on the shore just north of the North Village. We would check that the gypsum cutters who used to come from the main island of Bahrain had a valid permit issued by the government of Bahrain. The other guards were Rahma bin Rashid, Muhanna bin Hazeem,

> Abdullah bin Hazeem, Hazeem bin Muhanna, Hamad bin Mohammed, Mohammed bin Irhama, Afoor and his father, Faris and my father Makki. Rahma had a boat which was armed with a gun, which he would use to guard the islands. When I recently returned to the main Hawar Island I was able to recognise the spot where the guard hut used to be. (Nasr Al-Dosari, 16 September 1996 ¶ 19)

Another former resident of Hawar testified:

> The Ruler of Bahrain appointed local guards to keep watch over the coast. They kept a guard post on the coast until the Bahrain Government built the police fort just outside the North Village ...I remember one policeman who spent over 40 years on Hawar. His name was Juma. He was a Baluchi. He also used to tend to fishing traps on Braiber Head with the villagers from the North Village. (Hamoud Al-Dosari, 7 September 1996 ¶ 10)

In 1937–38, the Government of Bahrain established a police fort on the islands. That event, a response to developments in Zubarah reflecting the Bahrain government's fears of Qatar's expansionist ambitions, marked the beginning of a regular police presence on the Hawar Islands (Belgrave, 22 December 1938, 2; Belgrave, 19 August 1937). As the government explained, the fort "would be of military use in case of any emergency" (*Annual Report of the Government of Bahrain, March 1937–February 1938,* 16). Regular visits to the Hawars by Sheikh Khalifa bin Mohammed, the head of the Bahrain Police, commenced in the same year (Al-Ghattam, 15 September 1996 ¶ 19). In the summer of the following year, the fort was reinforced by stationing two full sections of soldiers there, to be rotated every fifteen days (Belgrave, 24 May 1938).

Following Qatar's armed attack on Zubarah, regulation of immigration into the Hawar Islands became stricter. Access by Qataris and other "foreigners" into the islands was forbidden, and the Chief Police Officer stationed on the Hawars was instructed as follows:

> On no account are any people, European or Arab, from Qattar coast to be allowed on any of the Hawar Islands. You are warned that there are people working opposite Hawar on shore and should

anyone land on Hawar islands you will be held responsible. (Belgrave, 10 November 1937)

These instructions were strictly observed. In the summer of 1938, when a Qatari attempted to land on Hawar in order to reclaim a boat that had earlier beached there, he was arrested and sent to the main Bahrain island. In the Ruler of Qatar's complaint, addressed to the British Political Resident, the incident was described as follows:

> [T]he residents of Hawar arrested and assaulted [the Qatari]... and took him to Bahrain where he was kept in prison for one day. (Abdullah bin Jasim Al-Thani, 8 July 1938)

Though Qatar had by the time of its Ruler's compliance already made its first claim to the Hawar Islands, it was clear that the Ruler of Qatar himself did not equate the residents of the islands to Qatari subjects—and he was well aware of their allegiance to the Ruler of Bahrain. For their part, the Government of Bahrain confirmed their jurisdiction in this case and explained that the Qatari had been "sent to Bahrain by the NCO in charge of Howar Fort for interrogation by the [Government of Bahrain's] Adviser after which he [had been] returned to Qatar" (Acting Adviser to Government of Bahrain, 17 July 1938).

A similar incident occurred later that summer: two Qataris landed on Hawar, only to be seized and sent under arrest to the main Bahrain island (PCL, 27 September 1938). The Ruler of Qatar took the matter up with the British Political Agent and protested that his two subjects had approached the Hawars "in order to make enquiries or to take water. The people of Hawar [had] suddenly arrested them in an awkward manner without hearing their statement or enquiring into their business and [had taken] them to Bahrain" (Abdullah bin Jasim Al-Thani, 12 July 1938, 1).

The Ruler of Qatar continued by comparing this incident to a hypothetical situation in which Bahraini ships might be seized on the Qatari coast (Abdullah bin Jasim Al-Thani, 12 July 1938, 1). Thus, though Qatar's Ruler expressed his dissatisfaction with the manner in which his subjects had been treated, he also acknowledged that the Hawars were under the Ruler of Bahrain's jurisdiction, as much as the Qatar coast was under his own authority. Significantly, in his letter the Ruler of Qatar described Hawar Islanders as the "people" and the "residents" of Hawar, thus recognizing both their permanent presence on the islands and the fact that their status differed from that of his subjects.

The Dowasir Incident

During 1923 a number of administrative and institutional reforms were introduced in Bahrain. These reforms represented changes from a "traditional" regime, and were to comprise the cornerstone of the new state bureaucracy. Among the measures introduced were: reorganization of the Customs Department, the drawing up of a Civil List, and implementation of a more egalitarian tax system (Khuri 1980, 88–107).

The Dowasir, loyal subjects of the Ruler of Bahrain, but also accustomed to a significant degree of autonomy, resisted the reforms. They particularly objected to the introduction of new pearling and other taxes applicable to all citizens of Bahrain, as the Dowasir had previously been exempt from direct taxation under the old regime. For the Dowasir, the new reforms meant the end of important economic privileges.

Trying to pressure the Ruler of Bahrain to stop the reforms, the Dowasir threatened to remove themselves from Bahrain. The Ruler, however, stood firm, and in early November 1923 a large section of the Dowasir left Bahrain, led by their chief, Ahmad bin Abdullah Al-Dosari. Most of those who left stayed away for about three and a half years; some were absent for a few years longer.

But their departure from Bahrain weakened them economically and politically. Additionally, the hardships they endured in their new settlement at Dammam—most notably, the imposition on them of *zakat* by the Wahhabi Amir—soon forced them to reconsider their position. In 1926, they appealed to the Ruler of Bahrain for permission to return to their base in Budaiya. The Ruler, Sheikh Hamad, who had never fully broken relations with the Dowasir, decided after some negotiations to allow them to return in March 1927.

The Dowasir returned to Bahrain under certain specific government-imposed conditions. They agreed to continue to recognize the authority of the Ruler of Bahrain, and of Bahraini legal and law enforcement authorities. They also agreed to pay taxes and accepted the Ruler of Bahrain's authority to nominate and remove their headmen. Moreover, they relinquished any claims to privileged status within Bahrain. They stated their acceptance of the Ruler of Bahrain's conditions in an express and public manner. On 27 March 1927, the British Political Resident, Lt.–Col. Haworth, described the meeting he had with Dowasir about their return:

> I informed them [the Dowasir] categorically that the whole matter rested with their acceptance of the laws of the country, that as long as they realized that they were as subject to law as any other person in Bahrain and had no privileged position Shaikh Hamad would naturally be glad to see them back in Bahrain. They accepted the condition without reserve and the interview ended amicably. (Haworth, 27 March 1927)

Having affirmed the authority of the Ruler of Bahrain and once again subjected themselves to the jurisdiction of the Bahrain government, the Dowasir returned to their homes on the main Bahrain island and the Hawar Islands. Their reintegration into Bahrain society was evidenced by their renewed participation in the political and social life of Bahrain. Many of them became distinguished figures in Bahrain's public life, including, for example, Yusuf bin Rahmah, who headed the Amiri Court for thirty years, and the remains of whose father's house can still be seen in the South Village of Hawar. Another prominent Bahraini was Abdullah bin Jabor Al-Dosari, secretary to Sheikh Hamad bin Isa Al-Khalifa in the 1930s (Volterra, 13 June 2000, 30 ¶ XVII)

16 British and Ottoman Recognition of Bahrain's Authority over the Hawars

As discussed in Chapter 14, the sovereignty of the Ruler of Bahrain over the Hawar Islands was exercised through the Bahraini Dowasir who lived in permanent settlements on both the Hawars and the main Bahrain island. The Hawars were continuously occupied by the Dowasir and governed by the Al-Khalifa and the Bahrain government. This fact was recognized not only by Bahrain authorities and the residents of the Hawars, but also by outside powers who had a presence in the Gulf at various times during the last two centuries. Among such powers, Britain and the Ottoman Empire were the most prominent players, and their involvement in the Gulf led them to take an acute interest in any territorial issue in the region.

British and Ottoman Recognition

Britain's Position (Nineteenth Century)

As the paramount power in the Gulf, Britain was involved not only in regulating relations among the sheikhdoms in the region, but also in supervising a variety of their domestic issues. The degree of its involvement was determined mainly by its concern with the safety of navigation in the Gulf, and—following the Ottomans' arrival on the Qatar peninsula—also by the maintenance of British political control over the remaining territories in the region. While Britain did not pursue a policy of active expansion into mainland Arabia, developments in those areas were closely monitored by the British government.

Throughout the eighteenth and nineteenth centuries, British authorities expressed no specific opinion as to the ownership of the Hawar Islands. They had no need to do so: the Dowasir who had established themselves on the islands were recognized as Bahraini subjects, and the title of the Al-Khalifa to the Hawars was unquestioned, either internally or by other powers in the region. Notably, no such claims were made by any tribal group or authority from the Qatar peninsula.

This being the state of affairs, any British involvement in aspects of the governance of the Hawars was deemed unnecessary. Moreover, as the islands were not contested territory, Britain felt little need to refer specifically to their political status. Britain, however, did—albeit indirectly—recognize the fact that it was the Ruler of Bahrain who exercised sovereign rights over the islands.

Such indirect recognition was contained, for instance, in the 1861 Friendly Convention and in the 1868 personal undertakings by the Ruler of Bahrain and the Sheikhs of Qatar. The importance of these documents lies in the fact that they made a critical distinction between the status of the Al-Khalifa and that of the Al-Thani. While the Ruler of Bahrain was described in the preliminary provision of the 1861 Convention as "Sheikh Mohammed bin Khaleefa, independent Ruler of Bahrain," Mohammed Al-Thani was referred to as "Mahomed bin Sanee, of Guttur." Significantly, the latter was not called a sheikh nor a chief; he was not described as independent; and no mention was made of him being a ruler. In short, the treaties implied no equality between the Al-Khalifa and the Al-Thani, and bestowed on the Al-Thani no attributes that would have fully qualified them as rulers of particular territories (*Terms of a Friendly Convention between Ruler of Bahrain and British Government,* 31 May 1861; *Agreement of Chief of El-Kutr,* 12 September 1868; *Agreement between Chiefs Residing in the Province of Qatar and Chief of Bahrain,* 13 September 1868).

The 1868 Al-Thani Agreement did, however, recognize that the Al-Thani exercised certain control over parts of the Qatar peninsula, though the exact nature of such control cannot be clearly deduced from the Agreement. History confirms that they were merchants and tax collectors rather than rulers in the full sense of the word—see Chapter 4, in "The Al-Thani Move toward Prominence." Regardless of the precise quality of the Al-Thani's influence, the Agreement shows that its territorial scope was, beyond doubt, limited to Doha and its environs.

Equally significant is the fact that the Al-Thani agreed, in their 1868 personal undertaking, to continue to act as subjects of the Al-Khalifa; thus they themselves confirmed the continuing title of the Ruler of Bahrain to the Qatar peninsula's southeastern areas.

The 1861 Convention and the 1868 Agreements both thus indirectly confirmed that the Ruler of Bahrain was still—at the end of the nineteenth century—sovereign over the Hawar Islands. The Al-Thani who were at that time just emerging in power in Doha, were far from asserting any claims over the northern reaches of the Qatar peninsula and even less over the Hawar Islands. Britain, who was author of and party to the three treaties, acknowledged and confirmed that fact.

The Ottoman Position (Nineteenth Century)

As discussed in Chapter 6, the Ottomans moved into the Arabian Peninsula during the latter half of the nineteenth century. They established themselves in Doha around 1871 on the invitation of Mohammed Al-Thani and his son Jasim, who was in turn granted the position of Ottoman assistant governor—*Kaimakam*—of the town of Doha and given Ottoman protection. The Ottomans and the Al-Thani shared a mutual interest in expanding their authority beyond Doha and its environs, and they made several attempts to establish their influence in the north and west of Qatar. All such attempts, however, proved unsuccessful and were rebuffed by Britain and Bahrain.

Ottoman authority on the Qatar peninsula was confined to areas under Al-Thani control, and the insecurity of their rule even in those areas prevented them from realistically considering further expansion. Thus, the Hawars were not part of the Porte's territorial ambitions. On the contrary, their existence as a territorial unit separate from and unrelated to the Doha confederation was uniformly recognized.

One example of such recognition can be found in an Ottoman Army political survey map drafted by a Captain Izzet in 1878. The map is a simplified but highly instructive tool, since it reflects the Ottoman understanding as to the status of various territories in the Arabian Gulf at the time. In the region that encompassed the Gulf of Bahrain (called the "Sea of Bahrain") and the Qatar peninsula, the features the map notes were grouped into two main areas. Not surprisingly, one was the Gulf of Bahrain, encompassing the Bahrain Islands, the Hawars, and Zubarah, while the other consisted of the two isolated settlements of the Doha

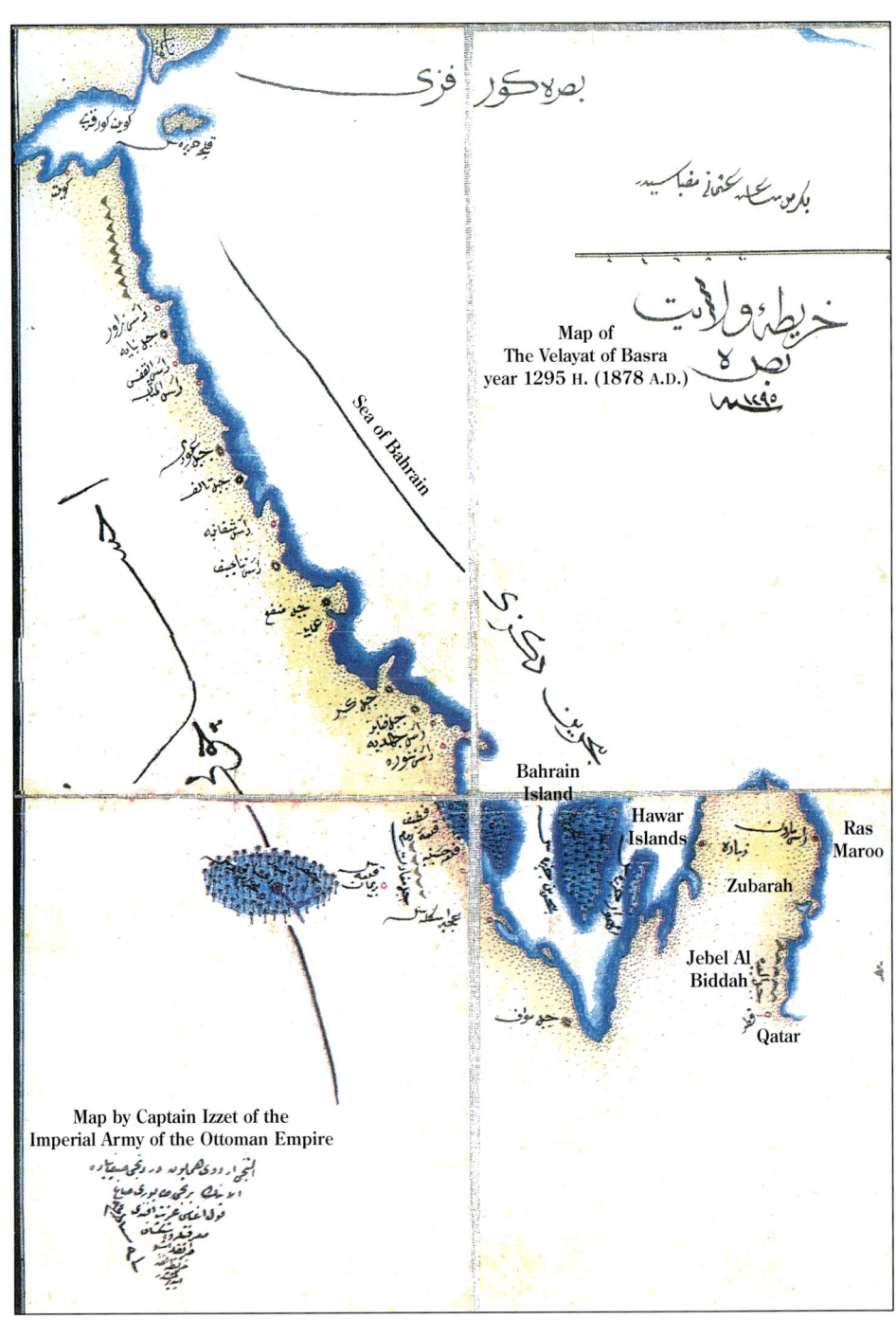

Map No. 5: Extract from Map by Captain Izzet of the Ottoman Imperial Army, 1878

confederation, in the far southeastern corner of the Qatar peninsula. Not only is it clear from the map that the Hawars formed an integral part of the social concentration that occurred in the Gulf of Bahrain, it is also evident that they were separated from Doha and what Izzet called "Qatar" by a large expanse of uninhabited land.

Throughout the period of Ottoman presence on the Qatar peninsula, neither the Ottomans nor the Al-Thani were in any way involved in the Hawars. And while the authority of the Ruler of Bahrain did effectively recede to the north and the west of the peninsula, his control over the Hawar Islands was never challenged. Although in 1909 the Porte made an attempt to extend its influence to another island, Zakhnuniya, the Ottomans never visited or claimed the Hawars.

The Zakhnuniya Incident (1909)

Zakhnuniya is an island in the Gulf of Bahrain, off the coast of today's Saudi Arabia. Like the Hawars, it was considered part of Bahrain, and was regularly occupied on a seasonal basis by the Bahraini branch of the Dowasir tribe who were loyal to the Al-Khalifa. On Zakhnuniya, the Dowasir lived "in two or three temporary huts at the southern extremity of the island and were engaged in fishing for sharks, swordfish etc...." On the west side of the island stood the remains of a fort built—according to Sheikh Isa (Bahrain's Ruler from 1869–1932)—by his father Sheikh Ali bin Khalifa (F. B. Prideaux, 20 March 1909).

In the spring of 1909, Ottoman troops landed on Zakhnuniya and declared that the island had been annexed by the Ottoman Empire. The residents of Zakhnuniya refused to cooperate on the grounds that they and the island were Bahraini:

> The Mudir [an official of the Ottoman Empire] the other day, told the Dowasir whom he found [on Zakhnuniya] that they should recognize themselves as Turkish subjects and he only asked them to haul up and lower the [Ottoman] flag each day. They replied that they could only follow their own headman who resided in Bahrain and resolutely declined to have anything to do with the [Ottoman] flag. (F. B. Prideaux, 20 March 1909)

The Dowasir then resorted to the Ruler of Bahrain, who in turn took the matter up with British authorities. As the British did not have sufficient information at the time, they began an investigation into the matter. Captain Francis Prideaux, the Political Agent in Bahrain, visited Zakhnuniya in 1909, and in his report, he noted that the Ottomans had indeed occupied Zakhnuniya and had raised their flag over the dilapidated fort. Prideaux also found sufficient evidence of the seasonal use of the island as fishing headquarters of the Dowasir of Budaiya and Zellaq (F. B. Prideaux, 20 March 1909).

The status of Zakhnuniya was essentially the same as that of the Hawars, Prideaux reported, and therefore concerns must arise that the Ottomans might be tempted to proceed to the Hawars also. Both Britain and Bahrain were worried at such a prospect, as their interests would have been seriously harmed by the expansion of the Ottoman Empire into territories that were considered exclusively Bahraini. In his report, Prideaux warned:

> I strongly deprecate letting the Turks keep Zakhnuniya as they will then naturally be encouraged to go on to Hawar... (F. B. Prideaux, 20 March 1909)

This concern was based on the similarities between the character of the Ruler of Bahrain's authority over the Hawar Islands and over Zakhnuniya. It was noted that if Bahrain would not assert its uncontested sovereignty over the Hawar Islands, difficulties would arise with the assertion of Bahrain's claim to Zakhnuniya, as they both were based on the Dowasir connection:

> ...if Shaikh Esa (the Ruler of Bahrain) doesn't want or dare assert his sovereignty over Hawar we shall be in rather a quandary. (F. B. Prideaux, 20 March 1909, 5)

Captain Prideaux's report thus provided the factual basis for formulating Britain's official response to the Ottomans. After examining the evidence, Britain then officially protested to the Porte, invoking the Ruler of Bahrain's sovereignty over Zakhnuniya. The British *Administration Report for Bahrain* for 1909 records:

> Representation as regards the soldiers and the flag were made to the Porte and the troops were withdrawn, after they had built a small house and had repaired the platform of the flagstaff. (*Administration Report for Bahrain for the Year 1909*, 69)

The Ottomans' withdrawal amounted to recognition that the Dowasir were subject to the Ruler of Bahrain. In 1911, British officials again investigated the situation, and published the results of this investigation in the *Administration Report for Bahrain for the year 1911*. The reports confirmed that the situation remained unchanged, and that the Bahraini Dowasir continued to demonstrate their allegiance to the Ruler of Bahrain, *inter alia*, by flying his flag:

> According to all reports received, no Turkish garrison has been stationed on the island during the year. The Dosoris [Dowasir] there at the end of the year were on occasions hoisting Shaikh Isa's flag [the flag of Bahrain] ... otherwise no flag was being flown. (*Administration Report for Bahrain for the Year 1911*, 99)

International Treaties (Early Twentieth Century)

The 1913 Unratified Anglo-Ottoman Convention

Four years after the Zakhnuniya incident the Ruler of Bahrain, in consultation with the British authorities in the Gulf, gave up his rights to Zakhnuniya Island. The Ottoman Empire considered Zakhnuniya of great political importance due to its location directly opposite the Ottoman port of Ojair. In a secret declaration annexed to the unratified 1913 Convention between Britain and Turkey, the British government took note of the decision of the Ottoman government to pay one thousand pounds to the Sheikh of Bahrain in compensation for the renunciation by him of all claim to the Island of Zakhnuniya (*Resolutions Approved at the Meeting of the Ottoman Cabinet Council on 19 April 1913*; *Secret Declaration Annexed to Convention between United Kingdom and Turkey*, 29 July 1913).

The Ottomans' willingness to pay compensation served once again as acknowledgement by the Ottomans of Bahrain's rights in Zakhnuniya. The source of Bahrain's authority over both Zakhnuniya and Hawar was similar—i.e., their inhabitation by the Bahraini Dowasir. Thus, Ottoman acceptance of Bahrain's authority over Zakhnuniya necessarily implied acceptance of Bahrain's authority over the Hawars.

This direct evidence of the Porte's recognition of the Ruler of Bahrain's continuing rights in the Hawar Islands is also indirectly corroborated by the text of the Convention itself. Although the status of the Hawars was not explicitly discussed in the context of Article 11, official British documents exist that dealt with the applicability of that Article to other areas neighboring Al-Thani territories. One such document is the memorandum, drafted by J. G. Laithwaite of the India Office, on "The Southern Boundary of Qatar and the Connected Problems." Among other issues, the Memorandum contained an evaluation of the dangers inherent in the extension of the Al-Thani's title over other areas of the peninsula. Referring to the 1913 Convention, Laithwaite noted that the wording of Article 11 "would justify the contention that the blue line was at once the eastern frontier of Nejd and the western frontier of Qatar." Laithwaite, however, continued:

> But there are definite objections to adopting this view. In the first place there is nothing to show that this was, in fact, the intent of HMG at the time when the Convention was concluded or that the provision had any object beyond limiting the eastern boundary of the Turkish possessions in this area. Secondly, there is no evidence of any claim to suzerainty by Qatar so far to the west or so far to the south. Thirdly, the Resident's telegram of 11 January 1934 emphasizes the absence of control by the Sheikh of Qatar over the interior of his state and *a fortiori* over regions so remote from Doha as are now under consideration. (Laithwaite, 5 March 1934, 2)

Thus even as late as in 1934 the Al-Thani were considered incapable of controlling various parts of their own dominions, much less of effectively extending their authority over other regions. Laithwaite continued:

> Fifthly, it is arguable that even in a formal document such as the 1913 Convention the fact that the blue line is spoken of as separating Nejd from the Qatar peninsula need not be regarded as determining the boundary of Qatar. The Qatar peninsula was the closest prominent geographical feature and the nearest adjoining Arab political entity on the mainland, and a reference to it for descriptive purposes was not unnatural. Finally, there is much to be said for giving no avoidable extensions to the boundaries of

Qatar, even if the consequence is that we have to deal with an area of indeterminate ownership between those boundaries and the blue line. (Laithwaite, 5 March 1934, 2)

Obviously, Laithwaite was making a clear distinction between the political and geographical entities of Qatar and the Qatar peninsula. In territorial terms, the former was not considered to coincide with the latter, and Laithwaite, along with other British officials, was aware of the dangers associated with equating the two entities. Qatar as a political unit was, once again, confirmed to comprise only certain areas of the peninsula. Neither at the beginning of the nineteenth century, nor at any other point in history, were the Hawar Islands formally or effectively considered part of those areas—despite their proximity to the geographical unit of Qatar.

The 1916 Treaty

The autonomy of the political entity of Qatar was for the first time recognized in the 1916 Treaty between Mohammed Al-Thani and the British government. The Treaty followed the withdrawal of Ottoman troops from the Qatar peninsula, and aimed to consolidate the territories under Al-Thani control by placing them under British protection. The Al-Thani chief was for the first time given the title of ruler of "Qatar" and was recognized as sovereign over what had been the Doha confederation and its environs.

But the Treaty contained no geographical definition of "Qatar," and no mention was made of the Hawar Islands. The Ottomans had never extended their control much beyond Doha and quite certainly had never reached the Hawars.

Consequently, the 1916 Treaty changed nothing in the well-established British view that the Hawar Islands were part of the dominions of the Ruler of Bahrain. Rather, the Treaty confirmed that despite the new political status of the Al-Thani, the geographical unit of Qatar (the whole peninsula) and the political unit of Qatar (Doha and its environs) still remained clearly distinct. Even in 1937, when Qatar expanded illegally through its attack on Zubarah, the Hawars remained outside the sphere of Al-Thani authority.

British Recognition in Official Reports (Early Twentieth Century)

Not only did Britain acknowledge that the territorial scope of the Al-Thani's influence in the Qatar peninsula was quite limited, it also continued to recognize the existence of Al-Khalifa rights to various areas in the Gulf of Bahrain, including parts of Qatar. British recognition of the sovereignty of the Ruler of Bahrain over the Hawar Islands was demonstrated in reports, maps, and correspondence between senior officials.

Mention has already been made of the Brucks report of the 1820s, published as part of the *Bombay Records* in 1856 (Brucks 1856). Also mentioned has been the fact that at the beginning of the twentieth century British authorities conducted a number of surveys in the region. Among these were the reports produced by Captain Prideaux during the 1909 Zakhnuniya incident and the 1911 reports of British officials about the situation on the Hawars. Those reports aimed to clarify the status of the islands to which Britain's attention had not been drawn previously. Uniformly, the investigations conducted by British officials established two basic facts: the Hawar Islands were inhabited and they belonged to Bahrain.

Those two facts were also reflected in the 1915 British Admiralty survey of the Arabian Gulf. The section entitled "El-Qatar" noted the following facts related to the Hawar Islands:

> An island, *Jezirah Hawar,* lies 5 miles W. of *Ras Abruruk* on the W. coast, with which it is roughly parallel; it is about 10 miles long, and has no permanent population, but the Dawasir of Zallaq in Bahrein have houses used as shooting-boxes in winter, and a cistern for rain-water. The islets *Rubadh* and *Janan* lie to N. and S. of Hawar, those of *Ajirah* and *Suwad* in the channel between it and the mainland. (*Handbook of Arabia* 1916, 326)

Thus, the Admiralty survey of 1915 furnished yet another proof of British recognition of the Al-Khalifa's ownership of the Hawar Islands. While it noted that the Hawars were located closer to the Qatar peninsula than to the main Bahrain island, it also emphasized the most significant fact in respect of the Hawars—namely, that they were inhabited by Bahraini subjects.

It should furthermore be stressed that not a single genuine historical document exists that describes the Hawars as belonging politically to the Al-Thani or to a "State of Qatar." While it was not uncommon to find references to the geographical proximity of the Hawars to the Qatar peninsula, none of the records ever gave that fact any political significance.

17 Oil Concessions in the Hawars

Britain and the U.S. Vie for Oil

Understandably, discussions over the Bahrain and Qatar oil concessions were characterized by passionate feelings on the part of all parties involved. For instance, Great Britain was adjusting to a New World Order that was to a significant extent shaped by oil after the First World War.

The world production of petroleum in 1936 was around 1,785,000,000 barrels. Of this amount, more than 61 percent was credited to the United States, with most of the American oil industry centered in Pennsylvania. Soviet Russia came second with around 11 percent. Third and fourth came Venezuela and Romania with about 9 and 7 percent, respectively (Seiden 1937, 44). This meant that the bulk of the world's oil supply was provided not by merely one country but by one U.S. state (Seiden 1937, 44; Yergin 1991, 56).

This gave the United States a degree of independence from world markets that Britain did not enjoy. To a large extent, Britain still depended on the raw materials derived from its colonies; this state of affairs forced it to maintain an "unrelaxing maintenance of direct lines of communication with the British crown lands and colonies" (Seiden 1937, 44)—a situation not only cumbersome but also expensive.

As noted earlier, the Gulf region provided Britain with strategic access to India—"the jewel in the Crown"—and it could not allow other factors (i.e., the United States and American oil companies) to interfere with this lifeline.

On the other hand, territorial disputes had arisen between the Rulers of Bahrain and Qatar over the Zubarah region and the Hawar Islands. In these, both Rulers had invested a great deal of emotional energy, as for them the issue was linked to a sense of pride and justice, not to mention the well-being of their states' financial reserves, should oil be found in any of the disputed regions.

Naturally, neither the British oil companies nor the Americans could be allowed to have access to these areas till the territorial disputes between the two countries were resolved. Having signed treaties with both Rulers, Britain had no choice but to be the mediating party between them.

Due to the evolving world order just described above, however, Britain placed its own commercial and strategic interests higher on the agenda than the local history of the area dictated. However, unlike Zubarah's case, the evidence in favor of Bahraini sovereignty over the Hawar Islands was too overwhelming for Britain to ignore.

Ruler of Bahrain's Assertion of Sovereignty throughout Negotiations

Simply claiming sovereignty over territory is not sufficient to prove it. As noted earlier, a Ruler can validate his claim in various ways. Externally, demonstrated ability to form treaties of alliance or commerce with foreign nations is among the characteristics that confer sovereignty. Internally, ability to make laws, to execute and to apply them, plus impose and collect taxes and levy contributions also demonstrates sovereignty.

The Ruler of Bahrain's actions in and regarding the Hawar Islands during the oil concession negotiations for that territory clearly indicate that he was indeed sovereign. A preliminary British investigation into the status of the Islands in 1936 found as much (see Section entitled "1936 British Opinion" later in this chapter).

Bahrain Concession of 1925 and Unallotted Area Concession 1928–33

Though the oil concession granted to EGS in 1925 (and later assigned to BAPCO) was valid for only two years, it came with the option of renewal—pending the satisfaction of the Sheikh (*Bahrain Oil Concession* 1925). In April 1933, BAPCO applied for such an extension of its license. As of yet, however, it had not exercised its option under the 1925 oil concession to choose the particular 100,000 acres for its oil lease. In addition, the matter of the unallotted area also remained undecided.

In its application, BAPCO argued that by virtue of the 1925 Concession "... the whole of the additional area including all the Territorial Waters of the Shaikh's Dominions..." was also granted to the company (Holmes, 17 May 1933, 1).

But the British Political Agency was wary of BAPCO's declaration:

> The phrase "all the Islands and all the territorial waters" is a dangerous one, for besides the well known Islands of Bahrain (the main Island, Muharraq and Sitra, and one or two islets) claims are still made to other islands and to areas on the Qatar coast... (Loch, 29 May 1933, 3)

At the heart of British concerns was this: if Bahrain were proved to be sovereign over the above areas, PCL would not be able to prospect for oil in the Hawar Islands (or the Zubarah region); thus, Britain would again lose out to an American oil company (BAPCO).

Bad feelings were already starting to develop over PCL activities:

> That... [Bahrain's] claims are not regarded locally as dead and gone is shown by the fact that I have heard mutterings that the explorers of the Anglo-Persian Oil Company Limited in Qatar have examined places to which the Ruler of Qatar had no right to allow them to go, and which people from Bahrain frequent to this day as a summer resort. (Loch, 29 May 1933, 3)

These feelings were exacerbated all the more, given that

> ... it is said that as late as last year (1932) the Ruler of Qatar admitted in public that certain areas on the Qatar coast pertain to Bahrain. (Loch, 29 May 1933, 3)

In June 1933 the Anglo-Persian Oil Company decided to join the bidding for the Bahrain unallotted area. This further complicated the matter for the British government: it wanted to protect its own commercial interests by limiting the territory which the 100 percent American-owned BAPCO could explore. As the British Political Resident stated:

> It would, as you will appreciate, be much more satisfactory from our point of view if remainder Island [*sic*] were to be developed by Anglo Persian Oil Company... (Fowle, 29 June 1933, 1)

In order to stave off BAPCO from the Hawar Islands, the British Political Resident maintained that

> It would... be prudent to name islands *i.e.* Bahrain Island, Muharraq and Sitrah (Umm Naasan and other islets near main island might be included if question is raised), otherwise controversy may arise over Hawar Island and Bahrain claim to certain places on the west coast of Qatar peninsula. (Fowle, 23 July 1933, 2)

The Ruler of Bahrain was apparently willing to exclude the Hawar Islands from the extension, but he stressed that the Hawar Islands were the dependencies of Bahrain, and that a ninety-year-old agreement somewhere attested to this effect. Thus, to avoid any misunderstanding by the omission of these islands, he stipulated that the area be called "Bahrain Islands" (Loch, 30 July 1933).

The British Political Resident accepted the Ruler of Bahrain's proposal, as in his view the "Hawar Island is clearly not one of the Bahrain group" (Fowle, 31 July 1933).

Bahrain and Qatar have advocated different interpretations as to what this phrase actually intended. The Qatari argument maintains that this constitutes British recognition that Hawar falls under Qatari sovereignty (Qatar 1996, 66 ¶ 3.46). On the other hand, Bahrain maintains that the British Political Resident's remarks reflect nothing more than geographic reality (Bahrain 1996, 98 ¶ 220).

In his evaluation of whether the 1925 Bahrain concession covered the Hawar Islands, Laithwaite from the India Office stated that the Concession would "presumably... exclude Hawar which belongs in any case geographically to Qatar" (Laithwaite, 9 August 1933, 5).

The key word here is "presumably." As will be shown in the next chapter, mere geographic proximity is insufficient to prove sovereignty; actual *effectivités* are required. Also, it should again be mentioned that prior to issuing this opinion, Laithwaite's admitted his lack of familiarity with the issue (Laithwaite, 9 August 1933, 4). Because of his unfamiliarity, Laithwaite would have been unaware of Bahrain's long history with the Hawar Islands.

Fortunately for Laithwaite and the India Office, however, no immediate decision regarding the Hawar Islands had to be taken, for in August 1933 BAPCO withdrew its offer for an additional concession to the Bahrain unallotted area.

The Ruler of Bahrain was "very angry and evidently... [felt]... that he has been 'done' by somebody" when he heard the news (Belgrave, 16 August 1933, 1). Members of the Bahrain Ruling Family were open with their views about who this "somebody" was:

> Sheikhs Abdulla and Sulman do not hesitate to say that the British Government has dissuaded Bahrain from coming to terms with the American company over the additional area in order to help A.P.O.C. [Anglo-Persian] to a get a footing in here... (Belgrave, 16 August 1933, 1)

In 1934, BAPCO ended up choosing 100,000 acres on the main island of Bahrain for its oil lease. This left the remaining area of the main island and all of the Sheikh's territories (including the Hawar Islands) as the unallotted area.

Qatar Concession 1935

Chapter 11 showed that the British agreed to give the Ruler of Qatar protection on the condition that he award the Qatar concession to the Anglo-Persian Oil Company. This the Ruler of Qatar did, thereby granting the British company the sole right to deal in any oil-related activity throughout the "principality of Qatr" (*Qatar Oil Concession* 1935).

However, the British did not make clear what territory this "principality" actually consisted of. This left the Ruler of Qatar with an open door to claim that the Hawar Islands belonged to him. He signed a map attached to the 1935 concession that showed the Hawar Islands to be part of Qatari territory (Skliros, 29 April 1936).

The Ruler of Bahrain immediately rejected the Ruler of Qatar's claims, instead stating that "the Hawar group of islands... is indisputably part of the State of Bahrain" (Belgrave, 28 April 1936).

It bears mentioning that during this period the Ruler of Qatar was still having trouble asserting his authority in Doha and its surrounding settlements. Discussing the Qatar Ruler's status vis-à-vis the oil concessions, the Foreign Office noted:

Although the Sheikh is to undertake in his agreement an obligation to protect the [Iraq Petroleum] Company, it will in practice be impossible for him to afford the Company effective protection unless we agree to his establishing far more effective forces than he at present possesses. This would probably in any case be impossible, since our accounts of the Sheikh are that he is little more than a large merchant and his territory is very sparsely inhabited by tribesmen over whom he appears to exercise a very loose control. (*India Office Memorandum*, 21 February 1934)

Definition of Ruler of Bahrain's Territory in Bahrain Concession

The 1925 exploration license granted to EGS (and then assigned to BAPCO) was not meant to represent the limits of Bahrain's territorial boundaries. It will be recalled that the concession provided an option to select a 100,000-acre area for an oil lease. Given that the total surface area of the main island of Bahrain was 142,000 acres, it was understood that it covered only a part of the Sheikh's territory, as evidenced by the provision made for the "unallotted area."

Nonetheless, Qatar has made much of the point that the 1925 Bahrain Concession made no specific mention of the Hawar Islands. Qatar maintains that this shows third-party recognition that the islands fell under the suzerainty of the Ruler of Qatar.

The exploration license did not include a map. It did however, rely on two maps drawn before the issuance of the 1925 concession: the draft concession map of 1923 and the "Map prepared by Major Holmes," also dated 1923. (*Provisional, not confirmed Bahrain Concession*, 1923; Qatar 1999, Map Atlas, Map no. 71).

On the first map, the areas called "The Bahrain Islands" (the proposed concession area) and the Hawar Islands are represented by two different colors. Qatar purports that this indicates that the Hawar Islands do not belong to Bahrain. But it must be noted that Article 1 of the draft concession explains that the purpose of the coloring was to define an area called "The Bahrain Islands." And the map refers to the defined area as being "Part of The Sheikh's Dominions"; not the "whole of" or "all of." Thus, this map does not purport to indicate the extent of the Ruler of Bahrain's territory.

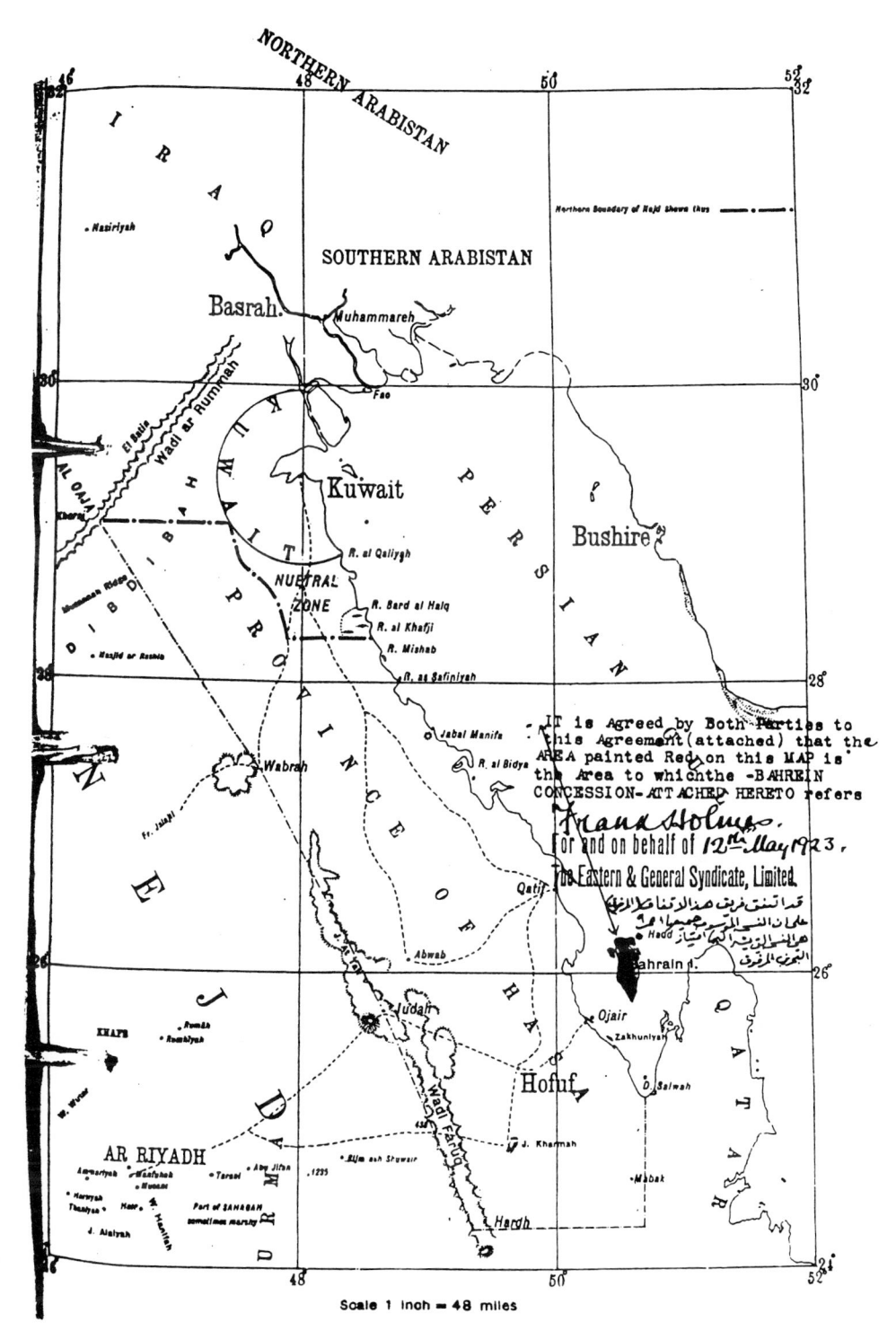

Map No. 6: Map Accompanying 1923 Draft Concession

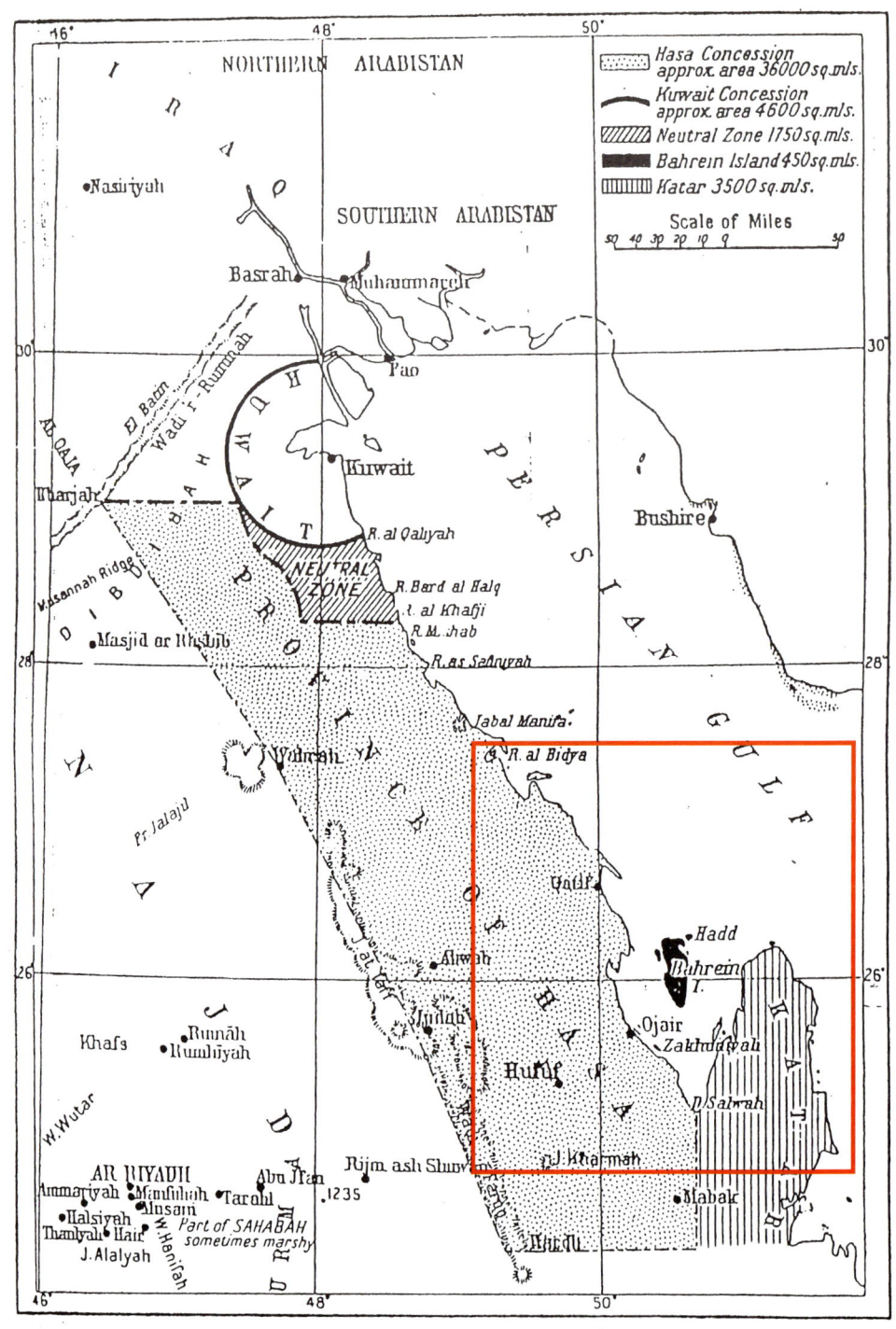

MAP PREPARED BY MAJOR HOLMES

Map No. 7: Map Prepared by Major Holmes, 1923 (See area of detail p. 276)

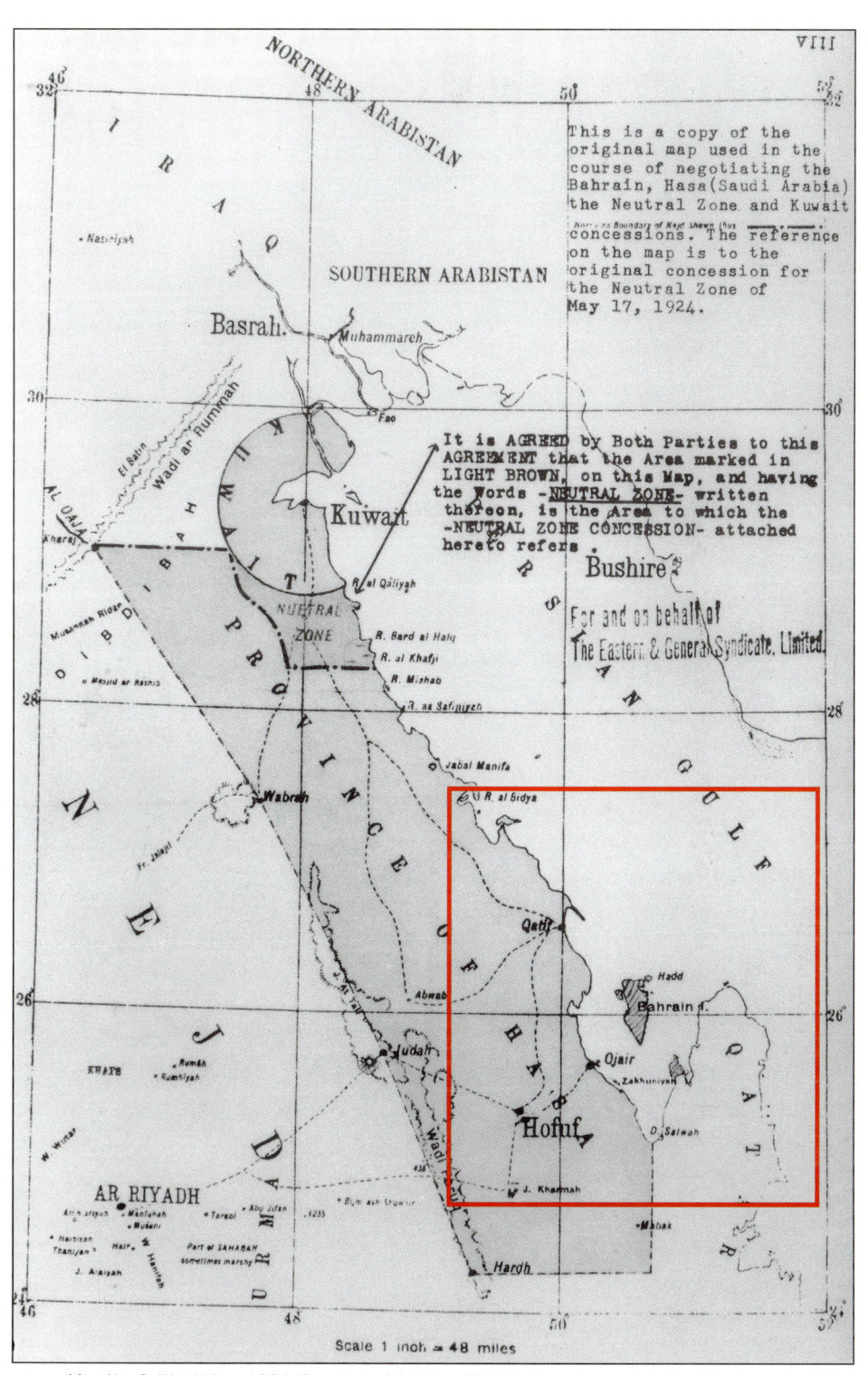

Map No. 8: Ward Map, 1924 (See area of detail p. 276)

276 | A LINE IN THE SEA

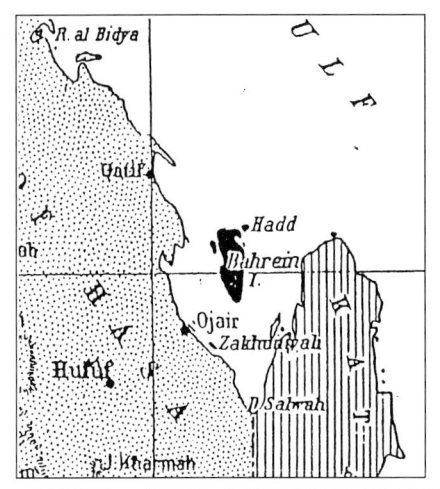

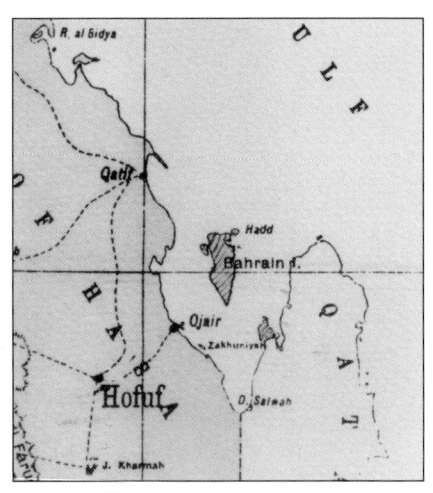

Details from Map No. 7: Map Prepared by Major Holmes, 1923 *(left)* and Map No. 8: Ward Map, 1924

The second map prepared by Holmes is similar to the first. And Holmes's position becomes even more clear when one considers a third map, produced by a close associate of his, Thomas Ward.

Ward played a key role in introducing Holmes to leading American oilmen, thus indirectly helping him secure the 1925 concession. In 1965, Thomas Ward published a book called *Negotiations for Oil Concessions in Bahrain, El Hasa (Saudi Arabia), the Neutral Zone, Qatar and Kuwait*, in which he reproduced a map that showed that the Hawar Islands were indeed a part of Bahrain.

A note on the map explains, "This is a copy of the original map used in the course of negotiating the Bahrain, Hasa (Saudi Arabia), the Neutral Zone and Kuwait oil concessions." The Hawar Islands are colored the same as the other Bahrain Islands (Ward 1965, viii).

Definition of Ruler of Qatar's Territory in Qatar Concession

In contrast to the 1925 Bahrain concession, the 1935 Qatar concession did include a map. The only boundary drawn on the map is across the south of the Qatar peninsula. As noted earlier, part of the agreement between the Ruler of Qatar and the British was that the British would afford him protection from Ibn Saud—but only if he granted the oil concession to APOC. This southern boundary, therefore, was designed to delineate Qatari territory from Saudi.

The British were vague about what exactly constituted the other areas to be included in the concession, however. Article 2 stated:

> ... the company can operate in any part of the State of Qatr as is defined below ... The State of Qatr means the whole area over which the Shaikh rules, and which is marked on the north of the line drawn on the map attached to this Agreement. (*Qatar Oil Concession* 1935, Article 2)

But nowhere in the Article, nor in the remainder of text for that matter, does the concession provide an exact definition of the extent of the Qatar Ruler's authority. Nonetheless, the General Manager of PCL, John Skliros, sought to extend the definition of the territory under the sovereignty of the Ruler of Qatar as far as possible. In 1936, he asked for clarification from the British government as to whether the Hawar Islands were under Qatari or Bahraini suzerainty, if one used the 1935 Concession map as evidence of Qatari sovereignty over the area:

> This island is, in fact, situated off the west coast of Qatar, from which it seems to be not more than [three-quarter] miles distant at its nearest point. The island is shown on the official map of Qatar which was signed by the Shaikh of Qatar ... and which forms part of the Qatar concession. This map, I believe, was seen and approved by the Political Resident and, perhaps, the India Office. All this points to its forming part of Qatar and not of Bahrain. (Skliros, 29 April 1936)

But all Skliros had to go on was geographic proximity. In addition, while the Hawar Islands were shown north of the line, so too was all of Bahrain, and Kuwait as well. Clearly the Ruler of Qatar had no sort of influence in these areas.

The British Political Resident, accordingly, dismissed Skliros's argument:

> The map in question showed not only Qatar, but part of the neighbouring territory including the Islands of Bahrain, so that the fact of Hawar appearing on it is of course no proof of ownership one way or the other. (Fowle, 25 May 1936, 1)

1936 British Opinion

The issue of sovereignty over the Hawar Islands still had to be resolved in order to progress on oil explorations in the region. Thus, in 1936, the British government further investigated the status of the Islands.

This time around the Ruler of Bahrain was more assertive, insisting on a more specific definition of the unallotted area—one that included the Hawar Islands. PCL was also aggressive, in that it threatened to instigate a territorial dispute over the Hawar Islands if it did not obtain the concession rights to them (Hickinbotham, 9 May 1936). It is interesting to point out that at this phase of the negotiations it was PCL, an oil company, and not the Ruler of Qatar, that was making the claim that the Hawar Islands were part of Qatari territory.

On 28 April 1936, Bahrain officially stated its position in writing (Belgrave, 28 April 1936). No such statement was received from Qatar. Initial findings supported the Ruler of Bahrain's position:

> I am inclined to think there is real substance in Sheikh Sir Hamad bin Isa's [the Ruler of Bahrain] claim. (Loch, 6 May 1936, 2)

Concern was expressed, however, that no word had yet been given on Qatar's position:

> I do not know what Sheikh Abdullah bin Jasim of Qatar's views about the Islands are, but I have never heard any protest from him against the activities of Bahrain's subjects there. (Loch, 6 May 1936, 2)

Absent an official position statement from Qatar, the British Political Resident had no choice but to go on the information available to him:

> ...it is beyond doubt that the [Hawar] Island has long been occupied by the Dowasir tribe of Bahrain (*vide* paragraph 7 of Letter No. 207 dated 4th April 1909 from the Political Agent, Bahrain to the Political Resident... and the reference to the Gazetteer of the Persian Gulf...), and it appears beyond doubt that the present Shaikh of Bahrain's father (who succeeded in 1869) and the Shaikh himself have exercised active jurisdiction in Hawar down to the present day (*vide* paragraphs 4–6 of Letter no. C/180 dated 28th April 1936 from the Adviser to the Government of

Bahrain to the Political Agent, Bahrain), apparently without interference or protest by the Shaikh of Qatar. (Fowle, 25 May 1936)

He concluded:

> In all the circumstances of the case, I incline to the view that Hawar should be regarded as belonging to the Shaikh of Bahrain and that the burden of disproving his claim lies on the Shaikh of Qatar. We have heard nothing on the subject from the Shaikh of Qatar, and it is quite possible that he may not dispute the claim of the Shaikh of Bahrain. (Fowle, 25 May 1936)

And it could not be ignored that this finding went against British commercial interests:

> H.M.G. would certainly prefer that P.C.L. should get this concession... (*Foreign Office Minute*, 26 June 1936)

Thus, the India Office tried to work out a plan through which they might convince the Ruler of Bahrain to give the unallotted area to PCL, since for all intents and purposes he was in control of the Hawar Islands:

> ...[His Majesty's] Government may consider it desirable to suggest to the Sheikh that it might be a good thing to give the remainder of the concession to Bahrain to [PCL]. Once BAPCO gets the whole area it will probably increase the difficulty of any arrangement being entered into between Standard Oil of California and the other big groups (which really means the Iraq Petroleum Company) over this territory with the object of securing a measure of British control. (Starling, 3 July 1936, 2)

On 9 July 1936, an interdepartmental (Foreign Office, Petroleum Department, Admiralty, and the India Office) meeting was held in London to discuss the issue. Again, it could not be denied that

> ...on the evidence at present available these Islands appear to belong to the Sheikh of Bahrein, and that the burden of disproving his claim lay on any other potential claimants. (*Minutes of a Meeting Held at the India Office*, 9 July 1936, 1)

It should be noted that at all times the British stressed that this decision was provisional. So, to be fair, they noted that

> . . . it would be impossible to give a final ruling without knowing whether the Sheikh of Qatar has a claim, and hearing it if he has one. (*India Office Minute*, 14 July 1936)

Not until 1939 did the Ruler of Qatar finally present his case, and as will be shown in the next chapter, the Islands were then still found to be part of Bahraini territory.

18 | British Adjudication of Sovereignty over the Hawars

In order to allow the oil exploration in the region to advance, and to resolve what was turning out to be a thorny issue between the two Gulf neighbors, Britain became enmeshed in activities designed to adjudicate the issue once and for all.

The Oil War Heats Up

That the Ruler of Qatar laid no claims to the Hawars until 1938 can easily be explained by the appearance in the 1930s of new factors that served as a powerful motive for Sheikh Abdullah to seek to include the islands among his possessions—the most significant of these was *oil*.

In 1936 British officials had identified the islands as a likely source of oil production:

> [The main Hawar Island] is a low, desolate looking place near to the mainland of Qatar, but it is possible that it may have considerable value now that oil has been found in Bahrain and is hoped for in Qatar. (Belgrave, 22 December 1938)

The Hawars were also considered potentially rich in oil by both BAPCO (Bahrain Petroleum Company) and PCL (Petroleum Concessions Limited)—the oil companies operating in Bahrain and Qatar respectively. At the time the Ruler of Qatar lodged his claim, the companies were competing with each other to obtain mineral rights in the Hawar Islands from the Government of Bahrain. In fact, Sheikh Abdullah made his first complaint about Bahrain's exercise of authority in the

Hawar Islands immediately after the Ruler was informed that Bahrain had entered into negotiations with the two oil companies for the granting of rights in the Hawars (Bahrain 1996, 174–75 ¶ 381).

Qatar's Motives

Qatar's 1935 Concession Agreement had been awarded to PCL—a British-dominated oil consortium—for rights in "the whole area over which the Shaikh rules and which is marked on the north of the line drawn on the map attached to [the] Agreement" (*Qatar Oil Concession 1935*). Though that formulation clearly referred only to such territory as was actually under the Ruler of Qatar, both Sheikh Abdullah and PCL had an interest in disregarding that statement and focusing on the fact that the area had been described as lying to the north of the line.

Thus PCL (as the concessionaire in Qatar) and Sheikh Abdullah (as the recipient of potential royalties) pointed to the Agreement as acknowledgement of the sovereignty of the Ruler of Qatar over the Hawars, as far as the Hawars fell to the north of the line. As was stressed in a letter from the British government to PCL, the line had been conceived to specify the southern boundary of the concession, but various territories that obviously did not belong to Qatar—including all of Bahrain—remained north of the line (Walton, 14 May 1936). Sheikh Abdullah's failure to receive British sanction in this case only increased his desire to pursue the fulfillment of his ambitions through other channels—notably through formal adjudication of the ownership of the Hawar Islands.

When Sheikh Abdullah at last raised his claim to the Hawar Islands, Qatar had no significant developed oil fields of its own. Oil deposits were discovered in the peninsula in 1939, but their commercial exploitation did not commence until after World War II. For its part, Bahrain was the first Arab state in which oil had been discovered, and was enjoying in the 1930s a period of unique prosperity. In contrast, Qatar, the envious neighbor, was plagued by poverty, hunger, and disease. The economic stagnation resulting (in both Bahrain and Qatar) from the decline of the pearling industry had been offset in Bahrain by the oil boom; but no comparable development had occurred in Qatar. Immigration from Qatar to Bahrain was on the rise, as Sheikh Abdullah's subjects tried to escape the desperate poverty in Qatar (Weightman, 5 December 1939, 1).

Qatar's weak economy had further been strained by the consequences of Qatar's armed 1937 attack on Zubarah. Not only had the Al-Thani's military campaign involved considerable expenditure of money and resources, it had also brought about an economic embargo by Bahrain. As the majority of Qatar's exports and imports had flowed till then through the port of Manama, the sanctions imposed by Bahrain had served to aggravate what was already a dire economic situation. In this context, Qatar's claim to the Hawars can also safely be viewed as a response to Bahrain's complaints about the invasion of Zubarah, and as an attempt to mitigate the consequences of the Bahrain embargo.

Not only was Qatar in the throes of economic disaster, the political situation on the peninsula was also unsettled. Al-Thani rule, which had traditionally been far from stable, was being further undermined by poverty and economic mismanagement:

> . . . the causes of dissatisfaction in Qatar are . . . [t]he Ruler's and his son Hamed's greed which makes them not only retain all the oil money but also control for their own benefit employment in the oil Co. Neither can see that Arab standards of life are changing and the rising generation with its contact with the outside world can no longer be deceived and repressed. (Weightman, 5 December 1939, 1)

> [The Ruler's] niggardliness in money matters and handling of employment in the oil Co. was losing him the support of the tribesmen he needed to control Qatar and his prospective oil field, and helping his Bahrain enemies to undermine his authority. (Weightman, 5 December 1939, 1)

The dispute over the Hawar Islands thus held the potential to alleviate Qatar's domestic economic and political problems. The attraction of such a dispute lay also in the fact that while it involved no risks to Qatar's interests, its outcome, if favorable to Qatar, would bring Sheikh Abdullah numerous benefits.

In 1938, Sheikh Abdullah submitted a formal claim to the islands to the British Political Agent. This set in motion proceedings that enabled both Qatar and Bahrain to present their arguments as to sovereignty over the Hawars, and led to an impartial evaluation by Britain of the evidence supporting both parties' claims.

The Arbitration

Basis for Britain as Arbitrator

The British government was empowered to act as arbitrator in the dispute between Qatar and Bahrain by virtue of the provisions of the 1861 Friendly Convention with Bahrain, as well as by the 1868 Agreement with the "Chief of El-Kutr." In Article 3 of the 1861 Convention, the Ruler further agreed to "make known all aggressions and depredations which may be designed, or have place at sea, against [himself], territories, or subjects, as early as possible, to the British Resident in the Persian Gulf, *as the arbitrator in such cases...*" (*Terms of a Friendly Convention between Ruler of Bahrain and British Government*, 31 May 1861, Article 3). [Emphasis added.]

The 1868 Agreement with the Chief of "El-Kutr" was similar in nature and contained a provision that the latter would "maintain towards Shaikh Ali bin Khalifeh, Chief of Bahrein, all the relations which [t]heretofore subsisted between [himself] and the Shaikh of Bahrein, and *in the event of a difference of opinion [with Bahrain] arising as to any question, whether money payment or other matter, the same [was] to be referred to the Resident*" (*Agreement of Chief of El-Kutr,* 12 September 1868). [Emphasis added.]

> This principle was re-confirmed in the 1916 Treaty between Qatar and Britain: "Whereas my grandfather, the late Shaikh Mohammed bin Thani, signed an agreement on the 12th September 1868 engaging not to commit any breach of the Maritime Peace, and whereas these obligations to the British Government have devolved on me his successor in Qatar...." (*Treaty between the British Government and Sheikh of Qatar,* 3 November 1916, preamble)

Thus both parties had formally committed—and agreed—to refer any disputes they might be engaged in with their neighbors to Britain as a third party. Under international law, such an agreement is uniformly construed as an agreement to arbitrate (Mustill and Boyd 1989, 15).

This was acknowledged also by the Ruler of Qatar himself, whose first formal claim to the Hawar Islands, submitted on 10 May 1938, stated in its opening paragraph:

I have the honour to refer to the firm friendship, good and strong relations *and the treaties which exist between me and H.B.M's Government*, upon which I rely, after God, in all my affairs. In view of this I submitted my protests and complaints to the Hon'ble the Political Resident in the Persian Gulf and to the Political Agent, Bahrain . . . (Abdullah bin Jasim Al-Thani, 10 May 1938) [Emphasis added.]

Stages

The adjudication undertaken by the British government involved examining the facts related to the two parties' exercise of sovereignty over the Hawars. Those claims were presented in the form of letters from the governments of Qatar and Bahrain which followed a sequence that typically characterizes arbitration procedures even today: Qatar's Claim was followed by Bahrain's Counter-Claim; that in turn was followed by Qatar's Rejoinder.

Qatar's Claim

Qatar's first claim to the Hawar Islands was advanced by Sheikh Abdullah in February 1938 when at a meeting with Hugh Weightman, the British Political Agent, the Ruler of Qatar complained about Bahrain's exercise of authority on the islands. Despite Weightman's urgings, however, Sheikh Abdullah failed to substantiate the validity of his claim and confined himself to the assertion that Bahrain had no "*de jure* rights" to the Hawars. In Weightman's report on the meeting, he remarked that the Al-Thani sheikh "changed the conversation immediately and it was evident that at that time he was by no means prepared to lay a formal claim to the Hawar group of islands" (Weightman, 15 May 1938). The British government nevertheless considered the possibility that Qatar might present such a formal claim in the future, and that issue was discussed among various British officials, both in the Gulf and in London (Fowle, 5 April 1938; Brenan, 13 April 1938).

But not until three months later did Sheikh Abdullah state his claim in writing. In a brief letter dated 10 May 1938, he explained:

Hawar is, by its natural position, a part of Qatar, and it is not hidden to anyone who is acquainted with geographical and natural condition and has seen the natural position of Hawar that it is,

> beyond doubt, a part of Qatar though it is a small Island separated by a shallow channel of water. But by its present position it is attached to Qatar, formed by it and belongs to it. (Abdullah bin Jasim Al-Thani, 10 May 1938)

That the Ruler of Qatar relied on no grounds other than geography in support of his claim was immediately noticed by the Political Agent (the official charged with conducting the on-site assessment for the British government):

> It remains to be seen whether the Shaikh of Qatar can in fact produce any evidence in support of his claim other than a mere reference to geographical location, which presumably will not by itself serve to contest the Bahrain claim supported as it is, by physical occupation. (Weightman, 15 May 1938)

Britain then fully assumed the function of adjudicator in the dispute. On 19 May 1938 it informed the Ruler of Bahrain that a claim had been advanced to the Hawar Islands by the Ruler of Qatar (Fowle, 19 May 1938). The next day, the British Political Agent wrote to Sheikh Abdullah, encouraging him to elaborate on his claim and assuring him that the British government would

> ... give the fullest consideration to any formal claim put forward by you [the Ruler of Qatar] to the Hawar Islands, provided that your claim is supported by a full and complete statement of the evidence on which you rely in asserting that you, as [Ruler of Qatar], possess sovereignty over them. (Weightman, 20 May 1938)

The British Political Agent further stressed "how important it is that your formal claim, supported by all the evidence which you can produce" be submitted (Weightman, 20 May 1938).

Sheikh Abdullah submitted another, slightly longer letter on 27 May 1938, describing the situation in similar—geographical—terms. The Ruler of Qatar's rhetoric was again strong, but offered no proof of either acts of administration in or historical title to the Hawars. The basis of Sheikh Abdullah's claim was presented as follows:

> In my capacity as Ruler of Qatar territory including coasts, islands, promontories and everything belonging to it, I have the right of ownership over these islands. (Abdullah bin Jasim Al-Thani, 27 May 1938, 3)

On 30 May 1938, Weightman visited Doha and met with Sheikh Abdullah, the Sheikh's two sons Hamad and Ali, and Secretary Saleh Al-Mana, who served as the Sheikh's advisors. The Political Agent "questioned [the Ruler] closely" regarding Qatar's claim. To Weightman's repeated enquiries as to whether the two letters put forward by the Ruler presented his claim "in all the detail he wished," or whether the Ruler had "any other evidence, documentary or otherwise, which he would wish to submit," Sheikh Abdullah inevitably stated that he had set out all he wished to say in the two letters and that "he had no other evidence to offer" (Weightman, 3 June 1938, 1–2). Reporting on the meeting, Weightman observed that:

> No evidence is offered of formal occupation by Qatar, no mention is made of collection of taxes, of sale of fishing rights, of the exercise of judicial authority, or indeed of the performance of any function which might denote sovereign rights. (Weightman, 3 June 1938, 3)

The Political Agent then summarized Qatar's claim as consisting of: "(1) a bare assertion of sovereignty; and (2) the affirmation that the Hawar Islands are part of the geographical unit of Qatar" (Weightman, 3 June 1938, 3).

At that same meeting, Sheikh Abdullah was given further explanation as to the arbitral proceedings his claim had initiated:

> [I explained to the Ruler of Qatar that] I could offer him no hope that His Majesty's Government would disturb the *status quo* while his claim was under consideration; it was common practice that when a person laid claim to property in the actual physical occupation of a second party, that party was left in possession until the new claimant had established his right before a tribunal. (Weightman, 3 June 1938, 2)

Bahrain's "Preliminary Statement" and Counter-Claim

Bahrain's amazement at the claim put forward by Sheikh Abdullah was communicated to the British Political Agent on 23 May 1938. In his letter to Weightman, Charles Belgrave, the Adviser to the Bahrain government, stated that proof of Bahrain's sovereignty over the Hawars could be provided on demand (Belgrave, 23 May 1938). A few days later, Bahrain submitted a "Preliminary Statement" containing evidence of the Ruler of Bahrain's authority over the Hawars. Referring to the statement, Weightman observed:

> I have not acknowledged receipt, since the Bahrain counter-claim has not yet been called for officially; nor should this document be regarded as a full and final compilation of the Bahrain evidence. (Weightman, 3 June 1938, 3)

When the Ruler of Qatar learned of Bahrain's initial submission, he demanded to be allowed access to the evidence, so Qatar's case could be framed more effectively:

> Perhaps, if I hear the statement which they consider it to be the ground on which they base their aggression, I may be able to rebut it and frustrate it and produce something which may prove my claim. (Abdullah bin Jasim Al-Thani, 15 June 1938)

This request appeared rather strange in light of Qatar's assertions that it alone had sovereign rights in the Hawars. Furthermore, at that stage Britain envisioned granting no such advantage to Qatar; so British officials in the Gulf were initially reluctant to pursue what threatened to become an endless series of claims and counter-claims:

> [Sheikh Abdullah] demanded the right to see the Bahrain Government's counter-claim, "in order to enable him to rebut it." I replied that I was unable to give him an assurance that His Majesty's Government would agree to such procedure, and that in my own opinion it was impossible to contemplate a procedure enabling each party in turn to rehearse the arguments, counter-arguments, rebuttal, counter-rebuttal and so on of the other, since this would render a decision impossible in his life-time or in mine. (Weightman, 3 June 1938, 2)

In line with this reasoning, the British Political Agent then recommended that the Ruler of Qatar's claim that new evidence might be available be disregarded, as such a claim would be "a complete contradiction of his previous very clear statement to me personally, in response to repeated questions, that he had produced all the evidence on which he relied. I do not consider that any notice need be taken of the new suggestion that further evidence might be available since he was very clearly instructed in my letter No. C/324–1.a/29 dated 20 May 1938 to produce at once all the evidence which he has" (Weightman, 21 June 1938). Weightman's recommendation was supported by Fowle, the British Political Resident and communicated to British officials in London (Fowle, 27 June 1938).

The British Government in London then carefully reviewed the arguments advanced by Sheikh Abdullah. British officials were aware that the Ruler of Qatar had been unable so far to marshal any genuine proof of his sovereignty over the Hawars; however, they felt that the role of adjudicator assumed by Britain required giving each party opportunity to comment on the submissions of the other party. This requirement was considered essential "when one [was] assuming an arbitral role of this nature," and the Foreign Office therefore recommended to the Secretary of State for India that the Ruler of Qatar be allowed to respond to Bahrain's Counter-Claim when that Counter-Claim was submitted:

> Under this procedure, the party who loses the case at least knows the grounds on which the decision was given, and has no opportunity of feeling that some erroneous statement, which he was able to controvert, has been relied upon in reaching a decision.
>
> We feel, therefore, that, even though the Sheikh of Qatar may not have any more really effective arguments to advance in support of his claim, a refusal on our part to accord him the same opportunity as was given to his rival might leave him with a genuine sense of grievance attributable to this cause alone. (*Foreign Office Letter to India Office*, 12 July 1938, 2–3)

The decision of British officials in the Gulf was thus overruled by London, the instructions given to the British Political Resident by the Secretary of State for India reading:

> HMG...while recognising that Sheikh of Qatar may be able to add nothing of substance to the statements he has already made, consider that on the whole it would be preferable to give him an opportunity to comment on the Bahrain reply. This would be in accordance with the normal procedures in such cases, and it is undesirable, if the eventual decision is in favour of Bahrein, that the Sheikh of Qatar should be left with a sense of grievance that he has not been fully heard... [P]lease communicate statement

of Bahrein Government when received to Sheikh of Qatar and allow him reasonable period for his comments and for the production of any further evidence in support of his claim. (Secretary of State for India, 21 July 1938)

On 14 August 1938, Bahrain was forwarded a copy of Qatar's Claim (Howes, 14 August 1938). Bahrain's Counter-Claim was submitted to the British Political Agent on 22 December 1938 and forwarded to Qatar on 5 January 1939 (Belgrave, 22 December 1938).

Bahrain's Counter-Claim provided numerous examples of the exercise of authority over the Hawar Islands by both the Ruler and the Government of Bahrain. It was fully consistent with Bahrain's position today, and summarized the basis of Bahrain's 1939 Claim as follows:

> The Hawar islands have been owned by the Ruler of Bahrain and occupied by his subjects for over a century... (Belgrave, 22 December 1938, 1)

> [The Hawar islands] have been under the rule of the Shaikhs of Bahrain since about the time when the Khalifah conquered Bahrain, in 1783. The Hawar Islands were held by the Ruling Family of Bahrain, Al Khalifah, for many years before the Al Thani family acquired any authority over the Qatar tribesmen. (Belgrave, 22 December 1938, 4)

The Counter-Claim stressed the permanent nature of the settlements on the Hawars. It referred to the Dowasir families who had stone houses there, and who resided on the islands "with their wives and families and their cattle, sheep and donkeys" (Belgrave, 22 December 1938, 2). It also pointed to numerous acts of administration by the Bahrain government:

> Shaikh Abdulla refers to "interference" by [the Ruler of Bahrain's] Government in Hawar. This is not a word which can be suitably used to describe the development by a Ruler of a part of his country. Admittedly the Government of Bahrain has built roads, fortifications, piers, landmarks and beacons and has experimented in artesian well drilling in the Hawar Islands in a similar manner as has been done in other parts of Bahrain. (Belgrave, 22 December 1938, 2)

References were also made to the exercise of judicial and police authority, also to the regulation of immigration and various economic activities (most notably, pearling and fishing) (Belgrave, 22 December 1938, 4–5; also, see Chapter 15).

Qatar's assertions, based on the geographical proximity of the Hawars to the Qatar peninsula, thus showed in stark contrast to the wealth of evidence of effective exercise of authority offered by Bahrain. The main themes that had emerged during the initial stages of the dispute between Qatar and Bahrain—i.e., the former's focus on geography and the latter's reliance on established historical facts and acts of administration— were further confirmed as the proceedings progressed.

Qatar's Rejoinder

Following the submission of Bahrain's Counter-Claim, Qatar was allowed almost three months to prepare its Rejoinder. Moreover, six months had already elapsed since Qatar filed its original Claim; during these months Qatar had been in a position to improve and refine its statements with respect to the Hawar Islands. Nevertheless, the Ruler of Qatar complained on 19 March 1939 about the time limit that had been imposed, to which the British Political Agent replied:

> ...you must remember that you had unlimited time in which to make your original claim which was expected to include all your arguments and evidence, and that at present you have been given an opportunity only to add any further comments that you may wish to make after seeing the Bahrain Government's reply. In other parts of the world when cases of this nature arise it is normal for such final statements as you are now preparing to be ready within two weeks or at the most a month. (Weightman, 22 March 1939, 1–2)

Qatar managed to comply with the time limit, but the Rejoinder it submitted on 30 March 1939 contained little to help its case: it again focused on geographical proximity as the main basis of Sheikh Abdullah's claim, and its fifteen pages were filled only with permutations of the geographical argument:

> ...[We] ask the Bahrain Government whether the Hawar Islands, from a geographical point of view, comprise a part of Bahrain

completing it from the south or a part of Qatar completing it from the north? ... The Hawar Islands are considered, from a geographical point of view, as a part which completes Qatar from the North. Any one who has the least primary knowledge of geography will agree with this. (Abdullah bin Jasim Al-Thani, 30 March 1939, 7–8)

Ironically, even Qatar's statements about facts of geography were incorrect. No one who had visited the Hawar Islands or who had "the least primary knowledge of geography" would, in fact, agree with Sheikh Abdullah as to the location of the Hawars. Rather than completing the Qatar peninsula from the north, the Hawars are located to the *west* of the peninsula—a fact that can easily be verified by referring to any geographical map of the region.

That the Ruler of Qatar had no clear idea even of the location of the Hawars may easily be attributed to the fact that he had never even visited the islands—either in an official or private capacity. Furthermore, though Qatar's Rejoinder contained assertions that "the [preceding Ruler of Qatar had] visited it many times and many others of the people of Qatar had visited it," no evidence was offered to support that statement (Abdullah bin Jasim Al-Thani, 30 March 1939, 9).

Nor did the attached affidavit of witnesses who testified that the Hawars were part of northern Qatar add more plausibility to Qatar's case (Abdullah bin Jasim Al-Thani, 30 March 1939, 16–17). The absence of evidence of exercise of Qatari authority over the Hawars was again striking. The only example given by Sheikh Abdullah referred to a Dowasir family from Zellaq in Bahrain who "used to frequent Qatar for fishing purposes" and who were during one such visit allegedly attacked. The Ruler of Qatar further stated that they complained to his father Sheikh Jasim, "who heard the complaint and decided against those who [had] attacked them on the ground that the attack [had taken] place in his own territory." Sheikh Abdullah claimed that there were witnesses who would "give their evidence about the same" event; however, no such evidence was produced (Abdullah bin Jasim Al-Thani, 30 March 1939, 12). Apart from that isolated—and unsupported—statement, Qatar's Rejoinder pointed to no acts of administration whatsoever by any Rulers of Qatar with respect to the Hawar Islands.

Qatar's Rejoinder did not contain any proof. Nor, significantly, did it even allege any particulars of Sheikh Abdullah or his predecessors' rule in the Hawar Islands. The Rejoinder abounded in rhetorical questions and appeals to irrelevant "logic." It attacked Bahrain's examples of exercise of sovereignty, but failed to provide any counter-examples of Qatari acts on the islands.

In conclusion, Sheikh Abdullah stated:

> ...I have explained my comments and remarks to Your Excellency *as fully as is required by the circumstances of this case*.... (Abdullah bin Jasim Al-Thani, 30 March 1939, 15) [Emphasis added.]

Britain's Decision

The decision taken by British officials in London as to the ownership of the Hawar Islands was preceded by a detailed examination of the arguments and the evidence submitted during the proceedings.

Britain's Hugh Weightman evaluated the evidence submitted by the Rulers of Qatar and Bahrain in his Report of 22 April 1939 (Weightman, 22 April 1939). The Report contained a record of the proceedings and a straightforward weighing of the evidence offered by the two Rulers. However, in his analysis Weightman went further than merely to comment on Qatar and Bahrain's submissions; he also referred to the facts he had himself established during the two visits he had made to the Hawars in relation to the case. The Report began with a summary of the proceedings and went on to review Qatar's claims. Unsurprisingly, it stated that:

> The Sheikh of Qatar's claim, as set out in [the letter of 27 May 1938], is based on the following:
> (a) A plain asseveration of sovereignty over this group of islands as over other islands adjacent to Qatar, the coasts, promontories and "everything belonging to Qatar."
> (b) A formal denial that Bahrain had, until recently, occupied these islands or exercised jurisdiction in any form therein.
> (c) A claim that the islands, by virtue of geographical propinquity, are an integral part of the Qatar State. (Weightman, 22 April 1939, 2)

As Qatar's Rejoinder obviously offered no new information or arguments apart from the affidavit attached at its end, Weightman only made an observation that the witnesses' testimony appeared to him "entirely valueless"—especially since all the witnesses' signatures were in the same handwriting, and no thumb impressions or seals were attached to their statement. In addition, the Political Agent noted that not only did affidavits contain no background of the witnesses or mention their actual places of residence, neither did they mention their reasons for having any special knowledge about the Hawars (Weightman, 22 April 1939, 2–3).

In paragraph 4 of his report, Weightman also examined the possibility of accepting "geographical contiguity" as valid grounds to award the Ruler of Qatar title to the Hawars. His conclusion was that the geographical principle was inapplicable, save in the case of unoccupied territories:

> Were this not so an equally valid claim to the whole of the Qatar Peninsula might presumably be raised by the Saudi Government! (Weightman, 22 April 1939, 3).

As Weightman had found "sufficient evidence to show that [the Hawars had been] occupied, whether temporarily or permanently, for the past 150 odd years," the Political Resident pointed out that the more relevant factors to consider would be "the circumstances attending the occupation, the nationality of the occupants, the authority they recognise and [the] evidence of the exercise of direct jurisdiction over them" (Weightman, 22 April 1939, 3). All these factors favored Bahrain.

Weightman's report continued with a detailed evaluation of the Ruler of Bahrain's claims, and of the evidence offered to support those claims. The Political Agent listed two earlier authoritative sources corroborating Bahrain's version of history: Lorimer's *Persian Gulf Gazetteer* (1908–15) and Captain Prideaux's reports during the Zakhnuniya incident. Weightman referred in particular to the 1800 grant of the Hawars to the Dowasir by the Qadi of Zubarah —an event that had been mentioned by Prideaux and been confirmed by the residents of the Hawars in Weightman's presence (Weightman, 22 April 1939, 4).

Weightman's own efforts to verify the other facts adduced to support Bahrain's claim he reported as follows:

> I have myself verified the accuracy of the statement made in the Bahrain counter-claim . . . that there are two villages in the main Hawar island. (Weightman, 22 April 1939, 4)
>
> The Bahrain Government claim, and the Shaikh of Qatar denies, that there is good grazing for flocks and herds in the Hawar main island. I can state, from personal knowledge, that in this respect the Bahrain Government are right. (Weightman, 22 April 1939, 5)
>
> Similarly it is quite true that the gypsum (or juss) which is found in Hawar is excavated under license from Bahrain. (Weightman, 22 April 1939, 5)
>
> Mention is also made in paragraph 9 of the Bahrain counter-claim of the pearling boats owned by the Dawasir of Hawar. I believe the Hawar owns only four, but these four were drawn up on the beach near the northern village during my visit there last week and they are admittedly registered in Bahrain. (Weightman, 22 April 1939, 5–6)

And so the report went. After submitting every significant statement to scrutiny, Weightman established both the authenticity and the relevance of Bahrain's evidence.

Weightman's report was submitted to Sir Trenchard Fowle, the British Political Resident in the Gulf. Fowle, in turn, forwarded the report to the British Government in London, calling it "a very clear statement of the case" (Fowle, 29 April 1939).

In London, the India Office undertook further analysis of the dispute and concluded that despite all the time that had passed

> The Sheikh of Qatar has been able to produce no evidence whatsoever in support of his claim. He relies solely on an assertion of sovereignty and on geographical propinquity. . . . (*India Office Minute*, 7 June 1939, 2)

An earlier Minute, prepared by C.E.M. Hemingway of the India Office, had put the geographical proximity issue in its proper context:

> . . . the Sheikh of Qatar adduces nothing positive in his own favour except the geographical contiguity of the islands to his undoubted territory. Even the geographical claim looks more plausible on

the map than in terms of travelling distances. The fact that the islands are separated by only five miles... of shallow water from the mainland is perhaps of less importance than that they are *separated by 50 miles of desert from the centre of the Qatar Sheikhdom at Doha*: whereas in so maritime an area as the South coast of the Persian Gulf *the 20 miles of easily navigable sea between them and Bahrein main island would be more of a link than a division.* The persistence of the Sheikh of Bahrein's interest in Zubara is an instance of the importance of this factor... (Hemingway, 22 May 1939, 2–3) [Emphasis added.]

The case was then reviewed by the Foreign Office, and, particularly by the Marquis of Zetland (Baxter, 13 June 1939) and Lord Halifax, who concurred in the India Office opinion that the evidence overwhelmingly favored Bahrain. A decision was then taken to confirm the sovereignty of the Ruler of Bahrain over the Hawar Islands and communicated to the British Political Resident in the Gulf (Baxter, 13 June 1939; Deputy Secretary to Government of India, 1 July 1939). On 13 June 1939, the Political Resident informed the Ruler of Bahrain and the Ruler of Qatar:

... I am directed by His Majesty's Government to inform you that, after careful consideration of the evidence adduced by [the Ruler of Bahrain] and the Shaikh of Qatar, they have decided that these islands belong to the State of Bahrain and not to the State of Qatar. (Fowle, 11 July 1939)

Significance of the Findings
Fair Proceedings
In addition to the above historical account, it would seem in order here to comment on the "between-the-lines" significance of several aspects of Britain's finding. First, the arbitration Britain undertook was formal and in every way met established criteria for the conduct of arbitral proceedings. Far from being an administratively imposed decision, the 1938–39 arbitration was conducted in accordance with principles still essential to the practice of international law today.

The arbitration involved adversarial submissions by both parties. It lasted thirteen months and allowed each of the parties sufficient opportunity to present its case, and also to comment on all statements and supporting documents presented by the other party. The parties' acknowledgement of Britain's authority to undertake such an adjudication, and the parties' consent to the procedures employed by British officials, was exemplified by their voluntary and active participation in the proceedings. In addition, that the Ruler of Qatar had himself initiated the arbitration and that both parties submitted evidence further confirmed their recognition of the validity of the British government's jurisdiction.

The final decision reached by the British government resulted from careful evaluation of the evidence submitted by Bahrain and Qatar regarding their involvement, or in the case of Qatar, its non-involvement, in the Hawar Islands. As should already be clear from the account of the adjudication, the dispute was decided after a thorough examination of the merits of the case, and after all relevant facts were taken into consideration.

Britain's remarkable lack of bias in awarding the Hawars to Bahrain is further confirmed by the political context of the adjudication. At this time when Bahrain had granted an oil concession to an American company while Qatar had granted oil exploration rights to a British company, Britain would have undoubtedly benefited by the Hawar Islands' inclusion into Qatar's territory. The fact that the British confirmed that the islands belonged to Bahrain only serves to reinforce the conclusion that Britain rendered the correct legal decision, even contrary to its own apparent self-interest.

The decision constituted a binding arbitral award, and at the time was so accepted by both Bahrain and Qatar. It confirmed the status quo—i.e., Bahrain's recognized sovereignty over and effective administration of the Hawars—and its validity was subsequently affirmed on a number of occasions.

Qatar's Inaccurate Statements and Lack of Evidence

As already mentioned, the claims made by the Ruler of Qatar in the course of the adjudication comprised mainly geographical arguments, and even these were characterized by inaccuracies and a complete lack of supporting evidence.

Such ignorance extended even to basic geographical facts. Despite Qatar's description of Bahrain's Counter-Claim as a "bold denial of firmly set facts" (Abdullah bin Jasim Al-Thani, 30 March 1939, 3),

Qatar's own statements contained striking inaccuracies, for instance, the assertion that the Hawar Islands "are islands whose extent is from 4 to 5 square miles approximately at high tide" (Abdullah bin Jasim Al-Thani, 30 March 1939, 3). Obviously, Sheikh Abdullah was referring to islands whose size was between one-fifth and one-quarter of that of the Hawar Islands, which comprise 20 square miles.

The inaccuracies in Qatar's statements can also be attributed to another possibility—that Sheikh Abdullah was in effect claiming a group of islands *other* than the Hawars—a hypothesis consistent with another assertion found in Qatar's Rejoinder:

> The Hawar Islands are considered, from a geographical point of view, as a part which completes Qatar from the North. Any one who has the least primary knowledge of geography will agree with this. (Abdullah bin Jasim Al-Thani, 30 March 1939, 8)

It has been pointed out that the Hawar Islands are located to the west of the Qatar peninsula rather than the north; however, there exists another group of islands located just off the northern tip of the Qatar peninsula: Ra's Rakan island and Umm Tays island, which perfectly fit the Ruler of Qatar's description as "completing" Qatar from the north, and which are, furthermore, much smaller than the Hawars. Sheikh Abdullah's confidence as to the location and the size of the islands furnishes further proof that the islands he was claiming did exist, though they were hardly the Hawars.

Such a conclusion is further supported by the physical descriptions of the islands provided by the two parties to the dispute. Notably, Qatar disagreed with Bahrain's statement that the islands contained "inhabited villages, established since a long time, with firmly built stone houses, permanently inhabited, for more than a century, by the subjects of the Ruler of Bahrain and the subjects of his ancestors with their wives, families, herds and boats." The Ruler of Qatar called such descriptions "concoctions" and expressed his understanding that the Hawar Islands were "barren, without water and unfit as pasturage for herds, and was in the past completely without inhabited buildings and by no any way can be called villages or anything that approaches the meaning of this word, and generally unfrequented except by fishermen who come from time to time..." (Abdullah bin Jasim Al-Thani, 30 March 1939, 3). Again,

Sheikh Abdullah's description can easily be applied to the small islands to the north of Qatar. Unlike those, the Hawars contained abundant evidence of more than a century's continuous habitation—a fact that the British Political Agent himself confirmed during his two inspections of the Hawars.

Aftermath of the Finding
Qatar's Protests
Three weeks after receiving Britain's decision, the Ruler of Qatar expressed his disappointment in letters to British officials dated 4 August 1939, 18 November 1939, and 7 June 1940 (Abdullah bin Jasim Al-Thani, 4 August 1939; Abdullah bin Jasim Al-Thani, 18 November 1939; Abdullah bin Jasim Al-Thani, 7 June 1940). The Ruler formulated his objections as follows:

> Is it acceptable to Your Honour to say that the islands which are considered the completing part of the Qatar State on the north side, belong to the Bahrain State and not to the State of Qatar ... that they do not belong to Bahrain according to their natural and geographical position. (Abdullah bin Jasim Al-Thani, 4 August 1939, 1)

Notable about these letters is this: Sheikh Abdullah did not seek, even at this stage, to present any further arguments or evidence in support of his claim. The strong rhetoric that had marked his submissions during the proceedings was still there; the substance, as had also been the case during the arbitration, was still missing. Another important fact: the Ruler's letter, while it questioned the merits of the British decision, contained no complaints about the fairness of the procedure or the binding nature of the decision.

In the British Political Agency's 1939 *Report on Qatar*, Sheikh Abdullah's protests were described as follows:

> The Shaikh of Qatar is protesting to the British Govt. against their decision that Hawar belongs to Bahrain. As regards an early delimitation of a boundary the Ruler [of Qatar] takes the somewhat "naïve" view that as Hawar belongs to Qatar the point cannot arise.

> *The Ruler [of Qatar]'s real conviction is that he must ultimately abide by the decision of H.M.G.* (Weightman, 5 December 1939, 5) [Emphasis added.]

That the Ruler of Qatar recognized the validity of the decision is demonstrated also by the fact that he did not mention the issue of the Hawar Islands again until 1947, when British enquiries regarding the maritime boundary caused his old grudges to resurface. Then, after 1948, the Ruler of Qatar remained silent for another seventeen years and voiced no interest either in the Hawar Islands or in the 1938–39 arbitration.

Qatar only renewed its claim in 1961 as a tactical response to Bahrain's continuing claim to Zubarah. And the years that had elapsed after the British adjudication did not help Qatar make its case claiming the Hawar Islands any more convincing than it had been in the 1930s. And again, the absence of any solid basis on which to lay their claim to Hawars led to numerous contradictions in their position. Thus, in February 1961, M.C.G. Man, the British Political Agent, reported about the Ruler of Qatar:

> Sheikh Ahmad [the Ruler of Qatar] told the Political Resident recently that he did not contest our decision on Hawar. (Man, 21 February 1961, 1)

Nevertheless, a month later the Ruler of Qatar stated that

> Qatar had never been satisfied with the award of this island in 1939 to Bahrain by the Political Resident and has only remained silent about it in deference to HMG. (*Qatar Diary No. 2 of 1961*, 4)

But fear of offending British sensibilities was hardly the main reason behind Qatar's silence. Rather, the truth was, the Hawar Islands were, in the aftermath of the adjudication—just as they had been prior to the adjudication—of little real interest to Rulers of Qatar. Not only were the Hawars in no way integrated with the center of the Qatar state at Doha, it had also become clear that they contained no significant economic resources (most notably oil). So a more likely explanation for the Ruler of Qatar's change of course in 1961 might be found in a statement made by the Ruler himself to the British Political Agent:

[The Ruler of Qatar] said that if Salman [the Ruler of Bahrain] persisted in pursuing his claim to Zubara he for his part would raise the question of Hawar Island. *(Qatar Diary No. 2 of 1961, 3–4)*

Affirmation of Validity of the 1939 Award

Despite Qatar's occasional protests against the 1938–39 British decision, Britain continued to consider the award valid and its conclusions accurate. Official British correspondence in the 1940s indicates that British officials consistently recognized that the evidence that had served as the basis for the award had unquestionably proven Bahrain's claims. Thus, in 1941 Sir Olaf Caroe of the Government of India's External Affairs Department noted that the weight of the evidence submitted during the 1938–39 proceedings had been and remained overwhelmingly in favour of Bahrain (Secretary to the Government of India, 19 November 1941). Other high-ranking officials in the Government of India also endorsed his view (Caroe, 19 November 1941).

British officials in the Gulf also consistently expressed their recognition of the importance of the 1939 award, and its definitive nature. Sir Rupert Hay, the British Political Resident, wrote to that effect in June 1946, noting that "the ownership of the Hawar Islands was definitively decided in 1939" (Hay, 4 June 1946, 1–2).

In 1946–47 Britain began to consider division of the seabed between Bahrain and Qatar in light of its dealings with the two countries' oil concessionaires. The line emerging from that exercise was not the product of any detailed examination or formal evaluation of the facts related to sovereignty over the Gulf of Bahrain's maritime features. However, it was in part based explicitly on the 1939 award, and British officials involved in the process were well aware of the status of the Hawars as belonging to Bahrain (C. J. Pelly, 23 December 1947; Bahrain 1996, ¶ 354 *et seq.*; Bahrain 1997, Sec. 3.5). Furthermore, the 1947 letter advising the Rulers of Bahrain and Qatar of Britain's position regarding the division of the seabed referred to the fact that the Hawar Islands were part of the territory of Bahrain (C. J. Pelly, 23 December 1947a; C. J. Pelly, 23 December 1947, 1).

Continued Development of the Hawars

Following the 1939 award, Bahrain continued to exercise its sovereignty over the Hawar Islands. It has been through the efforts of the Government of Bahrain that the islands have received the infrastructure and facilities to enable their ongoing occupation.

The Government of Bahrain has also made every effort to preserve the Hawars' historical heritage. Several government-sponsored projects have been designed to preserve the cemeteries and historic buildings—the mosque and the houses—in the North and South Villages of the main Hawar island.

Bahrain-Built Infrastructure

The Physical Planning Directorate of the Bahrain Ministry of Housing has commenced and/or completed numerous infrastructure development projects. Among these are housing projects, bird sanctuaries, and environmental preserves; holiday resorts, hotels, and campgrounds; a community center with elementary schools for girls and boys; a second mosque; recreational and commercial fishing marinas; commercial and light industry centers; markets, sewage, water, and power plants; hospitals, a domestic airport; and a causeway link between the main island of Bahrain and Jazirat Hawar (Extracts from the *Gulf Daily News*, 18 January 1997 onwards; extracts from the *Gulf Daily News*, 24 May 1997 onwards; extracts from the *Gulf Daily News*, 20 July 1997 onwards).

The Hawars' network of paved roads has expanded since 1980 (when the first such road was built to link the North Village to the south of Jazirat Hawar), and now these extend for more than 20 kilometers. Furthermore, the main Hawar island is integrated with the transportation structure of Bahrain through regular ferry service from the main Bahrain island. Four jetties have also been contracted to service the transportation needs of the main Hawar island.

Numerous amenities have made life on Jazirat Hawar more comfortable. The Bahrain government has taken care to provide the islands with a well-functioning water supply system comprising several fresh water wells (dug in the 1970s), a desalinization plant, storage facilities, and a distribution system established in 1982–83. The islands are supplied with electricity through their two 1.65 MW diesel electricity generators, and a contract has been concluded to increase the number of generators in light of growing power demands. Telecommunications on the Hawar Islands are provided by the Bahrain Telecommunications Company, BATELCO. The Hawars are served by a telephone exchange, a GSM mobile telephone station, a paging base station, and digital microwave lines. Public telephones are available in several locations.

A complex of new modern townhouses has been constructed in the north of the main Hawar island, as part of a housing project. The project was undertaken in view of the ever-expanding population of Bahrain that is expected to double in approximately 20 years (*UNDP Human Development Report State of Bahrain* 1998, 48). Bahrain, already the fifth-most densely populated state in the world (Bahrain 1996, 19 ¶ 54), views the Hawar Islands (constituting 6 percent of its small territory) as essential to meet its future needs.

The Hawar Islands are also important to the future development of Bahrain's tourist industry. A modern hotel facility has been built near the south village of Jazirat Hawar, and is reported to have attracted fifteen thousand visitors between 1997 and 1999 (Extracts from the *Gulf Daily News,* 18 January 1997 onwards). As well as being visited by Bahraini families and other tourists, the hotel has developed into a preferred venue for business events, conferences and weddings (Extracts from the *Gulf Daily News,* 29 September 1997 onwards; extracts from the *Gulf Daily News,* 25 October 1998 onwards).

Exploration Activities

Oil prospecting activities have been carried out on the Hawar Islands under the authority of the Government of Bahrain, but so far these have not led to discovery of any oil reserves on the islands or in the areas surrounding them.

Test drilling in the 1940s did not reveal the existence of any oil-bearing structures (Brown, 13 July 1949). Despite initial disappointing results, efforts were renewed in 1961, when a new geological program was launched involving exploration activities on Sawad Shamaliyah Island.

In 1965 concession rights in the Hawar Islands were granted to Conoco, but after initial studies the concession was relinquished that same year. Two years later, the Hawars were incorporated into another concession granted by the Bahrain government—this time to Superior Oil Company. In 1983 that concession was transferred to BANOCO.

Defense

The Hawars have been and remain an integral part of the State of Bahrain's defense system. All of the Hawar Islands, and their maritime areas, have been regularly patrolled by Bahrain. Furthermore, markers erected throughout the Hawar Islands in the 1930s have been maintained to the present day.

Today, a Bahraini military garrison is stationed on the main Hawar island. Although the garrison's capability is entirely defensive, it has been reinforced in response to numerous challenges from Qatar—most notably, Qatar's surprise 1986 attack on Fasht Al-Dibal, one of the maritime features constituting the Bahrain archipelago (Zahlan 1989; Crystal 1990).

That the Hawars have been essential to the security of Bahrain has also been demonstrated by their inclusion in the defense commitments undertaken by Bahrain on a bilateral, regional and international basis.

19 | Qatar's Version of the Hawar Situation

Highlights

Addressing the International Court of Justice on 8 June 2000, the Agent of Bahrain stated, "[I]f Qatar were to take the Hawar Islands from us ... not only would our country be amputated—but even the sovereignty remaining to us would be intolerably diminished" (Jawad Al-Arayed, 8 June 2000, 8 ¶ 6–7). Indeed, the Hawar Islands are not only an integral part of the modern-day State of Bahrain, they have been under uninterrupted Bahrain sovereignty for over two centuries:

Bahraini Events
- The Al-Khalifa brought the Gulf of Bahrain under their authority at the end of the eighteenth century.
- The highest Al-Khalifa official at Zubarah granted the Hawars to the Dowasir tribe (from Hasa) in 1800, whereupon the Dowasir became Al-Khalifa subjects. They occupied the Hawar Islands, and in 1845 they also established the settlements of Budaiya and Zellaq on the main Bahrain island.

Qatari Events
- The Al-Thani state did not exist at the end of the 18th century.
- The Al-Thani did not emerge as a power in southeast Qatar until the 1860s. The Dowasir of Hawar never had any contacts with the Al-Thani.

Bahraini Events

- The Dowasir migrated between their permanent settlements on the main Hawar island and the main Bahrain island on an annual basis.
- Bahrain continuously exercised and displayed jurisdiction in the Hawar Islands, as has been internationally recognized throughout the nineteenth and twentieth centuries.
- In the 1930s the Hawar Islands were considered potentially rich in oil.
- In 1938–39 the status of the Hawar Islands was formally adjudicated by Britain, and the islands were confirmed as belonging to Bahrain.
- The Hawar Islands have remained an integral part of the State of Bahrain.

Qatari Events

- No one from the Doha confederation ever reached the Hawar Islands.
- No contacts between the Hawar residents and any representative of the Al-Thani state ever occurred; the Al-Thani state, created at a great distance from the Hawars, centered on Doha.
- In 1938 the Ruler of Qatar raised his first claim to the Hawar Islands. His motive was oil.
- The 1938–1939 British adjudication was initiated by Qatar. Qatar relied exclusively on geographical proximity rather than on manifestations of sovereign activity to support its claim to the Hawars.
- Qatar's current claim to the islands has been raised to counter Bahrain's continued insistence on the restoration of Bahrain's rights in Zubarah.

Speaking perhaps most eloquently to the baselessness of Qatar's claim to the Hawar Islands was Qatar's submission of eighty-two forged documents to the International Court of Justice, for those forgeries were the only hope Qatar had to prove that its sovereignty had ever extended to the Hawars.

Qatar's Version of Events

Here, as with Zubarah, Qatar attempts by its arguments to deny both the historical and legal bases for Bahrain's claim to the Hawar Islands. Beyond that, it attempted to conceal its complete lack of evidence by inventing "supporting" evidence in the form of eighty-two forged documents which were submitted to the International Court of Justice. These latter documents will be dealt with in detail in Chapter 21. Here we will first outline the elements of Qatar's arguments and legal strategies set forth in support of its claim to the Hawars.

Geographical Proximity

Qatar's pleadings again "emotionally" raised the issue of the geographical location of the Hawar Islands, just off the western coast of the Qatar peninsula. Qatar asserted that the Hawar group of islands fit "neatly" with the general shape of the Qatar coast and were indeed a "direct continuation of the Qatar coast" (Qatar 1996, 49 ¶ 4.2). Qatar repeated this argument in different variations throughout its pleadings:

> ... Qatar pointed out that Qatar's western coast in the vicinity of the Hawar Islands is very ragged, and likened it to "a jigsaw puzzle with a few missing pieces." Those missing pieces are the Hawar Islands themselves which are needed to complete the curve of Qatar's western coast between Ras al Uwaynat and Ras Umm Hish... The geology and geomorphology of the area confirm this conclusion... consequence of this conclusion is that the area of the Hawar Islands can, in terms of coastal processes, be said to constitute an integral part of the Western Qatar coastal system. (Sinclair, 30 May 2000, 33–34 ¶ 2–3)

Qatar examined geological "facts" and made statements to the effect that the Hawars' geology was like Qatar's, not Bahrain's (Qatar 1996, 51 ¶ 4.6). Qatar's pleadings also pointed to the possibility that "over centuries" the Hawar Islands would probably be reunited with the Qatar mainland, as the zone between the islands and the mainland was characterized by sedimentation that was causing the intervening water to become "narrower and shallower" (Qatar 1996, 51 ¶ 4.6).

Naturally, Bahrain found it pointless to dispute these "facts" about the geology of the Qatar peninsula. It pointed out that these kinds of facts are irrelevant where inhabited territories are concerned. According to established principle in international law, possession and effective administration of a territory override proximity to it (for a more detailed discussion see *Bahrain Memorial* Section 4.3 and *Bahrain Counter-Memorial* ¶ 23–24).

Qatar also found it convenient to perceive the distance between the tail of the main Hawar island and the Qatar mainland as shorter than it actually is. Qatar claimed this distance is 250 meters (Sinclair, 21 June 2000, 40–41 ¶ 35–36) rather than 3 kilometers at low tide and 4 kilometers at high tide (Volterra, 28 June 2000, 52 ¶ 68). Bahrain produced photographs as well as marine survey data to back up its conclusion. Qatar stated that Bahrain had manipulated the image of Hawar's tail, but chose not to provide either photographs or maps of its own for the area (Sinclair, 21 June 2000, 41, ¶ 35).

Title

Qatar strongly disagreed with Bahrain's position regarding Bahrain's jurisdiction and control over the Hawar Islands.

First, Qatar contested the grant of the islands to the Dowasir by the Qadi of Zubarah. Qatar maintained that the historical sources invoked by Bahrain are unreliable and that the evidence contained in those does not prove Bahrain's thesis (Shankardass, 20 June 2000, 25–26 ¶ 2). Furthermore, Qatar chose to interpret Bahrain's arguments as amounting to a mere statement that Bahrain's jurisdiction over the islands commenced in 1800 with the grant by the Qadi (Shankardass, 20 June 2000, 25–26 ¶ 2). But this interpretation falls far short of what Bahrain has actually said—that by 1800 the Al-Khalifa were already sovereign over the Hawar Islands, and thus their official at Zubarah had the right to grant the islands to the Dowasir:

> ...here there was a *souverain* that existed prior to the arrival of the Dowasir in the Hawars, namely the Al-Khalifa Rulers of Bahrain. It was that *souverain* from whom the Dowasir obtained by grant the right to reside in the Hawars. (Lauterpacht, 8 June 2000, 24 ¶ 31)

But in its attempt to further undermine the above argument, Qatar also stated that even at the beginning of the nineteenth century—a time when the whole Qatar peninsula was recognized as belonging to

Bahrain—the authority exercised by the Al-Khalifa on the peninsula was ineffective (Shankardass, 20 June 2000, 26 ¶ 3). How effective their rule was in 1800 is inconsequential, the fact is that they were the *only* authority on the peninsula at that time. And even at the beginning of the 1900s—when Qatar emerged as a political unit—their sphere of influence was far from coextensive with the peninsula.

Even when the state of Qatar did finally emerge, it centered on Doha and the surrounding area in the southwest of the peninsula. Thus, no authority effectually competing with Bahrain ever emerged prior to the twentieth century in the northwestern parts of the peninsula. Nor did any authority originating from the peninsula ever displace, or even challenge, the historically established sovereignty of the Al-Khalifa over the Hawars (Bahrain 1996, 42 *et seq.*, 182 *et seq.* ¶ 104 *et seq.*, 406 *et seq.*; Bahrain 1999, 12 *et seq.*, 99 *et seq.* ¶ 25 *et seq.*, 193 *et seq.*).

And though Qatar maintained that the Hawar Islands belonged to the Al-Thani, it failed to show when or how the Al-Thani had ever acquired title to the islands. Throughout the pleadings, Qatar seemed to assume that certain territories inherently belonged to the state of Qatar—territories including not only the entire peninsula, but also the Hawar Islands. This argument is reminiscent of assertions made by Sheikh Abdullah Al-Thani in the 1930s:

> ...the Hawar Islands belonged to the Qatar State from the very day when God created them... they do not belong to Bahrain according to their natural and geographical position. (Abdullah bin Jasim Al-Thani, 4 August 1939)

In effect, Qatar strove to create a picture of an "inherent" geopolitical entity comprising the peninsula and the islands—an attempt seeming even more peculiar in the light of Qatar's own assertions that the Al-Thani state was a product of expansion and consolidation. What emerged from Qatar's pleadings was thus a confused theory based on unsupported assertions and assumptions of "manifest destiny."

Qatar's "Blank Slate" Theory

Qatar's theory culminated in the assertion that, prior to 1936, the Hawar Islands were uninhabited. Qatar dismissed outright all the evidence demonstrating Bahrain's display of governmental authority in the Hawars—and asserted that the islands had never had any permanent population. Qatar deemed as insignificant "the occasional and short-lived presence of itinerant fishermen on Hawar during the winter months, including some fishermen normally resident in Bahrain" (Qatar 1997, 78 ¶ 3.69).

Neither historical nor physical evidence of habitation of the islands were taken into account in Qatar's position. They chose to ignore the houses, mosques, and water cisterns—still to be seen on the islands today—which are several generations old (Belgrave, 22 December 1938).

Paradoxically, Qatar asked the Court to consider the existence of "cemeteries of those who happened to die in the distant past on the island, adult or children" as "fit[ting] into this past history" of sporadic human presence on the Hawars (Shankardass, 20 June 2000, 34 ¶ 31). But in so doing, Qatar itself confirmed that the islands had in fact been occupied for centuries:

> Even the witness statements, for what they are worth, speak of the past, of houses (or huts) in ruins, obviously having been abandoned, so that whatever the nature of their links they were only of a *number of generations ago*. (Shankardass, 20 June 2000, 34 ¶ 31) [Emphasis added.]

This statement plainly contradicts Qatar's main assertion denying long-term population on the islands—an assertion central to Qatar's version of history and given as one of the basic reasons behind Qatar's present claim to the Hawar Islands:

> It is a fact of nature that Hawar could not have been occupied permanently before Bahrain took it over in 1936/37. (Qatar 1996, 154 ¶ 6.174)

What Qatar alleges in the above statement is that the islands were occupied for the first time in the 1930s—an event Qatar interprets as related to the discovery of oil and the resulting "efforts to add to the territory of Bahrain" (Qatar 1996, 77 ¶ 5.57). In Qatar's view, the 1930s were the first time Bahrain made a claim to the Hawar Islands. Qatar's story went as follows:

> ...when Bahrain came seriously to press its claim to the Hawar islands in the 1930s, it did so through a clandestine occupation by moving a garrison to the islands. (Qatar 1997, 67–68 ¶ 3.50)

> In fact the evidence shows that Bahrain did not merely "increase its military presence" but illegally occupied the main Hawar island. (Qatar 1997, 68–70 ¶ 3.53)

In Qatar's pleadings, Britain was accused of affording Bahrain preferential treatment and backing these Bahraini activities on the Hawars (see Qatar 1997, 75 ¶ 5.55 *et seq.*). The forged documents Qatar submitted, and later withdrew, contained "evidence" supporting that version of events. Most notably, this "evidence" described a "plot" devised by the Adviser to the Bahrain government in collusion with British authorities to dispossess the Al-Thani of the Hawars (Qatar 1996, 77, 110, 159 ¶ 5.57, 6.64, 6.188). Even after Qatar abandoned the forged documents, its arguments continued to echo their earlier advanced theory of unfair treatment by the British.

Qatar's "blank slate theory" of the Hawars thus came to assume its final form: uninhabited islands, illegally occupied by Bahrain with British sanction, and settled thereafter with Bahraini subjects. With this theory, Qatar erased generations of peaceful long-term Hawar Island inhabitants from history.

History says otherwise. Rather than marking the beginning of Bahrain's presence on the Hawars, the events of 1937 were a manifestation of Bahrain's long-established and continuing sovereignty. So why did Bahrain feel it necessary to increase its military presence on the Hawars? Simply, it did not want to undergo another version of Qatar's armed attack on Zubarah.

Bahrain's actions in 1937 were nothing more or less than a reaction to Qatar's invasion of Zubarah. The Bahrain government was fully justified in stepping up the security of the Hawar Islands: as Qatar's expansionist ambitions had become abundantly clear that year, the defense of Bahrain's border regions naturally became a priority. The high volume of immigration from the Doha area (due to disaffection with the Al-Thani) gave yet another reason to tighten border controls. Rather than illegally extending its sovereignty to the islands, Bahrain was simply ensuring the defense of its territory.

The Dowasir Not Bahraini Subjects?

Another argument advanced by Qatar was that the Dowasir were not Bahraini subjects. Qatar's early pleadings contained statements and documents expressly "confirming" that claim. But all of that evidence was part of the forged documents set which Qatar subsequently withdrew.

In its later pleadings, Qatar modified its claim and insisted that the Dowasir's allegiance to the Ruler of Bahrain was not sufficiently constant—a fact that should, in Qatar's view, prevent the association of Dowasir presence on the Hawars with Bahraini presence there. Qatar invoked the autonomy of the tribe itself to support its argument that the Dowasir were not under Al-Khalifa authority, stopping just short of asserting that the Dowasir were a sovereign tribe in themselves (*cf.* Shankardass, 20 June 2000, 26 ¶ 4 *et seq.*; Qatar 1997, 39, 87 *et seq.* ¶ 2.70, 3.18 *et seq.*).

Bahrain admitted in its pleadings that relations between the Dowasir and the Ruler of Bahrain were sometimes problematic. Such tensions, however, never reached significant proportions other than during the short period of 1923–27, when some of the Dowasir left for Hasa in protest against the tax reforms introduced throughout Bahrain (the very fact that Bahrain collected taxes from the Dowasir demonstrated that the Bahrain government did hold jurisdiction over the Dowasir). The Dowasir's return in 1927 and their submission to the Ruler of Bahrain again confirmed their status as Al-Khalifa subjects. As Bahrain stated in its pleadings:

> . . . [E]ven if some Dowasir were occasionally unhappy, the fact remains that for many generations, year after year, season after season, all of their contacts were with Bahrain. No contacts were with Qatar. (Paulsson, 27 June 2000, 41 ¶ 46)

International Treaties

In keeping with its interpretation that the political entity of Qatar has been throughout history coextensive with the peninsula of Qatar, Qatar claimed that Mohammed Al-Thani's 1868 undertaking and the treaties of the early 1920s demonstrated the Al-Thani's sovereignty over the Hawar Islands. Qatar asserted that since at least the end of the nineteenth century, the Al-Thani sheikhs had ruled the entire peninsula—both "in [their] own right and as surrogate for the Ottoman Empire" (Bundy, 20 June 2000, 47 ¶ 24).

Qatar's analysis of the 1868 Agreements concluded that it was at that point that "Qatar" had for the first time been formally separated from Bahrain as a political entity. This separation, Qatar reasoned, meant acknowledgement of Al-Thani authority over the Hawars:

> ...[O]ne of the major objects of the Agreements of 1868 was to protect the territorial integrity of Qatar and its coasts, including its adjoining islands, against attacks from across the sea...As this recognition was in the context of the maintenance of maritime peace, it clearly covered the coasts and the islands adjoining mainland Qatar and therefore the Hawar islands, most of which lie within Qatar's territorial waters. (Qatar 1997, 56 ¶ 3.31)

Bahrain's detailed analysis of the 1868 undertakings demonstrated that the Agreements—far from extending the Al-Thani powers—spoke explicitly of Mohammed Al-Thani returning to Doha under the authority of the Al-Khalifa. Qatar's argument was simply another manifestation of its legally irrelevant theory of instant coast-to-coast sovereignty. A local chief/pearl merchant's promise to return to his town cannot logically be construed as amounting to recognition of his authority over islands which he had neither possessed nor acquired.

Qatar's wishful interpretations of history also marked its discussion of the unratified Anglo-Ottoman Convention of 1913 and the 1914 Treaty:

> Article 11 [of the 1913 unratified Convention] was also mentioned in the Anglo-Turkish Treaty of 1914 which was ratified, and contains no fewer than three references to the *peninsula* of al-Qatar. It is therefore quite clear that what was at stake here was the whole peninsula, without excluding the adjoining Hawar islands. (Qatar 1997, 59–60 ¶ 3.41)

As the significance of the Conventions mentioned above has been discussed at some length in Chapters 6 and 16, that analysis will not be repeated here. It will only be noted here that neither the 1913 Convention nor the 1914 Treaty had any need to exclude the Hawar Islands—it was well known at the time that the Hawar Islands had never been included among the Al-Thani's territorial possessions. The proximity argument was then, just as it is today, considered insufficient grounds on which to award territories recognized as belonging to a neighboring state.

Qatar also chose to see the 1916 Treaty establishing its independence from the Porte as further "proof" of its rights to the Hawars. The mere mention in the Treaty of the import and sale of arms, the ceding of land, and the regulation of customs duties was somehow twisted into being evidence that the Treaty "clearly applied to the entire peninsula of Qatar, its coasts, and its adjoining islands"(Qatar 1997, 64 ¶ 3.44[5]). Qatar also claimed:

> Most significantly, the obligation of the British Government under Article 10 to protect the Ruler and his subjects and territory "from all aggression by sea" *must necessarily cover* the whole peninsula and the adjoining islands including the Hawar islands just as much as did the Agreements of 1868. (Qatar 1997, 64 ¶ 3.44[5]) [Emphasis added.]

In truth, this represented merely another variation of Qatar's discredited "automatic coast-to-coast sovereignty" argument.

Oil Concession Maps

Qatar's examination of the oil concession maps aimed to show that oil companies considered the Hawars as belonging to Qatar. Basically, Qatar equated oil concession areas with territorial limits for Bahrain.

Qatar paid special attention to the map prepared by Major Holmes. As Qatar stated, the map had been created in 1928, therefore, after the 1925 Bahrain concession. Since the Hawar Islands were not included in the Bahrain concession area, Qatar asserted that Holmes knew the Hawar Islands belonged to the Al-Thani.

Qatar, however, confused the date of *publication* of the map with its date of *origin*. Major Holmes's map was, in fact, drafted in 1923, though not published until 1928. And the map was intended only to show a potential concession area—not the extent of the Ruler of Bahrain's authority (Shankardass, 30 May 2000, 21–22 ¶ 31; Paulsson, 27 June 2000a, 45 *et seq.* ¶ 71 *et seq.*).

"Provisional Decision"

Qatar argued that in 1936 British authorities had taken a "provisional decision" to award the Hawars to Bahrain. In line with its blank slate theory, Qatar maintained that the Hawars, which it claimed had been illegally occupied by Bahrain shortly before the decision was taken, were then awarded to Bahrain. That decision, Qatar said, predetermined the actual outcome of the formal 1938–39 arbitration regarding the status of the islands.

Qatar's pleadings contained numerous complaints regarding the British "decision." One such complaint concerned the oil companies' considerable arrogance and insensitivity in the mid-1930s toward Qatar's alleged rights over Hawar. It was pointed out that PCL initially viewed its concession over Qatar as covering the Hawar Islands, but then withdrew from that position on discovering that the British had "provisionally" decided that Hawar belonged to Bahrain.

Qatar charged British authorities themselves with numerous misdeeds. Qatar asserted that in 1936 British officials were aware of Qatar's interest in the Hawar Islands, but concealed that fact. Qatar invoked a May 1936 letter from the Political Agent, stating that he was unaware of the Sheikh of Qatar's views regarding Hawar, and that he had never heard of any protest from the Sheikh about activities of Bahrain's subjects there. Qatar then stated that given the state of affairs in the region at the time, the Political Agent had had a duty to find out what Qatar's views were, and he had not done so (Qatar 1996, 133–134 ¶ 6.122).

The Ruler of Qatar was said to have never previously had occasion to protest, as the activities of "Bahraini fishermen" on Hawar had not been inconsistent with what had been normal practice in the Gulf—i.e., the use of the islands by all fishermen of the region. Qatar claimed that British officials did everything possible, with the cooperation of interested oil company executives, to create the illusion that Bahrain held incontrovertible title to the Hawar Islands, while keeping the Ruler of Qatar in total ignorance of Bahrain's claim (Qatar 1997, 76 *et seq.* ¶ 3.65, 3.67 *et seq.*).

Qatar also brought up the issue of the map attached to the Qatar oil concession of 1935, purportedly showing the southern boundary of Qatar. In Qatar's interpretation, since the map contained no specific reference to the Hawar Islands belonging to anyone, this indicated that everything to the north of the southern boundary should be regarded as part of the state of Qatar. Qatar used this as evidence that the British government at the time had considered that the Hawars belonged to Qatar (Qatar 1996, 73, 97 ¶ 5.48, 6.26; Qatar 1997, 167 ¶ 5.25).

On the contrary, Bahrain pointed out, the map proved no such assertion. As the whole of Bahrain including the Hawars were depicted to the north of the line, Qatar's reasoning would imply that Kuwait and Bahrain were also part of Qatar's territory (Paulsson, 13 June 2000, 23 ¶ 54–56). Qatar went on to say that only when Bahrain had submitted a formal claim to the Hawar Islands had the India Office attempted to explain away the map attached to the Qatar concession by asserting that the map's purpose was simply to define the southern boundary of the concession (Shankardass, 30 May 2000, 30–31 ¶ 54; Shankardass, 21 June 2000, 20 ¶ 13). The India Office's dismissive reply to PCL's "Hawar is north and therefore Qatari" logic was a clear recognition of Bahrain's ownership of the islands (Walton, 14 May 1936).

A general theme running throughout Qatar's pleadings was the charge that British officials had been far from impartial in their dealings during oil concession negotiations. Qatar accused the British of trying to add to the territories of the Ruler of Bahrain, so the latter could maximize the benefits from his oil concessions. But why Britain would have done so was not convincingly explained by Qatar. Britain would have been better served by granting an Al-Thani claim, since PCL, a British company, had won the Qatar oil concession.

Qatar's inability to challenge the British award of 1939 on its merits led to Qatar's formulation of a number of other charges, mainly against the British officials who took part in the adjudication process. Qatar's pleadings accused the arbitrators of various faults and raised doubts as to their integrity. Qatar's initial assertions—that the Adviser to the Bahrain government had fabricated the evidence used in support of Bahrain's claim in 1938–39—were abandoned once it was discovered that those assertions were based entirely on forged documents (see Chapter 21).

Qatar characterized the arbitration as having had a number of procedural defects, which they saw as sufficient in and of themselves to invalidate the 1939 decision. Additionally, Qatar sought to prove that had it not been for the "suppression" of Qatar's evidence and the misconduct of certain British officials, the Qatar ruler would have been able to prove his claim. Qatar was constructing an essentially revisionist theory that equated the arbitration to a "sordid and indeed shameful" story (Sinclair, 31 May 2000), a cynical and "hypocritical" imposition of British interests (Shankardass, 31 May 2000).

Qatar's View on Defects of Award
No Consent
The first significant shortcoming of the 1938–39 decision, in Qatar's view, was the supposed absence of consent by its Ruler to participate in the proceedings:

> Qatar denies that its then Ruler gave his consent in 1938/39 to the determination by the British Government of his claim to sovereignty over the Hawar group of islands. (Qatar 1996, 130 ¶ 6.112)

> Obviously, there was no arbitration agreement authorising the British Government to act as arbitrator between Qatar and Bahrain in the matter of the dispute over title to the Hawar group of islands. (Qatar 1996, 131 ¶ 6.115)

By disagreeing with the interpretation of the various agreements which empowered Britain to act as arbitrator between the Rulers of Bahrain and Qatar (see "Basis for Britain as Arbitrator" in Chapter 18), Qatar sought to undermine the very premises on which the decision was based. In doing so, however, Qatar ignored the fact that its Ruler had himself requested and initiated the proceedings by raising a claim to the Hawar Islands. His referral of that claim to the British government only confirmed his submission to British jurisdiction under the "special treaty relations" between Britain and Qatar. Qatar also implicitly consented to the adjudication by actively participating in the proceedings.

No Equal Opportunity
Another criticism Qatar raised concerned the alleged violation of an essential rule in such procedures—that the parties should be given equal opportunity to present their cases.

Qatar traced the violation of that rule back to the 1936 "provisional decision" made by Britain, and stated that "the procedures were thus fundamentally flawed from the outset by the action taken in 1936" (Qatar 1996, 139 ¶ 6.136). For its part, Bahrain drew attention in its pleadings to the fact that British authorities had not taken a formal decision in 1936, but had rather formulated an advisory opinion for the purposes of the ongoing oil concession negotiations. That opinion had been explicitly labeled as "provisional," and had aimed to summarize already known facts related to the Hawar Islands. The significance of the "provisional decision" thus lay mainly in the fact that it only confirmed the well-known truth that the Hawars belonged to Bahrain. And, it will be recalled that it was two years after this decision, in 1938, that the Ruler of Qatar made his first claim to the Hawars.

Qatar also complained that the Al-Thani chief had been instructed to submit his claim "at the earliest possible moment," while no time limit had been placed on Bahrain for the submission of its Counter-Claim. Similarly, Qatar claimed it had not been afforded sufficient time to respond to Bahrain's Counter-Claim (Qatar 1996, 136–37 ¶ 6.130). In its pleadings, Bahrain pointed out that the Ruler of Qatar had had unlimited time to prepare his initial claim, as well as approximately ten months to present any additional evidence he might have had. Qatar's problem during the arbitration was not insufficient time; its problem was insufficient evidence.

Bias and Pre-judgment

Qatar's attempt to depict the arbitration as a "flagrant miscarriage of justice committed by the British government of the time on the basis of a slanted and flawed assessment" (Sinclair, 5 June 2000, 16 ¶ 15) also involved blackening the names of a number of British officials involved in the arbitration.

The primary offender in Qatar's eyes was Sir Hugh Weightman, who had authored the detailed report examining all available evidence on the Hawars, and who had reasonably concluded that the evidence overwhelmingly favored Bahrain. Weightman was depicted as a person motivated by an irrational and "paranoic" loathing for the Al-Thani (Sinclair, 5 June 2000, 14–15 ¶ 13; Qatar 1996, 114 ¶ 6.74). He was also accused of collusion with Belgrave (the Bahrain Government Adviser) on the basis of extracts that hardly supported such accusations.

In this respect, Qatar cited extracts from Belgrave's personal diaries which, it said, incontestably demonstrated the impropriety of the relations between Belgrave and Weightman:

1938

May 21: Went over to Agency, Shaikhs A and S came in with the Qattar shaikhs who we talked to, a pretty little intrigue which was my idea and which I hope will be successful.

May 22: Very busy, lots of people. Weightman re oil maps...

May 29: ...Weightman left in Bideford for Qattar and Trucial Coast...

1939

Jan 2: Went to Agency and there had a long talk with Davies ...Went to see Weightman again in the evening...

Jan 12: Went over to the Agency and had a talk with W[eightman], oil and other matters.

Jan 16: With Weightman to Sakhrir, all the shaikhs present. Oil talk. W left and I and the three shaikhs drove to Awali and had a long talk with Davies in his office about including Hawar. He was very upset...

Jan 18: Weightman back, had a talk to him about oil events since he left.

Jan 30: Went over to see Weightman and discussed the oil business.

Feb 2: Spent some time at Agency discussing oil
(Qatar 1996, 113–14 ¶ 6.72).

Qatar interpreted this and other similar entries as follows:

> It was clearly quite improper for Weightman, when acting in a quasi-judicial capacity, to discuss with the official representative of one of the parties, in the absence of an official representative of the other party, a visit which he had made to the islands in dispute. (Qatar 1996, 139 ¶ 6.136)

Qatar's other interpretations were equally far-fetched. Thus the entry below in Belgrave's personal diary, depicting a day in the office:

> Discussed oil & the new agreement & especially the question of our right of the Hawar Group of Islands which the Shaikhs fear the Agency will not allow. I think myself it is quite incontestable. (Qatar 1999, 137–38 ¶ 4.143)

This triggered the following comment:

> That the Bahrain Sheikhs should fear the British Political Agency would turn down a claim by the Ruler of Bahrain to the Hawar Islands is understandable. But why is Belgrave so confident that such a claim (to be made only five days later) will be backed by the Agency? Could it be that he had advance knowledge or at least a hint of what the reaction of the Agency to such a claim was likely to be? What other explanation is there, given, as Belgrave must have known, the very shaky grounds for a Bahraini claim to the Hawar Islands if those grounds were to be subjected to serious scrutiny? (Sinclair, 31 May 2000, 50 ¶ 10)

And another interpretation:

> We now also have Belgrave's entry in his diaries on 23 April 1936 ... that the Al-Khalifa Shaikhs, five days before the formal claim was made on 28 April 1936, did not in fact themselves believe that they had a sustainable claim to the Hawar Islands. (Shankardass, 5 June 2000, 27 ¶ 27)

Although the above extracts speak for themselves, it bears noting that the Ruler of Bahrain did indeed have reasons to fear that his *right* might be turned down by Britain—Britain's interests at the time lay with the British oil concessionaire in Qatar.

But Qatar's accusations of bias and pre-judgment were not directed at Weightman alone. According to Qatar, no fewer than six other British officials were implicated in the plot to dispossess the Al-Thani of the Hawars: Lt.-Col. Trenchard Fowle, British Political Resident; Lt.-Col. Percy Loch, British Political Agent prior to Weightman; R. T. Peel of the India Office; and C. W. Baxter of the Foreign Office (see Bahrain 1997, 119 ¶ 278; Sinclair, 5 June 2000, 13–14 ¶ 12[6]–12[7]). Qatar's claims of involvement by not only British officials in the Gulf, but also those in the India Office, implicated the British *government* in the "plot" against Qatar. Qatar's notion that British officials at different levels of government were biased against the Al-Thani amounted in Qatar's eyes to nothing less than "proof" that Britain had colluded with Bahrain against Qatar.

In addition, Qatar in its *Memorial* accused Abdul-Razzaq bin Rizoogi, British Residency Agent in the Trucial States, and Khan Bahador Isa Abdul-Lateef Al-Sarkal, Representative of the British government in Sharjah, of participating in the plot—the only "supporting evidence" for such assertions being the forged documents which it later withdrew (see, for example, Qatar 1996, 80–82, 111, 152–53 ¶ 5.63, 5.65–5.66, 6.67, 6.169, 6.173).

But Britain's aim in all this would still seem a mystery, since British interests would obviously have been better served by awarding the Hawars to Qatar. The fact that even under those circumstances the award had been made in favor of Bahrain only reinforces the argument that Britain's decision had been unbiased.

Subsequent Criticisms

Qatar placed significance on the fact that two British officials in the Gulf had shared its criticisms of the validity of the 1939 Award:

> What is remarkable in this story is that both Prior, the new Political Resident in the Gulf appointed to succeed Fowle in September 1939, and Alban, the new Political Agent in Bahrain appointed to succeed Weightman in 1940, should have expressed such unease and disquiet about the correctness of the British decision of 1939 on the Hawar islands. (Qatar 1996, 139 ¶ 6.137)

Bahrain, however, emphasized that both Prior and Alban had been appointed only after the 1939 decision, and thus had not been privy to any of the evidence used in support of Bahrain's and Qatar's arguments. These officials had expressed personal, and uninformed, opinions that had indeed been contrary to Britain's formal view.

As Bahrain pointed out, Prior's superiors had not only dismissed his views but had also stated that Prior had been influenced by personal animosity against Weightman and Belgrave (*Manuscript Minutes by Political Residency, August–September 1939;* Bahrain 1997, 123–30 ¶ 288–308). Prior also was known for his hasty opinions—as evidenced by the following extract, which relates that Prior was criticized by his superior, two years before leaving the civil service, for

> ...overgenerous use of explosives on paper. These defects give the impression of a certain immaturity...They are important in

that his position as Resident in the Gulf necessarily brings his work to the direct notice of the Secretary of State and of various high authorities in the Middle East. (Rich 1991)

The value of Prior's and Alban's opinions may also perhaps be judged by the fact that their backgrounds, as well as their further careers, were quite unremarkable. In contrast, Weightman, whose report on the Hawar Islands Prior and Alban had tried to challenge, went on to become Joint Foreign Secretary to the Government of India, where his position obviously involved working with high-ranking officials—a function Prior had been judged unable to perform. Thus, Prior's and Alban's claims, and Qatar's assertions that these claims undermined the validity of the 1939 Award, were relegated to mere wishful thinking by Qatar.

Resolution of the Dispute

20 | Steps toward Resolution

The dispute between Bahrain and Qatar continued to simmer—at varying levels of intensity—from the 1930s onward. While numerous attempts had been made to resolve the dispute during the years 1937–75, most notably by the British, none of these events had resulted in any improvement to the situation. Bahrain and Qatar remained irreconcilably divided, not only about what should be the just outcome to the situation, but also how to even begin discussing the dispute.

By the mid-1970s, the dispute was causing enough dissension between the parties that Saudi Arabia intervened to bring both countries into discussions aimed at resolution. By that time, the Arabian Gulf countries ranging from Oman on the south to Kuwait on the north, including both Bahrain and Qatar, were beginning negotiations to form the Gulf Cooperative Council (GCC), a union similar to the European Union. This dissension over borders between two of only six potential partner nations in the GCC needed a conclusion.

In 1976 new mediation efforts began under the auspices of Saudi Arabia and later the Gulf Cooperative Council. Throughout these discussions, the government of Saudi Arabia served as prime mediator between the two parties. Yet, those twelve years of discussions were largely unsuccessful, in good part because no definitions of the points involved in the dispute could be agreed upon.

Then, at the GCC Doha Summit Meeting of 1990, agreement on the scope of the dispute was finally achieved; a five-point statement defining the scope being arrived at. While this may seem now to have resolved a small matter, the agreement on this thirty-eight-word statement of the scope of the dispute was a key event in the final dispute resolution. The International Court of Justice later used this same five-point formulation in adjudicating the dispute.

Then, in July 1991, Qatar unilaterally filed the dispute with the International Court of Justice (ICJ) in The Hague, Netherlands. Over the course of the 1990s, the case moved through the international justice system, first to determine whether the Court had jurisdiction, and eventually through proceedings on the merits of the case, and final resolution.

GCC Mediation—1976 through 1990

Efforts by Saudi Arabia

In 1976, King Khalid bin Abdul-Aziz Al-Saud of Saudi Arabia undertook the role of mediator between the two states. After meetings with the Amirs of Bahrain and Qatar, he embarked on various initiatives to find a resolution to the outstanding territorial issues, as well as to prevent the escalation of tensions between the two states.

The mediation process was made possible by the acceptance by both parties of Five Principles proposed by Saudi Arabia. Those Principles defined the issues under discussion as "complementary, indivisible issues, [which were] to be resolved comprehensively together." The Principles and the ensuing negotiations reflected an understanding that the dispute was preferably to be settled by agreement, and that should such an effort fail, it would be submitted to arbitration (Bahrain 1992, 2–3 ¶ 1.4; *1978 Mediation Principles, as Amended in 1983*).

The Cooperation Council of Arab States of the Gulf, commonly known as the Gulf Cooperation Council (GCC), comprises Saudi Arabia, Bahrain, United Arab Emirates, Kuwait, Oman, and Qatar. Its mandate is to coordinate the economic, political, cultural, and security policy of the six states. Following the GCC's creation in May 1981, the Five Principles continued to serve as the basis for discussions within the framework of the Council and under the continuing patronage of Saudi Arabia. In 1983, Bahrain accepted Qatar's earlier proposal to amend the Fifth Principle, and a "Framework for reaching a settlement" was approved during a tripartite meeting in the same year (Bahrain 1992, 2 fn 6; *Press Communiqué* no. 94/16, 3).

The negotiations, however, produced no significant results. And relations between Bahrain and Qatar were further strained in 1986 when Qatar landed troops on Fasht Al-Dibal—one of the maritime features comprising the Bahrain archipelago—and seized workmen employed by Bahrain's contractors (Bahrain 1992, 30 ¶ 5.5). Saudi Arabia then stepped up its mediation efforts. However, even after the two states submitted detailed memoranda to Saudi Arabia the following year, their positions remained as irreconcilable as ever. Increasingly, the parties involved in the negotiations felt that the issues would be more successfully resolved by arbitration. The focus of the discussions then shifted to the possible terms of a joint submission of the case to the International Court of Justice in The Hague, the judicial body in which disputes between UN member states are resolved (Bahrain 1992, 3 ¶ 1.5).

The 1987 Agreement and the Tripartite Committee

In December 1987, King Fahd of Saudi Arabia advanced specific proposals toward submission of the case. In his letters to the Amirs of Bahrain and Qatar, he outlined the steps to be taken toward resolving the dispute. The letters stressed that:

> All the disputed matters shall be referred to the International Court of Justice, at the Hague, for a final ruling binding upon both parties, who shall have to execute the terms. (Al-Saud, 19 December 1987a; Al-Saud, 19 December 1987b)

The letters also emphasized the importance of maintaining the status quo, and provided for the establishment of a Tripartite Committee comprising representatives of the States of Bahrain and Qatar and the Kingdom of Saudi Arabia

> ... for the purpose of approaching the International Court of Justice, and satisfying the necessary requirements to have the dispute submitted to the Court in accordance with its regulations and instructions so that a final ruling, binding upon both parties, be issued. (*ICJ Judgment,* 1994, 6)

The Kingdom of Saudi Arabia further affirmed its willingness to continue its role as guarantor of the mediation process.

The Saudi proposals were adopted by Bahrain and Qatar respectively on 26 December 1987 and 21 December 1987 (Isa bin Salman

Al-Khalifa, 26 December 1987; Khalifa bin Hamad Al-Thani, 21 December 1987). This fact was also confirmed in the official announcement made by Saudi Arabia, which stated that:

> The contacts . . . have yielded a proposal . . . whereby the case should be referred to arbitration in accordance with the principles constituting the framework solution . . .
>
> Accordingly, agreement has been reached between the two parties, in accordance with the five principles to establish a committee . . . for the purpose of communicating with the International Court of Justice . . . (Bahrain 1992, 37 ¶ 5.19)

Thus, it was envisioned that the submission of the case to arbitration would be a collective effort involving the Tripartite Committee. The latter received a clear mandate to establish the requirements for approaching the International Court, and to facilitate the process of defining the terms of a "Special Agreement"—i.e., the formal application to the ICJ. That understanding was reflected in the draft agreements presented by both Bahrain and Qatar at the preliminary meeting of the Tripartite Committee during the 1987 GCC Summit Meeting in Riyadh (Bahrain 1992, 37–39 ¶ 5.21–5.23). Though Qatar was to argue—four years later—that the establishment of the Committee had been merely a procedural matter, at the time of its formation the Committee was clearly perceived by both parties to be an expression of their understanding that the case would be jointly submitted to the ICJ.

The Bahraini Formula

Between January and December 1988, the Tripartite Committee held six meetings, at which attempts were made to prepare the Special Agreement. Bahrain and Qatar each presented their draft proposals for such an Agreement in March 1988. However, these proposals revealed wide divergences in the parties' views as to the exact scope of the dispute. Bahrain's view was that the Court should be asked to determine Bahrain's rights in Zubarah, and to clarify the maritime boundary between the two states, while taking into account Bahrain's undisputed and well-established sovereignty over the Hawar Islands, Fasht Al-Dibal, and Qit'at Jaradah. For a more detailed discussion, see the section on "Maritime Delimitation" later in this chapter. Qatar, for its part, insisted that the Court should be asked to determine sovereignty over the Hawar

Islands, Fasht Al-Dibal, and Qit'at Jaradah, as well as the maritime boundary between the two states. Qatar furthermore raised objections to the inclusion of Zubarah among the issues to be adjudicated. These differences slowed the work of the Tripartite Committee. Despite a number of subsequent revisions to Bahrain's and Qatar's draft proposals, no mutually acceptable formulation of the dispute could be achieved during the first four meetings of the Committee (Bahrain 1992, 39–45 ¶ 5.24–5.33; Qatar 1992, 45–53 ¶ 3.34–3.47).

An important breakthrough occurred in October 1987 when, following an initiative by Saudi Arabia, Sheikh Hamad bin Isa Al-Khalifa, the Crown Prince of Bahrain, transmitted to Sheikh Hamad Al-Thani, the Crown Prince of Qatar, a broad definition of the subject matter of the dispute. The text, which came to be known as the "Bahraini formula," was an attempt to define "exhaustively the matters which would be referred to the Court," reads as follows:

1. The Hawar Islands, including the island of Janan
2. Fasht Al-Dibal and Qit'at Jaradah
3. The archipelagic baselines
4. Zubarah
5. The areas for fishing for pearls and for fishing for swimming fish and any other matters connected with maritime boundaries.
(*ICJ Judgment*, 1994, 7 ¶ 18)

Thus emerged the first definition of the dispute's scope. The International Court of Justice also used that same definition of the "whole of the dispute" in their proceedings.

The Bahraini formula employed a generalized approach to the task before the Court, to enable the two states to make progress toward the drafting of the Special Agreement. Again, the formula reflected an understanding that "[t]he Parties" were to submit the case jointly to the ICJ. Qatar apparently shared that view, as one of its delegates to the sixth committee meeting expressed Qatar's willingness to accept the formula after its possible reformulation by Bahrain, and further proposed:

> that the agreement which would be submitted to the Court should have two annexes, one Qatari and the other Bahraini. Each State would define in its Annex the subjects of dispute it wants to refer to the Court. (*ICJ Judgment*, 1994, 7 ¶ 18)

The two parties accepted the definition in principle and agreed to study the points raised during the discussions.

The dispute between Bahrain and Qatar was again discussed at the GCC Summit Meeting in December 1988; there it was decided that Saudi Arabia would continue its efforts to achieve an agreement between Bahrain and Qatar. But such efforts producing no conclusive results, it was decided the following year at the GCC summit that the period of Saudi mediation would be extended for an additional two months. A number of meetings were also held between the parties in the course of 1989 and 1990—none of which meetings achieved a settlement of the matter (Bahrain 1992, 47 ¶ 5.38).

Failure of the parties to adopt a Special Agreement for submission of the case to the International Court of Justice was largely due to the difficulties associated with defining the scope of the dispute. It will be recalled that Bahrain was initially reluctant to allow its sovereignty over the Hawar Islands to become a matter of discussion. Bahrain's eventual acquiescence to the possible inclusion of the Hawars among discussed issues was a result of Bahrain's confidence that its authority over the islands had been well established, as well as a reaction to the possibility of reasserting Bahrain's rights over Zubarah.

For its part, Qatar's positions were somewhat ambiguous regarding the inclusion of Zubarah: while at the sixth Tripartite Committee meeting Qatar consented to Zubarah becoming one of the subjects to be submitted to the Court, Qatar later qualified its position and stated that it was prepared to allow the determination of Bahrain's "private rights" in, rather than sovereignty over, Zubarah (Bahrain 1992, 47–48 ¶ 5.39; *ICJ Judgment*, 1994, 7 ¶ 18). Thus, the Bahraini formula and the five points adopted in principle at the sixth committee meeting failed to produce the necessary agreement.

The Doha Summit

The next GCC Summit meeting took place in Doha in 1990. Though the logical focus of the discussions was expected to be Iraq's recent invasion of Kuwait, Qatar brought up the issue of its dispute with Bahrain and stressed the urgency of submission of the matter to the International Court of Justice. Qatar further officially announced its acceptance of the Bahraini formula and insisted that Saudi Arabia's mediation efforts should terminate in April of the following year, whereupon the parties would be free to take the matter to the Court (Bahrain 1992, 4 ¶ 1.9).

As was later made clear, Qatar's objective was to secure an environment that would allow it to file a unilateral application to the Court. For that purpose, Qatar was to use—in July 1991—the Minutes of the Doha Meeting, which it chose to equate to an official agreement between the parties. In December 1990, Qatar's intentions were, however, unknown, and Bahrain acted on the assumption that the case would be jointly submitted to arbitration. Thus, Bahrain rejected two drafts of the minutes which included references to "each of [the parties]" or "either of the two parties" starting the proceedings, as that was seen as incompatible with the already agreed-upon joint submission to the Court. As a result, the final draft of the minutes provided for "the two parties" to take the dispute to the ICJ—words that had uniformly been used in the course of the negotiations (Bahrain 1992, 4–5 ¶ 1.10–1.11; Agreement of 25 December 1990). Furthermore, the Minutes noted that Saudi Arabia's mediation would continue until April 1991, after which the matter might be submitted to the Court. It was also noted that the mediation would continue even after possible referral of the dispute to the ICJ, and that the case would be withdrawn in the event of reaching a brotherly solution acceptable to both parties (*Press Communiqué* no. 94/16, 3).

Thus, the main achievement of the Doha meeting was agreement by the two parties to define the dispute between themselves in terms of the Bahraini formula advanced in 1988. Another important—though unforeseen by some of the parties—implication of the meeting was that it would serve as the basis for Qatar's unilateral submission of the case to the International Court of Justice.

ICJ Jurisdiction Phase

No notable developments occurred between Bahrain and Qatar in the months following the Doha Summit. Significantly, Qatar gave no indication to Bahrain that it was contemplating a unilateral application to the International Court of Justice.

Qatar's Application to the Court

The dispute between Bahrain and Qatar moved onto the international stage when Qatar made a unilateral submission on 8 July 1991 to the International Court of Justice in The Hague, entitled the *Case Concerning Maritime Delimitation and Territorial Questions Between Qatar and Bahrain*.

By virtue of its Application filed with the Registry of the Court, Qatar instituted proceedings against Bahrain without giving Bahrain any advance notice whatsoever. Qatar thus disregarded the principles that had undergirded the mediation process and placed Bahrain in a disadvantaged position—an action that also contradicted the established standards for the conduct of relations among Arab states of the Gulf. For its part, Bahrain—while remaining committed to submitting the case to the International Court of Justice—objected strongly to the manner in which Qatar had conducted itself.

Another serious shortcoming of Qatar's application was this: it failed to bring to the Court's attention the totality of the issues between Bahrain and Qatar. Significantly, the question of Zubarah—seen as critical by Bahrain—had not been included in Qatar's description of the case (Qatar 1991, 2–3 ¶ 11–25).

Qatar's application relied on the 1987 Agreement and the Doha Minutes, which it interpreted as fully fledged international treaties authorizing either party to bring the case before the ICJ (Qatar 1991, 5 ¶ 40). However, the 1987 Agreement pertained exclusively to the *joint* submission of the dispute to arbitration, nor did the Doha Minutes of 1990 mention *unilateral* submission of the case. Furthermore, the Doha Minutes had not been regarded at the time of their signature as amounting to anything more than a record of the negotiations—as was also evident by the fact that Qatar's UN registration of that document as a "treaty or international agreement" had taken place only twelve days before Qatar filed its Application with the International Court of Justice (Bahrain 1992, 8 ¶ 1.14.2).

Bahrain therefore contested the very basis of the Court's jurisdiction as invoked by Qatar. In its letters sent to the Court in July and August 1991, Bahrain pointed out that the 1987 Agreement and the 1990 Doha Minutes did not constitute sufficient grounds for conferring jurisdiction on the ICJ to adjudicate the matters between Bahrain and Qatar (Al-Baharna, 14 July, 18 August 1991).

Formal Pleadings

Following a meeting with the two parties in October 1991, the Court then decided to consider the questions of the Court's jurisdiction and the admissibility of Qatar's Application prior to proceeding with the merits of the case. An ICJ Order issued in the aftermath of the meeting emphasized the importance of bringing all matters of contention, as well as all relevant evidence, to the knowledge of the Court *(Order of 11 October 1991)*.

The two parties then proceeded with their formal pleadings before the ICJ on the issues of jurisdiction and admissibility. Their written submissions—all filed in 1992—comprised Qatar's *Memorial*, Bahrain's *Counter-Memorial*, Qatar's *Reply* and Bahrain's *Rejoinder*. A public hearing was then held between 28 February and 11 March 1994.

Throughout the pleadings, Qatar continued to refer to the agreement contained in the 1987 exchange of letters between the King of Saudi Arabia and the Amirs of Bahrain and Qatar, and to what it termed the "Doha Agreement," as international treaties. Qatar stated that the two documents together satisfied the necessary requirements for the institution of proceedings by Qatar. It also pointed out that the parties had committed themselves under the Agreement of 1987 to submit all matters of dispute to the ICJ, and that they had furthermore confirmed their decision in the "Doha Agreement" of 1990, where the scope of the dispute had been defined by reference to the Bahraini formula. Qatar also asserted that in view of the failure of the parties to produce a Special Agreement for submission of the case to the ICJ, the "Doha Agreement" had introduced a new approach to the Mediation process:

> [T]he Agreement reached at Doha in 1990 emerged as having the function of an *ad hoc* agreement containing a compromissory clause making it possible for each Party to submit an application to the Court presenting its own claims. (Qatar 1992a, 81 ¶ 4.84)

Qatar also stated that—insofar as the existence and the scope of the dispute had been already agreed upon—it was in a position to file a unilateral application in accordance with a provision in the Statute of the Court enabling unilateral submissions (Qatar 1992, 95 ¶ 4.64).

Bahrain accepted Qatar's interpretation of the 1987 Agreement as an undertaking by the parties to refer the case to the International Court of Justice. However, Bahrain pointed out that the 1987 Agreement was not sufficient to grant jurisdiction to the Court, since the submission of the matter to the ICJ had been conditional on the outcome of the work of the Tripartite Committee. The task of the Tripartite Committee had been to draft a Special Agreement for approaching the Court, and that task had not been altered at any stage of the mediation process. It was Bahrain's position, therefore, that in December 1990 Qatar had attempted—but failed—to change that condition (*cf.* Bahrain 1992a, 2 ¶ 1.04).

Bahrain also reiterated its position that the Doha Minutes had not constituted an international agreement but, rather, a record of a stage in diplomatic negotiations. Bahrain pointed out that neither party could have attributed any other meaning to the minutes since both Bahrain's and Qatar's Constitutions contained specific provisions related to international agreements concerning territory—conditions which had not been met in the case of the Doha Minutes (Bahrain 1992, 92 *et seq.* ¶ 6.91 *et seq.*).

Bahrain further pointed out that the words "*al-tarafan*" (the Parties) used in the Doha Minutes pertained to the two parties *together* rather than either of the parties *individually* submitting the matter to the Court. That this was the meaning intended by the words was borne out in the correct translation of their dual form from Arabic—a language that makes a distinction between the dual and the plural of nouns (Bahrain 1992, 54 *et seq.* ¶ 6.7 *et seq.;* Bahrain 1992a, 25 *et seq.* ¶ 5.05 *et seq.*)

Again Bahrain reiterated its preparedness, in principle, to submit to the Court's jurisdiction in relation to the dispute with Qatar. However, Bahrain strongly objected to Qatar's unilateral seizing of the Court and to the negative implications that such an act would have on the subsequent development of the pleadings. In particular, Bahrain was opposed to the Court proceedings placing the two states in the roles of plaintiff and defendant—a development that would negate the principles established earlier during the mediation process (Bahrain 1992a, 75 ¶ 7.22). Bahrain also insisted that the issue of Zubarah must necessarily form a part of the matters before the Court, in accordance with the parties' prior agreement—expressed on numerous occasions during the mediation process—that the issues outstanding between Bahrain and Qatar would be submitted to the ICJ in their entirety (Bahrain 1992a, 70 *et seq.* ¶ 7.12 *et seq.*).

Qatar's submission to the Court thus stressed that "[the Parties'] express commitments in the Agreements of December 1987...and December 1990...to refer their disputes to the...Court" furnished sufficient grounds for the Court "to exercise jurisdiction to adjudicate upon those disputes" (*Press Communiqué* no. 94/16, 4). Bahrain, for its part, considered that the provisions of the 1987 Agreement and the 1990 Minutes (which were, in any case, not viewed by Bahrain as legally binding treaties) contained no authorization for Qatar to unilaterally submit the case to the ICJ. Therefore, in Bahrain's view, the Court lacked jurisdiction.

The Court's Ruling

In its Judgment of 1 July 1994, the Court failed to decide either on its jurisdiction in the case or on the admissibility of Qatar's Application (*ICJ Judgment*, 1994).

The Court, however, reached a decision regarding the 1987 and 1990 texts, on which Qatar had based its Application. Considering the nature of the latter document, in particular, the Court noted that "international agreements may take a number of forms" (*ICJ Judgment*, 1994 ¶ 23) and concluded that:

> [The Doha Minutes] enumerate the commitments to which the Parties have consented. They thus create rights and obligations in international law for the parties. They constitute an international agreement. (*ICJ Judgment*, 1994 ¶ 25)

The Court also referred to the Bahraini formula as determining the "limits of the dispute with which the Court would be asked to deal." It went on to state:

> However, while the Bahraini formula permitted the presentation of distinct claims by each of the Parties, it nonetheless presupposed that the whole of the dispute would be submitted to the Court. (*ICJ Judgment*, 1994 ¶ 33)

The main problem identified in this context was the absence of the issue of Zubarah from the list of points brought to the ICJ's attention by Qatar. As the Court only had before itself Qatar's Application, it felt unable to make a determination as to the ICJ's jurisdiction until the "whole of the dispute" was submitted to it. The parties were therefore to be given an opportunity to present the entirety of their claims to the ICJ (*ICJ Judgment,* 1994 ¶ 41). Thus, for the first time in its history, the Court had issued an "interlocutory judgment" inviting the parties to further elaborate on their positions rather than disposing of the issue under consideration (*ICJ Judgment,* 1994—Oda dissenting opinion ¶ 3).

Following the Court's first decision, Qatar submitted, in November 1994, an "Act to comply with . . . the Judgment of the Court" (Al-Nuaimi, 30 November 1994). Qatar pointed out that the parties had failed to reach an agreement to act jointly and it was therefore submitting "the whole of the dispute . . . as circumscribed by . . . the 'Bahraini formula.'" Qatar listed the five points agreed upon at the sixth Tripartite Committee meeting and noted that Bahrain defined its claim to Zubarah as a claim to sovereignty (*Press Communiqué* no. 95/6, 2–3).

Bahrain, for its part, submitted a "Report . . . on the attempt by the Parties to implement the Court's Judgment." (Al-Baharna, 30 November 1994). Bahrain stated that it had welcomed the Court's Judgment of 1994, which Bahrain had interpreted as saying that the submission of the "whole of the dispute" would be "consensual in character." However, in Bahrain's opinion, Qatar's submissions had been made with a view to furthering its own case, and had therefore denied Bahrain "the right to describe, define or identify, in words of its own choosing, the matters which it [wished] specifically to place in issue." Bahrain furthermore noted Qatar's reluctance to include in the list of disputed matters the item of "*sovereignty* over Zubarah" (*Press Communiqué* no. 95/6, 3). [Emphasis added.]

Bahrain's comments on Qatar's "Act"—submitted in December 1994—confirmed this position and emphasized that

> . . . the Court did not declare in its Judgment of 1st July, 1994 that it had jurisdiction . . . Consequently, if the Court did not have jurisdiction at that time, then the Qatari separate Act . . . [could not] create that jurisdiction or effect a valid submission in the absence of Bahrain's consent. (*Press Communiqué* no. 95/6, 3)

The Court issued its final Judgment on 15 February 1995 (*ICJ Judgment,* 1995). By ten votes to five, it found that at Doha the parties had reaffirmed their consent to submit the dispute to the ICJ—jointly or unilaterally—and had determined its subject matter by the acceptance of the Bahraini formula. The Court was furthermore satisfied with the submission of the five-point list by Qatar (where Zubarah had been mentioned) and considered that it had been presented with the whole of the dispute. The Court therefore decided that it had jurisdiction to adjudicate the dispute and that Qatar's Application was admissible (*ICJ Judgment*, 1995 ¶ 44, 48).

The judges who had dissented from the Court's opinion pointed to the absence of clear consent by Bahrain to submit to the Court's jurisdiction (*ICJ Judgment*, 1995—Schwebel, Oda and Koroma dissenting opinions). The dispute over Zubarah had "not been submitted to the Court by or with the authority of Bahrain" (*ICJ Judgment*, 1995—Shahabuddeen dissenting opinion). There were also concerns that the Court had failed to give proper weight to the preparatory work of the Doha Minutes, in which Bahrain had expressed its clear opposition to the unilateral submission of the matter to the ICJ (*ICJ Judgment*, 1995—Schwebel dissenting opinion).

Despite these various concerns, however, the jurisdiction of the Court was confirmed, and the two parties were invited to submit their written pleadings on the merits of the case. Despite its original contention of lack of ICJ jurisdiction, Bahrain felt that its cause would be better served by active participation in the Merits phase and therefore began preparations for the next phase of the process.

ICJ Merits Phase

The Merits phase of the case before the International Court of Justice lasted from 1995 to 2000, and involved the simultaneous submission by both parties of *Memorials, Counter-Memorials,* and *Replies*. The final stage in this phase was a series of Oral Hearings that occurred in May and June 2000.

On 30 September 1996 Bahrain and Qatar submitted their *Memorials*, as the first stage in the Merits phase of the case. Qatar's *Memorial* was composed of one main volume of the arguments (often called *"the Memorial"*) of 375 pages, plus sixteen volumes of Annexes and Appendixes (including a Map Atlas)—a total of almost six thousand pages of materials. Bahrain's *Memorial* comprised seven volumes—one main volume of the arguments, five volumes of Annexes and a Map Atlas—almost two thousand pages of materials.

In its *Memorial*, Bahrain asked the Court to adjudge that:

- Bahrain is sovereign over Zubarah;
- ...over the Hawar Islands, including Janan and Hadd Janan;
- ...over all the insular and other features, including Fasht Al-Dibal and Qit'at Jaradah, comprising the Bahraini archipelago, and
- to draw the maritime boundary accordingly.

Qatar, of course, asked for the opposite.

As will be detailed in Chapter 21, Bahrain's analysis of the *Qatar Memorial* and the documents Qatar used to support its claims led to the compelling conclusion that Qatar had submitted eighty-one forged documents to the International Court of Justice. Subsequently, in Qatar's *Counter-Memorial* of 31 December 1997, it submitted yet another forged document, bringing the total number of forged documents to eighty-two. In September 1998, Qatar withdrew these forged documents from the case.

On 30 May 1999, as the last written stage in the Merits phase of the case before the Oral Hearings, Bahrain and Qatar submitted their *Replies*. Then in the final public segment, from 29 May through 29 June 2000, the International Court heard the Oral Pleadings of both parties. During the Oral Hearings, as he had during the entire Merits phase, His Excellency Jawad Salim Al-Arayed represented Bahrain as its Agent. Qatar was represented by His Excellency Abdullah bin Abdulatif Al-Muslemani, who had been appointed Qatar's Agent in June 1997.

Those interested in a more detailed recounting of the documentary history of the case will find it in the Court's Judgment (*ICJ Judgment*, 2001, 6–15).

Territorial Questions: the Hawar Islands and the Zubarah Region

The two distinct elements under consideration were the territorial questions between Bahrain and Qatar—namely sovereignty over Zubarah and sovereignty over the Hawar Islands—and the maritime delimitation to be made by the Court. During the pleadings, each state aimed to demonstrate that—in accordance with the relevant principles of international law—it had better title to the territories at issue than the other state.

Legal Foundations of Bahrain's Claims

Bahrain based its claims on four well-established principles of international law. The first of these principles states that *title is dependent on effective possession*. In international law, title to territory is intimately linked to possession. When there are only two claimants to the same territory, and both acknowledge that one of them and no other has title to it, the law recognizes the title claim of the party demonstrating the more effective occupation as evidenced by peaceful and continuous exercise of governmental authority—i.e., *effectivités*—appropriate for the type of territory in question. "The actual, continuous and peaceful display of State functions" is, according to the Island of Palmas Award, "the sound and natural criterion of territorial sovereignty" (*UN Reports of International Arbitral Awards*). Further, international law holds that unlawful possession cannot create title except in the case of prescription, i.e., right to title acquired through uninterrupted, customary usage over a long period of time. Thus, effective title depends on whether possession is acquired and maintained in accordance with the law prevailing at the time of the acquisition in question.

The second principle allows for the special context of Arab concepts of territory in areas where boundaries have not been formally drawn (areas of low habitation with nomadic or intermittent occupation), in which *allegiance to one claimant or the other* becomes an important determining factor.

The third principle Bahrain relied on was that *possession overrides proximity*. Proximity, adjacency, or contiguity of a disputed territory to the claimant's territory are not alone sufficient factors to vest title. This principle has been affirmed in several cases before the Court, such as the Island of Palmas case and the Minquiers and Echrehos case (*Minquiers and Echrehos, Judgment*, 1953).

The fourth principle is that of *res judicata*. This principle holds that once an issue of law or fact between two parties has been judicially examined and determined, that determination resolves the matter once and for all. Subject to the procedures of appeal or review as may exist within the framework of the original adjudicatory process, neither party is entitled subsequently to refuse to comply or to seek to reopen the issue in legal proceedings. (For a more detailed discussion of these four principles, see Chapter 3 of the *Bahrain Memorial*, 1996.)

Thus, respecting the Zubarah region, Bahrain claimed that it had maintained full and internationally recognized title from 1783 until 1937 by reference to the standard of contextually proportionate effective occupation. At the beginning of that period, the government of Qatar did not exist and—except for minor expansion into the southeast of the Qatar peninsula—the influence of the Al-Thani (Qatar's ruling tribe) during the Ottoman period never extended significantly beyond Doha Town and its environs. Following the government of Qatar's comparatively recent creation, it never established effective occupation in Zubarah, while Bahrain has continued to insist on its rights of two centuries' duration.

Bahrain also referred to the regional standard of the allegiance of the residents of Zubarah (most notably, the Al-Jabr branch of the Naim tribe, whose *dirah* comprised the Zubarah region). *Dirah* is the concept by which, in nomadic areas of the Gulf, a ruler establishes sovereignty over a territory within which his tribe moves. Bahrain further stressed that Qatar's 1937 attack on Zubarah had been an act of aggression inconsistent with the norms of international law prevailing at the time—particularly, the Covenant of the League of Nations and the Kellogg-Briand Pact. Thus, in Bahrain's view Qatar had never acquired lawful title to Zubarah, and Bahrain's sovereignty over the region had therefore not been effectively displaced.

In support of its claim to the Hawar Islands, Bahrain invoked the principle of *res judicata* and emphasized that Bahrain's ownership of the Hawars had been authoritatively recognized by Britain in 1939. In fact, the matter of sovereignty over the islands had been subject to formal, legitimate, and comprehensive review entered into willingly by both Qatar (whose Ruler had himself initiated the proceedings) and Bahrain. In and of itself, this was seen by Bahrain as sufficient to establish Bahrain's title under international law. In addition, Bahrain's *effectivités*—both during the period preceding British recognition and subsequent to the British award—had far surpassed the degree of exercise of authority required by international law. In contrast, Bahrain pointed out that prior to the 1930s, the Ruler of Qatar himself had been ignorant of the location of the islands. Even after the British award he had never extended his authority to the Hawars or, indeed, established effective authority over the part of the Qatar peninsula opposite the islands.

Legal Foundations of Qatar's Claims

Qatar, for its part, drew the Court's attention to the fact that a significant factor in establishing title to territory is the recognition by third parties of the extent of territory controlled by a certain state (Qatar 1996, 56 ¶ 5.9). This principle has been confirmed in a number of authoritative legal works, as well as in the *Delagoa Bay* case, the *Rann of Kutch* case and the *Dubai/Sharjah* case (Qatar 1996, 56–58 ¶ 5.10–5.14). In Qatar's *Memorial* and *Counter-Memorial*, the evidence it presented for external recognition was largely a series of documents by other Gulf, British, and Ottoman officials. These documents were later withdrawn, after being proved to be forgeries by Bahrain. (See Chapter 21 for further information about the forged documents submitted by Qatar.)

In addition, Qatar devoted considerable attention to analysis of arbitral awards and pointed to numerous characteristics necessary to establish the validity of such awards under international law. Four such characteristics—upheld in the *Dubai/Sharjah* Award—are: founding the arbitration on an existing arbitration agreement, affording the parties equal opportunity to present their arguments, ensuring that the arbitrators are independent, and providing reasons for the arbitral decision (Qatar 1996, 131 ¶ 6.114–6.115). The applicable fundamental rules in this respect were, in Qatar's view:

(1) the rule that both parties must have a proper and equal opportunity to present their case at all stages (the *audi alteram partem* rule);

(2) the rule that no one should be judge in his own cause *(nemo judex in causa sua);*

(3) the requirement that the proceedings should be free from corruption, fraud and bias; and

(4) the right of the parties to a reasoned decision.
(Qatar 1996, 133–34 ¶ 6.122)

These arguments by Qatar were attempting to show that the British Award of 1939, which had determined that the Hawar Islands were the property of Bahrain, was invalid and therefore not binding.

In respect to the Hawar Islands in particular, Qatar challenged the validity of the British Award of 1939 and asserted that the award had been flawed in many significant respects. In Qatar's view, consent had neither been sought from nor given by the Ruler of Qatar to the making of the British government determination concerning the Hawar Islands. Qatar further maintained that the procedure followed by the British government had been defective and that the evidence on which the decision had been based had been incomplete and otherwise suspect. The essential requirements for the validity of arbitral awards had thus, in Qatar's opinion, not been met; therefore the decision should not be permitted to stand.

Again, numerous forged documents were used to prove Qatar's assertions. However, even after their removal, Qatar continued to insist that the award had been vitiated on a number of grounds and should therefore have no legal effect with regard to sovereignty over the Hawar Islands.

Another notion Qatar made use of was that of a "critical date" or "critical period" in territorial disputes. That notion pertains to the approximate time of crystallization of a dispute, and gives significant weight to the acts of sovereignty performed by states before such territories become an issue of dispute. While displays of sovereignty subsequent to a "critical date" may be taken into consideration in such cases, that is done mainly for the purpose of illustrating or understanding "the situation as it was during the critical period" (Qatar 1997, 98 ¶ 3.100).

In formulating its territorial claims, Qatar also advanced the thesis that the integrity of the Qatar peninsula in effect bestowed title to the whole of the peninsula on the Al-Thani chiefs of Doha during the middle of the nineteenth century. Yet not only was such a claim legally and historically unsustainable, much of the evidence invoked in its support consisted of forged documents. (For a detailed discussion of the scope of Al-Thani authority, see Chapters 4 and 6; for a discussion of the forged documents, see Chapter 21.) A significant proportion of that "evidence" related to the recognition by third parties (notably, the Ottomans, the British, and regional rulers) of Al-Thani sovereignty over Zubarah and the Hawar Islands. While such evidence—had it been authentic—would have assisted Qatar's case, its removal when the documents were proved forged left Qatar with little on which to base its claims other than extravagant but unfounded assertions as to the extent of Al-Thani control.

Qatar implicitly recognized the importance of *effectivités* in establishing title, since many of the forged documents submitted to the Court purported to show the existence of such acts by the Al-Thani in relation to the Hawar Islands. However, following Qatar's announcement that it would disregard the forgeries, Qatar resorted to the "critical date" argument and attempted to demonstrate that Bahrain's *effectivités* had all taken place after the "critical period" of 1936–38 (i.e., after Bahrain had allegedly advanced its first claim to the Hawar Islands in 1936) and should therefore be disregarded (see also "Qatar's version" in Chapter 19, particularly "Blank Slate" section). In the absence of Qatari *effectivités*, Qatar relied—as had its Ruler in 1938–39—on proximity, itself an inapplicable principle when a territory is in the effective possession of another state (see also "Legal Foundations of Bahrain's Claims" in this chapter, as well as Chapter 11).

Maritime Delimitation

Both states recognized that the delimitation of the maritime boundary would be contingent on the outcome of the territorial part of the dispute. The established legal principle that "the land dominates the sea" therefore required that the Court make a pronouncement on the questions of sovereignty over Zubarah and the Hawar Islands before proceeding with the rather technical task of defining the maritime boundary between Bahrain and Qatar.

The adjudication of the two states' maritime claims was to be effected in accordance with the principles and rules of customary international law insofar as neither Bahrain nor Qatar were parties to any of the four Geneva Conventions governing maritime law (the Convention on the Territorial Sea and the Contiguous Zone, the Convention on the High Seas, the Convention on Fishing and Conservation of the Living Resources of the High Seas, and the Convention on the Continental Shelf). In addition, Bahrain had signed and ratified (while Qatar had signed but not ratified) the 1982 UN Convention on the Law of the Sea—a convention which therefore could not be considered as being in force between them, but which nevertheless was of the utmost importance in ascertaining the legal principles applicable to maritime delimitations.

Both states proposed that, following the determination of their territorial claims, the Court should effect a maritime delimitation by drawing a median line between their respective coasts. There was, however, considerable disagreement as to what coasts were relevant, and what methods should be employed to construct the median line. Most notably, Bahrain and Qatar disagreed as to the nature and extent of the Bahrain archipelago, and the status of certain features important to the delimitation of the maritime boundary.

The Bahrain Archipelago

Bahrain built its maritime claims on the concept of Bahrain as an archipelagic ensemble, contrasted with Qatar's existence as a continental state. Qatar, for its part, acknowledged that Bahrain was a "de facto archipelago," but its view as to that archipelago's extent differed from Bahrain's position (Qatar 1997, 72 *et seq.* ¶ 3.60 *et seq.*). Furthermore, Qatar chose to interpret Bahrain's status as an archipelago in geographical terms only, rather than attribute to it any significant legal weight.

Bahrain described the Bahrain archipelago as consisting of the largest island, Bahrain (sometimes referred to as Awal), the immediately adjacent islands of Sitra and Muharraq, other islands (including those of the Hawar group), and also more than twenty-two shoals (or, as they are referred to locally, *fasht*'s). Bahrain claimed further that as a state, it is composed of both the Bahrain archipelago and the continental Zubarah region (Reisman, 13 June 2000 ¶ 11). Since in Bahrain's view the Bahrain archipelago thus comprised all of the maritime features lying between the main island of Bahrain and the Qatar peninsula and since all such features had historically been subject to Bahrain's sovereignty, Bahrain asserted that the Court should confirm their total status as forming part of the State of Bahrain.

Bahrain demonstrated that its exercise of sovereignty had been consistent and continuous since the arrival of the Al-Khalifa in the region in 1783. Qatar, even at the time when it became a distinct entity and later a distinct state, had influence over only those parts of the continental peninsula where the Doha Sheikhs had exercised authority, namely the region around Doha.

But as Bahrain pointed out, the areas of sea, and the insular and other legally relevant formations situated between the peninsula and the main island of Bahrain, together with those peninsular areas that had been Bahraini, had continuously been part of the political entity of Bahrain.

This has always been Bahrain's official position, and was reflected even in the 1930s negotiations for oil concessions—negotiations that never met with any objections or reservations from the government of Qatar or from Petroleum Concessions Ltd., Qatar's concessionaire during that period.

Bahrain has historically carried out activities relating to, and indicating sovereignty over, specific maritime features, as well as over the entire Gulf of Bahrain. Bahrain activities have included maintaining coast guard patrols; providing aids to fishermen; erecting markers, monuments, and navigational beacons; and conducting maritime surveys in the area. (*Cf.* paragraphs 568 *et seq.* [pp. 249 *et seq.*] of the *Bahrain Memorial* 1996.) The Bahrain archipelago has thus existed during the last two centuries as not only an intrinsic geographical entity, but also as an integrated political and economic unit under the Al-Khalifa. This fact has been consistently asserted by the Bahrain government, as well as recognized by third parties on numerous occasions (*cf.* Lorimer 1908–15, II:234–35, 373–74; *Gazetteer of Arabia* 1915, 329; *Military Report on the Arabian Shores* 1933, 32; Belgrave 1934; Hay 1954).

Qatar has not disputed the above facts related to Bahrain's exercise of authority. Even more significantly, Qatar has been unable to point to any acts of exercise of authority by its own Rulers. What Qatar has done is challenge the significance of those acts and assert that they did not constitute valid grounds for title. However, as Bahrain pointed out:

> A continental State might see no particular significance in the beacons and cairns. For sea-going and archipelagic peoples, these are extremely important structures, vital for navigation and sometimes for survival itself. Hence, at the very least, the erection of the beacons and cairns by Bahrain (without any corresponding activity by Qatar) shows a strong interest in the maritime features. In *Grisbadarna*, the Tribunal noted that the effort and expense of these sorts of activities evidenced a perception of right and duty. Qatar manifestly did not feel a right or a duty to establish or maintain navigational aids in this area. (Reisman, 13 June 2000 ¶ 49)

The issue of the exercise of authority over the maritime features was directly related to the method to be employed in defining the maritime boundary. Thus, Bahrain claimed that its sovereignty over the maritime features in the Gulf of Bahrain did furnish sufficient grounds for Bahrain to insist that the median line delimiting its boundary with Qatar should take into account the outermost features of the Bahrain ensemble (Reisman, 13 June 2000 ¶ 6 *et seq.*).

Qatar, for its part, denied any legal significance to the numerous maritime features in the Gulf of Bahrain, equating these to "physical anomalies" (Quéneudec, 5 June 2000, ¶ 4). Qatar asserted that the median line should be drawn using the mainland-to-mainland method, i.e., taking into consideration only the coasts of the main Bahrain island and the Qatar peninsula. Qatar thus implied that a physical and legal "vacuum" existed in the Gulf of Bahrain, with the exceptions of the Hawar Islands, Fasht Al-Dibal, and Qit'at Jaradah. As Bahrain pointed out, however, Bahrain does not consist of a mainland with some lying-off islands, islets, and rocks; it is an insular and archipelagic ensemble, together with the continental territory of Zubarah. It would therefore be altogether inappropriate, claimed Bahrain, to draw a "mainland-to-mainland" median line and then to distribute the insular and other legally relevant features only according to whether these features were situated on the Bahraini or the Qatari side of that median line. According to Bahrain, the appropriate delimitation should be a delimitation between the coasts of the Bahrain ensemble, i.e., all the territories appertaining to Bahrain, on the one hand, and Qatar, on the other hand; not, as Qatar had requested, a median line dividing the maritime area between the coasts of the two "mainlands."

Status of Maritime Features

Aside from their disagreement in general as to whether the maritime features were relevant to the delimitation, Bahrain and Qatar took contrary views with respect to a number of specific features whose status would affect the maritime boundary. Most notably, such differences related to the basic distinction between islands and low-tide elevations (the legal term used to describe shoals, or *fasht*'s).

Under the 1982 Convention, an island is defined as "a naturally formed area of land, surrounded by water, which is above water at high tide" (*The Law of the Sea* 1983, art. 121[1]); while a low-tide elevation is defined as "a naturally formed area of land which is surrounded by and above water at low tide but submerged at high tide" (*The Law of the Sea* 1983, Article 13).

The legal implications of this distinction for the case were these: while both Bahrain and Qatar recognized the principle of international law holding that islands generate their own territorial waters, the two states disagreed as to the legal entitlements of uninhabited islands and low-tide elevations. Bahrain pointed out that islands—whether large or small, inhabited or uninhabited, or indeed uninhabitable—shared the same legal regime. In addition, Bahrain interpreted the principles of international law related to low-tide elevations as not precluding such formations from generating their own maritime entitlements. Qatar denied such entitlements both to small islands (which Qatar designated as islets or rocks—terms bearing no legal meaning) and to low-tide elevations.

Because the seas within the Bahrain archipelago contain a number of small islands, including Jazirat Ajirah, Al-Mu'tarid, Jazirat Mashtan, Jabbari, Umm Jalid, and Qit'at Jaradah, and low-tide elevations, including Fasht Bu Thur, Qita'a el Erge, Qit'at ash Shajarah, and Fasht Al-Dibal, the nature of the two parties' application of the law to the facts was of utmost significance to the maritime delimitation.

The divergence between Bahrain and Qatar's views as regards the following features were particularly notable:

Sitra island and Fasht Al-Azm
Sitra island is adjacent to the main Bahrain island, and is a component of the Bahrain archipelago. Fasht Al-Azm, which is an extension of Sitra island, is submerged at high tide. It nevertheless forms an integral part of Sitra island and has therefore been used by Bahrain to determine the basepoints from which the median line is to be drawn.

Qatar has chosen to see Fasht Al-Azm differently, and has stated that this is a feature separate from Sitra island. Qatar based its assertion on a claim that Fasht Al-Azm was divided from Sitra by a natural water channel, which was filled in during land reclamation activities in 1982, when an artificial canal was also dredged. While both Bahrain and Qatar agreed that the construction of the new canal had no legal significance, Qatar interpreted that canal as representing a replacement to the natural waterway that, in its view, had already existed between Sitra and Fasht

Al-Azm. The outcome of this controversy was to determine whether Fasht Al-Azm qualified as part of Sitra island, or whether—for the purposes of delimitation—it was to be considered a low-tide elevation separate from Sitra.

Naturally, Qatar claimed that the latter was the case. Invoking ambiguous evidence or tendentiously interpreting evidence that did not, in fact, support its conclusions, Qatar asserted that Fasht Al-Azm was indeed a low-tide elevation and thus, in Qatar's view, irrelevant to the delimitation of the maritime boundary. Qatar then proposed a boundary that cut across Fasht Al-Azm.

As Bahrain stressed, Qatar's position was contradicted by numerous hydrographical surveys, navigational charts, and marine pilot guides, none of which showed the existence of a navigable passage between Sitra and Fasht Al-Azm prior to 1982. Bahrain then submitted that the Fasht should be considered a part of Sitra island, with all the legal consequences deriving from that status (Reisman, 13 June 2000 ¶ 12 *et seq.*)

Qit'at Jaradah
Today, Qit'at Jaradah is an island. Evidence does suggest that it was for certain periods prior to the 1940s a low-tide elevation rather than an island. However, natural accretion caused its size and height to increase during the 1950s and subsequently, such that by the 1980s it had undoubtedly become an island.

Qatar asserted during the pleadings that Qit'at Jaradah still was a low-tide elevation, despite the fact that Qatar acknowledged that parts of Qit'at Jaradah were dry at high tide—a fact that qualifies it as an island under international law (Qatar 1996, 238 ¶ 10.55). The evidence adduced by Qatar in support of its assertions confirmed, rather than disproved, Bahrain's claim, as it included statements that Qit'at Jaradah was "exposed at all states of the tide" and comprised areas that were "permanently uncovered" (Bahrain 1997, 221–22 ¶ 512, 514).

In 1986, Qatari bulldozers removed the part of Qit'at Jaradah which had been exposed at high tide, thus attempting to alter its status to suit Qatar's position. Aside from this single instance, however, Qatar has exercised no manifestations of authority with respect to the island. Thus, as Bahrain stated:

It would be offensive to any notion of law or equity to allow Qatar to benefit from this intentionally unlawful act. (Bahrain 1999, 171 ¶ 332)

Furthermore, although Qatar's illegal activities in 1986 did artificially reduce Qit'at Jaradah to a low-tide elevation, in subsequent years, Qit'at Jaradah reverted to being an island once again, by means of natural accretion.

Bahrain insisted that Qit'at Jaradah had never been under Qatari control or jurisdiction. And while Bahrain could point to numerous *effectivités* in relation to Qit'at Jaradah, Qatar failed to show that their Ruler had exercised any measure of control with regard to Qit'at Jaradah. Bahrain pointed to numerous acts of exercise of Bahraini sovereignty over Qit'at Jaradah, such as conducting surveys, granting oil concessions, erecting a beacon in 1939, commissioning the drilling of an artesian well in 1940, maintaining coastguard patrols around the area of Qit'at Jaradah, and using Qit'at Jaradah for recreational purposes (Reisman, 13 June 2000, ¶ 32). Furthermore, Qit'at Jaradah's status as an island had been historically confirmed, most notably in the correspondence of British officials in the Gulf (Bahrain 1999, 167 *et seq.* ¶ 323 *et seq.*). Thus, it was Bahrain's position that Qit'at Jaradah should be considered an island and should, furthermore, be used in determining the maritime boundary between the two states.

Fasht Al-Dibal
Fasht Al-Dibal lies 2.08 nautical miles from the island of Qit'at Jaradah. This fact makes Fasht Al-Dibal relevant to the delimitation of the maritime boundary as this enables it to be used as a basepoint in the drawing of the median line. It will be recalled that Qatar disputed the significance of low-tide elevations to the maritime delimitation, and in this context, Qatar denied Bahrain's claim that Fasht Al-Dibal was a feature that could affect the course of the maritime boundary.

In 1986 Qatar launched an armed attack on Fasht Al-Dibal. Qatar deployed four armed helicopters, and detained and forcibly removed to Qatar the members of the construction crew operating on the Fasht under the authority of Bahrain. In deference to the mediation process that was ongoing at that time, Bahrain showed restraint in reacting to

Qatar's attack. That act had no material effect on the shoal's status as a possession of Bahrain.

As in the case of Qit'at Jaradah, Fasht Al-Dibal has historically been under the authority of Bahrain. Bahrain has conducted surveys, granted oil concessions, constructed cairns, constructed an artesian well, granted licenses for permanent fish traps, resolved navigational difficulties in the area, and carried out salvage operations during maritime emergencies (Reisman, 13 June 2000 ¶ 41 fn 2–8).

In 1946, the Political Agent wrote to the Rulers of Bahrain and Qatar asking whether they considered Fasht Al-Dibal and Qit'at Jaradah as part of their respective territories. In the event of an affirmative answer, the Rulers were invited to provide supporting evidence for their claims. The Ruler of Bahrain at that time stated that Bahrain's sovereignty over the Fasht derived from Bahrain's sovereignty over all the maritime features in the Gulf of Bahrain, as well as from Bahrain's exercise of effective control—such control having been manifested in the construction of artesian wells on Fasht Al-Dibal and Qit'at Jaradah and the erection of cairns.

The Ruler of Qatar's claim was based—as anyone familiar with the dispute might easily guess—on geographical proximity. The Ruler of Qatar's argument was that Fasht Al-Dibal was closer to his coast, and that his claim should be validated as a "consolation prize" for the injustice allegedly done by the British in awarding the Hawar Islands to Bahrain. Rather than grant Qit'at Jaradah or Fasht Al-Dibal to Qatar, however, the British confirmed Bahrain's sovereignty over the two features.

Bahrain's pearling banks
Bahrain's pearling banks are to the north and northeast of the Bahrain archipelago, and constitute the oldest and the richest pearl fisheries in the world. Principal among these are Fasht Naywah (Al-Amari), Abu Al-Kharb, Hayr Abu Al-Ja'al, Bin Zayaan, Bu Sawr, Naywah Al-Rumayhi, Naywah Al-Ma'awdah, Naywah Abdul-Qadr, Umm Al-Arshan, Khrais Al-Thayr, Umm Al-Qars, and Naywah Walid Ramadhan. Though many of Bahrain's pearling banks are, in fact, geographically closer to Qatar than to the main island of Bahrain, those pearling banks have always been Bahraini and under Bahrain's uninterrupted jurisdiction and control. (Qatar had its own pearling banks to the east of Doha.)

In the past, income from pearling provided not only most of the wealth of Bahrain, but also the major source of government revenue. Mainly Bahraini fleets worked the pearling banks, though tribes whose chiefs were on friendly terms with the Ruler of Bahrain were also permitted to operate in the region. The Bahrain government exercised exclusive authority over both the Bahraini and the foreign nationals working the banks.

With the development of cultured pearls by Japan in the 1920s, however, the Gulf's pearling industry declined in economic significance. Nevertheless, Bahrain continued to exercise control over the Gulf's pearling banks. To the present, Bahrain has continued to regulate the seasons for pearl diving, impose taxes on pearl diving boats, determine disputes related to pearling activities, and provide medical services on the banks through a hospital boat.

During the pleadings, Bahrain asserted that the pearling banks were relevant to the maritime delimitation and asked that the median line be adjusted to reflect Bahrain's sovereignty over them. Qatar treated Bahrain's claims with derision, yet Bahrain pointed out that its assertions were founded on legal principles: prior to the evolution of the contemporary continental shelf doctrine, the established view had been that a sovereign could assert ownership over the seabed and exclusive right to the "fructus" on proof of long established "occupation" of the beds and banks (Bahrain 1996, 275 ¶ 641). It was in this sense that Bahrain staked claim to the banks, over which Bahrain—and Bahrain only—had historically exercised any authority (Bahrain 1996, 274 *et seq.* ¶ 639 *et seq.*; Bahrain 1997, 279 *et seq.* ¶ 619 *et seq.*; Reisman, 13 June 2000 ¶ 55).

The 1947 Line

During the ICJ proceedings, Qatar claimed that the single maritime boundary should be drawn "with due regard to the line dividing the seabed of the two States as described in the British decision of 23 December 1947" (Qatar 1991). Qatar's claim rested on two letters sent on that date to the Rulers of Bahrain and Qatar respectively by C. J. Pelly, then British Political Agent in Bahrain. The letters, an attempt by British authorities to facilitate the operation of the oil companies in the area, had "forward[ed] . . . for [the Ruler's] information a copy of a map showing the line . . . which, His Majesty's Government considers, divides in accordance with equitable principles the seabed..." (C. J. Pelly, 23 December 1947).

Qatar stated:

> Qatar does *not* contend that the 1947 line is to be automatically regarded as *the* boundary line to be delimited between the maritime areas pertaining to Qatar and those pertaining to Bahrain. ...[Qatar] is not claiming a single maritime boundary drawn "along" that line... (Qatar 1996, 253 ¶ 11.19–11.20) [Emphasis in original.]

However, what Qatar proposed was, in effect, that the single maritime boundary to be drawn by the International Court of Justice should coincide with the line mentioned in the 1947 British letters—excepting those sections where it did not suit Qatar. (See Map No.1, p. xvii.) Thus, for instance, Qatar insisted that the line should be disregarded in that portion which enclaves the Hawar Islands (thus recognizing Bahrain's sovereignty over them), as well as in that part where it recognizes Bahrain's rights over Fasht Al-Dibal and Qit'at Jaradah.

In addition to being flagrantly self-contradictory, Qatar's position was legally flawed. Qatar's assertions that the British 1947 line should be considered a "circumstance highly relevant for the drawing of a single maritime boundary" and that the Court could "not act as if that line had never existed" (Qatar 1996, 253 ¶ 11.19) amount to equating the line with special or relevant circumstances. Such circumstances, however, are used in maritime delimitations to draw the dividing line; they do not in and of themselves constitute the dividing line.

In addition, the significance Qatar attributed to the line was quite unwarranted from both historical and legal perspectives. Unlike the 1939 British Award relating to the Hawar Islands, the 1947 British decision was not the result of a formal arbitration, but rather an attempt by British authorities to dispose of the issue of the division of the seabed for the purposes of ongoing oil concessions. As British authorities at the time and Qatar itself during the pleadings both consistently acknowledged, the 1947 line was merely a proposal submitted to the two Rulers; it was not a boundary delimited by means of a binding decision (Weil, 15 June 2000, 21 ¶ 133).

Thus, the line should hardly be regarded as a circumstance to be taken into consideration by the International Court of Justice. As Qatar itself stated in its 1991 Application to the ICJ, the Court was asked "to draw in accordance with international law a single maritime boundary between the maritime areas of seabed, subsoil and superjacent waters appertaining respectively to the State of Qatar and the State of Bahrain" (Qatar 1991). To base the maritime boundary between Bahrain and Qatar on a line drawn in 1947 in the context of oil concessions negotiations and not considered final by British authorities themselves, and then to alter those portions of the line that Qatar didn't like—such an exercise could hardly be marketed to the Court as one done in accord with international law.

In short, it would appear that Qatar's claims against Bahrain regarding numerous pertinent issues in this dispute would ignore—where it suited them—the established principles of international law, historic precedents, regional consensus, and even Qatar's own prior statements and stances in pursuit of their territorial aims.

21 | The Forged Documents

Before proceeding to describe the trial and judgment phase of this dispute between Bahrain and Qatar, we must relate in greater detail Bahrain's discovery of eighty-two aforementioned forged documents, submitted by the State of Qatar with its *Memorial* and *Counter-Memorial* to support its claims. This section demonstrates the exhaustive care taken by Bahraini analysts and distinguished international researchers to evaluate these disputed documents and eventually prove their lack of authenticity.

This chapter will lay out the sequence of events surrounding the forgeries—from initial suspicions to preliminary analysis, and then to detailed scholarly and forensic examination—that eventually resulted in Qatar's withdrawal of these documents. The chapter will conclude with a brief analysis of the effects of these documents' submission on the case, on the judicial process, and on the history of the Gulf region.

Discovery of the Forgeries

Submission of Memorials

The first stage in the ICJ Merits phase of the proceedings involved both parties' submission to the Court of "memorials"—statements of the facts and arguments accompanied by supporting documentation (called Annexes). The *Bahrain Memorial* (seven volumes) and the *Qatar Memorial* (sixteen volumes) were both submitted to the Court on 30 September 1996.

Initial Analysis of Evidence

While beginning work to help Bahrain's legal team to prepare the Bahrain *Counter-Memorial* a response to Qatar's *Memorial*—the next stage in the proceedings—Bahrain's Office of the Minister of State rigorously analyzed the arguments and supporting evidence in Qatar's *Memorial*. Very early in that process (by October 1996), Bahrain's analysts observed certain disturbing facts.

Particularly striking among these: that a substantial number of the documents included in the Annexes to Qatar's *Memorial* purported to describe past events and relations obviously inconsistent with the Gulf region's known history. Accepting Qatar's "evidence" in these documents as authentic would require wholesale reconsideration of the significance of various historical developments, and of the roles played by certain Rulers of Gulf nations, British officials, and other political personalities. And still another feature common to these documents was that they all seemed to have originated from Qatar's Diwan Amiri Archives—none was available from other public sources; none had previously been known to experts or historians; and none could be found in Bahrain's repositories.

The Office of the Minister of State assembled a team of researchers to study and examine Qatar's Annexes, and the claims and arguments these purported to prove, more thoroughly. The researchers' aim was to verify (if possible) the documents' authenticity and the accuracy with which they had been translated, and to compare the different versions Qatar had presented.

Initially, steps were taken to identify duplicate documents and determine where each document had been cited. Bahrain's team soon established that a large portion (almost one-third) of the documents included in the Qatar Annexes were never cited in Qatar's *Memorial*. After eliminating this third, plus the duplicates (where the same document had been submitted more than once with different Annex numbers), the researchers categorized the remaining documents and sought to determine whether the documents might be suspect—principally because they did not derive from publicly available sources. They identified eighty-one such documents, all sourced from the *Qatari Diwan Amiri Archives*, that is, the Qatari Amir's Court Archives.

Preliminary Investigation

Document Searches in Bahrain

Attempting to ascertain the authenticity of Qatar's "evidence," Bahrain's Office of the Minister of State requested that a number of Bahrain government agencies try to confirm certain documents' existence, and also to search for any materials that might relate to them.

Among the agencies active in this quest were the Bahrain Government Archives, the Amiri Court Archives, and the Bahrain Center for Studies and Research. They found that none of the suspect documents that should have been found in these depositories could be located. During the next two years while these forgeries were being investigated, the Bahrain Government Archives, which was the largest and most extensive of these repositories, acted in key partnership with the Office of the Minister of State. The Archives, which had been established by Charles Belgrave (the Adviser to the Amir of Bahrain from 1926 to 1957), held the bulk of all Bahrain government correspondence and records up to 1971.

The Ministry of Justice and Islamic Affairs also provided vital information relevant to the case. Based on well-documented information received from the Ministry of Justice and Islamic Affairs and the Bahrain Archives, the researchers established that the suspect Court judgments and land transactions Qatar invoked were indeed inauthentic, purportedly issued by persons who had never been judges in the Bahrain Court system.

The Ministry of Foreign Affairs was asked to use its existing contacts to obtain further information on documents related to persons or agencies in other GCC countries. Feedback from the Center for Documentation and Research in Abu Dhabi proved especially valuable. In addition to making available authentic sample letters of Rulers of Abu Dhabi and Dubai that bore the rulers' signatures and seals, the Center's experts in Abu Dhabi provided specific comments about a number of suspect documents' contents. In their report, the Center's experts mentioned that none of the questioned documents had been found in their holdings, and that they had observed many contradictions between issues discussed in the suspect documents and known historical facts. For example, among such contradictions was inclusion among the tribes of Qatar of five tribes well known to have recognized the authority of the Ruler of Abu Dhabi.

The Bahrain Government Archives also searched their collection, and the Office of the Minister of State searched historical sources at their disposal, trying to identify samples of genuine correspondence from any of the authors of the suspect documents. In the end, the Office of the Minister of State prepared a set of high quality original photographs of almost six hundred authentic documents (called internally the "Known Documents") by those suspect documents' "authors" who could be located. A list of these six hundred authentic documents, which had also been used by Bahrain's experts in preparing their reports, was supplied to the International Court of Justice in May 1998.

Additional searches were carried out to obtain biographical information, service records, or other related data about any persons who had purportedly written or received any of the Qatar-supplied doubtful documents. And additional historical facts were checked to identify other possible contradictions.

The researchers indeed found abundant contradictions in the suspect documents. Among these inconsistencies, documents supposedly related to the Ottoman administration of Hasa were dated as having been written before Hasa was ever annexed by the Ottomans. These documents also included numerous misplaced or anachronistic references, and were written in Arabic rather than in Ottoman Turkish (Osmanlica).

The researchers established that numerous suspect documents had been written either by or to persons who were in fact dead at the time of the supposed correspondence. The researchers found a letter supposedly written by an employee of the Adviserate in Bahrain *fourteen years before that person actually joined the Adviserate*. Had the person in question written the letter when it was dated, he would have been ten years old. Another document contained a reference to *"Her Majesty's Government"* at a time when the sovereign of Great Britain was King George VI.

The research team's findings more than confirmed suspicions about the non-authenticity of a large proportion of the documents attached as Annexes to Qatar's *Memorial*. A three-volume report on this research was presented to Bahrain's legal representatives, Freshfields, in February

1997. Bahrain's Office of the Minister of State also took the steps necessary to initiate a preliminary forensic document examination.

Analysis by Bahrain Criminal Investigations Directorate

In December 1996, Bahrain's Ministry of State requested the assistance of the Ministry of the Interior. Major Abdulla Abdul-Latif Hashim Al-Sadeh, a forgery and fingerprint expert with Bahrain's Criminal Investigations Directorate, was assigned to the project and began examining the "authenticity" of the suspect documents. His examination included linguistic and handwriting analysis, analysis of the seals and signatures, and comparison of the suspect documents with known authentic documents.

Because Qatar's Diwan Amiri Archive held the documents and made neither the originals nor color photographs of the originals available, Major Abdulla Al-Sadeh could review only photocopies of the suspect documents. These limitations prevented Major Al-Sadeh from using many techniques in his handwriting analysis that would have been possible with access to the original documents—such as study of the direction of the pen strokes, watermarks, breaks in the flow of the handwriting, ink color, pen impressions on the paper, document age, and ink age. Even so, he was able to draw conclusions from the positioning of the dates and signatures in the documents; the sizes and positions of various characters, words, and dots; and from the shape and style of the characters. His analysis included characters and words as they were found both within the same document and throughout the whole set of suspect documents.

First, Major Abdulla noticed similarities in the appearances of the phrase *"Bismillah Al-Rahman Al-Raheem"* throughout the suspect documents. He then discovered numerous similarities in other phrases, words and character combinations. Those observations led the expert to conclude it likely that in fact the very same individual had authored all of the documents under review. In addition, Major Abdulla identified numerous instances in which the author had attempted to disguise his natural handwriting by changing the first and the last letters of words—a fact that frequently resulted in the same characters appearing in obviously different styles within a single document.

In addition to the grammar and other characteristics of the suspect documents, Major Abdulla focused his linguistic analysis on consistencies of style and spellings of particular words. Similar spelling mistakes had been made in numerous documents, and words more appropriate to oral rather than written Arabic appeared throughout the suspect documents. Furthermore, the author's use of inappropriate local dialect and names pointed to the probability that the author was not of local origin. The documents employed references peculiar to Qatar but not to Bahrain, such as *"Al-Qatar"* instead of *"Qatar," "Bahrain"* instead of *"Al-Bahrain,"* or *"Bin Kanoo"* instead of *"Yousif bin Ahmed Kanoo"* or *"Beit Kanoo."*

Next, analysis of the seals on the suspect documents further confirmed Major Abdulla Al-Sadeh's suspicions regarding their authenticity. His examinations of the shape and size of the seals, of the position of dots and characters relative to each other, and of the styles (most notably, extensions) of the lines and characters inside the seals, showed the expert that modifications or copies of many individual seals had been used to signify more than one person throughout the set of documents. For example, he found that an unlikely "pair"—a Hawar resident and a Turkish naval captain—had supposedly used the same seal in 1930 and 1867 respectively. Another seal "had been used" by both a resident of Hawar in 1930 and by the Ruler of Abu Dhabi in 1937. And two different Rulers of Abu Dhabi had supposedly used identical seals, in 1927 and in 1937.

Comparing certain alleged signatures by Hawar residents found in the *Qatar Memorial* Annexes further cemented the expert's conviction that the "evidence" presented by Qatar was inauthentic. Major Abdulla Al-Sadeh's analysis was aided by samples of Hawar residents' signatures in the original of a 1938 written testimony—material publicly available from the India Office Archives and whose authenticity was unquestionable.

Other factors Major Al-Sadeh considered in his signature analysis included the general shape of signatures and their starting and ending points, pauses of the pen, readability, linking and decoration of the words, dot positions, and the shapes and styles of individual characters. The expert observed that within the suspect documents the same person obviously authored many unrelated individuals' signatures, while a considerable number of signatures seemed exact copies of genuine signatures appearing on the 1938 petition by Hawar residents.

Major Abdulla Al-Sadeh also studied two typewritten documents not included with the current suspect documents: a letter (known to be genuine) sent by the Ruler of Qatar to the Political Agent in Bahrain in 1939, and one of the testimonies—allegedly by Ḥawar residents—that had been affixed to the letter. It was noteworthy that the Political Agent in Bahrain at the time had questioned the authenticity of those very testimonies; he observed that the signatures were "in one handwriting, unsupported by thumb impressions or seals of the alleged signatories" (Weightman, 22 April 1939, 2–3).

Examining the typewritten documents, Major Abdulla looked for similarities in the typewriting faults (such as dislodged characters, characters leaning to one side, missing characters or dots, filled-in links and loops, added strokes, et cetera), and also in the typing styles (margins, indentations, spelling, et cetera). Major Abdulla found similarities in all the characteristics he studied—which led him to conclude that both documents had been typed on the same typewriter, very likely by the same typist. Thus it appeared that by even in the late 1930s, Qatar had begun to circulate inauthentic documents to shore up its ailing case for the Hawars.

Major Al-Sadeh conducted a final test to verify the authenticity of the suspect documents, which involved comparing these with genuine documents for characteristics like general format, handwriting, and signatures, and also the position of the date and repeated phrase *"Bismillah Al-Rahman Al-Raheem."* Once again, the analysis confirmed that the documents were forgeries. In addition, it was established that one document in particular—a 1938 written testimony by the subjects of the Ruler of Bahrain—had served as the model for forging names and signatures in numerous suspect documents appearing throughout Qatar's Annexes.

These anomalies identified in the course of the examination furnished sufficient grounds for Major Abdulla Al-Sadeh to reject the possibility that the eighty-one documents could be authentic. Whether compared with one another, or with known genuine documents, the suspect documents bristled with inaccuracies, linguistic and stylistic flaws, and historical inconsistencies (Al-Sadeh 1997).

Further Verification by International Experts

Armed with the above findings of Bahraini researchers, the Office of the Minister of State shared its suspicions with Freshfields, Bahrain's legal representatives in its case before the International Court of Justice. Bahrain's lawyers then proceeded to contact experts of international standing who might authoritatively assess the researchers' evidence about different aspects of the forged documents.

In May 1997, Bahrain requested that Qatar file the originals of the eighty-one suspect documents with the Court, for Bahrain's inspection (Jawad S. Al-Arayed, 29 May 1997). Bahrain asked that the documents be deposited at the Peace Palace in The Hague, and that they remain in the Court's custody until the conclusion of the case.

Although three weeks later Qatar agreed to produce the documents, they specified that the documents be examined only under certain conditions (Al-Muslemani, 12 June 1997). Qatar insisted on assurances that the documents would not be removed from the Registry; that the documents' inspection would not involve their destruction or deterioration; that a representative of the Court Registry be present during the examination; and that a representative of Qatar also be present at all times during the examination. Bahrain objected to the last condition, on the grounds that satisfying Qatar's request would amount to disclosing both the essence of Bahrain's suspicions and Bahrain's analytical approach. Bahrain also rejected attempts by Qatar to limit the duration of the inspection to one week; Bahrain requested to be allowed access to the originals for an entire month.

Three months after Bahrain's initial request the documents were delivered at the Peace Palace on 29 August 1997. However, six of the requested eighty-one originals were missing. Qatar explained that they would deliver the missing six as soon as the Diwan Amiri Archives could locate them. For nearly a year Bahrain filed repeated requests to examine those remaining six originals, but Qatar never made them available for inspection.

On 1 August 1997, Bahrain assembled a team in The Hague to conduct its evaluation of the suspect document originals. At that time the team included representatives from the Bahrain Office of the Minister of State, the Foreign Ministry of Bahrain, Freshfields, and an assemblage of distinguished international historians and forensics experts.

While all the experts present had been given copies of the eighty-one suspect documents early on to begin their analyses, this was their first opportunity to review the originals. Working nonstop over the next four weeks, the team prepared a comprehensive report of their findings—working against the thirty-day time limit which Qatar had given for the examination by Bahrain's team. The team's efforts at verification of the suspect documents assumed three broad categories: historical research, document searches, and forensic analysis.

Historical Research

The expertise of historians specializing in Gulf and Ottoman history was useful indeed to Bahrain's effort to eliminate any possibility that the eighty-one documents submitted by Qatar could be authentic.

Wilkinson

Among the key experts Bahrain had retained was Dr. John Wilkinson, *Ad Hominem* Reader in Middle Eastern Geography at the University of Oxford and Tutorial Fellow at St. Hugh's College, Oxford. Bahrain's lawyers asked Dr. Wilkinson to place the suspect documents in the framework of known historical facts. During his initial review, at which time Dr. Wilkinson was unaware of Bahrain's suspicions, both the appearance and the substance of the documents he was evaluating sorely perplexed him. In repeated calls to Freshfields, Dr. Wilkinson shared his concerns that a growing number of documents seemed "wrong." Only after Dr. Wilkinson stated his conviction that, taken as a group, the documents appeared to be forgeries, was he informed of Bahrain's similar suspicions.

Numerous examples can be given of the historical inconsistencies Dr. Wilkinson identified. For instance, two documents relating to the early history of Zubarah furnished descriptions of supposed tribal configurations that would not be appropriate until at least one and a half centuries later. Many of the suspect documents featured the word *"hijri"* (denoting the Islamic calendar, reckoned from Mohammed's flight from Mecca to Medina in A.D. 622). In the given context, this word's presence contradicted its customary usage, and could only be viewed as an attempt to draw a distinction between the Hijri and Gregorian calendars—which would have been an unlikely concern when the documents were supposed to have been written.

Another interesting—and anachronistic—feature of certain "Ottoman" documents was that these had supposedly been sealed and "OK"'d by British officials at the turn of the nineteenth century. While Dr. Wilkinson established that while the word "OK" was making its way into American English by that time, it was extremely unlikely that British officials would have incorporated it into their vocabulary.

"OK" and Purported British Seal on Forged Document QM III.7

Also, and significantly, the suspect documents contradicted known historical facts relevant to the Ottoman presence in Arabia. For example, some of the documents testified to Ottoman demarcations between Bahrain and the Qatar peninsula that Britain supposedly sanctioned. Yet at the time Britain was known to have actively opposed Ottoman policies in the region, and its ambassadors refused even to discuss sovereignty issues in Arabia. In truth, no contemporary references to demarcations can be found in the authentic communications or records of either of the two states.

Other examples of discrepancies noticed by Dr. Wilkinson included the dates of certain documents and the dates of the seals these contained. For instance, a British seal, signifying British approval, preceded an Ottoman seal on an "Ottoman" map; a seal on an "Ottoman" fleet report was dated approximately seventeen years after the report's given date; and numerous other documents were dated at least a decade earlier than their seals. Personal seals also held surprises for the researcher: one suspect letter had been sealed by a person other than the author;

on another suspect letter the spelling the author had used to sign his name differed from the spelling of the same name in his personal seal.

Documents related to Abu Dhabi appeared no more authentic than the others Dr. Wilkinson examined. One, a letter purportedly sent by Sheikh Zayed from "al-'Ayn," was dated at a time when no one referred to Abu Dhabi as "al-'Ayn"—and before Sheikh Zayed had even captured Abu Dhabi. Another document claimed that Sheikh Zayed applied his fingerprint as testimony that he would keep a certain promise—though in accordance with Shari'a law the appropriate way for local rulers to give testimony was by a signature witnessed by qualified Muslims.

Dr. Wilkinson also found various other problematic elements in Qatar's suspect documents relating to Abu Dhabi in the 1920s and 1930s. Those documents aimed to paint a picture of a grand plot—involving Charles Belgrave (Bahrain's Adviser), Britain, Bahrain, and Abu Dhabi—related to the Hawar Islands, Odaid, and an island situated between Qatar and Abu Dhabi. But Dr. Wilkinson found it impossible to reconcile any such alleged boundary dispute with well-documented history. Known records clearly show that the matter of Odaid and the islands was not an issue during the period to which these disputed documents referred. Dr. Wilkinson noted that only after World War II did the islands became an issue between Qatar and Abu Dhabi. Moreover, during the British arbitration over the islands in 1954, Qatar itself admitted that it had never previously raised a claim to them.

Dr. Wilkinson also rejected the historical logic of the events supposedly related to the Hawar aspect of the plot. He found it unlikely that Sheikh Shakhboot of Abu Dhabi would have sided with the Sheikhs of Qatar over Hawar—especially at a time when relations between the parties had been far from good, and when the Sheikhs of Qatar had historically described Sheikh Shakhboot as no less than a "[son] of Satan," and supported his rival in Abu Dhabi's dynastic struggles.

Dr. Wilkinson also confirmed the suspicions of the Office of the Minister of State (Wilkinson 1997) that a number of suspect documents related to Abu Dhabi were inappropriately dated. These documents made it appear as if Sheikh Sultan was still sending letters five months after he was assassinated; also that letters were being addressed to a well-known figure, Khan Bahador Isa Abdul-Lateef Al-Sarkal, the Residency Agent at Sharjah, four years after his death.

Dr. Wilson pointed out that the Abu Dhabi documents depicted Sir Charles Belgrave, Adviser to the Bahrain Government, as holding absurd opinions about his status relative to various Gulf authorities, and violating rules of standard protocol for both Bahrain employees and British nationals. Belgrave appeared from the disputed documents to have assumed that he had the authority of the British Residency Agent to interfere in actions toward local Rulers in the Trucial States. In documents supposedly written to another British official, Belgrave appeared to refer uncharacteristically casually to the British Political Resident. In certain other suspect letters, Belgrave was supposed to have assumed the title of a British Consul and to have used a seal bearing the British coat of arms—neither of which were accurate, acceptable, or ever done by Belgrave before or since.

Many of the disputed "Belgrave" documents depicted their author as perceiving himself a British official in the Gulf, though he was never part of the British administration. And interestingly, Belgrave supposedly wrote the majority of these suspect letters, including those to British officials, in Arabic; yet the few English words that do appear in this correspondence could hardly be attributed to a native speaker.

Wilkinson noted another discrepancy in Belgrave's suspect "correspondence": that despite the nature of Belgrave's historical position in Bahrain, he appeared to have been far from sufficiently informed about local events or general political affairs. For instance, in the suspect documents, Belgrave seems to have been unaware—for at least four years—of the death of the British Agent at Sharjah. He was apparently also unaware of the fact that British control over the region had been exercised—for over fifty years—through the Government of India at Delhi and Simla, rather than through the Bombay Residency as the disputed documents assert. And according to another suspect letter, the Bombay Residency itself was equally unaware of that fact, because they allegedly promptly replied to Belgrave's blatant misstatement of history.

In the suspect documents, not only did Belgrave appear to have been unclear as to his official function and title, but local personages also referred to or addressed Belgrave using inappropriate titles. For instance, some seemed to believe Belgrave was the *balyoz* (the British Representative in the Gulf), while others designated him as the *mustashar balyoz* (both the Adviser to the Ruler and the British Representative).

In summary, Dr. Wilkinson concluded that the cumulative weight of all the anomalies he discovered rendered the entire body of eighty-one suspect documents, in his words, "clearly absurd" (Wilkinson 1997).

Bostan and Finkel

Bahrain's team also referred the collection of "Ottoman" suspect documents for evaluation to Ottoman history experts Dr. Idris Bostan, Associate Professor in the Department of Modern History at Marmara University and Professor-elect in the Department of History at Istanbul University, and Dr. Caroline Finkel, an Ottoman historian and author of two books and fifteen papers on the subject. These two experts' analyses of the documents revealed the same anomalies discerned by Dr. Wilkinson, plus numerous additional historical discrepancies.

Among the first illogical features Dr. Bostan and Dr. Finkel observed was that these suspect Ottoman documents were written in Arabic. The two historians allowed that while for seven of the suspect documents Arabic might be explained, this fact was impossible to reconcile with official Ottoman practice for the other seventeen documents. The experts considered it particularly inexplicable that high-ranking Ottoman officials or captains in the Ottoman Navy (which was entirely Turkish-staffed) would use Arabic—especially if the purported documents' intended readers were other Ottoman officials. Also, this set of suspect documents was marked by a complete absence of standard honorifics and formulae—especially striking was the absence in any documents of customary praise to the Sultan.

Dr. Bostan and Dr. Finkel were disturbed by repeated references in the suspect documents to the Ottoman "Vali of Hasa." They pointed out that while British officials occasionally (and mistakenly) labeled as the "Vali" Ottoman officials lesser than the "Vali"—like the *Mutasarrif* or the *Kaimakam* in Hasa—it was unthinkable that the Ottomans themselves would ever have made such an error. For instance, it was highly unlikely that Barakah bin Era'ar, appointed *Mutasarrif* of Nejd in 1874, would appropriate the title of "Vali of Hasa" in 1873—a date at which he held no Ottoman administrative position.

Drs. Bostan and Finkel also found other titles utterly confused: in disputed documents a certain individual refers to himself as an "Exploratory Marine Captain"; another apparently believed himself to be a "Sultanic Marine Executive Manager." Yet, as the historians observed, no such titles existed in the Ottoman Empire. In another example, the recipient of a letter is addressed as both a "Vali" and an "Amir Alai"—a highly unlikely combination of functions, as the former title was civilian, the latter military.

The experts also found some of the disputed documents' usage of personal names absurd. In one, a person supposedly the Vice-Commander of the Sultanic Marine Fleet, gives Bash Jawish as his personal name. But Bash Jawish meant "Chief Petty Officer" in Ottoman Turkish; the Marine Fleet would never have been called Sultanic at the time; and the word *"tersane,"* translated "fleet" in the disputed documents, in fact meant "dockyard." Still another term drew the attention of the historians: they noted that *"Donamai Hamayoon"* (meaning "Imperial Ottoman Navy") was used in a document as the personal name of an "honorable judge."

So, if the suspect documents were to be taken as authentic, a number of Ottoman officials appear to have been unaware of the very sorts of actions and conduct that befitted their ranks. According to one disputed document, Saleh Pasha, a high-ranking Ottoman official, wrote a letter to Sheikh Jassim, an inferior, to ask his agreement to a certain action—Saleh Pasha also seeming (unthinkably) to perceive himself as a "brother" to that inferior.

In the disputed documents another important Ottoman Empire figure, Midhat Pasha, supposedly concluded a letter to the Ruler of Bahrain with a phrase implying that the recipient was not a Muslim—obviously a highly insulting implication. Still another person, designated in the disputed materials as the "Qadi" (a very high-ranking *religious* official) of the Imperial Ottoman Navy, was described as conducting surveys (then considered an utterly nonreligious task) in the Gulf.

But not only did high-ranking officials' correspondence seem strange: in Qatar's documents inferior officers seemed to have been equally unaware of their exact hierarchical positions. For example, one supposed Naval Captain obviously assumed it would be appropriate to write to his superiors in a rather casual tone.

Drs. Bostan and Finkel also found the format of some "Ottoman" letters unusual. According to standard Ottoman practice until the end of the nineteenth century, Ottoman officials would typically sign and affix their seals and indicate their ranks (and sometimes their names) on the originals of official documents. For copies of the original documents, they would only affix their seals—and also make sure to write the word *"suret"* (copy).

But the "Ottoman" documents in Qatar's collection seemed to comply with different standards of Ottoman correspondence. They were not designated as copies, and they also lacked numerous characteristics of original documents. On these documents the officials indicated their names, but not their ranks. Furthermore, the documents made no references whatsoever—as would be common practice in the Ottoman Empire—as to which institutions had been assigned the matters in question.

Certain "Ottoman" documents were also inappropriately dated with months and years, though the Ottomans customarily also indicated the weekday or the third of the month in which the document had been produced. And Drs. Bostan and Finkel echoed Dr. Wilkinson's observations regarding the appearance of the word *"hijri"* to designate the Islamic calendar as yet another element inappropriate to the letters' contexts.

Especially revealing to the researchers were the seals on a number of supposedly "official Ottoman" documents. Many featured a Sultanic *tughra* (official personal seal). But authentic *tughras* were never inscribed at the *feet* of official documents or used to indicate approval, as was the case in the Qatari documents. Until the middle of the nineteenth century, *tughras* were used only by Sultans and handwritten by special scribes at the *heads* of documents.

Furthermore, the experts found star-and-crescent seals inappropriately used to authenticate documents. They also found that certain documents—purportedly international demarcation agreements—had supposedly been authenticated by seals for a town fair in Northern Anatolia, the accountancy department in a north central Anatolian province, and the Imperial Land Registry. Seals of the Imperial Land Registry also figured in other disputed documents related to supposed international agreements—yet it was impossible that such authentication would have come from an agency involved entirely in land transactions between individuals.

The researchers found still another odd feature on the "Ottoman" documents: several contained the word *"Osmanli"* (meaning "Ottoman")—which came into use only around thirty years *after* the date of the documents. And even then, the appropriate reference in official communications would have been *"Bab-i Ali"* ("the Sublime Porte"). The documents also referred to Great Britain by its modern name, as opposed to *"Ingiltere Devleti"* ("the English State"), which would have been authentic usage at the time the disputed documents were supposedly written. Another anachronism they found was use of the word "Latin" to describe Western European letters. The experts pointed out that the Ottomans actually used another word—"Franskish"—in that sense until the early twentieth century.

Drs. Bostan and Finkel noted that the disputed documents' chronology of events was considerably flawed. They were amazed, for instance, to learn that Hafidh Pasha had supposedly received letters in his capacity of "Vali" of Baghdad—at a time when the actual Vali of Baghdad was Rauf Pasha. Similarly, the documents claimed that Saeed Bey received correspondence addressed to the "Vali" of Basrah—at a time when a "Mutasarrif" ruled Basrah and when that "Mutasarrif" was actually Halil Bey. The documents credited Midhat Pasha, a prominent historical figure, with supposedly sending letters from Hasa to the Ruler of Bahrain—a month *before* his well-documented first visit to Hasa.

Drs. Bostan and Finkel also found that the demarcation agreements (which many of the Ottoman documents purportedly represented or referred to) were difficult to explain. Dr. Wilkinson had commented in his independent analysis that it was unlikely that Britain would have engaged in such demarcations; Drs. Bostan and Finkel observed that it was equally unlikely that the Ottomans got involved in them during a period of Ottoman efforts to expand into Bahrain. In addition, the delimitation line depicted in one of the maps accompanying the purported agreement seemed to cross Nejd and Hasa—a fact hard to reconcile with the Ottomans' strategic interests in the region at that time (Bostan and Finkel 1997).

Schofield

Freshfields approached still another researcher about the disputed demarcation agreements, Dr. Richard Schofield, Deputy Director of the Geopolitics and International Boundaries Research Center and Teaching Fellow in Geography at the School of Oriental and African Studies at the University of London. Like Wilkinson, and Bostan and Finkel, this scholar was equally unable to find any reasonable explanation for the suspect "demarcation agreements" in their historical contexts. But Dr. Schofield's extensive background in the geography and history of Arab Gulf boundary matters did enable him to make valuable additional observations about the documents included in Qatar's Annexes.

First, Dr. Schofield noticed that the same seals supposedly used by the British Embassy in Constantinople also apparently signified that Embassy's approval of the suspect demarcation maps. The researcher found this most surprising, because the Embassy was known to have requested and received a new set of seals just before the date marked on the last map in the collection. And the seal used on these documents was not from the new set of seals.

Dr. Schofield's analysis strongly commented on the anomaly of the British engaging in, and supposedly agreeing to, demarcations with the Ottoman Empire. As the other historians had also observed, that simply had not occurred at the time. In addition, as Dr. Schofield established, the British Ambassador who supposedly approved at least two of the demarcation maps was the same British Ambassador who historically declared his refusal even to discuss sovereignty questions in Arabia.

Another confusing feature that Dr. Schofield commented on was a suspect demarcation map where the British Ambassador had supposedly endorsed the map on its signing date. Yet as Dr. Schofield commented, "Even for matters of the highest international priority, diplomacy in this era never worked remotely that fast."

The expert also noted that the suspect maps were poor in quality contrasted with known maps of that period. Furthermore, where maps used in negotiating territorial disputes would normally have included boundary claim lines appended to the actual formal claims, surprisingly, the maps in the Qatar collection stand alone—unsophisticated and inaccurate as they are. Even more surprising was the notion that Britain allegedly allowed such maps to become part of official records—at a time when not only the Persian Gulf chart, but also numerous other sketch maps of considerably finer quality, were readily available.

On one of the disputed maps, "Qatar" seemed to extend much farther than the lands its Ruler ever claimed—comprising, as well as land territories, an island that had always been recognized as belonging to Abu Dhabi.

Dr. Schofield echoed Drs. Bostan and Finkel's observation about one of the documents, a purported letter from Midhat Pasha to the

Ruler of Bahrain. Dr. Schofield noted, as they had, that not only was the tone of the letter undiplomatic, the letter also implied that its author believed the Ruler of Bahrain was an infidel. Dr. Schofield further noted that the letter, purportedly recognizing a boundary existing between Bahrain and the Qatar peninsula, was clearly inconsistent with Midhat Pasha's known intent at the time, which was to annex Bahrain to Nejd. Midhat Pasha had stated such intentions on numerous, well-documented occasions.

Dr. Schofield's expertise also came to bear on the authenticity of thirteen twentieth-century letters included in the *Qatar Memorial* Annexes. The researcher immediately observed that all thirteen letters—and most notably those between Belgrave and Abdul-Razzaq —could not have been exchanged using official channels. Belgrave could not correspond directly with the Residency Agent, but was rather expected to refer matters related to Britain to the Political Agent in Bahrain. Dr. Schofield therefore concluded that the letters could not have been official letters written by Belgrave.

The same reasoning applied to the replies "from the Residency Agent," Schofield determined. Further confirmation that the letters did not constitute official exchanges was the fact that in the disputed documents Belgrave did not use Abdul-Razzaq's full name, as would have been expected in formal correspondence. It also was equally unlikely that the suspect correspondence in question could have been unofficial, for in such a case, Belgrave would not have used the kind of stamp that appears in his letters.

Dr. Schofield also noticed that the clumsy language employed by "Belgrave" in the suspect documents contrasted sharply with the well-articulated and sophisticated letters and statements he produced on other, authenticated occasions. The scholar also noticed that "Belgrave" seemed in the suspect letters to have used inappropriate phrases such as "the praiseworthy, respected," "dignified, affectionate" and "honorable, respectable" to refer to Abdul-Razzaq, a *junior* British official (Schofield 1997).

Document Searches of U.S., French, and German Archives

Another expert approached by Freshfields was Dr. Henry Mattox, Adjunct Assistant Professor of History at North Carolina State University and former U.S. diplomat in Arabia. He sought to confirm the existence and authenticity of an "Ottoman" map purporting to have been approved by the U.S. government. The map bore a seal, a signature, and a written inscription on its back that appeared to have been affixed at Constantinople in the 1890s.

But Dr. Mattox's searches and inquiries with historians, archivists and officials (primarily with the U.S. National Archives and Records Administration in College Park, Maryland and Washington, D.C.) uncovered no evidence showing either that the Qatar-proffered map had ever previously existed, or that it had ever become part of official U.S. government records. Despite the expert's thorough survey of diplomatic and consular reports—particularly ones produced in Constantinople and dating from the period when the map was allegedly prepared and approved—no originals or copies of, or collateral references to the proffered map could be found. Furthermore, Dr. Mattox was assured by other qualified experts whom he consulted that none of them had seen or heard of any such document in any of the repositories where it should logically have been located.

Dr. Mattox also examined lists of all U.S. ministers, chargés, consuls general and acting consuls general who served in the 1890s and compared their signatures with the signature appearing on the purported Ottoman map. The expert observed that none of the historically authentic signatures even approximates the one on Qatar's map. Additionally, none of the officials who could possibly have been positioned to place their signatures to indicate U.S. approval was named "Murphy" (the supposed signer of the disputed document).

Nor did the seal design, attributed in the disputed document to the U.S. Department of State, match any design known to have been in use at the time. After examining the seals included in *The Eagle and the Shield: A History of the Great Seal of the United States*, Dr. Mattox established that the seal on the "Ottoman" map matched neither the official nineteenth century versions of the Department of State seal nor the designs of the nineteenth century Great Seal of the United States. As it is known that U.S. diplomatic missions in the 1890s used seals supplied by the Department of State, and as it is obvious that the seal on the "Ottoman" map conforms to none of the official designs approved at the time, the expert concluded that the seal could not have been placed on the map by any U.S. diplomatic or consular establishment (Mattox 1997).

With regard to the 1898 Ottoman survey map, purportedly signed by representatives of France and Germany, an exhaustive search of the archives of the French Ministry of Foreign Affairs and the Diplomatic Archives by Dr. Jean-Marc Thouvenin (Thouvenin 1997), and of the German Archives by Dr. Grupp found no such document or any references to it (Grupp, 20 June 1997).

Forensic Analysis

To conduct further forensic analysis of the suspect documents, the Government of Bahrain engaged the services of three additional expert document examiners, who scrutinized the original documents at The Hague: Mr. Mokhtar Amin, former Head of the Egyptian Forgery and Falsification Identification Department of the Ministry of Justice; Dr. Mohammed Ezz-El-Din Sobhi, former Head of the Assiut branch of the same Egyptian forgery department; and Mr. Peter Tytell, an independent American forensic examiner, diplomate of the Forensic Science Society and board member of the *International Journal of Forensic Document Examiners*.

They conducted an initial review of the documents from May to July 1997, based on copies of the documents included as Annexes to Qatar's *Memorial*. In September 1997, the originals of seventy-five of the suspect documents, plus photocopies of the six undelivered documents, were made available to Mr. Amin, Dr. Sobhi, and Mr. Tytell at the Peace Palace in the Hague. Following their detailed independent analyses—and despite certain limitations on the testing methods applied (due to the sealed plastic covers in which Qatar had placed the documents)—the experts reached conclusive determinations about the documents' genuineness.

The experts conducted four types of examinations: intercomparison of the suspect documents; comparisons of certain documents with known authentic documents by the same authors; a natural handwriting examination; and examinations of the inks, papers, and other characteristics of the documents.

The intercomparison of suspect documents involved nondestructive optical techniques such as magnification, transited incidental and oblique illumination, long-wave and short-wave ultraviolet radiation, et cetera. Devices used included stereoscopic microscopes, hand magnifiers, specialized viewing filters, a closed circuit television system for viewing infrared and reflected infrared luminescence, a paper micrometer, and other precision measuring devices. During each stage of the examination, the experts were also careful to apply standard principles of document examination and identification.

The examiners' intercomparison focused on several characteristics—most notably seal impressions, stamps, and papers. Like the findings of Major Adbulla Al-Sadeh's preliminary examination in Bahrain, the analyses by Mr. Amin, Dr. Sobhi, and Mr. Tytell established that the documents in the suspect collection were interrelated. After examining the documents using computerized Visual Spectral Comparitor (VSC) equipment, computer image processing, and electronic and/or photographic superimposition, the experts determined that numerous features pointed to the documents' non-authenticity.

Seals and Stamps

All the disputed documents contained numerous seal impressions, some in ink, some in wax. Many of the seals featured Arabic alphabet characters. Of such seals, a number were attributed to more than one individual, which contradicted the very nature of seals' use as a means of personal authentication. In the disputed documents it appeared that impressions of the same seal, or that seals produced by the same master, had been used over a period of sixty-six years, in unrelated documents. These included: a letter dated 1937, supposedly by Shakhboot bin Sultan (Ruler of Abu Dhabi); a letter by Hamad bin Isa bin Ali Al-Khalifa dated 1935; two Ottoman maps respectively dated 1874 and 1891; and a testimony by Hawar residents dated 1930. Thus, with the original documents now in hand, these international forensic experts were able to confirm the initial analysis made by Major Abdulla, Bahrain CID's forgery expert.

The experts also noted that numerous Ottoman emblem seals had been "reused" on various documents encompassing long periods of time. Thus, the same seal figured on four purportedly Ottoman maps dated over a twenty-four-year period, while another seal was noted on three other maps dated over thirty-one years. Two suspect Ottoman maps dated over a twenty-three-year period featured yet another seal. The experts also identified a set of seven suspect Ottoman maps and letters, from three different individuals, which were dated over three decades, yet bore the same seal.

They also observed impressions in the form of Latin alphabet initials—supposedly signifying approval by Western powers—in a number of suspect documents. Thus, they found an ornate initial "R" in six documents; a floral initial "D" on three maps; a floral initial "F" on two maps; and a floral "G" (together with a floral "F") on one map. Judging by the content of the documents, the latter two seals were attributed to the ambassadors of France and Germany respectively. The experts noted that whatever German official purportedly "approved" these documents with the floral "G" seal, had apparently adopted the *English*, not the German (*Deutschland*), designation for his own country.

Floral "G" Seal Attributed to German Ambassador on Forged Document QM III.46

Mr. Amin, Dr. Sobhi and Mr. Tytell also found problematical numerous patterns in the black ink typographic stamp impressions on the suspect documents. Some of these disturbing elements included: retouched "C. Dalrymple Belgrave" signature stamp impressions and a similarly retouched purported "British Consulate in Bahrain" stamp. The experts also observed chronological sequences of stamped reference numbers on certain documents at odds with the sequence of the dates stamped on the same documents. For example, a purported judgment by Judge Salmeen bin Rabee was date-stamped "18TH MAY 1939" and given the reference number "459/7BH/QT"; another purported judgment by the same judge was date-stamped "11 MAR 1939," i.e., approximately two months earlier, yet given the reference number "460/7BH/QT."

Paper Anomalies

In addition to the seal and stamp anomalies found throughout the collection of suspect documents, the experts found the paper used in their production still another factor inappropriately linking different documents to each other. Mr. Amin, Dr. Sobhi, and Mr. Tytell noted that the suspect collection abounded in examples of "recycled" stationery. They found numerous suspect documents apparently written on paper previously used or intended for other uses. Commonly, at least one edge of the particular papers was torn; indicating that the paper had originally been part of other, larger sheets of paper.

Two letters (QM III.20 and QM IV.9) written more than four years apart, by two different people, were both written on sheets shorn from the same larger piece of paper. This was evidenced by the continuation of the same elaborate Ottoman inscription across the back of both letters, the watermark across the sheets, and an exact alignment of the torn edges.

QM III.20   QM IV.9
Script Continuation and Matching Edges on Separate Forged Documents

Similarly, a letter by Sharq bin Ahmed (a person allegedly involved in the Belgrave conspiracy) contained an Osmanlica passage, the final stroke of which continued in a suspect letter purportedly authored by Belgrave (QM III.201 and QM III.215). In another indication that the two documents were part of the same larger whole, their torn edges also matched perfectly.

For another pair of documents with Osmanlica writing (QM III.25 and QM IV.11), two letters supposedly written by Barakah bin Era'ar

378 | A LINE IN THE SEA

QM III.201　　　　QM III.215
Script Continuation and Matching Edges on Separate Forged Documents

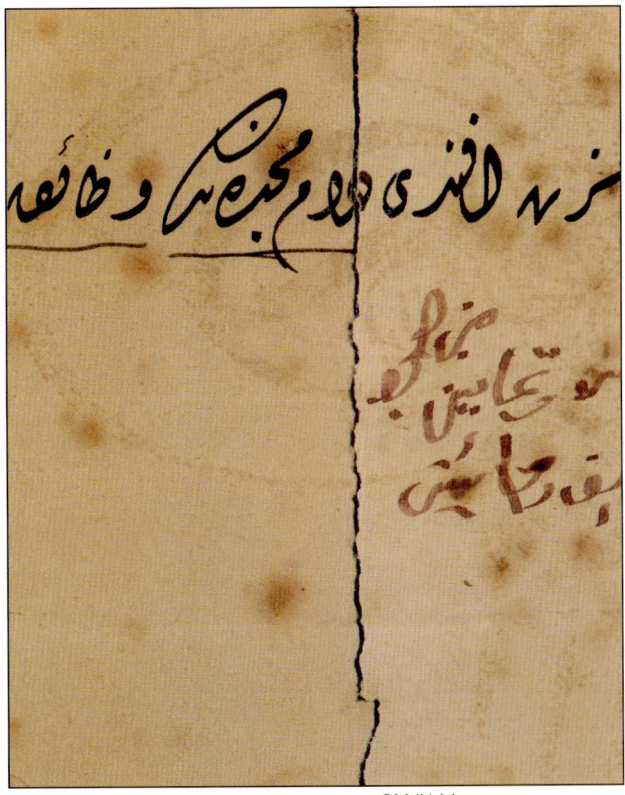

QM III.25　　　　QM IV.11
Script Continuation and Matching Edges on Separate Forged Documents

(Ruler of Hasa), it appeared that the author used parts of the same torn sheet of paper to produce both—despite the fact that they are dated almost four years apart. As was the case with the other pairs of documents, the Osmanlica writing in one of these continued in the other, and their physical fit revealed that their edges also perfectly matched.

The experts observed two other instances of documents obviously taken from larger sheets of paper. One involved two letters supposedly from Sheikh Hamad bin Isa bin Ali Al-Khalifa, Ruler of Bahrain (QM III.100 and QM III.69). That the two letters were dated nine years apart seemed strikingly at odds with the continuity of their watermark, two strips of mending tape in common, and with their perfectly matched edges.

QM III.100

QM III.69
Matching Edges on Separate Forged Documents

QM III.100

QM III.69
Detail Showing Matching Edges and Watermark Continuation on Separate Forged Documents

The other instance involved four documents, all of which had been prepared using pieces torn from the same sheet of paper. These documents supposedly were authored by different individuals: a former owner of property in Hawar, two Bahraini judges, and the Adviser to the Bahrain Government (QM III.186, III.202, III.96, and III.214).

Examining the originals at the Peace Palace also enabled the experts to establish that various suspect documents had been prepared using paper from books, agendas, or other bound volumes. Among these spurious documents were four maps, one statement, and twenty-nine letters allegedly written by numerous unrelated individuals. Typically, these documents each had three clean-cut edges and one raggedly torn or unevenly cut edge. The experts observed brown discoloration at the even edges, though paper at the torn edges appeared fresh. In addition, the smoothly trimmed edges of some of the documents contained remnants of golden "gilt edging," while the uneven edges bore marks of binding, such as holes from stitching or stapling or remnants of glue.

Mr. Amin, Dr. Sobhi, and Mr. Tytell also determined that six other documents had probably also been produced on paper taken from books or other bound volumes. The examiners further observed that certain "recycled" documents possessed the same kinds of features, such as length, width, type of paper, thickness, gilt edging, et cetera, while others shared the same individualizing features, such as patterns of discoloration, staining, or physical damage.

The experts also noted that six of the documents had been prepared on paper with indented (scored) lines. Such paper was of a type the experts knew was used by scribes and calligraphers, whose writing typically followed the indented lines. Yet this was not the case with the documents in the Qatar collection: in all those, the writing violated the lines—a fact that led the experts to conclude that the six documents represented still another set of documents written on paper originally intended for different purposes.

The examiners also established that in numerous instances the writing on the documents and the physical features of the paper on which they had been prepared intersected in ways that would have been impossible had the documents been genuine. For instance, the right margins on three documents conformed to unevenly cut paper edges, indicating that the text was written *after* the paper had been unevenly trimmed.

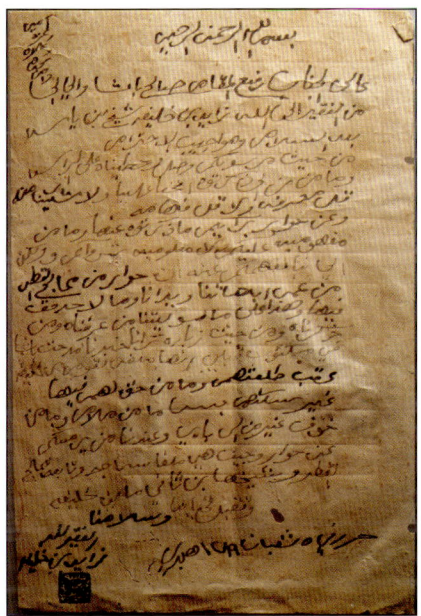

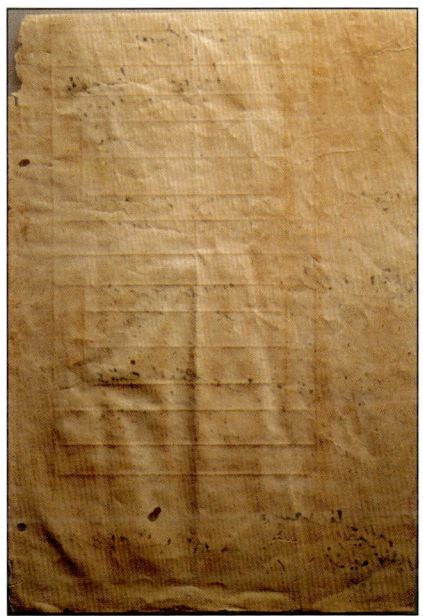

Document QM III.21 (Front)   Document QM III.21 (Reverse)
Document with Indented Lines where Writing Violates Lines on Forged Document

In other documents, the intersections between the writing and the physical features of the paper—folds, holes, or cuts—indicated that such folds, holes, or cuts predated the writing. In cases where pen strokes intersected with folds or holes, the ink had "bled" to the other side of the paper. In other cases, where the writing attempted to avoid such features, clean borders of paper appeared around the holes or along the folds.

Comparisons

Mr. Amin, Dr. Sobhi, and Mr. Tytell also compared the purported authorship of forty-six of the disputed documents with genuine documents produced by those same authors. The Office of the Minister of State had organized a collection of genuine exemplars from a variety of sources, including the Bahrain Archives, the Archives of the Bahrain Ministry of Justice and Islamic Affairs, the Abu Dhabi Center for Documentation and Research, the India Office Library and Records within the British Museum, private document collections, and certain recognized primary document compilations and journals. These were all historical documents authenticated as genuine by relevant institutions or by the authors of relevant books or journals.

For one important figure, Charles Belgrave, the Adviser to the Ruler of Bahrain (whose signature appears in twenty-six of the suspect documents), the examiners were able to compare signatures found in some two hundred fifty authentic documents. The experts established that one original signature, from one of the authentic documents dated 1938 (the original of which resided in the British Archives), was probably used to produce *all* signatures appearing in the suspect set.

Belgrave Genuine Signature—Likely Used to Produce Forged Signatures

III.140

III.151

IV.59

Examples of Belgrave Signatures from Qatar Forged Documents

Comparison of Genuine and Forged Belgrave Signatures

Further examination of the genuine documents revealed that Belgrave's signatures showed much natural variation, while the signatures on the suspect documents all looked identical—but also failed to match any known Belgrave signature stamps. The experts observed two other elements in the suspect Belgrave documents but not in the genuine ones: a stamp that read "THE ADVISER BAHRAIN GOV." and a circular foil seal with a British coat of arms. It should also be noted that the latter seal had previously drawn the attention of historians Drs. Wilkinson and Schofield, who concluded it was unthinkable that a person of Belgrave's standing would have appropriated the British emblem when he was not in fact a British administrator in the Gulf.

The experts determined that certain letters purportedly produced by Rulers of Abu Dhabi and included in the Qatar Diwan Amiri Archives collection also deviated from the standards with which known correspondence from the same Rulers had been noted to comply. The general layout of authentic letters, the positioning and orientation of different elements, and the balanced and fluent writing style employed by Abu Dhabi scribes differed sharply from both the untidy appearance of the suspect documents and the inharmonious handwritings of their authors.

And the known seals of individual Rulers of Abu Dhabi were completely different from the ones appearing in the suspect collection. The examiners observed that the authentic seals of Sheikh Zayed bin Khalifa, Sheikh Tahnoon bin Zayed, and Sheikh Sultan bin Zayed all had stylized ornamentation modeled on the Ottoman *tughra* emblem, while the seals in the suspect collection were much more primitive in quality, and their morphology and readable content bore no similarity to known originals. In addition, a seal attributed to Sheikh Sultan bin Zayed was also found on documents purportedly authored by Sheikh Shakhboot bin Sultan. Moreover, the experts established that within the suspect documents a seal attributed to Sheikh Shakhboot was identical to seals appearing on two Ottoman maps, a purported testimony by a Hawar resident, and a letter from a "Ruler of Bahrain" (QM III.128, QM III.100, QM III.77, QM III.46, and QM III.29).

Not only Sheikh Shakhboot's seal, but also his signature, was established as inauthentic. Sheikh Shakhboot's genuine signatures on a number of known documents led the experts to conclude that the Ruler's handwriting demonstrated a primitive writing skill level—a quality not reflected in the suspect documents. The highly stylized signatures on two suspect documents, together with handwriting consistent with the signatures, could not, the experts said, have been produced by the person who had signed the genuine letters.

The experts made similar observations about the purported correspondences of Rulers of Bahrain. For example, the experts found that Sheikh Isa bin Ali Al-Khalifa's seal on the forged documents was different from the seal used in his known authentic letters. The experts also established that neither the general format nor the writing style of the suspect letters attributed to Sheikh Hamad bin Isa bin Ali Al-Khalifa conformed with patterns observed in his authentic correspondence.

Mr. Amin, Dr. Sobhi, and Mr. Tytell also compared authenticated letters by numerous other local figures with suspect documents these figures supposedly produced. This comparison established enough critical differences to conclude that neither the handwriting nor the signatures in any of the suspect documents agreed with those in the authentic documents prepared by the same authors. In certain cases, the experts also noted that even purported signatures by the same individuals on different suspect documents bore little resemblance to each other.

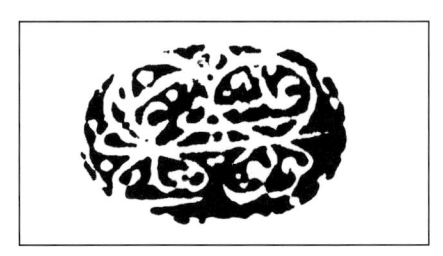

Purported Seal of Sheikh Isa from Forged Document QM III.49

Seal from Authentic Letter by Sheikh Isa

Comparison of Genuine and Forged Seal Impressions by Sheikh Isa bin Ali Al-Khalifa

Handwriting

The experts also studied the Qatar Diwan Amiri Archive suspect documents and established that without exception the documents in the suspect collection contained evidence of "disguised" handwriting. Clearly trying to hide his true identity, the suspect documents' author evidently resorted to a variety of means to alter his more prominent writing characteristics—a common feature of forged handwriting. As the document examiners observed, this resulted in several unusual features common to the suspect documents.

One such anomaly involved numerous variations in the formation of identical or similar characters within individual documents. The experts acknowledged that it is very rare, especially in Arabic handwriting, for a person to form certain characters in more than two or three ways. The experts found the variety of character forms within each suspect document so large that these could not have occurred naturally.

To help identify the elements of disguise in the suspect documents, the experts also considered the peculiarities of different Arabic writing styles that reflect different levels of handwriting skill development and sophistication. In particular, the examiners found two writing styles, Naskh (commonly referred to as undeveloped) and Rykaa (referred to as developed) most relevant to the case. The experts' extensive document analysis experience told them that Arabic writers seeking to disguise their natural handwriting often resort to use of elements of both Naskh and Rykaa styles. Most commonly, such intermixing occurs with the characters *jiim, haa, khaa, ayn, ghayn,* and *miim*. Other attributes of Naksh, such as the use of arched and/or sloped strokes, characters, and ligatures, and the separation of the dots of the characters *ta, tha, shiin,* and *yaa,* may also be associated with attempts to disguise.

In the suspect documents, the shapes of certain characters were so abnormal, it proved impossible to associate those characters with any Arabic writing style. Asymmetrical characters and character connections violating basic Arabic calligraphy rules were among features common in the documents included in the Qatar Diwan Amiri Archives collection. For instance, within a letter purportedly written by Ali bin Khadim Al-Hamily, an Agent of Sheikh Shakhboot, the extent of variation in the designs and sizes of certain characters was far too large to be attributed to natural handwriting patterns. Moreover, the shapes of certain characters seemed so unusual that the experts were unable to identify them as belonging to *any* Arabic writing style.

The majority of the suspect documents also featured abnormally long or truncated character extensions. Occasionally, such forms can be observed within the same words, such as in the case of a letter purportedly from Sheikh Shakhboot. There, a number of words are not only formed differently throughout the document, but are also unnaturally extended.

Furthermore, the experts found signs of unnatural retouching and overwriting in numerous documents. These the experts interpreted as evidence that the writer had attempted to alter characters where he realized he had inadvertently shown his natural handwriting. One example of such overwriting is a purported letter from Charles Belgrave, where the connections between *alif* and *lam* appear in both natural and retouched forms.

Mr. Amin, Dr. Sobhi, and Mr. Tytell also examined the suspect documents for patterns of handwriting similarities. One expert observed that the collection seemed meant to masquerade as a variety of documents, prepared by disparate authors in various locations and at different time periods. And the documents' author employed numerous deceptive techniques to create an impression of authenticity. Among such techniques, the document examiners identified the use of varying amounts of ink on the pen, use of different writing instrument nib widths, altered document formats, and varied shapes and sizes of certain characters and/or words.

But the use of such techniques failed to prevent the experts from identifying numerous handwriting similarities throughout the documents. They established that certain features appeared consistently in the collection. Numerous occurrences, such as the "look" of the invocation *"Bismillah Al-Rahman Al-Raheem"* across the set of suspect documents, revealed these anomalies.

Where in certain documents natural handwriting patterns did show through their disguises, these patterns were found to be not only similar to each other, but also comparable to the characteristics of undisguised natural handwriting in other documents. Mr. Amin, Dr. Sobhi, and Mr. Tytell were thus able to identify a considerable number of "individualizing" features—enough to furnish sufficient grounds for the experts to conclude that all the documents in the suspect collection originated from the same source—likely from the same author (Amin, Sobhi and Tytell 1997, 137).

Submission of Experts' Reports to the Court

The international experts' investigations, plus a number of others, were assembled into a series of volumes. On 25 September 1997, the Agent of Bahrain before the Court, H.E. Minister Jawad Al-Arayed, submitted these findings to the Court in an eighteen-page letter, together with two volumes of appendixes totaling approximately 750 pages (Jawad S. Al-Arayed, 25 September 1997).

The letter told the Court of:

- Bahrain's discovery of eighty-one suspect documents cited one hundred times by Qatar in its *Memorial,* and the scale and scope of these
- Details and results of Bahrain's investigations that verified that all eighty-one documents were in fact forgeries
- Bahrain's wishes that the Court take whatever action it deemed advisable

Appendix I to the letter consisted of a document-by-document summary of the evidence Bahrain had collected about each of the suspect documents. Appendix II consisted of detailed research reports by the sixteen experts involved, describing their procedures, protocols and results. Bahrain also informed the Court that it would disregard these eighty-one documents in preparing its *Counter-Memorial*.

The initial report of 25 September 1997 merely summarized the forensic examination results. But over the following months, Amin, Sobhi, and Tytell prepared a complete forensic report on all the suspect documents. On 31 December 1997, Bahrain submitted this complete expert forensic examination of all eighty-one suspect documents to the Court, in a letter from Bahrain's Agent Jawad Al-Arayed (Al-Arayed, 31 December 1997). The report consisted of six volumes and eighteen hundred pages: a cover letter from the Agent along with the main report, and five volumes of the experts' detailed findings. The report concludes:

> Having examined originals of 75 of the 81 and photocopies of the remaining 6, it is our expert opinion that the entire Qatar Diwan Amiri Archives collection of 81 documents submitted for examination is not genuine. (Amin, Sobhi and Tytell 1997a, I-2)

As the next stage of written proceedings, both sides submitted *Counter-Memorials* on 31 December 1997. When Bahrain examined Qatar's *Counter-Memorial*, it was found that Qatar had included yet another forged document.

Bahrain submitted a further report to the Court on 28 March 1998, detailing evidence which showed that Qatar's *Counter-Memorial* Map No. 1 was also clearly a forgery (Jawad S. Al-Arayed, 26 March 1998).

The report also included additional findings that had come to light since the submission of the Bahrain's September and December 1997 Expert reports on the forgeries. First was a report by the UK College of Arms—the official British body which deals with authorized government insignia—that gave further evidence on the non-authenticity of certain British heraldic devices used throughout the documents (College of Arms [Great Britain], 1998).

A second report, by Stuart Houghton Ltd., revealed that wax and seal impressions used on the many of the eighty-one forged documents had been produced by a set of seals designed, registered, and manufactured by Stuart Houghton in 1990 (Houghton 1998)—long after the dates on the suspect documents.

Houghton Seal

Seal Found on Forged Document QM IV.10
Dated in 1870

Comparison of Houghton's Seal Originally Designed in 1990, with a Seal Used on a Qatari Forged Document Dated 120 Years Earlier

The Bahrain Agent's letter to the Court asked that all eighty-two disputed documents be withdrawn from the record and that the Court hold further proceedings to consider how to treat this matter. Eventually it was agreed that Qatar would conduct its own examination of the disputed documents and issue an interim report on their findings by no later than the end of September 1998.

Withdrawal of Documents

On 30 September 1998, Qatar issued its *Interim Report* (Qatar 1998). In this report, Qatar cites its experts' examination of the documents as yielding uncertain results.

In numerous letters to the Court, Bahrain had repeatedly asked Qatar to explain the provenance of these suspect documents, but in its *Interim Report* Qatar declined to comment on provenance, except to say that, given the paucity of Qatar's archives, Qatar has tried since independence to acquire pertinent documents through academic and private channels—among those, the challenged documents. It was through such channels, Qatar averred, that it had acquired these documents, and it had then submitted them to the Court in good faith. Where these documents had actually originated, Qatar never ventured to explain.

Qatar sought opinions from five examiners, but particularly telling was a report submitted by Qatar's experts David Crown and Brian Carney. To their credit, these eminent U.S. forensic document examiners sided with Bahrain's expert examiners about the non-authenticity of the seventy-seven suspect documents that they had been able to examine meaningfully. Their report confirmed many of the results of the Bahrain forensic experts about the suspect documents, including: use of stamps which had never been used by British Diplomatic staff, matching torn edges on separate and incongruous documents, use of Queen Elizabeth II's seal on documents from the 1800s, incongruous use of a Belgrave rubber signature stamp on all, inappropriate use of stamps and seals on Ottoman documents, and that many of the documents had been written on paper which originally was cut from a book and the writing added later.

These experts were also allowed to test the ink on the documents—a test which was not available to the Bahrain experts because of the plastic document sealing. Crown and Carney found that a substantial number of the suspect documents were written in ballpoint or other "modern ink" which they said "was not available when the document was allegedly written" (Crown and Carney 1998, 7). In their conclusion, Qatar's experts stated that:

> Out of the 81 documents... 77 documents contain faults or flaws which cannot be refuted or rebutted.
>
> Mr. Peter Tytell, et al. regarded all 81 documents to be fabrications. At this juncture, we cannot show this to an erroneous or poorly reasoned conclusion even though we might dispute a few points... (Crown and Carney 1998, 14)

Qatar's introduction to the *Interim Report* concluded:

> ... after reviewing these various experts' reports and in the light of the conflicting views amongst the Parties' experts, Qatar has decided that it will disregard all the 82 challenged documents for the purposes of the present case so as to enable the Court to address the merits of the case without further procedural complications. It does so, however, with the proviso that it does not accept Bahrain's distortions of the historical facts or its exaggerations of the effect of the challenged documents on Qatar's case. (Qatar 1998, 17)

In other words, Qatar withdrew all the challenged documents, while at the same time holding that the claims the spurious documents supported were nonetheless still valid. Qatar effected its formal withdrawal of the forged documents by a letter to the Court from Qatar's Agent in December 1998 (Al-Muslemani, 15 December 1998). On 15 December 1998, Qatar expressed its "regret at the situation that [had] arisen and the inconvenience that [it had] caused the Court and Bahrain" (Al-Muslemani, 15 December 1998). However, this fact remained: Qatar's *Memorial* and *Counter-Memorial* were both filled with arguments and document references contaminated by these eighty-two forged documents.

Qatar's actions placed Bahrain in an awkward posture to prepare its Reply. Bahrain was obliged to reply to a case whose contents had been fundamentally altered by Qatar's decision to disregard the eighty-two forged documents found in its *Memorial* and *Counter-Memorial*. Bahrain's efforts to identify and disregard the arguments contaminated by those documents resulted in Bahrain's reproducing a version of Qatar's *Memorial* and *Counter-Memorial* in which it highlighted Qatar's tainted arguments in another color (Qatar 1996a; Qatar 1997a). Subsequently, Qatar produced its own, slightly altered "highlighted" versions of its *Memorial* and *Counter-Memorial* and submitted these to the Court (Qatar 1996b; Qatar 1997b).

Yet even in the last phase of the Court proceedings, the Oral Hearings, Bahrain's legal representatives were forced to call the Court's attention to numerous references to and arguments based on the forged documents by Qatar's legal team during the hearings. So even at this stage of the proceedings the forgery-contamination continued (Lauterpacht, 8 June 2000, 12–14, ¶ 7–12).

Qatar Claims Supported by the Forgeries

Qatar's use of these eighty-two forged documents to support its case can best be shown by Qatar's own words in its *Counter-Memorial*. There, Qatar states in the introductory summary what it calls "the central elements" of its case. Qatar asserts that its evidence achieved the following:

1. "demonstrated" the territorial integrity of Qatar as comprising the whole peninsula and the Hawar Islands;
2. "showed" that this alleged territorial integrity was recognized "at least" since the mid-nineteenth century by Britain, the Ottoman Empire, local rulers, and indeed Bahrain;
3. "showed" the worthlessness of Bahrain's evidence regarding the Hawar Islands in the arbitration that resulted in the British Award of 1939, which included the "Belgrave conspiracy" involving British officials, other local Gulf rulers, and the Naim; and
4. "provided evidence" of Qatar's own "acts of sovereignty" on the Hawar Islands (Qatar 1997, 1–3, ¶ 1.2–1.8).

Analysis revealed that the eighty-two forged documents were designed to portray the following:

1. that Sir Charles Belgrave, Bahrain's Adviser, engaged in a criminal conspiracy with British officials to tamper with evidence relating to the Hawar Islands and to Zubarah, leading to Britain's 1939 Award in Bahrain's favor,
2. that prior to that conspiracy, Qatar had engaged in acts of sovereignty in the disputed territories, and
3. that a number of Rulers and officials, as well as Britain and the Ottoman Empire, had recognized that the Hawar Islands and the Zubarah region were part of Qatar.

Thus, the immediate significance of Qatar's withdrawal of the eighty-two forged documents that three out of four of their original arguments were no longer supported—the only argument remaining was physical proximity. Their case now disastrously undermined, Qatar was forced to find new rationale for their arguments for the Hawars and Zubarah—namely proximity, cartography, faulty arbitration, and *ad hominem* attacks on Bahrain's case.

But Qatar's actions, which so abused the judicial process, had an even wider significance—the entire history of the Gulf region was tarnished (Jawad S. Al-Arayed, 25 September 1997).

Wider Significance of the Forgeries

To assess the effects of Qatar's abuse of the judicial process and of the Court's integrity and its administration of justice, it will be useful to cite the opening statement of Bahrain's Agent, His Excellency Jawad Al-Arayed, given during the oral phase of the hearings in The Hague in June 2000.

Referring to the fact that Qatar's weak case led it to rely on forged documents to substantiate its claims, Mr. Al-Arayed points out the gravity of that action: "Imagine the damage that would have been done to the administration of international justice—indeed to the very position of this Court—if *Bahrain had not* exposed those forgeries" (Jawad S. Al-Arayed, 8 June 2000, 9 ¶ 12).

The only mention of the eighty-two forged documents in the Court's final Judgment was a brief narrative of the events surrounding their discovery and subsequent withdrawal (*ICJ Judgment,* 2001, 8–10, ¶ 15–23). However, in a separate opinion as part of the final Judgment, Judge Fortier commented on the issue of the forged documents, which he believes, "should have been commented upon in the Judgment. Since the Court chose not to address this issue, I have decided that it was my duty to do so" (*ICJ Judgment,* 2001—Fortier Dissenting opinion, 1, ¶ 1). He goes on to make the following comments about what he terms "this extraordinary incident":

> I believe that the Court should not simply disregard and fail to take into consideration this unprecedented incident. In my opinion, these documents have "polluted" and "infected" the whole of Qatar's case (CR 2000/11, pp. 12 and 14 [i.e., Lauterpacht, 8 June 2000, 12, 14]).
>
> Some of them resurface, directly or indirectly, at various stages of Qatar's written and oral pleadings. They remain in the record and some of them linger and are invoked occasionally in support of Qatar's alternative argument.
>
> ... Qatar's case today is not the same case as when it was first set out in [their] Memorial in September 1996.
>
> ... Qatar's Counter-Memorial contained a summary of what it called "the central elements" of its case and asserted that Qatar's evidence had achieved [them] ... I observe that all of these "central elements" of Qatar's case depended on the use of the 82

documents. These documents were later abandoned by Qatar... [and] Qatar then adopted a new argument to support the maintenance of its claim to the Hawar Islands.

...I believe the Court, in considering the Parties' conflicting versions of the facts in this case, had a duty to do more than merely narrate the Parties' respective exchange of letters following Bahrain's challenge of the authenticity of 82 documents which loomed as central to Qatar's case. I regret that it has elected not to do so. (*ICJ Judgment,* 2001—Fortier Dissenting opinion, 1–2 ¶ 4–11)

Here, articulately and forcefully stated, we see the broader significance of Qatar's action to the administration of justice and the history of the Gulf region, where, just as those forged documents did during the conduct of the case of *Qatar v. Bahrain,* they continue to distort historical fact and international justice.

22 | The Judgment

The Merits phase of the ICJ case ran for more than six years. It began on 15 February 1995 when the Jurisdiction phase Judgment was issued, and its first major documentation landmark was the joint submission of written *Memorials* on 30 September 1996. This was followed by the submission of *Counter-Memorials* by both parties on 31 December 1997. The last major submission was of *Replies* on 30 May 1999, followed by submission of *Supplemental Documents* on 1 March 2000. The culminating event in the proceedings was the Oral Hearings, which took place in the Great Hall of Justice in the Peace Palace at The Hague, from 29 May to 29 June 2000 (see the *Verbatim Record of the Public Sitting 2000*).

On 16 March 2001, the International Court of Justice issued its Judgment in the case of *Qatar v. Bahrain*. The case had been not only the longest in duration and most extensively documented in the International Court's history, but had also involved a number of unprecedented developments, most notably the introduction by Qatar of eighty-two forged documents in support of its case. This Judgment brought closure to a dispute of more than seventy years.

The Court's Decision

Before reviewing the Court's decision and reasoning in the case of *Qatar v. Bahrain* it is helpful to first understand the philosophy which underlies the International Court of Justice and its role in international law.

In documents prepared by the International Court to describe its history and goals, the Court states its purpose clearly:

> The ultimate aim of the Court, where there is a conflict, is to open the road to international harmony... [T]he mere fact that the case has been submitted to the Court means that... good arguments exist on both sides... [I]t is clearly impossible for [the Court] to please everybody, still less to favour any party. This is, indeed, inherent in the role of a Court. (International Court of Justice 1996, 73–74)

Thus, the International Court's aim in such cases is revealed as twofold: "deciding legal disputes between States" and "thereby, contribut[ing] to the maintenance of peace and to the development of friendly relations among States" (International Court of Justice 1996, 89). But these two purposes have not always proved complementary. Typically, and especially given the Court's mandate to ensure peaceful relations between countries, decisions emanating from the Court do not totally favor just one side in a dispute; nor do such decisions always follow a "literal" interpretation of the law. The Court's decisions have often been tempered according to the principle of equity, and, thus, have tended to deliver things to both sides.

And so the International Court of Justice did in their decision in this case, rendered on 16 March 2001. It might be said that, in terms of the Hawars and Zubarah at least, the Judgment gave twenty-first century political legitimacy to a kind of *modus vivendi* that had been arrived at between the two Parties and that had persisted for several generations.

After recounting the complex history of the dispute and the arguments presented by the Parties in their various written pleadings, the Judgment's findings were:

- Qatar was awarded sovereignty over Zubarah, Janan Island, and the low-tide elevation of Fasht Al-Dibal;
- Bahrain was awarded sovereignty over the Hawar Islands and the island of Qit'at Jaradah;
- A single maritime boundary between the two states was drawn (*ICJ Judgment,* 2001, 71–72)

For purposes of comparison and contrast, the final maritime line rendered in the Judgment, the maritime delimitations requested by Bahrain and Qatar at the Court, and the 1947 British decision line (which had been the de facto border until the Judgment had been rendered) are all portrayed on Map No. 9, p. 398. It can be seen by examining the map that Bahrain has gained considerable maritime territory to the east of the 1947 British decision line, despite the loss of Fasht Al-Dibal and Janan.

Aware of the Court's tendency to give something to each party in a dispute, it was not unexpected that Qatar would gain Zubarah, in counterpoint to the Court's confirmation of Bahraini sovereignty over the Hawars. Zubarah had been under Qatari control since their invasion of 1937, no population remained there, and Zubarah was a geographical part of the Qatari peninsula. In contrast, on the Hawars, not one bit of evidence provided by Qatar—other than forged documents—indicated that Qataris had ever set foot on Hawar, much less held any authority there. Let us now proceed to examine in detail the reasoning behind the Court's decision, and also how the ICJ accomplished the maritime division.

The Court's Reasoning

The Court's Judgment first reviewed the history of the case and the dispute (*ICJ Judgment*, 2001, 6–15 ¶ 1–34) and the general history of the area (*ICJ Judgment*, 2001, 15–25 ¶ 36–69). Then, for each of the issues of the dispute, the Court reviewed the logic and pleadings of both parties; followed by its reasoning and its decision on that issue. Finally, any judge who so wished was allowed to present separate opinions about any issues involved in the case. In some cases these opinions involved quite dissimilar reasonings about the outcomes, disagreements with the final outcomes, and/or comments on other issues not mentioned in the final Judgment.

Zubarah

Regarding Zubarah, the Court summarized its reasoning as follows: "In the period after 1868, the authority of the Shaikh of Qatar over the territory of Zubarah was gradually consolidated; it was acknowledged by the 1913 Anglo-Ottoman Convention, and was definitely established by 1937" (*ICJ Judgment*, 2001, 30 ¶ 96).

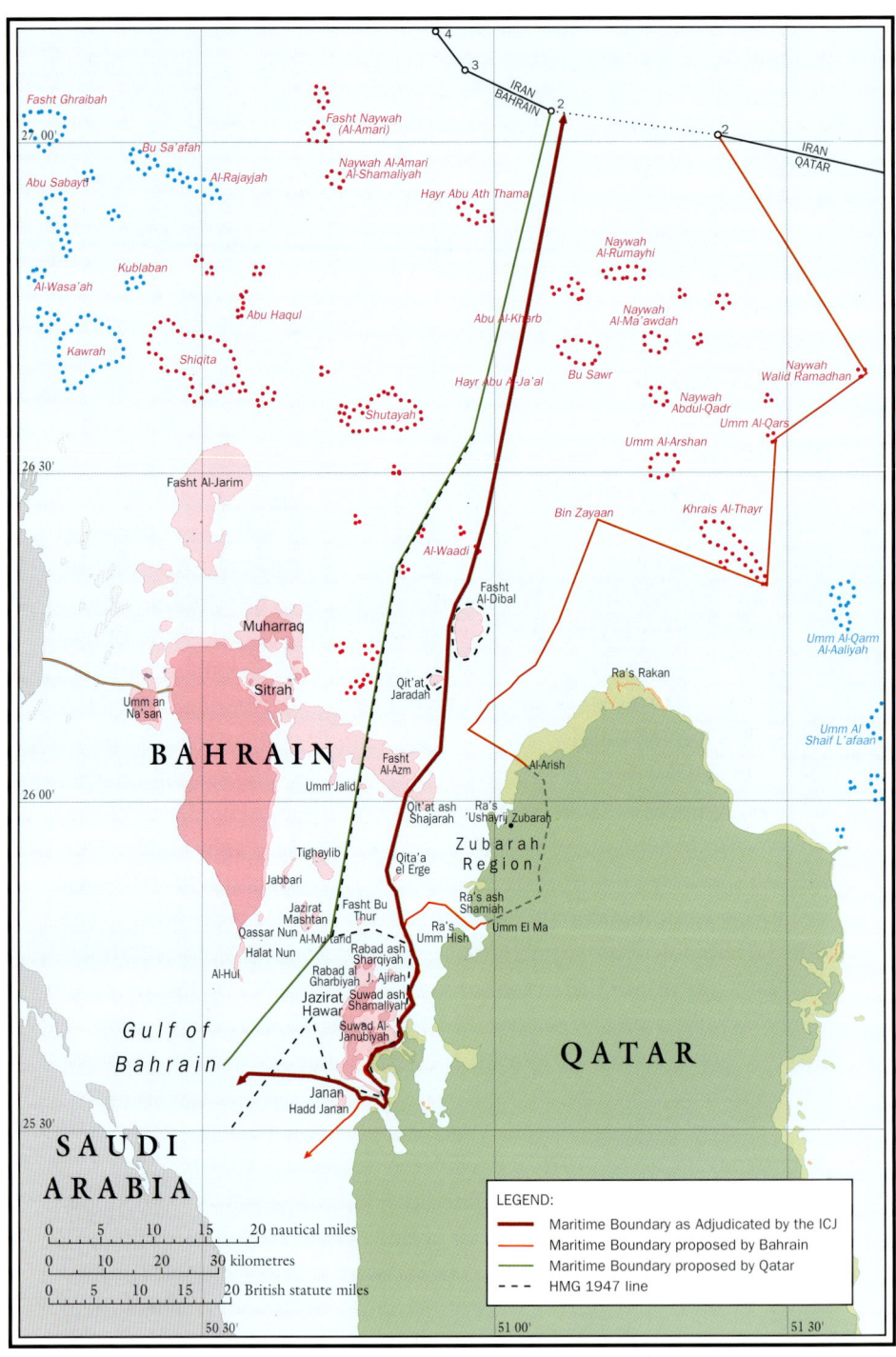

Note: According to 1947 HMG Line, Qit'at Jaradah and Fasht Al-Dibal were Bahrain enclaves on the east of the Line.

Map No. 9: Bahrain and Qatar—Various Maritime Boundary Lines

The Court denied that the Naim tribe had exercised sovereign authority on behalf of the Bahrain Sheikhs within Zubarah. Further, the Court said that it could not accept Bahrain's contention that Britain "had always regarded Zubarah as belonging to Bahrain," noting in particular the 1868 Agreements, the 1913 unratified Anglo-Ottoman Convention, and the 1937 correspondence between the Political Resident and the Secretary of State for India (*ICJ Judgment*, 2001, 30 ¶ 95).

The Court's Judgment made no comment on the evidence regarding British recognition of Bahrain's sovereignty over Zubarah (see Chapter 10, section entitled "Recognition by Third Parties—Great Britain"; Bahrain 1996, 104–5 ¶ 241; Bahrain 1997, 98–115 ¶ 246–52 for further discussion). Nor did they comment on why the British—if they indeed did not believe that Bahrain had any rights there—were so actively involved in June and July 1937, just prior to Qatar's invasion, in negotiations between Qatar and Bahrain regarding Zubarah. Taken in conjunction with the three British acts the Court chose to comment on, at a minimum this surely should indicate British dissonance on the issue.

Yet the Court reasoned that "the terms of the 1868 agreement show that any attempt by Bahrain to pursue its claims to Zubarah through military action at sea would not be tolerated by the British" (*ICJ Judgment*, 2001, 28 ¶ 84). The remainder of the Court's reasoning makes no comment on any of the evidence of sovereign acts by Bahrain, of British acknowledgement of Bahrain's authority, lack of Ottoman presence or control, or Al-Thani written confirmations that they had no control of the area. In fact, it would seem that the Court virtually ignored all of Bahrain's evidence dealing with events after 1868.

In support of their reasoning, the Court gave credence to a number of Qatari contentions that seemed utterly unsupported by evidence. In one section, the Court cites the Qatari claim that:

> A town existed in the area of Zubarah well before . . . [the Al-Khalifa] left Kuwait for Bahrain and thence for Zubarah. In Zubarah, the local sheikhs laid down a condition for their settlement: payment of the usual taxes in exchange for the right to trade in the area. (ICJ Judgment 2001, 26 ¶ 77)

However, the only "evidence" that Qatar presented concerning this supposed "pre-existing" Zubarah town, or about any "conditions for settlement" during that period, was contained in the forged documents, which were to be "disregarded." How then did the Court allow this reasoning enter into its final Judgment?

Further, the Court's Judgment noted that, "[a]ccording to Qatar, no official acts had been performed by Bahrain in Zubarah since 1868, while Qatar has carried out many acts of sovereignty there." The Court made no comment on Bahrain's evidence showing that neither the Ottomans nor the Al-Thani had any authority in Zubarah prior to 1937, and that the Al-Thani ruler repeatedly through the late 1800s disclaimed any responsibility for the northern peninsula. Yet in its final reasoning, the Court noted that the "[Naim] came under the jurisdiction of the local territorial sovereign, which was not Bahrain and had not been Bahrain at least since the events of 1868" (*ICJ Judgment 2001*, 28 ¶ 86; see also *Bahrain Memorial*, Chapter 1, *Bahrain Counter-Memorial*, Chapters 1 and 3). This despite the fact that Qatar had supplied no evidence of the Al-Thani's being the "local territorial sovereign," and no evidence of having held any authority over the Naim or the area until Qatar overran the town in 1937.

The Hawars

A number of different legal arguments were put forward regarding the Hawars. Qatar put forward two, the first being *original title*—basically the position that Qatar owned the Hawars by default because they ruled the geographical peninsula. In support of this contention, Qatar put forward a number of maps created by various world publishers in the 1700s and 1800s, which Qatar said showed the Hawars in the same colors as the Qatar peninsula.

In the case's Oral Hearings, Bahrain supplied a number of maps of the same vintage, all showing that the Qatar *peninsula* did not even exist at the time. This illustrated that mapmakers then working from great distances could certainly not be relied on for accuracy. Additionally, Bahrain showed maps drawn by persons who actually visited the area during that time period; these maps all showed the Hawars as part of Bahrain.

The second argument put forward by Qatar was *proximity*—which basically says that because the Hawars are physically closer to the Qatar peninsula than they were to the main Bahrain island, and because they are geomorphologically part of the peninsula, that they should belong to Qatar. In response, Bahrain detailed international case law examples showing that, historically, "proximity, adjacency or contiguity... is not sufficient to vest title."

In its turn, Bahrain put forward several legal arguments of its own regarding Bahrain's sovereignty over the Hawars. First, Bahrain showed that it had exercised continuous and uninterrupted sovereignty over the Hawars for the last two centuries. To illustrate this, Bahrain cited numerous examples of its exercise of authority, legally called *effectivités*, both before and after 1938. Paragraphs 101–4 of the final Judgment detail some of these acts of authority, beginning in the early 1800s and continuing through the present day.

A second argument Bahrain put forward is that the British decision of 1939, which determined that the Hawar Islands belonged to Bahrain, is a *binding arbitral decision*. Legally this contention rests on a principle called *res judicata*, meaning that legally made decisions are binding, and cannot be continuously re-adjudicated. Qatar contended that the British decision of 1939 was null and void because Qatar did not consent to the decision and was not given fair hearing; therefore, the decision was biased, and procedurally incorrect.

Finally, Bahrain also put forward the argument of *uti possidetis juris*. This legal principle basically says that states born of decolonization should remain intact, i.e., that the territorial limits drawn at the time of independence must be respected.

The Court's Judgment ruled on only one of these legal arguments— whether the 1939 British decision was binding:

> Turning to the Hawar Islands, the Court states that the decision by which the British Government found that those islands belonged to Bahrain does not constitute an arbitral award, but that this does not mean that it is devoid of legal effect. It notes that Bahrain and Qatar consented to Great Britain settling their dispute at the time and found that the 1939 decision must be regarded as a decision that was binding on those same states after 1971. Rejecting Qatar's arguments that the decision was null and void, the Court concludes from the foregoing that Bahrain has sovereignty over the Hawar Islands. (*Press Release* 2001/9, 16 March 2001, 2)

The Court thus found it unnecessary "to rule on the arguments of... original title, *effectivités,* and the principle of *uti possidetis juris* in the present case" (*ICJ Judgment,* 2001, 42–43 ¶ 148).

Janan
The Court recognized that both parties had supplied considerable evidence regarding whether or not Britain considered Janan to be part of the Hawar Islands. Bahrain, for its part, cited among other evidence the British adjudication of 1938–39, in which Janan was considered part of the Hawar group awarded to Bahrain. Qatar discounted this consideration as having been due to lack of clear understanding by Britain at the time as to the exact composition of the Hawars, a matter "corrected" in the 1947 maritime delimitation which set forth what became the de facto maritime boundary between the two states, known as "HMG's 1947 line."

Regarding Janan, the Court ruled that the British 1947 decision was "an authoritative interpretation of the 1939 decision" and ruled that "Qatar has sovereignty over Janan Island including Hadd Janan on the basis of the decision taken by the British Government in 1939, as interpreted in 1947" (*ICJ Judgment,* 2001, 47–48 ¶ 164–65).

Fasht Al-Dibal, Qit'at Jaradah, and the Maritime Boundary
We will not attempt here to explain much of the highly technical detail involved in maritime delimitations. Instead, we will focus only on the key issues as they involve the territory under dispute in this case. The Court's Judgment stated, "the Court has made clear that maritime rights derive from the coastal State's sovereignty over the land, a principle which can be summarized as 'the land dominates the sea'" (*ICJ Judgment,* 2001, 53 ¶ 185).

Thus the Court's first task in the maritime delimitation was to determine which islands should come under Bahrain's sovereignty. The Court had ruled above that the Hawars belonged to Bahrain, and that Janan was allocated to Qatar. The remaining marine features involved three highly contentious issues: Fasht Al-Azm, Fasht Al-Dibal, and Qit'at Jaradah.

During the proceedings, Bahrain presented evidence showing that Qit'at Jaradah was an island, rather than a low-tide elevation. While Qatar contested that characterization, in the Court's Judgment it "considers that it [Qit'at Jaradah] should be considered as an island because it is above water at high tide; the Court adds that the activities which have been carried out by Bahrain are sufficient to support its claim of sovereignty over the island" (*Press Release* 2001/9, 16 March 2001, 2).

Regarding Bahrain's archipelagic status, the Court observed that since Bahrain "has not made this claim [for archipelagic status] as one of its formal submissions... the Court is therefore not requested to take a position on this issue" (*ICJ Judgment,* 2001, 53 ¶ 183). But Bahrain could not have formally applied for archipelagic status while the question of Zubarah remained unresolved. Thus the Court did not, in our opinion, take into sufficient account the special considerations that apply to low-tide elevations in archipelagic states.

The Court observed that it could make no determination between the arguments of the parties as to whether or not Fasht Al-Azm was an extension of Sitra Island (*ICJ Judgment,* 2001, 54 ¶ 190). The Judgment also noted that international treaty law is silent on the question of whether low-tide elevations should be regarded as territory (*ICJ Judgment,* 2001, 57 ¶ 205). However, the Court decided that special circumstances justified choosing a delimitation line passing between Fasht Al-Azm and Qit'at ash Shajarah (*ICJ Judgment,* 2001, 59 ¶ 218).

The Judgment noted that "the Court has sometimes been led to eliminate the disproportionate effect of small islands" (*ICJ Judgment,* 2001, 60 ¶ 219). Thus, based on the fact that Qit'at Jaradah is a very small island, the Court decided that a special circumstance existed and chose to draw the maritime delimitation line between Qit'at Jaradah and Fasht Al-Dibal, without giving the island of Qit'at Jaradah the benefit of any territorial sea.

It is of interest to note that when the Court ruled on the issue of Janan Island, it used the British 1947 decision—which had given Janan to Qatar—as a valid and binding interpretation of its 1939 decision. That 1947 decision had also given sovereignty over Qit'at Jaradah and Fasht Al-Dibal to Bahrain—showing Bahrain's clear sovereignty over these features by making them Bahraini enclaves within what Britain decided was Qatar's territorial sea. However, in ruling on those two maritime features now, the Court was silent about the 1947 decision.

In the end, while Bahrain lost possession of Fasht Al-Dibal, a shoal that had previously been under its sole sovereignty, the new maritime delimitation gave considerably more seabed to Bahrain than it had previously enjoyed. (see Map No. 9, p. 398)

Significance of the Judgment

Judgments of the International Court are considered final, without appeal, and binding for the two parties. However, as the Court has no enforcement arm, it relies on the good faith of both parties for implementation of its decisions. "By signing the Charter, a State Member of the United Nations undertakes to comply with any decision of the International Court of Justice in a case to which it is a party" (International Court of Justice 1996, 73).

Speaking to the nation on television after the Judgment's reading, Sheikh Hamad bin Isa Al-Khalifa, Bahrain's Amir, said, "We salute the ICJ over its wise verdict and declare our complete acceptance of its ruling. We have given orders to take the necessary measures to ensure its implementation, taking into consideration that the outcome of the verdict is a joint gain for both the brotherly states of Qatar and Bahrain. We have jointly won the battle of the future and the time has come to open a brighter, new chapter in our relations and to accomplish the dreams and aspirations of generations of Bahrainis and Qataris."

For his part, Sheikh Hamad Al-Thani, the Amir of Qatar, also addressing his people on television, admitted that recognition of Bahrain's sovereignty over the Hawar Islands "was not easy upon us . . . However, despite the pain we feel, we think that the Court award has put an end to the dispute . . . It will enhance the security and stability of our Gulf states and contribute to strengthening the GCC . . . I extend [to Bahrain] a hand that has always been full of fraternity and cordiality so that we can close that page and open a new chapter where the two brotherly people take part in planning and deepening our future relations."

Both Rulers have pointed to the settlement of this long-standing dispute as an example for other countries of the world to follow in resolving conflicts by calm and peaceful means.

With this long, complex dispute now settled, both parties can look forward to improved relations and a new era of ties which will bring mutual economic and social benefit.

The Future

Curiously, in the very midst of this dispute, relations between Bahrain and Qatar began taking a turn for the better. In December 1999 Qatari Amir Sheikh Hamad visited Bahrain to thrash out the disputed issues. This visit led to the establishment of a Joint Bahraini–Qatari High Committee, headed by the Crown Princes of the two countries.

Since then, the parties have established diplomatic relations at the ambassadorial level, allowed citizens use of mere personal identity cards to travel freely between the two countries, and Qatar's airline now operates to and from Bahrain.

Beyond these, many additional ideas have been put forth concerning issues of mutual concern. Chief among these has been discussion of the building of a causeway linking both countries.

For its part, Bahrain has developed plans to exploit the mineral resources of Hawar, and also to develop the area as a site for tourism.

Relations between the two countries have been further cemented since the visit of Sheikh Hamad of Qatar to Bahrain early in 2001. He congratulated Bahrain's ruler, Sheikh Hamad, for successfully completing the referendum on the new National Action Charter, and for the overwhelming support demonstrated by the people of Bahrain for Sheikh Hamad's efforts to modernize the country by means of political, economic and social reforms.

Prominent Personalities

Al-Jabor, Nasir bin—Bahrain-appointed governor of Zubarah and chief of the Naim tribe; Sheikh Isa bin Ali at his accession in 1869 acknowledged to the PR that Al-Jabor was his subject, remaining loyal after some tribes in the Qatar peninsula, like the Al-Thani, rebelled against him in 1867.

Al-Jabr, Rashid bin Mohammed—Headman of the Naim tribe resident in Zubarah and loyal to the RB; warned the RB of Qatar's intentions in the 1930s and, following the attack of 1937, fled with his fellow tribesmen to Bahrain.

Al-Khalifa, Sheikh Hamad bin Isa—Ruler of Bahrain, 1932–1942; ruled Bahrain during the period of oil discovery.

Al-Khalifa, Sheikh Isa bin Ali—Ruler of Bahrain, 1869–1932; from June 1921 Sheikh Hamad was his Agent.

Al-Khalifa, Sheikh Mohammed bin Abdullah—Resided in Dammam and was a rival of Sheikh Mohammed bin Khalifa in the 1840s; member of the triumvirate that ruled for three months in 1869 until succeeded by Sheikh Isa bin Ali.

Al-Khalifa, Sheikh Mohammed bin Khalifa—Ruler of Bahrain jointly with Sheikh Abdullah bin Ahmed, 1834–1842, when driven out by the latter; restored in 1843 and ruled to 1868 when ousted by the British; member of the triumvirate that ruled for three months in 1869 until succeeded by Sheikh Isa bin Ali.

Al-Khalifa, Nasir bin Mubarik—Head of a rival branch of the Al-Khalifa family who went into exile in Qatar with members of the Bani Hajir tribe. Allied himself with Sheikh Mohammed bin Khalifa and Sheikh Mohammed bin Abdullah to overthrow Sheikh Ali bin Khalifa in 1869; ruled with them for a three-month interregnum until forced out by the British and replaced by Sheikh Isa bin Ali. Sometimes cited simply as Nasir bin Mubarik.

Al-Thani, Sheikh Jasim bin Mohammed—became de facto Chief of Doha under the Ottomans when they established their garrison there in 1871; formally succeeded his father, Sheikh Mohammed, as Chief of Doha in 1876.

Alban, Major Reginald G. E.—Political Agent, Bahrain (April–November 1927; October 1940 to January 1942); expressed, along with Prior, unease with British decision of 1939 awarding Hawar Islands to Bahrain.

Ballantyne, H. K.—London Solicitor to BAPCO and to the Ruler of Bahrain; appointed as the Ruler's London legal representative in May 1949. He was "the recognized channel of communication between Bapco and the British Government."

Belgrave, Sir Charles Dalrymple—Adviser to the Government of Bahrain (from 1926 to 1957); carried on the reforms begun by Daly and founded the governmental structure that eventually came to exist at independence in 1971; possessed of a strong character, he was responsible for all Bahrain's internal affairs. As such he vigorously supported Bahrain's territorial claims.

Brucks, Captain George—Captain in Britain's Indian Navy; responsible for the first Arabian Coast Survey (1821–1829) which included the Hawar Islands (then known as Warden's Islands).

Cox, Sir Percy—Political Resident, Bushire (1904–1914); Resident during the critical period when the Ottomans were negotiating to withdraw from the Qatar peninsula. Throughout his long career in the Arab world he exercised much influence on behalf of British imperial policy, particularly regarding Bahrain.

Darwish, Abdullah—Close advisor to Sheikh Ali, the RQ, during the 1950s; the forged documents portrayed him as a co-conspirator with Charles Belgrave.

Fowle, Sir Trenchard—Political Resident, Bushire (1936–1940); key player in the British attempts to resolve the problem resulting from Qatar's attack on Zubarah in 1937. With Hickinbotham, active in British efforts to settle the Zubarah dispute in late 1930s.

Galloway, Lt.-Col. Arnold—Political Agent, Bahrain (1945–1947); tried unsuccessfully to negotiate a solution to the Zubarah problem during the mediation efforts of the late 1940s.

Gaskin, J. C.—Political Assistant of the Bushire Residency, based in Bahrain (1900–1914); first British official to be permanently based in Bahrain; studied and reported on extent of Al-Thani authority; recommended Bahrain have Zubarah region and keep a representative there.

Hay, Lt.-Col. (later Sir) William Rupert—Political Resident, Bushire (1946–1953); involved in British efforts to settle the Zubarah dispute in the late 1940s.

Hickinbotham, Major Thomas—Political Agent, Bahrain (1937–1944); with Fowle, active in British efforts to settle the Zubarah dispute in late 1930s.

Holmes, Major Frank—New Zealand oil concession entrepreneur in the Middle East from early 1920s. Acted for Eastern and General Syndicate and later for Petroleum Concessions Limited as negotiator for Bahrain Additional Area, 1938. Headquartered in Bahrain, he exercised much influence there and was instrumental in persuading Sheikh Hamad to allow exploration for oil—resulting in the first discovery of oil in the Gulf.

Jaber, Rahmah bin—the Sheikh of Khor Hassan who allied himself with the Wahhabis and became their chief tool for carrying out their piratical activities. His occupation of Zubarah and alliance with Muscat represented a threat to the Ruler of Bahrain.

Kemball, Lt. (later Capt.) Arnold Burrowes—Officiating Political Resident, Bushire (April 1843–December 1843; March 1852–July 1855); actively involved in the mid-nineteenth century in implementing the first of a series of treaties in the Gulf intended to suppress piracy.

Kemball, Col. Charles Arnold—Political Resident, Bushire (1898–1904; Acting, April 1900–April 1904); staunch advocate of Bahrain's rights in the Zubarah region.

Loch, Percy Gordon—Political Resident, Bushire (1933–1935; Political Agent, Bahrain, November 1916–February 1918, November 1932–April 1937); advocated Bahrain's claims on the western shores of the Qatar peninsula and to the Hawar Islands.

Lorimer, John G.—Indian civil servant in the early 1900s and, later, Political Resident in Bushire (December 1913–February 1914); undertook on behalf of the British government the compilation of the *Gazetteer of the Persian Gulf, Oman and Central Arabia*, an historical and geographical dictionary intended to serve as a reference handbook for British officers and civil servants in India and the Gulf.

Pelly, Cornelius J.—Political Agent, Bahrain (1947–1950); architect of the 1950 "verbal agreement" regarding Zubarah.

Pelly, Capt. J. H.—Commander and Senior Naval Officer in the Gulf (1890s); expelled Al-Thani from Zubarah in 1895 in one of their attempts to wrest it from Bahrain.

Pelly, Lt.-Col. Lewis—Political Resident, Bushire (1867–1869); effected the 1868 Agreement between the Chiefs residing in Doha and the Ruler of Bahrain, confirming Britain's view of the Qatar peninsula as a dependency of Bahrain.

Prideaux, Lt.-Col. Francis B.—Political Agent, Bahrain (October 1904–May 1909; Political Resident, Bushire, April 1924–January 1927); undertook a detailed study in 1905 of the Qatar peninsula and its tribes for Lorimer's *Gazetteer*; recognized Al-Thani authority as limited to the environs of Doha; advocated Bahrain's rights to Zakhnuniya when the Ottomans occupied it.

Prideaux, Lt.-Col. William F.—Acting Political Resident, Bushire (May 1876–1877).

Prior, Sir Geoffrey—Political Agent, Bahrain (1929–1932; Political Resident, Bushire, 1941–1945); along with Alban expressed unease at the British decision of 1939 awarding the Hawar Islands to Bahrain.

Ross, Lt.-Col. Edward C.—Political Resident, Bushire (1872–1891); strongly urged British government to keep Ottomans from occupying Zubarah region.

Sa'id, Sayid—The Imam of Muscat who in 1810 allied himself with the RB to expel the Wahhabi forces from the Bahrain Islands and the eastern coast of the Qatar peninsula. In 1815 and 1828, when relations between the two states had deteriorated, undertook two unsuccessful expeditions against Bahrain.

Saldanha, Jerome A.—Judge in the Bombay Provincial Civil Service who compiled the eighteen-volume *Persian Gulf Précis* summarizing the records of the Bombay and Calcutta archives back to 1600.

Skliros, John—PCL's London executive, 1936 onwards. As PCL's agent in the negotiations for the 1936 Qatar oil concession he was eager to extend the territory under Qatar's sovereignty as far as possible.

Tarif, Isa bin—Head of the Al bin Ali tribe resident in the Zubarah region. Appointed by the RB as governor of Doha, he intrigued against Sheikh Mohammed bin Thani and eventually against the RB himself.

Weightman, Sir Hugh—Political Agent, Bahrain (1937–1940); actively advocated Bahrain's claims to Hawar Islands in the 1939 British adjudication.

Rulers of Bahrain and Qatar

Al-Khalifa Family Rulers in Qatar

H.H. Sheikh Khalifa Al-Khalifa [Al-Awal] (in Kuwait)	until 1708
H.H. Sheikh Mohammed bin Khalifa Al-Khalifa (Qatar Peninsula)	1708–1772
H.H. Sheikh Khalifa bin Mohammed Al-Khalifa (Qatar Peninsula)	1772–1783

Rulers of Bahrain

H.H. Sheikh Ahmed Al-Fatih Al-Khalifa	1783–1795
H.H. Sheikh Salman bin Ahmed Al-Khalifa	1795–1825
H.H. Sheikh Abdullah bin Ahmed Al-Khalifa	1825–1843
H.H. Sheikh Mohammed bin Khalifa Al-Khalifa	1843–1868
H.H. Sheikh Ali bin Khalifa Al-Khalifa	1868–1869 (Sept.)
H.H. Sheikh Mohammed bin Abdullah Al-Khalifa[1]	1869
H.H. Sheikh Isa bin Ali Al-Khalifa	1869–1932
H.H. Sheikh Hamad bin Isa Al-Khalifa	1932–1942
H.H. Sheikh Salman bin Hamad Al-Khalifa	1942–1961
H.H. Sheikh Isa bin Salman Al-Khalifa	1961–1999
H.M. Sheikh Hamad bin Isa Al-Khalifa[2]	1999–

---

[1] There was a three-month interregnum from September until November 1869 following the death of Sheikh Ali bin Khalifa during which a triumvirate consisting of Mohammed bin Abdullah, Mohammed bin Khalifa, and Nasir bin Mubarik governed (the first named seemed to have been in the ascendancy). This was followed by the accession of Sheikh Isa bin Ali in November 1869.

[2] On 14 February 2002, the State of Bahrain officially reverted to the traditional title of *Mamlakat*, or Kingdom, of Bahrain. From that date forward, His Highness the Amir became known as His Majesty King Hamad bin Isa Al-Khalifa.

Chiefs of Doha/Rulers of Qatar

Sheikh Mohammed bin Thani (Chief of Bidda/Doha)[3]	–1876
Sheikh Jasim bin Mohammed Al-Thani (Chief of Doha)	1876–1913
Sheikh Abdullah bin Jasim Al-Thani (Chief of Doha/Ruler of Qatar)[4]	1913–1948
Sheikh Ali bin Abdullah Al-Thani	1948–1960
Sheikh Ahmed bin Ali Al-Thani	1960–1972
Sheikh Khalifa bin Hamad Al-Thani	1972–1995
Sheikh Hamad bin Khalifa Al-Thani	1995–

---

[3] Sheikh Mohammed bin Thani remained the nominal Chief of Doha until 1876 when he retired from public life. He died in 1878. His son, Sheikh Jasim, became de facto Chief of Doha following the establishment of the Ottoman garrison in Doha in 1871 and formally succeeded in 1876.

[4] In 1916, Britain signed a treaty with the Chief of Doha, calling him the "Sheikh of Qatar."

Rulers of Bahrain: Periods of Rule

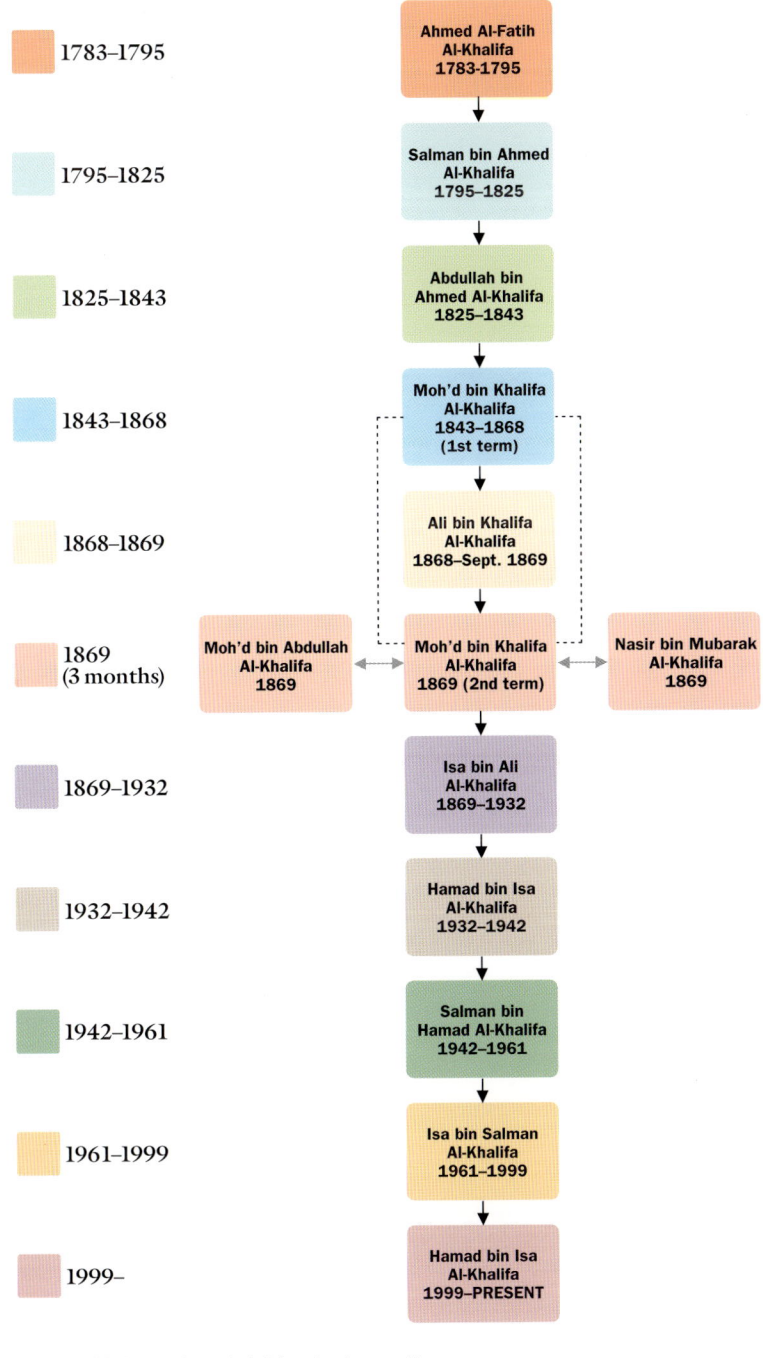

Color	Period
■	1783–1795
■	1795–1825
■	1825–1843
■	1843–1868
■	1868–1869
■	1869 (3 months)
■	1869–1932
■	1932–1942
■	1942–1961
■	1961–1999
■	1999–

Succession of rulers:

- Ahmed Al-Fatih Al-Khalifa, 1783–1795
- Salman bin Ahmed Al-Khalifa, 1795–1825
- Abdullah bin Ahmed Al-Khalifa, 1825–1843
- Moh'd bin Khalifa Al-Khalifa, 1843–1868 (1st term)
- Ali bin Khalifa Al-Khalifa, 1868–Sept. 1869
- Moh'd bin Abdullah Al-Khalifa, 1869 ⟷ Moh'd bin Khalifa Al-Khalifa, 1869 (2nd term) ⟷ Nasir bin Mubarak Al-Khalifa, 1869
- Isa bin Ali Al-Khalifa, 1869–1932
- Hamad bin Isa Al-Khalifa, 1932–1942
- Salman bin Hamad Al-Khalifa, 1942–1961
- Isa bin Salman Al-Khalifa, 1961–1999
- Hamad bin Isa Al-Khalifa, 1999–PRESENT

Periods of Rule are shown in left hand column. All rulers during that time period are shown with the same color coding, as indicated.

Key:
⟷ Joint Rule
------ Non-Consecutive Terms as Ruler

Bibliographical Note

Principal Reference Sources Used

A study of this kind necessarily relies primarily on unpublished archival resources, especially the archives of the powers that dominated the Gulf historically—the British and Ottomans—and those of the oil companies involved in early exploration and the acquiring of petroleum concessions. For those readers wishing to pursue the subject further the following sources are especially useful:

- Chevron Archives, San Ramon, California
- India Office, London
- Administration Reports of the Political Agency (R 15/2)
- Political and Secret Memoranda and Related Files (L/P+S/18)
- Records of the Political Agency (R 15/2)
- Records of the Political Residency (R 15/1)
- Public Records Office, London
- Foreign Office Papers (FO 371)
- The Ottoman Archives, Istanbul

The great bulk of the references cited here are to these primary sources. It should be noted that many of them are also available as Annexes to the pleadings of the *Case Concerning Maritime Delimitation and Territorial Questions Between Qatar and Bahrain (Qatar v. Bahrain)* heard in May and June 2000 before the International Court of Justice in The Hague. These Annexes are cited in the list which follows.

In addition, many have been published in compilations such as the *Records of Bahrain*, the *Records of Qatar*, and Saldanha. Reference to these sources is also cited. The pleadings themselves along with related documents submitted to the International Court of Justice by the two parties to the case, as well as transcripts of the oral presentations and the judgment, are available on the Internet at the Court's website: www.cij-icj.org. It should be pointed out that the pertinent documents of the earlier jurisdiction and admissibility phase are, likewise, available on the Court's website.

With regard to published sources, the following stand out as being especially useful for study of this subject.

1. The Gazetteer of the Persian Gulf, Oman and Central Arabia (Lorimer)
The *Gazetteer*, compiled by John Gordon Lorimer (1870–1914), an Indian Civil Servant in the early 1900s and, later, British Political Resident in Bushire, was a British government project originally intended to produce a handbook for British agents and policymakers.

Volume 1 (published in 1915) is a detailed history of the Persian Gulf region and its surrounding countries based on Lorimer's own notes and on copious summaries of archival and printed material produced by British officers and civil servants in India and the Gulf.

Volume 2 (published in 1908) is a geographical dictionary, much of the material presented here having been gathered by Lorimer and his assistants during their field trips, covering the same area. It provides not only a detailed history and geography of the area but much insight into political, social and economic matters as well. It is a monumental factbook described by the *Times Literary Supplement* as being "without any modern substitute."

2. Précis of Bahrein Affairs and *Précis of Katar Affairs (Saldanha)*
The eighteen volumes of Saldanha's *The Persian Gulf Précis*, 1903–8, comprise a comprehensive summary of British records relating to the Gulf from the earliest East India Company operations to the beginning of the twentieth century. Each geographic area is treated separately. Like Lorimer, these volumes were produced to see that British officials concerned with administration and policy making were well informed on the areas of their concern. The précis were compiled by Jerome A. Saldanha, a judge in the Bombay Provincial Civil Service who summarized and explained the treaties, reports, letters, memoranda, and other records in the government archives in Bombay and Calcutta back to 1600, producing a mass of information, much of which was relied on by Lorimer for his *Gazetteer*.

Among the geographic volumes produced were: *Précis of Bahrein Affairs, 1854–1904* and *Précis of Katar Affairs, 1873–1904*. Originally published in Simla between 1903–8, the entire work was reprinted in eight volumes by Archive Editions in 1986.

3. *The Records of Bahrain* and *The Records of Qatar*

The *Records of Bahrain* is an eight-volume set of facsimiles of documentary materials covering the period from 1820 through 1960, selected from important archival sources and arranged according to broad subjects. Published by Archive Editions, it is designed to provide a comprehensive survey of the origins and development of the State of Bahrain. The documents, drawn mainly from the India Office Records in London, cover not only political developments but such areas as economic growth, tribal movements and Al-Khalifa rule and succession. Continuation volumes cover the period 1961 through 1965.

The *Records of Qatar*, also an eight-volume set covering the period 1820 through 1960, is similar to the *Records of Bahrain*, and, like its companion set, makes available a comprehensive selection from British archives of the most important documents relative to Qatar's history. Similarly, continuation volumes covering the years 1961 through 1965 supplement it.

4. *Selections from the Records of the Bombay Government, New Series, No. XXIV, 1856*

This volume is a collection of reports received by the Government of Bombay and was designed, like Lorimer's *Gazetteer*, to serve as a reference book for officers working in the area. It covers the years from 1805 through 1856 and contains a great deal of information that Lorimer omitted. Originally printed in Bombay in 1856, it has been reprinted by Oleander Press as *Arabian Gulf Intelligence: Selections from the Records of the Bombay Government, New series, no. XXIV, 1856, Concerning Arabia, Bahrain, Kuwait, Muscat and Oman, Qatar, United Arab Emirates and the Islands of the Gulf.*

5. *Annual Administration Reports of the Persian Gulf Political Residency, 1873–1947*

These have been reprinted and published in ten volumes entitled *The Persian Gulf Administration Reports* by Archive Editions in 1986.

6. *The Bahrain Government Annual Reports, 1924–1970*

Published in eight volumes by Archive Editions.

7. A Collection of Treaties, Engagements and Sanads Relating to India and Neighbouring Countries (Aitchison)

This work, compiled by C. U. Aitchison and published in fourteen volumes in Delhi, has gone through many editions and reprintings. It is an important source of treaties and similar documents for the part of the world covered.

List of References

Abbreviations Used

Ann: Annex
BCM: *Bahrain Counter-Memorial* (1997)
BCM (1992): *Bahrain Counter-Memorial* (Jurisdiction phase) (1992)
BM: *Bahrain Memorial* (1996)
BR: *Bahrain Reply* (1999)
BRej: *Bahrain Rejoinder* (Jurisdiction phase) (1992)
BSD: *Bahrain Supplemental Documents* (2000)
FO: Foreign Office
IO: India Office
IOR: India Office Records
PAB: Political Agent, Bahrain
PCL: Petroleum Concessions Limited
PR: Political Resident, Persian Gulf
QCM: *Qatar Counter-Memorial* (1997)
QM: *Qatar Memorial* (1996)
QM (1992): *Qatar Memorial* (Jurisdiction phase) (1992)
QR: *Qatar Reply* (1999)
QR (1992): *Qatar Reply* (Jurisdiction phase) (1992)
RB: Ruler of Bahrain
RQ: Ruler of Qatar

Abbas, Hajj [Chief of Police, Bahrain], 14 April 1936, Letter to Bahrain Court. (BM Ann 245)

Abdullah bin Hasan [Messenger of Hamad bin Isa bin Ali Al-Khalifa (RB)], 22 June 1937, IOR R/15/2/203. (BM Ann 131)

Acting Adviser to Government of Bahrain, 17 July 1938, Letter to Hugh Weightman [PAB], IOR R/15/2/1858. (BM Ann 267)

Administration Report for Bahrain Political Agency for the Year 1909. In *The Persian Gulf Administration Reports, 1843–1947*, 6:69–73. Gerrards Cross: Archive Editions, 1986. (BM Ann 237)

Administration Report for Bahrain Political Agency for the Year 1911. In *The Persian Gulf Administration Reports, 1843–1947*, 6:97–108. Gerrards Cross: Archive Editions, 1986. (BM Ann 240)

Administration Report for Bahrain Political Agency for the Year 1923. IOR R/15/1/713/4. In *The Persian Gulf Administration Reports, 1843–1947*, 8. Gerrards Cross: Archive Editions, 1986. (BM Ann 89)

Agreement between Chiefs Residing in the Province of Qatar and Chief of Bahrain, 13 September 1868. In *A Collection of Treaties, Engagements and Sanads Relating to India and Neighbouring Countries,* compiled by C. U. Aitchison, 2:193. 5th ed. 14 vols. in 11. Delhi: Manager of Publications, 1929–33. (BM Ann 13) Also in *Records of Bahrain,* 2:15–16.

Agreement Entered into by Shaikh Mahomed bin Khalifah, Chief of Bahrain, for the Abolition of the African Slave Trade, 1847. Translation. *Records of Bahrain,* 1:584.

Agreement of Chief of El-Kutr (Guttur) Engaging Not to Commit Any Breach of the Maritime Peace, 12 September 1868. In *A Collection of Treaties, Engagements and Sanads Relating to India and Neighbouring Countries,* compiled by C. U. Aitchison, 11: 183–84. 5th ed. 14 vols. in 11. Delhi: Manager of Publications, 1929–33. (BM Ann 12) Also in *Records of Bahrain,* 2:15.

Agreement of 25 December 1990: The Minutes Signed by the Foreign Ministers of Qatar, Bahrain and Saudi Arabia on 25 December 1990. (QM (1992) Ann II.32)

Agreement Signed by Ruler of Qatar and Ruler of Bahrain on 17 June and 23 June 1944 Respectively, IOR R/15/2/205. (BM Ann 167)

Agreement Signed by the Chief of Bahrain, 22 December 1880. Translation. In *A Collection of Treaties, Engagements and Sanads Relating to India and Neighbouring Countries,* compiled by C. U. Aitchison, 11:237. 5th ed. 14 vols. in 11. Delhi: Manager of Publications, 1929–33. (BM Ann 37) Also in *Records of Bahrain,* 2:409.

Al-Arayed, Jawad S. [Agent for the State of Bahrain], 29 May 1997, Letter to the President of the Court, Submitted by the Agent for the State of Bahrain in re Maritime Delimitation and Territorial Questions between Qatar and Bahrain.

———, 25 September 1997, Letter to the President of the Court, Submitted by the Agent for the State of Bahrain in re Maritime Delimitation and Territorial Questions between Qatar and Bahrain. 3 v.

———, 31 December 1997, Letter to the President of the Court, Submitted by the Agent for the State of Bahrain in re Maritime Delimitation and Territorial Questions between Qatar and Bahrain. 6 v.

———, 26 March 1998, Letter to the President of the Court, Submitted by the Agent for the State of Bahrain in re Maritime Delimitation and Territorial Questions between Qatar and Bahrain.

———, 8 June 2000. Opening Statement. In *Verbatim Record of the Public Sitting Held on Thursday, 8 June 2000...in the Case Concerning Maritime Delimitation and Territorial Questions between Qatar and Bahrain (Qatar v. Bahrain).* The Hague: International Court of Justice. (CR 2000/11:8–11)

Al-Arayed, Salim A., 2001. *Islamic Law as Administered in British India and in Joint British Courts in the Arabian Gulf, 1857–1947.* Bahrain: Al Ayam Press.

Al-Baharna, Hussain M., 14 July, and 18 August 1991, Letters to the International Court of Justice. Cited in *ICJ Judgment,* 1994, ¶ 4.

———, 30 November 1994, *Report of the State of Bahrain to the International Court of Justice on the Attempt by the Parties to Implement the Court's Judgment of 1st July 1994.* Cited in *ICJ Judgment,* 1995, ¶ 13.

Al-Dosari, Hamoud bin Muhanna bin Hamad, 7 September 1996, Translation of Statement. (BM Ann 313[a])

Al-Dosari, Nasr bin Makki bin Ali, 16 September 1996, Translation of Statement. (BM Ann 314[b])

Al-Dosari, Salman bin Isa bin Ahmad bin Saad, 15 September 1996, Translation of Statement. (BM Ann 315[a])

Al-Ghattam, Ibrahim bin Salman bin Ahmed, 15 September 1996, Translation of Statement. (BM Ann 316[a])

Al-Hafidh Abi Abdullah Mohammed Bin Yazid Al-Qazwini, *Sunan Ibn Maja*, Part I, 187 (translation and Arabic version). (QM Ann II.68)

Al-Jabor, Rashid bin Mohammed [Chief of Naim tribe], 24 April 1937, Translation of Letter to Hamad bin Ali Al-Khalifa [RB]. (BM Ann 120)

Al-Khalifa, Abdulla bin Khalid and Ali Aba Hussein, 1984. "Some of the History of al-Utoob in the Eighteenth Century: the Immigration of al-Utoob from al-Hadar in Najd." Originally published in Arabic in *al-Watheeka* 4:12–52. (BCM Ann 118[b])

Al-Khalifa, Hamad bin Isa [RB], 3 May 1930, Proclamation no. 1889/17 of 1348 (corresponding to 3 May 1930) (Bahrain Archives/Proclamation file)

———, 14 April 1937, Letter to Capt. Tom Hickinbotham [PAB], IOR R/15/2/202. (BM Ann 115)

———, 1 July 1937, Letter to Capt. Tom Hickinbotham [PAB], IOR R/15/2/203. (BM Ann 135)

———, 6 July 1937, Letter to Capt. Tom Hickinbotham [PAB]. (BM Ann 143[a])

———, 6 July 1937a, Letter to Capt. Tom Hickinbotham [PAB], IOR R/15/2/203. (BM Ann 144)

———, 26 April 1939, Letter to Capt. Tom Hickinbotham [PAB], IOR R/15/2/204. (BM Ann 162)

Al-Khalifa, Isa bin Ali [RB], 2 September 1873, Translated Purport of Statement. (BM Ann 19) Also in *Records of Qatar*, 2:523.

———, 17 December 1874, Letter to Lt.-Col. Edward C. Ross [PR]. (BM Ann 26)

———, December 1877, Letter to Maj. Charles Grant [First Asst. PR]. Cited in J. A. Saldanha, *Précis of Katar Affairs, 1873–1904*. Gerrards Cross: Archive Editions, 1986, 9.

———, 15 January 1911, Translation of Letter to Maj. Percy Z. Cox [PR]. (BM Ann 239[a])

———, 14 May 1914, Letter to Lt.-Col. Arthur P. Trevor [PAB], IOR R/15/1/740. Also in *Records of Bahrain*, 3:583.

Al-Khalifa, Isa bin Salman [RB], 26 December 1987, Letter to King Fahd of Saudi Arabia; translated into English by Qatar. (BCM (1992) Ann I.4)

Al-Khalifa, Salman bin Hamad [RB], 14 September 1944, Letter to Maj. Tom Hickinbotham [PAB]. (BM Ann 170)

———, 3 February 1945, Letter to Maj. Tom Hickinbotham [PAB], IOR R/15/2/205. (BM Ann 177)

———, 5 March 1947, Letter to Cornelius J. Pelly [PAB], IOR R/15/2/605. (BM Ann 183)

———, 2 March 1948, Letter to Cornelius J. Pelly [PAB], FO 371/68324. (BM Ann 186)

Al-Khalifa, Salman bin Hamad [RB], 24 June 1948, Letter to Ernest Bevin [British Foreign Secretary], FO 371/68324 96694. (BM Ann 189)

———, 18 March 1953, Letter to Lt.-Col. Rupert Hay [PR], FO 1016/266 XC 148 248. (BM Ann 202)

———, 8 February 1961, Letter to Sir George Middleton [PR], FO 371/156721. (BM Ann 218)

Al-Meri, Ali bin Fetais, 30 May 2000. "The Ottoman Administrative Structure in Qatar." In *Verbatim Record of the Public Sitting Held on Tuesday, 30 May 2000... in the Case Concerning Maritime Delimitation and Territorial Questions between Qatar and Bahrain (Qatar v. Bahrain)*. The Hague: International Court of Justice. (CR 2000/6 [translation]: 2–6)

Al-Muslemani, Abdullah A. [Agent for the State of Qatar], 12 June 1997, Letter to the International Court of Justice.

———, 15 December 1998, Letter to the International Court of Justice.

Al-Naimi, Mohammed bin Mohammed bin Theyab, 6 September 1996, Translation of Statement. (BM Ann 233[a])

Al-Naimi, Saleh bin Muhammed Ali bin Ali, 14 September 1996, Translation of Statement. (BM Ann 234[a])

Al-Nuaimi, Najeeb, 30 November 1994. Act to Comply with Paragraphs (3) and (4) of Operative Paragraph 41 of the Judgment of the Court Dated 1 July 1994. Cited in *ICJ Judgment*, 1995, ¶ 12.

Al-Sadeh, Abdulla, 1997. ICJ Counter-Memorial Analysis: Qatar Suspect Document Forgery Report. Bahrain. (prepared for the Office of the Minister of State; unpublished)

Al-Saud, Fahd bin Abdul-Aziz [King of Saudi Arabia], 19 December 1987a, 1987b, Letters to Isa bin Salman Al-Khalifa [RB] and Khalifa bin Hamad Al-Thani [RQ]. Translation. Cited in *ICJ Judgment*, 1994, ¶ 17.

Al-Thani, Abdullah bin Jasim [RQ], 23 April 1937, Translation of Letter to Lt.-Col. Percy G. Loch [PAB], IOR R/15/2/202. (QM Ann III.120)

———, 9 June 1937, Letter to Lt.-Col. Trenchard Fowle [PR], IOR R/15/1/369. (BM Ann 129)

———, 11 July 1937, Translation of Letter to Capt. Tom Hickinbotham [PAB], IOR R/15/2/203. (BM Ann 149)

———, 17 July 1937, Letter to O. Kirkpatrick Caroe [PR], IOR R/15/2/203. (BM Ann 153)

———, 10 May 1938, Translation of Letter to Hugh Weightman [PAB], IOR R/15/1/690. (BM Ann 256)

———, 27 May 1938, Translation of Letter to Hugh Weightman [PAB], IOR L/P+S/R/3895. (BM Ann 260)

———, 15 June 1938, Extract from Letter to Hugh Weightman [PAB], IOR R/15/1/690. (BM Ann 263)

———, 8 July 1938, Translation of Letter to Hugh Weightman [PAB]. (BM Ann 265)

———, 12 July 1938, Translation of Letter to Hugh Weightman [PAB]. (BM Ann 266)

———, 30 March 1939, Rejoinder (in the form of a letter) to Hugh Weightman [PAB]. (BM Ann 279) Also in *Records of Bahrain*, 5:281–95.

———, 4 August 1939, Letter to Lt.-Col. Trenchard C. Fowle [PR]. (BM Ann 289) Also in Records *of Bahrain*, 5:302–4.

———, 18 November 1939, Letter to Lt.-Col. Charles G. Prior [PR], IOR R/15/2/547. (BM Ann 291)

———, 7 June 1940, Letter to Hugh Weightman [PAB], IOR R/15/2/547. (BM Ann 294)

———, 30 January 1945, Letter to Salman bin Hamad Al-Khalifa [RB], IOR R/15/2/205. (BM Ann 175)

Al-Thani, Jasim bin [Chief of Doha Town], 24 November 1880, Letter to Lt.-Col. Edward C. Ross [PR], Bombay Archives, Political Department File No. 1680, Vol. 158, IOR P/1741. (BCM Ann 15)

———, 9 March 1881, Letter to Lt.-Col. Edward C. Ross [PR]. (BM Ann 38)

Al-Thani, Khalifa bin Hamad [RQ], 21 December 1987, Letter to King Fahd of Saudi Arabia. (QM (1992) Ann II.16)

Amery, L. S. [Secretary of State for the British Colonies], 19 June 1928, Letter to Lt.-Col. Lionel B. Haworth [PR], COC.59115/28 [No. 2], BSA. Cited in Angela Clarke, *Bahrain: Oil and Development, 1929–1989*. London: Immel, 1990, 82.

Amin, Mokhtar Mohamed, Mohammed Ezz-el-Din Sobhi, and Peter V. Tytell, 1997. *Expert Forensic Document Examination Report*. In Jawad S. Al-Arayed, 25 September 1997, Vol. 3, App. II.8.

———, 1997a. *Expert Forensic Document Examination Report*. Revised. In Jawad S. Al-Arayed, 31 December 1997.

Annual Report of the Government of Bahrain, March 1937–February 1938). Bahrain: n.p. (BM Ann 253) (*The Bahrain Government Annual Reports, 1924–1970* have been published in 8 vols. by Archive Editions, Gerrards Cross, England.)

Anscombe, Frederick F., 1994. "The Ottoman Gulf and the Creation of Kuwayt, Sa'udi Arabia, and Qatar, 1871–1914." Ph.D. diss., Princeton University.

———, 1997. *The Ottoman Gulf: the Creation of Kuwait, Saudi Arabia, and Qatar*. New York: Columbia University Press.

Bahrain, 1992. *Case Concerning Maritime Delimitation and Territorial Questions between Qatar and Bahrain (Qatar v. Bahrain). Counter-Memorial Submitted by the State of Bahrain. Questions of Jurisdiction and Admissibility*. n.p., 3 vols.

———, 1992a. *Case Concerning Maritime Delimitation and Territorial Questions between Qatar and Bahrain (Qatar v. Bahrain). Rejoinder Submitted by the State of Bahrain. Questions of Jurisdiction and Admissibility*. n.p.

———, 1996. *Case Concerning Maritime Delimitation and Territorial Questions between Qatar and Bahrain (Qatar v. Bahrain). Memorial Submitted by the State of Bahrain (Merits)*. n.p., 7 vols.

———, 1997. *Case Concerning Maritime Delimitation and Territorial Questions between Qatar and Bahrain (Qatar v. Bahrain). Counter-Memorial Submitted by the State of Bahrain (Merits)*. n.p., 3 vols.

———, 1999. *Case Concerning Maritime Delimitation and Territorial Questions between Qatar and Bahrain (Qatar v. Bahrain). Reply Submitted by the State of Bahrain (Merits)*. n.p., 2 vols.

Bahrain Counter-Memorial, 1992. *See* Bahrain, 1992.

———, 1997. *See* Bahrain, 1997.

Bahrain Court Record for Case no. 264/1351, 1932. (BM Ann 243)

Bahrain Memorial, 1996. *See* Bahrain, 1996.

Bahrain Oil Concession, 1925, IOR R/15/1/649. (BM Ann 90) Also in *Records of Bahrain*, 4:279–85.

Bahrain Order in Council, 12 August 1913. (BSD Ann 2) Also in *Records of Bahrain*, 5:446–69.

Bahrain Rejoinder, 1992. *See* Bahrain, 1992a.

Bahrain Reply, 1999. *See* Bahrain, 1999.

Ballantyne, H. K. [Solicitor to BAPCO and RB], 2 June 1948, Letter to Charles Belgrave [Adviser to Government of Bahrain]. (BM Ann 188)

———, 2 June 1948a, Letter to L. Pyman [FO]. (BM Ann 187[a])

Baxter, C. W. [FO], 13 June 1939, Transcript of Letter to Secretary of State, India Office, IOR R/15/2/547. (BM Ann 284[b])

Beatty, Jerome, 1939. "Is John Bull's Face Red?" *American Magazine* (January). Cited in Daniel Yergin, *The Prize*. New York: Simon and Schuster, 1991, 817, note 4.

Belgrave, Charles D. [Adviser to Government of Bahrain], 16 August 1933, Letter to Lt.-Col. Percy G. Loch [PAB], IOR R/15/2/390. (BCM Ann 64)

———, 1934. "Pearl Diving in Bahrain." *Journal of the Royal Central Asia Society* XXI (July): 450.

———, 28 April 1936, Letter to Lt.-Col. Percy G. Loch [PAB], IOR R/15/1/688. (BM Ann 246)

———, 20 June 1937, Letter to Capt. Tom Hickinbotham [PAB]. (BM Ann 130[a])

———, 2 July 1937, Letter to Capt. Tom Hickinbotham [PAB], IOR R/15/1/370. (BM Ann 139)

———, 6 July 1937, Letter to Capt. Tom Hickinbotham [PAB], IOR R/15/2/203. (BM Ann 145)

———, 19 August 1937, Letter to Capt. Tom Hickinbotham [PAB], IOR R/15/2/204. (BM Ann 158)

———, 10 November 1937, Letter to Head Natur. (BM Ann 249)

———, 31 January 1938, Letter to E. V. Packer, PCL. (BM Ann 250)

———, 23 May 1938, Letter to Hugh Weightman [PAB], IOR R/15/2/547. (BCM Ann 87)

———, 24 May 1938, Police Orders. (BM Ann 259)

———, 29 May 1938, Note Entitled "The Hawar Islands," IOR R/15/2/547. (BM Ann 261)

———, 22 December 1938, Bahrain Counter-Claim in the Form of a Letter to Hugh Weightman [PAB], IOR R/15/2/547. (BM Ann 274)

———, 20 April 1939, Letter to Hugh Weightman [PAB]. (BM Ann 280)

———, 11 June 1942, Memorandum to Edward Wakefield [PAB], IOR R/15/2/204. (BM Ann 164)

———, 26 June 1950, Letter to R. Andrew [PAB]. (BM Ann 199)

———, 15 April 1952, Letter to W. Laver [PAB]. (BM Ann 200)

———, 1960. *Personal Column*. London: Hutchinson.

Bentinck, William, 1834. Quotation cited in Alvin J. Cottrell, *The Persian Gulf States*. Baltimore: Johns Hopkins University Press, 1980, 75.

Bibby, Geoffrey, 1970. *Looking for Dilmun*. London: Collins.

Biscoe, Hugh V. [PR], 7 June 1932, Letter to the Foreign Secretary of India, FO 371/16000. (BCM Ann 56)

Bostan, Idris and Caroline Finkel, 1997. *Expert Ottoman Report*. In Jawad S. Al-Arayed, 25 September 1997, Vol. 3, App. II.2.

Brenan, T. V. [FO], 13 April 1938, Letter to J. P. Gibson [IO], FO 371/21822 97609. (BM Ann 255)

Brown, R. M. [BAPCO Chief Local Representative], 13 July 1949, Letter to Charles D. Belgrave [Adviser to Government of Bahrain]. (BM Ann 298)

Brucks, George B., 1856. "Memoir Descriptive of the Navigation of the Gulf of Persia, 1821–1829." In *Arabian Gulf Intelligence: Selections from the Records of the Bombay Government, new ser., No. 24, 1856*, compiled by R. Hughes Thomas, 531–634. Bombay: Bombay Education Society's Press, 1856. Reprint, Cambridge: Oleander Press, 1985. (BM Ann 7)

Bundy, Rodman, 31 May 2000. "The Cartographic Evidence in the Case." In *Verbatim Record of the Public Sitting Held on Wednesday, 31 May 2000...in the Case Concerning Maritime Delimitation and Territorial Questions between Qatar and Bahrain (Qatar v. Bahrain)*. The Hague: International Court of Justice. (CR 2000/7:8–25)

———, 20 June 2000. "The Territorial Integrity of Qatar [Part I]." In *Verbatim Record of the Public Sitting Held on Tuesday, 20 June 2000...in the Case Concerning Maritime Delimitation and Territorial Questions between Qatar and Bahrain (Qatar v. Bahrain)*. The Hague: International Court of Justice. (CR 2000/17:42–53)

———, 21 June 2000. "The Territorial Integrity of Qatar [Part II]." In *Verbatim Record of the Public Sitting Held on Wednesday, 21 June 2000...in the Case Concerning Maritime Delimitation and Territorial Questions between Qatar and Bahrain (Qatar v. Bahrain)*. The Hague: International Court of Justice. (CR 2000/18:8–16)

The Buraimi Memorials, 1955. 1987. Memorial of the Government of Saudi Arabia. Gerrards Cross: Archive Editions.

Burrows, B. [PR], 5 May 1954, Letter to Salman bin Hamad Al-Khalifa [RB]. (BM Ann 209)

Caroe, Olaf K., 19 November 1941, Letter to R. T. Peel [Government of India], containing a handwritten annotation by Peel, IOR L/P+S/12/3895. (BCM Ann 107)

Chief of Naim Tribe, 25 April 1937, Letter to Hamad bin Ali Al-Khalifa [RB]. (BM Ann 121)

Chisholm, Archibald H. T., 1975. *The First Kuwait Oil Concession Agreement: a Record of the Negotiations*. London: Frank Cass. Cited in Daniel Yergin, *The Prize*. New York: Simon and Schuster, 1991, 817, notes 1, 4.

Clarke, Angela, 1990. *Bahrain: Oil and Development, 1929–1989*. London: Immel.

College of Arms (Great Britain). 1998. *Report of David Vines White*. London: The College. In Jawad S. Al-Arayed, 26 March 1998.

Commander of the Sphinx, 1898. [Report on the Arab Rising in Qatar.] Cited in J. A. Saldanha, *Précis of Katar Affairs, 1873–1904*. Gerrards Cross: Archive Editions, 1986, 45–46.

Constable, Capt. C. G. and Lt. A. W. Stiffe, 1864. [Abu Dhabi to Ras Tanura.] Chaps. 7–8 in *The Persian Gulf Pilot, 1864*. London: Admiralty Hydrographic Office. Reprint, Gerrards Cross: Archive Editions, 1989. (BM Ann 11) Also in *Records of Qatar*, 2:5–45.

Convention between United Kingdom and Turkey Regarding the Persian Gulf and Adjacent Territories, 29 July 1913. (BM Ann 81) Also in *Records of Qatar*, 4:1–4, 323–325.

Costa, Paolo M., 1995. "Archeological Report on the Hawar Islands—Hawar Project: Final Report." Unpublished. (BM Ann 310)

Crown, David A. and Brian B. Carney, 1998. *Forensic Document Examination Report*. In Qatar Interim Report, Ann III.

Crystal, Jill, 1990. *Oil and Politics in the Gulf: Rulers and Merchants in Kuwait and Qatar*. Cambridge: Cambridge University Press.

———, 1995. *Oil and Politics in the Gulf: Rulers and Merchants in Kuwait and Qatar*. Updated ed. Cambridge: Cambridge University Press.

David, Eric, 5 June 2000. ["History of the Origins of Zubarah."] In *Verbatim Record of the Public Sitting Held on Monday, 5 June 2000...in the Case Concerning Maritime Delimitation and Territorial Questions between Qatar and Bahrain (Qatar v. Bahrain)*. The Hague: International Court of Justice. (CR 2000/8–9 [translation]: 49–54, 2–19)

———, 21 June 2000. "Zubarah." In *Verbatim Record of the Public Sitting Held on Monday, 21 June 2000...in the Case Concerning Maritime Delimitation and Territorial Questions between Qatar and Bahrain (Qatar v. Bahrain)*. The Hague: International Court of Justice. (CR 2000/18 [translation]: 39–55)

Deputy Secretary to Government of India, 1 July 1939, Letter to Lt.-Col. Trenchard C. Fowle [PR], Records of Political Department, India Office. (BM Ann 286)

Dickson, Maj. Harold [PAB], 6 December 1919, Memo to Deputy PR, IOR L/P+S/10/850. (BM Ann 86)

———, 17 January 1920, Memo to Deputy PR, IOR L/P+S/10/850. (BM Ann 87)

Draft Memorandum to Turkish Ambassador, July 1911, FO 371/1234. (BM Ann 78)

Draft Telegram under Cover of Letter from India Office to T. V. Brenan, 10 July 1937, FO 371/20783XC/132657. (BM Ann 148)

Dubai/Sharjah Arbitration Award, 19 October 1981, 91 *International Law Reports*, 1993. (QM Ann III.295)

Elphinstone, Mountstuart, 1819. Quotation cited in John B. Kelly, *Britain and the Persian Gulf, 1795–1880* (Oxford: Clarendon Press), 162–163.

Exclusive Agreement of the Shaikh of Bahrain with the British Government, 13 March 1892. In *A Collection of Treaties, Engagements and Sanads Relating to India and Neighbouring Countries*, compiled by C. U. Aitchison, 11:238. 5th ed. 14 vols. in 11. Delhi: Manager of Publications, 1929–33. (BM Ann 318) Also in *Records of Bahrain*, 2:456.

Expenditure Summary for the Government of Bahrain for 1358H (1939). (BM Ann 293) Also in *Records of Bahrain*, 5:432–41.

Extract from Ottoman Map Entitled *The Velayat of Basra* by Capt. Izzet of the Imperial Army of the Ottoman Empire, 1878. (BM Map No. 2)

Extracts from *Gulf Daily News*, 18 January 1997 onwards. (BR Ann 6)

———, 24 May 1997 onwards. (BR Ann 7)

———, 20 July 1997 onwards. (BR Ann 8)

———, 29 September 1997 onwards. (BR Ann 10)

———, 25 October 1998 onwards. (BR Ann 12)

Ferdinand, Klaus, 1993. *Bedouins of Qatar*. Copenhagen: Rhodos.

Foreign Office Discussion Paper and Draft Letter Attached Thereto, 21 July 1948, FO 371/68324. (BM Ann 191)

Foreign Office Letter to India Office, 12 July 1938. (QM Ann III.165)

Foreign Office Letter to Lt.-Col. Rupert Hay [PR], 3 September 1949, FO 371/74971 96754. (BM Ann 194)

Foreign Office Minute, 26 June 1936, FO 371/19973. (BCM Ann 75)

Foreign Office Minutes entitled "Eastern and Southern Frontiers of Arabia," 25 June 1937, FO 371/30777 XC/132657. (BM Ann 133)

Foreign Secretary, 20 April 1895, Telegram No. 783-E to Col. Frederick A. Wilson [PR]. *Records of Qatar*, 3:581.

Fortier, L. Yves. In *ICJ Judgment*, 2001, *Dissenting Opinion*.

Fowle, Lt.-Col. Trenchard C. [PR], 29 June 1933, Letter to Lt.-Col. Percy G. Loch [PAB], IOR R/15/2/389. (BCM Ann 62)

———, 23 July 1933, Telegram to Colonial Secretary, IOR R/15/1/653. (QM Ann III.85)

———, 31 July 1933, Telegram to the Secretary of State for India, IOR R/15/1/653. (QM Ann III.88)

———, 12 March 1934, Note of Meeting with Abdullah bin Jasim Al-Thani [RQ]. (BCM Ann 122) Also in *Records of Qatar*, 5:419–23.

———, 11 May 1935, Letter to Abdullah bin Jasim Al-Thani [RQ]. (BM Ann 103)

———, 25 May 1936, Express Letter to Secretary of State for India, IOR L/P+S/12/3895. (QM Ann III.107)

———, 5 May 1937, Memorandum to Secretary of State for India, IOR R/15/2/202. (BM Ann 127)

———, 23 June 1937, Telegram to Secretary of State for India, IOR R/15/1/370. (BM Ann 132)

———, 2 July 1937, Telegram to India Office, London, IOR R/15/2/203. (BM Ann 138)

Fowle, Lt.-Col. Trenchard C. [PR], 9 July 1937, Telegram to Secretary of State for India and Government of India External Affairs Department, IOR R/15/2/203. (BM Ann 147)

———, 5 April 1938, Note, FO 371/21822. (BM Ann 254)

———, 19 May 1938, Telegram to Hugh Weightman [PAB], IOR R/15/1/690. (QM Ann III.153)

———, 27 June 1938, Letter to the Secretary to the Government of India and copied to Hugh Weightman [PAB], IOR R/15/2/547. (BM Ann 264)

———, 29 April 1939, Letter to Secretary of State for India. (BM Ann 282) Also in *Records of Bahrain*, 5:300.

———, 11 July 1939, Letter to Hamad bin Isa Al-Khalifa [RB]. (BM Ann 287)

———, 11 July 1939a, Letter to Abdullah bin Jasim Al-Thani [RQ]. (BM Ann 288)

Fraser, Lt. E. A. [Officiating Second Asst. PR], 18 December 1874, Letter to Lt.-Col. Edward C. Ross [PR]. (BM Ann 27)

———, 1875, Report. Cited in J. A. Saldanha, *Précis of Katar Affairs, 1873–1904*. Gerrards Cross: Archive Editions, 1986, 11.

———, 8 March 1875, Letter to Lt.-Col. Edward C. Ross [PR], IOR P/775. (BCM Ann 12)

Fripp, M. [BAPCO Representative], 10 August 1941, Letter to Charles Belgrave [Adviser to Government of Bahrain]. (BM Ann 295)

Fromkin, David, 2001. *A Peace to End All Peace: the Fall of the Ottoman Empire and the Creation of the Modern Middle East*. New York: Holt, 1989 (An Owl book).

Further Engagement Entered into by Shaikh Mahomed bin Khalifah with the British Government for the More Effectual Suppression of the Slave Traffic, 1856. Translation. *Records of Bahrain*, 1:586.

Galloway, Lt. Col. Arnold C. [PAB], 11 June 1946, Letter to Lt.-Col. Rupert Hay [PR], IOR R/15/2/605. (BM Ann 180)

Gaskin, J. C. [Assistant PAB], 22 March 1902, Letter to Lt.-Col. Charles A. Kemball [PR], IOR R/15/2/26. (BCM Ann 29)

———, 29 March 1902, Letter to Lt.-Col. Charles A. Kemball [PR], IOR R/15/2/26. (BCM Ann 30)

Gazetteer of Arabia, 1915. [Bombay]: Government of India. (BM Ann 323)

General Treaty with the Arab Tribes of the Persian Gulf, 23 February 1820. In *A Collection of Treaties, Engagements and Sanads Relating to India and Neighbouring Countries*, compiled by C. U. Aitchison, 11:245–249. 5th ed. 14 vols. in 11. Delhi: Manager of Publications, 1929–33. (BM Ann 2) Also in *Records of Bahrain*, 1:194–95.

Government of India, 20 May 1870, Letter to Secretary of State for India. Cited in J. G. Lorimer, *Gazetteer of the Persian Gulf, Oman and Central Arabia*. Calcutta: Superintendent Government Printing, 1908–15, I:905.

———, 14 February 1881, Despatch to Secretary of State for India. Cited in J. A. Saldanha, *Précis of Bahrein Affairs, 1854–1904*. Gerrards Cross: Archive Editions, 1986, 68.

———, 10 July 1902, Despatch to Secretary of State for India. Cited in J. A. Saldanha, *Précis of Katar Affairs, 1873–1904*. Gerrards Cross: Archive Editions, 1986, 50.

———, 31 March 1904, Letter to Secretary of State for India. Cited in J. A. Saldanha, *Précis of Katar Affairs, 1873–1904*. Gerrards Cross: Archive Editions, 1986, 56.

Government of India Foreign Department Memorandum No. 127, 22 May 1879. (BM Ann 36) Also in *Records of Qatar*, 3:31–38.

Grant, Maj. Charles [First Asst. PR], 16 August 1873, Précis of Conversation with Sheikh Esau bin Ali Al-Khalifa [RB], IOR L/P+S/9/23. (BM Ann 17) Also in *Records of Qatar*, 2:519.

Grupp, T., 20 June 1997, Letter to Robert Volterra [Freshfields]. In Jawad S. Al-Arayed, 25 September 1997, App. II.6.

Hakki Pasha, 25 February 1913, Translation of Note from Hakki Pasha, former Grand Vizier, A.AMD.HV. 103/19 Inner File 59. (Ottoman Archives) (BCM Ann 37[b])

A Handbook of Arabia, 1916. Vol. I, General. Compiled by the Admiralty War Staff, Intelligence Division. Reprint, Gerrards Cross: Archive Editions, 1988. (QM Ann III.296, at 326)

Haworth, Lt.-Col. Lionel B. [PR], 27 March 1927, Despatch to Foreign Secretary of the Government of India, IOR R/15/2/87. (QM Ann III.73)

———, 2 April 1928, Letter to Secretary of State for the Colonies. (BM Ann 94)

Hay, Lt.-Col. William R. [PR], 19 November 1941, Letter to Secretary to Government of India, L/P+S/12/3806a. (BM Ann 296) Also in *Records of Qatar*, 6:559–61.

———, 4 June 1946, Express Letter, FO 371/52254. (BCM Ann 108)

———, 7 February 1950, Letter to Foreign Office, FO 371/82091 96754. (BM Ann 196)

———, 1954. "The Persian Gulf States and Their Boundary Problems." *Geographical Journal* 120 Part 4 (December): 437.

———, 1959. *The Persian Gulf States*. Washington: Middle East Institute. (QM Ann III.303)

Hemingway, C.E.M., 22 May 1939, *India Office (Political Department) Minute*, IOR L/P+S/12/3895. (BM Ann 163)

Hendry, W., 15, 19 September 1925, Letter to Sheikh Hamad bin Isa Al-Khalifa, attaching 1925 Bahrain Civil Lists. (BCM Ann 55)

Hennell, Lt. Samuel [PR], 25 July 1839, Letter to East India Company in London. Quoted in LeQuesne, q.v., 85. (BCM Ann 110–12)

———, 30 August 1839, Letter to H. M. Consul General in Egypt. Quoted in LeQuesne, q.v., 85. (BCM Ann 110–12)

Hennell, Lt. Samuel [PR], 28 February 1849, Transcription of Letter to A. Malet [Chief Secretary to Government, Bombay]. *Records of Bahrain*, 1:594.

Herbert, Aubrey, 1924. *Ben Kendim, a Record of Eastern Travel*. London: Hutchinson. (BSD Ann 3)

Hickinbotham, Capt. Tom [PAB], 9 May 1936, Letter to Lt.-Col. Trenchard C. Fowle [PR], IOR R/15/1/688. (BCM Ann 73)

Hickinbotham, Capt. Tom [PAB], 23 April 1937, Telegram to Lt.-Col. Trenchard C. Fowle [PR], IOR R/15/2/202. (BM Ann 119)

———, 30 April 1937, Telegram to Lt.-Col. Trenchard C. Fowle [PR], IOR R/15/1/309. (BM Ann 124)

———, 3 May 1937, Letter to Lt.-Col. Trenchard C. Fowle [PR], IOR R/15/1/309, enclosing a Report Entitled "Zubarah Incident," IOR, R/15/1/309, and a Memorandum, "Possible Basis for Compromise," IOR R/15/2/202. (BM Ann 126)

———, 29 May 1937, Note, IOR R/15/1/369. (BM Ann 128)

———, 1 July 1937, Note of Interview with C. Belgrave [Adviser to Government of Bahrain], IOR R/15/2/203. (BM Ann 136)

———, 2 July 1937, Telegram to Lt.-Col. Trenchard C. Fowle [PR], IOR R/15/1/370. (BM Ann 137)

———, 16 September 1937, Letter to Lt.-Col. Arnold C. Galloway [Secretary to PR], IOR R/15/2/204. (BM Ann 159)

———, February 1944, Proposal for the Settlement of the Zubarah Dispute, IOR R/15/2/205. (BM Ann 166)

———, 8 February 1944, Letter to Abdullah bin Jasim Al-Thani [RQ], IOR R/15/2/205. (BM Ann 165)

———, 6 March 1945, Letter to Salman bin Hamad Al-Khalifa [RB]. (BM Ann 178[a])

Holmes, Maj. Frank [BAPCO], 17 May 1933, Letter to Lt.-Col. Percy G. Loch [PAB], IOR R/15/1/652. (BCM Ann 58)

Houghton, Stuart, 1998. *Statement*. In Jawad S. Al-Arayed, 26 March 1998.

Howes, Capt. J. B. [Officiating PAB], 14 August 1938, Letter to Acting Adviser to Government of Bahrain. (BM Ann 270)

Ibn Al-Athir, *Al-Nihayat fi Gharib Al-Hadith Wa Al-Athar*, Vol. 4, 80 (Translation and Arabic version). (QM Ann II.71)

Ibn Saad, *Al-Tabaqat Al-Kubra*, Vol. 3, 28 (Translation and Arabic version). (QM Ann II.72)

ICJ Judgment, 1994. *See* International Court of Justice, 1994.

———, 1995. *See* International Court of Justice, 1995.

———, 2001. *See* International Court of Justice, 2001.

India Office Memorandum, 11 January 1934, FO 371/17813. (BCM Ann 66)

———, 21 February 1934, FO 371/17798. (BCM Ann 67)

———, 14 July 1937, FO 371/20783. (BM Ann 152)

India Office Minute, 14 July 1936, IO L/P+S/12/3895. (QM Ann III.111)

———, 7 June 1939, FO 371/23185. (BM Ann 283)

"Industrial City on a Tropical Island: the Story of Bahrein," 1937. *World Petroleum* (Oct.): 32–41.

International Court of Justice, 1994. *Maritime Delimitation and Territorial Questions between Qatar and Bahrain. Jurisdiction and Admissibility. Judgment*. The Hague.

———, 1995. *Maritime Delimitation and Territorial Questions between Qatar and Bahrain. Jurisdiction and Admissibility. Judgment*. The Hague.

———, 1996. *The International Court of Justice: a Guide to the History, Composition, Jurisdiction, Procedure, and Decisions of the Court*. The Hague.

———, 2001. *Case Concerning Maritime Delimitation and Territorial Questions between Qatar and Bahrain (Qatar v. Bahrain). Judgment*. The Hague. (A summary of the Judgment is given in the Court's *Press Communiqué* no. 2001/9bis, to which a summary of the opinions is annexed. The full text of the Judgment and of the opinions, as well as other documentary materials relating to this case, are available on the Court's website [http://www.icj-cij.org.]).

Joffé, George. 1994. "Concepts of Sovereignty in the Gulf Region." In *Territorial Foundations of the Gulf States*, edited by Richard Schofield, 78–93. New York: St. Martin's Press.

Jones, James F. [PR], 8 February 1862, Letter to Ameer Fysul [Ruler of Wahabees]. (BM Ann 9)

Justamond, John O., 1776. *A Philosophical and Political History of the Settlements and Trade of the Europeans in the East and West Indies*. New ed. Edinburgh: Caddel. This work, by the Abbé Raynal, translated from the French by Justamond, is cited as Justamond's *History of the East and West Indies* and quoted in *Extracts from Brief Notes Containing Historical and Other Information Connected with the Province of Oman*, by Robert Taylor. In *Arabian Gulf Intelligence: Selections from the Records of the Bombay Government, new ser., No. 24, 1856*, compiled by R. Hughes Thomas, 1–40. Bombay: Bombay Education Society's Press, 1856. Reprint, Cambridge: Oleander Press, 1985. Also in *Records of Bahrain*, 1:89–90.

Kelly, John B., 1968. *Britain and the Persian Gulf, 1795–1880*. Oxford: Clarendon Press. (BCM Ann 114)

———, 1980. *Arabia, the Gulf and the West*. London: Weidenfeld and Nicolson.

Kemball, Lt. Arnold B., 1844. "Chronological Table of Events." In *Arabian Gulf Intelligence: Selections from the Records of the Bombay Government, new ser., No. 24, 1856*, compiled by R. Hughes Thomas, 121–165. Bombay: Bombay Education Society's Press, 1856. Reprint, Cambridge: Oleander Press, 1985. Also in *Records of Bahrain*, 1:3–18.

———, 1844a. "Observations on the Past Policy of the British Government towards the Arab Tribes of the Persian Gulf." In *Arabian Gulf Intelligence: Selections from the Records of the Bombay Government, new ser., No. 24, 1856*, compiled by R. Hughes Thomas, 61–74. Bombay: Bombay Education Society's Press, 1856. Reprint, Cambridge: Oleander Press, 1985.

———, 1856. "Memoranda on the Resources, Localities, and Relations of the Tribes Inhabiting the Arabian Shores of the Persian Gulf." In *Arabian Gulf Intelligence: Selections from the Records of the Bombay Government, new ser., No. 24, 1856*, compiled by R. Hughes Thomas, 91–119. Bombay: Bombay Education Society's Press, 1856. Reprint, Cambridge: Oleander Press, 1985. (BM Ann 6) Also in *Records of Qatar*, 1:87–100.

Kemball, Lt.-Col. Charles A. [PR], 26 April 1902, Letter. Cited in J. A. Saldanha, *Précis of Katar Affairs, 1873–1904*. Gerrards Cross: Archive Editions, 1986, 49.

———, 23 March 1903, Letter to Government of India, FO L/P+S/19. (BM Ann 67)

Keyes, Maj. Terence H. [PAB], 23 August 1915, Letter to Lt.-Col. Percy Z. Cox [PR], IOR R/15/2/30. (BM Ann 82)

Khuri, Fuad I., 1980. *Tribe and State in Bahrain: The Transformation of Social and Political Authority in an Arab State*. Chicago: University of Chicago Press. (BM Ann 227)

Koroma, Abdul G. In *ICJ Judgment*, 1995, *Dissenting Opinion*.

Laithwaite, J. G. [IO], 9 August 1933, Letter to Petroleum Department, Board of Trade, IOR R/15/1/653. (QM Ann III.91)

———, 15 December 1933, Note on Conversation with G. W. Rendel [FO], on Qatar. Cited in Jill Crystal, *Oil and Politics in the Gulf*. Cambridge: Cambridge University Press, 1990, note 7.

———, 5 March 1934, Memorandum revised to 5 March 1934, IOR R/15/1/628. (QCM Ann III.40)

Lauterpacht, Elihu, 8 June 2000. ["Qatar's Claim to Hawar."] In *Verbatim Record of the Public Sitting Held on Thursday, 8 June 2000...in the Case Concerning Maritime Delimitation and Territorial Questions between Qatar and Bahrain (Qatar v. Bahrain)*. The Hague: International Court of Justice. (CR 2000/11:11–43)

Laver, W. S. [PAB], 19 May 1952, Letter to C. Belgrave [Adviser to Government of Bahrain], FO 1016547. (BM Ann 201)

The Law of the Sea: Official Text of the United Nations Convention on the Law of the Sea, 1983. New York: United Nations.

Lease between Ruler of Bahrain and BAPCO, 29 December 1934, IOR, R/15/1/661. (BM Ann 102)

LeQuesne, C. M. 1953, *The LeQuesne Report on the Boundary between Saudi Arabia and the Shaikhdoms of Qatar and Abu Dhabi and the Sultanate of Muscat and Oman*. n.p. (BCM Ann 110–12)

Loch, Lt.-Col. Percy G. [PAB], 29 May 1933, Letter to Lt.-Col. Trenchard C. Fowle [PR], IOR R/15/1/652. (BCM Ann 59)

———, 13 June 1933, Memorandum, IOR, R/15/2/10/23. (BM Ann 99)

———, 25 June 1933, Letter to Lt.-Col. Trenchard C. Fowle [PR], IOR R/15/1/626. (BM Ann 100)

———, 30 July 1933, Despatch to Lt.-Col. Trenchard C. Fowle [PR], IOR R/15/1/653. (QM Ann III.87)

———, 6 May 1936, Letter to Lt.-Col. Trenchard Fowle [PR], IOR R/15/1/688. (BM Ann 247)

———, 13 March 1937, Note, IOR R/15/2/202. (BM Ann 109)

Longrigg, Stephen H. [PCL], 16 August 1937, Letter to J. C. Walton [IO]. (BM Ann 157)

———, 1968. *Oil in the Middle East: Its Discovery and Development*. London: Oxford University Press.

Lorimer, John G., 1908–15. *Gazetteer of the Persian Gulf, Oman, and Central Arabia*. 2 vols. in 6. Calcutta: Superintendent Government Printing.

Madgwick, T. George, 1926. *Report*. Quoted in Ward 1965, q.v., 29–32.

———, 16 January 1927, Letter to Eastern and General Syndicate. Quoted in Clarke 1990, q.v., 66–7.

Man, M. [PR], 21 February 1961, Letter to R. Beaumont [FO], FO 371/1567 21 26336. (BM Ann 299)

Manuscript Minutes by Political Residency (August–September 1939), IOR R/15/1/693. (QM Ann III.212)

Mattox, Henry E. 1997, *Expert Research Report*. In Jawad S. Al-Arayed, 25 September 1997, Vol. 3, App. II.7.

Military Report on the Arabian Shores of the Persian Gulf, Kuwait, Bahrain, Hasa, Qatar, Trucial Oman and Oman, 1933. Calcutta: Government of India Press.

Minquiers and Echrehos, Judgment, 1953. ICJ Reports, 47.

Minutes of a Meeting Held at the India Office, 9 July 1936, IOR 371/19973. (BCM Ann 77)

Montigny-Kozlowska, Anie, 1985. Evolution d'un groupe bédouin dans un pays producteur de pétrole: les al-Na'im de Qatar. Ph.D. diss., Université Paris V René Descartes, Sciences Humaine—Sorbonne. (BM Ann 229)

Muharram Pasha [Vali of Basra], 5 December 1908, modern translation of Ottoman Arabic telegram. (Ottoman Archives) (BM Ann 73[a])

Mustill, M. J. and S. C. Boyd, 1989. *The Law and Practice of Commercial Arbitration in England*. Second ed. London: Butterworths.

Nabhani, Muhammad ibn Khalifah, 1923. "The Battle of Umm Suwayya." In *Tuhfah al-Nabhaniyah fi ta'rikh al-Jazirah al-'Arabiyah*. Cairo: al-Mahmudiya Press. (BCM Ann 52[b])

News Agent, Bahrain, 14 October 1874, Letter to Lt.-Col. Edward C. Ross [Acting PR], R/15/2/E/10. (BCM Ann 11)

———, 9 February 1875, Translated Purport of Letter to Lt.-Col. Edward C. Ross [PR], IOR P/775. (BM Ann 28)

———, 16 March 1875, Letter, IOR P/775. (BCM Ann 13)

1978 Mediation Principles, as Amended in 1983; translated into English by Qatar. (BCM (1992) Ann I.1)

Oda, Shigeru. In *ICJ Judgment*, 1994, *Dissenting Opinion*.

———, In *ICJ Judgment*, 1995, *Dissenting Opinion*.

Official Report of the Ottoman Council of Ministers, 1 February 1914, Translation, MV. 233, 50. (Ottoman Archives) (BCM Ann 43[b])

Order of 11 October 1991. The Hague: International Court of Justice.

Ottoman Ambassador to London, 28 February 1913, Translation of document to Ottoman Council of Ministers. (BCM Ann 38[b])

Ottoman Arabic Cabinet Minutes, 27 November 1889, modern translation. (Ottoman Archives) (BM Ann 45[a])

Ottoman Arabic Report, 27 January 1909, modern translation of original. (Ottoman Archives) (BM Ann 75[a])

Ottoman Arabic Report by Governor of Sanjak of Akka, 24 December 1907, modern translation. (BM Ann 72[a])

Ottoman Arabic Report from Province of Basra to Ministry of Interior, 25 September 1909, modern translation. (BM Ann 76[a])

Ottoman Arabic Report on Zubarah Affair, 3 May 1897, modern translation. (Ottoman Archives) (BM Ann 63[a])

Ottoman Minister of the Interior, 11 December 1908, Translation of Note to Council of Ministers/Vizier, BEO no. 259726. (Ottoman Archives) (BCM Ann 33[b])

Ottoman Ministry of the Interior, 30 November 1911, Translation of Letter to Basra Province, H. R.HMS.ISO 39/2–2. (Ottoman Archives) (BM Ann 79[a])

Ottoman Report Concerning Bahrain, Qatar, Nejd and Basra, 29 May 1917, Translation, HR. HMS.ISO 29/2–1. (Ottoman Archives) (BCM Ann 47[b])

Ottoman Report Concerning Zubarah and Bahrain, 12 February 1896, Translation, HR. HMS.ISO 39/2–2. (Ottoman Archives) (BCM Ann 27[b])

Ottoman Report on Bahrain, 16 September 1895, Translation, HR. HMS.ISO 39/2–2. (Ottoman Archives) (BCM Ann 26[b])

Ottoman "Report on Bahrein" from the Ottoman Council Chamber, 22 April 1900, Translation. (BM Ann 64[a])

Ottoman Report on Qatar, 22 September 1893, Translation. (BCM Ann 25[b])

Palgrave, William G., 1877. *Personal Narrative of a Year's Journey Through Central and Eastern Arabia (1862–1863).* London: Macmillan. Cited in Jill Crystal, *Oil and Politics in the Gulf.* Updated ed. (Cambridge: Cambridge University Press, 1995), 28.

———, 1877a. *Personal Narrative of a Year's Journey Through Central and Eastern Arabia (1862–1863).* London: Macmillan. Cited in Nanette Pilkington, *Territorial Integrity of Qatar* (The Hague: International Court of Justice, 29 May 2000 [CR 2000/5]), 49, ¶ 17.

Particulars of Case in the Bahrain Court between Bahrain Subjects Living in Hawar, no. 264/1351, 1932, IOR R 15/2/547. (BM Ann 242)

Paulsson, Jan., 8–9 June 2000. "The Events of the 1930s in Their Context." In *Verbatim Record of the Public Sitting Held on Thursday, 8 June 2000...in the Case Concerning Maritime Delimitation and Territorial Questions between Qatar and Bahrain (Qatar v. Bahrain).* The Hague: International Court of Justice. (CR 2000/11–12:43–50, 8–43)

———, 13 June 2000. "Petroleum Maps." In *Verbatim Record of the Public Sitting held on Tuesday, 13 June 2000...in the Case Concerning Maritime Delimitation and Territorial Questions between Qatar and Bahrain (Qatar v. Bahrain).* The Hague: International Court of Justice. (CR 2000/14 [translation]: 14–28)

———,. 27 June 2000. "A Summary of Bahrain's Position on Issues of Sovereignty." In *Verbatim Record of the Public Sitting Held on Tuesday, 27 June 2000...in the Case Concerning Maritime Delimitation and Territorial Questions between Qatar and Bahrain (Qatar v. Bahrain).* The Hague: International Court of Justice. (CR 2000/21:8–20)

———, 27 June 2000a. "Five Factual Topics Relating to the 1939 Award." In *Verbatim Record of the Public Sitting Held on Tuesday, 27 June 2000...in the Case Concerning Maritime Delimitation and Territorial Questions between Qatar and Bahrain (Qatar v. Bahrain).* The Hague: International Court of Justice. (CR 2000/21:33–53)

———, 28 June 2000. "Zubarah." In *Verbatim Record of the Public Sitting Held on Wednesday, 28 June 2000 ... in the Case Concerning Maritime Delimitation and Territorial Questions between Qatar and Bahrain (Qatar v. Bahrain)*. The Hague: International Court of Justice. (CR 2000/22 [translation]: 22–26)

Petroleum Concessions Limited, 27 September 1938, Letter to Hugh Weightman [PAB], IOR R/15/2/547. (BM Ann 271)

———, 30 June 1939, Letter to Under-Secretary of State for India, IOR R/15/2/547. (BM Ann 285)

Pelly, Cornelius J. [PAB], 23 December 1947, Letter to Abdullah bin Jasim Al-Thani [RQ], IOR R/15/2/430. (BM Ann 297)

———, 23 December 1947a, Letter to Salman bin Hamad Al-Khalifa, FO 371/68325. (QM Ann III.257)

———, 20 March 1950, Letter to Rupert Hay [PR], FO 371/56091. (BM Ann 197)

Pelly, Capt. J. H., 9 July 1895, Copy of Letter to Lt.-Col. Frederick A. Wilson [PR], IOR R/15/1/314. (BM Ann 58)

———, 23 July 1895, Letter to Mahomed Effendi at Zubarah, IOR R/15/1/314. (BM Ann 59)

———, 7 September 1895, Letter to Col. Frederick A. Wilson [PR], IOR R/15/1/314. (BM Ann 60)

———, 7 September 1895a, Letter to Abdullah bin Jasim Al-Thani [RQ]. (BM Ann 61) Also in *Records of Qatar*, 3:619.

Pelly, Lt.-Col. Lewis [PR], 13 April 1863, Letter to H. L. Anderson [Chief Secretary of Government of Bombay]. (BM Ann 10)

———, 11 September 1868, Letter to Mahomed bin Sanee [Thani]. (QM Ann II.27) Also in *Records of Bahrain*, 2:14.

Pilkington, Nanette, 29 May 2000. "Territorial Integrity of Qatar." In *Verbatim Record of the Public Sitting Held on Monday, 29 May 2000 ... in the Case Concerning Maritime Delimitation and Territorial Questions between Qatar and Bahrain (Qatar v. Bahrain)*. The Hague: International Court of Justice. (CR 2000/5:46–63)

Preliminary Treaty between Britain and the Sheikhs of Bahrain, 5 February 1820. In *A Collection of Treaties, Engagements and Sanads Relating to India and Neighbouring Countries*, compiled by C. U. Aitchison, 11:233. 5th ed. 14 vols. in 11. Delhi: Manager of Publications, 1929–33. (BM Ann 1)

Press Communiqué no. 94/16, 1 July 1994. The Hague: International Court of Justice.

——— *no. 95/6*, 15 February 1995. The Hague: International Court of Justice.

Press Release 2001/9, 16 March 2001. The Hague: International Court of Justice.

Prideaux, Capt. Francis B. [PAB], 16 July 1905, Letter to Maj. Percy Z. Cox [Officiating PR] (attached to a despatch from Maj. Cox to S. M. Fraser [Secretary to the Government of India], IOR R/15/2/26). (BM Ann 71)

———, 23 December 1905, Memorandum to Maj. Percy Z. Cox [PR], IOR R/15/2/26. (BCM Ann 31)

Prideaux, Capt. Francis B. [PAB], 20 March 1909, Transcript of a Letter to Maj. Percy Z. Cox [PR], IOR R/15/2/25. (BM Ann 235) Also in *Records of Bahrain*, 3:383–87.

———, 4 April 1909, Letter to Maj. Percy Z. Cox [PR], IOR R/15/2/547. (BM Ann 236)

Prideaux, Capt. William F. [Officiating PR], 7 October 1876, Letter to T. H. Thornton [Officiating Secretary to Government of India]. (BM Ann 34)

Prior, Lt.-Col. Charles G. [PAB], 18 June 1944, Memorandum of Meeting with Abdullah bin Jasim Al-Thani [RQ], IOR R/15/2/205. (BM Ann 168)

Projected Ottoman Council of Ministers Decision Concerning Qatar re Negotiations with Britain, 11 March 1913, Translation, A.AMD.MV 1093/19 Inner File 57–58. (Ottoman Archives) (BCM Ann 40[b])

Provisional, not Confirmed Bahrain Concession, 1923, IOR R/15/1/664. (QM Ann III.66) (Drawn up by Frank Holmes of EGS, with accompanying map.)

Qatar, 1991. *Application Instituting Proceedings Filed in the Registry of the Court on 8 July 1991*. Maritime Delimitation and Territorial Questions between Qatar and Bahrain (Qatar v. Bahrain). n.p.

———, 1992. *Case Concerning Maritime Delimitation and Territorial Questions between Qatar and Bahrain (Qatar v. Bahrain). Memorial Submitted by the State of Qatar. Questions of Jurisdiction and Admissibility*. n.p., 3 vols.

———, 1992a. *Case Concerning Maritime Delimitation and Territorial Questions between Qatar and Bahrain (Qatar v. Bahrain). Reply Submitted by the State of Qatar. Questions of Jurisdiction and Admissibility*. n.p., 2 vols.

———, 1996. *Case Concerning Maritime Delimitation and Territorial Questions between Qatar and Bahrain (Qatar v. Bahrain). Memorial Submitted by the State of Qatar (Merits)*. n.p., 17 vols.

———, 1996a. *Case Concerning Maritime Delimitation and Territorial Questions between Qatar and Bahrain (Qatar v. Bahrain). Memorial Submitted by the State of Qatar (Merits)*. Highlighting by Bahrain. n.p.

———, 1996b. *Case Concerning Maritime Delimitation and Territorial Questions between Qatar and Bahrain (Qatar v. Bahrain). Memorial Submitted by the State of Qatar (Merits)*. Highlighting by Qatar. n.p.

———, 1997. *Case Concerning Maritime Delimitation and Territorial Questions between Qatar and Bahrain (Qatar v. Bahrain). Counter-Memorial Submitted by the State of Qatar (Merits)*. n.p., 6 vols.

———, 1997a. *Case Concerning Maritime Delimitation and Territorial Questions between Qatar and Bahrain (Qatar v. Bahrain). Counter-Memorial Submitted by the State of Qatar (Merits)*. Highlighting by Bahrain. n.p.

———, 1997b. *Case Concerning Maritime Delimitation and Territorial Questions between Qatar and Bahrain (Qatar v. Bahrain). Counter-Memorial Submitted by the State of Qatar (Merits)*. Highlighting by Qatar. n.p.

———, 1998. *Case Concerning Maritime Delimitation and Territorial Questions between Qatar and Bahrain (Qatar v. Bahrain). Interim Report (Merits)*. n.p., 3 vols.

———, 1999. *Case Concerning Maritime Delimitation and Territorial Questions between Qatar and Bahrain (Qatar v. Bahrain). Reply Submitted by the State of Qatar (Merits).* n.p., 7 vols.

Qatar Counter-Memorial, 1997. *See* Qatar, 1997.

Qatar Diary No. 2 of 1961—for the Period February 2–March 1, 1961, FO 371/156974 9536. (BM Ann 300/301)

Qatar Interim Report, 1998. *See* Qatar, 1998.

Qatar Memorial, 1992. *See* Qatar, 1992.

———, 1996. *See* Qatar, 1996.

Qatar Oil Concession, 1935, IOR R/15/1/633. (BM Ann 104)

Qatar Reply, 1992. *See* Qatar, 1992a.

———, 1999. *See* Qatar, 1999.

Quéneudec, Jean-Pierre, 5 June 2000. "Maritime Delimitation." In *Verbatim Record of the Public Sitting Held on Monday, 5 June 2000 ... in the Case Concerning Maritime Delimitation and Territorial Questions between Qatar and Bahrain (Qatar v. Bahrain).* The Hague: International Court of Justice. (CR 2000/9–10 [translation]: 29–53, 2–11)

Rasul, Haji Ahmad bin Abdul [PAB], 27 June 1888, Letter to Lt.-Col. Edward C. Ross [PR], IOR P/3276. (BM Ann 43)

Recent Photographs of the Hawar Islands and Bahrain's Maritime Features. (BSD Ann 12)

Reisman, Michael, 13 June 2000. "Maritime 1." In *Verbatim Record of the Public Sitting Held on Tuesday, 13 June 2000 ... in the Case Concerning Maritime Delimitation and Territorial Questions between Qatar and Bahrain (Qatar v. Bahrain).* The Hague: International Court of Justice. (CR 2000/14–15:33–59, 8–16)

Report entitled "Note on Developments in the Zubarah Case," 1948, FO 371/68324. (BM Ann 185)

Report from Ottoman Council of State Department of Internal Affairs, 18 January 1887, modern translation. (Ottoman Archives) (BM Ann 39)

Report from the Office of Assistant to the Governor of Katar, 7 November 1891, modern translation. (Ottoman Archives) (BM Ann 48[a])

Report to British Political Resident, 1 May 1870. (Bombay Archives, Political Department, Vol. 105 [1869]). (BCM Ann 8)

Representations on Zubarah to Foreign Office, 4 August 1949. (BM Ann 193)

Request for Registration of Property in Zubarah Region in Bahraini Land Registration Directorate, 23 April 1937. (BM Ann 118)

Resolutions Approved at the Meeting of the Ottoman Cabinet Council on 19 April 1913, Translation, BEO no. 266331. (Ottoman Archives) (BM Ann 240A[a])

Rich, Paul, 1991. *The Invasions of the Gulf: Radicalism, Ritualism and the Sheikhs.* Cambridge: Allborough. Cited in Paulson, 27 June 2000, 50 ¶ 43 fn 43.

Ross, Lt.-Col. Edward C. [PR], 13 September 1873, Letter to Mohammed bin Thani [Chief of Bidda/Doha]. Cited in J. A. Saldanha, *Précis of Katar Affairs, 1873–1904*. Gerrards Cross: Archive Editions, 1986, 3.

Ross, Lt.-Col. Edward C. [PR], 12 September 1874, Letter to Secretary to Government of India, IOR L/P+S/9/25. (BM Ann 21)

———, 10 November 1874, Letter to Secretary to Government of India. (BM Ann 24) Also in *Records of Qatar,* 2:556–557.

———, 12 December 1874, Letter to Isa bin Ali Al-Khalifa [RB], IOR R/15/1/370. (QM Ann III.30)

———, 19 December 1874, Letter. Cited in J. A. Saldanha, *Précis of Katar Affairs, 1873–1904.* Gerrards Cross: Archive Editions, 1986, 7.

———, 24 December 1880, Report on Proceedings to Government of India. Cited in J. A. Saldanha, *Department of Bahrein Affairs, 1854–1904.* Gerrards Cross: Archive Editions, 1986, 67.

———, 1881, Note of Secret Interview with Nasir bin Mubarak at Guttur, IOR L/P+S/9/66A. (BCM Ann 17)

———, 1886–1887. *Report on the Administration of the Persian Gulf Political Residency and Muscat Political Agency for the Year.* Calcutta: Foreign Department Press. (BCM Ann 18–19)

———, 24 December 1887, Letter. Cited in J. A. Saldanha, *Précis of Katar Affairs, 1873–1904.* Gerrards Cross: Archive Editions, 1986, 32.

———, 12 March 1888, Telegram to Foreign Department, Government of India, IOR P/3276. (BM Ann 40)

———, 12 March 1888b, Letter. Cited in J. A. Saldanha, *Précis of Katar Affairs, 1873–1904.* Gerrards Cross: Archive Editions, 1986, 34.

———, 17 March 1888, Correspondence between PR and Secretary to Government of India, IOR P/3276. (BM Ann 41)

Saldanha, Jerome A.,1904. *Précis of Bahrein Affairs, 1854–1904.* Simla. Reprinted as: *The Persian Gulf Précis, Vol. 4: Précis of Bahrein Affairs–Katar Affairs, 1854–1904.* Gerrards Cross: Archive Editions, 1986.

———, 1904a. *Précis of Katar Affairs, 1873–1904.* Simla. Reprinted as: *The Persian Gulf Précis, Vol. 4: Précis of Bahrein Affairs–Katar Affairs, 1854–1904.* Gerrards Cross: Archive Editions, 1986. (BM Ann 70)

Salmon, Jean, 30 May 2000. "Introduction II: General Themes in the Present Case." In *Verbatim Record of the Public Sitting Held on Monday, 29 May 2000 . . . in the Case Concerning Maritime Delimitation and Territorial Questions between Qatar and Bahrain (Qatar v. Bahrain).* The Hague: International Court of Justice. (CR 2000/5 [translation]: 22–32).

Savory, Roger M., 1980. "A.D. 600–1800." In *The Persian Gulf States: A General Survey,* edited by Alvin J. Cottrell, 14–40. Baltimore: Johns Hopkins University Press.

———, 1980a. "The Ancient Period." In *The Persian Gulf States: A General Survey,* edited by Alvin J. Cottrell, 3–13. Baltimore: Johns Hopkins University Press.

Schofield, Richard,. 1997. *Expert Research Report.* In Jawad S. Al-Arayed, 25 September 1997, Vol. 3, App. II.4.

Schwebel, Stephen M. In *ICJ Judgment,* 1995, *Dissenting Opinion.*

Secret Declaration Annexed to Convention between United Kingdom and Turkey Regarding the Persian Gulf and Adjacent Territories, 29 July 1913. (BM Ann 240B)

Secretary of State for India, 21 July 1938, Letter to Lt.-Col. Trenchard C. Fowle [PR], IOR R/15/1/691. (BM Ann 269)

Secretary to the Government of India, 19 November 1941, Letter to India Office, R/15/2/547. (QM Ann III.230)

Seiden, Rudolf, 1937. "Iraq and Bahrein—Factors in British Foreign Policy." *World Petroleum* (July): 44–45.

Shahabuddeen, Mohamed. In *ICJ Judgment, 1995, Dissenting Opinion.*

Shankardass, R.P.K., 30 May 2000. "Limited Extent of Bahrain and the Impact of Oil Concessions on Qatar/Bahrain Territories." In *Verbatim Record of the Public Sitting Held on Tuesday, 30 May 2000 ... in the Case Concerning Maritime Delimitation and Territorial Questions between Qatar and Bahrain (Qatar v. Bahrain)*. The Hague: International Court of Justice. (CR 2000/6:13–31)

Shankardass, R.P.K., 31 May 2000. "Oil Concession—History of the 1936–1939 Decisions." In *Verbatim Record of the Public Sitting Held on Wednesday, 31 May 2000 ... in the Case Concerning Maritime Delimitation and Territorial Questions between Qatar and Bahrain (Qatar v. Bahrain)*. The Hague: International Court of Justice. (CR 2000/7:25–44)

———, 5 June 2000. "Rebuttal of the Alleged Effectivités pre-1936 (Legal and Factual)." In *Verbatim Record of the Public Sitting Held on Monday, 5 June 2000 ... in the Case Concerning Maritime Delimitation and Territorial Questions between Qatar and Bahrain (Qatar v. Bahrain)*. The Hague: International Court of Justice. (CR 2000/8:17–34)

———, 5 June 2000a. "Zubarah—Disclaimers: Not a Serious Dispute." In *Verbatim Record of the Public Sitting Held on Monday, 5 June 2000 ... in the Case Concerning Maritime Delimitation and Territorial Questions between Qatar and Bahrain (Qatar v. Bahrain)*. The Hague: International Court of Justice. (CR 2000/9:26–33)

———, 20 June 2000. "Rebuttal of Bahrain's Effectivités pre-1936." In *Verbatim Record of the Public Sitting Held on Tuesday, 20 June 2000 ... in the Case Concerning Maritime Delimitation and Territorial Questions between Qatar and Bahrain (Qatar v. Bahrain)*. The Hague: International Court of Justice. (CR 2000/17:25–41)

———, 21 June 2000. "Territorial Extent of Qatar and Bahrain and the Oil Concession History." In *Verbatim Record of the Public Sitting held on Wednesday, 21 June 2000 ... in the Case Concerning Maritime Delimitation and Territorial Questions between Qatar and Bahrain (Qatar v. Bahrain)*. The Hague: International Court of Justice. (CR 2000/18:16–32)

Sharaf bin Ahmad, 1909. Translation of a Judgment Made by the Qadi of Shara Court, Bahrain in the Year 1327 Hejrah (1909). (BM Ann 238) Also in *Records of Bahrain*, 5:244.

———, 1910. Translation of a Judgment Made by the Qadi of Shara Court, Bahrain in the Year 1328 Hejrah (1910), IOR R/15/2/547. (BM Ann 238A)

Sinclair, Ian, 30 May 2000. "Geography of the Hawar Islands and the Principle of Proximity." In *Verbatim Record of the Public Sitting Held on Tuesday, 30 May 2000 ... in the Case Concerning Maritime Delimitation and Territorial Questions between Qatar and Bahrain (Qatar v. Bahrain)*. The Hague: International Court of Justice. (CR 2000/6:32–54)

Sinclair, Ian, 31 May 2000. "1936 and 1939 British Decisions on Hawar." In *Verbatim Record of the Public Sitting Held on Wednesday, 31 May 2000... in the Case Concerning Maritime Delimitation and Territorial Questions between Qatar and Bahrain (Qatar v. Bahrain)*. The Hague: International Court of Justice. (CR 2000/7:45–54)

———, 5 June 2000. "Decisions on Hawar." In *Verbatim Record of the Public Sitting Held on Monday, 5 June 2000... in the Case Concerning Maritime Delimitation and Territorial Questions between Qatar and Bahrain (Qatar v. Bahrain)*. The Hague: International Court of Justice. (CR 2000/8:8–16)

———, 21 June 2000. "Qatar's Positive Case on Hawar." In *Verbatim Record of the Public Sitting Held on Wednesday, 21 June 2000... in the Case Concerning Maritime Delimitation and Territorial Questions between Qatar and Bahrain (Qatar v. Bahrain)*. The Hague: International Court of Justice. (CR 2000/18:23–42)

Skinner, K. [BAPCO], 5 December 1936, Letter to H. Ballantyne [BAPCO]. (BM Ann 108)

Skliros, J. [PCL], 29 April 1936, Letter to IO, IOR, R/15/1/688. (QM Ann III.104)

Smith, Maj. S. [Asst. PR], 20 July 1871, *Report from Biddah*, R/15/2/E/110. (BCM Ann 9)

Starling, F. C. [Petroleum Department], 3 July 1936, Letter to M. J. Clauson [IO], IOR R/15/2/400. (BCM Ann 76)

Stegner, Wallace E., 1971. *Discovery! The Search for Arabian Oil*. Beirut: Middle East Export Press.

Sultan bin Mohamed bin Salamah, Letter to Col. Frederick A. Wilson [PR], 25 April 1895, *Records of Qatar*, 3:584.

Takvimi Vekayi [Official Ottoman Gazette], 8 June 1871, English translation of extract. (Ottoman Archives) (BM Ann 16[a])

Talbot, Lt.-Col. Adelbert C. [PR], 7 May 1893, Letter to Secretary to Government of India, IOR/P+S/7/70. (BM Ann 51)

Terms of a Friendly Convention between Ruler of Bahrain and British Government, 31 May 1861. In *A Collection of Treaties, Engagements and Sanads Relating to India and Neighbouring Countries*, compiled by C. U. Aitchison, 11:234–36. 5th ed. 14 vols. in 11. Delhi: Manager of Publications, 1929–33. (BM Ann 8)

Thouvenin, Jean-Marc, 1997. *Expert Research Report*. In Jawad S. Al-Arayed, 25 September 1997, Vol. 3, App. II.5.

Treaty between the British Government and Sheikh of Qatar, 3 November 1916. In *A Collection of Treaties, Engagements and Sanads Relating to India and Neighbouring Countries*, compiled by C. U. Aitchison, 11:258–61. 5th ed. 14 vols. in 11. Delhi: Manager of Publications, 1929–33. (BM Ann 84)

Trevor, Lt.-Col. Arthur P. [PR], 13 May 1921, Letter to Foreign Secretary of India, FO 371/7724. (BCM Ann 48)

———, 13 May 1921a, Letter to Foreign Secretary of Government of India, enclosing Letter from Shaikh Abdullah bin Jasim Al-Thani, and Reply, 8 August 1921, *Records of Qatar*, 5:13–18.

———, 10 November 1922, Despatch to Denys de S. Bray [Foreign Secretary to the Government of India], IOR L/P+S/11/222. (BCM Ann 51) Also in *Records of Qatar*, 5:19–23.

Tuson, P., 1973. *The Records of the British Residency and Agencies in the Persian Gulf*. London: India Office Records. (QM III.313)

UN Reports of International Arbitral Awards, Award of 4 April 1928, Island of Palmas Case (Netherlands/U.S.A.), Vol. II, 831, at 840.

Understanding between Representative of the Ruler of Bahrain and Representative of the Sheikhs of the Doha Confederation, 10 April 1869, IOR L/P+S/9/15. (BCM Ann 5)

UNDP Human Development Report State of Bahrain. 1998, 48. (BR Ann 11)

Vali of Basra, 12 April 1888, Letter to Head Clerk of the Padishah, modern translation. (Ottoman Archives) (BM Ann 42[a])

Verbatim Record of the Public Sitting Held…in the Case Concerning Maritime Delimitation and Territorial Questions between Qatar and Bahrain (Qatar v. Bahrain), 2000. The Hague: International Court of Justice. (CR 2000/5–2000/19, 2000/21–2000/22; 2000/25)

Viceroy of India, 19 January 1903, Telegram No. 83, to HM Secretary of State for India, London. In Saldanha, *Précis of Katar Affairs, 1873–1904*. Simla: 1904, 51.

Volterra, Robert, 13 June 2000. "The Uninterrupted Continuum of Bahrain's Sovereignty over the Hawar Islands as Evidenced by Its Effectivités and the Conduct of the Residents of Hawar." In *Verbatim Record of the Public Sitting Held on Tuesday, 13 June 2000…in the Case Concerning Maritime Delimitation and Territorial Questions between Qatar and Bahrain (Qatar v. Bahrain)*. The Hague: International Court of Justice. (CR 2000/13:8–34)

———, 28 June 2000. "Qatar has Failed in Its Attempt to Discredit the 80 Examples of Bahraini Activities on the Hawar Islands." In *Verbatim Record of the Public Sitting Held on Wednesday, 28 June 2000…in the Case Concerning Maritime Delimitation and Territorial Questions between Qatar and Bahrain (Qatar v. Bahrain)*. The Hague: International Court of Justice. (CR 2000/22:34–52)

Wakefield, Edward [PAB], 11 January 1948, Letter to Lt.-Col. Geoffrey Prior [PR]. (BM Ann 184)

Walton, J. C. [IO], 14 May 1936, Letter to J. Skliros [PCL], IOR R/15/1/688. (BM Ann 248)

Ward, Thomas E., 1965. *Negotiations for Oil Concessions in Bahrein, El Hasa (Saudi Arabia), the Neutral Zone, Qatar, and Kuwait*. New York: privately printed. Cited in Daniel Yergin, *The Prize*. New York: Simon and Schuster, 1991, 817, note 1.

Warden, Francis, 1856. Historical Sketch of the Uttoobee Tribe of Arabs (Bahrein). In Arabian *Gulf Intelligence: Selections from the Records of the Bombay Government, new ser., No. 24, 1856*, compiled by R. Hughes Thomas, 361–425. Bombay: Bombay Education Society's Press, 1856. Reprint, Cambridge: Oleander Press, 1985. (BM Ann 5) Also in *Records of Bahrain*, 1:19–83.

Weightman, Hugh [PAB], 15 May 1938, Letter to Lt.-Col. Trenchard C. Fowle [PR]. (BM Ann 257) Also in *Records of Qatar*, 6:19–22.

———, 20 May 1938, Letter to Abdullah bin Jasim Al-Thani [RQ], IOR R/15/2/547. (BM Ann 258)

———, 20 May 1938a, Letter to Charles Belgrave [Adviser to Government of Bahrain], IOR R/15/2/547. (QM Ann III.154)

———, 3 June 1938, Letter to Lt.-Col. Trenchard C. Fowle [PR], IOR R/15/2/547. (BM Ann 262)

———, 21 June 1938, Letter to Lt.-Col. Trenchard C. Fowle [PR], IOR R/15/2/547. (QM Ann III.162)

———, 22 March 1939, Letter to Abdullah bin Jasim Al-Thani [RQ], IOR R/15/2/547. (QM Ann III.190)

———, 22 April 1939, *Report* (in the form of a letter) to Lt.-Col. Trenchard C. Fowle [PR]. (BM Ann 281). Also in *Records of Bahrain*, 5:252–59.

———, 5 December 1939, *Report entitled "Qatar,"* IOR R/15/2/142. (BM Ann 292)

Weil, Prosper, 15 June 2000. "The Maritime Delimitation. Part II." In *Verbatim Record of the Public Sitting Held on Thursday, 15 June 2000... in the Case Concerning Maritime Delimitation and Territorial Questions between Qatar and Bahrain (Qatar v. Bahrain)*. The Hague: International Court of Justice. (CR 2000/16 [translation]: 2–33)

Wilkinson, John C., 1991. *Arabia's Frontiers: the Story of Britain's Boundary Drawing in the Desert*. London: Tauris.

———, 1997. *Expert Historical Report*. In Jawad S. Al-Arayed, 25 September 1997, Vol. 3, App. II.1.

Wilson, Col. Frederick A. [PR], 17 April 1895, Telegram to the Foreign Secretary, *Records of Qatar*, 3:581.

———, 2 May 1895, Telegram to the Foreign Secretary, *Records of Qatar*, 3:581.

———, 4 May 1895, Letter to Secretary to the Government of India, Foreign Department, IOR R/15/1/314. (QM Ann II.39) Also in *Records of Qatar*, 3:582.

———, 18 May 1895, Letter to Secretary to the Government of India, Foreign Department, Records *of Qatar*, 3:586.

Yapp, Malcolm, 1980. "British Policy in the Persian Gulf." In *The Persian Gulf States: A General Survey*, edited by Alvin J. Cottrell, 70–100. Baltimore: Johns Hopkins University Press.

———, 1980a. "The Nineteenth and Twentieth Centuries." In *The Persian Gulf States: A General Survey*, edited by Alvin J. Cottrell, 41–69. Baltimore: Johns Hopkins University Press.

———, 1994. *The Making of the Modern Middle East, 1792–1923*. London: Longman.

Yergin, Daniel, 1991. *The Prize: the Epic Quest for Oil, Money and Power*. New York: Simon and Schuster.

Zahlan, Rosemarie S., 1979. *The Creation of Qatar*. London: Routledge.

———, 1989. *The Making of the Modern Gulf States: Kuwait, Bahrain, Qatar, the United Arab Emirates and Oman*. Reading: Ithaca Press.

Index

Note: Page numbers in italics indicate illustrations or tables; *def* indicates definitions; *map* indicates maps; *n* indicates notes; *q* indicates quotations

Numerals

1868 Agreements, 45–46, 69–70, 86, 111–12, 256–57, 284
 Qatar's interpretation of, 111, 207–8, 312–13
1875 Treaty: India Office reinterpretation of, 194
1878 Ottoman–Al-Thani attack on Zubarah, 145, 210
 Qatar's version, 210
1895 Ottoman–Al-Thani attack on Zubarah, 146–48, 210
 Qatar's version, 210
1913 Convention. *See* Anglo-Ottoman Convention
1916 Treaty (Anglo–Al-Thani Treaty), 98–100, 117, 284
 and the Hawars, 263
 Qatar's interpretation of, 116, 187, 314
 on the territorial extent of Qatar, 99–100, 159, 187
1937 Qatari attack on Zubarah, 189–90
 aftermath, 191–95
 Bahrain's version, 340
 British nonintervention policy, 189, 191
 economic consequences for Qatar, 192–93, 283
 events preceding, 181–89
 See also taxation of Zubarah by the RQ
 Qatar's version, 214–17
 RB's protest and request for British help, 190–91, 192
1938–39 Hawar Islands sovereignty arbitration, xvi, 221, 222, 284–301
 Bahrain's Counter-claim, 290–91
 Qatar's request to see, 288–90
 Bahrain's Preliminary Statement, 287–88
 Britain's decision, 293–96
 as binding, 401–2
 British criticisms of, 321
 correspondence affirming, 301
 Qatar's interpretation of, 314–17
 Qatar's protests following, 299–301
 as unbiased, 297, 321
 Janan as included in, 222, 223–25
 oil concessions and, 224
 process, 285
 as fair proceedings, 296–97
 Qatar's version, 316, 317–18
 Qatar's allegations of collusion in, 311, 315, 316, 318–21
 Qatar's claim and Rejoinder, 285–87, 291–93, 294
 inaccuracies in, 292, 297–99
 Qatar's consent to, 284–85, 317
 Qatar's version, 317
 Qatar's request to see Bahrain's Counter-claim, 288–90
1944 Agreement (on Zubarah), 195–97, 217
 Qatar's interpretation of, 217
1947 maritime boundary decision, xvi, 222–23, 301, 351–53
1950 Agreement (on Zubarah), 200–2
1987 Agreement (on an ICJ appeal), 327–28
 Bahrain's interpretation of, 333–34
 Qatar's interpretation of, 332, 333

A

Abbasids: and Bahrain, 8
Abdul-Aziz ibn Saud. *See* Al-Saud, Abdul-Aziz (Ibn Saud)
Abdul-Razzaq bin Rizoogi. *See* Rizoogi, Abdul-Razzaq bin
Abdul-Wahhab, 27, 78
Abdulla Abdul-Latif Hashim Al-Sadeh. *See* Al-Sadeh, Abdulla Abdul-Latif Hashim

| 445

Abdullah bin Ahmed. *See* Al-Khalifa, Sheikh Abdullah bin Ahmed
Abdullah bin Hasan, 188–89
Abdullah bin Jabor Al-Dosari, 254
Abdullah bin Jasim. *See* Al-Thani, Sheikh Abdullah bin Jasim
Abu Dhabi:
    border dispute with Qatar, 365
    Isa bin Tarif's secession to, 33
    ruler(s). *See* Ruler(s) of Abu Dhabi
    suspect documents relating to, 365, 382–83
Adeed. *See* Odaid
Aden: Portuguese capture of, 11
adjudication of Hawar Islands sovereignty. *See* 1938–39 Hawar Islands sovereignty arbitration
Adviser to Bahrain. *See* Belgrave, Sir Charles
Agent of Bahrain. *See* Al-Arayed, Jawad Salim
Agreement between Chiefs in ... Qatar and Chief of Bahrain, 45–46*q*, 69–70*q*
agreements. *See* treaties and agreements
agriculture (Bahrain Islands): administration of, 22–23
Ahmed bin Ali. *See* Al-Khalifa, Sheikh Ahmed bin Ali; Al-Thani, Sheikh Ahmed bin Ali
Ahmed bin Mohammed. *See* Al-Khalifa, Sheikh Ahmed bin Mohammed Al-Fatih; Al-Thani, Sheikh Ahmed bin Mohammed
Ahmed the Conqueror. *See* Al-Khalifa, Sheikh Ahmed bin Mohammed Al-Fatih
Aitchison, C. U.: *A Collection of Treaties, Engagements and Sanads...*, 420
Al bin Ali tribe, 43
    Al-Thani as part of, 43
    attack on pearl fishers near Doha, 95
    breaks with the RB, 33, 110, 146
    settlement attempt in Zubarah, 146–47

Sheikh Sultan bin Mohammed Salamah, 146, 147
See also Isa bin Tarif
Al bu 'Ainain tribe: break with Sheikh Abdullah, 33, 110
Al-Arayed, Jawad Salim, 338
    on the Hawars as part of Bahrain, 305*q*
    suspect document reports submission letter, 386–87
Al-bu-Kawarah, 88
Al-Dowasir. *See* Dowasir tribe
Al-Furaiwah. *See* Furaiwah
Al-Ghattam, 231
Al-Idrisi, 9*q*
Al-Jabar, Nasir bin. *See* Nasir bin Jabar
Al-Jabor. *See* Rashid bin Mohammed bin Jabor
Al-Jabr (Naim tribe branch), 139, 182
    dirah (territory), 132–33
Al-Jalahimah, 18–19, 20
    and the Al-Khalifa, 18, 19–20, 28, 29, 125
    Bushir bin Rahmah, 30, 64
    possession of and expulsion from Zubarah, 28, 29
    See also Rahmah bin Jaber
Al-Khalifa (ruling family of Bahrain):
    and the Al-Jalahimah, 18, 19–20, 28, 29, 125
    and the Al-Musallam, 18–19
    authority in the Hawars, 226–29, 241–43, 308–9
        British recognition of, 255–57, 264–65, 268
        effectivités, 243–53, 343, 401
        Ottoman recognition of, 257–59, 261
        Qatar's version, 308–9
    authority in the Qatar peninsula, 18–19, 20, 109–10, 207, 309
        Al-Thani recognition of, 109, 156–57, 269
        British recognition of, 109–10, 115, 207
        in Ottoman-ruled Qatar, 46, 90
        Qatar's version, 109, 308–9

Al-Khalifa *(continued)*
  authority in the Qatar peninsula *(continued)*
    as recognized by regional powers, 109–10, 115
    in Zubarah. *See* authority in Zubarah, *below*
  authority in Zubarah, 121, 125, 127, 141, 142–43, 145, 206–7, 210–11
    Al-Thani recognition of, 156, 269
    British recognition of. *See under* Zubarah (region)
    Ottoman recognition of, 155–56
    Qatar's version, 206
  authority over pearling tribes, 23, 24
    Qatar's version, 112–13
  the British and, 13, 61–62, 87, 174–75
  and the Dowasir, 226–27, 228–29
  dynastic struggles, 32–35, 64–65, 71
    Qatar's version, 112
  establishment on Bahrain main island, 20
  external challenges to, 27–32
  governance:
    of the Bahrain Islands, 22–24, 26
    by coalition with local tribes, 22, 23–24, 24–27, 227, 241
    by direct administration, 22–23
    of the Qatar peninsula, 24–27, 44
    international responsibilities, 25–26
  migration to/establishment of Zubarah, 18–19, 124–25
  and the Naim, 21, 25, 39–40, 40, 121, 125, 128–29, 135–39, 142, 183–84, 208–9
    Qatar's version, 208, 215–16
  origins in Kuwait, 18
  piracy suppression, 25–26
  return to Zubarah, 27, 126
  rise, 17, 18–20
  taking of the Bahrain Islands, 19–20, 27–28, 125–26
  and the Wahhabis, 25, 27–28, 28–29, 30–32, 35–37, 126
  See also Ruler(s) of Bahrain; *and individual Al-Khalifa Sheikhs*

Al-Khalifa, Sheikh Abdullah bin Ahmed (RB: 1796–1843), 32–33, 413*n*, 413
  blockades of Qatif, 31
  family dissatisfaction with, 33
  and the Huwailah secessionists, 33
  move to Khor Hassan, 33–34
  move to Muharraq, 34
  vs. Muscat, 29–30
  rebuilding of Zubarah, 34
  removal from power, 34–35, 64, 413*n*
  settlement in Dammam, 35
  vs. Sheikh Mohammed bin Khalifa, 32, 34–35, 64, 65, 413*n*
  and the slave trade, 54
  vs. the Wahhabis, 30–31
Al-Khalifa, Sheikh Ahmed bin Ali: meeting with Sheikh Jasim, 90–91
Al-Khalifa, Sheikh Ahmed bin Mohammed Al-Fatih (RB: 1783–96), 19, 413
Al-Khalifa, Sheikh Ali bin Khalifa (RB: 1868–69), 69, 413*n*, 413
  assassination of, 71
  vs. Sheikh Abdullah, 34, 413*n*
Al-Khalifa, Sheikh Hamad bin Isa (RB: 1932–42), 407, 413
  Bahraini formula initiative, 329
  Belgrade on the death of, 203*q*
  claims to Zubarah, xvi, 181, 192, 195
    British nonintervention policy, 193–95
    modified renouncement, 186–87
  protest of Qatar's attack on Zubarah and request for British help, 190–91, 192
  suspect letters from, 379, 383
Al-Khalifa, Sheikh Hamad bin Isa (RB: 1999–), 413
  on the ICJ verdict, 404*q*
Al-Khalifa, Sheikh Isa bin Ali (RB: 1869–1932), 407, 413*n*, 413
  British choice as RB, 71
  and the Naim, 135–36
  on the Naim, 138–39*q*, 144*q*
  palace, 238
  port plans for Zubarah, 160–61
  suspect seal, 383, *384*

Al-Khalifa, Sheikh Isa bin Salman (RB: 1961–1999), *413*
Al-Khalifa, Sheikh Khalifa bin Salman (RB: 1825–34), 33, 413*n*, *413*
Al-Khalifa, Sheikh Mohammed bin Abdullah (RB: 1869), 35, 407, *413*
  as joint RB, 413*n*
Al-Khalifa, Sheikh Mohammed bin Khalifa (founder of Zubarah), 18, 129
Al-Khalifa, Sheikh Mohammed bin Khalifa (RB: 1834–42/1843–68/1869), 407, 413*n*, *413*
  blockades of the Hasa coast, 35, 36
  and the British, 66, 67–68, 69
  departure from Bahrain, 69
  expedition against Doha and Wukra, 25, 45, 69
  vs. Isa bin Tarif, 65–66
  as joint RB, 413*n*
  vs. Sheikh Abdullah, 32, 34–35, 64, 65, 413*n*
Al-Khalifa, Sheikh Nasir bin Mubarik. *See* Nasir bin Mubarik Al-Khalifa, Sheikh
Al-Khalifa, Sheikh Salman bin Ahmed (RB: 1796–1825), 32–33, *413*
Al-Khalifa, Sheikh Salman bin Hamad (RB: 1942–61), *413*
  agreements on Zubarah, 195–97, 200–2
  claims to Zubarah, 198, 202
  offer on Zubarah, 199–200
Al-Khuwayr. *See* Khor Hassan
Al-Manasir (Bedouin tribe), 42
Al-Murrah (Bedouin tribe), 42
Al-Musallam, 124
  and the Al-Khalifa, 18–19
Al-Muslemani, Abdullah bin Abdulatif, 338
Al-Naim. *See* Naim tribe
Al-Naimi, Saleh bin Muhammed Ali bin Ali: on Qatar's attack on Zubarah, 190
Al-Qais, 8

Al-Ramzan (Naim tribe branch), 139, 184
Al-Sabah, 19
Al-Sadeh, Abdulla Abdul-Latif Hashim: suspect document analysis, 359–61
Al-Sarkal, Isa Abdul-Lateef, Khan Bahador:
  Qatar's allegations against, 321
  suspect letters to, 365
Al-Saud, Abdul-Aziz (Ibn Saud), 78
  the British and, 160, 164–65, 176, 194
  influence in Qatar, 101, 157, 174, 175
  influence in Zubarah, 183, 215
  port plans for Jubail, 160
  and Sheikh Jasim, 92
Al-Saud, Fahd, King: letters to the Amirs of Bahrain and Qatar, 327
Al-Saud, Khalid bin Abdul-Aziz, King: Bahrain–Qatar border dispute mediation efforts, 202, 326–27
Al-Saud, Mohammed, 27, 78
Al-Saud, Turki bin Abdullah, 30
"al-tarafan" (Doha Minutes term), 334
Al-Thani (ruling family of Qatar), 86
  alienation of other tribes from, 88–89, 174
  attack on Bahrain foiled, 148
  attacks on Zubarah:
    1937 attack. *See* 1937 Qatari attack on Zubarah
    Ottoman–Al-Thani attacks, 121, 144–45, 145, 146–48, 210–11
  authority in the Qatar peninsula, 46–47, 88, 90–91, 95–96, 96–98, 107–8, 110–11, 114, 115, 153–54, 262
    Palgrave on, 110
    Qatar's version, 107–8, 113–14, 312–14
    in Zubarah. *See* authority in Zubarah, *below*
  authority in Zubarah, 208, 209–11
    Qatar's version, 206, 207–8, 209–11, 214–15
  Bedouin hostility to, 174
  the British and, 13, 87, 93–96, 154

Al-Thani *(continued)*
  checks on the expansion of, 82
  diminished power under the Ottomans, 87–88
  expansion attempts in Zubarah, 83, 121, 143–49
    attacks, 121, 144–45, 145, 146–48, 210–11. *See also* 1937 Qatari attack on Zubarah
    failure of, 149–52
    resettlement plans/occupation efforts, 145–46, 148–49, 153, 197–98
  and the Ottomans, 80, 82, 86–90, 150–51
  rebellion of 1893, 91–93, 93–94
  recognition of Bahrain's authority in the Qatar peninsula, 109, 156–57, 269
  rise, 17, 43–47
  status in Doha, 44, 45, 46–47, 136, 256
  and the Wahhabis, 36, 174
  See also Chiefs/Chief of Doha; Ruler(s) of Qatar; *and individual Al-Thani Sheikhs*
Al-Thani, Sheikh Abdullah bin Jasim (CD/RQ: 1913–1948), *414*
  agreement on Zubarah, 195–97
  Anglo–Al-Thani Treaty with, 98–100, 117
  attack on Zubarah. *See* 1937 Qatari attack on Zubarah
  claims to Zubarah, 179, 181, 187
  family dissidents, 157, 175, 193
  lack of control in Qatar, 100–2, 157, 175
  and the Ottoman surrender, 98
  port plans for Zubarah, 182
  on Qatari landing incidents in the Hawars, 252–53
  as Ruler of Qatar, 98
  taxation of Zubarah. *See* taxation of Zubarah by the RQ
  Weightman on, 283*q*, 285*q*
Al-Thani, Sheikh Ahmed bin Ali (RQ: 1960–1972), *414*
Al-Thani, Sheikh Ahmed bin Mohammed:
  as *Kaimakam* of Qatar, 92, 96

  request for treaties with the British, 94
  and the *Vali* of Basra, 91–92
Al-Thani, Sheikh Ali bin Abdullah (RQ: 1948–1960), *414*
  agreement on Zubarah, 200–2
Al-Thani, Sheikh Hamad bin Khalifa (RQ: 1995–), *414*
  on the ICJ verdict, 404*q*
Al-Thani, Sheikh Jasim bin Mohammed (CD: 1876–1913), 407, 414
  attack on Bahrain foiled, 148
  attacks on Zubarah, 144–45, 145, 146–48, 210–11
  authority in the Qatar peninsula, 47*q*, 88, 90–91, 95–96, 96–97, 114, 115*q*, 128, 156–57
    Qatar's version, 113–14
  battle with the *Vali* of Basra, 92
  and the British, 94
  discouragement, 157
  expulsion of the Indian traders of Doha, 86–87
  as Governor of Doha, 88, 90
  and Ibn Saud, 92
  as *Kaimakam* of Qatar, 88, 89, 92, 128
  Kelly on, xiii*q*
  meeting with Sheikh Ahmed bin Ali Al-Khalifa, 90–91
  and Nasir bin Mubarik, 90, 145–46
  and the Ottomans, 47, 80–81, 82, 86, 87, 88–90, 94, 145–48
  suspect letter from Saleh Pasha, 368
Al-Thani, Sheikh Khalifa bin Hamad (RQ: 1972–1995), *414*
Al-Thani, Sheikh Mohammed (CD: –1876), 414
  1868 Agreements, 45–46, 69–70, 111–12
  and the Ottomans, 80, 87–88
  Palgrave on, 110
  as a Wahhabi agent, 36, 44
Al-Utub tribe, 18
Alban, Reginald G. E., 321–22, 408
Ali bin Abdullah. *See* Al-Thani, Sheikh Ali bin Abdullah
Ali bin Khalifa. *See* Al-Khalifa, Sheikh Ali bin Khalifa

allegiance, tribal: and territorial claims, 133*q*, 339
  See also Naim tribe: and the Al-Khalifa
Amair tribe, 36
American oil companies in the Gulf: BAPCO, 168–72, 173, 269
  British concerns about, 173–75, 200
  Gulf Oil, 170
  Standard of California (Socal), 171
  Standard Oil, 170, 174, 176
Amery, L. S., 171
Amin, Mokhtar Mohammed: suspect document analysis, 374–86
Amir of Bahrain. *See* Ruler(s) of Bahrain (RB)
Amir of Qatar. *See* Ruler(s) of Qatar (RQ)
Anglo–Al-Thani Treaty. *See* 1916 Treaty
Anglo-Ottoman Convention (1913), 96–97, 313–14
  and the Hawars, 261–63
  Qatar's interpretation of, 115–16, 313
  secret declaration annexed to, 261
  as unratified, 97–98
Anglo-Persian Oil Company (APOC), 177
  and the Bahrain concession, 169, 174
  and the Bahrain unallotted area, 269
  oil exploration in Qatar, 176
  oil exploration in Zubarah, 269
  Qatar concession awarded to, 271
  See also Petroleum Concessions Limited (PCL)
Anglo-Turkish Convention (1914), 116, 313
Annexes to *Memorials* in *Qatar v. Bahrain*, 355
Arabia:
  the British and, 77
  Ottoman expansion into, 77–80
  Ottoman expeditions against the Wahhabis, 30, 31, 78–79
  See also Al-Saud; Wahhabis
Arabian Gulf:
  American influence in, 173–74
  authority (control) in the Gulf region, 20–21, 207
  border disputes in. *See* border disputes in the Gulf
  British banning of hostilities in, 59
  British influence in, 13, 36, 37, 49, 52, 61–62, 62, 80, 87
    decline, 164–65
  British interests in, 14, 49–50, 77, 80, 160–61, 162–63, 267
    in Bahrain, 62, 63
    in Qatar, 101, 163, 174, 175, 191, 194
    in Zubarah, 148*q*
  British mediation of local disputes, 58–59
  British presence in, 13–14, 51, 59–60
  early lower-Gulf history, 3–10
  environment, 3
  Ibn Saud's influence in Qatar, 101, 163, 174, 175
  India and, 51
  Islamic emergence in, 8–9
  neutral zone, 59, 60–61
    enforcement of, 63–67
  oil as a major force in, 162–79
  oil companies in. *See* oil companies in the Gulf
  Ottoman influence in, 13, 37, 80, 87
  Ottoman interests in, 78, 80
  Ottoman presence in, 11–12, 37
  piracy in, 15, 50
  place names, 4*map*
  political instability in, 14–15
  Portuguese presence, 11–13, 49
  security improvement in, 60
  trade centers, 8
    Bahrain, 5, 9, 12
    Zubarah, 19
  trade routes around, 6–7
  tribes in. *See* tribes in the Gulf
  wars in. *See* wars in the Gulf
  Western powers advent, 11–15, 49, 73, 173–74
Arabian Gulf Intelligence: Selections from the Records of the Bombay Government, 419
Arabic writing in suspect documents: Belgrave letters, 366
  character seals, 375

Arabic writing in suspect documents: *(continued)*
  as disguised, 384–85
  Ottoman documents, 367
  styles, 384–85
Araij (Qatar peninsula): Wahhabi attack on, 36
arbitration:
  of Hawar Islands sovereignty. *See* 1938–39 Hawar Islands sovereignty arbitration
  standards, 341–42
Armstrong, Thomas R., 170
authority (control) in the Gulf region, 20–21, 207
  dirah (nomadic tribal territory), 21, 132
    of the Naim tribe, 132–33
    ICJ recognition of, 133
  vs. Western sovereignty, 21
  See also under Al-Khalifa; Al-Thani; Ottomans
Awal: Bahrain main island as, 8–10, 344

B

Baghdad:
  and Bahrain, 9
  Suleiman's capture of, 11
Bahrain:
  administrative reforms of 1923, 253
  Adviser to. *See* Belgrave, Sir Charles Dalrymple
  Agent of. *See* Al-Arayed, Jawad Salim
  Al-Thani attack on foiled, 148
  archives. *See* Bahrain Government Archives
  authority in disputed territories. *See under* Al-Khalifa
  and Baghdad, 9
  border dispute with Qatar. *See* Bahrain–Qatar border dispute
  British administration of, 74–75
  British influence on, 13, 37, 61, 80
  British interests in, 49–50, 62, 63
  British intervention in internal affairs, 70–72
  British protection of, xv, 60–61, 62–70
  Friendly Convention, 36, 67–69, 256–57, 284
  protectorate status proposal, 66
  British recognition of, 61
  British regulation of foreign relations, 73–75
  British relations with, 62, 63, 72–73
    as a piratical port, 52, 54
    with the RB, 53, 60, 62
    with Sheikh Mohammed, 66, 67–68, 69
  claims to the Hawars, 268, 269, 270, 271, 340
    British recognition of, 278–80, 297, 321
    effectivités, 243–53, 401
    legal arguments, 339–40, 401–2
    Qatar's version, 308–9
  claims to Zubarah, xvi, 181, 192, 195, 198, 202
    British nonintervention policy, 193–95
    British recognition of. *See under* Zubarah (region)
    historical explanation, 203–5
    legal arguments, 339–40
    modified renouncement, 186–87
    Qatar's version, 205
  Counter-Memorials, 333, 356, 387, 395
  determining characteristics, 9–10, 27, 63
  Dilmun civilization in, 5–7
  emergence as a modern political entity, 17, 18–20, 61, 67, 80, 105–6
  as entrepôt for pirated goods, 51–52, 53–54
  fresh water system, 167, 167–68
  Fuwairat as part of, 115
  governance. *See under* Al-Khalifa
  Hawars as part of, 270–71, 272–77
    Al-Arayed on, 305*q*
  independence from Britain, xv
  interests in Zubarah, 128, 141–42
  Islamic emergence in, 8–9
  Kurshid Pasha's threat against, 31
  legal counsel in *Q. v. B.*, 362
  and the Maritime Truce, 60
  Memorial (1996), 337–38, 355

Bahrain: *(continued)*
  Muscat attacks on, 27, 29–30, 126
    expulsion of the Wahhabis, 29, 127
  Muscat expedition by, 30
  Muscat expulsion from, 27–28, 126
  Muscat-Bahrain peace treaty, 30, 58–59
  Naim payment records, 161
  neutral zone extension to, 60–61
  oil concession. *See* Bahrain oil concession
  oil discovery in, 161, 172
  oil exploration in, 169, 170
  Ottoman attack on, 12
  Ottoman influence on, 13, 37, 80
  and the Ottomans, 12, 36, 65
  pearling banks, 350–51, 398*map*
  pearling in, 9, 126, 351
    Al-Khalifa administration, 23–24, 351
    demise, 161–62, 351
  pearls of, 126
  Persian control of, 7, 13, 14–15, 124–25, 125
  Persian defense against Muscat, 27
  Persian expulsion from, 19, 126
  Political Agent in. *See* Political Agent in Bahrain
  population migration from Zubarah/Qatar peninsula, 132, 162, 191–92
  Portuguese presence in, 11–13
  prosperity from oil revenues, 161, 172
  Qatar peninsula as part of, 46, 57–58, 61, 68–69, 70
  Rejoinder (1992), 333
  Reply (1999), 338, 395
  ruler(s). *See* Ruler(s) of Bahrain (RB)
  ruling family. *See* Al-Khalifa
  sanctions on Qatar, 192–93, 283
  sovereignty in the Gulf of Bahrain, 345
  sovereignty in the Hawars:
    assertion of during oil concession negotiations, 268–72
    reluctance to submit to the ICJ, 330
  See also Al-Khalifa: authority in the Hawars; claims to the Hawars, *above*
  sovereignty in Zubarah. *See* Al-Khalifa: authority in Zubarah; claims to Zubarah, *above*
  Tarut Island as part of, 7, 31
  territorial extent, 9–10, 20, 28
  trade as disturbed by dynastic struggles, 35
  as a trade center in the Gulf, 5, 9, 12
  "unallotted area". *See* unallotted area (Bahrain oil concession)
  vulnerability to attack, 27, 63
  Wahhabi alliances against, 64, 66–67
  Wahhabi attacks on:
    expulsion of Muscat, 27–28, 126
    later attacks, 36
  Wahhabi presence in and expulsion from, 28–29, 127
  Wahhabi tribute payments by, 28, 30, 31–32, 36–37
  Yaaribah tribe's capture of, 15
  Zubarah as part of, 115*q*, 159–62
  See also Bahrain Archipelago; Bahrain Islands; Hasa coast; Hawar Islands; Zubarah (region)
Bahrain Archipelago:
  islands and shoals, 344
    See also maritime features (Bahrain Archipelago)
  and the maritime boundary between Bahrain and Qatar, 344–46
  ICJ on, 403
  navigational structures, 345
  See also Bahrain Islands; Gulf of Bahrain
Bahrain Counter-Memorial (1992), 333
Bahrain Counter-Memorial (1997), 356, 387, 395
The Bahrain Government Annual Reports, 419
Bahrain Government Archives: suspect document searches, 357, 358
Bahrain Islands, 122*map*
  Al-Khalifa governance of, 22–24, 26
  Al-Khalifa taking of, 19–20, 27–28, 125–26
  Hawars as not in, 270–71

Bahrain Islands *(continued)*
  individual islands, xvii*map*, 122*map*, 269, 398*map*
    See also Bahrain main island; Muharraq
  Ottoman claims to, 71–72
  as a socio-economic unit with the Hawars and Zubarah, 225, 296
  See also Bahrain Archipelago
Bahrain main island, xvii*map*, 122*map*, 398*map*
  as the Al-Khalifa seat of government, 20, 126
  as Awal, 8–10
  as a commercial center, 229
  Dilmun cities on, 5–6
  Dowasir settlement on, 228–29
  environment, 3, 5
  Manama, 34
  oil concession on, 271
  trade as disturbed by dynastic struggles, 35
  as Tylos, 7
  See also Bahrain Islands
Bahrain Memorial (1996), 337–38, 355
Bahrain oil concession, 166–68
  allotted area chosen, 271
  assignment to BAPCO, 168–72
  British nationality clause in, 163
  British oil companies' disinterest in, 167, 168–69
  and British recognition of Bahrain's authority in Zubarah, 163, 173–75, 176–79
  draft concession map, 272, *273*
  extension of, 268–71
  and the Hawars, 268–71
  maps pertaining to, 272–76, *273, 274, 275, 276*
  territorial extent, 272–76
  unallotted area. *See* unallotted area (Bahrain oil concession)
Bahrain Order in Council (1913), 74
Bahrain Petroleum Company Limited (BAPCO):
  Bahrain concession assignment to, 168–72, 173
  unallotted area claims, 269
Bahrain Rejoinder (1992), 333

Bahrain Reply (1999), 338, 395
Bahrain–Qatar border dispute, xvi–xviii
  1987 Agreement, 327–28, 332
  Bahraini formula (1987), 328–30
  British arbitration of Hawars sovereignty. *See* 1938–39 Hawar Islands sovereignty arbitration
  British mediation efforts, xvi, 186–87, 195–97, 200–2, 217, 268
  Doha Minutes/Agreement (1990), 331, 332
  Doha Summit (1990), 330–31
  Five Principles (1978/1983), 326
  Hawar Islands issues/history. *See* Hawar Islands
  historical context, 1–117
    Qatar's version, 107–17
  ICJ case. *See Qatar v. Bahrain*
  joint ICJ submission plans, 327, 328, 329, 331, 334
  maritime boundary. *See* maritime boundary between Bahrain and Qatar
  oil and, xi, xvi, 162–79, 191, 267–68
  Qatar's falsification of the historical record, xiii
    See also forged documents; Qatar's version of events, *below*
  Qatar's unilateral ICJ submission, 331, 332, 333, 335
    Bahrain's objection to, 334–35
  Qatar's version of events:
    in the Hawars, 307–22
    in the historical context, 107–17
    in Zubarah, 203–17
  roots, xi
  Saudi proposals (1987), 327–28
  Saudi–GCC mediation efforts, xvi–xviii, 202, 325, 326–31
  scope definition, 328–31
  Special Agreement, 328, 330
  status quo: importance of maintaining, 327
  Tripartite Committee, 327, 328, 328–29, 334
  Zubarah issues/history. *See* Zubarah (region)
Bahraini formula (1987), 328–30
  ICJ on, 335

Ballantyne, H. K., 199, 408
  Zubarah proposal, 199
Bandar Abbas (Persia/Iran), 4*map*, 14
Bani Abdul-Qais tribe, 8
Bani Hajir tribe (Beni Hajir), 42, 151
  attacks on Zubarah, 137–38, 144–45, 190
  maritime violations, 84, 95
  Nasir bin Mubarik and, 407
Bani Khaled tribe: influence in the Gulf, 124
BANOCO (oil company), 303
BAPCO. *See* Bahrain Petroleum Company Limited
Barakah bin Era'ar: suspect letters by, 377–79
"Bash Jawish": suspect document misusage, 368
Basra (Iraq), 4*map*, 8, 14
  Persian occupation of, 19
Baxter, C. W., 320
Bedouin tribes:
  and the Al-Thani, 174
  as nomads, 6
  in the Qatar peninsula, 39–40, 41
  Al-Khalifa and, 24–25
  territory, 3
  See also Bani Hajir tribe; nomadic tribes
Belgrave, Sir Charles Dalrymple, 357, 408
  on the death of Sheikh Hamad (1942), 203*q*
  Qatar's allegations of collusion in the Hawars arbitration, 311, 318–20
  on Qatar's attack on Zubarah, 189*q*, 190
  on the RQ's claim to the Hawars, 287
  signature stamp, 376, 382, 389
  suspect correspondence, 366, 372
benefit system for nomadic tribes (*ikrimiyah*), 21, 135–36, 183
Beni Hajir tribe. *See* Bani Hajir tribe
Bibby, Geoffrey: on Zubarah as not an ancient city, 129–30*q*

Biddah. *See* Doha
Bin Saud. *See* Al-Saud, Abdul-Aziz
bin Tarif. *See* Isa bin Tarif
"*Bismillah Al-Rahman Al-Raheem*":
  suspect document appearances, 359, 361, 386
"blank slate" theory on the Hawars, 309–11
border disputes in the Gulf:
  Foreign Office–India Office policy disagreements, 164–65
  Qatar–Abu Dhabi border dispute, 365
  See also Bahrain–Qatar border dispute
Bostan, Idris: Ottoman suspect document analysis, 367–70
Britain (British):
  1868 Agreements. *See* 1868 Agreements
  administration of Bahrain, 74–75
  and the Al-Khalifa, 13, 61–62, 87, 174–75
  and the Al-Thani, 13, 87, 93–96, 154
  and Arabia, 77
  arbitration of Hawars sovereignty. *See* 1938–39 Hawar Islands sovereignty arbitration
  as arbitrator of Gulf disputes, 284–85
  and Bahrain, 62, 63, 72–73
  as a piratical port, 52, 54
  Bahrain unallotted area concerns, 269–70
  banning of hostilities in the Gulf, 59
  decline as a world power, 162, 165, 173–74
  foreign policy: diplomacy vs. colonial rule, 165–66, 194
  and Ibn Saud, 160, 164–65, 176, 194
  influence in the Gulf, 13, 36, 37, 49, 52, 61–62, 62, 80, 87
    decline, 164–65
  interests in the Gulf, 14, 49–50, 77, 80, 160–61, 162–63, 267
  in Bahrain, 62, 63
  in Qatar, 101, 163, 174, 175, 191, 194
  in Zubarah, 148*q*

Britain (British): *(continued)*
  intervention in Bahrain's internal affairs, 70–72
  intervention in Ottoman-ruled Qatar's internal affairs, 93–96
  loss of India, 165
  Maritime Truce, 59–60, 62
  mediation of Gulf disputes, 58–59
    Al-Thani–Ottoman conflict, 93–94
    Bahrain–Qatar border dispute, xvi, 186–87, 195–97, 200–2, 217, 268
  nonintervention in Zubarah, 189, 191, 193–95
  and the Ottomans, 79–80, 87, 93, 96, 143, 149, 155–56, 260–61
  Palestine policy, 164–65
  Piracy Agreements. *See* General Treaty
  piracy suppression, 52–53
    Qawasim expeditions, 50, 54
    See also 1868 Agreements; General Treaty; Maritime Truce
  Preliminary Treaty with the RB, 54–55
  presence in the Gulf, 13–14, 51, 59–60
  protection of Bahrain, xv, 60–61, 62–70
    Friendly Convention, 36, 67–69, 256–57, 284
    protectorate status proposal, 66
  protection of British oil companies in the Gulf, 173–75
  protection of Qatar, xv, 98, 100, 175
  protection of Zubarah, 143–49
  Qatar peninsula policy options (1905), 154–55
  Qatar's allegation of collusion in the Hawars arbitration, 311, 315, 316
    charges against officials, 316, 318–21
    officials charged, 321
  and the RB, 53, 60, 62, 271
    advice to keep clear of the Qatar peninsula, 86, 212
    Sheikh Mohammed, 66, 67–68, 69
  recognition of Al-Khalifa authority: in the Hawars, 255–57, 264–65, 268
    in the Qatar peninsula, 109–10, 115, 207
    in Zubarah. *See under* Zubarah
  recognition of Bahrain, 61
  recognition of Bahrain's sovereignty: in the Hawars, 278–80, 297, 321
    in Zubarah. *See under* Zubarah
  recognition of Qatar, 98–99
  regulation of Bahrain's foreign relations, 73–75
  slave trade suppression, 54, 62–63
British East India Company, 13–14
  fleet, 49–50
British Foreign Office (FO):
  India Office takeover, 165, 166
  India Office–FO Gulf policy disagreements, 164–65
  on the RQ's request see Bahrain's Counter-claim to the Hawars, 289–90*q*
British nationality clause (in oil concessions), 163, 175
British oil companies in the Gulf:
  British protection of, 173–75
  D'Arcy Exploration Company, 176
  disinterest in the Bahrain concession, 167, 168–69
  See also Anglo-Persian Oil Company (APOC); Petroleum Concessions Limited (PCL)
British Political Agents. *See* Political Agent in Bahrain; Political Agent in Qatar
British Political Resident. *See* Political Resident in the Persian Gulf
British seals on suspect documents, 364, 371, 389
  College of Arms report, 387
Brucks, George, 408
  on Al-Khalifa authority in the Qatar peninsula, 109, 207
  on the Al-Khalifa taking of the Bahrain Islands, 126
  on the Hawars, 228*q*
  on Zubarah, 128*q*
Bushir bin Rahmah:
  vs. Sheikh Abdullah, 64
  and the Wahhabis, 30

456 | A LINE IN THE SEA

Bushire (Persia/Iran), 4*map*
Bushire Residency, 51
   reorganization of, 56–57

C

Carmathian movement/empire, 8–9
Carney, Brian: suspect document analysis, 388–89
Caroe, Sir Olaf, 301
Center for Documentation and Research (Abu Dhabi): suspect document searches, 357
Chiefs/Chief of Doha:
   1868 Agreements with, 45–46, 69–70, 86, 111–12
   lineage, *414*
   Ottoman invitation by, 80
   RB expedition against, 45, 69
   as Ruler of Qatar, 98
   See also Al-Thani, Sheikh Jasim bin Mohammed; Al-Thani, Sheikh Mohammed
civil lists (of Bahrain): Naim records, 161, 216
coalition rule (indirect governance): by the Al-Khalifa, 22, 23–24, 24–27, 227, 241
coastal tribes (Arabian Gulf), 6
   in the northwest Qatar peninsula, 39–40
A Collection of Treaties, Engagements and Sanads...(Aitchison), 420
College of Arms (UK): suspect document British insignia report, 387
colonial rule vs. diplomacy in British foreign policy, 165–66, 194
Conoco (oil company), 303
control in the Gulf region. *See* authority (control) in the Gulf region
Cooperation Council of Arab States of the Gulf. *See* Gulf Cooperation Council
Costa, Paolo: on Hawar Island villages, 233, 238
Counter-Memorials (in *Q. v. B.*), 387, 395
   Bahrain's, 333, 356, 387, 395
   Qatar's. *See Qatar Counter-Memorial*
Cox, Sir Percy, 408
Criminal Investigations Directorate (Bahrain): suspect document analysis, 359–61
critical date/period: and territorial claims, 341, 342
Crown, David: suspect document analysis, 388–89

D

D'Arcy Exploration Company, 176
Dammam (Hasa coast):
   as ceded and recovered by the Al-Khalifa, 30–31
   Dowasir settlement at, 253
   Sheikh Abdullah's settlement in, 35
Darin (Tarut Island): Bahrain and, 7
Darwish, Abdullah, 408
date discrepancies in suspect documents, 358, 364, 365, 369, 370, 371
dead persons: suspect letters to/from, 358, 365
demarcation suspect documents, 364, 370, 370–72
Dilmun civilization, 5–7
diplomacy vs. colonial rule in British foreign policy, 165–66, 194
dirah (nomadic tribal territory), 21, 132, 340
   of the Naim tribe, 132–33, 134*map*
   Qatar's version, 208
direct administration: by the Al-Khalifa, 22–23
diwan (ruler's council) (Bahrain Islands), 23
Diwan Amiri Archives, 356, 359
Doha (Biddah) (Qatar peninsula), 41, 122*map*
   1868 Agreements with the Al-Thani chiefs, 45–46, 69–70, 86
   Al bin Ali attack on pearl fishers near, 95

Doha (Biddah) (Qatar peninsula) *(continued)*
  Al-Khalifa governance, 25
  Al-Thani authority as confined to, 46–47, 88, 107–8, 110–11, 128
  Al-Thani status in, 44, 45, 46–47, 136, 256
  British East India Company punishment of, 57
  British survey description, 41–42*q*
  Chiefs. *See* Chiefs/Chief of Doha
  Governor. *See* Governor of Doha (*Kaimakam* of Qatar)
  Hawar contacts, 242
  Ibn Saud's influence in, 101
  Indian traders as expelled from, 86–87
  museum in, xiii
  Ottoman presence in. *See* Ottomans in the Qatar peninsula
  pearling, 41
  power vacuum in, 94–95
  RB expedition against, 25, 45, 69
  rebellions:
    against the Al-Khalifa, 25, 69, 110
    against the Ottomans, 91–93
  seceders from, 88, 128
  Sheikh Nasir in, 90
  Sudan tribe in, 124
  Wahhabi influence in, 36
Doha Affair (1867–68), 25, 45, 69–70
Doha Minutes/Agreement (1990), 331
  Bahrain's interpretation of, 333–34
  ICJ ruling on, 335
    dissenting opinion, 337
  as an international agreement, 332, 333, 335
  Qatar's interpretation of, 332, 333
Doha Summit (1990), 325–26, 330–31
"*Donamai Hamayoon*": suspect document misusage, 368
Dowasir Incident (1923–27), 253–54
Dowasir tribe, 23, 41
  and the Al-Khalifa, 226–27, 228–29
    governance, 227, 241
  as Bahraini subjects, 242–43, 311–12
    Qatar's version, 311–12
  departure from the Hawars, and return, 253–54

  distinguished individuals, 254
  fishing activities, 235–36
    government regulation of, 243–44
  Hawars as granted to, 226, 294
    Qatar's version, 308
  pearling activities, 236–37
    government regulation of, 244–45
  seasonal migration, 230–31
  settlement at Dammam, 253
  settlement on the Bahrain main island, 228–29
  settlement on the Hawars, 226
  settlement on Zakhnuniya, 259, 261
Dubai, ruler(s), 69, 87
Dubai/Sharjah Arbitration, 133*q*
Dukhan region (Qatar peninsula), 122*map*, 226
dynastic struggles among the Al-Khalifa, 32–35, 64–65, 71
  Qatar's version, 112

E

Eastern and General syndicate (EGS):
  and the Bahrain oil concession, 167–68, 171
economic sanctions: by Bahrain on Qatar, 192–93, 283
effectivités:
  Bahrain's *effectivités* in the Hawars, 243–53, 401
  Qatar on, 343
  and territorial claims, 270, 339
EGS. *See* Eastern and General syndicate
Elphinstone, Sir Mountstuart: on British piracy policy, 53
embargo: Bahrain's sanctions on Qatar, 192–93, 283
Emir of Bahrain. *See* Ruler(s) of Bahrain (RB)
Emir of Qatar. *See* Ruler(s) of Qatar (RQ)
equity principle in ICJ decisions, 396
  in the "*Q. v. B.*" Judgment, 397
Exclusive Agreements (1880, 1892), 72–75
  as implemented for Qatar, 98

F

Fahd Al-Saud, King: letters to the Amirs of Bahrain and Qatar, 327
Failaka Island (Kuwait), 7
Faisal (Wahhabi Amir), 32
falsification of the historical record by Qatar, xiii
 See also forged documents; Qatar: version of dispute-related events
Fasht Al-Azm, xvii*map*, 398*map*
 ICJ Judgment on, 403
 and Sitra, 347–48
Fasht Al-Dibal, xvii*map*, 349–50, 398*map*
 ICJ Judgment on, 396, 403
 Qatar's attack on, 304, 327, 349–50
fingerprints as seals on suspect documents, 365
Finkel, Caroline: Ottoman suspect document analysis, 367–70
fishing:
 in the Hawars, 235–36
 government regulation of, 243–44
 in Janan, 223
 See also pearling
Five Principles (1978/1983), 326
Foreign Office. *See* British Foreign Office
forensic analyses of suspect documents, 359–61, 374–86, 388–89
 comparisons among documents, 359–60, 374–81
 devices used, 374–75
 comparisons with known authentic same-author documents, 360, 361, 381–84
 handwriting analysis. *See* handwriting in suspect documents
 paper analysis. *See* paper of suspect documents
forged documents (from Qatar): early example, 361
 See also forged documents (in Qatar's ICJ case)
forged documents (in Qatar's ICJ case), 306, 307, 355–93
 ICJ on, 392

Judge Fortier on, 392–93*q*
 origin (provenance) as unexplained, 388
 Qatar's case as dependent on, 390–91, 392–93
 Qatar's report on, 388, 389–90
 sole source, 356
 submissions of, 338
 as suspect. *See* suspect documents
 wider significance, 391, 392–93
 withdrawal of, 338, 388–90
Fortier, Judge (ICJ): on the forged documents, 392–93*q*
Fowle, Sir Trenchard, 295, 320, 408
 on the RB's claims to Zubarah, 193, 195
Freshfields, 362
Friendly Convention (1861), 36, 67–69, 256–57, 284
Furaiwah (Qatar peninsula): Qatar's attack on, 191
Fuwairat (Qatar peninsula), 41, 122*map*
 Doha seceders move to, 88
 Ma'adhid tribe in, 124
 as part of Bahrain, 115
 Sheikh Mohammed's base in, 34

G

Galloway, Arnold, 197, 408
Gaskin, J. C., 408
 on Al-Thani authority in the Qatar peninsula, 153–54
Gazetteer of the Persian Gulf... (Lorimer), 418
 on the Al-Thani, 43*q*
 on the Bedouin tribes of the south Qatar peninsula, 42*q*
 on the General Treaty as applicable to the Qatar peninsula, 57–58
GCC. *See* Gulf Cooperation Council
General Treaty (Piracy Agreements) (1820), 54–56
 effects, 58–59, 61, 62
 implementation of, 56–59
 spirit, 55–56
 Trucial flag requirement for Arab vessels, 55, 56, 57–58

General Treaty *(continued)*
   war vs. plunder and piracy in, 55, 56, 57, 58
Geneva Conventions on maritime law, 343
geographical proximity:
   in the RQ's claims to the Hawars, 285–86*q*, 291–92*q*, 307
      Hemingway on, 295–96*q*
      inaccuracies in, 292, 297–99, 308
      Weightman on, 294*q*
   and territorial claims, 294, 307–8, 339, 400–1
Ghariyeh (Qatar peninsula), 122*map*
   Bahrain–Qatar negotiations in, 189
   settlement in, 88–89
Gilgamesh: Dilmun as described in, 5
Government of India Office (IO):
   Foreign Office takeover of, 165, 166
   Foreign Office–IO Gulf policy disagreements, 164–65
   on the RB's claims to Zubarah, 194*q*
   on the RQ's claim to the Hawars, 295*q*
Governor of Doha (*Kaimakam* of Qatar), 25, 44
   Isa bin Tarif, 65, 137
   Sheikh Ahmed, 92, 96
   Sheikh Jasim, 88–90, 92, 128
   Sheikh Nasir bin Mubarik, 90
Governor of Zubarah, 207
   RB's change of, 143
Great Britain. *See* Britain (British)
Gulf. *See* Arabian Gulf
Gulf Cooperation Council (GCC):
   Bahrain–Qatar border dispute mediation efforts, xvi–xviii, 325, 326–31
Gulf of Bahrain, 225
   Bahrain's sovereignty in, 345
   as a link between Bahrain main island and the Hawars, 296*q*
   See also Bahrain Archipelago
Gulf Oil: and the Bahrain oil concession, 170–71
gypsum mining in the Hawars, 238–39
   government regulation of, 245–46

H

Hadd Janan (Hawar Islands), 222–23
   ICJ Judgment on, 402
Hafidh Pasha: suspect letters to, 370
handwriting in suspect documents:
   analyses, 359, 360, 383–84, 384–86
   in Arabic, 366, 367, 375, 384–85
   as disguised, 384–85
   overwriting, 385
   See also signatures on suspect documents
Hasa coast (of Arabia):
   Al-Khalifa blockades on, 31, 35, 36
   Bahrain and, 6, 7
   Dammam, 30–31, 35
   environment, 150
   Ottoman annexation of, 31, 71
   Ras Tanura, 150
   See also Qatif
Hasan, Abdullah bin, 188–89
Hawar Islands, xvii*map*, 122*map*, 221–322, 398*map*
   1916 Treaty and, 263
   Al-Khalifa authority in, 226–29, 241–43, 308–9
      British recognition of, 255–57, 264–65, 268
      effectivités, 243–53, 343, 401
      Ottoman recognition of, 257–59, 261
      Qatar's version, 308–9
   Anglo-Ottoman Convention and, 261–63
   animal husbandry, 237–38
   Bahrain oil concession and, 268–71
   Bahrain's claims to, 268, 269, 270, 271, 340
      British recognition of, 278–80, 297, 321
      effectivités, 243–53, 343, 401
      legal arguments, 339–40, 401–2
      Qatar's version, 308–9
   "blank slate" theory on, 309–11
   commercial activity, 230, 235–36
   defense measures, 251, 304, 311
   development projects, 247–48, 302–3
   dispute resolution (judicial authority) in, 244

Hawar Islands *(continued)*
  Doha contacts with, 242
  Dowasir departure from, and return, 253–54
  Dowasir settlement on, 226
  economic activities, 234–39
    government regulation of, 243–46
  electricity generators, 302–3
  ferry service, 302
  fishing, 235–36
    government regulation of, 243–44
  geography, 221
  governance, 227, 241
  government regulation, 243–46, 253
  as granted to the Dowasir, 226, 294
    Qatar's version, 308
  gypsum mining, 238–39
    government regulation of, 245–46
  habitation patterns/evidence, 230–34
    Qatar's version, 309–11
  history (c.1780–) (summary), 305–6
  hotel, 303
  housing project, 303
  ICJ Judgment on, 396, 400–2
  immigration regulation, 251–53
  inhabitants:
    Al-Dowasir. *See* Dowasir tribe
    Al-Ghattam, 231
  island names and sizes, 222
  Janan. *See* Janan
  law enforcement, 249–51
  mosques, 247–48
  as not in the Bahrain Islands, 270–71
  oil concessions in, 267–80, 281–82, 303
  oil exploration, 303
  oil potential, 281
  as part of Bahrain, 270–71, 272–77
    Al-Arayed on, 305*q*
  PCL's claims to for Qatar, 277, 278, 282
    Qatar's complaint about, 315
  pearling, 236–37
    government regulation of, 244–45
  plot allegedly related to, 365
  Qatar oil concession and, 271–72
  Qatar's claims to, 223, 271, 282, 283, 300–1, 309

1938-39 arbitration claim and Rejoinder, 285–87, 291–93, 294, 297–99
  as applicable to other islands, 298–99
  economic and political motives for, 282–83
  inaccuracies in, 292, 297–99, 308–9
  legal arguments, 341–43, 400–1
  oil and, 281–82
  proximity issue. *See* geographical proximity
Qatar's version of events in, 307–22
Qatari landing incidents, 252–53
RB's claims to. *See* Bahrain's claims to, *above*
RB's visits to, 241–42
roads, 302
RQ's claims to. *See* Qatar's claims to, *above*
seasonal migration, 230–31
as a socio-economic unit with the Bahrain Islands and Zubarah, 225, 296
sovereignty in:
  Bahrain's assertion of during oil concession negotiations, 268–72
  Bahrain's reluctance to submit to the ICJ, 330
  British arbitration of. *See* 1938–39 Hawar Islands sovereignty arbitration
  ICJ judgement, 396, 400–2
  See also Al-Khalifa authority in, *above*; Bahrain's claims to, *above*; Qatar's claims to, *above*
suspect correspondence on, 365
telecommunications facilities, 303
villages, 232–33
water supply systems, 232, 233–34, 247, 302
Hawar residents: alleged testimonies, 361
Hay, Sir Rupert, 301
Hay, William, 409
  on the Qatar peninsula interior, 42–43*q*

Hemingway, C. E. M.: on the geographical proximity issue in the RQ's claims to the Hawars, 295–96*q*

Hickinbotham, Thomas, 409
   on the 1875 Treaty, 194–95, 194*q*
   mediation of Zubarah dispute, 195–97

"*hijri*": suspect document misusage, 363, 369

historical analysis of suspect documents, 363–72

HMG line between Bahrain and Qatar, xvi, xvii*map*, 351–53, 398*map*

Holmes, Frank, 409
   and the Bahrain oil concession, 166–72

Holmes map, 272, *274*, 276, *276*
   Qatar's interpretation of, 314

Hormuz:
   Ottoman attack on, 12
   Portuguese capture of, 11

Hossein Effendi: voyage to Zubarah, 144

Huwailah (Qatar peninsula), 122*map*, 124
   chiefs' break with Sheikh Abdullah, 33

I

Ibn Saud. *See* Al-Saud, Abdul-Aziz

ICJ. *See* International Court of Justice

ikrimiyyah (ruler benefit system for nomadic tribes), 21, 135–36, 183

Imam of Muscat (Sayid Sa'id), 410
   alliances with the RB, 29, 36
   and the Huwailah chiefs, 33
   intervention in Bahrain, 29–30, 33, 64
   and Rahmah bin Jaber, 29
   See also Muscat

immigration regulation:
   in the Bahrain Islands, 162
   in the Hawars, 251–53

imperial rule vs. diplomacy in British foreign policy, 165–66, 194

India:
   British loss of, 165
   and the Gulf, 51

India Office. *See* Government of India Office

Indian traders of Doha: as expelled by Sheikh Jasim, 86–87

indirect governance. *See* coalition rule

"*Ingiltere Devleti*": suspect document misusage, 370

ink on suspect documents, 389

Interim Report (Qatar 1998), 388, 389–90

interlocutory judgment in *Qatar v. Bahrain*, 335–36

International Court of Justice (ICJ):
   Bahrain–Qatar border dispute case. *See Qatar v. Bahrain*
   on the forged documents, 392
   philosophy, 395–96
   purpose, 396
   recognition of tribal authority/control in the Gulf region, 133
   suspect document reports submitted to, 386–87, 388–89

international experts' suspect document analyses, 362–86
   reports submitted to the ICJ, 386–87, 388–89

international law:
   ICJ role in, 395–96
   principles on territorial claims, 339–43, 400–1

Iraq Petroleum Company, 177

Isa bin Ali. *See* Al-Khalifa, Sheikh Isa bin Ali

Isa bin Tarif, 33, 43, 410
   vs. the RBs, 64, 65–66, 137
   requests to attack Bahrain, 33, 64
   secession to Abu Dhabi, 33

Islam:
   Al-Qais conversion to, 8
   Carmathian movement/Empire, 8–9
   emergence in the Gulf, 8–9
   Wahhabi movement. *See* Wahhabis

Island of Palmas Award, 339

islands, 346*def*
  legal status (entitlements), 347
Isa Abdul-Lateef Al-Sarkal. *See* Al-Sarkal, Isa Abdul-Lateef, Khan Bahador
Izzet map (Ottoman map), 83, 213, 258

J

Jabar. *See* Nasir bin Jabar
Jaber. *See* Rahmah bin Jaber
Jalahimah tribe. *See* Al-Jalahimah
Janan (Hawar Islands), xvii*map*, 222–23, 398*map*
  demarcation as separate from the other Hawars, 222–23
  fishing, 223
  ICJ Judgment on, 396, 402
  as included in the 1938-39 arbitration, 222, 223–25
Janson, Edward, 171
Jasim bin Mohammed. *See* Al-Thani, Sheikh Jasim bin Mohammed
Jubail (Hasa coast): port plans of Ibn Saud, 160

K

Kaimakam of Qatar. *See* Governor of Doha
kaza of Qatar. *See* Ottoman-ruled Qatar
Keir, Sir W. G., 54
Kelly, J. B.:
  on diplomacy vs. colonial rule in British foreign policy, 165–66, 194
  on Foreign Office–India Office Gulf policy disagreements, 164–65
  on Qatari falsification of the historical record, xiii
Kemball, Arnold Burrowes, 409
Khalid (Wahhabi pretender), 31
Khalid bin Abdul-Aziz Al-Saud. *See* Al-Saud, Khalid bin Abdul-Aziz, King
Khalifa bin Ghatam (Naim chief), 143
Khor Hassan (Khuwayr) (Qatar peninsula), 33, 40
  Al-Jalahimah in, 20
  Sheikh Abdullah's move to, 33–34
  Sheikh Abdullah's reprisals against, 34
  Sheikh of. *See* Rahmah bin Jaber
Khuwayr. *See* Khor Hassan
"Known Documents" collection, 358
Kurshid Pasha of Egypt: threat against Bahrain, 31
Kuwait: settlement of, 18

L

Laithwaite, J. G.:
  on the Hawars, 270
  on the southern boundary of Qatar, 262, 263
"land dominates the sea" principle, 343, 402
"Latin": suspect document misusage, 370
Latin initial seals on suspect documents, 376
Law of the Sea, UN Convention on, 343
linguistic analysis of suspect documents, 359–60, 382–83
local councils *(majlis)* (Bahrain Islands), 22–23, 23–24
Loch, Percy Gordon, 320, 409
Lorimer, John G., 409
  See also Gazetteer of the Persian Gulf...
low-tide elevations, 346–47*def*
  legal status (entitlements), 347

M

Ma'adhid tribe, 43, 124
  Al-Thani as, 43, 45
Madgwick, T. George: on oil exploration in Bahrain, 169, 170
main island of Bahrain. *See* Bahrain main island
majlis (local councils) (Bahrain Islands), 22–23, 23–24
Man, M. C. G., 300

Ottomans (Porte): *(continued)*
recognition of Bahrain's (Al-Khalifa) authority in the Hawars, 257–59, 261
recognition of Bahrain's (Al-Khalifa) authority in Zubarah, 155–56
Sheikh Jasim bin Mohammed and, 47, 80–81, 82, 86, 87, 88–90, 94, 145–48
Suleiman the Magnificent, 11
Zakhnuniya occupation, 259–60
Zakhnuniya payment, 261

Ottomans in the Qatar peninsula:
administration, 84–86
arrival, 37, 71–72, 80–81
authority, 81, 82–83, 84–86, 209–11
Qatar's version, 209–11
checks on the expansion of, 82
expansion attempts in Zubarah, 83, 121, 143–49
attacks, 144–45, 145, 146–48, 210–11
diplomacy, 144
failure of, 149–52
resettlement plans/occupation efforts, 145–46, 148–49, 153
piratical acts, 87
withdrawal, 85, 98
See also Ottoman-ruled Qatar

P

PAB. *See* Political Agent in Bahrain

Palestine: and declining British influence in the Gulf, 164–65

Palgrave (British traveler):
on Al-Khalifa vs. Al-Thani authority in the Qatar peninsula, 110
on the Qatar peninsula interior, 42*q*

paper of suspect documents, 377–81
ink, 389
matching torn edges of unrelated documents, 377–80, 389
physical damage–writing correlations, 380–81
recycled papers, 377, 380–81, 389

PAQ. *See* Political Agent in Qatar

PCL. *See* Petroleum Concessions Limited

pearl divers: government protection of, 245

pearling:
Al bin Ali attack on pearl fishers, 95
in Bahrain, 9, 126, 351
administration of, 23–24, 351
demise, 161–62, 351
in Doha, 41
in the Hawars, 236–37
government regulation of, 244–45
in Zubarah, 18
Ottoman interests in, 144, 145–46

pearling banks of Bahrain, 350–51, 398*map*

pearling season, 236
British banning of war/hostilities during, 59
vulnerability of pearling tribes during, 135

pearling tribes:
Al bin Ali in Zubarah, 146–77
Al-Khalifa authority over, 23, 24
Qatar's version, 112–13
in the Qatar peninsula, 23, 40, 41
vulnerability during pearling season, 135

pearls of Bahrain, 126

Peel, R. T., 320

Pelly, C. J., 198, 409
1947 maritime boundary decision, 222–23, 301, 351–52

Pelly, J. H., 410
attack on the Al-Thani fleet at Zubarah, 148

Pelly, Lewis, 138, 410
visit to Doha, 45

pension lists (of Bahrain): Naim records, 161

Perpetual Treaty of Peace (Trucial chiefs), 60
as implemented for Qatar, 98–99

Persia:
attacks on Zubarah, 19, 125
control of Bahrain, 7, 13, 14–15, 124–25, 125
defense of Bahrain against Muscat, 27
expulsion from Bahrain, 19, 126

oil: *(continued)*
  exploration:
    in Bahrain, 169, 170
    in Zubarah, 269
    world production in 1936, 267
    See also oil concessions
  oil companies in the Gulf:
    in the Hawars, 303
      Qatar's allegation of collusion in the 1938–39 arbitration, 315
    Red Line Agreement, 170, 171
    See also American oil companies in the Gulf; British oil companies in the Gulf
oil concessions:
  and the 1938–39 Hawar Islands arbitration, 224
  in Bahrain. *See* Bahrain oil concession
  and British recognition of Bahrain's authority in Zubarah, 163, 173–75, 176–79, 200, 217
  in the Hawars, 267–80, 281–82, 303
  in Qatar. *See* Qatar oil concession
  Saudi oil concession, 176
oil exploration:
  in Bahrain, 169, 170
  in Zubarah, 269
"OK": suspect document misusage, 364
Oman:
  Wahhabi attacks on, 31, 36
  Yaaribah tribe's capture of Bahrain, 15
Oral Hearings (in *Q. v. B.*), 337, 395
  agents, 338
original title: and territorial claims, 400
"*Osmanli*": suspect document misusage, 369
Ottoman maps:
  Izzet map, 83, 213, *258*
  suspect maps, 371, 372–74
Ottoman seals on suspect documents, 369, 375, 389
Ottoman suspect documents, 367–70
  Arabic writing in, 367
  date discrepancies, 369, 370
  format anomalies, 368–69
  mistaken terms, 367–68, 369, 369–70
  seal anomalies, 369, 375, 389
Ottoman-ruled Qatar *(kaza)*, 258 *map*
  Al-Khalifa authority in, 46, 90
  Al-Thani authority in, 95–96, 96–98, 114
    Palgrave on, 110
    Qatar's version, 113–14
  British intervention in internal affairs, 93–96
  Kaimakam:
    Sheikh Ahmed as, 92, 96
    Sheikh Jasim as, 88, 89, 92
  rebellion of 1893, 91–93, 93–94
  territorial extent, 99–100, 114–15, 159, 187
    Qatar's version, 114
  tribes and settlements, 41–42
  vs. Zubarah's inhabitants, 142
  See also Doha; Ottomans in the Qatar peninsula
Ottomans (Porte):
  administrative failures, 151
  administrative system, 79
  and the Al-Thani, 80, 82, 86–90, 150–51
    rebellion of 1893, 91–93, 93–94
  and Bahrain, 12, 36, 65
  and the British, 79–80, 87, 93, 96, 143, 149, 155–56, 260–61
  claims to the Bahrain Islands, 71–72
  expansion into Arabia, 77–80
  expeditions against the Wahhabis, 30, 31, 78–79
  fear of European encroachment, 77–78
  financial troubles, 84
  Hasa coast occupation, 31, 71
  influence in the Gulf, 13, 37, 80, 87
  interests in the Gulf, 78, 80
  interests in Zubarah, 144, 145–46, 155–56
  presence in the Gulf, 11–12, 37
  protest of British intervention in Bahrain, 71
  in the Qatar peninsula. *See* Ottomans in the Qatar peninsula

Murair Fort (Zubarah):
  building of, 125
  Sheikh Mohammed bin Khalifa's capture of, 34
  strengthening of, 127
Muscat:
  attack on Zubarah, 127, 206
  attacks on Bahrain, 27, 29–30, 126
    expulsion of the Wahhabis, 29, 127
  Bahrain expedition against, 30
  expulsion from Bahrain, 27–28, 126
  peace treaty with Bahrain, 30, 58–59

N

Naim tribe, 131–39
  and the Al-Khalifa, 21, 25, 39–40, 40, 121, 125, 128–29, 135–39, 142, 183–84, 208–9
    Qatar's version, 208, 215–16
  in Bahrain records, 161, 216
  branches, 139
  defense of Zubarah, 19, 65–66, 137–38
    against Qatar's attack, 184, 185, 188, 190
  dirah (territory), 132–33, 134*map*
    Qatar's version, 208
  flight from Zubarah, 191–92
  as guardians of the Qatar peninsula, 25, 40, 136
  ICJ Judgment on, 399, 400
  migration to Bahrain, 132, 162, 191–92
  origin, 131
  as pastoral nomads, 131–32
  plebiscite proposal, 216–17
  RB payments to, 135–36
  RB's supplying of, 142, 184–85, 185
  report on Qatar's attack on Zubarah, 190
  return to Zubarah, 201
  RQ's taxation of, 182–83, 184
    Naim responses to, 183–85, 187–88
  seasonal migration, 132
  settlement in Zubarah, 18, 121, 131
  Sheikh Isa bin Ali on, 138–39*q*, 144*q*
  smuggling charge by Qatar, 214–15
  split (rift), 139, 182
  tax payments to the Al-Khalifa, 136
Nasir bin Jabar (Naim chief), 135, 143, 407
  reply to Hossein Effendi, 144*q*
Nasir bin Madhkur (Nasir of Bushire and Bahrain):
  attacks on Bahrain, 27
  attacks on Zubarah, 19, 125
Nasir bin Mubarik Al-Khalifa, Sheikh, 145, 151, 153, 407
  attack on Zubarah, 145
  as Governor of Doha, 90
  as joint RB, 407, 413*n*
  and Sheikh Jasim, 90, 145
Nasir of Bushire and Bahrain. *See* Nasir bin Madhkur
navigational structures in the Bahrain Archipelago, 345
Nearchus, 7
neutral zone in the Gulf, 59
  armed operations as restricted in, 59, 63
  enforcement of, 63–67
  extension to Bahrain, 60–61
nomadic tribes:
  and pearling tribes, 40
  ruler benefit system *(ikrimiyah)*, 21, 135–36, 183
  territory. *See dirah*
  See also Bedouin tribes

O

Odaid (Adeed) (Qatar peninsula), 41, 122*map*, 258*map*
  British survey description, 42*q*
  as outside Ottoman control, 82–83
  suspect correspondence on, 365
Office of the Minister of State (Bahrain): suspect document investigation, 356, 357–61
oil:
  and the Bahrain–Qatar border dispute, xi, xvi, 162–79, 191, 267–68
  discovery:
    in Bahrain, 161, 172
    in Qatar, 204

Manama (Bahrain main island), 122*map*
  Sheikh Abdullah's reprisals against, 34
  Sheikh Abdullah's suspected piracy in, 64
  Sheikh Mohammed vs. Sheikh Abdullah in, 34
Manasir tribe:
  attack on Zubarah, 190
  British reprisals for piracy, 57
maps:
  Bahrain oil concession draft map, 272, *273*
  Holmes map, 272, *274*, 276, *276*
    Qatar's interpretation of, 314
  ICJ evidence submitted by Qatar, 213
  Izzet map, 83, 213, *258*
  Qatar oil concession map, 271, 276, 277
    Qatar's interpretation of, 315–16
  suspect maps, 371, 372–74, 387
  Ward map, *275*, 276, *276*
maritime boundary between Bahrain and Qatar, 343–53, 398*map*
  Bahrain Archipelago and, 344–46
  ICJ on, 403
  HMG line, xvi, xvii*map*, 351–53, 398*map*
  ICJ Judgment on, 396, 398*map*, 402–4
  mainland-to-mainland line, 346
  Qatar on, 346, 351
maritime features (Bahrain Archipelago), xvii*map*, 344, 346–51, 398*map*
  Fasht Al-Azm, 347–48
  Fasht Al-Dibal, 349–50
  legal status (entitlements), 347
  pearling banks, 350–51
  Qit'at Jaradah, 348–49
maritime law: Geneva Conventions on, 343
Maritime Truce (1835), 59–60, 62
  as implemented for Qatar (1916 Treaty), 98–99
Mary Tudor (Queen of England), 203*q*

Mattox, Henry: suspect document analysis, 372–74
Memorials (in *Q. v. B.*), 333, 355, 395
  Annexes to, 355
  Bahrain's, 337–38, 355
  Qatar's. *See Qatar Memorial* (1992); *Qatar Memorial* (1996)
Mesopotamia: and Dilmun, 5–6
Midhat Pasha, 79, 85, 149–50, 151
  suspect letters from, 368, 370, 371–72
Ministry of Foreign Affairs (Bahrain): suspect document searches, 357
Ministry of Justice and Islamic Affairs (Bahrain): suspect document searches, 357
Ministry of State. *See* Office of the Minister of State (Bahrain)
Ministry of the Interior (Bahrain): suspect document analysis, 359–61
Moberly, John C., 205
Mohammed Al-Thani. *See* Al-Thani, Sheikh Mohammed
Mohammed Ali (of Egypt): Ottoman expeditions against the Wahhabis, 30, 31, 78–79
Mohammed bin Abdullah. *See* Al-Khalifa, Sheikh Mohammed bin Abdullah
Mohammed bin Khalifa. *See* Al-Khalifa, Sheikh Mohammed bin Khalifa (founder of Zubarah); Al-Khalifa, Sheikh Mohammed bin Khalifa (RB: 1834–42/1843–68/1869)
Mohammed ibn Saud, 27, 78
Monasoor tribe: attack on Zubarah, 137–38
mosques on the Hawars, 247–48
Muharraq (Bahrain island), xvii*map*, 122*map*, 398*map*
  as the Al-Khalifa seat of government, 126
  as a commercial center, 229
  Sheikh Abdullah and, 34
  Sheikh Isa bin Ali's palace, 238

Persia: *(continued)*
  occupation of Basra, 19
  protest of British intervention in Bahrain, 71
  Safavid dynasty, 14–15
  Sassanian Empire, 7
  Seleucid state, 7
Persian Gulf. *See* Arabian Gulf
The Persian Gulf Administration Reports, 419
The Persian Gulf Précis (Saldanha), 418
Petroleum Concessions Limited (PCL), 177
  and Bahrain's unallotted area, 177–79, 269, 279
  claims to the Hawars for Qatar, 277, 278, 282
    Qatar's complaint about, 315
  operations in Qatar, 191
  Qatar concession transfer to, 177
  requests for Qatar border information, 176–77
Piracy Agreements. *See* General Treaty
piracy in the Gulf, 15, 50
  "acknowledged war" vs. "plunder and piracy" in the General Treaty, 55, 56, 57, 58
  Al-Khalifa suppression of, 25–26
  Bahrain as entrepôt for pirated goods, 51–52, 53–54
  British suppression of, 52–53
    Qawasim expeditions, 50, 54
    See also 1868 Agreements; Friendly Convention; General Treaty; Maritime Truce
  Manama incident, 64
Pirate Coast (Trucial Coast), 50, 59
Political Agent in Bahrain (PAB), 74
  on the 1875 Treaty, 194 *q*
  1947 maritime boundary decision, 222–23, 301, 351–52
  on Al-Thani authority in the Qatar peninsula, 153–54
  on British options in the Qatar peninsula, 154
  compromise proposal on Zubarah, 186–87
  on the Hawars, 223–25

  mediation of Zubarah dispute, 195–97
  on the RQ's claim to the Hawars, 286 *q*, 287 *q*, 293–95
  and request to rebut Bahrain's Counter-claim, 288–89 *q*
  turnover problem, 198
  warning on Zubarah, 181 *q*
Political Agent in Qatar (PAQ): as not appointed until 1953, 99, 101–2
Political Resident in the Persian Gulf, 51
  on Al-Thani authority in the Qatar peninsula, 95–96 *q*
  on the Bahrain unallotted area, 269–70
  on the expulsion of the Indian traders of Doha, 86–87, 93
  mediation of the Al-Thani–Ottoman conflict, 93–94
  naval operation against Bahrain, 71
  on Ottoman authority in the Qatar peninsula, 85 *q*
  on Ottoman–Al-Thani expansion attempts in Zubarah, 145, 146–47, 148, 153
  on Qatar's insecurity, 100 *q*
  RB assurances to, 53
  on RB authority in Zubarah, 142–43, 145
  on RB piracy suppression, 26 *q*
  on RB tribute payment to the Wahhabis, 31–32 *q*
  on the RB's claims to Zubarah, 193, 195
  visit to Doha, 45
Porte. *See* Ottomans
Portuguese: presence in the Gulf, 11–13, 49
possession: and territorial claims, 339
Précis of Bahrein Affairs (Saldanha), 418
Précis of Katar Affairs (Saldanha), 418
Preliminary Treaty (1820), 54–55
Prideaux, Francis B., 410
  on British options in the Qatar peninsula, 154
  on the Dowasir, 227 *q*
  on Zakhnuniya, 260

Prideaux, William F., 410
Prior, Sir Geoffrey, 321–22, 410
proximity. *See* geographical proximity

Q

"Qadi": suspect document misusage, 368
Qadi of Zubarah:
  Hawars grant to the Dowasir, 226, 294
  Qatar's version, 308
Qatar:
  archives. *See* Diwan Amiri Archives
  attack on Fasht Al-Dibal, 304, 327
  attack on Zubarah. *See* 1937 Qatari attack on Zubarah
  Bahrain's sanctions on, 192–93, 283
  "blank slate" theory on the Hawars, 309–11
  border dispute with Abu Dhabi, 365
  border dispute with Bahrain. *See* Bahrain–Qatar border dispute
  British influence on, 13, 80
  British interests in, 101, 163, 174, 175, 191, 194
  British protection of, xv, 98, 100, 175
  British recognition of, 98–99
  claims to the Hawars, 223, 271, 282, 283, 300–1, 309
    1938-39 arbitration claim and Rejoinder, 285–87, 291–93, 294, 297–99
    as applicable to other islands, 298–99
    economic and political motives for, 282–83
    inaccuracies in, 292, 297–99, 308–9
    legal arguments, 341–43, 400–1
    oil and, 281–82
    proximity issue. *See* geographical proximity
  claims to Zubarah, 179, 181, 187
    Bahrain's interpretation of, 340
    legal arguments, 341–43
  Counter-Memorial. *See Qatar Counter-Memorial* (1997)
  economic hardship, 193, 282–83
  emergence as a modern political entity, 17, 80, 98–100, 102, 105–6

  falsification of the historical record, xiii
    See also forged documents; version of dispute-related events, *below*
  forged documents. *See* forged documents (from Qatar)
  Hawars as not considered part of, 263
  Ibn Saud's influence in, 101, 157, 174, 175
  ICJ case against Bahrain. *See Qatar v. Bahrain*
  independence from Britain, xv
  instability, 100–2, 157, 174, 283
    and the Qatar oil concession, 101, 175–76, 271–72
  Interim Report (1998), 388, 389–90
  landing incidents in the Hawars, 252–53
  maritime boundary proposal, 351
  Memorials. *See Qatar Memorial* (1992); *Qatar Memorial* (1996)
  national museum, xiii
  oil concession. *See* Qatar oil concession
  oil discovery in, 282
  Ottoman influence on, 13, 80
  Political Agent in, 99, 101–2
  population concentration, 43
  Rejoinder (1939), 291–93, 294
  Replies (in *Q. v. B.*), 333, 338, 395
  resettlement of Zubarah attempt, 197–98
  ruler(s). *See* Ruler(s) of Qatar (RQ)
  ruling family. *See* Al-Thani
  southern boundary, 262, 263
  sovereignty in disputed territories. *See* claims to the Hawars, *above*; claims to Zubarah, *above*
  territorial extent, 99–100, 114–15, 159, 187, 262–63, 277
    Qatar's version, 114
  unilateral application to the ICJ, 331, 332, 333, 335
    Bahrain's objection to, 334–35
  version of dispute-related events:
    in the Hawars, 307–22
    in the historical context, 107–17
    in Zubarah, 203–17
  See also Ottoman-ruled Qatar; Qatar peninsula

Qatar Counter-Memorial (1997), 338, 387, 395
   Bahrain's version, 390
   as contaminated by the forgeries, 390, 392–93
"Qatar" in historical documents: Qatar's version, 108
Qatar Memorial (1992), 333
Qatar Memorial (1996), 337, 338, 355
   Bahrain's version, 390
   as contaminated by the forgeries, 390, 392–93
   initial analysis, 356
   See also forged documents (in Qatar's ICJ case)
Qatar oil concession, 175–77
   award to APOC, 271
   British nationality clause in, 175
   and British recognition of Bahrain's authority in Zubarah, 163, 173–75, 176–79, 200, 217
   and the Hawars, 271–72
   instability of Qatar and, 101, 175–76, 270–71
   map attached to, 271, 276, 277
      Qatar's interpretation of, 315–16
   territorial extent, 276–77
   transfer to PCL, 177
Qatar peninsula, 122*map*
   Al-Khalifa authority in, 18–19, 20, 109–10, 207, 309
      Al-Thani recognition of, 109, 156–57, 269
      British recognition of, 109–10, 115, 207
      in Ottoman-ruled Qatar, 46, 90
      Qatar's version, 109, 308–9
      as recognized by regional powers, 109–10, 115
      in Zubarah. *See under* Zubarah
   Al-Khalifa governance of, 24–27, 44
   Al-Thani authority in, 46–47, 88, 90–91, 95–96, 96–98, 107–8, 110–11, 114, 115, 128, 153–54, 262
      Palgrave on, 110
      Qatar's version, 107–8, 113–14, 321–24
      in Zubarah. *See under* Zubarah
   Anglo-Ottoman Convention on, 96–98
   British advice that the RB keep clear of, 86, 212
   British influence in, 36
   Dilmun and, 6
   Dukhan region, 122*map*, 226
   early historical insignificance, 7–8
   environment, 3
   General Treaty as applicable to, 57–58
   geography as a strategic impediment, 149–50
   human geography, 39–43
   interior, 42–43
   northwest tribes and settlements, 39–41
   Ottoman expansion attempts in Zubarah. *See under* Zubarah
   Ottoman presence in. *See* Ottomans in the Qatar peninsula
   Ottoman-ruled region. *See* Ottoman-ruled Qatar
   as part of Bahrain, 46, 57–58, 61, 68–69, 70
   pearling tribes, 23, 40, 41
   population (late 18th Cent., 1940s), 129
   population migration to Bahrain from, 132, 162
   Portuguese disinterest in, 12
   power vacuum in, 84
   as a refuge, 27, 40–41
   southeast tribes and settlements, 41–42
      See also Ottoman-ruled Qatar
   southern nomadic tribes, 42
   Wahhabi attack/influence on, 36, 100
   See also Doha; Zubarah
Qatar Reply (1992), 333
Qatar Reply (1999), 338, 395
Qatar v. Bahrain (ICJ case), xviii, 395
   beneficial results, 405
   Counter-Memorials. *See Counter-Memorials* (in *Q. v. B.*)
   Judgment, 396–97
      acceptance by the parties, 404
      as binding, 404
      dissenting opinion, 392–93*q*

Qatar v. Bahrain (ICJ case) *(continued)*
  Judgment *(continued)*
    equity, 397
    reasoning, 397–404
    significance, 396, 404–5
  Jurisdiction phase, 331–37
    Bahrain's contestation, 332
    formal pleadings, 333–35, 336
    interlocutory judgment, 335–36
    ruling and dissenting opinions, 336–37
  Memorials. *See* Memorials (in *Q. v. B.*)
  Merits phase, 337–53, 355, 395
    forged documents. *See* forged documents (in Qatar's ICJ case)
    formal pleadings, 337–38, 395
    maritime boundary, 343–53
    territorial disputes, 338–43
  Oral Hearings, 337, 338, 395
  Qatar's case as dependent on the forged documents, 390–91, 392–93
  Qatar's *Interim Report* (1998), 388, 389–90
  Qatar's unilateral application, 331, 332, 333, 335
    Bahrain's objection to, 334–35
  Replies, 333, 338, 395
  Supplemental Documents, 395
Qatar–Bahrain border dispute. *See* Bahrain–Qatar border dispute
Qatif (Hasa coast):
  Al-Khalifa blockades of, 31, 35, 36
  shallows, 150
Qawasim tribe:
  British expeditions against, 50, 54
  pirate fleets, 50
  and the Wahhabis, 28, 50
Qit'at Jaradah, xvii*map*, 348–49, 398*map*
  ICJ Judgment on, 396, 402–3

R

Rahmah bin Jaber, 409
  British mediation between the RBs and, 58
  and the Imam of Muscat, 29
  taking of and expulsion from Zubarah, 28, 29
  and the Wahhabis, 28

Ras Al-Kaimah (Trucial Coast/UAE), 4*map*, 50
  British capture of Qawasim headquarters, 50, 54
Ras Tanura (Hasa coast), 150
Rashid, Sheikh (of Ras Al-Kaimah), 19
Rashid bin Mohammed Al-Jabor, 216, 407
  RQ on, 216*q*
  RQ's demand on, 182–83, 184
RB. *See* Ruler(s) of Bahrain
Records of Bahrein, 419
Records of Qatar, 419
Red Line Agreement (among oil companies), 170, 171
reference sources, 417–20
religions: on Tylos, 7. *See also* Islam
Replies (in *Q. v. B.*), 333, 338, 395
res judicata: and territorial claims, 339, 401
Residencies (British East India Company), 14, 51
  Bushire Residency, 51, 56–57
Restrictive Line. *See* neutral zone in the Gulf
Rizoogi, Abdul-Razzaq bin:
  Qatar's allegations against, 321
  suspect correspondence with Belgrave, 372
Ross, Edward C., 410
RQ. *See* Ruler(s) of Qatar
ruler benefit system for nomadic tribes *(ikrimiyah)*, 21, 135–36, 183
Ruler(s) of Abu Dhabi:
  1868 Agreement, 69
  alliances with the RB, 25, 36, 45, 64–65
  intervention in Bahrain, 29–30, 64
  Isa bin Tarif and, 33
  recognition of Al-Khalifa authority in the Qatar peninsula, 110
  Sheikh Zayed, 213, 365, 383
  suspect letters from, 365, 382–83
  suspect seals, 383
  agreement to arbitrate the Hawars dispute, 284

Ruler(s) of Bahrain (RB):
  agreements on Zubarah, 195–97, 200–2
  Al-Thani as agents of, 44, 46, 136
  alliances with the Imam of Muscat, 29, 36
  alliances with the Ruler of Abu Dhabi, 25, 36, 45, 64–65
  authority in disputed territories. *See under* Al-Khalifa
  and the British, 53, 60, 62, 271
    British advice to keep clear of the Qatar peninsula, 86, 212
    Sheikh Mohammed and, 66, 67–68
  British mediation between Rahmah bin Jaber and, 58
  claims to the Hawars. *See under* Bahrain
  claims to Zubarah. *See under* Bahrain
  council *(diwan)*, 23
  dynastic struggles, 32–35, 64–65, 71
    Qatar's version, 112
  Hawar visits, 241–42
  interests in Zubarah, 128, 141–42
  joint rulership, 32–33, 413*n*
  lineage, *413*
  offer on Zubarah, 199–200
  payments to the Naim, 135–36
  periods of rule, *415*
  Preliminary Treaty with Britain, 54–55
  Qatar's allegation of collusion in the Hawars arbitration, 316
  supplying of Zubarah, 142, 184–85, 185
  suspect letter from Midhat Pasha to, 368, 371–72
  tribute payments to the Wahhabis, 28, 30, 31–32, 36–37
  See also Al-Khalifa; *and individual Al-Khalifa rulers*
Ruler(s) of Dubai, 69, 87
Ruler(s) of Qatar (RQ):
  agreement to arbitrate the Hawars dispute, 284–85
    Qatar's version, 317
  agreements on Zubarah, 195–97, 200–2
  attack on Zubarah. *See* 1937 Qatari attack on Zubarah
  claims to the Hawars. *See under* Qatar
  claims to Zubarah. *See under* Qatar
  lineage, *414*
  as proclaimed in the Anglo–Al-Thani Treaty, 98, 99
  recognition of Al-Khalifa authority in Zubarah, 269
  See also Al-Thani; *and individual Al-Thani rulers*

S

Sa'id, Sayid. *See* Imam of Muscat
Saeed Bey: suspect correspondence to, 370
Safavid dynasty (Persia), 14–15
Saldanha, Jerome A., 410
  The Persian Gulf Précis, 418
Saleh bin Muhammed Ali bin Ali Al-Naimi: on Qatar's attack on Zubarah, 190
Saleh Pasha: suspect letter to Sheikh Jasim, 368
Salman bin Ahmed. *See* Al-Khalifa, Sheikh Salman bin Ahmed
Salman bin Hamad. *See* Al-Khalifa, Sheikh Salman bin Hamad
sanctions: by Bahrain on Qatar, 192–93, 283
Sassanian Empire: and Bahrain, 7
Saudi Arabia:
  Bahrain–Qatar border dispute mediation efforts, xvi–xviii, 202, 325, 326–31
    Five Principles (1978/1983), 326
    proposals (1987), 327–28
Saudi oil concession, 176
Saudis. *See* Al-Saud
Sayid Sa'id. *See* Imam of Muscat
Schofield, Richard: suspect document analysis, 370–72, 382
sea: as a buffer between Bahrain and Qatar (1868 Agreements), 111
  See also maritime boundary between Bahrain and Qatar

seals on suspect documents:
   analyses, 360, 364–65, 375–76
   Arabic characters, 375
   British seals, 364, 371, 387, 389
   fingerprints, 365
   individual seals used in unrelated documents, 375, 383
   Latin initials, 376
   Ottoman seals, 369, 375, 389
   of Rulers of Abu Dhabi, 383
   of Sheikh Isa bin Ali, 383, *384*
   Stuart Houghton Ltd. seals, 387, *388*
   U.S. seal, 373

Selections from the Records of the Bombay Government, 419

Seleucid state: and Bahrain, 7

Shakhboot bin Sultan, Sheikh, 365
   suspect seal and signature, 383

Sharjah (Trucial Coast/UAE), 4*map*, 50
   British blockade of, 57

Sharq bin Ahmed: suspect letter by, 377

shoals. *See* low-tide elevations

signatures on suspect documents, 360, 373, 383–84
   Belgrave stamp, 376, 382, 389

Sitra (Bahrain island), xvii*map*, 122*map*, 398*map*
   and Fasht Al-Azm, 347–48

Skliros, John, 410
   claim to the Hawars for Qatar, 277

slave trade: British suppression efforts, 54, 62–63, 99

slavery: Zinj slave revolt, 8
   See also slave trade

Sobhi, Mohammed Ezz-El-Din: suspect document analysis, 374–86

Socal (Standard of California): and the Bahrain oil concession, 171

sovereignty:
   Gulf notions vs. Western notions, 21
   See also authority (control) in the Gulf region
   in the Hawars. *See under* Hawar Islands
   in Zubarah. *See under* Zubarah (region)

Special Agreement (ICJ application), 328, 329, 330, 333

stamps in suspect documents, 376, 382, 389

Standard of California (Socal): and the Bahrain oil concession, 171

Standard Oil, 170, 174, 176

Stuart Houghton Ltd. seals, 387, *388*

Sublime Porte. *See* Ottomans

Sudan tribe, 124

Suleiman the Magnificent, Sultan, 11

Sultan bin Mohamed Salamah, Sheikh, 146, 147

Sultan bin Zayed, Sheikh:
   suspect letters from, 365
   suspect seal, 383

Sultan of Nejd. *See* Al-Saud, Abdul-Aziz (Ibn Saud)

Sumerian inscriptions: Dilmun as described in, 5

Superior Oil Company, 303

Supplemental Documents (in *Q. v. B.*), 395

suspect documents (in Qatar's ICJ case):
   Abu Dhabi documents, 365
   Arabic writing in, 366, 367, 375, 384–85
   "authors'" known authentic documents collection, 358
   authorship by one person, 359, 360, 384–86
   Bahrain's evaluation team, 362–63
   Belgrave correspondence, 366, 372
   comparisons among, 359–60, 374–81
   devices used, 374–75
   comparisons with known authentic same-author documents, 360, 361, 381–84
   contradictions in: generally, 357–58, 358
   date discrepancies in, 358, 364, 365, 369, 370, 371

suspect documents (in Qatar's ICJ case): *(continued)*
   to/from dead persons, 358, 365
   demarcation documents, 364, 370, 370–72
   discovery of, 356
   document searches:
      in Bahrain and other GCC countries, 357–59, 381–82
      in U.S., French, and German archives, 372–74
   forensic analysis. *See* forensic analyses of suspect documents
   as forgeries. *See* forged documents (in Qatar's ICJ case)
   handwriting in. *See* handwriting in suspect documents
   historical analysis, 363–72
   initial analysis, 356
   ink, 389
   international experts' analyses, 362–86
   linguistic analysis, 359–60, 382–83
   maps, 371, 372–74, 387
   originals: as requested and delivered, 362
   Ottoman documents, 367–70
   paper, 377–81, 389
   preliminary investigation, 357–61
   reports submitted to the ICJ, 386–87, 388–89
   seals. *See* seals on suspect documents
   signatures on. *See* signatures on suspect documents
   stamps, 376, 382, 389

T

Tahnoon bin Zayed, Sheikh: suspect seal, 383
Talbot, Adelbert C., 93–94
Tarif. *See* Isa bin Tarif
Tarut Island (Hasa coast):
   Ghariyeh settlers' move to, 88–89
   as part of Bahrain, 7, 31
   Sheikh Mohammed's blockade of, 35
taxation of Zubarah by the RQ, 182–83, 184
   Bedouin incursions in support of, 188–89

   compromise proposal, 186–87
   Naim and RB responses to, 183–85, 187–88
   negotiation breakdown, 189–90
territorial claims:
   international law principles on, 339–43, 400–1
   Ottoman claims to the Bahrain Islands, 71–72
   See also under Hawar Islands; Zubarah (region)
territorial integrity: and territorial claims, 342
territory of nomadic tribes. *See dirah*
"*tersane*": suspect document misusage, 368
third party recognition: and territorial claims, 341
timeline of key events, 103
title: original title and territorial claims, 400
   See also sovereignty
trade centers in the Gulf, 8
   Bahrain, 5, 9, 12
   Zubarah, 18
trade routes around the Gulf, 6–7
treaties and agreements:
   1868 Agreements, 45–46, 69–70, 86, 111–12, 256–57, 284
      Qatar's interpretation of, 111, 207–8, 312–13
   1875 Treaty, 194
   1916 Treaty. *See* 1916 Treaty (Anglo–Al-Thani Treaty)
   1944 Agreement (on Zubarah), 195–97, 217
      Qatar's interpretation of, 217
treaties and agreements:
   1950 Agreement (on Zubarah), 200–2
   Anglo-Ottoman Convention. *See* Anglo-Ottoman Convention
   Anglo-Turkish Convention, 116, 313
   Doha Minutes/Agreement. *See* Doha Minutes/Agreement
   Exclusive Agreements, 72–75, 98

treaties and agreements: *(continued)*
  Friendly Convention, 36, 67–69, 256–57, 284
  General Treaty (Piracy Agreements), 54–56
    implementation of, 56–59
  Maritime Truce, 59–60, 62, 98–99
  Muscat-Bahrain peace treaty, 30, 58–59
  Perpetual Treaty of Peace, 60, 98–99
  Preliminary Treaty, 54–55
  Qatar's interpretation of, 111–12, 115–17
  slave trade suppression agreements, 62–63
tribes in the Gulf:
  allegiance: and territorial claims, 133*q*, 339
    See also Naim tribe: and the Al-Khalifa
  Bani Khaled, 124
  coastal tribes, 6, 39–40
  nomadic tribes, 21, 40
    See also Bedouin tribes
  pearling tribes, 23, 40, 41
  in the Qatar peninsula, 39–42, 124
    alienation from the Al-Thani, 88, 174
    recognition of Al-Khalifa authority, 110
tribute (zakat), 133
  payments to the Wahhabis by Bahrain, 28, 30, 31–32, 36–37
Tripartite Committee, 327, 328, 328–29, 334
Trucial Coast (Pirate Coast), 50, 59
Trucial flag: as required for Arab vessels, 55, 56, 57–58
Trucial system, 50–51
"*tughra*": suspect document misusage, 369
Turki bin Abdullah Al-Saud, 30
Turks. *See* Ottomans (Porte)
Tylos: Bahrain main island as, 7
Tytell, Peter: suspect document analysis, 374–86

U

Udaid. *See* Odaid
Umayyad caliphs: and Bahrain, 8
UN Convention on the Law of the Sea, 343
unallotted area (Bahrain oil concession), 168, 271
  APOC and, 269
  BAPCO claims to, 269
  BAPCO withdrawal from, 271
  British concerns, 269–70
  PCL and, 177–79, 269, 279
  Zubarah as an addition to, 173–75
United States:
  advent in the Gulf, 173–74
  emergence as a world power, 162, 165, 173–74
  oil production in 1936, 267
  suspect seal, 373
  See also American oil companies
uti possidetis juris: and territorial claims, 401

V

Vali of Baghdad: suspect document misidentification of, 370
Vali of Basra:
  battle with Sheikh Jasim, 92
  in Ottoman-ruled Qatar, 91–92
  suspect document misusage, 370
"Vali of Hasa": suspect document misusage, 367
villages on the Hawars, 232–33

W

Wahhabis, 27–28, 78
  Abdul-Aziz ibn Saud. *See* Al-Saud, Abdul-Aziz (Ibn Saud)
  Abdul-Wahhab, 27, 78
  and the Al-Khalifa, 25, 27–28, 28–29, 30–32, 35–37, 126
  and the Al-Thani, 36, 174
  alliances against Bahrain, 64, 66–67
  attack on the Qatar peninsula, 36, 100
  attack on Zubarah, 127, 206
  attacks on Bahrain:
    expulsion of Muscat, 27–28, 126
    later attacks, 36

Wahhabis *(continued)*
  attacks on Oman, 31, 36
  and the Bani Hajir, 42
  and Bushir bin Rahmah, 30
  Huwailah chiefs and, 33
  Ibn Saud. *See* Al-Saud, Abdul-Aziz
  Khalid, 31
  Mohammed ibn Saud, 27, 78
  Ottoman expeditions against, 30, 31, 78–79
  presence in and expulsion from Bahrain, 28–29, 127
  Qawasim and, 28, 50
  and Rahmah bin Jaber, 28
  recognition of Al-Khalifa authority in the Qatar peninsula, 110
  tenets (aspects), 78
  tribute payments by Bahrain to, 28, 30, 31–32, 36–37
  Turki bin Abdullah Al-Saud, 30
Ward, Thomas, 170, 276
Ward map, 275, 276, *276*
wars in the Gulf, 63
  "acknowledged war" vs. "plunder and piracy" in the General Treaty, 55, 56, 57, 58
  banning of hostilities during pearling season, 59
  as restricted in the neutral zone, 59, 63
water supply systems in the Hawars, 232, 233–34, 247, 302
Weightman, Sir Hugh, 411
  on the Dowasir, 237*q*, 237–38*q*
  on the Hawars, 223–25
  on Janan, 224
  Qatar's allegations of collusion in the Hawars arbitration, 318–20
  on the RQ, 283*q*, 285*q*
  on the RQ's claim to the Hawars, 286*q*, 287*q*, 293–95
    and request to rebut Bahrain's Counter-claim, 288–89*q*
Western notions of sovereignty: Gulf notions vs., 21
Western powers: advent in the Gulf, 11–15, 49, 73, 173–74
  See also Britain (British); Ottomans; United States

Wilkinson, John C.: suspect document analysis, 363–67, 370, 382
Wukra (Qatar peninsula), 41, 122*map*
  British survey description, 42
  RB expeditions against, 25, 26, 45, 69
  seceders from, 88–89

Y

Yaaribah tribe (Oman): capture of Bahrain, 15
Yusuf bin Rahmah, 254

Z

zakat. *See* tribute
Zakhnuniya (island, Hasa coast), 122*map*, 259
  Dowasir settlement on, 259, 261
  Ottoman occupation of, 259–60
    British response to, 260–61
  Ottoman payment for, 261
Zakhnuniya Incident, 259–61
Zayed bin Khalifa, Sheikh, 213
  suspect fingerprint and letter from, 365
  suspect seal, 383
Zinj slave revolt, 8
Zubarah (region) (Qatar peninsula), xvii*map*, 121–217, 122*map*, 134*map*, 258*map*, 398*map*
  1944 Agreement on, 195–97, 217
  1950 Agreement on, 200–2
  Al-Jalahimah possession of and expulsion from, 28, 29
  Al-Khalifa authority in, 121, 125, 127, 141, 142–43, 145, 206–7, 210–11
    Al-Thani recognition of, 109, 156–57, 269
    British recognition of. *See* British recognition of Bahrain's sovereignty in, *below*
    Ottoman recognition of, 155–56
    Qatar's version, 206
  Al-Khalifa migration to, 18, 124–25
  Al-Khalifa return to, 27, 126
  Al-Thani authority in, 208, 209–11
    Qatar's version, 206, 207–8, 209–11, 214–15

Zubarah (region) *(continued)*
  Al-Thani expansion attempts, 83, 121, 143–49
    attacks, 144–45, 145, 146–48, 210–11. *See also* 1937 Qatari attack on Zubarah
    failure of, 149–52
    resettlement plans/occupation efforts, 145–46, 148–49, 153, 197–98
  Al-Thani recognition of Bahrain's authority in, 109, 156–57, 269
  Bahrain's claims to, xvi, 181, 192, 195, 198, 202
    British nonintervention policy, 193–95
    British recognition of. *See* British recognition of Bahrain's sovereignty in, *below*
    historical explanation, 203–5
    legal arguments, 339–40
    modified renouncement, 186–87
    Qatar's version, 205
    See also Al-Khalifa authority in, *above*
  Bahrain's interests in, 128, 141–42
  Ballantyne proposal, 199
  Bani Hajir attacks on, 137–38, 144–45, 190
  British interests in, 148*q*
  British mediation efforts on, xvi, 268
    1944 Agreement, 195–97, 217
    1950 Agreement, 200–2
    compromise proposal, 186–87
  British nonintervention policy, 189, 191, 193–95
  British protection of, 143–49
  British recognition of Bahrain's sovereignty in, 86, 152–55, 212–13
    change of attitude on, 160–61, 163, 173–75, 176–79, 200, 212, 217
    Qatar's version, 211–12, 213
  decline/desertion of, 34, 40, 127–28, 207
  development of, 206–7
  establishment of, 18–19, 125
  forts:
    Murair Fort, 125, 127, 142
    RQ's fort, 195, 201
  founder, 18, 129
  geography, 121–23
  history (pre-1762) (origins), 123–24
    Qatar's version, 205–6
  history (1762–1937), 203–5
    Qatar's version, 205
  Ibn Saud's influence in, 183
  ICJ Judgment on, 396, 397–400
  Manasir attack on, 190
  Muscat attack on, 127, 206
  Naim defense of, 19, 65–66, 137–38
    against Qatar's attack, 184, 185, 188, 190
  Naim flight from, 191–92
  Naim return to, 201
  Naim settlement in, 18, 121, 131
    dirah (territory), 132–33, 134*map*
  Nasir bin Madhkur's attacks on, 19, 125
  oil exploration in, 269
  Ottoman expansion attempts, 83, 121, 143–49
    attacks, 144–45, 145, 146–48, 210–11
    diplomacy, 144
    failure of, 149–42
    resettlement plans/occupation efforts, 145–46, 148–49, 153
  Ottoman interests in, 144, 145–46, 155–56
  Ottoman recognition of Bahrain's authority in, 155–56
  Ottoman-ruled Qatar vs. Zubarah's inhabitants, 142
  as outside Ottoman control, 82–83
  as part of Bahrain, 115*q*, 159–62
  pearling, 18
    Ottoman interests in, 144, 145–46
  Persian attacks on, 19, 125
  Political Agent's warning on, 181*q*
  population:
    at its height, 129
    migration to Bahrain, 132, 162, 191–92
    See also Naim tribe
  port plans:
    of the RB, 160–61
    of the RQ, 182
  principal settlement. *See* Zubarah (town)

Zubarah (region) *(continued)*
  prosperity as a trading center, 129
  Qadi: Hawars grant to the Dowasir, 226
  Qatar's attack on. *See* 1937 Qatari attack on Zubarah
  Qatar's claims to, 179, 181, 187
    Bahrain's interpretation of, 340
    legal arguments, 341–43
  Qatar's resettlement attempt, 197–98
  Qatar's version of events in, 203–17
  RB's claims to. *See* Bahrain's claims to, *above*
  RB's offer on, 199–200
  RB's supplying of, 142, 184–85, 185
  RQ's claims to. *See* Qatar's claims to, *above*
  RQ's taxation of. *See* taxation of Zubarah by the RQ
  settlements, 123, 134*map*
  as a socio-economic unit with the Bahrain and Hawar Islands, 225, 296
  sovereignty in:
    ICJ judgement, 396, 397–400
    issue as submitted to the ICJ, 335–36
    See also Al-Khalifa authority in, *above*; Al-Thani authority in, *above*; Bahrain's claims to, *above*; Qatar's claims to, *above*
  town "pre-existing" in, 399–400
  as an unallotted oil concession area for Bahrain, 173–75
    PCL and, 177–79
  Wahhabi attack on, 127, 206
Zubarah (town) (Qatar peninsula), 124
  archaeological evidence on, 129–30
  destruction of, 127, 145, 206
  fortification of, 125, 127, 142
  Governor, 207
    RB's change of, 143
  rebuilding of, 34